G000150907

A Sense of Purpose

A Sense of Purpose was the title of a – now famous – letter sent by Larry Fink, Founder and Chairman of Blackrock Inc, one of the largest global institutional investors. In it he urges CEOs to consider the societal implications of their business decisions and to focus on their long-term plans. "To prosper over time, every company must not only deliver financial performance, but also show how it makes a positive contribution to society. Companies must benefit all of their stakeholders, including shareholders, employees, customers, and the communities in which they operate."

Through our global initiative Business. For Good™, launched many years before Larry Fink's letter was published, we encourage business leaders to 'think and act long-term' in order to enhance business performance and pursue profit responsibly for the mutual benefit of companies, their stakeholders and society at large. Businesses are at the heart of value creation. They have a major part in promoting prosperity and acting in true Mazars' style, as stewards for future generations.

At a time when many auditors are lost and confused about their role in society, we can and need to give a renewed sense of purpose to our work. As part of our work, we are at the heart of business, at the connection between shareholders and the companies they invest in. We must play our part in helping the companies that we audit be sustainable. I like to call it "futureproofing their business".

But as a pre-condition we also need to futureproof our business. We are investing to deliver quality, to be more efficient hence financially sustainable and relevant to the needs of our stakeholders. We are also at the forefront of various campaigns to bring change in our profession through challenging the way companies report, promoting the need for a more open, less concentrated audit market, and encouraging better regulation.

Real impact only comes through action. Be part of the transformation of audit.

David Herbinet
Global Head of Audit and Assurance

MAZARS | business. for good

The Trillion Dollar Shift

Achieving the Sustainable Development Goals;
Business for Good is Good Business

Routledge
Taylor & Francis Group

LONDON AND NEW YORK

MARGA HOEK

Colophon

First published 2018
by Routledge
2 Park Square, Milton Park, Abingdon, Oxon OX14 4RN

and by Routledge
711 Third Avenue, New York, NY 10017

Routledge is an imprint of the Taylor & Francis Group, an informa business

Routledge is the world's leading academic publisher in the Humanities and Social Sciences and has partnered with many of the most influential societies and academic bodies to publish their journals and book series. Routledge is proud to publish across all areas of sustainability and the environment bringing the latest research on climate change, natural resources, sustainable energy, business and development to a global audience of researchers, students, sustainable practitioners and anyone interested in creating a sustainable future for all.

© 2018 Marga Hoek

Chief Editor: Amie de Jeu
Business analyst & researcher: Theresa McCarty
Printer: EcoMedia
Design and lettering: I am Creative - EcoMedia

This book is printed on Agriwaste from PaperWise, highly qualified paper made from agricultural waste. The production of this book is based on a 100% IPA (solvent) free print process with cradle-to-cradle (gold standard) biodegradable, toxin free bio-inks (green4print.nl) and sustainable plates that eliminate chemistry, gum and water used in the conventional plate production process. Based on a certified climate calculation this book is 100% carbon free (production, materials, distribution). The eco-laminate used for the cover is made from wood waste and is biodegradable.

British Library Cataloguing-in-Publication Data
A catalogue record for this book is available from the British Library

Library of Congress Cataloguing-in-Publication Data
A catalogue record has been requested for this book

ISBN: 978-0-8153-6431-3 (hardback)
ISBN: 978-1-351-10729-7 (e-book)

Publisher's Note
This book has been prepared from camera-ready copy provided by the author.

Acknowledgments

I dedicate this book to my three beautiful children Faye, Boyd and Gray. They endured my mission to write this book throughout the last two years and especially the last months. My mission in that sense was theirs. And it will be, since it is actually their future and the future of their children to be, that is at stake. I sincerely hope that this book will inspire many parents around the world to ensure children have a safe and hopeful future in a world that is theirs to sustain.

I can only be incredibly thankful for the ongoing support, inspiration, humor, incredible professionality and perseverance of my chief editor Amie de Jeu. This book would not have seen the light of day without her. My mission was definitely hers and she has supported my voice giving life to that, every step of the way. I also thank Theresa McCarty, business analyst & researcher enormously for her dedication to this project and making sure all research was done with perfectionism on accuracy, facts and the right numbers and references. I also thank all the companies profiled in this book for their inspirational work in creating sustainable business cases.

I am thankful to Paul Polman, in collaboration with whom the inspiration rose and the enthusiasm grew for this book and who supported me all the way. I thank Feike Sijbesma for his inspiration and support and Gérard Mestrallet for his inspiring visionary leadership he shared with me. All three leaders wrote a beautiful foreword for this book, for which I am grateful. Last but certainly not least, the team of EcoMedia who helped me to make this book a showcase for sustainability with paper made of agricultural waste and endured ongoing drive to improve, redo and further improve. I thank my publisher Rebecca Marsh at Routledge for believing and trusting in me, especially to publish the book in an open access, free online version since I do not want to put a price on access to knowledge that is crucial for the world we all want.

This book is a book of many, and any recognition of this book should go to all. But most importantly, it is a book with a mission. To inspire people to lead the way to find, create and scale up solutions for our Global Goals, and achieve the world we all want. With business that is a power for good. For a world that is fair to all and that can and will sustain.

Marga Hoek

Contents

Preface
Forewords

3 TRILLION DOLLAR SHIFT **IN SECTORS**

4 SCALING UP FOR A TRILLION DOLLAR SHIFT

Preface

MARGA HOEK

It's been over two years since the course was set to a better world via the Paris Agreement, the establishment of the Sustainable Development Goals (SDGs) and the Financing for Development conference in Addis Ababa. Taken together, these three conferences and agreements represent a much-needed holistic paradigm shift, and a fundamental change in the way we approach the task of creating a better world. The global movement started a journey, or better said a next journey, since that actually already started with the Millennium Goals. Now, the SDGs are a global compass guiding us all, in a language we all understand and interpret the same way.

While we are in the first phase of this journey, we must be very aware that this journey is more crucial and more difficult than we could have imagined. The world is experiencing hurricanes, floods, droughts, and storms like we have never seen before, with enormous consequences for people, planet and economy. In the previous decade, the world's economy suffered an estimated loss of US $2.7 trillion because of natural disasters. This decade will no doubt show an exponential increase, and inaction on climate change comes with the huge comprehensive cost estimated at US $24 trillion. At the same time, inequalities among people across the world are growing instead of diminishing, resulting in dangerous divides, conflicts, and social unrest. Despite the fact that we have been able to lift millions of people out of poverty, half of the world's population is still living on less than US $2 a day and nearly 800 million people still go to bed hungry every day. Thirty percent of the world's 1.8 billion young people are neither employed nor in school or training programs; and over 61 million children of primary school age are not in school. Progress on gender equality also still lags far behind, and women continue to face significant economic, social, and even legal barriers to equality.

It is increasingly clear that the way forward on our journey towards 2030 needs to use the power of business as leverage to grow a stable, sustainable global economy and society. Consider that business corporations account for many of the largest economies operating around the world. Many corporations have a balance sheet outranking countries' GDPs. And consider the investment potential of private capital which is a much larger percentage than public investment potential by now, as the percentage of total capital flows of donor countries' ODAs into emerging markets has decreased, while private capital flows have increased and grown. Last but not least, consider the power of business needed to safeguard consistency in policy, as business was crucial to creating the Climate Agreement and the Sustainable Development Goals, and is equally important to maintaining them.

Let's engage business in a new purpose. Business that embeds the Goals into the heart of companies, strives to not only serve its own goals, but the Global Goals at the same time. Since there is no business if there is no planet, there are also no business opportunities in a world of exponentially growing risks, increasing poverty, climate change, and resource scarcity. Wise leaders understand this and know that navigating towards the Goals means safeguarding the planet and its inhabitants, and securing a sustainable business and economic future. The growth of business for good incorporates a new meaning of growth which we must embrace, disconnecting negative impact from growth, and connecting growth with positive impact on the world.

At a business level, there is every reason to engage with the SDGs. This book demonstrates that business for good is good business, and aims to show how business and capital can have a positive impact on the SDGs, while improving their competitiveness. You will read how new markets, worth up to US $12 trillion, can be unlocked by 2030. Returns on sustainable business cases are getting better by the year or even the month, with businesses working against climate change performing almost 20% better than their peers. In this context, not engaging with the SDGs becomes the risk, especially since customers and employees will demand that companies be part of the solutions, rather than the problem. Markets are changing

radically, and products and services that do not create real value will soon be phased out.

Since the scale of our collective solutions must meet the scale of our Goals, let this book be an inspiration to all businesses to venture beyond the comfort zone, and explore new ways to create profitable business cases while also safeguarding and positively impacting people and the environment. For that reason, I have endeavored to create a comprehensive, yet inspirational book that provides an overview of the SDGs, what they mean to business and capital, and how to engage. You will read what shared value is, and how to use it as a leading business principle. You will gain insights into industry sectors and read business cases of companies all over the world. And you will get an overview of research and collaborations exploring sustainability.

This book is an extension of my personal mission to contribute to the repurposing of business and capital. Repurposing to do good for the world must become a primary mission for all; it can be done, and must be done. Our future depends on it. To spread this message, I have made all content digitally available with an open access model. So, spread the word and spread the mission, because together we can achieve our Goals.

Forewords

PAUL POLMAN
CEO UNILEVER

The Sustainable Development Goals (SDGs), adopted in September 2015 in New York by 193 countries are a true beacon of hope, and have rightly sparked great interest from business and investors. Its goal is simply to leave no-one behind. To irreversibly eradicate poverty and do so in a more sustainable and equitable way. The world needs it now more than ever, if we want it to function for everyone, including for those yet to come.

The role business can, and must play in achieving the Goals cannot be overestimated, as governments will not be able to change the world for the better merely by themselves.

The reality is that the Goals need business, and at the same time business also needs the Goals, because the SDGs provide the potential to unlock new markets and bring about a business opportunity of staggering magnitude. The latter is estimated at no less than US $12 trillion by 2030 with 380 million new jobs created. Indeed, implementing the SDGs is one of the biggest business opportunities of our time.

So, for business, the question is not 'why', but 'how' to develop solutions which are both good for business and which create positive SDG impact. This requires transformational change throughout sectors.

We need to quickly learn, both individually and collectively, how to undertake this crucial journey. It starts with awareness of the SDGs, and how each business can positively contribute. Businesses that understand this and put themselves to the service of society, will have a long and prosperous future. Businesses that don't, will be voted out, and this is happening with increased frequency.

The good news is that we can adapt: we are an intelligent species, and the challenge ahead will be finding a way to put our resources to good use. A combination of human willpower and knowledge of the subject matter can make it happen.

This new publication by Marga Hoek goes a long way in providing us with such required knowledge. *The Trillion Dollar Shift* provides a comprehensive overview of SDG opportunities across sectors, and shows the reader how to engage and create economic and social impact on each of the 17 SDGs. Throughout the book, you will find useful examples of companies that have already embarked on this journey.

In order to maximize accessibility, the author has decided to make *The Trillion Dollar Shift* a digital open access publication, available free of charge, and I would like to thank Marga for that.

We can therefore be sure this inspiring book will reach interested readers across the globe, and rightly so, as its important message can help bring us one step closer to the better world we all aspire to by 2030. It will hopefully unlock the purposeful leader inside of you, and make you part of a growing movement to ensure we leave no one behind.

" WE CANNOT CLOSE OUR EYES TO THE CHALLENGES THE WORLD FACES **AND BUSINESS MUST MAKE AN EXPLICIT POSITIVE CONTRIBUTION TO ADDRESSING THEM.**"

PAUL POLMAN, CEO UNILEVER

FEIKE SIJBESMA
CEO-CHAIRMAN
DSM

Sustainability should, by now, be considered a core value and business driver. It should be embedded in the business strategy of all companies. Large, multinational companies, like DSM, have tremendous global reach and impact, and must therefore demonstrate societal responsibility by becoming part of the solution to our global challenges rather than part of the problem. DSM embraces this responsibility and, as a global leader in its industry, has committed itself to the Sustainable Development Goals (SDGs).

Increasingly, companies are setting out to help solve society's big problems with innovative solutions, their technological capabilities, their outreach to consumers, and their investments. At DSM, we repositioned our business from a chemical company into a Life Sciences & Materials Sciences company. The core of our strategy is "Bright Science, Brighter Living". We aim to make food healthier and more nutritious, engineer more sustainably, develop materials that can benefit the environment, convert agricultural waste, and invest in sustainable solutions. At DSM, innovations must be able to demonstrate positive impact on people and planet to ensure that we contribute to a better world with our products.

This book by Marga Hoek offers business leaders many insights, ideas and practical cases on how business can contribute to a sustainable world, making use of the navigating power of the SDGs. Its comprehensiveness, global orientation and inspirational cases offer great value to the reader. Most importantly it demonstrates that the process of businesses creating solutions to the world's challenges is both a responsibility and a business model. I hope this book will inspire many business leaders to take on that responsibility, and address these challenges with business solutions that will both improve our world and strengthen their company.

Today, both companies and government hold a responsibility to achieve the Sustainable Development Goals (SDGs) in order to fight poverty in its many forms as well as climate change. Business by now has come to the conclusion that fighting global problems like climate change is in the best interest of companies and thus: shareholders. Climate change is not only an ecological but also an economical catastrophe, and business has become aware of that especially the last three to four years.

The world of energy is changing, we're moving towards a less centralized, less carbon-intensive energy world, away from the centralized world of yesterday. Both business and government hold the keys to achieve this. From the perspective of government: One of the best ways to speed the energy transition is a carbon tax. It is absolutely key to discouraging investment in fossil fuels. Such a strategy would quantify climate risks, as each ton of carbon emissions would come at a hefty price. It would also undercut profits for big polluters and push investment toward low and no-carbon alternatives like solar and wind.

But then, business needs to actively engage in these societal challenges, with their products, business models and investments, throughout the world. Multinational companies specifically, must engage since they can be both global and locally present. At ENGIE, our challenge consists of finding new ways to provide power to more people, sustainably. Recently, we were awarded several solar and wind projects in Mexico, which demonstrates both ENGIE competitiveness in carbon-free generation and our commitment to support Mexico, a country rapidly growing which is resolutely engaged in liberalizing its economy while fueling it with responsible energy. More globally, we aim to provide sustainable energy to 20 million people worldwide by 2020. This means we invest in new solutions through our venture capital and many other initiatives. We engage in local programs, for instance in Brazil's Salto hydroelectric plant, and collaborate with all relevant stakeholders in many countries. One of our most recent projects is to build photovoltaic smart micro-grids for 3,000 villages in the province of Papua, which is consistent with our vision of leading the global energy transition. The drive for decarbonization will significantly contribute to powering the country's energy needs in a sustainable way, in partnership with local companies.

On this transformational journey, we discover and learn while we meet many challenges. And there are many more to overcome. In this sense, I am happy that Marga Hoek provides us with such a thorough yet inspirational book about the synergy between business, capital and the SDGs. Knowledge and leadership by example are key for transformation.

GÉRARD MESTRALLET
CHAIRMAN
ENGIE

1 NO POVERTY

2 ZERO HUNGER

3 GOOD HEALTH AND WELL-BEING

4 QUALITY EDUCATION

5 GENDER EQUALITY

6 CLEAN WATER AND SANITATION

7 AFFORDABLE AND CLEAN ENERGY

8 DECENT WORK AND ECONOMIC GROWTH

9 INDUSTRY, INNOVATION AND INFRASTRUCTURE

SUSTAINABLE DEVELOPMENT GOALS

10 REDUCED INEQUALITIES

11 SUSTAINABLE CITIES AND COMMUNITIES

12 RESPONSIBLE CONSUMPTION AND PRODUCTION

13 CLIMATE ACTION

14 LIFE BELOW WATER

15 LIFE ON LAND

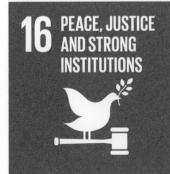

16 PEACE, JUSTICE AND STRONG INSTITUTIONS

17 PARTNERSHIPS FOR THE GOALS

" THERE IS NO PLAN B BECAUSE

WE DO NOT HAVE A PLANET B."

BAN KI-MOON
FORMER UN SECRETARY-GENERAL

50 Cases

Throughout the world

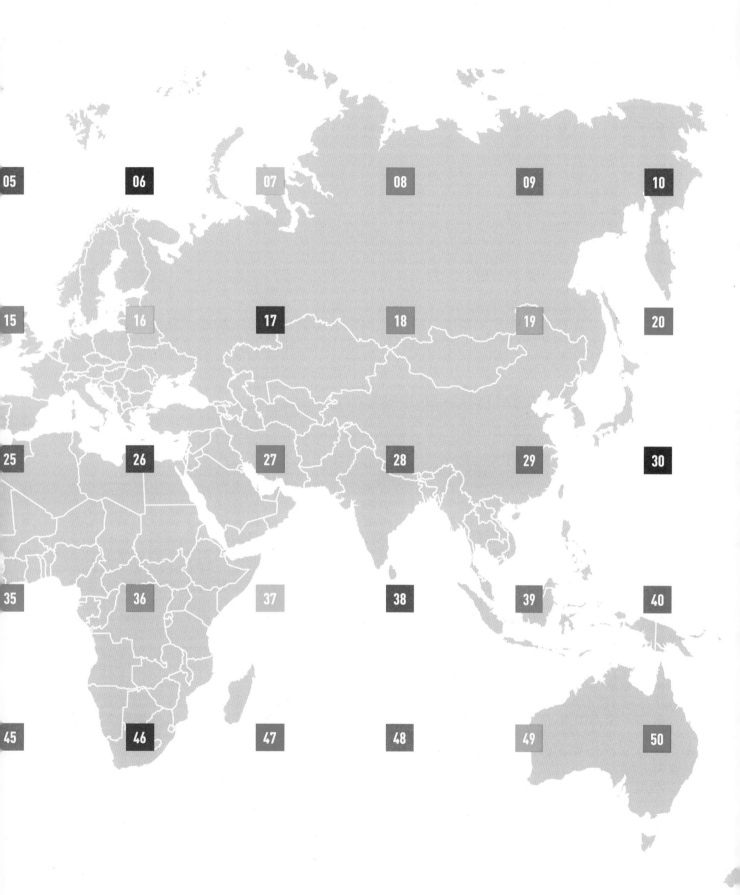

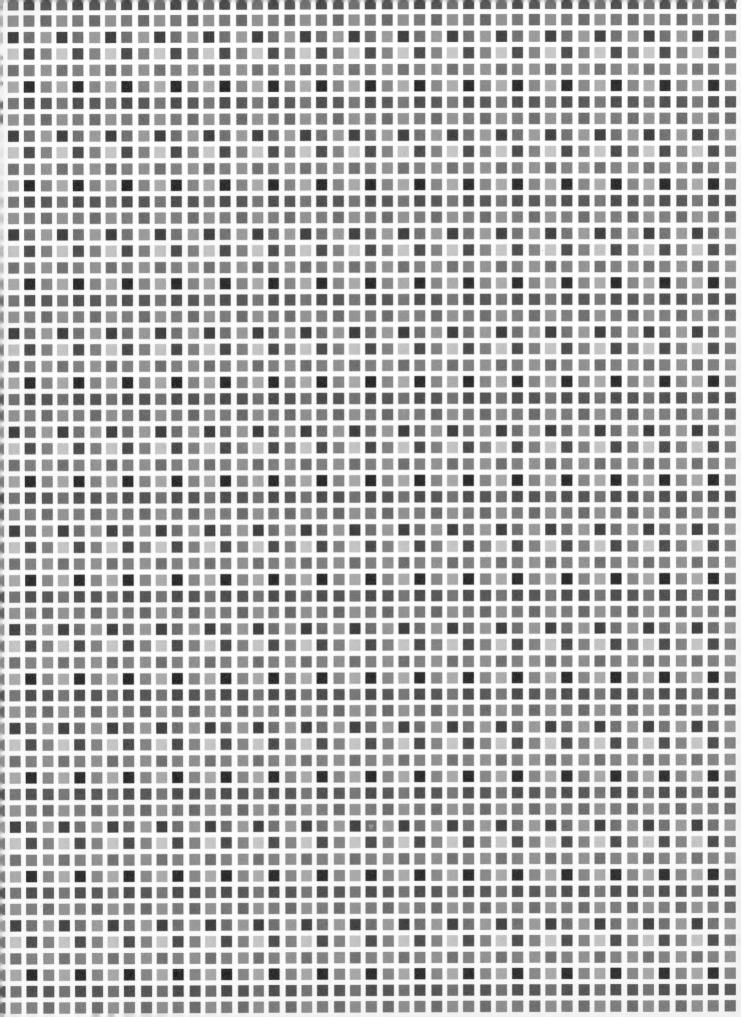

PART 1 | BUSINESS'S CONTRIBUTION TO THE TRILLION DOLLAR SHIFT

INTRODUCTION

Business is the engine of the economy, growth, innovation and job creation. Every company, large and small, has the potential to make a significant contribution towards economic, social and environmental progress.

The United Nations carefully created 17 Sustainable Development Goals (SDGs) that identify what we all should be striving towards, and what we should reach by 2030 for the benefit of mankind. This is a call to action for both business and capital. Frontrunners are gearing their business practices to help achieve the Goals. If the SDGs make anything clear to business, it is that business for good is good business.

Business has the power to accelerate the achievement of the Sustainable Development Goals, and realizing the Goals will in turn also improve the ecosystem for doing business. Trillions of dollars in public and private funds are to be redirected towards the SDGs, creating huge opportunities for responsible companies to deliver solutions. Engaging and innovating today means a stronger continuity for resilient business and industry in the future.

Since the creation of the SDGs, there has been a substantial increase in the number of companies that are able to measurably demonstrate the transformative impact of their technologies, products, services and business models. But the movement must grow and scale, since its impact is still too small to reach the Goals in time.

In Part 1, you will learn more about the Sustainable Development Goals, the progress that has been made thus far by business and government, the new meaning of growth, and the shared value model. You will also begin to read about some of the opportunities that will emerge. Markets worth trillions of dollars are waiting to be unlocked. Unlocking these markets is not only a great opportunity, it is a necessity.

ACHIEVING THE SUSTAINABLE DEVELOPMENT GOALS
THE GREATEST CHALLENGE AND BIGGEST OPPORTUNITY

Our world today, in many ways, offers people greater opportunity to live prosperous lives than in any other time in history. The unprecedented social improvements and technological advances have truly revolutionized many aspects of daily life. Although these modern achievements have been beneficial to the world – lifting millions out of poverty, giving people access to basic services and enabling innovations – there is still a long way to go to meet some of the greatest challenges the world has ever faced. With the imminent dangers of the consequences of climate change and the mounting inequalities among populations, it is now more than ever we need a viable long-term solution. Business and capital are answering this call to action and providing the solution. The SDGs present a unique roadmap to set financial flows and development initiatives on a directed course that addresses not only our personal financial objectives, but also our worldwide environmental and social needs. Supporting sustainable development and meeting our Global Goals will take efforts from all sectors in every nation and require new levels of market participation. For the SDGs to be realized in entirety, we will need major participation from business and capital, and conversely businesses will need the achievement of the SDGs to thrive and prosper.

1.1 THE NEW MEANING OF BUSINESS IN SOCIETY

"Ours can be the first generation to end poverty – and the last generation to address climate change before it is too late." This compelling ambition, stated concisely by the former UN Secretary-General Ban Ki-moon, is at the core of the Sustainable Development Goals (SDGs). As the world faces momentous challenges, there is an accelerating urgency to create sustainable solutions.

In our fast-changing world, we have seen great social improvements and technological advances over the past 30 years. We have experienced a significant number of people being lifted out of poverty. Technology has been developing at an unprecedented pace. And, more than ever before, people are connected to each other and to knowledge through sophisticated shared global networks.

Yet, despite the steps that have been taken and the vast amount of knowledge available, our global problems are growing and there has not been enough large-scale movement to turn the tide. According to a study conducted by the UN Food and Agricultural Organization in 2015, natural disasters triggered by climate change have doubled since the 1980s,[1] threatening the global population environmentally, socially as well as financially. In the previous decade, the world's economy suffered an estimated loss of US $2.7 trillion because of natural disasters. This decade will no doubt show an exponential increase – which has already begun with hurricanes, floods and earthquakes devastating so many areas. It is estimated that inaction on climate change comes with the huge comprehensive cost of US $24 trillion.

OUR GLOBAL PROBLEMS ARE GROWING IN PROPORTION.

The World Economic Forum reports that violence and armed conflict now cost more than 13% of GDP. And obesity has become a global issue costing 2.8% of GDP[2] according to a recent McKinsey analysis.[3] Despite the fact that millions have been lifted out of poverty, half of the world's population is still living on less than two dollars a day. There are also many reports of social inequality and youth unemployment increasing around the world: 30% of the world's 1.8 billion young people are neither employed nor in school or in any other training, and over 57 million children of primary age are not in school at all. Women still face economic, social and even legal barriers to equality as progress on gender equality lags far behind.

PART OF THE SOLUTION, RATHER THAN THE PROBLEM

Business and capital have contributed to these problems. But we have come to a point where we are starting to recognize that neither businesses, nor investments, nor the world will survive if we continue down this path. Not only is it a societal dead-end street, but it is also an economic road-block when global GDP is eaten up by huge percentages due to environmental and social costs.

WE NEED A STRONG CONTRIBUTION FROM BUSINESS.

As this book will demonstrate, there is only a future for businesses that will be a part of the solution instead of the problem. As we will explain throughout this book, those businesses that will engage with the solutions and thus engage with the Sustainable Development Goals, will have a secure future for themselves and secure the future of our world at the same time. They will produce products and services that we need in order to solve the greatest challenge of our times: the achievement of the Sustainable Development Goals.

A MATTER OF TRUST

We need a strong contribution from business. Because, to add to the risks and challenges, we live in what we could define as a vacuum in political leadership and short-term orientated political systems. The "social contract" among politics, government, and society as a whole is becoming increasingly damaged, and connections that need to be tighter than ever are actually loose or even lacking. This is a huge threat to long-term planning and overall coherence among all parties in society. And most of all, it damages trust immensely. Trust, however, is something we need desperately. But trust has never been so low, and the lack of trust has never been so broad, related to politics, government and other institutions, and business. Much of the current public disillusionment is closely tied to the impact of the global economic crisis, the lack of vision in political leadership, and the effects of pervasive corruption. Even within companies, trust in leadership is low.

CONSIDER THAT BUSINESS CORPORATIONS ACCOUNT FOR 69 OF THE LARGEST ECONOMIC ENTITIES.

With only a little over twelve years to go to meet the Global Goals by 2030, which is crucial to maintaining - or better said creating - a stable and fair world, the time is running out. To accelerate our actions to achieve the Goals, we need trust and that trust will grow when we achieve the Goals. Both are interdependent: accelerating for the achievement of the Goals means building trust and vice versa. It is not a coincidence that Goal 17 is about the partnerships for the Goals as you will see and read later on.

PUBLIC-PRIVATE PARTNERSHIP FOR THE GOALS

It is increasingly clear that the way forward is one that must be paved by both business and government, but definitely not by government alone. And this is not a matter of trust, but a matter of roles and numbers. For one thing, governments lack the necessary means to bring about the level of change that is needed. We need to consider that the power of business has grown tremendously and should be leveraged to develop a stable, sustainable global economy and society. Consider that business corporations account for 69 of the largest economic entities, operating throughout the entire planet. And consider the investment potential of private capital, which is a much larger percentage than public investment potential by now. For instance, the percentage of total capital flows of donor countries' Official Development Assistance (ODA) into emerging markets has decreased from over 50% to less than 10%, while private capital flows have increased and grown. And last but not least, consider the power of business needed to safeguard consistency in policy. Business was crucial to creating the Climate Agreement and the Sustainable Development Goals and is equally important to maintaining them. Therefore, governments need business like never before.

Equally, business needs government to develop the right frameworks, tax systems, and support for internalizing external costs – all of which are necessary for a system-wide change. Just pricing environmental externalities across the value chain for food waste prevention alone adds an estimated 92% to the value of business opportunities addressing food waste.[4] To open up markets, create real and fair business cases, and to scale up solutions, business needs good government to set these frameworks and to create stability, direction, and trust.

BUSINESS CAN AND MUST STEP UP

As business begins to embrace the Goals, there is the risk of business becoming too proud of itself for being part of the solution rather than the problem, while in fact business is not growing these solutions at the speed it needs to and the scale it must. If it is really to contribute to the achievement of climate action, our Goals, and the new meaning of capital, business must accelerate and scale up the solutions.

> BUSINESS WAS CRUCIAL TO ACHIEVING THE CLIMATE AGREEMENT AND THE SUSTAINABLE DEVELOPMENT GOALS AND IS EQUALLY IMPORTANT TO MAINTAINING THEM. THEREFORE, GOVERNMENTS NEED BUSINESS LIKE NEVER BEFORE.

A 2017 Global Scan Sustainability Survey, titled *Evaluating Progress Towards the Sustainable Development Goals*, found that while corporate respondents say their business is responding to the SDGs by developing products or services that will provide solutions, and nearly all report that they are currently contributing or planning to contribute to the SDGs, all respondents agree that society's progress on sustainable development and the SDGs has been poor thus far. Although more than 75% of the companies that took part in the survey have already started addressing the Global Goals, it also raises the question of exactly how companies are integrating the Global Goals into their business strategies. This needs clarification, as only a few companies are actually measuring the societal impact of their work with the Ten Principles and the Global Goals, as was set up by the UN.

> COMPANIES ALL OVER THE WORLD ARE REALIZING THAT CONTRIBUTING TO THE WORLD IS ALSO IN THEIR BEST INTEREST.

REPURPOSING: THE NEW MEANING OF BUSINESS

This book is meant as a guide; as an inspiration to engage with the SDGs when developing business strategy. Let's create a new meaning for business: business that functions with purpose and puts the Goals at the heart of the company, and business that serves both its own interests and those of the world at the same time. Consider also the higher impact of business on society: business should de-risk the political process and give political leaders the full backing to reform policy for the better. Engage in public-private initiatives, like the Open Government Partnership (OGP), for example, that aims to secure concrete commitments from governments to promote transparency, empower citizens, fight corruption, and harness new technologies to strengthen governance. Engaging is definitely beneficial for both business and government and is crucial for a wider system change creating new markets, built on sustainable principles, and thus building trust.

Business can and must be a key participator in achieving the Global Goals, and in the rebuilding

THE TEN PRINCIPLES OF THE UN GLOBAL COMPACT:

Human rights
- **Principle 1:** Businesses should support and respect the protection of internationally proclaimed human rights; and
- **Principle 2:** make sure that they are not complicit in human rights abuses.

Labor
- **Principle 3:** Businesses should uphold the freedom of association and the effective recognition of the right to collective bargaining;
- **Principle 4:** the elimination of all forms of forced and compulsory labor;
- **Principle 5:** the effective abolition of child labor; and
- **Principle 6:** the elimination of discrimination in respect of employment and occupation.

Environment
- **Principle 7:** Businesses should support a precautionary approach to environmental challenges
- **Principle 8:** undertake initiatives to promote greater environmental responsibility
- **Principle 9:** encourage the development and diffusion of environmentally friendly technologies.

Anti-Corruption
- **Principle 10:** Businesses should work against corruption in all its forms, including extortion and bribery.

of trust throughout the world: by demonstrating trust, by giving trust, and by deserving trust. The SDGs bring business the huge gift of learning to be much more holistic and think at a much broader system level, which is key to being successful in the multi-stakeholder era we are in now and which is also key to rebuilding trust. So be aware, and even, be inspired as we enter an era that will need business to fulfill a constructive role at the highest system level. Join in a more holistic and fundamental approach of "doing good, by doing business." Although awareness and knowledge of how to act differently is still lacking, companies all over the world are realizing that contributing to the world is also in their best interest. And so should you.

" **THE POST-2015 DEVELOPMENT AGENDA PRESENTS A HISTORIC OPPORTUNITY FOR BUSINESS** TO ENGAGE MORE DEEPLY AS A STRONG AND POSITIVE INFLUENCE ON SOCIETY."

PETER BAKKER, PRESIDENT & CEO, WORLD BUSINESS COUNCIL FOR SUSTAINABLE DEVELOPMENT

1.2 THE SDGs: THE WORLD'S GOALS FOR 2030

For guidance and clarity, the United Nations created 17 Sustainable Development Goals (See Figure 1), which are a set of aspirational goals introduced as a plan of action for "people, planet and prosperity." The Sustainable Development Goals are often referred to as SDGs and as our collective *Global Goals*. They are the broader successor to the Millennium Development Goals, which were adopted in September 2000. The 17 Sustainable Development Goals apply not only to all members of the UN, but to business and capital as well. They are broad and ambitious in scope and focus on all three dimensions of sustainable development: social, economic and environmental.

September 2015 marked the historic moment when 193 countries agreed on the UN's 17 Sustainable Development Goals. The creation of the SDGs resulted from a process that was more inclusive than ever, with governments involving business, civil society, and citizens from the outset. According to Ban Ki-moon, governments and businesses have never before had such a concrete "to-do list for people and planet." The Goals were introduced and adopted with the ambition to achieve a better future for all – laying out a path over the next 15 years to end extreme poverty, fight inequality and injustice, and protect our planet. The 17 Goals are defined further by 169 specific Targets, which are supported by 230 Indicators that address the most important social, economic, environmental and governance challenges of our time.

GOALS – TARGETS - INDICATORS

The Goals outline clear objectives for 2030. But more specifics were needed to guide governments and companies towards achieving the Goals. As shown in Figure 2, in addition to the 17 broad, ambitious and comprehensive Sustainable Development Goals, 169 Targets associated with these Goals have been specified to give further clarity on *what* is meant exactly and *how* to achieve the Goals. Furthermore, 230 Indicators were established on March 11, 2016 by the United Nations Statistical Commission's Interagency and Expert Group on SDG Indicators (IAEG-SDGs)[6] to guide companies, cities, and countries on *monitoring* their progress and making concrete steps towards achieving the Targets and ultimately the Goals.[7]

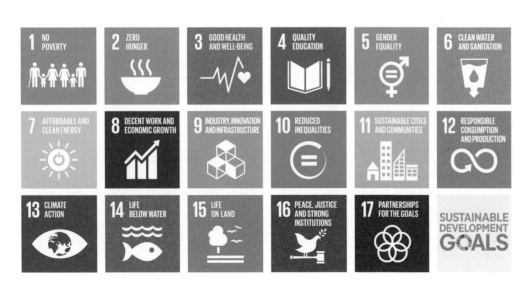

Figure 1

The Sustainable Development Goals

Figure 2
SDG Goals, Targets, Indicators

To explain how the Goals, Targets, and Indicators relate to each other, let's take a few examples.

 SDG 1: No Poverty; This is an ambitious Goal when you consider that in the year 2000, there were 1.75 billion people living in poverty. This number has decreased to 900 million, but we are still a long way off from the goal of no poverty by the year 2030. To get there, seven Targets have been set to give guidance on how to start to eliminate poverty. And twelve Indicators are specified to guide measurements of the Targets. As an example, for SDG 1, we will look at Target 1.1 which reads: "By 2030, eradicate extreme poverty for all people everywhere, currently measured as people living on less than US $1.25 a day." This is a more clearly defined Target than the overall Goal. Then, Indicator 1.1.1 for Target number 1.1 gives guidance on how to measure the progress, namely that countries, cities, and companies should break down their target areas and measure poverty according to the "Proportion of population below the international poverty line, by sex, age, employment status and geographical location (urban/rural)." So the Targets and Indicators define

and measure, ultimately helping to structure concrete Key Performance Indicators (KPIs)[8] towards achieving the Goals.

 SDG 2: Zero Hunger; Again, an extremely ambitious Goal considering in the year 2000, there were 198 million children stunted through malnutrition. By 2016 this number had decreased a bit to 155 million.[9] Globally the stunting rate fell from 33% in 2000 to 23% in 2016[10], but progress made in those sixteen years is a mere fraction of what must be achieved in the next twelve to thirteen years. How the world will approach this Goal has been broken down into eight Targets and 14 Indicators. Looking at Target 2.1, it states: "By 2030, end hunger and ensure access by all people, in particular the poor and people in vulnerable situations, including infants, to safe, nutritious and sufficient food all year round." And the two associated Indicators for this Target ask for progressive measurements to be checked for: "Prevalence of undernourishment" (Indicator 2.1.1) and the "Prevalence of moderate or severe food insecurity in the population, based on the Food Insecurity Experience Scale (FIES)" (Indicator 2.1.2).

SDG 7: Affordable and Clean Energy; From the 169 total Targets that have been specified for all of the SDGs, there are five Targets for SDG 7, related to energy efficiency and renewable energy. And there are six Indicators. Now let's take the first two Targets that have been laid down for SDG 7, specifically 7.1: "By 2030, ensure universal access to affordable, reliable and modern energy services" and 7.2: "By 2030, increase substantially the share of renewable energy in the global energy mix." For Target 7.1, there are two Indicators: 7.1.1 "- Proportion of population with access to electricity", and 7.1.2 "- Proportion of population with primary reliance on clean fuels and technology." And for Target 7.2, there is one Indicator, namely, 7.2.1 "Renewable energy share in the total final energy consumption." These Targets and Indicators are acutely relevant as there are still 1.2 billion people living without access to electricity and more than 40% of the world's population is still relying on polluting and unhealthy fuels for cooking.[11]

THE GOALS: COMPREHENSIVE AND INTERDEPENDENT

The SDGs are often described as a network of Goals since all 17 are interconnected and interdependent.[12] Impact on one SDG almost always means impacting several others, both in terms of risk and negative impact, and in terms of positive impact. When starting to work with the SDGs, it is crucial to bear this interdependency in mind and be aware of cross effects, since it is relevant for business innovation and strategy purposes. It is equally important not to get lost, or get overly theoretical and end up with trying to impact all the SDGs. Prioritizing is the key to a focused strategy, while keeping in mind the cohesion.

For that reason, the SDGs often get structured, for instance into groups of SDGs relating to ecological, social and economic goals with SDG 17 - partnerships for the goals - as the overarching and connecting factor. Also, grouping the SDGs according to the kinds of capital they represent can be helpful. Another way of structuring the SDGs is by hierarchy. The Stockholm resilience center[13] did this for the SDGs' impact on food, distinguishing different levels of necessity and impact.

THE SDGs ARE THE BIG PICTURE GOALS. THE TARGETS AND INDICATORS ARE MORE SPECIFIC AND DETAILED.

Whatever method you choose, make sure it is functional. All ways of clustering, reworking or dividing the SDGs are a means to an end, enabling you to: determine and grow your impact on the SDGs, connect with all parties throughout the supply chain, and combine impact with relevant stakeholders.

ENGAGING THE PRIVATE SECTOR

It is expected that the SDGs will engage business far more than the preceding Millennium Development Goals did. Business contributed to the creation of the SDGs, and business will be crucial for the achievement of them as well. As a result, the link between the SDGs and business is closer than it was between the Millennium Development Goals and business. PricewaterhouseCoopers (PwC) mapped in 2015 the MDGs to the SDGs and explored where business thinks it has impact, shown in Figure 3.

A UNIVERSAL LANGUAGE FOR OUR GLOBAL CHALLENGES

It is no doubt that one of the biggest strengths of the SDGs, besides being comprehensive, is the fact that they provide the world with one set of Goals, Targets, and Indicators – which translates easily to business Key Performance Indicators (KPIs), and thus provides one language for all. A true universal language. And the Goals are in fact universal, which I believe is a great achievement. They apply to all parts of the world, but bring different challenges and gaps depending on the part of the world, the state of the economy, country specifics and so on.

Figure 3
MDGs & SDGs

2000	2015		
MDGs	**SDGs**	**How business thinks it impacts the SDGs**	**Which SDGs business sees as an opportunity**
Poverty/Hunger	Decent work and economic growth	●	●
	Zero hunger	●	●
	No poverty	●	●
Education	Quality education	●	●
Equality/Women	Gender equality	●	●
	Reduced inequalities	●	●
Child Mortality	Good health and well-being		
Maternal health		●	●
HIV/AIDS/Malaria			
Environment	Climate action	●	●
	Clean water and sanitation	●	●
	Life on land	●	●
	Sustainable cities and communities	●	●
	Peace and justice Strong institutions	●	●
	Life below water	●	●
Partnership	Partnerships for the goals	●	●
	Industry, innovation and infrastructure	●	●
	Affordable and clean energy	●	●
	Responsible consumption and production	●	●

● Least impact/opportunity (mean index score <15)   ● Moderate impact/opportunity (mean index score 15-20)
● Greatest impact/opportunity (mean index score >20)
Source: PwC SDG Engagement Survey 2015.

It should therefore also become the universal responsibility to achieve the Goals around the world, not only in our own region, country, city, household or to the benefit of our own company. In a 2016 report by the SDG Fund,[14] the "principle of universality" is described as the foundational value of the SDGs. The report states: "The 'principle of universality' has been widely characterized as a foundational value of the SDGs– and also one of its more innovative ones. It has a long-standing tradition in the UN system and underlies much of its normative work, for instance in the realm of human rights. However, its application has usually been confined to specific regulatory frameworks, not to an all-encompassing programmatic agenda. Unlike the previous MDGs, which were conceived mainly as an agenda for development centered on attaining a set of basic, minimum living standards in developing countries, the 2030 Agenda is universal in scope. Universal means that the subject belongs or extends to all countries and their people. The SDG Agenda is no longer about developed and developing countries, the rich and the poor; it now extends worldwide. The Agenda commits all countries to contribute towards a comprehensive effort for global sustainability in all its dimensions – social, economic and environmental – while ensuring equity, peace and security. These goals show that our society, from each individual to every collective organization, has an agenda to achieve and that sustainable development has become a must for all if the world is to survive and progress is to be shared."

ONE LANGUAGE FOR ALL

The SDGs, Targets, and Indicators outline a common agenda, clear guidance and measurement markers. They also provide all players with a common language. This communication tool is vital in the global movement, and successful implementation will require everyone to champion this agenda and communicate accordingly. So much effort has turned to dust, or has been delayed, simply because stakeholders or people around the world weren't able to fully understand each other. Progress has been impeded just because of communication breakdowns due to language, or narrative, or, most importantly, definitions.

The SDGs have provided us all - governments, business, NGOs, science, and private citizens alike - with one language to discuss our common ground. This is a major step and pathway to gather strength from around the world.

For the first time, great effort has been put into creating the Goals' structure, its language, its presentation and visualization, and to making it very attractive and inspiring. The colors of the icons are positive, the Targets are short and clear, and the Indicators are concrete and easily translated to an organization's own KPIs. Over the last couple of years, the language of the SDGs has become widespread and has served as an inspiration to many, including this book. For companies, it is great to profile the SDGs visually on websites and other forms of communication: people recognize the icons and know straight away what they mean; they communicate your contribution. And that is tremendously effective for your reputation indeed.

Companies like IKEA, Unilever, DSM and many others are using the Goals, Targets, and Indicators as a common language when creating their own KPIs. Although each industry and company can and does interpret the Goals and Targets according to their own business needs, the common language helps them collaborate with others for greater efficiency and impact.

> THE SDGs, TARGETS, AND INDICATORS OUTLINE A COMMON AGENDA, CLEAR GUIDANCE AND MEASUREMENT MARKERS. THEY ALSO PROVIDE ALL PLAYERS WITH A COMMON LANGUAGE.

Unilever is a great example of a company really living the SDGs in every way they can. While admitting implementation is a matter of perseverance, as strategy shifts for large companies are not achieved overnight, Unilever recognizes it is absolutely worthwhile to make the shift. With commitment and dedication, success can be achieved with long-term benefits. Unilever's CEO, Paul Polman, stands steadfast in his commitment and consistently points out that you truly can "do good business by doing good." Unilever created a business-focused "master plan" called the Sustainable Living Plan. It is an exemplary model of how a leading company is taking responsibility for achieving the SDGs and tackling several Goals at the same time. Polman succinctly stated, "Every business will benefit from operating in a more equitable, resilient world if we achieve the SDGs. We have an opportunity to unlock trillions of dollars through new markets, investments and innovation. But to do so, we must challenge our current practices and address poverty, inequality and environmental challenges."[15]

CASE NO.

UNILEVER

Unilever Sustainable Living Plan
A Brighter Future; A Better Business

Case applied in: Global
Headquarters located in: The Netherlands /
England
www.unilever.com

IMPACT SDGs

SDG 3 & SDG 6

By 2020 Unilever aims to help more than a billion people improve their health and hygiene to reduce the incidence of life-threatening diseases like diarrhoea. Handwashing, Oral care and Nutrition are major drivers.

SDG 5 & SDG 8

Unilever drives fairness in the workplace, by implementing the UN Guiding Principles on Business and Human Rights, by advancing opportunity for women, and developing inclusive business and increasing the participation of young entrepreneurs in their value chain.

SDG 2 & SDG 12

Unilever aims to reduce the waste associated with the disposal of their products by 50%, as well as sourcing 100% of their agricultural raw materials sustainably, by 2020.

SDG 13

Become carbon positive for their own operations by 2030.

WE CANNOT CLOSE OUR EYES TO THE CHALLENGES THE WORLD FACES.
BUSINESS MUST MAKE AN EXPLICIT POSITIVE CONTRIBUTION TO ADDRESSING THEM. AFTER ALL, BUSINESS CANNOT SUCCEED IN SOCIETIES THAT FAIL.
PAUL POLMAN, CEO UNILEVER

Unilever believes that business must be part of the solution to global challenges. As CEO Polman often states "Businesses cannot be bystanders in a system that gives it life in the first place". In 2010, they launched the Unilever Sustainable Living Plan, which was created as a blueprint for sustainable business. By the end of 2016, they achieved and exceeded their original target of reducing their CO2 emissions, cutting emissions by 43% per ton of production compared to their 2008 baseline (SDG 13). Their other goals for 2020 include helping over 1 billion people improve their health and well-being (SDG 3 & 6) and they have already reached 538 million people through programs on handwashing, sanitation and safe drinking water. They also aim to enhance the livelihoods of 5.5 million people across their value chain, for example with their Project Shakti and other initiatives to improve safety, and equal opportunity (SDG 8), especially for women entrepreneurs (SDG 5). In 2015, they announced their plans to become 'carbon positive' in their operations by 2030, meaning that they aim to eliminate coal from their energy mix entirely (SDG 13). They also aim to directly support the generation of more renewable energy than they consume, making the surplus available to the markets and communities where they operate, and source 100 % of the company's agricultural raw materials sustainably by 2030 (SDG 12).

Already in 2015, Unilever reached another significant milestone when its global factory network of over 240 factories sent zero non-hazardous waste to landfills. This was achieved by using the 'four R approach' of Reducing, Reusing, Recovering, or Recycling. From a financial standpoint, since 2008, Unilever's waste program has contributed to costs avoided of over €250 million, and it has resulted in the creation of hundreds of jobs. By cutting waste and reducing the use of energy, raw materials and natural resources, Unilever has created efficiencies and cut costs, while becoming less exposed to the volatility of resource prices. With their Sustainable Living Plan, Unilever has achieved cumulative cost avoidance of over €700 million since 2008 and created value for people and the planet. They have set out a clear vision: "decoupling growth from environmental impact, while increasing our positive social impact". Now seven years into the plan, Unilever is proving that there is no contradiction between sustainable and profitable growth. In fact, total shareholder return since CEO Polman announced the Sustainable Living Plan is 290%.

The company has been well recognized for its efforts and leadership role, receiving numerous awards. For the last seven years, for example, it has been named the number one company in the annual Globe Scan / Sustainability ranking, based on a survey of 1,000 sustainability experts around the world. Unilever has also regularly topped the relevant category of the prestigious Dow Jones Sustainability Index (DJSI), including in 2017 in the Personal Products sector. Oxfam's latest Behind the Brands report recognized Unilever as the number one company in its sector for its sustainability commitments, while CDP (Climate Disclosure Project), the non-profit global environmental disclosure platform, identified the company as a global leader in corporate sustainability, with a position on this year's A List for climate, water and forests.

CHALLENGE

To improve the health and wellbeing of one billion people whilst decoupling environmental impact from growth; sustainably source 100% of their raw materials, become carbon positive by 2030; enhance livelihoods for millions by 2020 with special focus on women.

OPPORTUNITIES FOR SCALE

Sustainability will continue to be integrated into every corner of the business, and has the opportunity to generate new opportunities and growth: more people are choosing purpose-driven brands, such as Axe, Knorr, Dove, Domestos and Lifebuoy; as consumers' needs adjust due to changes in the environment, Unilever is innovating with new products, such as laundry products that use less water. They are also training more smallholder farmers in sustainable practices, which is making their supply chain more secure. Increasingly, Unilever is using its size and scale (2.5 billion consumers globally use their products daily) to drive more transformative change across the industry. The company is seen as a global leader in the fight on climate change and is leading many global initiatives around deforestation, human rights, sanitation, food waste and transparency amongst other things.

Sources and further information

- https://www.unilever.com/news/news-and-features/2016/Why-the-SDGs-are-the-greatest-growth-opportunity-in-a-generation.html
- https://www.unilever.com/sustainable-living/the-sustainable-living-plan/reducing-environmental-impact/waste-and-packaging/towards-a-zero-waste-business/
- http://businesscommission.org/
- https://www.hul.co.in/sustainable-living/
- https://www.hul.co.in/sustainable-living/a-call-to-action/
- https://www.unilever.com/Images/uslp-unilever-sustainable-living-plan-scaling-for-impact-summary-of-progress-2014_tcm244-481642_en.pdf
- https://www.youtube.com/watch?v=utSYAkQi5hY
- https://www.unilever.com/news/Press-releases/2017/unilevers-sustainable-living-brands-continue-to-drive-higher-rates-of-growth.html

" UNILEVER IS PROVING THAT THERE IS NO CONTRADICTION BETWEEN SUSTAINABLE AND PROFITABLE GROWTH. "

1.3 THE SDGs: FIRST YEARS OF UNFOLDING

In 2015, two significant events took place: the signing of the UN's Sustainable Development Goals and the COP21 Paris Agreement. These two events made it clear that we are on the threshold of a new era. The world's challenges are clear and companies, nations, and industries have embarked on a purposeful journey. We will see, and you will experience by reading this book, that business and capital have a new direction: contributing to a better world, being part of the solution instead of the problem, and creating an enduring – and profitable - business case and sustainable strategy.

The Goals are a new, objective definition of what sustainability stands for. Achieving the Goals means we have made tremendous strides towards developing a better world; a more stable, just and sustainable world. Although there will still be problems to overcome and challenges to face, we'll be at a much better starting point to take on a new set of challenges in 2030 if we can achieve the SDGs by that time.

The launch of the SDGs has had significant impact already. Immediately after their establishment, the SDGs garnered support from the global business community. Word spread and many people learned about the SDGs and frontrunners were quickly committed and involved.

GATHERING THE BUILDING BLOCKS 2015 - 2016

From the establishment and expanded definition of the SDGs in 2015, we saw in 2016 the gathering of the building blocks and the laying of groundwork, with numerous coalitions being formed. At a UN meeting in October 2016, Judith Rodin, then President of the Rockefeller Foundation explained, "To realize the SDGs, we need to foster a new era of collaboration and coordination, and the United Nations Secretary-General has unprecedented convening pow-er to do this by bringing together leaders from different sectors."[16] To that end, many practical platforms were launched by the United Nations, including a private sector partnership platform to scale up innovative finance solutions, a Pioneers' Program to profile SDG champions throughout the world, as well as a number of new business solutions for 2030.

> **"TO REALIZE THE SDGs, WE NEED TO FOSTER A NEW ERA OF COLLABORATION AND COORDINATION."**
>
> PRESIDENT EMERITA, UNIVERSITY OF PENNSYLVANIA & FORMER PRESIDENT, THE ROCKEFELLER FOUNDATION

In addition to the UN initiatives, partnerships involving businesses, industries, and national governments have been established to address the SDGs on a large scale. Global business partnerships such as the Business Commission was launched by Unilever's CEO Paul Polman during the World Economic Forum in Davos in January 2016, urging the private sector to prioritize and make advancements on sustainable development initiatives. Unilever also joined a host of industry partners to create an open platform called Paragon, combining their market research forces in addressing key global development and sustainability challenges. 2016 was also declared "The Year of Green Finance" in the UK, with financial leaders convening to encourage sustainable investments and the divestment from polluting industries such as fossil fuels.

Nations are forming pacts and coalitions as well. Costa Rica, for example, is bringing together a broad cross-section of society including entrepreneurs of large and small companies as well as academics, and civil organizations - all working towards building dynamic links to approach their own challenges regarding things like improving public transportation, and doing this with the

SDGs firmly in mind. And the Netherlands saw seventy signatories from business and civil society including AkzoNobel, Philips, numerous banks, universities, and foundations such as UNICEF all join together in an SDG Charter[17] to provide innovative solutions based on knowledge and technology.

PREPARING A SOUND FOUNDATION 2016 - 2017

In addition to the collaborations mentioned above, assessments and measurement tools have been put in place to get a clear picture of where we are now and what still needs to be achieved. Reports and research have also been done, as mentioned earlier, on how business can contribute to achieving the goals and what new markets are opening up. The World Business Council for Sustainable Development produced an *SDG Compass*[18] to guide companies on how they can align their strategies, and measure and manage their contribution to the realization of the SDGs.

The UN, together with over 6,000 business leaders from all over the world, co-created a *Global Opportunity Report* identifying 15 new sustainable markets. And the Organization for Economic Cooperation and Development (OECD) produced a report in July 2016 on their pilot assessment of the starting positions of six OECD countries related to the SDGs and the distance still needed to go. In the report, they used 86 Indicators for 73 Targets covering all 17 Goals.[19] The intent was to help governments as they prepare to take on the SDG challenges. One of their observations was that, "On average, OECD members have made the most progress on health, water and energy, and have furthest to go on gender equality."[20] Specifically, "health and water are the two Goals where OECD countries are in the best starting position, with nearly 70% of the distance to the SDGs' finish lines already traveled. OECD countries have already traveled at least 50% of the distance to the end level Targets for poverty, food, energy, sustainable cities and oceans. By contrast, gender equality scores are low, with members averaging only around one-third of the progress needed to meet the Target."

Data collection, interpretation, and communication remain key areas for improvement. In the United Nations' *Sustainable Development Goals Report 2016*, it became evident that there was a significant data gap.[21] "Many national statistical systems across the globe face serious challenges in this regard. As a result, accurate and timely information about certain aspects of people's lives are unknown, numerous groups and individuals remain invisible." In their report, they recommend that in order "to fill data gaps and improve international comparability, countries will need to adopt internationally agreed upon standards, while the international statistical community will need to work closely with development partners and other stakeholders to strengthen national statistical capacities and improve reporting mechanisms. New data sources and technologies for data collection and the integration of different sources of data will need to be explored, including through partnerships with civil society, the private sector and academia."[22]

DATA COLLECTION, INTERPRETATION, AND COMMUNICATION REMAIN KEY AREAS FOR IMPROVEMENT.

Research into business intentions and practices is being conducted as well, for example, PwC — one of the world's largest financial consultancy firms — surveyed nearly one thousand businesses about their plans to address the SDGs. They found that while 71% of the companies are planning how they will engage with the SDGs, only 10% are planning to assess their impact on the SDGs that are relevant to their industry, or even understand how to do this. Clearly, there is work to be done to continue to educate and guide businesses.

In July 2016, The Sustainable Development Solutions Network (SDSN) and Bertelsmann Stiftung launched the *SDG index and Dashboards — Global Report* "to provide a report card for tracking SDG progress in countries throughout the world and ensuring accountability." They measured over-

Figure 4
The SDG index
sdgindex.org

	Rank	Country	Score	Rank	Country	Score
	1	Sweden	85.6	41	Argentina	72.5
	2	Denmark	84.2	42	United States	72.4
	3	Finland	84.0	43	Armenia	71.7
	4	Norway	83.9	44	Chile	71.6
	5	Czech Republic	81.9	45	Uzbekistan	71.2
	6	Germany	81.7	46	Kazakhstan	71.1
	7	Austria	81.4	47	Uruguay	71.0
	8	Switzerland	81.2	48	Azerbaijan	70.8
	9	Slovenia	80.5	49	Kyrgyz Republic	70.7
	10	France	80.3	50	Cyprus	70.6
	11	Japan	80.2	51	Suriname	70.4
	12	Belgium	80.0	52	Israel	70.1
	13	Netherlands	79.9	53	Costa Rica	69.8
	14	Iceland	79.3	54	Malaysia	69.7
	15	Estonia	78.6	55	Thailand	69.5
	16	United Kingdom	78.3	56	Brazil	69.5
	17	Canada	78.0	57	Macedonia, FYR	69.4
	18	Hungary	78.0	58	Mexico	69.1
	19	Ireland	77.9	59	Trinidad and Tobago	69.1
	20	New Zealand	77.6	60	Ecuador	69.0
	21	Belarus	77.1	61	Singapore	69.0
	22	Malta	77.0	62	Russian Federation	68.9
	23	Slovak Republic	76.9	63	Albania	68.9
	24	Croatia	76.9	64	Algeria	68.8
	25	Spain	76.8	65	Tunisia	68.7
	26	Australia	75.9	66	Georgia	68.6
	27	Poland	75.8	67	Turkey	68.5
	28	Portugal	75.6	68	Vietnam	67.9
	29	Cuba	75.5	69	Montenegro	67.3
	30	Italy	75.5	70	Dominican Republic	67.2
	31	Korea, Rep.	75.5	71	China	67.1
	32	Latvia	75.2	72	Tajikistan	66.8
	33	Luxembourg	75.0	73	Morocco	66.7
	34	Moldova	74.2	74	Jamaica	66.6
	35	Romania	74.1	75	Paraguay	66.1
	36	Lithuania	73.6	76	Belize	66.0
	37	Serbia	73.6	77	United Arab Emirates	66.0
	38	Greece	72.9	78	Barbados	66.0
	39	Ukraine	72.7	79	Peru	66.0
	40	Bulgaria	72.5	80	Jordan	66.0

all performance across the SDGs and gave a rating based on how well the country is presently doing related to meeting the SDGs. For example, "Sweden's overall index score of 84.5 signifies that Sweden was on average 84.5% of the way to the best possible outcome across the 17 SDGs at this point in time (See Figure 4). This preliminary measurement became the first of many and was an inspiration to measure not only countries' performance on the SDGs, but also cities, business sectors, and individual companies. The World Bank also released their *Atlas of SDGs*, which includes over 150 maps and data visualizations to assist with efforts to track progress in achieving the Goals.[23] Countries are at different stages regarding measuring and monitoring SDG pro-

Rank	Country	Score	Rank	Country	Score
81	Sri Lanka	65.9	120	Bangladesh	56.2
82	Venezuela, RB	65.8	121	Zimbabwe	56.1
83	Bhutan	65.5	122	Pakistan	55.6
84	Bosnia and Herzegovina	65.5	123	Rwanda	55.0
85	Gabon	65.1	124	Swaziland	55.0
86	Lebanon	64.9	125	Kenya	54.9
87	Egypt, Arab Rep.	64.9	126	Ethiopia	53.5
88	Colombia	64.8	127	Cote d'Ivoire	53.3
89	Iran, Islamic Rep.	64.7	128	Lesotho	53.0
90	Bolivia	64.7	129	Uganda	52.9
91	Guyana	64.7	130	Cameroon	52.8
92	Bahrain	64.6	131	Tanzania	52.1
93	Philippines	64.3	132	Burundi	51.8
94	Oman	64.3	133	Mauritania	51.1
95	Mongolia	64.2	134	Zambia	51.1
96	Panama	63.9	135	Congo, Rep.	50.9
97	Nicaragua	63.1	136	Angola	50.2
98	Qatar	63.1	137	Togo	50.2
99	El Salvador	62.9	138	Burkina Faso	49.9
100	Indonesia	62.9	139	Sudan	49.9
101	Saudi Arabia	62.7	140	Yemen, Rep.	49.8
102	Kuwait	62.4	141	Djibouti	49.6
103	Mauritius	62.1	142	Benin	49.5
104	Honduras	61.7	143	Mozambique	49.2
105	Nepal	61.6	144	Guinea	48.8
106	Timor-Leste	61.5	145	Nigeria	48.6
107	Lao PDR	61.4	146	Mali	48.5
108	South Africa	61.2	147	Malawi	48.0
109	Ghana	59.9	148	Gambia, The	47.8
110	Myanmar	59.5	149	Sierra Leone	47.1
111	Namibia	59.3	150	Afghanistan	46.8
112	Guatemala	58.3	151	Niger	44.8
113	Botswana	58.3	152	Haiti	44.1
114	Cambodia	58.2	153	Madagascar	43.5
115	Syrian Arab Republic	58.1	154	Liberia	42.8
116	India	58.1	155	Congo, Dem. Rep.	42.7
117	Turkmenistan	56.7	156	Chad	41.5
118	Iraq	56.6	157	Central African Republic	36.7
119	Senegal	56.2			

gress. Some have assessed the availability of data for each of the global SDG indicators. Uganda reported in July 2016, that it had approximately 35% of its data readily available to measure progress on the 230 global indicators. Estonia also had approximately 14% of its indicators measurable in 2016. And countries such as Colombia, Finland, France, Samoa, Sierra Leone and Switzerland also reported in 2016 that they had aligned or made plans to align their national indicators to the global SDG indicators. Business frontrunners created their own tracking systems to monitor their progress on the SDGs, such as IKEA with their annual *Sustainability Reports*[24] (See Case 2). IKEA's report updates stakeholders on their progress in their People & Planet Positive Strategy.

02

CASE NO. IKEA

People & Planet Positive Strategy
Make a positive difference for people and the environment, today & tomorrow

Case applied in: Global
Headquarters located in: The Netherlands
www.ikea.com

IMPACT SDGs

SDG 7
Affordable and Clean Energy
Become energy independent by being a leader in renewable energy and improving energy efficiency in all operations. By August 2020, IKEA aims to produce as much renewable energy as it consumes in their operations.

SDG 12
Responsible Consumption and Production
Strive to make all home furnishing materials renewable, recyclable or recycled and turn waste into resources. Develop reverse material flows for waste material, ensure key parts of range of products are easily recycled, and take a stand for a closed loop society.

SDG 13
Climate Action
Tackling climate change by committing to produce as much renewable energy as they consume in operations by 2020, and switching their entire lighting range to LED. IKEA is joining with others to take a stand, call for positive change, and inspire others, including customers, to take action.

THE UN SUSTAINABLE DEVELOPMENT GOALS ARE THE MASTER PLAN FOR A CLEANER, FAIRER WORLD. WE WANT TO LEAD WITH PASSION AND PURPOSE TO HELP MAKE THAT WORLD POSSIBLE.
STEVE HOWARD, CHIEF SUSTAINABILITY OFFICER IKEA GROUP

IKEA is committed to helping their customers live more sustainably. They are also one of the signatories to the United Nations Global Compact set of principles - based on human rights, labor, environment and anti-corruption - which are associated with the SDGs. IKEA measures their sustainability impact by tracking the sales of products that are categorized as enabling a more sustainable life at home. They report their progress towards their goals and specify how they are impacting all of the SDGs and working towards fulfilling the Global Compact Principals in their annual Sustainability Report.

Their goals include a fourfold increase in the sales of products geared toward a more sustainable production and consumption (SDG 12) by the end of FY20, compared with FY13. Already by FY15, these sales had more than doubled compared to FY13, to €1,311 million. IKEA is also focused on climate change with a commitment of €400 million through 2020 to support communities most affected (SDG 13). Aiming to offset their energy use, IKEA endeavors to produce as much renewable energy as it consumes in its operations by 2020 in addition to becoming 30% more energy efficient in that same timeframe. IKEA has committed to investing €600 million in renewable energy, which includes sizeable investments in wind farms, solar panels and biomass generators (SDG 7).

As one of the largest retailers in the world, IKEA 's products are resource intensive. As noted by Steve Howard, Chief Sustainability Officer IKEA Group, "The UN Sustainable Development Goals are the master plan for a cleaner, fairer world. We want to lead with passion and purpose to help make that world possible." While protecting the raw materials that go into products, IKEA endeavors to ensure a sustainable supply chain, which they consider vital to their long-term success. IKEA's progress toward the SDGs regarding responsible production and consumption includes 2020 targets aimed at sourcing 100% of wood, paper, and cardboard from more sustainable sources and reusing these materials in the creation of new products. By August 2015, IKEA successfully achieved the target of sourcing 100% of cotton used in products from sustainable sources. To help meet their goals on climate action, IKEA is taking the lead in developing and promoting products and solutions that inspire people to lead more sustainable and climate-friendly lives. Sales performance of such products in 2016 rose to €1,802 million, nearly twice as much as 2013 sales of €641 million. IKEA now has approximately 1,138 products that fall under its range of offerings designed to enable more sustainable and healthier lifestyles. From LED light bulbs to water efficient taps and indoor gardening equipment, IKEA tracks sales of these products to measure their overall impact, and is 70% of the way towards their sales targets in this genre.

CHALLENGE

To develop and revise all products to enable customers to save or generate energy, conserve and re-use water, reduce waste and live healthier lives.

OPPORTUNITIES FOR SCALE

IKEA's work with social entrepreneurs creates livelihood opportunities for women and minority groups, with the ability to expand production capacity and sell the collections in more countries. IKEA will start several new partnerships that will enable IKEA countries and stores to take a consistent approach, while developing partnerships that make real and relevant difference in their local communities. This will expand the delivery of market-specific products to a diverse range of customers.

Sources and further information

- www.ikea.com/ms/en_US/img/ad_content/ IKEA_Group_Sustainability_Report_FY16.pdf
- www.unglobalcompact.org/what-is-gc/mission/ principles
- www.ikea.com/ms/en_US/img/ad_content/ IKEA_Group_Sustainability_Report_FY16.pdf https://www.unglobalcompact.org/what-is-gc/ mission/principles

" IKEA MEASURES THEIR SUSTAINABILITY IMPACT BY TRACKING THE SALES OF PRODUCTS THAT ARE CATEGORIZED AS ENABLING A MORE SUSTAINABLE LIFE AT HOME."

In many respects, 2016 was quite a year. There was a firm SDG breeze: A lot of preparation and analysis took place leading to the clear formulation of ambitions. We saw a lot happen on a positive track, and a foundation was laid. In addition to research, in 2016, the ambitions of sectors and companies that are at the forefront of engaging with the SDGs started to come to life. Those realizing the enormous impact and opportunities for business engaging with the SDGs started pledging, collaborating and formulating individual and collective commitments. However, there were also events in 2016 that shook the foundation, whether we talk about the Brexit, the US elections, or terrorist threats, that could make us doubtful, skeptical or fearful. But in the words of Christiana Figueres, a Costa Rican diplomat and the leading lady in the 2015 Paris Agreement, we need to "stay calm and transform on." The world has chosen a sustainable course and recognized what needs to be done for the long-term benefit of the world and people. This movement will not be stopped by political swings or any other current affairs.

THE WORLD HAS CHOSEN A SUSTAINABLE COURSE AND RECOGNIZED WHAT NEEDS TO BE DONE FOR THE LONG-TERM BENEFIT OF THE WORLD AND PEOPLE.

In October 2016, The World Economic Forum (WEF) assessed the developments thus far by asking a selection of Forum experts to comment on the progress of the individual Goals. Publishing their findings in an article entitled "Sustainable Development Goals: one year on but are we any closer?"[25] they drew five conclusions. Firstly, it is evident that momentum is growing with over 50 countries already integrating the Goals into their national strategy plans. Secondly, the interconnectivity of the Goals is leading to opportunities for greater impact such as "Target 12.3 regarding food loss and waste, which links a range of ambi-

> ## "STAY CALM AND TRANSFORM ON."
> CHRISTIANA FIGUERES, DIPLOMAT – COSTA RICA

tions such as zero hunger, sustainable consumption, land, water, and forestry." Thirdly, although it is clear that strong leadership is needed, at the time of their study there were still only a few good examples. By now, fortunately, leaders are emerging who are making the SDGs a serious focus. They also determined that "one of the great challenges for the next 12 months will be to develop viable business models that attract private investment – sometimes matched with public funding." And lastly, they concluded that better measurement is needed. "Recognizing which businesses are incorporating social and environmental considerations into their business models; which countries have proactive policy practices to share; and – especially – which approaches have not delivered results, is the only way to guarantee efficient, accountable delivery of the Goals."

2016 was a year of tremendous groundwork on which we can build; groundwork in terms of collaborations founded, research and insights gathered, awareness created and initiatives started. Nevertheless, let's not be naive: still only a small minority of businesses are really aware of the Goals, and there is a need for private investment of US $2.5 trillion a year. So, we have only just begun our journey. As the WEF report shows, we need many others to help create a sound foundation on which to build the bridge, so we can all walk the path. There is an urgent need to speed up and scale up, since the scale of our solutions must meet the scale of our goals.

BUILDING THE BRIDGE 2017

The year 2017 as I see it, had to be the year to prepare for acceleration – to move on from the groundwork to building the bridge everyone can walk on. Both the private and the public communities should be able to scale up initiatives by

UN GLOBAL COMPACT PLATFORMS

Early in 2017, the UN Global Compact launched four new platforms to accelerate the achievement of the Goals. These partnerships and platforms form a value chain in the SDG process, involving all the relevant links along the journey from ambition to action. The intention is to coordinate their work in order to make the chain as strong as possible. The platforms focus on activating the SDGs in business worldwide by developing the following perspectives:

1. new solutions
2. new financing
3. new reporting
4. new innovation

The New Solutions Platform is a "comprehensive mapping of solid and scalable sustainable solutions." Sources for this platform comprise of the UN Global Compact´s global network of companies, 80 country networks and more than 600 business schools and 2.5 million students enrolled in the Principles for Responsible Management Education (PRME).

For New Financing, Global Compact has partnered with the Principles for Responsible Investment (PRI) and UNEP-FI to create a platform on "catalyzing financial innovation to identify innovative financial products that have the potential to redirect towards critical infrastructure and sustainable solutions."

Regarding the initiative for New Reporting, Global Compact will concentrate its efforts on developing a widely accepted reporting practice with special focus on "making the reporting useful and relevant for small and medium-sized companies."

And lastly, the concentration on New Innovation will manifest in what is called "Project Breakthrough" in partnership with Volans. The concept is to "connect companies with exponential thinkers and innovators – advancing the understanding of how disruptive technologies can be developed and form new business models." Global Compact has also developed several Apps to help businesses understand the SDGs.

2018, while continuing to develop new ones. In other words: The bridge should be built and ready to support large-scale solutions in 2018 and beyond. Building and maintaining this bridge is a significant task, as it must be firm and far-reaching. And with a long way still to go to achieve the Goals by 2030, we need all businesses and institutions to join in with full participation.

Scale and great impact are crucial if we are to make significant headway towards the Goals. Consider where we currently stand and where we are aiming. In 2016, hunger still affected nearly 800 million people[26] while the goal for 2030 is to end all hunger. CO_2 emissions grew significantly from 2000 to 2015, indexing at a little over 24 million kilotons of CO_2 emissions in the year 2000 to over 36 million kilotons in 2015.[27] Although there has been movement in the right direction with a slowdown in CO_2 emissions since 2015, a more dramatic reduction is still needed if we are to limit the warming of the Earth to 2 or preferably 1.5 degrees as stipulated in the Paris Agreement. In 2006, on average men earned nearly double what women earned, and in 2015, although all incomes have risen, men still earned nearly double compared to women's earnings. And in 2015, there were nearly 60 million young children who did not receive an elementary education.[28] The goal for 2030 is for all children to receive quality education. The bridge we are building must lead to solutions for all of these great challenges and everyone needs to work towards them together.

STILL…795 MILLION PEOPLE AFFECTED BY HUNGER, 36 MILLION KILOTONS OF CO2 EMISSIONS, MEN EARN MORE THAN WOMEN, 60 MILLION CHILDREN NOT IN SCHOOL … THERE IS MORE WORK TO BE DONE.

As global movement to implement the Goals is gaining traction, and the groundwork is being set, countries have started to integrate the SDGs into their national policies, plans and programs. The concrete identification of the shared Global Goals, and assessments of where we stand

now, gives clarity to what still needs to be done. Quite a number of countries around the world are already setting definitive goals and creating a course of action to achieve the goals set by the SDGs and the Paris agreement.

The High-Level Political Forum (HLPF) is the main United Nations platform on sustainable development, established in 2012, and has a central role in the follow-up and review of the 2030 Agenda for the SDGs at the global level. The Forum meets annually and addresses different SDGs each year. (See Figure 5). At the 2017 meeting, HLPF focused on the theme of "Eradicating poverty and promoting prosperity in a changing world." The themes that have been declared for 2018 and 2019 are: "Transformation towards sustainable and resilient societies"; and "Empowering people and ensuring inclusiveness and equality" respectively. In addition to representatives of Member States, 77 Ministers, Cabinet Secretaries, Deputy Ministers, and nearly 2500 stakeholders participated. Twenty-two UN Member States sent a powerful message when, not even a year after the adoption of the 2030 Agenda, they presented their national voluntary reviews at the 2016 High-Level Political Forum. The voluntary reviews explain how each country intends to integrate the SDGs into their national strategies and budget processes.[29] In 2017, the

Figure 5
HLPF Timeline
sustainabledevelopment.un.org

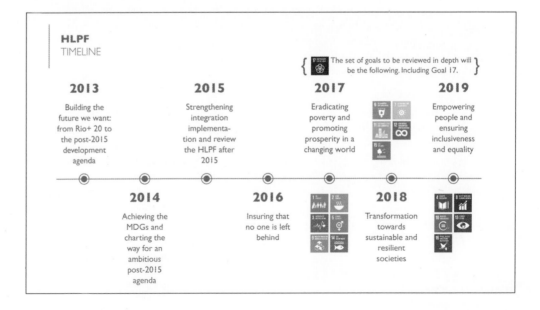

number of countries voluntarily reporting their progress and results nearly doubled to 43, and there are 48 planned for 2018. According to UN General Assembly resolution 70/299, the voluntary reviews aim to "facilitate the sharing of experiences, including successes, challenges and lessons learned."[30] If we take a journey through some of the continents, we can see action in many areas. The following examples of countries' progress and attention to the SDGs shows their commitment to creating a sustainable future.

Asia: The Chinese government has been implementing the 2030 Agenda in all sectors and has made progress on many of the SDGs. In 2016, China's GDP increased by 6.7%, or 74.4 trillion RMB, contributing to more than 30% of global growth.[31] Employment also grew at a fast pace, adding a total of 13.14 million urban jobs and lifting 12.4 million people out of poverty. Living conditions also improved with per capita disposable income increasing by 6.3% in real terms. At this rate, China is expected to achieve the SDG on poverty eradication ten years ahead of schedule. Also in Asia, the Indonesian government is promoting sustainability in business and private-sector organizations, and has been among the most active partners in launching SDG-related activities in the country. Collaborative organizations have brought government, NGOs, philanthropic foundations, and businesses together to improve conditions for their population of 255 million, and their environment which includes 17,000 islands. Indonesia has successfully reduced poverty from 17.75% in 2006 to 10.7% in 2016.[32] Their great challenge now is to reduce poverty even further and improve the welfare of the population. Japan is also looking to improve aspects of their society, namely gender equality, health, and disaster risk reduction. Japan aims to become a role model for the world on implementation of measures to achieve the SDGs, and will work with countries worldwide to achieve the Goals globally. Three cities in Asia rank in the top 10 of smartest cities in the world: Seoul, Hong Kong, and Singapore, with their attention to environmental and economic sustainability. Seoul, for instance has created the "Sharing City Seoul Initiative." Under this initiative, Seoul promotes the shared use of both public and private resources, while at the same time boosting civic engagement and supporting local businesses, and helping to make Seoul more resource-efficient, accessible and sustainable. The economic savings of sharing parking spaces, opening public facilities, and sharing cars in 2015 was nearly US $42 million, according to the city government.[33] South Korea also partnered with Norway to make progress on SDG 4 and encouraged educational institutions to include the SDGs as part of schools' curriculum, and South Korea carried out nationwide campaigns for the implementation of the Goals. Furthermore, the Asia-Pacific SDG Partnership has launched the SDG Data Portal, showing the current status and progress towards the 17 SDGs for the 58 member states of ESCAP (the UN Economic and Social Commission for Asia and the Pacific).

Africa: In Uganda, the government, in collaboration with the UN, organized a national SDG launch event, including an exhibition of the 17 SDGs by stakeholders, and appointed five eminent Ugandans to serve as SDG ambassadors to help raise awareness of the Goals. In both Uganda and Sierra Leone, SDG trainings were provided to journalists. Sierra Leone also prepared an SDG communication strategy to bring attention to and simplify the messages of the SDGs, and organized SDG exhibitions in Freetown as well as campaigns at various universities by engaging with mayors, university teachers and students. And in Kenya, they are currently in the process of integrating climate change into the curriculum for primary and secondary levels of education.[34] The Kenyan government has also directed all Ministries, Departments and Agencies (MDAs) to mainstream the SDGs into policy, planning, budgeting, monitoring and evaluation systems and processes, and they have already established several programs to meet the Goals, including: Mobile health clinics, Water ATMs, and Social protection programs. In many other countries throughout Africa, attention is focused on reducing and ultimately eliminating food insecurity and poverty.

"THE SDGs EXPLICITLY RECOGNIZE THAT WE CANNOT HOPE TO ACCOMPLISH THIS AMBITIOUS AGENDA IF HALF THE WORLD'S POPULATION IS NOT INCLUDED IN DECISIONS, IN POWER, AND IN OPPORTUNITIES."

CANADA'S STATEMENT TO THE 2017 UN HIGH LEVEL POLITICAL FORUM ON SUSTAINABLE DEVELOPMENT

North America: Canada is committed to advancing the SDGs domestically and internationally. Domestically, they are striving to reduce inequality by growing the middle class; investing CA $120 billion in infrastructure over the next decade; renewing their relationships with indigenous peoples; and promoting gender equality and women's empowerment.[35] For gender equality, Canada is taking many concrete steps. They have included a Gender Statement as part of the federal budget, which contains more than 60 measures and investments that are identified as having differential gender impacts.

Tangible actions include CA $101 million towards establishing a national strategy to address gender-based violence, a CA $7 billion investment over 11 years for early learning and childhood development, and providing more flexible maternity and paternity leave. In their work abroad, SDG 5 (achieving gender equality and empowering all women and girls) will be the entry point under Canada's new Feminist International Assistance Policy, and will drive progress on the other SDGs. Gender equality and the empowerment of women and girls has now been placed at the heart of their international assistance efforts, marking a significant shift in their focus and practices. To address climate change, Canada has established the Pan-Canadian Framework on Clean Growth and Climate Change, a concrete plan that will allow them to meet their international commitments. Their Federal Sustainable Development Strategy also addresses the environmental aspects of the SDGs, which they firmly support. And to help bridge the capital gap in funding the SDG

agenda, Canada and Jamaica co-lead a Group of Friends on SDG Financing at the UN, which seeks new sources of public, private, and philanthropic financing for the SDGs. Mexico implemented MY World Mexico in April 2016, gathering nearly 200 volunteers and 60 organizations to work towards spreading awareness of the SDGs and strengthening accountability measures. Mexico also established a "Green Plan" to tackle the intense pollution problem in Mexico City. The strategy has resulted in a set of programs to improve and expand public transportation systems, as well as offer more cycling and walking options. Citizens are being educated about the importance of sustainable mobility's role in fostering a healthier, more mobile, and safer environment. In the United States, there is support for climate action among many States. After it was declared that the United States would withdraw from the Paris climate deal, 14 state governors vowed to continue upholding the agreement and press ahead with policies to fight global warming. California, Colorado, Connecticut, Delaware, Hawaii, Massachusetts, Minnesota, New York, North Carolina, Oregon, Rhode Island, Vermont, Virginia, and Washington formed an alliance together with Puerto Rico to use their knowledge, resources and considerable economic sway to propel sustainable environmental policies.[36] These 14 members represent US $7 trillion of the total $18 trillion US GDP, and generate 1.3 million jobs in clean energy.

South America: In its 2016 Voluntary National Review (VNR) at the HLPF meeting, Colombia reported that it had aligned the SDGs with the peace agreement between the Government and the Revolutionary Armed Forces of Colombia (FARC). It added that the agreement would be the first of its kind with a focus on sustainable development and the SDGs would become a tool for peace-building in Colombia. In Central and South America, nations are also making headway on the Global Goals. The current Five-Year Development Plan (2014 -2019) in El Salvador calls for the implementation of several of the Global Goals including SDG 8 (decent work and economic growth), SDG 4 (quality education) and SDG 16 (peace, justice and strong institutions). This action clearly embodies the three main priorities defined in the Plan: 1. productive employment generated through sustained economic growth; 2. inclusive and equitable education; and 3. effective citizen security. The development of the first phase of SDG mainstreaming in El Salvador is guided by a commitment to building on the results already achieved and on the perspectives shared by more than 4,000 Salvadorans about the "El Salvador We Want" as part of the UN SDG Action Campaign. The Government of Brazil has been a long-standing champion of sustainable development. The Brazilian Institute of Geography and Statistics (IBGE) has represented the Mercosur countries and Chile on the Inter-Agency and Expert Group on Sustainable Development Indicators and has been elected as the new Chair of the UN Statistical Commission, actively contributing to the task of developing the SDG indicators at the global level. The country has also put in place a Post-2015 Agenda Task Force that publishes available national indicators as input for the follow-up process on the SDG targets.

Europe: The European Union will invest €222 million in the fields of environment and resource efficiency, nature and biodiversity, environmental governance and information, and projects supporting climate change adaptation and mitigation. The European sustainable economy projects include: testing an Italian prototype that could cost-effectively convert petrol cars into hybrid vehicles, creating bio-based products from waste-

water sludge in the Netherlands, and applying a new biological treatment to remove pesticides and nitrates from water in southern Spain. In the area of climate action, the EU's projects support their target to reduce greenhouse gas emissions by at least 40% by 2030 compared to 1990 levels. Individual countries in Europe are also aligning their strategies to the SDGs, such as Finland who is pursuing "The Finland We Want by 2050: Society's Commitment to Sustainable Development" which is tied to the 2030 Agenda as well as its Development Policy. Among other countries, Switzerland has also incorporated the SDGs into its Foreign Policy Strategy 2016-2019.

TO ACCELERATE THE CHANGE NEEDED, NOT ONLY BUSINESS AND GOVERNMENTS MUST BE ENGAGED, BUT CAPITAL AS WELL.

And Germany too is a vocal proponent of the SDGs. In addition to campaigning for ambitious implementation by the EU of the SDGs, and calling for a new EU Sustainable Development Strategy, Germany is implementing numerous concrete targets domestically.[37] Countries are also forming new coalitions to advance the SDGs, like Denmark, Iceland, Norway, Sweden and Finland who together launched an initiative called: Nordic Solutions to Global Challenges on May 30, 2017. Their aim is to spread their knowledge and experience related to sustainable solutions. Specifically, their six flagship projects include: energy solutions, sustainable cities, gender effect at work, health and welfare solutions, food policy lab, and climate solutions.[38] Representatives of the Nordic countries point out that much of what they are doing affects all of the SDGs. Furthermore, Sweden has set their own goal to become carbon-neutral by 2045. France is also involved in many private-public partnerships for the Goals, including: The 10YFP Sustainable Food Systems Programme, Climate and Clean Air Coalition and the Sustainable Ocean Initiative.

CASE NO.

TRINE SOLAR

Crowdfunded Solar Investments for the Global South
Innovative financing model for solar projects in the developing world

Case applied in: Africa
Headquarters located in: Sweden
www.jointrine.com

IMPACT SDGs

SDG 1
No Poverty
Helped finance projects worth over €2.5 million, alleviating energy poverty.

SDG 3
Good Health and Well-Being
Replacing kerosene improves indoor air quality and reduces deaths. Pilot investment reduced kerosene use by 72%.

SDG 7
Affordable and Clean Energy
Funds cleaner and decentralized electricity from solar panels by a low interest loan system, delivering electricity and reducing CO2 emissions by 58,000 tons.

SDG 11
Sustainable Cities and Communities
Delivers solar power to more than 194,000 people early on during the urbanization transit to facilitate a sustainable urban growth trajectory.

SDG 13
Climate Action
Estimates saving 3.7 million tons of CO2 annually by 2026.

1 IN 5 PEOPLE ON THE PLANET IS USING KEROSENE AND DIESEL FOR ENERGY, AND **YOU WANT TO HAVE A SOLUTION TO THAT PROBLEM.** IF YOU WANT FUNDING FOR CLEAN ENERGY, **CROWD INVESTING IS THE SCALE PLATFORM NEEDED.**
SAM MANABERI, FOUNDER AND CEO TRINE SOLAR

Since its launch in 2015, TRINE's crowd-investing model for financing solar energy solutions has provided electricity to communities that cannot bear the upfront costs themselves, while delivering a financial return for investors (SDG 11). With an investment minimum of only € 25, even small-scale investors can profit from their impact investment. Many solar energy entrepreneurs in developing countries are waiting to be able to scale their business with fair loans at reasonable interest rates. The loans are paid back with interest by the value of electricity produced from the solar energy system. The model also improves livelihoods for both the investors and the energy recipients and mitigates CO2 emissions. Energy poverty is a critical issue for over a billion people in remote communities around the world. Investors contribute to a set of rigorously vetted potential solar projects. Once raised, the money is transferred to the local partner as a loan, and the interest generated is eventually split between TRINE and the funders. TRINE combines their for-profit business model with positive social and environmental impact to attract individual and corporate investors, who often match sums raised from the "crowd". TRINE's solution fills a financing gap and democratizes financing of solar energy (SDG 7).
TRINE gets its name from a "trifold mission of achieving ROI, social and environmental goals." This innovative crowdfunding investment platform makes an positive impact and generates a return on investment.

Growing access to solar energy is allowing families across Africa to stop using kerosene as an energy source and start using cleaner, cheaper solar energy. It is more environmentally friendly by reducing carbon emissions and is also a far less costly option (SDG 3). However, bringing solar technology to the majority of Africans without electricity remains difficult. Small start-ups are becoming more prevalent and can catalyze sustainable economic growth by providing cheap and clean electricity, bypassing the challenges of expensive power transmission and distribution infrastructure. But they often lack the capital needed to cover manufacturing and shipping costs, making it hard to scale renewable energy. TRINE is also creating opportunities for local industry. In Sidonge, Kenya, for example, plans for solar-powered bottling and refrigeration services would allow locals to sell purified water and milk. TRINE's solar initiative in this region has 16 investors contributing to the €30,000 total amount, helping 250 people and reducing 146 tons of CO2 (SDG 13).

TRINE has helped initiate more than a dozen projects and given over 194,000 people greater access to energy (SDG1). These include a US $25,000 initiative to provide solar lights to fishermen in Jinja, Uganda, expected to generate 6.75% annual returns after a 1.5-year payback period. The company expects to be cash flow positive in two years. If successful, its five-year plan would see one million people gain access to clean energy.

CHALLENGE

To provide the 1.1 billion impoverished people around the world access to electricity by closing the financing gap.

OPPORTUNITIES FOR SCALE

If this investment model gains widespread adoption to 15% of the target group, it has the potential to deliver energy access to 48 million people and save 3.7 million tons of CO_2 emissions annually by the year 2026. TRINE's model is on track to eliminate energy poverty for 66 million people within the next five years and expects its crowd-investment platform for solar energy projects will raise around €100 million by mid 2019.

Sources and further information

- www.jointrine.com/projects
- explorer.sustainia.me/solutions/crowdfunded-solar-investments-for-the-global-south
- www.pv-magazine.com/2017/06/29/swedens-trine-raises-6-million-in-funding-round-for-solar-projects
- www.crunchbase.com/organization/trine#/entity
- report.businesscommission.org
- www.jointrine.com/news/trine-guesting-bbc-business-live

" MANY SOLAR ENERGY ENTREPRENEURS IN DEVELOPING COUNTRIES ARE WAITING TO BE ABLE TO SCALE THEIR BUSINESS WITH FAIR LOANS AT REASONABLE INTEREST RATES."

These countries and many others recognize that the SDGs and sustainability is good for economic growth, as the rest of this book will demonstrate as well. As shown, the SDGs have not only been adopted by countries all over the world, but they are being internalized into policies and programs. However, the general consensus at the HLPF was if the world is to stay on target and achieve the SDGs by 2030, key stakeholders, including governments, must drive implementation at a faster rate. The recent Cop23 climate change summit in Bonn, Germany confirms this conclusion. The UN presented *The Emissions Gap Report 2017* just before the summit. "The overarching conclusions of the report are that there is an urgent need for accelerated short-term action and enhanced longer-term national ambition, if the goals of the Paris Agreement are to remain achievable – and that practical and cost-effective options are available to make this possible."[39]

2018: TIME TO SPEED UP AND SCALE UP

In reference to the latest progress report on the SDGs, UN Secretary-General Antonio Guterres warns: "Implementation has begun, but the clock is ticking…the rate of progress in many areas is far slower than needed to meet the targets by 2030."[40] This most recent report found that while progress has been made over the past decade across all areas of development, the pace of progress has been insufficient and advancements have been uneven to fully meet the implementation of the SDGs.

To accelerate the change needed, not only business and governments must be engaged, but capital as well. Many studies have recently been conducted regarding capital and the SDGs, and awareness of the capital gap has grown. It has become clear that we need an additional US $2.5 trillion a year to reach the Goals, which means private capital needs to shift in investment focus, and blended finance must be developed wisely and utilized more. Public funds, especially in developing countries are often not sufficient to invest in the solutions that will ultimately benefit them. Therefore, blended finance – that is a combination of public and private funding – offers a way forward. Conversely, developed countries, where governments do have money to invest, but want to encourage private investors to engage as well in order to really propel advancements, can use public capital to attract private capital.

PRIVATE CAPITAL NEEDS TO SHIFT IN INVESTMENT FOCUS, AND BLENDED FINANCE MUST BE UTILIZED MORE.

In the case of Trine Solar, the company came up with a modern innovative solution to the lack of capital needed to implement sustainable energy solutions in Africa. They initiated crowd-investing to offer experienced investors as well as people from around the world a pathway to impact investing. Investors can invest as little as US $25 in a worthwhile investment to help developing communities gain access to energy through solar solutions. This model not only provides a much-needed utility to communities that lack access to energy, it also provides investors with a profitable venture and a green one at that (See Case 3).

In the capital world, the SDGs came out at the time that research was already showing that sustainable investing was increasingly paying off. The Organization for Sustainable Investors determined from a study they conducted that "during a period of three years (2009-2011) financial returns in terms of stock rate were 30% higher in 10 high-sustainability companies listed on the AEX, compared to 10 low-sustainability companies in the AEX."[41]

WE NEED MORE ACTIVE INVESTMENTS IN SUSTAINABLE SOLUTIONS.

Capital investors, including large pension funds such as APG and PGGM[42] in the Netherlands, and other asset management organizations throughout the world, have started to turn their attention to the SDGs. They are tracking and reporting their investments according to sustainability and corporate governance performance. Some are joining other investors and organizations like the Global Real Estate Sustainability Benchmark (GRESB) to create standards such as the Global Standard for Portfolio-Level Sustainability Assessment in Real Estate and develop and establish a consistent global sustainability framework.

JOIN TOGETHER TO HELP MEET THE GREATEST CHALLENGE AND BIGGEST OPPORTUNITY OF ALL TIME.

Institutional investors at scale have been divesting from fossil fuel companies. Between 2015 and 2016, the fossil fuel divestment movement doubled, with the value of assets held by divesting institutions and individuals now exceeding US $5 trillion.[43] In May 2017, thousands of people attended over 260 events in 45 countries on six continents during the Global Divestment Mobilization (GDM) organized by the grassroots organization 360.org to call for divestment from the fossil fuel industry. UK universities have emerged as world leaders on fossil fuel divestment as the total global value of funds being withdrawn by higher education institutions tips GBP £80 billion.[44]

In order to achieve the Goals, divestment alone is not enough, we need to level the playing field by eliminating subsidies to fossil fuels. By the end of 2016, more than 50 countries had committed to phasing out fossil fuel subsidies, but this is far from a global commitment. In addition, we need more active investment in sustainable energy solutions. Investment in renewable energy is gaining ground, but again, much more needs to be done.

So if 2017 was the year of preparing to cross the bridge, we definitely have to make sure that regardless of growing risks and instability around us, we have to, like Christiana Figueres said, "stay calm and transform on" with a solid commitment to promote more solutions at a higher speed and a greater scale.

WRAP UP

If we all contribute, we can use the groundwork to build this bridge, and we can look forward to us all crossing it to a sustainable future. Building it will be rewarding and gratifying. And it will be successful business-wise as well. You will see when we look back to admire the bridge we have built, and when we look ahead in anticipation, business, capital, civil society, and governments will be crossing the bridge we have all built together. So, take everybody with you that you can to join together to help meet the greatest challenge and biggest opportunity of all time, for all of us. ■

2

BUSINESS FOR GOOD: A TRILLION DOLLAR BUSINESS CASE

The misallocation of resources, as well as the drive for profitable returns at the expense of humanity and the environment, has all begun to reveal that doing business and employing capital in this way is a costly proposition. The SDGs offer a growth potential of enormous magnitude that, when implemented, could mobilize trillions of dollars. Business and capital have the power, and are well positioned, to take advantage of this unprecedented opportunity. While unlocking markets and guiding trends, capital expenditures for new markets that respond to the SDGs will become sound investments with stable returns. The power of the private sector to innovate and devise solutions is unmatched, and it must be harnessed to steer us in the right direction. By embedding SDG solutions into business models and directing capital toward the common Goals, businesses can scale up their impacts significantly. Shared value is an important model for both business and capital to create value not only for themselves, but for the environment and society as well.

2.1 THE CALL TO BUSINESS AND CAPITAL

The adoption of the SDGs and the Paris Agreement were, in addition to a call on governments, a message from and for the business and capital world. And the message is clear: businesses and capital must aim to create a positive impact on all the assets of the world. They must contribute to developing an economy that is here for the world, and leave behind the exploitation of a world serving the economy.

While business has contributed to the mass destruction of our resources, it also holds the key to the solutions. Therefore, the call to business is necessary as corporations are in fact some of the largest economies in the world, transcending borders with far-reaching influence. Responsible business models are good for the world and they can open many opportunities as well. There is simply no reason not to incorporate the SDGs in business and capital strategies, innovations, products and services throughout the supply chains.

The UN has specifically urged the financial industry to play a larger role in impact investing with the goal of aiding the SDGs. This too is a necessary call to action as capital plays a pivotal role in driving the world towards achieving the Goals.

And a significant shift in investment strategy is needed. The financial sector has created a chasm between the economic and real value of money. For years, maximizing the return on investment has been the name of the game and has been an adrenalin rush that has surged through the entire financial sector. This phenomenon, however, is not solely responsible for the economic crises that ensued, the failing economic system as a whole is to blame.

The financial sector has come to the realization that action is necessary and sustainable practices present a great opportunity. Achim Steiner, director of the United Nations Environmental Program proclaimed 2016 the "Year of Green Finance." During that year, several countries issued strategies for greening their financial systems. China, for example, launched a 35-Point Program[1] with guidelines for establishing a more robust green financial plan. China also became the largest green bond market with issuance of US $30.2 billion.[2] Leading insurance regulators also decided to work together on how to respond to sustaina-

> ## "ETHICS IS THE NEW COMPETITIVE ENVIRONMENT."
>
> PETER ROBINSON, FORMER CEO MOUNTAIN EQUIPMENT CO-OP

bility challenges like climate change. In all, the UN estimates that the number of policy measures to green the financial system has more than doubled to over 200 measures across 60 countries.[3] These policy changes were closely connected with the rapid growth of green finance in the marketplace.

A similar movement can be seen in the traditional shelters of capital: the stock exchange. In 2015, 30 stock exchanges worldwide - including Euronext and Qatar - joined the Sustainable Stock Exchanges initiative, thereby committing themselves to a set of best practices to promote sustainable investment; today that number is up to 56 stock exchanges. Ten years ago, the phenomenon of green bonds didn't even exist. In the meantime, and particularly in 2016, the issuance of green bonds grew rapidly with over US $81 billion in green bonds being issued, showing significant growth of nearly double what it was in 2015.[4] The total cumulative issuance of green bonds has grown tremendously since 2007 and is now over US $215 billion. A further US $19 billion was issued during the first two months of 2017. In fact, Moody's estimates the market for green bonds moving to US $206 billion in total issuance in 2017 alone[5].

THE FINANCIAL SECTOR HAS COME TO THE REALIZATION THAT ACTION IS NECESSARY AND SUSTAINABLE INVESTING PRESENTS A GREAT OPPORTUNITY.

China is especially active in the pursuit of their sustainable economic plan. It is based on their concept of an "Ecological Civilization" (ECZ) which steers investment towards endeavors to conserve energy and resources and protect the environment. Researchers estimate that it would take US $274 to $468 billion of this type of "green investment" each year from 2014 to 2020 to shift the Chinese economy toward an ECZ.[6] All in all, the amount of sustainable investments has increased significantly since 2014. According to the *Global Sustainable Investment Review 2016*, global sustainable investment assets reached US $22.89 trillion at the start of 2016, a 25% increase from 2014,[7] with two-thirds of that growth in Europe, and significant strides in China. This movement, together with the unmistakable trend to divest from fossil fuels, makes it clear that there is a shift in the right direction.

A MESSAGE TO AND FROM BUSINESS

The rise of sustainable business is also visible by the groundbreaking success of the COP21 climate summit in Paris and its successor, COP22. Governments and businesses widely recognize that they share responsibility for what undoubtedly is the greatest challenge in our history: to combat climate change and establish a world economy that is fundamentally sustainable. Over 500 companies and more than 180 investors, representing trillions of dollars in revenue and assets under management, have made more than 1,000 commitments to reduce greenhouse gas emissions.[8] Despite the decision by the United States federal government to retract their collaboration with this agreement, nearly every other country in the world has signed on, and remains committed. In addition, individual cities and states in the US as well as many American businesses also remain committed, and are forming partnerships and significant initiatives to further the goals of the agreement.

Paul Polman put it very well when he aptly said that the Paris summit was "a message to business." And in my opinion, we should also add that it is a message from business! Businesses see the opportunities to unlock markets and innovate. Leading companies are excited to work towards achieving the Global Goals and the Paris agreement reinforces the SDGs. It is not a surprise that 79 large multinational companies signed an open letter supporting the Paris agreement and pledging their commitment to do their part in the efforts to curb climate change.[9] And when US President Trump withdrew from the Paris Agreement, 25 leading American companies signed a letter urging him not to pull out of this historic

> **"WE ARE CEOs FROM 79 COMPANIES AND 20 ECONOMIC SECTORS WITH OPERATIONS IN OVER 150 COUNTRIES AND TERRITORIES, TOGETHER WE GENERATED OVER US $2.1 TRILLION OF REVENUE IN 2014. WE AFFIRM THAT THE PRIVATE SECTOR HAS A RESPONSIBILITY TO ENGAGE ACTIVELY IN GLOBAL EFFORTS TO REDUCE GREENHOUSE GAS EMISSIONS, AND TO HELP THE WORLD MOVE TO A LOW-CARBON, CLIMATE-RESILIENT ECONOMY."**
>
> OPEN LETTER SIGNED IN ADVANCE OF THE PARIS CLIMATE AGREEMENT IN DECEMBER 2015. WEFORUM.ORG

accord. Although the agreement was originally aimed at governments, many members of the business community see the benefits and potential.

The SDGs are a good compass for the business community to develop sustainable business models in various sectors. Companies in virtually all industries see climate action (SDG 13) as one of the five most important SDGs to act on. If businesses worldwide use their power and scale to positively influence the environment and eliminate negative impacts, then we will be well on our way to achieving the SDGs.

Achieving all of the Sustainable Development Goals by 2030 is an ambitious vision. But it is a vision that offers huge growth potential for business and capital. It is a game changer that requires business and capital to be a driving force. Lise Kingo, CEO and Executive Director of the United Nations Global Compact, urges business and capital to contribute to the SDGs. Summarizing the part business plays in the Global Goals, Kingo states "The private sector has the power of innovation and ability to create many of the solutions needed to address the challenges the world is facing today. To meet the SDGs, we need to mobilize businesses to scale up their impacts significantly. The private sector will play an essential role in achieving the Sustainable Development Goals. The most important contribution a company can make is to do business responsibly, and then find opportunities to innovate around these ambitious

global goals. Smart companies and industries that readily embrace this new agenda will be the leaders of tomorrow." [10][11]

An innovative start-up called Sanivation took these words to heart and created a business aimed at solving two of the most pressing issues facing people in developing countries: lack of sanitation due to poor infrastructure, and expensive polluting fuel options. The need to address these issues is significant as diseases caused by unsafe water and the lack of basic sanitation kill more people every year than all forms of violence, including war. Therefore, solutions for these problems are crucial. Sanivation's business model has the potential to unlock a multi-million dollar market, while helping people improve their health and dignity and giving them access to a better, more sustainable and more affordable fuel source (See Case 4).

> **"SMART COMPANIES AND INDUSTRIES THAT READILY EMBRACE THIS NEW AGENDA WILL BE THE LEADERS OF TOMORROW."**
>
> LISE KINGO, CEO & EXECUTIVE DIRECTOR OF THE UNITED NATIONS GLOBAL COMPACT [12]

" THE OPPORTUNITY TO RAISE THE QUALITY OF LIFE IS THE BIGGEST BUSINESS OPPORTUNITY GOING."

ANAND MAHINDRA, CHAIRMAN AND MANAGING DIRECTOR MAHINDRA & MAHINDRA

SANIVATION

Helping people in urbanizing communities throughout Kenya live a modern and healthy life
Addressing the sanitation and fuel need in East Africa

Case applied in: East Africa
Headquarters located in: Kenya
www.sanivation.com

IMPACT SDGS

SDG 3
Good Health and Well-Being

Provides a hygienic place to use the toilet and removes infectious waste from communities, helping to reduce diarrheal disease. Benefits the 70% of Africa's nearly one billion people that do not have access to hygienic sanitation facilities, and the 30% that practice open defecation or use communal pit latrines, which are unsanitary and often dangerous.

SDG 6
Clean Water and Sanitation

Prevents the contamination of local water sources.

SDG 7
Affordable and Clean Energy

Using the briquettes saves up to 15% on monthly fuel costs because of improved performance and efficiency.

EVEN WITH AN AMBITIOUS GROWTH PLAN, SANIVATION MIGHT [ONLY] BE ABLE TO REACH 0.5% OF THE MARKET IN THE NEXT FIVE YEARS. **THAT'S [STILL] ABOUT US $5 MILLION IN ANNUAL REVENUE FROM WHAT USED TO BE A WASTE PRODUCT.**

ANDREW FOOTE, CEO AND CO-FOUNDER SANIVATION

Sanivation was launched in 2014 as a comprehensive program, offering a range of services from toilets and waste collection to the production and sale of waste-based fuel briquettes. The company's mission responds to fuel shortages, water contamination, and health issues. Sanivation's innovative idea to use human waste as a source of fuel, offers many benefits. It saves people money, reduces CO_2 emissions, saves 88 trees per ton used, improves health by improving sanitation and decreases the contamination of water caused by poor sanitation.

Demand for household fuel alternatives is high in many parts of the world, especially in developing regions. In Kenya, over 80% of urban households rely on charcoal for energy. Since 2004, charcoal use has gone up by more than 50% while prices have almost tripled. Moreover, charcoal is a dirty fuel and is responsible for two million deaths annually, and the production of charcoal is a leading cause of forest degradation across the world. The briquettes that are created from feces offer a safer, and longer lasting alternative to charcoal. This innovative idea not only provides safe, affordable and clean energy (SDG 7), it unlocks a whole new market. In Kenya, feces-based briquettes have the potential to meet 50% of the country's energy demand.

Furthermore, adequate hygiene and sanitation is severely lacking in Kenya and other parts of devel-

oping nations. 2.4 billion people across the globe lack access to a decent toilet and live without sufficient sanitation facilities. Nine out of ten people living in rural areas of developing countries still practice open defecation with 90% of human waste being disposed into the environment before being treated. This has caused diarrheal disease to be the second-leading cause of death in the world for children under five, killing 1.5 million children each year. Adequate sanitation alone can reduce diarrheal illness by 37.5%.

Sanivation's solution to both of these issues is to provide toilets and a waste collection service, and use this waste to create a fuel source. The waste collection venture offers a subscription-based sanitation service, where customers pay a monthly fee of 600 Kenyan shillings (about US $6.50) for a Sanivation employee to install a toilet and then pick up the waste twice a week and transport it to the work site (SDG 9). The toilet service helps to prevent the contamination of local water sources and promote good health and well-being (SDGs 6 & 3). Sanivation captures the waste in sealable containers which is transported to treatment facilities. During treatment, valuable resources are recovered before the waste is disposed of in an ecologically friendly manner. The usable resources are treated and turned into briquettes to be used as fuel, which Sanivation then sells at a lower price than charcoal.

CHALLENGE

To solve two pressing issues in Kenya: dependence on charcoal, and inadequate sanitation facilities.

OPPORTUNITIES FOR SCALE

Human waste has the potential to create electricity for 138 million homes and become a US $9.8 billion market globally. The portability and modularity of the container-based model may enable governments to finance improved sanitation in informal settlements without the political issues that come along with piped infrastructure. The combination of income from user fees, sales of recovered resources and government investment could provide a new sustainable financial model.

Sources and further information

- http://www.sanivation.com
- demandasme.org/waste-not-addressing-the-fuel-and-sanitation-need
- solutions.sustainia.me/solutions/toilet-service-offers-sanitation-and-clean-fuel
- www.businessinsider.com/kenya-startup-turns-poop-into-fuel-2016-6
- www.who.int/water_sanitation_health/monitoring/jmp-2015-key-facts/en

" THIS INNOVATIVE IDEA NOT ONLY PROVIDES SAFE, AFFORDABLE AND CLEAN ENERGY, IT UNLOCKS A WHOLE NEW MARKET."

The challenges presented by the 17 Global Goals are all challenges that impact business and capital. Rather than seeing them as problems or growth limiters, companies should see the challenge to meet the Goals and Targets as a huge growth opportunity. Business, capital, and the SDGs are mutually dependent and businesses need the goals as much as the goals need businesses.

> "BY REDUCING THEIR CARBON EMISSIONS, BUSINESSES ARE SAVING MONEY, THEY'RE BUILDING THEIR BRANDS, AND THEY'RE ATTRACTING CONSUMERS THAT WANT TO BUY FROM BUSINESSES THAT ARE ACTING IN THE MOST SUSTAINABLE WAY."
>
> JOHN HOLDREN, FORMER SENIOR SCIENCE AND TECHNOLOGY ADVISOR TO PRESIDENT OBAMA[13]

While some governments are working towards achieving the goals, business can have an even greater impact since business transcends borders and therefore has the power and potential to accelerate the SDGs. Business is also at the heart of creating innovative solutions for the SDGs. For instance: reducing food waste or using more energy efficient alternatives for lighting and fuel are challenges that business can tackle. But innovations and scaling up solutions needs capital.

CAPITAL SUPPORT

Private capital is needed to support business in tackling the global challenges and to finance the innovations that will facilitate the solutions. The additional annual investments needed add up to US $2.5 trillion, whereas only $1.4 trillion is on the table right now (See Figure 6). Solutions for

health, nutritional food, drinkable water and other basic needs require adequate financing, entrepreneurship, and creative business thinking. They need scale as well, since the scale of the business solutions must meet the scale of the Global Goals.

PUTTING THE SDGs AT THE HEART OF CORPORATE STRATEGY DEMANDS A CHANGE IN MINDSET.

Shifting the business model and mindset to meet the SDGs and present sustainable and valuable solutions socially, environmentally as well as financially is, in fact, a model that creates prosperous opportunities. Orientation towards solving the Global Goals creates an innovation driver for companies. It enhances the repurposing of the company to be an innovative part of global solutions, instead of a contributor to global problems. It means companies will reinforce themselves to create enduring, sustainable business models and thus strengthen their existence. Directing your business and capital towards the Global Goals is ensuring your company's own prosperous future.

USING THE GLOBAL GOALS AND THE TARGETS AS A COMPASS TO DIRECT SUSTAINABLE BUSINESS CASES IS PROVING PROFITABLE FOR MANY COMPANIES ALREADY.

Recognizing the many challenges faced throughout the world, and using the Global Goals and the Targets as a compass to direct sustainable business cases is proving profitable for many companies already, and is having a positive impact on people in all parts of the world. For example, the global retailer Gap, Inc. concentrates its efforts on SDG 5: Gender equality, and addresses several Targets within this Goal that not only enhance the company's position but also hold potential to unlock new markets (See Case 5). The McKinsey

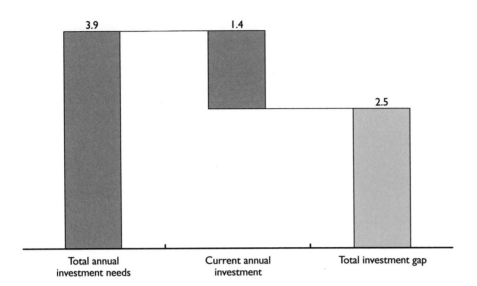

Figure 6 **Estimated Investment Gap in Key SDG Sectors 2015 – 2030 (trillions of USD, annual average)**[14]

Global Institute estimates that the market impact of products and services that focus on gender equality could add up to US $28 trillion, or 26% of annual global GDP by 2025.[15] Increasing the reach of these products and services will have three types of impact: Social, Consumer, and Market. Not only is achieving gender equality an essential human right – it also has the ability to unleash a range of positive economic and development outcomes. Although women and girls have made significant gains in the past decade in terms of education, health, economic participation, and political leadership, gender equality continues to lag in many critical areas. This prevalent inequality comes at the cost of substantial and unrealized social and market benefits. In the majority of the world's wealthiest countries, women are still not paid the same amount as men, essentially leading to less buying power. In the U.S., for example, on average a woman makes 80 cents for every dollar a man earns. What a man makes in 12 months, a woman must work 15 months or more to earn the equivalent amount.[16] The missing 20 cents or 20% adds up.

By focusing on the Global Goals, companies are directing their business behavior towards creating sustainable workforces and sustainable markets. Business and capital, when assuming the responsibility as a force for good, create many exciting prospects and opportunities for growth and endurance. Innovation, technological advances, and using the SDGs as drivers are propelling businesses and capital investors on a new trajectory. This new direction will benefit people and the planet, and will benefit the company's bottom line in the process. The Sustainable Development Goals are truly the world's greatest challenge and biggest opportunity. The response by business and capital to this has the potential to make transformational change that will set the stage for a sustainable future.

CASE NO.

GAP, INC.

Accelerating Gender Equality
Introducing and enhancing training and
education for female garment workers

**Case applied in: Asia, Latin America and
Caribbean**
Headquarters located in: USA
www.gapinc.com

IMPACT SDGS

SDG 1

No Poverty

Employ more women to
improve gender equality, which
is a global issue that Gap
believes is a precondition to
the elimination of poverty.

SDG 5

**Achieve gender equality
and empower all women
and girls**

Provide equal opportunity
to 50,000 women in the
workplace, marketplace and
community in 12 countries,
empowering women with
the skills and confidence to
advance at work and at home.

GAP INC. IS COMMITTED TO A CULTURE OF EQUALITY, **WHERE EVERYONE
HAS THE OPPORTUNITY TO STAND AS EQUALS AND THRIVE.**
ART PECK, PRESIDENT AND CEO OF GAP INC.

Gap, Inc. operates with a strong stance on businesses needing to recognize the opportunity to enhance performance and returns by having more diversity in their workforce. Gap shows how gender equality can pay dividends both for their core business, as well as for society at large. It is the first and only Fortune 500 Company to disclose and validate its pay equality practices. Women make up 73% of the Gap, Inc. workforce, including store managers and the CEO's leadership team. In 2014 Gap, Inc. displayed unprecedented transparency by releasing data confirming that women and men in their workforce are paid equally across all company facilities.

The Gap Inc. P.A.C.E. program (Personal Advancement and Career Enhancement) empowers women with the skills and confidence to advance at work and at home. Designed as an education program offering life-skills classes to female garment workers, the curriculum provides 80 hours of instruction in nine subject areas including communication skills, financial literacy, time and stress management, and problem solving and decision-making. Since GAP launched P.A.C.E. in 2007, more than 50,000 women in 12 countries have participated in the program. Overall, participants reporting higher self-esteem rose by 49% by the end of the program, while women reporting improved self-efficacy and belief in their ability to produce desired results increased by 150%.

The P.A.C.E. program has not only empowered thousands of women, it has also had a strong business impact by reducing turnover and absenteeism, improving work efficacy, higher productivity and retention rates. In Cambodia, for example, retention rates were 66% higher for P.A.C.E. participants than other workers. And at a factory in India, productivity was 15% higher for P.A.C.E. participants. GAP has progressively expanded the program from focusing solely on the women who make its clothes to also include women in surrounding communities, and is also committed to develop new curricula and pursue licensing agreements with NGOs, corporations, and schools to deliver tailored training to more than 500,000 women and adolescent girls in geographies and sectors beyond those where the company has a direct interest. The expansion of P.A.C.E. in workplace and community settings will allow women and girls to acquire the confidence, life skills, and technical abilities needed to enhance their career opportunities and socio-economic mobility. As a broad success, P.A.C.E. reveals participants' significant gains in efficiency, along with improved cost savings and personal benefits to the workers. Through the expansion of the program, there have been improvements in attendance and productivity as well as a general boost in confidence among participants. P.A.C.E. has generated a positive return on the company's investment, with an estimated total value of US $52 million.

CHALLENGE

To improve gender equality in company operations and beyond; relieve financial strain for women by equalizing pay structures and improving women's position in the workforce.

OPPORTUNITIES FOR SCALE

In September 2015, GAP announced a commitment to expand their program to reach one million women around the world by 2020. Their dedication to end discrimination against women is represented at the very highest levels with actions such as CEO, Art Peck, signing the UN Women's Empowerment Principles. P.A.C.E is now being offered to global partners and peer corporations in an effort to broaden its reach and impact for women's empowerment

Sources and further information

- http://www.businessfor2030.org/goal-5-achieve-gender-equality http://www.gapinc.com/content/gapinc/html/media/pressrelease/2016/med_pr_epd_41116.html
- http://sdg.responsiblebusiness.com/wp-content/uploads/sites/2/2016/11/Detailed-Briefing_SDG5.pdf
- http://www.gapincsustainability.com/people/pace-changing-one-million-lives
- https://hbr.org/2017/03/how-companies-can-champion-sustainable-development
- https://adressed.gapinc.com/blog/2017/3/22/gap-inc-history-of-equality-equal-pay-day
- https://www.clintonfoundation.org/clinton-global-initiative/commitments/pace-academy-learning-programs-advance-women-and-girls
- http://www.gapinc.com/content/gapinc/html/media/pressrelease/2016/med_pr_gapinc_catalyst_2016.html

" GAP SHOWS HOW GENDER EQUALITY CAN PAY DIVIDENDS BOTH FOR THEIR CORE BUSINESS, AS WELL AS FOR SOCIETY AT LARGE."

2.2 THE NEW MEANING OF GROWTH

The SDGs support a new vision for growth. In recent times, growth has had quite a negative connotation, as the growth of companies, and economic growth in a wider sense, meant a negative impact on our world: more greenhouse gasses, more resources used, more destruction and more pollution. But now, growth is taking on a new meaning, accelerated and further clarified by the SDGs. Sustainable growth, positive impact, and responsible corporate ambition have entered the stage of world business. While keeping a keen eye on the Goals – and the ambition to meet the SDGs by 2030 – businesses are concentrating on not only minimizing their negative impact but creating positive impact as well. Thus, we must disconnect growth and negative impact, a connection that has existed since the industrial revolution. And we must latch on to a new revolution – one of positive impact for people and planet. Thanks to digital and technological development and the repurposing of business endeavors, we have an unprecedented opportunity to attach a new meaning to growth, namely: sustainable growth ensures societal and environmental benefits and an enduring business.

NET POSITIVE IMPACT

"Net Positive is a new way of doing business which puts back more into society, the environment and the global economy than it takes out."[17] Trailblazing companies are embracing the ambition to "double the business but halve the impact." This can mean that companies increase their positive impact on some goals, and at the same time decrease their negative impact on others. Becoming net positive requires organizations to be ambitious and plan for long-term success. They have to go beyond risk avoidance and incremental improvements and start to innovate. In 2013, Forum for the Future worked with The Climate Group and WWF to convene the Net Positive Group (NPG). This collaboration set out to develop principles, guidance and a measurement framework to help companies achieve net positive impact and plan for long-term success.

RECONNECTING: GROWTH AND IMPACT

Keep in mind that the disconnection of growth and negative impact is not the final destination of the journey. It is a focal point along the way. After disconnecting growth and negative impact, we must then connect growth to positive impact in order to reach real sustainable growth.

> WE MUST DISCONNECT GROWTH FROM NEGATIVE IMPACT AND RECONNECT GROWTH TO POSITIVE IMPACT ON OUR GLOBAL GOALS. THEN WE CAN SPEAK OF GROWTH AS A FORCE FOR GOOD.

Carpet manufacturer Interface changed course years ago to create a positive impact with its growth (See Case 6). They are eliminating their negative impact and creating positive impact as they strive to put more back into society and the environment than they take out, like becoming CO_2 positive by developing more renewable energy than they need themselves and therefore being in a position to supply energy to others in their surroundings. In these cases, growth is good. The examples show that growth in this respect makes a positive impact on the world. We can then truly speak of business as a force for good, and we can look at growth as something that contributes to the world rather than takes from it. As Jay Gould, CEO of Interface clearly states: "Business is the most powerful entity in the world and with power comes responsibility. To have a purpose-driven business you need to pinpoint the crossroads between what the world needs and where your company excels. At Interface, we have been committed to addressing environmental issues for more than two decades, and are approaching our Mission Zero goal to eliminate any negative impact on the environment by 2020. We are now focused on becoming a restorative business through our Climate Take Back mission as we work to address global warming. By transparently discussing our regenerative approach our hope is it will inspire other businesses to challenge their own Sustainable Development Goals and contribute to creating a climate fit for life."

In the coming decades growth must, at the very least, be disconnected from negative impact associations and connected instead to positive impact. This transition is necessary to ensure that we reach our goals in 2030. As the Institute for Human Rights and Business so aptly puts it "Growth should be understood not as an objective in itself, but rather as a means to an end by providing decent livelihoods, increasing security and improving the welfare of all citizens. If growth does not deliver these, it has limited value from a development perspective."[18] The value of growth is the creation of value for society and the environment, and certainly not the exploitation of the world's assets. Exploitive growth with insular financial gain can no longer be tolerated and will, in fact, lead to its own demise eventually as it is simply not sustainable. Growth as a force for good, positive impact, and scaling up sustainable activities is the new meaning of growth.

Greenbiz reports that several companies have directly or indirectly started developing approaches towards net positive impact.

- Rio Tinto: one of the first companies to take on net positive impact approach on biodiversity. The company's framework focuses on avoidance, mitigation and offsetting the negative impacts of its operations. This goal set a benchmark within the mining industry and with other extractive sectors that other companies are now aspiring to emulate.
- The Consumer Goods Forum, an independent global network of retail and manufacturing companies, is showcasing its ability to develop standard approaches with members through its intention to mobilize its collective resources to help achieve zero net deforestation by 2020.
- Puma is developing an Environmental, Social and Economic profit & loss statement that will assess the benefits of their business against their environmental and social costs.

Greenbiz.com The Next Smart Sustainability Idea: A Net Positive Impact Business

06
CASE NO. # INTERFACE

Mission Zero; Net-Works; Climate
Take Back
Moving from negative impact to positive impact

Case applied in: Global
Headquarters located in: USA
www.interface.com

IMPACT SDGS

SDG 7
Affordable and Clean Energy
87% of the energy used at all manufacturing comes from renewable sources.

SDG 8
Decent Work and Economic Growth
Added another revenue stream to fishing businesses by buying their used nets.

SDG 12
Responsible Consumption and Production
Recycled and bio-based materials used globally is 58% and the average carbon footprint has been reduced by 60% compared to the 1996 baseline.

SDG 13
Climate Action
GHG emissions have been reduced by 95% compared with a baseline year of 1996.

SDG 14
Life below water
Reduced pollution in the oceans by repurposing old fishing nets that would otherwise have been discarded into the waters.

WE WANT TO CREATE **A CLIMATE FIT FOR LIFE.**
JAY D. GOULD, PRESIDENT AND CEO INTERFACE

Mission Zero is an initiative that Interface started over 20 years ago. It represents their promise to eliminate any negative impact their company may have on the environment by the year 2020, which is the condition to become restorative. Since they started this initiative, they have reduced their greenhouse gas emissions by 95% (SDG 13), are obtaining 87% of their energy from renewable sources (SDG 7), are producing their products with up to 58% recycled and bio-based materials and have reduced their carbon footprint by 60% (SDG 12).

Net-Works is a cross-sector initiative that Interface began in 2012, when they joined the Zoological Society of London (ZSL) to form a unique partnership to source material in a way that would benefit communities and the environment, and develop a new model of community-based conservation, one that would bring immediate benefits to local people. Net-Works is an innovative business that empowers people in coastal communities in the developing world to collect and sell discarded fishing nets, thereby removing these nets from the ocean where they wreak havoc with marine life (SDG 14). The nets are sold into the supply chain and recycled into yarn to make carpet tile. Since 2012, over 125 tons of nets that would otherwise have been waste have been collected through Net-Works. For context, approximately 640,000 tons of fishing nets are wasted in the world's oceans. Coastal communi-

ties in the developing world are almost entirely reliant on the ocean for their livelihood. Interface aims through the Net-Works model to empower these communities to better protect and manage their local marine resources and to diversify their livelihoods so they are not solely reliant on fishing (SDG 8). Building on the trust that they have developed in these regions, Interface is able to explore and develop other domains such as providing banking and financial services to the fishing communities, many of whom have limited access to financial facilities.

Climate Take Back is Interface's newest endeavor to make a positive impact and take steps to reverse climate change. Interface sees the SDGs as the concrete building blocks for a continuation of what it already started to do in the 1990s. Climate Take Back's positive mission is based on 4 principles and points of attention:

1. **Live Zero:** Making sure no more carbon is put into the atmosphere.
2. **Love Carbon:** Using the carbon that is already in the atmosphere as a building block to make products and resources.
3. **Let Nature Cool:** Running their business in such a way as to not interfere with nature's ability to cool itself.
4. **Lead the Industrial Re-revolution:** Sharing what they are learning, and have learned, to change how business is done.

CHALLENGE

To eliminate any negative impact Interface's companies may have on the environment by the year 2020 and move towards creating positive impact.

OPPORTUNITIES FOR SCALE

Interface will scale up Mission Zero by extending the goals to suppliers in their Suppliers to Zero initiative. In keeping with the vision of Interface Founder, Ray Anderson, that business innovations should give back to the planet, Interface has taken steps to create ProofPositive, a carbon-negative carpet tile. Whilst in its infancy, the ProofPositive tile concept is the first step on the Climate Take Back journey to commercialize products that use bio-based materials and reverse climate change.

Sources and further information

- http://www.interface.com/US/en-US/campaign/climate-take-back/Climate-Take-Back
- https://www.youtube.com/watch?v=4JcfZAjS9Jk
- http://www.thenaturalstep.de/about/interface-case-study/
- Interface Global, 2015 Annual Report
- https://www.greenbiz.com/article/inside-interfaces-bold-new-mission-achieve-climate-take-back
- http://www.interfaceglobal.com/Sustainability/Our-Progress/AllMetrics.aspx
- http://www.interface.com/US/en-US/campaign/negative-to-positive/Climate-Take-Back?cm_mmc=social-organic-_-2016June-_-GreenBiz-_-mission#395291081
- https://issuu.com/sustainia/docs/sustainia100_2016/158
- www.net-works.com
- The Global Findex Database 2014 World Bank
- Fishing's Phantom Menace (2014)

" CLIMATE TAKE BACK IS INTERFACE'S NEWEST ENDEAVOR TO MAKE A POSITIVE IMPACT AND TAKE STEPS TO REVERSE CLIMATE CHANGE. "

2.3 THE SHARED VALUE MODEL

Building on the ambition to move from reducing negative impact to creating a positive impact, the model of Shared Value has become the current, business-driven, sustainable model pervading sustainable global business and capital. The shared value model supports a positive impact for society, the environment, finance, and for all parties involved. It is characterized by the principle: Doing well and doing good are not mutually exclusive. Meaning financial success does not need to come at the expense of society or the environment. And creating a positive impact on society and the environment does not need to come at the expense of profit.

> **"SHARED VALUE IS BASED ON "POLICIES AND OPERATING PRACTICES THAT ENHANCE THE COMPETITIVENESS OF A COMPANY WHILE SIMULTANEOUSLY ADVANCING THE ECONOMIC AND SOCIAL CONDITIONS IN THE COMMUNITIES IN WHICH IT OPERATES."** [19]
>
> **MICHAEL PORTER AND MARK KRAMER**

Financial, societal and environmental benefits can be achieved simultaneously. In fact, at the core of shared value are societal and environmental issues which serve as the drivers in propelling profitable shared value business cases across a wide spectrum of companies and industries. In this regard, shared value is the ideal business model to support the realization of the Sustainable Development Goals.

The trailblazing researchers and business strategists Michael Porter and Mark Kramer first introduced shared value in an article they wrote for the *Harvard Business Review* in 2006 and later expanded upon the concept in 2011 with their article: "Creating Shared Value: Redefining Capitalism and the Role of the Corporation in Society."[20] They defined the concept of shared value as "policies and operating practices that enhance the competitiveness of a company while simultaneously advancing the economic and social conditions in the communities in which it operates."

SHARED VALUE IS:

1. Reconceiving Products and Markets to meet societal needs and address unserved or under-served customers.
2. Redefining productivity practices to better utilize resources, employees, and business partners.
3. Enabling Local Development by improving the available skills, supplier base, and supporting community institutions to boost productivity, innovation, and growth.

Companies of all sizes throughout the world are embracing shared value. At the 2017 Shared Value Summit, over 400 leaders from companies, nonprofits, and governments came together to help shape strategies and discuss innovative ideas that will accelerate this model. These companies and many others are recognizing the benefits of shared value and are ready to move forward away from negative impact avoidance and toward positive impact creation.

Nestlé is one such company that has made shared value a priority in their business strategy and has embedded its principles across all parts of their business, listing an impressive 169 examples on their website of how they are creating shared value.[21]

CORPORATE SOCIAL RESPONSIBILITY CSR	CREATING SHARED VALUE CSV
Adressing societal needs and challenges by giving back + doing no/less harm	Adressing societal needs and challenges with a business model
Doing good	Doing well by doing good
Discretionary or in response to external pressures, no relation with competitiveness	Integral to competing: propels competitive advantage in new, unlocked markets
Separate from profit maximizing, philanthropy	Integral to profit maximizing
Agenda determined by external factors and often personal or departments' preference	Agenda company, sector and market specific
No real influence on innovation, other than incremental	Initiates radical innovation and incremental innovation at scale
Operational and tactical issue	Strategical priority, at the heart of business
Scalable, but from cost perspective	Scalable, with profit increasing
Seen as costs and legitimization of operations for investors	Seen as commercial opportunities for investors

Figure 7 **CSR vs. CSV**
Based on multiple sources

Companies can indeed contribute in a meaningful way. For large food and beverage companies such as Nestlé, shared value involving farmers in developing countries can have substantial impact (See Case 7). Porter and Kramer have assessed the impact of shared value in agricultural cases, saying, "while Fair Trade can increase farmers' incomes by 10% to 20%, shared value investments can raise their incomes by more than 300%."[22] Lifting people from poverty is one way that creating shared value can help achieve the Global Goals. Shared value business cases often touch many Global Goals at the same time, as illustrated by the following Nestlé case.

07 CASE NO. NESTLÉ NESPRESSO

Nespresso - The Positive Cup
Sustainably Sourced Coffee

Case applied in: Europe, South America, Africa
Headquarters located in: Switzerland
www.nestle-nespresso.com

IMPACT SDGS

SDG 8
Decent Work and Economic Growth
Engage 63,000 farmers in 11 countries, representing over 82% of Nestlé's total coffee supply, growing the share of "AAA Sustainable Quality" certified coffee volume from zero to 41% in 8 years.

SDG 11
Sustainable Cities and Communities
Help develop thriving, resilient communities and improve 30 million livelihoods in communities connected to Nestlé's business activities.

SDG 12
Responsible Consumption and Production
Create efficiencies and reduce waste, Nestlé employed new techniques that save an estimated 144 million gallons of water annually.

SDG 17
Partnerships for the Goals
Leverage investments through a series of public-private partnerships channeling US $87 million into regions where AAA coffee is sourced.

> OUR AIM IS TO CREATE MORE VALUE FOR FARMERS, BUSINESS PARTNERS AND CONSUMERS, WHILST AT THE SAME TIME CARING FOR THE ENVIRONMENT. **THROUGH OUR ENGAGEMENT [IN SUSTAINABILITY] WE AIM TO SHOW THE IMPORTANT ROLE THE PRIVATE SECTOR CAN PLAY.**
>
> JEAN-MARC DUVOISIN, CEO NESTLÉ NESPRESSO SA

Nestlé's ambitions are to create shared value by having a positive impact on society and the environment, improving farmer welfare, and driving environmental sustainability in coffee farming and consumption. They believe that in order for their business to prosper in the long term, so too must the communities with which they work. Nestlé describes itself as a "catalyst for change going beyond its own operations."

Nestlé has set 42 commitments to creating shared value. Their commitments are linked to three overarching ambitions: "Enable healthier and happier lives; Help develop thriving, resilient communities; And steward resources for future generations." The company's ambitious goals are rolled into The Positive Cup initiative that addresses these commitments. As part of this vision, their subsidiary Nespresso set new goals in the areas of coffee sourcing and social welfare. In this regard, they are concentrating efforts in a few key areas - aluminum sourcing, resource use, product disposal, and resilience to climate change — which have become important drivers in the company's commitment to play its part in achieving the SDGs.

Nestlé puts these objectives into place with their many shared value projects. One example from their 169 projects is how they are "Improving the skills, opportunities, well-being and productivity of employees, contractors and suppliers" by working with the coffee bean farmers to provide training to improve their practices. This leads to higher qual-

ity beans, higher yields, and higher revenues while leaving a smaller environmental footprint. (SDG 11) This shared value strategy helps these bean farmers improve growing techniques and farm management and become more resilient.

Nestlé's strong stance on innovation has supported volume growth, with 30% of sales coming from products introduced or renovated in the last three years. By creating efficiencies and reducing waste, together with focusing on innovation in responsible production and consumption (SDG 12) Nestlé works towards creating a positive impact on the working conditions in areas where they get their coffee beans. For example, Nestlé Nespresso is creating jobs and economic growth (SDG 8) by pursuing innovative solutions to farmer welfare, including the expansion of their AAA Farmer Future Program through a retirement savings plan for farmers in Colombia, and the provision of training and engagement of 63,000 farmers across 11 countries. Nestlé Nespresso also trained a team of over 300 highly skilled agronomists, and they created shared value for their value chain partners with an extensive agroforestry program, and land management training initiatives in the AAA regions.

Additionally, in 2015, the Nespresso Sustainability Innovation Fund was launched to initiate and attract blended financing solutions — to find new financial mechanisms to interest investors in socio-environmental projects that result in positive impacts (SDG 17).

CHALLENGE

To deliver greater value for society and the environment including the use of only 100% sustainably sourced coffee, 100% sustainably managed aluminum, and 100% carbon efficient operations by 2020.

OPPORTUNITIES FOR SCALE

Nestlé is committed to building on the Nespresso – Positive Cup program, expanding the program in Ethiopia, Kenya and South Sudan, investing over CHF 15 million in these countries over six years, and 500 million in the program overall.

Sources and further information

- https://www.nestle-nespresso.com/sustainability/the-positive-cup
- https://www.nestle.com/asset-library/documents/library/documents/corporate_social_responsibility/nestle-in-society-summary-report-2016-en.pdf
- Nestle In Society: Creating Shared Value and Meeting Our Commitments, 2016 report
- https://www.nespresso.com/positive/us/en#!/sustainability/commitments/coffee
- https://www.nestle-nespresso.com/asset-library/documents/nespresso-positive-cup-csv-report-interactive.pdf
- http://www.carbon49.com/2016/06/nestle-creating-shared-value-environmental-sustainability/
- http://www.nestle.com/csv/what-is-csv
- http://www.eco-business.com/opinion/shifting-markets-and-mindsets-financing-the-sustainable-development-goals/

" NESTLÉ BELIEVES THAT IN ORDER FOR THEIR BUSINESS TO PROSPER IN THE LONG TERM, SO TOO MUST THE COMMUNITIES WITH WHICH THEY WORK. "

Although the awareness of shared value and its implementation into business practices has been growing, it still needs to become common practice. Mark Kramer sees potential in the SDGs. In an interview, he said: "We look at the SDGs and say, 'There is a market here.' You can actually quantify the market potential of for-profit business to meet the needs of the SDGs. Getting business to understand that this is about new markets, new business opportunities, and new business models – instead of charity or the mandate of the development agencies, the government, and the NGOs is a fundamental shift that can be very empowering."[23]

BUSINESS CASES THAT CREATE PROFIT, WHILE ALSO CREATING VALUE FOR STAKEHOLDERS, SOCIETY AND THE ENVIRONMENT, MOVE THE WORLD CLOSER TO SOLVING THE SDGS; THAT IS THE SHIFT WE NEED.

Mark Kramer explains the link between business, the shared value model, and the SDGs as "a new revenue model for business."[24] Business cases that create profit for a company's bottom line, while also creating value for stakeholders, society and the environment, move the world closer to solving the Sustainable Development Goals; that is the shift we need.

This shift, this *Trillion Dollar Shift*, is as much about mindset as it is about business and capital strategy. Positive societal or environmental impact and positive financial results have been considered two separate concepts for a long time. It has been generally accepted that you could have one or the other, but not both. Shared value is all about having both. Shared value is a synergy of positive impact on society, the environment, and the company's bottom line. It combines positive impact and profit by creating economic value and societal value at the same time. It is a sustainable model which I am convinced will sustain us in the future.

CORPORATE SOCIAL RESPONSIBILITY TO CREATING SHARED VALUE

The emergence of shared value was based on Porter and Kramer's observance that, despite the incorporation of Corporate Social Responsibility (CSR), the communities in which companies operated often felt little benefit from their growth and profit. Instead, people tended to perceive that corporate profits came at their expense. The evolution of CSR was a reaction to this consumer perception and a move in the direction to behave more responsibly. Over the years, there has been a gradual acceptance of CSR which "promotes a vision of business accountability to a wide range of stakeholders, besides shareholders and investors, and the key areas of concern are environmental protection and the wellbeing of employees, the community and civil society in general."[25] The underlying idea is that "corporations can no longer act as isolated economic entities operating in detachment from broader society."

SHARED VALUE IS A SYNERGY OF POSITIVE IMPACT ON SOCIETY, THE ENVIRONMENT, AND THE COMPANY'S BOTTOM LINE.

CSR is certainly aimed in the right direction, but has often manifested in philanthropic endeavors with companies making donations to worthy charities or supporting local social clubs and the like. While these are worthy and admirable endeavors, making societal contributions and creating impact that benefit communities, CSR has not been embedded in the fabric of the financial model for profit. It is often viewed as an expense, or an investment in goodwill. Again, the concept that you can have a synergetic model of both positive social and environmental contributions *and* financial gain was not woven into this model. "The common strategy of CSR is that a company maximizes shareholder value, then uses some of those profits for social good. The problem is the first part of maximizing shareholder value often brings a certain level of harm to the environment, their suppliers and customers, and the local communities. With shared value, a company creates economic value in a way that also creates social value."[26] Porter and Kramer draw a distinction between the common activities related to CSR and their business concept of shared value.[27] They explain that "Shared value is not social responsibility, philanthropy, or sustainability, but a new way for companies to achieve economic success." The difference between CSR and Creating Shared Value (CSV) can be seen in Figure 7.

DOING WELL AND DOING GOOD IS NOW EVEN MORE FEASIBLE, THANKS TO THE GUIDING FRAMEWORK OF THE SDGs AND THE SHARED VALUE MODEL.

Porter and Kramer also stated that, "Not all profit is equal. Profits involving a social purpose represent a higher form of capitalism, one that creates a positive cycle of company and community prosperity." The Shared Value Initiative was launched in 2012 by mission-driven consulting firm FSG as a Clinton Global Initiative Commitment to Action.[28] With conferences taking place annually, this Initiative endeavors to bring awareness to the difference between shared value and CSR: "Shared value is a management strategy in which companies find business opportunities in social problems. While philanthropy and CSR focus efforts on *giving back* or minimizing the harm business has on society, shared value focuses company leaders on maximizing the competitive value of solving social problems in new and existing markets while achieving cost savings, talent retention and more. With the help of NGOs, governments, and other stakeholders, business has the power of scale to create real change for monumental social problems."[29] With this in mind, and given the very nature of shared value, it has the inherent potential of making significant headway towards achieving the SDGs. The Sustainable Development Goals go hand in hand with this business model and present concrete objectives for shared value cases. Providing affordable and clean energy (SDG 7) is

one of the objectives set out by the SDGs and is a main driver for many energy companies that recognize that the exploitation of non-renewable resources is not a sustainable model for the long-term. The Italian company Enel has been a traditional energy company with sizable coal, oil, and natural gas assets for the past 55 years. But they have been utilizing the shared value model in recent years to facilitate their transformation to a more sustainable business model. Enel is therefore working to align long-term socio-environmental sustainability goals with its business objectives. They are also responding to investor requests for green assets by broadening their capital market offerings (See Case 8).

SHARED VALUE AS AN INVESTMENT MODEL

Creating Shared Value is not only a business model, it also serves as an investment model as investors look for ways to maximize their financial returns while simultaneously contributing to sustainable activities. Investors utilize Socially Responsible Investing (SRI) and Impact Investing, as well as Shared Value Investing (SVI) strategies. Investment can and does hold enormous sway, and these kinds of investment strategies have great impact as we will explore later on in this book. Figure 9 shows how investment focus can vary and how the shared value strategy inspires investors and Corporate Venture Capital to seek profitable opportunities in solving societal and environmental issues.

Shared value can be incorporated in distinctive ways across a range of contexts, assigning a business strategy that addresses competitive positioning, profit margins as well as the SDGs. Examples of shared value business and investment can be found in a number of areas and sectors. An example from the Health sector is profiled in Case 9 which shows how a company that has a shared value business model and a focus on solving one of societies issues, namely the rise in obesity and unhealthy diets that are fed to US school children, attracted investment that also focuses on supporting businesses with a purpose.

In the United States, weight gain and health issues among children is partly due to unhealthy food

CASE NO. ENEL

Shared Value
Open Power

Case applied in: Global
Headquarters located in: Italy
www.enel.com

IMPACT SDGS

SDG 4
Quality Education
Supported 84,000 educational activities as of 2015, reached 300,000 people in 2016 with projects such as Powering Education in Kenya, Ubuntu in South Africa and scholarship programs in Latin America.

SDG 7
Affordable and Clean Energy
By 2020, Enel aims to generate 1 kWh of electricity while producing less than 350g of CO2 emissions.

SDG 8
Decent Work and Economic Growth
Embedded shared value throughout its value chain. Initial target of 500,000 people exceeded in 2016 with the reach of 1.1 million. New target for 2020 is 1.5 million beneficiaries.

SDG 13
Climate Action
Set several interim targets such as <350gCO2 eq/KWh by 2020, and is on the way to fully decarbonizing the Group's energy mix by 2050.

FOR ENEL, A SHARED VALUE APPROACH IS KEY TO OPENING NEW BUSINESS OPPORTUNITIES BY ADDRESSING SOCIAL AND ENVIRONMENTAL CHALLENGES IN ALL PHASES OF THE VALUE CHAIN.
FRANCESCO STARACE, ENEL CEO AND GENERAL MANAGER

As global energy consumption increases, not only in percentage terms, but also in absolute terms, over 1 billion people still have no access to energy, or have it to only a limited extent. It is becoming increasingly important to attract various industrial sectors and create new opportunities and competitive challenges, while developing the use of renewable energy.

Enel strives to give people access to affordable, reliable and clean energy (SDG 7) by reducing energy poverty, protecting the environment, and protecting local communities. The company is committed to promoting affordable, sustainable and modern energy via its Enabling Electricity initiative, which will benefit three million people, mainly in Africa, Asia and Latin America.

The "Open Power" shared value model began in response to the need to expand the company's long-term presence in emerging-market countries. Enel has now spread this model throughout its organization as they are implementing a shared value model across all business and investment strategies with four main pillars: Engaging the local communities; Engaging the people they work with; Aiming at operating efficiency and innovation; Decarbonizing the energy mix.

Enel engages the local communities by: expanding access to energy with the target to reach three million beneficiaries by 2020 (SDG 7); promoting social and economic development for 1.5 million people by 2020 (SDG 8); and providing quality education to 0.4 million people by the same year (SDG 4).

In their effort to achieve operating efficiency and innovation, Enel promotes global partnerships and supports high-potential start-ups. They have selected 40 innovative start-ups for development projects (SDG 17). And they have deployed Ultra-broad band to 250 municipalities (9.5 million homes) in Italy.

Decarbonizing the energy mix is being realized with their development of renewable capacity, reduction of thermal capacity, specific CO2 emissions reduction, and environmental retrofitting of selected plants (SDG 7 & 13).

As of the first half of 2016, Enel applied the shared value methodology on 528 assets, including plants and distribution networks, while amassing US $82.7 (€75.5) billion in revenue in 2015, and a 17% increase in net income for 2016 (2,570 million euros in 2016 from 2,196 million euros in 2015). In 2016, Enel recorded a share price increase of around 8% - 12%. 68% of the institutional investors are long-term investors, confirming the appreciation of a business model which is sustainable over time.

CHALLENGE

To link the business strategy of Environmental, Social, and Governance (ESG) to concrete values and conduct, and prepare for the challenge of increased demand for energy.

OPPORTUNITIES FOR SCALE

Enel's targets include decommissioning of 13 GW of fossil power plants in Italy, which is a milestone in the long-term goal to operate in carbon neutrality by 2050. Enel will also form partnerships with stakeholders to provide electricity to 3 million people by 2020, assist 1.5 million people socially and economically, increase production of renewable energy, finance the transition to a low carbon economy, and diversify their investor base - targeting investments towards environmentally conscious projects.

Sources and further information
- http://sustainability.thomsonreuters. com/2017/02/22/executive-perspective-enel-climate-leader-and-energy-producer/
- http://sharedvalue.org/resources/enel-redefining-value-chain
- 2015 revenue figures from Enel 2015 annual report
- https://www.enel.com/en/investors/a201608-sustainability.html
- Enel Group Green Bond Framework 2016
- https://www.enel.com/content/dam/ enel-com/investors/2017/ENG_ BDS2016_20170502_4WEB.pdf

" ENEL PROMOTES GLOBAL PARTNERSHIPS AND SUPPORTS HIGH-POTENTIAL START-UPS. "

offerings and is especially prevalent in the lunches supplied in public schools. In reaction to this societal failing and to improve nutrition for young people (SDGs 2 & 3), Revolution Foods was born (See Case 9). This start-up required funding to scale. Investors such as DBL and the Kellogg Foundation recognize the opportunities in Shared Value Investing, and thus helped Revolution Foods accelerate and scale to their present capacity of generating US $130 million in revenue.

Although shared value practices and related investment strategies are growing, the consumer impression that corporate success comes at the expense of communities and the environment still prevails. It has become even stronger in the recent economic recovery, in which rising corporate earnings have done little to offset high unemployment, local business distress, and severe pressures on community services.[30] For this reason, it is cru-

cially important that the shared value model permeates economic strategy. I believe, as Porter and Kramer do, that "shared value could reshape capitalism and its relationship to society. It could also drive the next wave of innovation and productivity growth in the global economy."[31] Shared value is profitable for business and investors. It is good business sense and at the same time helps meet the Sustainable Development Goals. It is a significant step in the right direction, but far more needs to be done. Although the shared value model is the future strategy for business at the micro or meso (sector) level, it cannot carry the necessary shift in financial structure all by itself. We still need impactful system changes at the macro level, such as changes to the short-term shareholder system, realistic and fair pricing and tax systems, and appropriate laws and legislations that facilitate the unlocking of markets. In parts 2 and 3 of this book, I will discuss these points further.

Figure 8 **Shared Value Investing**[32]

Maximize Shareholder Value	Socially Responsible Investing (SRI)	Impact Investing	Shared Value Investing
The fiduciary duty of investors is to focus on economic return	Desire to invest in "good" companies	Business can have both economic and social purpose	Opportunity to drive economic value through social impact
	■ Good social and environmental performance signals good management and mitigates risk ■ Introduces a negative screen into investment analysis	■ Invest in entities that generate social returns along with economic returns	■ All companies can create shared value ■ Shared value expands the opportunity set ■ A natural extension of traditional investment analysis

"GDP IS NOT A GOOD MEASURE OF ECONOMIC PERFORMANCE, IT'S NOT A GOOD MEASURE OF WELL-BEING."

JOSEPH STIGLITZ, ECONOMIST

CASE NO. REVOLUTION FOODS

Shared value investing
Providing Healthy School Lunches

Case applied in: USA
Headquarters located in: USA
www.revolutionfoods.com

IMPACT SDGS

SDG 3

Promote Healthy Lifestyles

Serves over 1.5 million freshly prepared, healthy meals to students across the country each week; the healthy meals ensure more productive, more attentive, better motivated and better performing students.

SDG 8

Decent work and Economic Growth

Provides over 2000 jobs to local inner-city residents.

IT'S SUPER CRITICAL TO HAVE FUNDERS WHO ARE **FOCUSED ON MISSION-BASED COMPANIES.**

KRISTIN RICHMOND, FOUNDER AND CEO REVOLUTION FOODS

Two mothers, Kristin Richmond and Kirsten Saenz Tobey, who had the professional background needed, set out to promote health and well-being within communities (SDG 3) by enhancing school lunch offerings using locally sourced, healthy alternatives. The result was the foundation of Revolution Foods.

The company's mission is to provide every child a healthy meal free of artificial colors, flavors, preservatives, or high-fructose corn syrup. This mission is gaining traction and, with a compound annual growth rate of 125%, Revolution Foods has quadrupled revenue over the past five years. It supports local economies by providing jobs to inner-city employees (SDG 8) who prepare a million meals a week (breakfast, lunch, snack, and dinner) across 25 cities in 10 states and Washington D.C. Each meal costs approximately US $3 and about 85% of Revolution Foods' meals reach children who are in free or reduced-price meal programs. Over 50% of the schools they serve have reported tangible academic improvements since starting with Revolution Foods.

Revolution Foods uses ingredients that students are familiar with – engineering a healthier hot dog, for example. The company's chefs visit classrooms to do taste tests, providing children with colored cards to express themselves. Revolution Foods also caters to regional tastes, depending on the location of the schools. The company sells its product to schools that provide free or reduced-price meal programs via federal funding, which means it needs to keep costs down. It does that in part by cooking in a centralized kitchen and then delivering the meals to schools, where school employees serve the children.

Revolution Foods attracted impact investors. Both DBL Investors, a San Francisco based venture capital fund management firm, and Kellogg saw the opportunity for a shared value investment. Kellogg invested US $5,750,000 in this small company, and together with the funds invested by DBL and other like-minded sources, Revolution Foods had the necessary capital to grow from a small start-up to a thriving company. They currently serve 1600 schools, generated US $130 million in revenue in 2016 – an increase of 25% from 2015 - and employ over 2000 people (SDG 8). Revolution Foods is making a significant impact already and, with 100,000 public schools across the country, has the potential to scale even more. The company expects to continue its growth trajectory, with its dedication to providing healthy foods and creating jobs, enabling it to create economic growth and shared value.

CHALLENGE

To promote healthy lifestyles and change the school lunch structure in the USA by offering a locally sourced, healthy alternative within school budgets.

OPPORTUNITIES FOR SCALE

There is significant potential to scale up for more impact as there are 100,000 public schools in the US. The company is also moving into new markets with its newest venture which is a high-quality packaged meal competing against Kraft Food's Lunchables in supermarkets. They are aiming to provide busy working parents with a quick meal for their families without artificial colors, flavors, or preservatives.

Sources and further information

- http://www.huffingtonpost.com/entry/our-global-goals-need-all-businesses_us_58a76c36e4b0b0e1e0e20aac
- http://haas.berkeley.edu/IBSI/ouralumni/revolution_foods.html
- http://www.dblpartners.vc/
- https://www.forbes.com/sites/geristengel/2016/07/27/revolutionizing-an-industry-by-building-an-empire-based-on-values/2/#2061ee6c3b72
- https://www.fastcompany.com/3039619/revolution-foods

" REVOLUTION FOODS EXPECTS TO CONTINUE ITS GROWTH TRAJECTORY, WITH ITS DEDICATION TO PROVIDING HEALTHY FOODS AND CREATING JOBS, ENABLING IT TO CREATE ECONOMIC GROWTH AND SHARED VALUE."

2.4 UNLOCKING SDG MARKETS AND THEIR POTENTIAL

The Sustainable Development Goals present tremendous opportunities to unlock new markets. Created with a key difference from their predecessor, The Millennium Development Goals, the SDGs were founded in consultation with representatives from the business community. In this regard, the SDGs and the associated Targets and Indicators are tools to be used by business to shape sustainable business cases and it is widely recognized that business is integral to achieving the Goals. As mentioned in the previous section, Mark Kramer describes the fundamental shift to shared value and the unlocking of markets and opportunities as being empowering. This shift is empowering, it is exciting, and it holds enormous potential!

Figure 9 **Four Trends Affecting Business Opportunities**

TRENDS

Changing demographics, Income growth, Technological advances, and International collaborations are the current trends making business opportunities compelling, according to *The SDG Industry Matrix* a report produced by KPMG and Global Compact.[33] Demographically, the population in developing regions is projected to increase from 5.9 billion in 2013 to 8.2 billion in 2050 while the population of developed regions will remain around 1.3 billion. This inspires companies to look to developing regions for potential growth markets. Income growth is developing worldwide, and we can expect to see the bottom 40% nearly double their spending power by 2020 from US $3 trillion to $5.8 trillion. This may be especially visible in countries like India, Indonesia, and Nigeria which are seeing a robust rise in the middle class.[34] Technological innovation and its pervasive implementation is helping to connect to new markets and "catalyzing improved market analysis, knowledge sharing, product and service design, renewable energy sources, distribution models and operational efficiencies. Technology is also lowering market entry costs for non-

traditional actors and start-ups with innovative disruptive business models." Collaborations, as discussed in chapter one, between governments, businesses, international financial institutions, the United Nations, civil society, and academia are developing new ways of working with each other in pursuit of compatible objectives. These collaborations have tremendous power to unlock new markets, even the playing field for sustainable activities, and encourage innovative solutions that pave the way for a more sustainable economy and at the same time work towards achieving the Sustainable Development Goals.

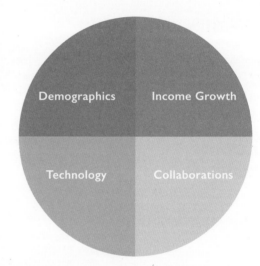

NECESSARY CONDITIONS

Although business is the main driver in achieving the Global Goals and has the means to move the world in the right direction, it cannot achieve the shift alone. There are conditions that need to be met in order to create conducive environments for business to break through established models and constraints and facilitate this shift.

The conditions include:
- Capital and investment cohesion
- Adapted laws and legislation
- Adjusted shareholder model – from short-termism to long-term strategies
- Incorporation of externalities to reflect real pricing

Firstly, innovative financing from both private and public sources will be required to unlock the estimated US $5 to $7 trillion of annual investment needed worldwide. According to the WEF, in developing countries there is US $3.9 trillion in capital and business investment required annually to achieve the SDGs.[35] Presently, there is US $1.4 trillion on the table, leaving a shortfall of US $2.5 trillion yearly.[36] The call to capital will be discussed further in Chapter 4.

Secondly, a new "social contract" between business, government, and society is essential to defining the role of business in a new, fairer economy. Law and legislation changes are often needed to unlock and enable SDG markets and sustainable business.

INVESTMENT CAN AND DOES HOLD ENORMOUS SWAY.

Thirdly, the current short-term shareholder model undermines sustainable strategies. A report by the McKinsey Global Institute[37] showed that firms focused on the long term faired significantly better than those focused on short-term results. Long-term strategy compared to short-term business and investment practices will be discussed in other chapters of this book.

Lastly, if externalities are priced - such as ecological footprint, and social impact - and are incorporated into the accounting, new markets are dominant to the current ones! Pricing externalities, and adjusting capital strategies will be expanded on in Chapter 4.

EMERGING OPPORTUNITIES

Using the 17 Global Goals together with the 169 Targets and 230 Indicators gives guidance and specifics on where to look for opportunities. The SDGs shine a light on the world's challenges, and the Targets make clear what solutions need to be sought. For example, a Danish pump manufacturer, Grundfos, focused their attention on SDG 6: Clean Water and Sanitation, and two of the associated Targets: "By 2030, achieve universal and equitable access to safe and affordable drinking water for all" (Target 6.1), and "Support and strengthen the participation of local communities in improving water and sanitation management" (Target 6.b). Grundfos recognized a need in Kenya for clean water and set out to provide a sustainable solution that adds value to the standard of living for people in Nairobi (See Case 10)[38] and opens up a market for innovation including their new product, the AQtap water dispenser. Their endeavors in Nairobi have been so successful, they are expanding to other developing countries, such as India.

CASE NO. GRUNDFOS

AQtap Water Dispenser
Water ATMs - accessible clean water to
Nairobi's poorest residents

Case applied in: Africa
Headquarters located in: Denmark
www.grundfos.com

IMPACT SDGS

SDG 6
Clean Water and Sanitation
Provides access to clean drinking water to nearly 100,000 residents in Kenya with 40 projects that have been implemented in the country since 2009.

SDG 11
Sustainable Cities and Communities
AQtap dispenser uses mobile technology to provide data on water consumption to the local water board, helping the city's water board plan for the amount of water needed for the local population.

SDG 16
Peace, Justice and Strong Institutions
Liberated people from the control cartels have had on water, initiated freedom to people by ensuring them access to water when they need and want it.

WATER IS ACTUALLY IN EVERYTHING. TO SOME PEOPLE THIS MAY BE OBVIOUS, BUT TO MANY IT COMES AS A SURPRISE. THIS ALSO APPLIES TO THE SUSTAINABLE DEVELOPMENT GOALS. **WATER IS LINKED TO 15 OF THE 17 GOALS.**
MADS NIPPER, GROUP PRESIDENT CEO GRUNDFOS

In Kenya, more than 16 million people – 36% of the population – do not have access to clean drinking water. To solve this problem, a partnership between Grundfos Lifelink and Nairobi City Water and Sewerage Company (NCWSC) was formed in 2015. The goal was to help Nairobi's local water board improve the capacity of its water services and provide low-cost, safe drinking water to consumers.

The lack of access was due to poor water and sewage infrastructure as well as corruption and black market cartels that, without the structure of public water utilities, are able to control the prices of water thereby resulting in high costs for the consumers and potential health risks because of unregulated water sources. In 2015, water consumption in the region was reduced by 2% compared to 2014, and compared to 2008 the consumption has been reduced by 34%. Assisting local communities with water initiatives has been a key factor for Grundfos in reducing water consumption while at the same time increasing access to safe drinking water not only in Nairobi, but also around the globe.

Grundfos recognized the opportunity to grow their business across Africa, responding to water contamination issues (SDG 6), the stability of vulnerable communities (SDG 11), and people's inability to access water due to violence and other dangers (SDG 16). Thus, Grundfos developed an innovative water distribution channel using their recently launched AQtap water dispenser. Now, 100,000 residents can access a water ATM, which uses the company's AQtap technology, and pay a nominal price for their water use via mobile technology provided in partnership with Safaricom. Using this method and technology also provides useful data on water consumption, which in turn helps the city's water board plan for the amount of water needed for the local population.

This innovative solution has a significant impact on the community by providing safe access to clean water. With this access to water, people in Nairobi are able to have a newfound independence. They have the freedom to get water when they want to without fear of danger or disease.

CHALLENGE

To facilitate access to clean drinking water. Worldwide: 663 million people (1 in 10) lack access to safe water.

OPPORTUNITIES FOR SCALE

In the next five years, Grundfos aims to reach 2 million people worldwide, using a similar approach in places like India, Thailand and Bangladesh.

Sources and further information

- http://www.grundfos.com/cases/find-case/water-atms-offer-low-priced-water-to-nairobis-poorest-residents.html
- https://sustainabledevelopment.un.org/partnership/?p=10977
- http://magazines.grundfos.com/Grundfos/SU/UK/GrundfosSustainabilityProgressReport2015
- http://ceowatermandate.org
- https://sustainabledevelopment.un.org/partnership/?p=10977
- http://magazines.grundfos.com/Grundfos/SU/COM/UK/Gmagazineno30
- http://www.grundfos.com/cases/find-case/grundfos-lifelink-projects-in-kenya.html
- http://water.org/water-crisis/water-sanitation-facts

" ASSISTING LOCAL COMMUNITIES WITH WATER INITIATIVES HAS BEEN **A KEY FACTOR FOR GRUNDFOS IN REDUCING WATER CONSUMPTION.**"

Although progress has been made in recent years on improving access to clean drinking water, there is still more to be done. As stated in a report published by *National Geographic*, "Nearly 2.6 billion people have gained access to clean drinking water in the last 25 years. That still leaves about 663 million without sanitary water." The Millennium Development Goals had set the target to halve the proportion of people without access to safe drinking water. The world achieved this goal in 2010. Now, in order to achieve the Goal number 6, set in the Sustainable Development Goals – to "Ensure availability and sustainable management of water and sanitation for all", - there is work to do, and opportunities to explore. Africa, in particular, holds great potential for new markets. At a recent Better Business, Better World conference hosted by Safaricom, on February 23, 2017 the commission found that across the African continent, there is potential for inclusive green growth and development that remains untapped. In Africa alone, sustainable business models could open up an economic prize of at least US $1.1 trillion and create over 85 million new jobs by 2030.[39]

SWEET SPOTS

Developing countries constitute more than half of the total value of opportunities and new markets; US $12 trillion a year and up to 380 million jobs can be generated by 2030, according to a landmark report launched by the Business & Sustainable Development Commission (BSDC) titled: *Better Business, Better World*.[40] The 60 biggest SDG opportunities identified in the report are associated with four main areas, namely: food and agriculture, cities, energy and materials, and health and well-being. These "sweet spots" have the potential to grow 2 to 3 times faster than average GDP over the next 10 to 15 years. According to another report by the Business Commission, *Valuing the SDG Prize*,[41] the 15 largest opportunities are in: (1) affordable housing, (2) circular models in automotive, (3) improving energy efficiency in buildings, (4) the expansion of renewables, (5) circular models in appliances, (6) risk pooling in healthcare, (7) remote patient monitoring, (8) reducing food waste in the value chain, (9) forest

ecosystem services, (10) circular models in electronics, (11) telehealth, (12) electric and hybrid vehicles, (13) improving energy efficiency in non–energy intensive industries, (14) low-income food markets, and (15) energy storage systems."

IN AFRICA ALONE, SUSTAINABLE BUSINESS MODELS COULD OPEN UP AN ECONOMIC PRIZE OF AT LEAST US $1.1 TRILLION AND CREATE OVER 85 MILLION NEW JOBS BY 2030.

The shift to a shared value business model, innovation, and a focus on developing trends directs businesses toward unlocking new markets and developing new ones. A leading report by John Elkington called *The Breakthrough Forecast – Market Sweet Spots 2016 to 2025* also identifies areas in which markets can grow significantly or be unlocked. In this report, 21 areas (sweet spots) are identified, namely: 3D printing, accounting, air conditioning, biomimicry, business education, calming (stress reduction), clean water, construction, data, drones, electric vehicles, finance, food, genomics, geoengineering, Internet of Things, materials, robotics, solar power, space, visualization.[42] Some of these areas coincide with the Business Commission report. For instance, Elkington's mention of air-conditioning as one of the "sweet spots" for growth, shares elements with number 3 listed above from the Business Commission report regarding improving energy efficiency in buildings. Identifying these opportunities, recognizing the global trends of an expanding middle class and an increased demand for indoor cooling due to rising temperatures, and keeping the SDGs in mind, has given way to an innovative business case in air-conditioning, energy use and service management.

A Singapore based company, Kaer Water and Air, has developed a breakthrough business model to lower consumption while increasing their profit. Recognizing that air conditioning is a burden to the environment and energy efficiency is increasingly important to their client base, the company has created a system that alleviates the burden on building owners of managing energy efficiency (See Case 11). Instead of simply capitalizing on an increased demand for their product, Kaer thoughtfully implements an enduring business model that will allow them to increase their sales for the short and long term. Benjamin Lai, General Manager at Kaer, stated succinctly: "Instead of trying to get building owners excited about energy efficiency, Kaer will focus on that, as we now pay the bill under the Kaer Water model. They can focus on their core business and leave sustainability targets to us."[43]

BREAKTHROUGHS

Technological areas such as robotization, drones, 3D printing, and the Internet of Things (IoT) are innovative breakthroughs poised for an explosion of uses in our daily lives. And with these technological advances, there are new opportunities to connect people to knowledge that was previously inaccessible. The technological breakthroughs will have unprecedented ability to break open new

> ## "THE FASTEST-GROWING CAUSE FOR SHAREHOLDERS IS SUSTAINABILITY."
>
> GEORGE SERAFEIM HARVARD BUSINESS REVIEW[44]

markets and reach new target groups. Take for example the case of GSMA and the Airtel Green SIM (See Case 36 Chapter 6) who developed a mobile phone platform to bring information and personal advice to smallholder farmers. Farmers using the Airtel Green SIM with their mobile phones can learn about weather, crop prices, and relevant news, and they can receive customized advice on smart crop combinations, effective and cost-efficient fertilizers, and many other important agricultural points. With their provision of this information, GSMA and their partners tap into the market of 500 million smallholder farmers worldwide.

11

CASE NO.

KAER

Air-Conditioning as a Service (ACaaS)
Revolutionizing the performance of green
buildings with a breakthrough business model

Case applied in: Asia
Headquarters located in: Singapore
www.kaer.com

IMPACT SDGS

SDG 7

**Affordable and Clean
Energy**

Reduce energy costs by 50%.

SDG 11

**Sustainable cities and
communities**

ACaaS helps make cities
sustainable by giving all
buildings access to the best
cooling technologies and
services that reduce the
energy consumed by these
systems by 50-70%.

SDG 12

**Responsible Consumption
and Production**

Reducing the energy
consumed by air-conditioning
systems by 50-70%.

SDG 13

Climate Action

Buildings account for 30%
of the global energy demand
and, in tropical climates,
air-conditioning can account
for up to 50% of a building's
energy requirements.

SIMILARLY TO OTHER PRODUCT-AS-A-SERVICE OFFERINGS LIKE SPOTIFY AND NETFLIX, KAER AIR SPARES CONSUMERS HIGH UPFRONT COSTS AND INSTEAD ALLOWS THEM TO SIMPLY ENJOY A SERVICE WITH BETTER PERFORMANCE, **MORE FLEXIBILITY AND REDUCED RISK. IN THIS CASE: AIR-CONDITIONING.**

JUSTIN TAYLOR, CEO, KAER

Kaer endeavors to assist the world in gaining easy access to the very best cooling services and technologies. No matter the size of business, or industry sector, Kaer's Air-Conditioning as a Service (ACaaS) business model delivers indoor cooling to suit their customer's needs. Kaer Air, the latest service offering from Kaer, allows building owners to purchase air-conditioning on a consumption basis without the need to invest in, maintain or operate any air-conditioning equipment.

Kaer assumes all financial and operational responsibility for the entire air-conditioning system to deliver the ideal environment. Building owners simply dictate the temperature and humidity conditions they want to achieve and Kaer will deliver this wherever and whenever required. This service has no upfront cost and is provided at a fixed monthly fee or a pay-as-you-use rate (SDG 7). In

providing this service, Kaer is responsible for all costs associated with running the air-conditioning system including the electricity and water used by the chiller plant equipment.

Kaer Air is a win-win business model. It lowers demand for the product it sells and delivers the highest performing, most reliable air-conditioning systems for its customers. Reducing this demand allows Kaer to offset the surging demand that urbanization brings (SDG 11). Because Kaer pays for the electricity used by the system this model incentivizes Kaer to operate as efficiently as possible (SDG 12). This incentive drives Kaer to improve the system day after day, resulting in Asia's most efficient systems. Getting better as time goes on, Kaer Air is leading in climate action by allowing building owners to meet their operational, financial and sustainability goals (SDG 13).

CHALLENGE

To help manage the surging global demand for indoor cooling that is driven by rising temperatures and a rapidly expanding middle class.

OPPORTUNITIES FOR SCALE

As the climate warms, there are vast economic and robust business opportunities for cooling systems. Consequently, Kaer is able to expand its markets, locations and offerings. Kaer has predominantly operated in Singapore and Malaysia, yet its potential market is spread throughout the world. It recently moved into India where air conditioning use is expected to rise, already accounting for around 40% of Mumbai's power consumption. Even in cooler Britain, almost 20% of total electricity used goes into air conditioning.

Sources and further information

- http://report.businesscommission.org/case-studies/kaer-case-study
- http://www.eco-business.com/news/game-changing-business-models-for-green-buildings/
- http://www.eco-business.com/news/how-much-do-singapore-businesses-care-about-sustainability/

" BY 2100, CLIMATE CHANGE ALONE COULD PUSH DEMAND FOR AIR-CONDITIONING UP 72%."

> **"WHEN WE THINK ABOUT BREAKTHROUGHS, ONE WAY OF FRAMING IT IS TO THINK ABOUT MINDSETS, TECHNOLOGIES, AND BUSINESS MODELS."**[45]
>
> JOHN ELKINGTON

Consider that mobile subscriptions in Africa have gone from almost no subscribers in 2000 to around 900 million today.[46] Mobile phones have already allowed for dramatic breakthroughs in e-finance and e-health, overcoming long-standing gaps in access to facilities such as bank branches and clinics. John Elkington presented reliable numbers in *The Breakthrough Forecast* showing the market for big data applications having increased by US $39 billion in 2015 with the forecast to further increase to US $76 billion by 2020. A recent report by the Global e-Sustainability Initiative (GeSI) and Accenture Strategy showed that ICT companies could realize an additional US $2.1 trillion in revenue by focusing on services that lead to the achievement of the SDGs. And there are countless other "sweet spots" in various markets where the ICT sector can make a real difference. For example, in less developed parts of the world, billions of people - including many farmers –still do not have access to a banking system. ICT is crucial to facilitating that access and rapidly expanding the accessibility to finance as well as knowledge on a large scale, as we will explore in Chapter 3 ICT and Technology.

THE NEED TO EVOLVE

While Elkington presents many interesting sweet spots to look for business opportunities, and breakthroughs that are opening up markets and possibilities, he also argues that capitalism, markets and business must evolve profoundly by 2025. Gender equality (SDG 5) is one area in which such an evolution must take place. With new business opportunities arising due to the catalysts for implementation of the SDGs, there is an increasing need to drive gender participation as well as women's contribution in the workforce and access to education. Women and girls still lag behind men and boys in opportunities for social and economic growth. For example, participation rates for women in universities in India and China remain at a low 42 to 48%; women are likely to spend 4.5 more years in retirement than men; and only 4.8% of CEOs of Global Fortune 500 companies are women. Accenture Strategy recently published a report entitled *Corporate Disruptors: How Business is Turning the World's Greatest Challenges into Opportunities*[47] that illuminates how gender diverse businesses are more likely to show superior performance in the marketplace. Some of the metrics validating this concept include how gender-diversity likely 1) increases market share, as companies are 45% more likely to witness market share growth; 2) grow market size, as companies are 70% more likely to successfully capture new markets; 3) enhance equity, as companies are likely to achieve 53% higher returns on equity.

GENDER DIVERSE BUSINESSES ARE MORE LIKELY TO SHOW SUPERIOR PERFORMANCE IN THE MARKETPLACE.

YES Bank is one such company that recognizes the need to develop financial products that respond to women's needs. Through the expansion of financial access and business opportunities, YES promotes skill development and technology access for the empowerment of women. Creating an employee value proposition to achieve diversity goals, YES thereby contributes to market evolution while also generating new business models for women (See Case 12).

" SHARED VALUE COULD RESHAPE CAPITALISM AND ITS RELATIONSHIP TO SOCIETY. **IT COULD ALSO DRIVE THE NEXT WAVE OF INNOVATION AND PRODUCTIVITY GROWTH IN THE GLOBAL ECONOMY."**

MICHAEL PORTER AND MARK KRAMER

CASE NO.

YES BANK

Say YES to Inclusive and Social Banking
Empowering women

Case applied in: India
Headquarters located in: India
www.yesbank.in

IMPACT SDGS

SDG 1
No Poverty
YES LEAP reached over 1.3 million women customers across 5,000 villages and disbursed a total of US $500 million in loans.

SDG 5
Gender Equality
YES Bank offers financing to women in order to equalize gender opportunities in India and its LEAP program has been in contact with approximately 40,000 women's groups as of 2014.

SDG 10
Reduced Inequalities
The Inclusion and Social Banking division specializes in serving the 600 million unbanked people India.

SDG 17
Partnerships for Goals
YES Bank has 42 partner business correspondents, with over 700 branches across 19 states in the country.

YES BANK SUPPORTS FINANCING **TO WOMEN ENTREPRENEURS IN INDIA** TO DRIVE FUTURE ECONOMIC GROWTH AND JOB CREATION.
RANA KAPOOR, MANAGING DIRECTOR & CEO, YES BANK

YES Bank reaches out to rural areas to provide banking services to the poor in India, which remains a highly unbanked country, with more than half of the population financially excluded. In 2004, Mr. Rana Kapoor left his job at a multinational bank and started YES Bank with a vision of driving inclusiveness and sustainability across India. The bank uses sophisticated financial tools and adopts advanced technologies that are traditionally available only to big businesses, to develop offerings for the marginalized poor (SDG 1).

YES Bank launched the Livelihood Enhancement Action Programme (YES LEAP) in 2011 to help Indian women (SDG 5). Women's economic participation, educational attainment and health and survival in India is lacking. Although women make up around half of the population, much of the talents, human capital and economic potential of women remain untapped in India as women are still a marginalized and vulnerable group. An estimated three million women-owned businesses in India employ over eight million people. However, only about a quarter of them are able to get the financing they need to grow and create jobs.

YES LEAP provides comprehensive financial services, including credit, savings and micro-insurance to women Self Help Groups (SHG). These groups are typically comprised of 10 to 20 women from local villages that make small regular contributions to a common fund. As the fund grows, money can be lent back to group members to meet their needs. While micro-finance institutions offer a lower interest rate than usuries, it is still difficult for women in rural villages to access credit as individuals because collateral is often needed. YES LEAP closes this gap through providing an unsecured group loan to women SHGs, offering an interest rate comparable to or even lower than micro-finance institutions. The nature of SHGs also ensures that each woman involved in these groups can have access to the fund when needed (SDG 10).

YES LEAP's business correspondents, which include NGOs, Self Help Promoting Institutions and small to medium size enterprises that had already established long-term and credible connections with the SHGs, serve as an important point for the facilitation of YES Bank's financial inclusion services (SDG 17).

The program has made immeasurable impact on the women involved, contributing to the social empowerment and financial security of women, as well as enabling women entrepreneurs to compete with their male counterparts and develop and grow their own businesses.

CHALLENGE

To help bridge the gender gap in India, which ranks among the bottom 30 in gender equality out of 142 countries worldwide.

OPPORTUNITIES FOR SCALE

YES Bank will continue its efforts in innovative inclusive and social banking – not only in relation to technology, but also in understanding the ever-changing demands of customers. YES Bank has set a target to double the amount of loan disbursement under YES LEAP every year over the next 3 to 5 years, aiming to reach out to as many women as possible.

Sources and further information

- http://csr-asia.com/report/Oxfam_CSR_Asia_17.11.15.pdf
- https://www.accenture.com/_acnmedia/PDF-4/Accenture-Strategy-Corporate-Disruptors.pdf
- https://www.yesbank.in/pdf/glocalizing_responsible_banking_mind_share_outcomes_in_india.pdf
- https://www.yesbank.in/media/press-releases/yes-banks-chief-sustainability-officer-receives-leading-women-awards-from-the-world-business-council-for-sustainable-development
- http://www.deccanchronicle.com/business/companies/140717/yes-bank-opic-and-wells-fargo-tie-up-to-support-women-entrepreneurs-smes.html

" THERE IS AN INCREASING NEED TO DRIVE GENDER PARTICIPATION AS WELL AS **WOMEN'S CONTRIBUTION IN THE WORKFORCE AND ACCESS TO EDUCATION.**"

SUSTAINABLE BUSINESS

In addition to new markets emerging, current markets are fading. Markets for products such as non-sustainable energy sources and sugary refreshments are diminishing as demand for these products falls with consumer awareness. At the same time, environmental changes and the development of economies are initiating new demands and opening opportunities for businesses to reach new target groups and develop solutions. Incorporating the Global Goals and the associated Targets in business initiatives and strategies helps companies shape their strategies for enduring success. For many companies, embedding sustainable business practices into operations, business models, and missions is no longer optional, it is imperative in order to remain competitive. Further validating this point, new case studies and data are emerging all the time. A new report published by WWF and ISEAL titled *SDGs Mean Business: How Credible Standards Can Help Companies Deliver the 2030 Agenda*[48] illustrates how forward-thinking businesses can unlock new market opportunities by implementing intelligent and credible sustainability standards across their operations. It also calls attention to how such standards can deliver direct benefits to companies and small-scale producers, while also accelerating progress on the SDGs.

ALTHOUGH THE AWARENESS AND ACCEPTANCE OF CSV AND ITS IMPLEMENTATION INTO BUSINESS HAS BEEN GROWING, THE SHARED VALUE BUSINESS MODEL STILL NEEDS TO BECOME COMMON PRACTICE.

Sustainability standards translate the broad concept of sustainability into specific, concrete measures for companies and their suppliers. With broad uptake, these standards can move whole sectors toward improved social, environmental and economic performance. They are also an important mechanism to help companies reach their targets by scaling-up sustainable practices, and can be used at every point in the value chain – enabling producers, harvesters, and processors to achieve a recognized level of sustainability, and traders, manufacturers and retailers to address the impacts of their supply chains. This can make a major contribution to the SDGs.

EMBEDDING SUSTAINABLE BUSINESS PRACTICES INTO OPERATIONS, BUSINESS MODELS, AND MISSIONS IS NO LONGER OPTIONAL; IT IS IMPERATIVE IN ORDER TO REMAIN COMPETITIVE.

In terms of agriculture, for example, adoption of sustainability standards has encouraged productivity and quality improvements and consequently accounted for net increases in farmers' income. Identifying the societal trends, new hotspots, and sector related opportunities are the necessary components to unlocking the markets associated with the SDGs. These markets are large and plentiful and they have the potential to grow fast and strong.

2.5 A CALL TO ALL BUSINESSES (LARGE, SMEs, START-UPS AND SCALE-UPS)

The journey towards achieving the SDGs by 2030 needs all businesses - large, mid-sized and small - to join in. If they do not, we will fail to reach our destination in time, or we may never arrive at our destination at all. The key to businesses successfully accelerating towards these Goals is a positive synergy between businesses of all kinds and all sizes. This has to do with the value of scale being equally as important as the value of innovation. Let us explore the spectrum of:

1. Large companies – multinationals
2. Start-ups and Scale-ups
3. SMEs – small and mid-sized enterprises

LARGE COMPANIES

Large multinationals are notoriously difficult to turn and are often compared to large ships which take time, and often a seemingly gradual approach, to change course. But because of their sheer size, these conglomerates can have a large net positive impact by reducing their negative impact in some

business areas while creating a positive impact in others. For instance, Nike's Chief Sustainability Officer, Hannah Jones, explained the company's target: "We've set a moonshot challenge to double our business with half the impact. It's a bold ambition that's going to take much more than incremental efficiency – it's going to take innovation on a scale we've never seen before. It's a challenge we are setting for ourselves, our collaborators and our partners as we move toward a circular economy future." [49]

Nike, like Ikea and Unilever, recognize their influence and understand that there is a fundamental change they will need to undergo. They will invariably need time to change their course completely, but change their course, they will. And with clarity of vision and determination, these large multinational companies can have a major positive impact on the environment and on societies all over the world (See Case 13).

> ## "INCREMENTAL CHANGE WON'T GET US THERE FAST ENOUGH."
>
> **MARK PARKER CEO NIKE** [50]

13

CASE NO. **NIKE**

Double Business Growth, Half the Impact
Minimizing Environmental Impacts While
Expanding Profits

Case applied in: Global
Headquarters located in: USA
www.nike.com

IMPACT SDGS

SDG 6
Clean Water and Sanitation
Increased water efficiency by 18% per unit in apparel dyeing and finishing and 43% in footwear manufacturing.

SDG 7
Affordable and Clean Energy
Reduced carbon emissions with continued growth - revenue increased 64% since 2008 and limited absolute emissions to 20%.

SDG 8
Decent Work and Economic Growth
86% of contract factories demonstrated an investment in workers, progressing toward the goal of 100% by FY20.

SDG 12
Responsible Consumption and Production
Designed products that provide superior performance with a lower environmental impact.

SDG 13
Climate Change
In FY15, footwear factories diverted 92% of waste and delivered substantial water reductions.

> I BELIEVE THAT ANY COMPANY DOING BUSINESS TODAY HAS TWO SIMPLE OPTIONS: **EMBRACE SUSTAINABILITY AS A CORE PART OF YOUR GROWTH STRATEGY OR EVENTUALLY STOP GROWING.**
> **MARK PARKER, PRESIDENT AND CEO, NIKE, INC.**

With sustainable growth at the forefront of its business goals, the sportswear giant plans to continue to decrease its total energy use and reduce CO2 emissions, while increasing its clean energy portfolio. As part of its mission to "accelerate toward a low-carbon growth economy", Nike presents its sustainability efforts with three core goals: minimize its environmental footprint (SDG 7 & 13), transform its manufacturing (SDG 6 & 12) and "unleash human potential" (SDG 8). At the same time, they recognize that the two leading drivers of environmental and socio-economic impact across their value chain are the materials used in products and the outsourced manufacturing of those products. Since 2008, the company's contract footwear manufacturers have cut energy use per unit by around 50%. That means in the past decade the company used half the energy and generated around half the emissions to make its shoes. In FY15, Nike reported it had significantly reduced carbon emissions during a period of continued growth – shipping more than 1 billion units and seeing sales rise 52% (from FY11 through FY15).

In 2012, Nike launched its Sustainable Manufacturing and Sourcing Index (SMSI), a system for combining factory ratings with lean manufacturing and human resource management, as well as for health, safety and the environment. Using the SMSI, the company continues to drive factory performance through sound measurements and

metrics. Not only has there been steady progress in factory performance, but Nike's sustainability initiatives have also contributed to the retailer's financial success. Known as a heavy polluter for much of the 1990s, Nike has cleaned up its operations and now boasts some of the highest returns on sustainable investments among North American apparel and footwear companies. According to an in-depth study for investors from Morgan Stanley - measuring a brand's performance on environmental, social, and governance issues -, the expansion of Nike's sustainability initiatives has paid off and it scores at the top of the list among its peers. For example, by embedding sustainability into its innovation process, Nike created the US $1 billion-plus Flyknit line, which uses a specialized yarn system, requiring minimal labor and generating large profit margins. Flyknit reduces waste by 80% compared with regular cut and sew footwear. Since its launch in 2012, Flyknit has reduced 3.5 million pounds of waste.

Nike is an enormous company with over 600 manufacturing partners outside the US, many in developing countries, and as such has an opportunity to have a tremendous environmental sustainability impact on the world. If they can work with their partners and hold them to higher environmental standards (beyond local government requirements) – Nike can impact a significant part of the global supply chain.

CHALLENGE

To reduce overall negative impact and reach 100% renewable energy by the end of FY25 in owned or operated facilities where energy purchase decisions are made on site.

OPPORTUNITIES FOR SCALE

Moving forward, Nike has set a goal of nearly doubling its business to US $50 billion while halving its environmental impact even further by 2020. Nike generated US $30.6 billion in FY15 and promises to add US $20 billion over a five-year period. Nike's eventual vision is to shift its entire supply chain to a "closed loop" ecosystem, embedding sustainable innovation from design to finish.

Sources and further information

- https://rctom.hbs.org/submission/nike-innovating-with-sustainability/
- http://footwearnews.com/2016/business/retail/nike-plans-double-business-environmental-impact-2015-sustainability-report-220481/
- Nike Inc. Sustainable Business Report, Sustainable Innovation is a Powerful Engine for Growth, FY14/15
- https://www.theatlas.com/charts/Vy5fcle2
- https://s1.q4cdn.com/806093406/files/doc_financials/2016/ar/docs/nike-2016-form-10K.pdf

" DOUBLING GROWTH AND HALVING NEGATIVE ENVIRONMENTAL IMPACT IS NOT ONLY A SUSTAINABILITY MEASURE, IT IS A BUSINESS MATTER."

Doubling growth and halving negative environmental impact is not only a sustainability measure, it is a business matter. The challenges we face to combat climate change at this stage need proactive, positive action. It is simply too late for merely a gradual reduction protocol. Because many businesses and governments were too slow and stymied to act when they needed to, we are now at a tipping point. And we need more positive action to make an impact, thereby tipping us in the right direction. However, as mentioned earlier, for large multinationals it is hard to change course quickly and drastically. For this very reason, they should have set their course in the direction of sustainability a long time ago. But I am encouraged that many of them are doing it now. Large multinationals must now step up their actions further, wield their power, and use their force for good.

SCALE HAS IMPACT

Corporations are some of the largest economic entities in the world, ranking higher than many countries. So imagine, if one of those companies reduces their waste and lowers their negative footprint, it already has a huge impact. Now imagine if those giants create positive societal and environmental value, it can turn the tide. If such large multinationals adopt new solutions for the SDGs throughout their product lines, then the scale grows exponentially as does its impact. For example, as shown in chapter 1, the Swedish company IKEA has committed to investing 600 million euros in renewable energy, and aiming for 100% renewable energy as well as producing the total amount of energy they consume by 2020. Unilever is another multinational mentioned in Chapter 1 as being greatly inspired by the SDG timeline to become CO2 positive by 2030.

Large purpose driven companies like these and others, such as Interface, Nestlé, Nike, and DSM have the SDG vision in place for all of their business and product development. At DSM, it means that new innovation must show a positive impact on either the planet or the people, or preferably both, in order to be developed for the global market. For instance, DSM uses its Nutrition Improve-

MANY OF THE TOP 100 ECONOMIC ENTITIES ARE CORPORATIONS, NOT COUNTRIES. WALMART, APPLE, SHELL ARE RICHER THAN RUSSIA, BELGIUM, SWEDEN

ment Program to develop innovative solutions to help fight hunger and malnutrition. The company is committed to improving the nutrition of the two billion people at the bottom of the economic pyramid who are suffering. Their program leads to innovative products such as high-quality micronutrients tailored to the needs of pregnant women as well as to all other segments of developing societies (See Case 42 in Chapter 8).

SMALL COMPANIES AND THEIR GIANT IMPACT

While large companies often transition slowly to a sustainable business model, small companies can move faster. A lot of innovative start-ups and scale-ups are incorporating this new meaning of growth from the floor of their foundation. Their business models are often based on creating a positive impact on the world and bringing about solutions for the SDGs. This makes sense, since they come right off the drawing board, and from the beginning aim directly to be part of the solution for the Global Goals, with more radical innovations enabling faster net positive impact. Large and mid-sized companies, however, often have to combine a longer-term strategy for incremental innovations of their current business model (less bad, reducing the footprint). This is exactly why the SDGs are a call to *all* business: large, mid-size and small. The large and mid-sized companies are impactful because of their volume, but their actions are not quick and encompassing enough. Small companies have the bold solutions, can act swiftly, and they fashion their businesses to wholly support the SDGs and engage in business for good. Now the objective is to link mid-sized and large companies and their capital and networks to these small companies to scale the innovative models and solutions.

START-UPS AIM AT THE HEART OF THE SDGs AND THEIR MARKET POTENTIAL

We have great examples from multinationals effectively addressing the SDGs. But, at the same time, large companies often need disruptive start-ups and scale-ups to be able to reorient from established sectors into SDG growth markets. A tanker simply doesn't shift course as easily as a speedboat does. There are currently many highly innovative, very creative start-ups with high growth potential arising around the globe. These start-ups are born from the orientation towards these new markets and the solutions to the problems facing our world. In other words, their products and services focus on the issues and opportunities presented in the SDGs.

AN EFFECTIVE WAY FOR LARGE AND SMALL COMPANIES TO CONNECT IS THROUGH INVESTMENT, SUCH AS CORPORATE VENTURE CAPITAL FUNDS.

An example of an innovative start-up focused on social impact is found in a unique solution to a problem facing people in Uganda. Pneumonia kills 27,000 children under the age of five every year. Most of these cases are due to pneumonia being misdiagnosed as malaria. Therefore, Ugandan engineer Brian Turyabagye created Mama-Ope[52], a biomedical "smart jacket" to quickly and accurately diagnose pneumonia. The smart jacket can diagnose pneumonia three to four times faster than a doctor and eliminates most possibility for human error. This example and many others like it focus on the pressing issues faced in developing countries as the need for impact on the Goals is the highest there. At the same time, it is in these countries that the biggest business opportunities

are at hand. The Business Commission's report mentions that half of the value of the SDG business opportunities arise in developing countries. And equally important, it states that the majority of jobs, almost 90%, will be created in developing countries. This includes 85 million jobs in Africa and 220 million jobs in developing Asia.

WHEN SMALL MEETS BIG – THE IMPACT IS GREAT

Good things happen when small meets big. Large companies can benefit from the innovation and purpose driven culture of the start-up, and the start-up can benefit from the network of the large company to scale up faster. There are different ways that large companies and small are coming together. One way involves the large companies using the Ambidextrous business model to nurture breakthrough innovation. An Ambidextrous Organization keeps their regular business endeavors going at the same time while creating or incorporating business units that have their own unique processes, structures, and cultures. These business units either identify new opportunities, develop new products or services, or protect a new venture within the umbrella of the large company.

BMW, for instance, is working on their established product by producing more energy efficient and electric cars, and at the same time it is getting into the car sharing arena with their ReachNow enterprise. During the first weeks of operation, over 13,000 people signed up. It has proven successful and BMW is currently expanding to more cities in the United States. Mercedes-Benz owner Daimler has also been tremendously successful with their car-sharing subsidiary, Car2go, which serves eight countries. Mercedes has also recently launched a new car sharing service that approaches the market from a different angel – facilitating peer-to-peer sharing. The project is embedded into Mercedes-Benz Cars' CASE strategy, which focuses on the important topics for the future including connectivity, autonomous driving.

An effective way for large and small companies to connect is through investment, such as Corporate Venture Capital Funds. John Elkington describes

Corporate Venture Capital (CVC) as "a discrete investment activity into an independent company or a portfolio of companies with the objective of achieving both financial and strategic return to the parent company." The strategic return is particularly essential. The companies receiving CVC investment are often innovative start-ups or scale-ups, and the investment also serves to give them access to new knowledge and core competencies. Further reading on this in Chapter 4 regarding business capital. A comparable synergy arises when start-ups are strengthened by Foundations from large corporations, as we saw earlier in Case 9 with the American start-up Revolution Foods receiving financing from the Kellogg Foundation to provide healthy school meals with locally produced foods.

SMALL AND MID-SIZED ENTERPRISES (SMEs) - STUCK IN THE MIDDLE

We have seen how large companies can make a big splash when they redirect their business practices to be more sustainable, and we know that start-ups have infinite possibilities to innovate, but what about the established small and medium sized companies? According to the *World Trade Report 2016* by the World Trade Organization, small and mid-sized companies make up 93% to 95% of the total enterprises in countries all over the world, and account for approximately two-thirds of all employment, representing the largest part of both business and the economy. In Mexico for example, SMEs account for 99.8% of Mexico's total economy. In Britain, mid-sized companies are outperforming both smaller and larger businesses, according to the *Financial Times*.

SMEs must turn their attention to the SDGs since they are a worldwide force and have tremendous power. SMEs can, and often do, embrace social, environmental and economic sustainability as part of their business operations. SME owner-managers are often interested in ensuring a strong, positive legacy for their business, especially if the business is a family firm. Their smallness can be an advantage: owner-managers can strongly influence employee behavior and a lack of extensive management structures can make change easier. SMEs can also adapt quickly and agilely when it suits them, leaving them well-positioned to take advantage of new niche markets for products or services with socially responsible aspects.

Mid-sized companies are also showing - as I interpret it - a new orientation towards their business development processes and recognizing the potential for product innovation in developing countries. This makes sense: in those countries, it is often very clear what problems need to be solved. The situation is often poignant in terms of child illnesses and death, labor conditions, illness due to lack of hygiene and clean water, and lack of education opportunities. There are currently 385 million children living in poverty worldwide and in developing countries, 20% of the children live in poverty stricken conditions.

SMEs and social enterprises are finding solutions. Moyee Coffee, for example, is using a revolutionary "Fair chain" approach to build a thriving business while at the same time breaking through the cycle of poverty and benefitting people at the bottom of the pyramid (See Case 14).

SMEs REPRESENT MORE THAN 90% OF GLOBAL BUSINESSES AND ACCOUNT, ON AVERAGE, FOR ABOUT 50% OF GROSS DOMESTIC PRODUCT OF ALL COUNTRIES AND FOR 63% OF THEIR EMPLOYMENT.[53]

(ACCA 2010)

" CREATIVITY IN SUSTAINABILITY IS THE KEY TO UNLOCKING MANY STRUCTURAL BARRIERS **IN OUR DAILY ENVIRONMENTAL CHALLENGES AND TO IDENTIFYING THE GROWTH INDUSTRIES OF THE FUTURE."**

VICTOR CHU, CHAIRMAN AND CEO OF FIRST EASTERN INVESTMENT GROUP

CASE NO. **14**

MOYEE COFFEE

FairChain Coffee Production
Business model based on producing coffee in
the countries where it is harvested.

Case applied in: Ethiopia
Headquarters located in: The Netherlands
www.moyeeethiopia.com

IMPACT SDGS

SDG 1
No Poverty
Aims to increase percentage of
value to 50% staying in coffee
producing countries.

SDG 8
**Decent Work and Economic
Growth**
Thanks to the Ethiopian
Government's granting Moyee
the special status as a
FairChain exporter, Moyee will
source all of its coffee directly
from smallholders.

SDG 10
Reduced Inequalities
60% of all the beans sold
by Moyee will come from its
Ethiopian roaster.

SDG 11
**Sustainable Cities and
Communities**
Moyee will move to in Addis
Ababa to meet both local and
international demand, creating
business and jobs in the
country.

SDG 12
**Responsible Consumption
and Production**
Collaborates with several
agricultural institutes with the
aim to explore sustainable and
climate smart agriculture in
Ethiopia.

WE DON'T SELL COFFEE, WE SELL IMPACT. FAIR CHAIN IS ABOUT THREE THINGS:
ECONOMIC IMPACT; SOCIAL IMPACT; AND ECOLOGICAL IMPACT.
GUIDO VAN STAVEREN VAN DIJK, FOUNDER MOYEE COFFEE

Coffee is crucial to Ethiopia's economy, with one in four Ethiopians relying on it for their livelihoods. Most small-scale family farmers live in remote locations and lack access to credit and financing. They are therefore vulnerable to middlemen who offer cash for their coffee at a fraction of its value. There is a need for farmers to earn better incomes, allowing them to keep and maintain their land (SDG 11). Guido van Staveren van Dijk, Founder of Moyee Coffee developed the "FairChain" system which sets out to create an equal split between Moyee (the reseller) and the farmers, so each receives 50% (SDG 1). Moyee aims to roast 900,000 kilograms a year and to be recognized throughout Europe and the US as a Mpremium coffee brand with a serious social and economic message.

By roasting and packaging coffee beans in their land of origin, local farmers can earn more. Moy-

ee works with approximately 350 smallholders to help them improve their yields and the quality of their beans. Moyee Coffee's ambition is to create shared value by distributing products that bring to its local growers as much as it brings to its Dutch shareholders, (SDG 10) while remaining price competitive to their customers.

The company has successfully responded to its impact goals by educating and empowering Ethiopians to roast their own beans and setting the stage for ethical industrialization (SDG 8). Employing this innovative new business structure of roasting and packaging Ethiopian coffee in Ethiopia instead of the West, Moyee was able to increase its revenue more than ten-fold in two years from US $80,000 in 2014 to US $900,000 in 2016. The company has also become the first ISO certified coffee roasting facility in Ethiopia and one of the very first in Africa (SDG 12).

CHALLENGE

To improve the livelihoods of farmers in developing countries by changing the business model so the product is produced in the country where the raw materials are grown.

OPPORTUNITIES FOR SCALE

Moyee Coffee has grown into a leading internet based coffee retailer. They have expanded their operations to include sales points in Belgium, France and Germany; and are planning to develop production in Panama and Columbia to grow their FairChain network.

Sources and further information
- http://africabusinesscommunities.com/features/interview-debritu-mogesse-lusteau-founding-partner-moyee-coffee-the-netherlands.html
- http://www.conservation.org/stories/sustainable-coffee-challenge/Pages/partners.aspx
- http://impact.moyeecoffee.com/impact-report-2016#!/home-copy-copy-copy-copy-copy-2-copy/item/1
- http://degroenezaak.com/wp-content/uploads/2016/09/Publicatie-SDGs-2016_De-Groene-Zaak.pdf
- https://issuu.com/dionpielanen/docs/moyee_impact_report_pages_bs_250x17
- https://moyeecoffee.com/emerce/
- callthefarmer.moyeecoffee.com

" THE COMPANY HAS SUCCESSFULLY RESPONDED TO ITS IMPACT GOALS BY EDUCATING AND EMPOWERING ETHIOPIANS TO ROAST THEIR OWN BEANS AND SETTING THE STAGE FOR ETHICAL INDUSTRIALIZATION."

SMEs MUST TURN THEIR ATTENTION TO THE SDGs SINCE THEY ARE A WORLDWIDE FORCE AND HAVE TREMENDOUS POWER.

While some SMEs are able to shape their business models to respond to the SDGs, others run into difficulties when transitioning to more sustainable behaviors and most SMEs have been slow to adopt environment-related improvements. For instance, in the EU, only 29% of SMEs have introduced measures to save energy or raw materials (compared with 46% of large enterprises).[54] This is especially the case for well-established companies that have been doing business in a certain way for a long period with a loyal client and supplier base. If they don't have large sums of money to push a transition or absorb costs while shoring up a more sustainable approach, they are sometimes forced to continue non-sustainable practices for longer than they would like to. For example, a company relying on packaging for their products may find a more sustainable option but encounter resistance from their clients due to higher costs or a less premium look and feel. Fortunately, SMEs are persevering and moving forward with sustainable initiatives as an ethical business driver and a strategic differentiator for their brand.

Given the importance of SMEs for the world economy and their impact on social and environmental issues, it is necessary that SMEs shift to sustainable business practices and that they are supported by their business partners and clientele. The business advisory group Grant Thornton conducted a study and calculated that the UK mid-market comprises of 34,000 companies, making up more than a fifth of private sector turnover. With the large share that mid-sized companies represent, it is vital that they too take aim at achieving the SDGs.

WRAP UP

We can clearly conclude that we need all businesses. Large, mid-sized, small, start-ups and scale-ups; they all bring unique assets to the table and create the necessary scale together. It is the case that large companies and start-ups tend to dominate the attention, but more attention should be paid to SMEs and scale-ups to bring them into the conversation regarding achieving the SDGs. Large companies should also realize their value to SMEs, start-ups and scale-ups and should make partnering with them a cornerstone of their strategy. We need them all: they all count, they all will profit, and our world will too. ∎

PART 2 | THE TRILLION DOLLAR SHIFT ACCELERATED

INTRODUCTION

The SDGs present an exciting opportunity for innovation in both the capital mobilization and the technological capacity of today's world. Businesses that solve problems and create solutions for today's challenges represent the leaders of tomorrow.

As the fastest growing industry today, Information and Communications Technology (ICT) represents the future of the way we conduct our daily lives. There is no greater disruptive force or catalyst for unprecedented improvements. If harnessed efficiently, the power of ICT can truly be a large component of our strategy to meet he 2030 Goals. Information and Communications represents just one aspect of the potential for technology. Other types of technological advancements, such as big and small data, Internet of Things, and artificial intelligence will influence our lives and the way we do business. Opportunities for technological innovation and integration offer a new trajectory in the trade and movement of goods and services, finance and investment, and institutional capabilities. Thus, both ICT and Technology with be required in our journey to reach our collective Goals. For the purposes of brevity in this chapter, ICT and technology is used to refer to ICT and other advanced technologies.

In addition to technology underpinning today's business, capital investment remains the foundation of the economy. Achieving the SDGs will require funding and cooperation on an unprecedented scale. The private sector will play an essential role in achieving the Global Goals and is integral to meeting the financial need. With the estimated necessary investment of US $5 to $7 trillion per annum, the SDGs will require the redirection of private capital to fill the gap of available public funds. Businesses and investors that embrace this new challenge to fill the gap will lead the way toward a more sustainable future. The shared value opportunities are vast, while blended finance initiatives are paramount to success.

We need all capital and creative investments to make progress on the SDGs, not to mention our need for the multiple parties and services that will be required to disseminate these funds. The private sector holds a pivotal position in advancing ICT and Technology as well. The efficient allocation of resources through breakthroughs in financial and technological advancements will drive growth and become the winning formula for business success, investment returns, and the achievement of the SDGs.

ICT AND TECHNOLOGY

The impact and value of Information and Communication Technology (ICT) and other technological breakthroughs in societies today can hardly be overestimated. It is a driving force behind innovation, connectivity, productivity and efficiency in nearly every sector. It is responsible for enormous changes in how we live and how we work. Because of this influence, the main focus should be the creation of a positive impact for all business areas. ICT is used in all business sectors and its strength lies in the fact that it is embedded in nearly all business activities. The challenges and opportunities for ICT and technology are unique, as technology is the fastest growing industry in current times. Telecommunications and Technology are now part of nearly everything we do, and this will only increase exponentially in the coming years. ICT and technology pervades all areas of business and technological solutions can be applied effectively to every other sector. ICT has entered our lives and has already changed the way we live, work and communicate. We have entered the 'Fourth Industrial Revolution', and can expect more sweeping changes to come in rapid succession.

3.1 ICT, TECHNOLOGY AND THE SDGs

With the emergence of the concrete Sustainable Development Goals, the urgency for the ICT sector to direct its course towards contributing to their achievement is palpable. Past generations were empowered by steam engines, the telegraph, automobiles, aviation and mass communications. Ours benefits from the extraordinary surge of information brought by the internet and from the other technological breakthroughs. These benefits can and should be directed towards the Global Goals. 'ICT for good' is good for the world and good for the ICT business.

USING ICT FOR GOOD IS THE KEY TO FAST-FORWARDING THE SDGs.

Using ICT for good is the key to fast-forwarding the SDGs. Many companies and startups are utilizing current and evolving technology to create sustainable enterprises, but the domain itself can and must do everything in its power to lead the way towards achieving positive impacts on society and the environment. ICT has the potential to significantly accelerate every one of the 17 Sustainable Development Goals.

The impact that ICT and technology can have on the SDGs and economic sustainability is immense. According to a report called *ICT & SDGs by The Earth Institute Columbia University and Ericsson*, "ICTs have the potential to increase the rate of diffusion of a very wide range of technologies across the economy. Key sectors in which technology diffusion can be accelerated include: healthcare, education, financial services, electrification, and high-yield agriculture. The accelerated uptake of these technologies, and others empowered by ICTs, constitute the key to achieving the Sustainable Development Goals by their target date of 2030."[1]

The report identifies five ways ICTs can accelerate the uptake of SDG-related technologies:

1. The first is that ICTs themselves diffuse with remarkable speed. The uptake of mobile phones, computers, the internet, and social media, have been the fastest adoptions of technology in human history.

2. The second way is that the ICTs can markedly reduce the cost of deploying the needed technologies. In health care, for example, ICTs make possible a greatly expanded role for low-cost Community Health Workers (CHWs), enabling many diagnoses and treatments to be made at the community level rather than at high-cost facilities;

in education, ICTs enable students to access quality online teaching even when no qualified teachers are locally available; and online finance allows individuals to obtain banking services even when no banks are present.

3. The third way is that the ICTs can dramatically speed the public's awareness of the new technologies, and therefore the demand and readiness for those technologies.

4. The fourth is that national and global information networks can support the rapid upgrading of new applications.

5. The fifth way is that ICTs can accelerate technology diffusion by providing low-cost online platforms for training workers. The revolution of Massive Open Online Courses (MOOCs), for example, enables students anywhere to gain free access to high-quality university courses.

ICT is clearly a key driver in accelerating and scaling the solutions to the SDGs and is the newest powerful tool we have for solving the world's major challenges. The many technological advancements that have debuted and evolved in recent years can each affect the SDGs profoundly.

 Mobile communication and internet connectivity permeate our everyday lives and open the door to untold opportunities for positive impact.

 Social media lets people connect and facilitates the power of the people.

 Big and small data allows computational analysis, revealing trends, patterns and behaviors which can help in achieving many of the SDGs.

 Smart grids facilitate the highly efficient distribution of locally generated energy, even in remote areas.

 3D-printing and innovative manufacturing optimizes the use of resources and energy, with 3D printing allowing for parts or tools to be tailor-made and only manufactured when needed.

 Robotics and Artificial Intelligence (AI) will transform sectors such as manufacturing and health care, and have a huge influence on jobs.

 Driverless vehicles will influence infrastructure and disrupt industries such as public transportation.

 Drones will help facilitate information gathering and introduce innovative distribution of goods.

 The Internet of Things (IoT) holds exponential opportunities and can accelerate the circular economy.

 Blockchain facilitates secure and transparent financial transactions, and has the potential to rock economic foundations.

TECHNOLOGY IS A DRIVING FORCE BEHIND INNOVATION, CONNECTIVITY, PRODUCTIVITY AND EFFICIENCY IN NEARLY EVERY SECTOR.

IMPACT ON EVERY SDG

ICT and technology form the backbone of today's digital economy and have tremendous potential to improve people's lives in fundamental ways and therefore are crucial to achieving the SDGs by 2030. Each SDG is impacted by ICT and technology.

SDG 1: No Poverty; As internet access spreads worldwide, the 'digital divide' becomes less, affording people across the globe access to knowledge and financing – especially relevant for people living in remote areas of the world, like smallholder farmers in developing countries. There are more than 2 billion unbanked people in the world.[2] Due to digital financial services, many are participating in the digital economy for the first time; and access to financial services has proven to be a pivotal step in helping people out of poverty.[3] Transforming economies at every level, ICTs are helping society to overcome infrastructure issues, lift productivity and enable innovation that boosts incomes. Digital identity management systems, enabled by ICTs, are allowing countries to close these gaps. Promoting inclusive innovation and better education and jobs for the poor, via online work and education opportunities will provide further opportunities to impoverished people.[4]

SDG 2: Zero Hunger; ICT is providing opportunities to connect people in need with people with excess. It is also providing much needed information to farmers to improve crop yields. Big and small data analytics are helping to eliminate waste. ICT and technology offers opportunities to benefit farmers and agricultural production via better access to useful information - weather forecast, market prices; monitoring environmental and soil conditions to make farming more profitable and sustainable - water management, pest/disease control; tracking food supplies and mapping agricultural production and food shortages to establish comprehensive data systems.[5] ICT and technological applications play an important role in fostering local, national and global food security and inclusive rural development by enhancing production and productivity, lowering operating costs, facilitating access to markets, information, credit, and improving the lives of many poor rural people.

SDG 3: Good Health and Well-Being; Robotic assistance in health care; big and small data providing better analysis tools; big data analytics can provide the necessary information to analyze trends, and make projections about disease outbreaks, health service usage, patient knowledge, attitudes, and practices. ICT developing access to health information, enabling patients to contact health care services remotely, regardless of their proximity to a health care center; informing health care workers - for example, helping to learn and prepare for disease outbreaks, identify patient symptoms, follow established treatment protocols, perform remote diagnostics, and access expert support.

> **"WE MAKE THE FUTURE SUSTAINABLE WHEN WE INVEST IN THE POOR, NOT WHEN WE INSIST ON THEIR SUFFERING.**
>
> BILL GATES

SDG 4: Quality Education; ICT is making education available to more people than ever before and thus assisting in progress towards realizing the SDGs pledge to 'leave no one behind'. In developing countries such as Tanzania where schools are scarce, families are making it a priority to have a smart phone so the children can learn and develop themselves. The number of internet users in Tanzania alone rose 52 percent to 17.26 million in 2015 from 2014.[6] Internet and mobile learning is helping to help break down economic barriers, divides between rural and urban, as well as the gender divide. In addition to ICT facilitating educational opportunities for people worldwide, the Goal to improve quality education for all also applies to the need for improved technological education. Globally, there will be a talent gap for at least 10 million jobs requiring advanced digital skills by 2020.

SDG 5: Gender Equality; ICT is providing equal access to information. Schooling and information have long been withheld from women in some areas of the world as a way to keep them subservient. With internet access to knowledge and information, women around the world have opportunities for emancipation. For example, apps developed for smallholder farmers are reaching women and facilitating their ability to participate in the agriculture industry in developing countries on a more equal footing to men. It is estimated that 103 million youths worldwide are devoid of basic literacy skills, and more than 60 % of them are women. It is predicted that 90 % of future jobs will require ICT skills, and about 2 million new jobs will be created in the computer, mathematical, architecture and engineering fields in which women can play a big role. UN Women is currently developing a Virtual Skills School to ensure that no woman or girl is left behind and to offer a second chance at learning to those who had to leave formal education. Initiatives such as these provide women and girls with learning pathways that facilitate their integration into formal schooling, allow them to progress into technology sectors as either job seekers or job creators, and enable them to enter and grow in all fields.

> **AN INCREASE IN INTERNET ACCESS FOR 600,000 WOMEN IN DEVELOPING COUNTRIES WOULD CONTRIBUTE US $13-US $18 BILLION TO THOSE COUNTRIES' COMBINED ANNUAL GDP.**
>
> RELIEFWEB.INT

SDG 6: Clean Water and Sanitation; Big and small data is providing necessary information for solutions to be found to improve water purity and sanitation. Robots are being used in sanitation processing fa-

cilities to reduce CO_2 emissions and pollution. Technological innovations such as AQtap (See Case 10 in Chapter 2) help people in poor or remote areas access clean drinking water.[7] As agriculture accounts for approximately 70 % of global water withdrawals, advanced wireless sensors are being used in the fields to monitor humidity levels and soil moisture, and can automatically turn on irrigation systems when needed. Online, real-time monitoring systems are showing national progress towards the goal of communities becoming 'open defecation-free'. The public nature of these system helps participating communities to contextualize the changes they are implementing and serves as inspiration to other communities.

SDG 7: Affordable and Clean Energy; Smart grids are creating pathways for consumers to participate in energy production, e.g. with the use of private solar panels. Developments in computer graphics, 3D visualization and models, distributed networks and wireless capabilities, coupled with more powerful enterprise software applications, make it possible to apply ICT in all phases of an energy facility's lifecycle. Progressive cities, such as Singapore and Barcelona, are managing energy flows by implementing many new data-driven services, including intelligent parking solutions, smart trash collection and intelligent lighting.[8] Green technologies and processes have the potential to play a significant role in reducing global greenhouse gas emissions.

SDG 8: Decent Work and Economic Growth; The internet has enabled the rapid growth of E-commerce; reducing the trade costs associated with physical distance, allowing a larger number of businesses to access the global marketplace, reaching a broader network of buyers and participating in global value chains. Despite the continued slow pace of global trade growth, E-commerce has increased steadily, supported by increasingly fast and efficient technologies which help to lower barriers to trade for both businesses and consumers. E-commerce in goods and services was worth US $22.1

trillion dollars in 2015, a 38 % increase since 2013. For businesses, the internet promotes inclusion of firms in the world economy by expanding trade, raising productivity of capital, and intensifying competition in the marketplace, which in turn induces innovation.[9] Automated productivity created by technology allows talent to become one new form of capital, as the knowledge economy drives people towards higher-paying forms of work that manage new technologies.[10]

> **PRIVATE BUSINESSES ARE BECOMING INCREASINGLY AWARE OF THEIR IMPACT ON THE ENVIRONMENT AND ARE USING SMART SYSTEMS TO IMPROVE THEIR PROFITABILITY IN A SOCIALLY RESPONSIBLE WAY. FOR EXAMPLE, UPS' SMART TRANSPORTATION SYSTEM IS SAVING THEM 10 MILLION GALLONS OF FUEL ANNUALLY (US $300 MILLION IN COSTS) WHILE REALIZING ANNUAL REDUCTIONS OF 100,000 METRIC TONS OF CO2 EMISSIONS.**
>
> UNCTAD.ORG

SDG 9: Industry, Innovation and Infrastructure; Smart grids modernize electricity transmission in order to meet increased demand. ICT can be used for building resilient infrastructure and fostering innovation; Infrastructure is controlled, managed and optimized by ICTs, for example, power networks, water supplies, transportation systems, and telecommunication networks all use ICT. The technology sector is and should continue

to be concentrated on expanding internet access around the world. Other technological advancements also contribute to making cities smarter and more sustainable while improving quality of life. Driverless vehicles and electric vehicles for example, will have a considerable impact on infrastructure and transportation. Industrialization and the increase in productivity highly depends on the effective use of ICTs.[11] Innovations in technology facilitated financial systems, such as the M-Pesa digital payment platform, which is a commonly used financial payment system in Kenya and other countries, facilitates innovation and has spawned a host of startups in Nairobi.[12]

SDG 10: Reduced Inequalities; ICTs can assist governments with the movement of people across borders, balancing security and other policy interests with the needs and rights of individual migrants. Technology advancements help promote safer, legal forms of migration, and enhance the benefits that migration offers to migrants and the societies they move between. Transformative connectivity initiatives put in place by a number of public and private sector partners have been supporting the Global Strategy for Connectivity for Refugees. The West Nile region, for example, has expanded mobile network coverage and 3G connectivity reaching at least 150,000 refugees.[13]

SDG 11: Sustainable Cities and Communities; ICT can improve public services by leveraging open data and inclusive smart governance models. Sensor networks, digital data and urban dashboards, as well as data accessibility, are becoming common concepts as part of urban development worldwide. Examples include the United for Smart Sustainable Cities Initiative (U4SSC) and a pilot project to monitor urban-environments which promotes the use of information ICT to facilitate and ease transitions to smart sustainable cities.[14] Development of an E-governance platform to guide urban planners' efforts will collect and analyze data on the impacts of smart-city projects. Big data projects such as 'Connecting Cities and Communities' analyze lessons from the implementation of smart living, mobility and protection of the environment in cities around the world. Smart grids facilitate distributed power generation allowing for greater local contribution and control of energy.

 SDG 12: Responsible Consumption and Production; Cloud computing, smart grids, smart metering, and reduced energy consumption of ICTs all have a positive impact on reducing consumption. They offer increased dematerialization and virtualization as well as innovative ICT applications enabling sustainable production and consumption. 3D printing can reduce waste, challenge global supply chains (through localized manufacturing) and offer flexibility in the manufacturing process.[15] New business models for small scale and customized production are expected to rapidly expand through the 3D technology's applications for both industrial and consumer uses. The technology sector as a whole can help to salvage an estimated 52 billion dollars per year through reusing, repurposing and creating new value from old technology, according to Project MainStream, a circular economy initiative led by the CEOs of nine global corporations and backed by the Ellen MacArthur Foundation.[16]

 SDG 13: Climate Action; Technological capabilities such as drones, AI and big data applications enhance observations and numerical weather prediction to better prepare for severe weather conditions. Integration of available data into long-term climatic datasets is essential to weather forecasting for climate impact. New chip sensors providing small data can be integrated with high-quality measurements (i.e. observations of air quality at high resolution) and new indirect measurements obtained from communication technologies (e.g. rainfall inferred from operational efficiencies of mobile phone networks) are examples of the opportunities to integrate technology.[17]

SDG 14: Life Below Water; Internet and satellite maps can be used to track migration patterns of endangered

sea-animals and better understand lifetimes, loss and predation. Monitoring of global fish-stocks, oxygen levels, algal blooms, pollution, temperature and currents will be increasingly accurate through digital systems. Big data can be used to analyze the oceans, in terms of biodiversity, pollution, weather patterns or ecosystem evolution.[18] Data collection and analysis also forms the foundation for the development of models and strategies to address issues that concern the health of the oceans. Addressing the issue of ship strikes - the collision of vessels and whales - the International Whaling Commission developed a global ship strike database: an online data entry tool for submitting reports of strikes to identify and prioritize hot spots where collisions occur. This helps develop an understanding of the numbers of collisions, movements of cetaceans (whales, dolphins and porpoises) and circumstances surrounding collisions with the aim to reduce these events and maintain healthy and safe waters.

 SDG 15: Life on Land; Various technologies and ICTs are being used extensively to observe, monitor, track and protect terrestrial wildlife from poachers as well as other destructive activities. Wildlife management using tracking collars is an important tool in conservation efforts. Animals are fitted

ICTs OFFER MASSIVE POTENTIAL TO DEVELOP GAME CHANGING SOLUTIONS. WITH BIG DATA AND TECHNOLOGIES, THE TIME FOR COMPANIES AND GOVERNMENTS UNDERPLAYING DEFORESTATION, WILDLIFE TRADE, POACHING OR ILLEGAL FISHING IS OVER.

ITU.INT

with satellite tracking collars enabling researchers and conservationists to monitor individual movements and chart habitat and landscape connectivity. WWF has trained indigenous populations in the use of cutting-edge software, smartphones and GPS to gather data and map local communities to report on the status of their land.[19] Additionally, remote sensing based natural capital assessments are used to help conservation organizations target investments in forest restoration, guide jurisdictional development planning, and map supply risks for corporate sourcing decisions.[20]

SDG 16: Peace, Justice and Strong Institutions; Blockchain increases financial inclusion and transparency, as blockchain is essentially a global ledger storing all transactions.[21] Big data analytics are already being used to predict where crimes may occur in order to help solve them by deploying police, etc. Social media is used by citizens to unite and contest injustice. Smart services and the Internet of Things help governments optimize the use of natural resources and improve the delivery of citizen services. Smart systems can also help governments identify and manage threats,[22] for example, remote sensors and RFID tags, generate rich sets of highly accurate georeferenced digital data about the land, waterways, transport routes and settlements in a country. This data also contributes to the understanding of environmental trends and activities taking place within and surrounding a country that would impact its citizens.

SDG 17: Partnerships for the Goals; Implementation and use of ICTs require coordinated partnerships. In crisis situations, ICT and technological solutions have demonstrated their power to help governments and partners craft responsive and resilient systems to meet the needs of children, youth and adults[23]. The Emergency Telecommunications Cluster (ETC) is a global partnership of humanitarian, government and private sector organizations. Led by WFP, it works to ensure that all those responding to emergencies – including people affected by disaster – have access to vital communication services. Corporate organizations within the ICT field are increasingly participating in the development of new solutions. Ericsson Response, for example, has been working closely with the ETC in the design and development of 'WIDER' (Wireless LAN in Disaster and Emergency Response), a mechanism designed to enable humanitarian workers to access the internet from any suitable device in any emergency-affected area. Other partnerships include ITU/UNESCO Broadband Commission for Sustainable Development (2010) ; Alliance for Affordable Internet (2013); Connect 2020 (2014); Global e-Sustainability Initiative - SMARTer2030 (2015); OECD/G20 work on Digitization (2015); Global Connect (2016); Partnership for Sustainable Development Data (2016); Digital Impact Alliance (2016); World Bank's Digital Partnership for Development (2016); WEF's Future Internet for All initiative (2016); ITU/UN Women EQUALS: The Global Partnership for Gender Equality in the Digital Age (2016).

> **"I BELIEVE THAT, IF MANAGED WELL, THE FOURTH INDUSTRIAL REVOLUTION CAN BRING A NEW CULTURAL RENAISSANCE, WHICH WILL MAKE US FEEL PART OF SOMETHING MUCH LARGER THAN OURSELVES: A TRUE GLOBAL CIVILIZATION. I BELIEVE THE CHANGES THAT WILL SWEEP THROUGH SOCIETY CAN PROVIDE A MORE INCLUSIVE, SUSTAINABLE AND HARMONIOUS SOCIETY. BUT IT WILL NOT COME EASILY."**
>
> KLAUS SCHWAB, FOUNDER AND EXECUTIVE CHAIMAN, WEF

" **IF WE CAN EXTEND THE INTERNET TO MORE PEOPLE, WE INCREASE VOICE... WE INCREASE ECONOMIC OPPORTUNITY... AND WE INCREASE EQUALITY.** "

SHERYL SANDBERG, CHIEF OPERATING OFFICER AND MEMBER
OF THE BOARD, FACEBOOK, USA

3.2 RESPONSIBILITY FOR TOMORROW'S WORLD

There are several crucial responsibilities related to this industry. The world today and certainly, the world tomorrow revolves around ICT and technology. And, frankly, for the world to continue to revolve with us living on it - for human beings to have a sustainable future here on Earth - we need to stop all negative impact on our environment and society and scale up the positive impact. ICT and technology, our Fourth Industrial Revolution, has the momentum and the potential to turn the tide.

The predominant responsibility of this sector is the greening of and through ICT and technology. This essentially entails the pursuit of sustainability within the ICT and technology sector. So the greening of the sector means tech companies should be watching and reducing their own environmental footprint, especially related to energy use and production of products. This is an important responsibility to take on now and not later as ICT and technology has already permeated much of the day-to-day lives of people throughout the world. And the prospect is that our use and dependence on ICT and technology will continue to grow. Therefore, the industry itself must endeavor to be environmentally sustainable and be critical of energy sources. The International Energy Agency (IEA) forecasts that by 2020 the ICT industry will account for more than 14 percent of global energy consumption. The ICT and technology industry is already the fifth largest industry in energy consumption: It accounts for 2 - 4 % of global energy consumption and carbon emissions, with an increase of 4 - 5 % per year. Research shows that if no action is taken, by 2020 the ICT industry's CO2 emissions will be double the amount of 2007.

Therefore, the companies within this sector should by now be well on their way towards a zero impact goal, and should preferably already be working towards creating a positive impact like Unilever is doing by producing more sustainable energy than they use themselves. Companies in this field must make this a priority and create sustainable work facilities and practices. The ICT and technology industry makes a positive impact on people and societies, but they need to step up their game when it comes to setting the right example and making a positive environmental impact as well.

Furthermore, 'greening through' ICT and technology is the facilitation through technological solutions of other industries and companies to become sustainable and make a positive impact. This is certainly where ICT and technology excels and provides opportunities as far as the imagination can go.

THE PREDOMINANT RESPONSIBILITY OF THIS SECTOR IS THE GREENING OF, AND THROUGH, ICT AND TECHNOLOGY.

Secondly and most importantly, this sector has the ability and thus the responsibility to have a widely shared, radical new look at the opportunities that digitalization offers. The emphasis is on the words "widely shared" because without this, the extremely ambitious targets that the SDGs have set will never be achieved in time. And because of its ubiquitous permeation worldwide and throughout all sectors, ICT and technology have the power to revolutionize businesses and propel sustainable innovation.

Currently, apart from a few leading multinationals, radical innovation comes from inspired startups, and since they are growing quickly - scale-ups. There are still too many established players in the ICT sector who are mainly geared towards solving problems that come up and are focused on the mantra: 'You ask, we deliver'. While a better credo would be: 'We take our responsibility for tomorrow's world', with the underlying driver to contribute to sustainability by focusing on independent innovation, connectivity, productivity and efficiency. This resolute commitment to sustainability should be implemented together with the users as well. Industry partners throughout the world should also aim for this.

An example of a company that is taking their responsibility for tomorrow's world is Ushahidi[24], an open-source software platform dealing with social issues by enabling vulnerable citizens to share, in real-time, testimonies of human rights violations or crisis. They can reach out to people and inform them of what is happening, where and when. This initiative helps to support SDG 16 – Peace, Justice and Strong Institutions. It is currently being used in the slums of Kibera, Kenya and India and has the potential to be used anywhere in the world (See Case 15).

The educational video platform Nafham[25] is another example of a responsible business model. Their business case is shown in Chapter 7.

Figure 10 **Components to leverage ICT for sustainable economic development. Source: ICCWBO.org SDGs Diagram**

15

CASE NO. **USHAHIDI**

Syria Tracker and SafeCity
Humanitarian Trackers - Helping people raise
their voices through technology

Case applied in: Syria and India
Headquarters located in: Nairobi
www.ushahidi.com

IMPACT SDGS

SDG 5
Gender Equality
Since 2012, collected over
10,000 stories from over
50 cities in India, Kenya,
Cameroon and Nepal
to create awareness on
harassment and abuse against
women and disadvantaged
communities.

SDG 10
Reduced Inequalities
Given people a voice
through 10 million posts or
testimonials.

SDG 11
**Sustainable Cities and
Communities**
Deployed information over
120,000 times.

SDG 16
**Peace, Justice and Strong
Institutions**
Allowed 25 million people
to be reached in critical
situations.

SDG 17
Partnerships for the Goals
Partner with leading
foundations and organizations
to increase access to
information, empower citizens,
and protect marginalized
communities.

THE MOBILE APP IS EASY TO USE AND IS A LONG-AWAITED ADDITION TO THE
SOLUTION. WE LOOK FORWARD TO FURTHER DEVELOPMENTS FROM USHAHIDI TO
**HELP ORGANIZATIONS LIKE OURS TO USE TECHNOLOGY FOR GOOD IN
A VERY ECONOMICAL MANNER.**

ELSAMARIE D'SILVA, FOUNDER AND CEO OF RED DOT FOUNDATION (SAFECITY)

Ushahidi, which in Swahili means "testimony", is an application that was created to report the violence in Kenya after the post-election conflict in 2008. Since then, thousands have used this crowdsourcing tool to defend democratic values and raise their voice for freedom. Media sources and newspapers are using Ushahidi today in order to survey strikes all over the world by using data and live communication tools. Ushahidi is a social enterprise that provides software and services to numerous sectors and civil society to help improve the bottom up flow of information. The company believes that "if marginalized people are able to easily communicate to those who aim to serve them, then those organizations and governments can more effectively respond to their communities' immediate needs, while simultaneously bringing global attention to their problems through the aggregation of their voices."

Ushahidi's solutions help people live in a safer and more just society (SDG 16). Two of these notable solutions, Syria Tracker and SafeCity, are instances where Ushahidi technology has been used to deploy innovative products that benefit society. The first is the humanitarian crowdsourcing platform Syria Tracker, which has used Ushahidi technology for over 6 years to collect first-hand reports of the violence going on in Syria. Years of violence has disrupted Syria and about 40% of its people have been displaced, including millions who have fled the country. Syria Tracker has now gathered

over 5,700 reports from people on the ground, helped trigger alerts to those nearby, and brought transparency to the instability of a region in crisis (SDG 10). It is the longest standing reporting tool in Syria, and the reports they have helped to surface have been used by The Washington Post, the United Nations, and USAID.

The second solution is SafeCity, which uses Ushahidi technology to help make cities in India safer for women, giving them a way to anonymously and safely report on harassment and abuse (SDG 5). UN Women states that 1 in 3 women face some kind of sexual assault at least once in their lifetime, and in India a rape occurs every 20 minutes. SafeCity has gathered nearly 10,000 reports over the past few years. This real-time reporting of danger or potential danger to women has allowed SafeCity to advocate to cities for more street lighting, awareness campaigns, and improved city resources to protect women.

The Ushahidi tool facilitated the creation of these two organizations and allowed them to dedicate their resources to solving these problems, instead of having to spend them building technology from scratch. Syria Tracker and SafeCity, created with the use of Ushahidi technology, are helping to protect civilians in Syria and bring transparency to human rights abuse of women in India (SDGs 11 & 17).

CHALLENGE

To help people connect and raise awareness of danger or crises.

OPPORTUNITIES FOR SCALE

Ushahidi partnered with Devex to contribute to #DataDriven which explores the power of data to achieve development outcomes in every sector. Ushahidi contributes with data collection and developmental visualization to further the deployment of the SDGs. Ushahidi has created other digital platforms including RollCall for teams to reach each other during crises; BRCK to connect to internet no matter where you are; SMSsync turning phones into an SMS to URL gateway; and CrisesNet which helps to format and expose crisis data in a simple, intuitive structure. Ushahidi continues to develop new ways for technology to contribute towards safer communities.

Sources and further information

- https://www.ushahidi.com/about
- https://www.ushahidi.com/blog/2016/07/19/ushahidi-partners-with-devexs-datadriven-campaign
- https://www.ushahidi.com/blog/2016/09/26/two-ushahidi-deployers-selected-for-un-solutions-summit
- https://syriatracker.crowdmap.com/
- http://safecity.in/
- https://www.washingtonpost.com/world/syrian-refugee-crisis-map/2013/12/13/f45b570e-645b-11e3-a373-0f9f2d1c2b61_graphic.html?utm_term=.7f218cd3c62f
- https://pages.devex.com/about-devex

" **USHAHIDI'S SOLUTIONS HELP PEOPLE LIVE IN A SAFER AND MORE JUST SOCIETY.** "

" GOALS ARE ONLY WISHES UNLESS YOU HAVE A PLAN."

MELINDA GATES, BILL & MELINDA GATES FOUNDATION

3.3 SETTING THE COURSE COMES WITH A TREMENDOUS PRIZE

The list of startups, and fast growing scale-up initiatives is long, as technology is inspiring a plethora of applications across all sectors. It is an exciting time as the technological possibilities are explored. There is tremendous potential for innovation. But what is currently lacking is large-scale contributions by big, financially strong ICT companies towards tackling the flaws in our current economic, social and ecological system.

For large-scale positive impact, underpinned by the ICT and technological tools at our disposal, there needs to be more focus on the SDGs. The entire ICT industry, companies big and small, should set their course towards contributing to the realization of the SDGs. Some large companies, such as Nokia and Huawai, are setting their course in the right direction as they recognize that business for good is good business, and contributing to the realization of our Global Goals comes with a trillion dollar prize.

As estimated by the Business and Sustainable Development Commission, "Delivering the SDGs could generate over 12 trillion dollars' worth of business opportunities." So strong focus on busi-ness solutions for the SDGs not only serves the world, it serves the companies as well. It unlocks markets, connects to both current and future needs of customers and is thus not only a profita-ble but also sustaining business strategy.

DELIVERING THE SDGs COULD GENERATE OVER 12 TRILLION DOLLARS' WORTH OF BUSINESS OPPORTUNITIES.

Fortunately, there is some movement in this direction by big companies such as Nokia.[26] In 2015, for example, Nokia focused on the SDGs to use their technology to "improve public safety and the resilience of communities to extreme weather changes; connect the unconnected; explore the possibilities around digital health; and launch products that decrease CO_2 emissions from network infrastructure." They have estimated that there will be 50 billion connected devices in 2025, which makes SDG 9 (Infrastructure, Industry and Innovation) the most material one in terms of improving people's lives with technology. Huawai also sees many opportunities and is involved as well in expanding connectivity worldwide, so people around the globe can benefit from ICT and technological solutions. One of Huawai's projects along the SDG pathway was to facilitate mobile access to health care in China (See Case 16).

16 CASE NO. HUAWEI

Enable full connectivity and create a more sustainable future.
Deliver innovative ICT solutions that drive the digital transformation of all industries

Case applied in: Asia
Headquarters located in: China
www.huawei.com

IMPACT SDGS

SDG 3
Good Health and Well-Being
Provided a telemedicine platform for people in remote areas of China to access medical care.

SDG 9
Industry, Innovation and Infrastructure
Supported 1,500 customer networks. Provided mobile signals to Mount Everest Camp; Deployed 100G submarine network in the Arctic Circle to meet communications needs in Greenland.

SDG 11
Sustainable Cities and Communities
Increased energy efficiency of major products by 23%. Used green packaging in 60% of products to reduce the use of wood by over 123,000 m³.

SDG 13
Climate Action
Reduced CO2 per unit of sales revenue by 20.6% in 2016; Guaranteed network stability during 200 major events and natural disasters worldwide.

TODAY, MOST VITAL INFRASTRUCTURE IS CONTROLLED BY ICT: POWER GRIDS, WATER SUPPLIES, TRANSPORTATION HUBS, AND MORE, **THIS MAKES ICT INFRASTRUCTURE AN ECONOMIC CORNERSTONE**, NOT JUST FOR UTILITIES AND LOGISTICS, BUT FOR EMPOWERMENT. BROADBAND ACCESS ENABLES PEOPLE TO OBTAIN EDUCATION, START BUSINESSES, CREATE JOBS, AND MUCH MORE.
KEVIN (JINGWEN) TAO, CHAIRMAN, CORPORATE SUSTAINABLE DEVELOPMENT COMMITTEE, HUAWEI TECHNOLOGIES CO LTD.

Huawei believes investment in technology is a key accelerator to help nations achieve the SDGs. Maintaining a strategic focus to incorporate the SDGs into its core business, the company has built over 1,500 networks in partnership with telecom carriers, creating value for customers and helping connect over one-third of the world's population (SDG 9). Their primary goal is to build a robust ecosystem to sustain long-term development and deliver innovative ICT solutions that drive the digital transformation of all industries (SDG 11 & SDG 13).

In addition to focusing on boosting economic growth in areas where they operate, their own profit margins have grown as a direct result of their sustainable activities. Huawei's annual revenue was CNY 521,574 million (US $77 billion), up 32% year-on-year. Over the past five years Huawei has increased its revenue by 24%, operating profit by 23%, and cash flow from operating activities by 18%. One of Huawei's endeavors to utilize their technological expertise to help accelerate the SDGs is their solution to a problem in the Henan province of China where healthcare resources are inaccessible in a timely fashion for many people. To address this issue, Huawei has provided a professional telemedicine solution, enabling remote consultations and remote diagnoses for patients as well as distance training for doctors (SDG 3). In partnership with the First Affiliated Hospital of Zhengzhou University and the Henan Health and Family Planning Commission, Huawei has deployed a telemedicine platform that

covers hospitals across the province's cities, counties, townships, and villages. The system uses high-quality video conferencing systems (also known as telepresence systems) to connect the provincial hospital, 18 city-level hospitals, 130 county-level hospitals, ambulances throughout the province, and hospitals in townships and villages which are now in trial operation. The telemedicine platform can offer all nine remote medical services suggested in the national telemedicine standards, making it China's largest, most comprehensive telemedicine system. Each year, the hospital provides more than 10,000 remote consultations and 30,000 remote diagnoses.

With the hospital's data growing dramatically, it is becoming increasingly important to effectively handle and apply this data. To meet this need, Huawei has built a big data platform that enables the hospital to store and process huge volumes of data. This platform allows the hospital to access data more quickly and provide more efficient management. It also enables easy and rapid analysis of data to turn it into critical insights. The result of the project is more effective remote consultations and better care for patients. Huawei is committed to providing leading telemedicine solutions to address inequalities and inefficiencies in healthcare, and is thus working with the First Affiliated Hospital of Zhengzhou University to establish a joint innovation center to promote and develop the use of telemedicine and big data so as to improve health outcomes.

CHALLENGE

To use technology to help achieve many SDGs, and address healthcare inequalities, inefficiencies, and inaccessibility in China.

OPPORTUNITIES FOR SCALE

Huawei's telemedicine solution can be expanded to other regions. Additionally, the company plans to invest in four key areas to drive technology breakthroughs: devices, connectivity, cloud computing and chipsets. Huawei partners with more than 20 global players to look at how mobile technology can promote various vertical industries. The company recently launched X Labs which will comprise of three new research labs that will explore various use cases for mobile applications, drive innovation, and promote an open industry ecosystem.

Sources and further information

- http://www.huawei.com/en/news/2017/6/Critical-Role-UN-SDGs
- http://www-file.huawei.com/-/media/CORPORATE/PDF/Sustainability/2016-Huawei-Sustainability-Report-en.pdf?la=en
- https://www.fastcompany.com/company/huawei
- http://www.huawei.com/en/sustainability/digital-divide/digital_technology#China-Telemedicine-Initiative-en-ru
- http://www.activetelecoms.com/news/telecom-industry/telecom-vendors/huawei-consumer-business-group-ceo-addresses-plans-for-future-ai-development
- http://www-file.huawei.com/-/media/CORPORATE/PDF/publications/winwin/27/win-win-27-en.pdf

" HUAWEI BELIEVES INVESTMENT IN TECHNOLOGY IS A KEY ACCELERATOR TO HELP NATIONS ACHIEVE THE SDGs. "

THE LEARNING CURVE TO IMPACT AND PRIZE

Each new technology goes through a learning curve in which the technology passes through several "generations" of improvement. Each of these generations often carries lower costs, greater resilience, easier use, and wider applicability. ICT has the unprecedented potential to speed up these generational cycles. Because of enhanced information flows, open sourced applications and inter-operability, gains made by one developer can be picked up and improved by others.[27] This type of upgrading process has accelerated, with the 'winners' of this intense competition often carrying home the 'prize' of a large dominance over much of the global market. While globalization has blurred the boundaries of country borders for business transactions and technological development, individual countries can and should speed up their own learning curves and shorten the time of each technology generation, especially for ICT-based solutions that have a strong local content (e.g. education, healthcare, agriculture, and environmental management).

> "ICTs WILL BE ABSOLUTELY CRITICAL TO MEETING EACH OF THE 17 SDGs AND MOBILE TECHNOLOGY WILL CONTINUE TO BE AT THE VERY HEART OF FUTURE DEVELOPMENT."
>
> HOULIN ZHAO, SECRETARY-GENERAL, INTERNATIONAL TELECOMMUNICATION UNION

To reach the Goals set by the SDGs and to reap the trillion dollar prize, employing SDG paths rather than continuing business-as-usual (BAU) is vital. As illustrated in figure 11, the BAU path will support partial achievement of the Goals but will not be sufficient to facilitate full achievement. A concerted shift is needed in the business strategy to reach the Goals and reach the prize.

Figure 11 **Comparison of BAU and SDG Paths**

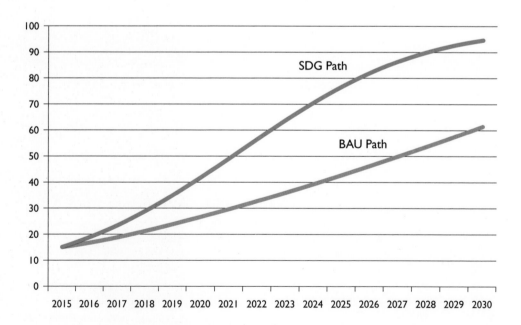

3.4 THE DIGITAL DIVIDE

The possibilities for improving people's lives through technological solutions are endless, but let's not lose sight of the current reality that 3.9 billion people have no – or minimal- access to the internet. More than half of the global population remains cut off from Information and Communication Technology (ICT), according to the International Telecommunications Union's (ITU) report ICT Facts & Figures 2016. In developed countries, 81 % of the population has internet access, compared with 40 % in developing countries and 15 % in the least developed countries. Furthermore, despite falling prices for ICT services, research shows that mobile broadband growth is slowing.[28] Internet usage rates are also higher for men than for women in all regions of the world. The global internet user gender gap grew from 11% in 2013 to 12 % in 2016. Africa makes up the largest regional gender gap at 23 %, and the smallest being in the Americas at only 2 percent. Although almost one billion households in the world now have internet access (of which 230 million are in China, 60 million in India and 20 million in the world's 48 LDCs), there are still large differences around the globe. Figures for household access show the large gap in the digital divide, with 84 % of households connected in Europe, compared with 15.4 % in the African region.

FOR ICT TO IMPACT THE WORLD, THE WORLD MUST BE CONNECTED.

More needs to be done to make internet available to everyone and close the digital divide. For ICT to impact the world, the world must be connected. At the rate ICT is developing, this digital divide will become more pronounced if it is allowed to continue. Without internet connection, people will be left behind. They will not be able to benefit from so many of the innovations that could positively affect their lives and their communities. Looking at figure 13 there are big things in store in the ICT and technology realm. But people need

to be connected to the internet, and there needs to be more widespread internet availability especially to rural areas and in developing nations. The "Tipping Points" shown in the figure below are exciting but also integral parts of the fourth industrial revolution. And those without internet access will not be able to participate in terms of progress, nor will they be able to take advantage of innovative solutions to the challenges they face. The course is clear: the ICT and technology sector must create large-scale solutions, focus on the SDGs, and expand internet connectivity.

REVOLUTIONIZING BUSINESS BY ICT & TECHNOLOGY

The ICT and technology sector is characterized by innovation and rapid development. The uptake of technological innovations usually follows an S-shaped curve as explained in the Ericsson report ICT and the SDGs[29] and shown in figure 12. "The diffusion (or uptake) of the technology typically starts at a very low level, and initially will increase only gradually. After some time, the uptake of the technology will accelerate. Later on, as the coverage rate approaches 100 %, the growth will slow again and finally come to a halt when coverage is complete."

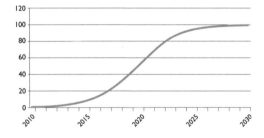

Figure 12

S- shaped technology diffusion curve.

Given this typical trajectory, projections have been made about new technologies that are emerging but have not yet taken hold universally. Some of these projections were illustrated as "Tipping Points" in a recent WEF report called Technology Tipping Points and Societal Impact.[30] As shown in Figure 13, in the next ten years we can expect explosions in the use of Robotics, Internet of Things, Blockchain, 3D Printing, AI, Driverless Cars, and more.

Figure 13 **Average Year Each tipping Point is Expected to Occur**

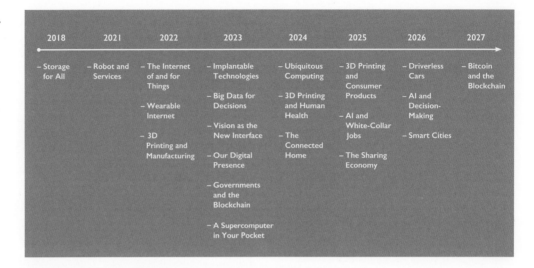

2018	2021	2022	2023	2024	2025	2026	2027
– Storage for All	– Robot and Services	– The Internet of and for Things	– Implantable Technologies	– Ubiquitous Computing	– 3D Printing and Consumer Products	– Driverless Cars	– Bitcoin and the Blockchain
		– Wearable Internet	– Big Data for Decisions	– 3D Printing and Human Health	– AI and White-Collar Jobs	– AI and Decision-Making	
		– 3D Printing and Manufacturing	– Vision as the New Interface	– The Connected Home	– The Sharing Economy	– Smart Cities	
			– Our Digital Presence				
			– Governments and the Blockchain				
			– A Supercomputer in Your Pocket				

3.5 THE FOURTH INDUSTRIAL REVOLUTION & TEN BREAKTHROUGH OPPORTUNITIES

The explosiveness of technological innovation and usage are signs that we have entered a new era. It has been called the "Fourth Industrial Revolution." In the first industrial revolution, water and steam power was used to mechanize production; the second used electric power to create mass production; and the third used electronics and information technology to automate production. Now the fourth industrial revolution is building on the third, and is characterized by "a fusion of technologies that is blurring the lines between the physical, digital, and biological sphere."[31]

Klaus Schwab, Founder and Executive Chairman of the World Economic Forum, and author of the book: *The Fourth Industrial Revolution* calls for leaders and citizens to "together shape a future that works for all by putting people first, empowering them and constantly reminding ourselves that all of these new technologies are first and foremost tools made by people for people."[32] Elon Musk and others have also been vocal recently about the advancements in Artificial Intelligence (AI), warning governments and industry to regulate AI

to protect human civilization.[33] Leaders who are watching the rapid technological advancements closely know that technology has the very real potential to serve good or bad. Cyber-security is a growing and critical concern. In the thrust to connect the entire world's population to the internet, and create more automated devices, we need to recognize the vulnerability that comes with that.

> **THE FOURTH INDUSTRIAL REVOLUTION HAS THE POTENTIAL TO BRING ABOUT GREAT CHANGES, BUT ALSO PERILOUS ONES AS WELL.**

Developers and regulators must keep a close eye on the ramifications of technological advances and implementation. Caution should not be thrown to the wind in order to embrace the next great thing. Cyber-security is vital as is cautious and ethical progress. The fourth industrial revolution is by definition a fundamental and rapid change. The fast-paced changes that we are experiencing are exciting but should be done with positive purpose. Let's all keep our eye on the ball, focus, and take responsibility to ensure that this revolution helps mankind to achieve positive change for societies and our environment. The SDGs are the guiding light to keep us on the right track.

TEN TECHNOLOGICAL BREAKTHROUGHS: OPPORTUNITIES FOR POSITIVE IMPACT

The technological breakthroughs have come and are still coming in rapid succession, and they often use a blend of ICT and technology in their designs. The following list categorizes technologies with the greatest influence on how we live, work and achieve the SDGs.

	Mobile Telephones & Internet Communication
SOCIAL MEDIA	Social Media and E-commerce
	Big Data and Small Data
SMART	Smart Grids
3D	3D Printing (also known as Additive Manufacturing)
	Robotics & Artificial Intelligence (AI)
	Driverless Vehicles
	Drones
IoT	Internet of Things (IoT)
BLOCK CHAIN	Blockchain and Cyber-Security

1. Mobile and Internet Communication have connected the world and impacted societies in all countries. Mobile communication has evolved into internet connectedness which has opened the door to infinite possibilities and knowledge. Mobile phones are steadily being replaced by smartphones, extending the functionality of this technological innovation to facilitate not only telephone communication but internet communication as well. This extension of mobile access to internet holds the potential to unlock a variety of markets including the growth of small-holder farms in developing nations, and peer-to-peer commerce. Internet access has grown substantially over the last decade and by 2015,

3.2 BILLION INTERNET USERS IN 2015

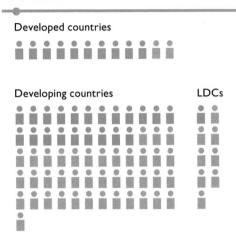

3.2 billion people globally were online. While in developed countries about 80 % of the population was using the internet in 2015, only one-third of the population in developing countries was online, and merely one out of ten people in the Least Developed Countries (LDCs) are currently using the internet (figure 14 above). Internet user penetration rate was about 11 % lower for females than for males, globally (figure 15).

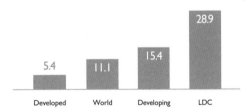

The gap in internet user penetration rate between males and females in 2015

2. Social Media has increased the ability for people all over the world to easily communicate with their personal networks. Organizations have increased efforts to take advantage of their online presence in order to gain greater access to their customers, and to gather information on customers' needs and preferences so as to customize and enhance the quality of services offered. Gathering and communicating information from surrounding communities, and reporting the results through the use of SMS or internet-based applications,

Figure 14 & 15

Internet users 2015 & Gap in Internet user penetration rate between males and females[34]

has engendered a new level of transparency and accountability within the systems and structures that affect the lives of even the most vulnerable populations. Social media creates new and faster ways to communicate and share information; it gives a voice to all people including those in low resource settings, increasing their confidence and ability to influence decisions and structures that impact their communities and families.

3. Big Data and Small Data are the various data that are collected and then analyzed to give insights into behavior, trends, and patterns. Big data is the technological facilitations of information collection. It provides the statistics needed for reporting, pattern analysis, and strategic planning. Big data analytics is helpful regarding the SDGs as this technology makes it feasible to identify trends and gather information pertinent to measuring how close or how far we are from achieving our Global Goals. Small data is a specific set of information that is characterized as accessible, inform-

ative and actionable. Small data provides details of specific behavior or current situations that are locally relevant, it augments and complements big data at the micro and citizen level.

4. Smart grids are part of the digitization of the energy sector and allow for two-way traffic of energy. That is to say that in contrast to current energy grids, which supply energy to consumers, smart grids can also collect energy from consumers. Smart grids also facilitate internet communication by creating multi-pathways for communication to flow from and to several sources and contact points. By connecting generation and consumption and enabling the multidirectional flows of energy and information, smart grids improve the efficiency of the overall energy system. Digital technologies can use information on the consumption patterns to ease transmission congestion by dispatching distributed power, as opposed to tapping into distant power resources through the transmission grids.

> **SERVICES THAT WILL BE NEEDED AS SMART GRIDS BECOME MORE COMMONPLACE INCLUDE: HOME ENERGY MANAGEMENT, ADVANCED METERING INFRASTRUCTURE, DISTRIBUTION AND SUBSTATION AUTOMATION COMMUNICATIONS, ASSET MANAGEMENT AND CONDITION MONITORING, DEMAND RESPONSE, SOFTWARE SOLUTIONS, AND ANALYTICS.**
>
> TECHREPUBLIC.COM

5. 3D printing, which is also referred to as Additive Manufacturing is an evolving technology which is still in its early stages. There is a lot of experimental innovation in 3D printing especially related to different kinds of filaments from plastics to human tissue to food. Also, reduction of price to produce 3D printers and sustainable and cheap energy to run the printers are being explored in order to make 3D printing a solution to many of the problems faced in developing countries. This type of manufacturing allows for a product to be made at multiple locations anywhere in the world, eliminating many traditional supply chain and production costs associated with traditional manufacturing. It also reduces waste associated with traditional manufacturing processes and allows non-traditional raw materials to be combined with mainstream materials as a means to mitigate raw material shortages and reduce environmental impact.

6. Robotics and AI development has surged in both industrial and consumer robot applications. There is an integration of advanced robotics into the IoTs that are helping to solve some

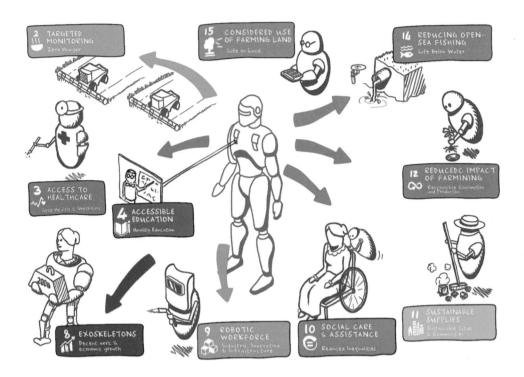

Figure 16

**Robotics and the SDGs
PA Knowledge Ltd;
Global Compact
Source: breakthrough.
unglobalcompact.org
Robots**

> "IT IS ESTIMATED THAT SELF-DRIVING CARS COULD REDUCE DEATHS ON THE ROAD BY 90%. THAT IS ALMOST 30,000 LIVES SAVED EACH YEAR IN THE US ALONE AND US $190 BILLION DOLLARS SAVED EACH YEAR IN HEALTHCARE COSTS ASSOCIATED WITH ACCIDENTS."
>
> MCKINSEY.COM

of the world's most challenging issues. One main breakthrough that is also driving the robotics revolution is artificial intelligence (AI) and enhanced machine learning more generally. Machine learning algorithms are enabling rapid breakthroughs in robotics pattern recognition, voice recognition, natural language capabilities, and problem-solving capacities. Robots not only have the capacity to handle many menial tasks, they are moving into areas of more advanced capabilities to enter the high-tech service economy in legal analysis, medical diagnostics, and other areas of complex problem solving that will assist in achieving progress.

7. Driverless Vehicles have made significant advances over the past five years, with the potential to offer huge societal advantages. This technology eliminates vehicle collisions by making roads safer, optimizing the movement of vehicles by reducing congestion and improving efficiency, and freeing time for drivers to do other things. Pilot projects are well underway, and once the technology is perfected and accepted, driverless vehicles have the potential to become widespread and have significant impact on people's lives. Autonomous road vehicles are also opening up new business opportunities. Changing ownership models, as people buy mobility only when they need it, allows vehicle assets to be used more which results in a reduction in transport costs. Although current activity in this area is focused on the developed world, there is also great potential in the developing world and these areas could perceivably jump ahead in implementation.

8. Drones have proven to be a good way to generate low-cost data that can provide insights such as crop health so farmers can make more informed decisions. To gather this information, drones are often equipped with infrared cameras to analyze photosynthetic levels; the higher the photosynthetic levels, the healthier the crops. In this way, they enable farmers to make informed decisions on effective pesticide use. Drones are also starting to be used at the sub-national and local levels for other purposes. Officers from protected areas, environmental managers, ecologists, wildlife researchers, and rangers have all been engaged to explore the use of drones in their work. Drones provide real-time information and are therefore extremely useful in crisis situations such as forest fires and are being integrated into disaster preparedness and response operations. Information captured by drones can help prepare for extreme weather intensified by ongoing shifts in climate.

> **ANNUAL DISASTER LOSSES NOW AVERAGE US $200 BILLION DOLLARS GLOBALLY.**
>
> DOCUMENTS.WORLDBANK.ORG

9. Internet of Things (IoT) technology has the potential to help us create a more sustainable world. IoT is both communicative and analytical and therefore has the capability to help solve the SDGs. For example, ecosystems – both technological and environmental – are too complex for analysis and action by any single technology. Thus, technology-to-technology communication and action means there are fewer missed opportunities for conservation. IoT technology provides society with a more connected future. Sensors within technologies will monitor products throughout their life cycle and alert users when older products can be easily repaired or refurbished. There is potential for these sensors to signal to manufacturers which components can be repurposed and reused, saving both the environment and possibly trillions of production dollars.

10. Blockchain and Cyber-Security are important developments resulting from our dependence on technology and the need for transparency but also privacy. Blockchain is an open sourced digital ledger that allow users to record and trace all types of transactions. Blockchain is mainly used for financial transactions, and provides an alternative to conventional banking by allowing users to keep track of financial payments. Blockchain is also used for energy transactions in smart grids providing a means to keep track of electricity consumed and delivered. It transforms the role of business in the energy transaction from that of the service provider to that of the consumer enabler. Additionally, blockchain is used as an integral part of cyber-security. The technology's codes allow people all over the world to take control of their digital identities. The sophisticated record-keeping databases of blockchain can help people verify their identity, get access to banking services, to insurance, and many other financial products. Blockchain's ability to give people control over their digital identities makes it an increasingly important tool in mitigating inequality around the world, and helps to protect people from fraud. Cyber-security is essentially ICT protecting itself against infiltration. This is important for our privacy, and our sense of trust in technological devices and software. Improvements in the sophistication of cyber-security goes hand-in-hand with advances in ICT and technology.

These ten technologies are poised to shape the way we do business. Technological innovations and applications can be incorporated in all sectors to expand and enhance products and services. As you read more about these technological advances and consider how they can be integrated in your field, consider too how they can be applied for positive impact of the SDGs. Let's explore the ten technological breakthroughs and find inspiration in their continued development.

1. NEW TECHNOLOGIES: MOBILE TELEPHONES AND INTERNET COMMUNICATION

The emergence of mobile telephones took some years to become affordable and mainstream. Motorola produced the first handheld mobile phone in 1973. It weighed 1.1 kg and you could only use it for 30 minutes before needing to recharge it for 10 hours. The first touch screen smartphone was introduced by Apple in 2007. In just 10 short years, the amount of people with smartphones has shot to 2.5 billion, that is a third of the world's entire population![35] And the amount of people with mobile phone subscriptions was 4.7 billion in 2016 with the expectation that this number will grow to 5.6 billion in 2020.[36] That is nearly everyone in the world with a mobile phone! Mobile phones have quickly become the standard throughout the world, and this technology has even overcome the fact that in developing countries, many areas do not have access to telephone land lines, making mobile phones a tremendous asset. However, while mobile phones are prevalent throughout the world, and most people even have smartphones which could grant them access to the internet, the connectivity with internet still needs to be improved and made more widely available. Phone access has reached areas in the world previously unconnected, but internet access, in many cases, has not become as widespread. Look at the figures below and you can see that mobile phone subscriptions seem to have even exceeded global population by this measure, caused undoubtedly by people having more than one subscription in some parts of the world, but internet access – while showing dramatic growth – is still lagging.

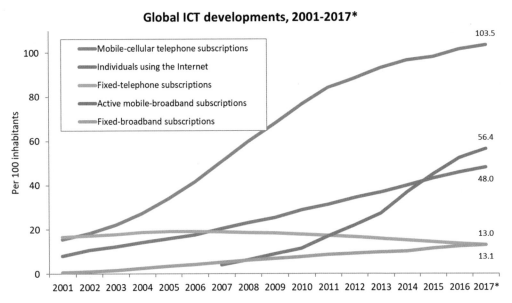

Global ICT developments, 2001-2017*

- Mobile-cellular telephone subscriptions
- Individuals using the Internet
- Fixed-telephone subscriptions
- Active mobile-broadband subscriptions
- Fixed-broadband subscriptions

Per 100 inhabitants

103.5

56.4

48.0

13.0

13.1

2001 2002 2003 2004 2005 2006 2007 2008 2009 2010 2011 2012 2013 2014 2015 2016 2017*

Figure 17
**Global ICT development 2001-2017
Source: itu.int**

Figure 18 (right)
Most adults in advanced economies use the internet, developing countries less so
Source: pewglobal.org

Internet connectivity is now a necessary utility. As shown in the overview of technological developments, new technologies all depend on, or are enhanced by, internet connectivity. With internet connectivity, people throughout the world can tap into the developments taking place; without it, they cannot. Furthermore, with the development of apps and knowledge sharing platforms, people, rich and poor, in every corner of the world, have the potential to gain access to each other, to knowledge, to products and to finances. Internet connectivity also brings with it the connection to social media. News apps, discussion platforms, internet shopping, and crowd sourcing, all of which have come on the scene relatively recently, yet they are so well-known and commonly used by people with internet access, that it is hard to remember what life was like without them. This access to information and to each other is invaluable and has become part of the daily lives for many people in the developed world and a part of businesses as well. Companies are regularly hiring people whose job is to control their online presence and monitor and steer social media campaigns and interactions with customers.

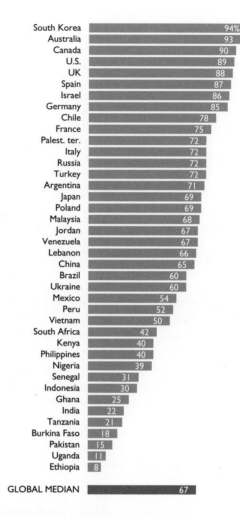

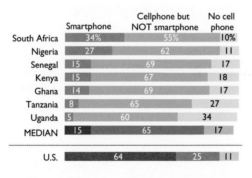

Figure 18 (right)
Most adults in advanced economies use the internet, developing countries less so
Source: pewglobal.org

Figure 19 (left)
Few Own Smartphones in Africa, But Cell Phones Common
Source: blogs.unicef.org
How Mobile Phones are Changing the Developing World

While mobile phone saturation globally covers most of the population even in developing countries, and internet connectivity is growing, internet connectivity must still catch up to the mobile phone levels. The ICT industry has a responsibility to play a key role in improving internet access. This is, in fact, one of the SDG Targets – Target 9c which reads: "Significantly increase access to Information and Communications Technology and strive to provide universal and affordable access to the internet in Least Developed Countries by 2020."

In the report produced by GSMA called *2016 Mobile Industry Impact Report: Sustainable Development Goals*[37], Mats Granryd the Director General of GSMA pointed out that while it is predicted that by 2020 nearly 60 % of the world's population will have access to the internet, this still leaves 40 % without. This 40 % represents people who need this connectivity the most. Granryd emphasized that this must change and the mobile industry is very focused on "extending network coverage to rural areas, improving affordability of mobile services, delivering locally relevant content and increasing digital skills and literacy." Granryd recognizes the industry's important opportunity to "leverage the mobile networks that we have built and the services we deliver to help achieve the Sustainable Development Goals."

This commitment to the SDGs was strongly asserted when the mobile industry became the first sector to commit to the Sustainable Development Goals in February 2016. And it is reaffirmed in the *2016 Mobile Industry Report* while also recognizing the challenges that still lay ahead: diminishing the digital divide, making internet and mobile telephone access universal, and at the same time creating sustainable shared value.

As shown earlier in this section, ICT and technology impact all of the SDGs and according to the GSMA report, there are four SDGs for which the greatest impact from the mobile and internet communication sector is felt: SDG 9: Industry, Innovation & Infrastructure which relates to the ICT industry's endeavors to connect and include all communities, stimulating economic participation. SDG 1: No Poverty, by providing equal access to economic resources including financial services. SDG 4: Quality Education, by providing access to educational content and digital resources, as was shown in the previously mentioned Nafham case. SDG 13: Climate Action, by helping to improve emergency communication and warning systems.

2. NEW TECHNOLOGIES: SOCIAL MEDIA, AND E-COMMERCE

Internet connectivity also facilitates social platforms. Worldwide, there are 1.86 billion people on Facebook, and between the years 2012 and 2013, the amount of local businesses with their own Facebook page doubled from 8 million to 16 million and by the end of 2015, that number had jumped to 50 million. The opportunities for businesses to use mobile technology are exponential. Facebook is the poster child of the social media explosion. Since the emergence and popularity of Facebook, other social media platforms have flourished as well. Social media, is now commonplace for people worldwide. We use it to connect to friends, but also to connect to business contacts, with platforms such as LinkedIn.

Greater connection among people on a larger and broader scale inspires innovations associated with this. For example, online customer reviews is a phenomenon that has also been prompted by these extensive connections. And because of these review systems, companies such as ebay can function and grow. People would otherwise be wary of sending money to a total stranger on the promise that the advertised product will be sent to them in return. But due to the reviews and rating system, a feeling of trust and a sense of guarantee is cultivated which correlates with the same feeling we have when ordering something from a company. Thus, business based on peer-to-peer sales is now a growing, flourishing business model.

We have seen many companies sprouting up for peer-to-peer car rentals such as SnappCar in Europe and Getaround in the US, for example. This disrupts the hold that car rental agencies have had over the market. And we have seen peer-to-peer lodging rentals with Airbnb disrupting the hotel industry. In a study conducted by BrightLocal,[38] 88 % of consumers trust online reviews as much as personal recommendations. Customer reviews and social media have also facilitated more trust in e-commerce. This has also caused disruptions such as retail stores closing down in favor of online shops. Some e-commerce companies are using their business model to not only make money but to also make a positive impact and contribute to the SDGs. Alibaba is one such company, as you can read in Case 17.

> ## 88 % OF CONSUMERS TRUST ONLINE REVIEWS AS MUCH AS PERSONAL RECOMMENDATIONS.
>
> BRIGHTLOCAL

17

ALIBABA GROUP

Rural Taobao; E-Commerce
Using a digital platform to expand access to
goods and services in China and worldwide

Case applied in: China
Headquarters located in: China
www.alibabagroup.com/en

IMPACT SDGS

SDG 10
Reduced Inequalities
Generated over RMB20 billion
for merchants in over 800
designated poverty counties
on Alibaba's China retail
marketplaces during the
twelve-month period ending in
March 2016.

SDG 11
**Sustainable Cities and
Communities**
Set up operations in over
16,500 villages in 333
counties, covering 27
provinces in China, with Rural
Taobao Service Centers,
connecting these rural areas
to urban through e-commerce
interaction.

SDG 17
Partnerships for the Goals
Cooperate with local
governments and populations
through Rural Taobao Partners
and support the estimated 600
million Chinese that live in
rural areas.

OUR STRATEGY IS TO SELL GOODS FROM URBAN AREAS TO VILLAGES, AS WELL AS HELP FARMERS SELL FARMER PRODUCTS TO PEOPLE LIVING IN THE CITIES. THIS WE BELIEVE **WILL HAVE A HUGE POTENTIAL IN THE FUTURE.**
DANIEL YONG ZHANG, DIRECTOR AND CEO ALIBABA

In China, the giant country's future business movements will have enormous impact globally. Companies like Alibaba are beginning to look into this opportunity by focusing on how eco-efficiency and a "Lean" agenda could save or make money through better management of the energy and resource flows of commerce. Despite reports of slowing growth in the Chinese economy, E-commerce giant Alibaba exceeded expectations, reporting that in the fiscal year ending March 31, 2017 revenue had an increase of 56% year-over-year. .

Alibaba's new consumer E-commerce business, Taobao, is hoping to reach consumers from the lower income demographic in rural parts of China who face limited choices, high prices and poor quality of products. Given the dispersed population and poor logistical infrastructure in these areas, there is a critical need for better services and retail offerings. In addition to Taobao, which is similar to eBay, China's largest E-commerce company presides over a collection of online platforms including Tmall and the payment service Alipay. All together, these platforms create one of the most sophisticated and lucrative online retail ecosystems in the world. With nearly half of China's population living in rural areas, there is significant opportunity for digitization and big data infrastructure, urban-rural integration and entrepreneurial and employment expansion (SDG11).

One of the main reasons for the company's high 2016 earnings was the continued expansion and

reach into rural China. As Alibaba expands to these rural areas, they are helping rural farmers market their products to urban consumers, and has created opportunities for people living in poverty to elevate their income levels (SDG 10). Alibaba sees rural China as a vast and largely untapped growth opportunity. At the end of 2014, there were just 178 million internet users in rural China, fewer than one in three residents. By December 2016, the rural coverage was up to 201 million.

Alibaba has invested 10 billion yuan over the past few years (US $1.5 million) in logistics, hardware and training to expand its e-commerce model to 100,000 villages, setting up rural service centers where it provides computers and monitors, training local residents to serve as its representatives in the centers. Traditional business models employed by Alibaba include E-Commerce, Layer Player and Long Tail. This involved creating Rural Taobao Service Centers, where Alibaba provides internet connections along with purchasing and delivery services that provide goods to consumers in these areas, and allows them to sell their products to other parts of China.

Rural Taobao also leverages the reach of its local partners to build a structure for young people to go back to their hometowns to start their own businesses (SDG 17). Rural Taobao Partners run the service centers that provide purchasing and delivery services.

CHALLENGE

To provide access to a broad variety of goods and services and to help farmers earn more by selling agricultural products directly to urban consumers.

OPPORTUNITIES FOR SCALE

Alibaba estimates that consumption in rural China will reach RMB1 trillion by 2020. Eventually, as part of the Lean dimension, Alibaba has ambitions to repurpose excess capacity by using this same infrastructure and digital platform to sell vegetables and fruits to the cities to further increase incomes for farmers.

Sources and further information

- http://www.reuters.com/article/
  us-development-goals-finance-
  idUSKCN0RQ0RD20150926
- https://www.devex.com/news/business-leaders-
  call-for-new-socially-focused-business-model-
  that-embraces-sdgs-89437
- https://www.brookings.edu/research/
  links-in-the-chain-of-sustainable-finance-
  accelerating-private-investments-for-the-sdgs-
  including-climate-action/
- http://www.bbc.com/news/
  technology-40509405
- http://fortune.com/2016/01/28/alibabas-rural-
  china/
- http://www.alibabagroup.com/en/ir/
  pdf/160614/09.pdf
- http://www.alibabagroup.com/en/ir/
  article?news=p150710
- http://www.alibabagroup.com/en/news/press_
  pdf/p170518.pdf
- http://cnnic.com.cn/IDR/
  ReportDownloads/201706/
  P020170608523740585924.pdf

" DESPITE REPORTS OF SLOWING GROWTH IN THE CHINESE ECONOMY, E-COMMERCE GIANT ALIBABA EXCEEDED EXPECTATIONS."

Customer reviews, peer-to-peer platforms, E-commerce, and social media not only serve as technological facilitators to new innovative businesses, they also facilitate grassroots movements. As mentioned in chapter 1, people do not have to wait for governments and even businesses to initiate sustainable practices. The SDGs belong to us all. And we can make our voices heard. Social media is far reaching and powerful. Companies now have whole departments designated to social media. Businesses can utilize social media to promote their business and advertise in a whole new way. Recommendations or 'word of mouth' explodes in volume with digital connectivity. On platforms such as Twitter, companies invite feedback from their customers and are obliged to respond as that feedback is public; social media is thus ensuring a higher level of integrity and transparency from companies. So if people encourage the companies they do business with to be more sustainable and strive towards achieving the SDGs, then companies will be more inspired to do so, to meet their customers' demands.

3. NEW TECHNOLOGIES: BIG DATA AND SMALL DATA

Big data is the collection of a large volume of data using hardware and software technology and can be used to gain insights into trends. It can be very helpful in strategic decision-making. It facilitates monitoring and evaluation and is therefore very useful in the analysis of the progress on the SDGs. Big data provides much needed statistics to know where and what the greatest challenges are as well as the impact that is being generated. It can supply information about where interventions are needed and monitor the process and progress.

Big data technology has several applications. For instance, the large-scale farming market has the potential to be worth US $145 to US $180 billion dollars by 2030 with the help of big data. Large-scale farms (farms with more than two hectares of land) account for an estimated 70 % of global land under cultivation. Research from the Business and Sustainable Development Commission has shown their yields can be improved by a further 40 % over the next 20 years (SDG 12).[39] One

of the key strategies to reach this goal is to improve the diffusion of technologies. For example, the Brazilian Agricultural Research Corporation, known as Embrapa, has pioneered more than 9,000 technology projects to develop Brazilian agriculture, including using big data techniques to optimize crop yields.[40]

Small data is information often collected to give specific information. For example, big data would collect information from health care data centers on diabetes trends in a particular country or among a certain demographic. Small data would collect information through sensors on a diagnostic tool of a patient's blood sugar levels over a given year. Small data is collected in many ways. It could be the data collected by surveys or observations. It can also be collected using technology such as sensors. Small data is integral in drones as they are designed to collect certain data, and integrated in AI to respond to certain cues, and small data helps drive the progress and integration of IoT. Small data collection is seen in watches that count our steps or parking garages to tell us if there are any spots available and where they are. Big and small data serves many purposes: among them, they promote transparency and help verify progress of SDG action. Data also helps businesses identify how they can realistically commit to the SDGs. Let's take Southwest Airlines and its Evolve project as an example. One of the key elements of the project was fuel efficiency. This action combined two issues simultaneously that addressed cost - fuel efficiency and environmental impact. When the airline replaced seat covers and other interior elements with lighter-weight, more environmentally friendly materials, it reduced the weight of each aircraft by more than 600lbs, saving fuel and reducing emissions.[41] These outcomes had objective measures that could be validated through data collection, which made the impact of the project comprehensible to managers, external stakeholders and observers. With sharply focused objectives and measurable outcomes, companies can give managers the opportunity to track progress and see success in the numbers. In this case, we also see that reducing fuel consumption delivers shared value: it saves money for the airline and reduces emissions (SDG 13) while also utilizing data for impactful advancements of the Global Goals.

Data collection enables systematic criteria-setting that makes a company's progress tangible. It allows managers to track performance against their stated goals and make adjustments when needed. Big and small data facilitate a data-driven conversation and give a structured analysis of what actions are beneficial and also which ones may not be working. In addition, external observers have the opportunity to monitor how closely the company is adhering to its public commitments. It makes the company's engagement with the SDGs deeper by facilitating investments in complementary initiatives. With the added element of transparency, data can help build trust among a company's stakeholders. It facilitates a clear and comprehensive dialogue on how the business is saving money, enhancing its brand value, and achieving its goals.

BIG AND SMALL DATA FACILITATE A DATA-DRIVEN CONVERSATION AND GIVE A STRUCTURED ANALYSIS OF WHAT ACTIONS ARE BENEFICIAL AND ALSO WHICH ONES MAY NOT BE WORKING.

Big and small data complement each other and businesses are making good use of both. For example, Disney provides their guests with a wristband fitted with sensors so they can easily check into their hotel room, buy their lunch and go through turnstiles. The wristband tracks the movements of the visitor using small data applications and feeds it to a big data collection facility for the company to analyze total visitor traffic which they can use to make appropriate adjustments to accommodate more visitors and ensure smooth flows. In other applications, small data technology can be applied to collecting information about a family's energy use, for example, while big data analytics would be used to collect data from an

entire region. The collection of both types of data is important in understanding the behavior of people and overarching influences that affect energy use. When small and big data are applied to issues relating to the SDGs, the insights gained can be used to focus on strategic and practical applications and innovations to move us forward towards achieving the Global Goals.

4. NEW TECHNOLOGIES: SMART GRIDS

Smart grids enhance and modernize existing energy grids. The standard energy grid was originally designed for one-way traffic - supplying energy from an energy plant to consumers. Now, smart grids are being designed to support two or multi-way traffic. They provide an electricity supply network that uses digital communications technology to detect and react to local changes in usage.

The system is a network of sensors that enable the remote monitoring of equipment and resources on an energy smart grid. Smart grid sensors are generally used to collect information from electrical meters, fault detectors, voltage generators and other connected devices. They are also used to monitor weather conditions and power line temperature. This information is then used to calculate energy use as well as the line's carrying capacity. When the data is analyzed and used to adjust the system, the power flow of existing transmission lines for power companies is increased significantly. A smart grid sensor can also be used within homes and businesses to increase energy efficiency.

A smart grid meta-analysis of 30 business cases for smart meter projects in 12 countries in 4 continents, found that on average, the Net Present Value (NPV) of project benefits exceeded the NPV of costs by nearly two to one. The International Renewable Energy Agency (IRE) reports that studies have found smart grid technology to be financially beneficial in several areas of the world. This technology is particularly beneficial in the Middle East and North Africa where investments could save the region US $300 million to

" THE 2030 AGENDA RECOGNIZES THE GREAT POTENTIAL OF GLOBAL CONNECTIVITY TO SPUR HUMAN PROGRESS."

ANTÓNIO GUTERRES, UN SECRETARY GENERAL

one billion dollars annually while helping to realize the potential for solar power.[42] Potential investments in sustainable technologies in the US, such as smart grid and renewables, have an NPV of 20 billion to 25 billion dollars based solely on benefits to utilities.

Smart grids monitor and help address several important issues, namely: increasing energy consumption; global climate change; utilization of renewable energy sources; and more efficient electricity management. With smart grids, energy generation is becoming decentralized, with people generating solar energy at their own homes, and personal electric vehicles being used as an energy source as well. Because of this multi-direction flow of energy, these systems require increased sophistication in the management of energy supply and demand. People are moving from their traditional role as consumers – consuming what the energy companies provide – to become 'energy prosumers' as they both produce and consume energy. An energy prosumer is a consumer of energy who also produces energy to provide for their own needs, and when their production exceeds their requirements, sells, stores or trades the surplus energy.

KT Corporation is an example of a company that has used smart grids to develop its KT-MEG (Micro Energy Grid).[43] The KT-MEG platform was implemented in 2015 as a total energy management solution that has 1,700 client sites along with 1,400 electric car charging sites across Korea. On the supply side, the KT-MEG monitoring center has managed to increase generation efficiency by 20 % through an integrated system that enhances the efficiency of various energy sources. On the demand side, the system has helped domestic hospitals save up to 72 % of energy costs.

Smart grids and the IoT work together to manage electricity systems. Research shows that the implementation of smart grid systems has the potential of lowering carbon emissions by approximately 12 %[45] because of the grid's response to information collected. For example, if the smart grid senses that there is no recent electrical activity in a certain home, high-energy devices such as water heaters are automatically turned off. Smart grids in combination with other technologies can change the way we consume and 'prosume' energy, and this can go a long way towards helping to achieve SDG 7 – the provision of affordable and clean energy to all.

Figure 20 **Smart grid**

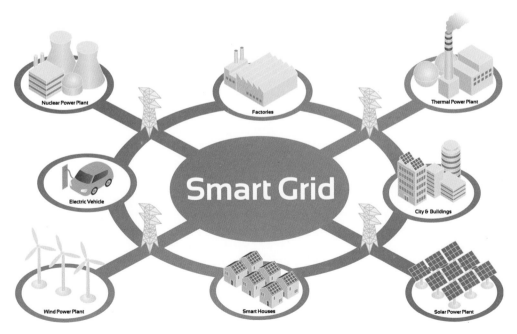

18

CASE NO.

SIEMENS

Smart Grid Integration
Energy management - rethinking power for the better

Case applied in: Australia and New Zealand
Headquarters located in: Germany
www.siemens.com

IMPACT SDGS

SDG 8

Decent Work & Economic Growth

Australia's Climate Change Authority has identified energy efficiency as the best way to reduce CO2 emissions while improving productivity and creating jobs. And the federal government is working with Siemens to improve energy productivity by 40% by the year 2030.

SDG 9

Industry, Infrastructure & Innovation

Cumulatively, Australia and New Zealand will invest $ 6.1 billion in smart grid infrastructure over the next decade.

BY FAILING TO PREPARE, YOU ARE PREPARING TO FAIL
– ESPECIALLY IN AN INCREASINGLY COMPLEX ENERGY SYSTEM.

DR. MICHAEL WEINHOLD, CTO OF SIEMENS ENERGY MANAGEMENT

Siemens' commitment to the SDGs is embedded in their focus areas on electrification, automation and digitalization. The company is one of the world's largest providers of energy- and resource-efficient technologies. Their concentration on smart grid investments will focus on improving the smart electricity metering, battery storage, advanced storage and grid communications sectors to help utility firms improve their energy billing, clean energy portfolios and management of grid networks. Power outages have an immediate and significant impact across all infrastructure domains. Avoiding them requires sensible planning and timely investment in the right technologies. For example, in 2006 when 250,000 customers in Auckland had their power supply disrupted when a transmission circuit failed, the disruption cost the New Zealand economy approximately AUD $70 million of GDP. Siemens' smart grid solutions make it possible to modernize and adapt existing power grids to future expectations (SDG 9). They enable power operators to manage energy more efficiently, react more flexibly to changing demand and incorporate electricity from distributed and renewable sources.

Australia and New Zealand are together predicted to invest AUD $6.billion in smart grid infrastructure between 2017 and 2027. The two countries are well positioned to develop and expand projects such as smart metering, battery energy storage, advanced sensors and grid communications (SDG 8). Strong utilities, unsubsidized power prices and high consumption rates com-

bined with high per-capita income and positive policy environments for clean technology offer an encouraging environment for smart grid implementation.

Australia and New Zealand have abundant energy sources and benefit from a reliable energy supply. However, power grids still face growing challenges: rising demand, vulnerability to severe weather, and the tricky integration of renewables. Boosting efficiency and resilience improves the affordability of power and helps get the grid ready for the future. As of March 2017, New Zealand has completed a significant majority of its national smart metering rollout, and the Australian state of Victoria has completed its statewide rollout. Regulations in other Australian states and at the national level have been more limited. But Siemens' investments will particularly benefit the state of South Australia, which has recently suffered from statewide blackouts. New Zealand has accomplished its smart grid rollout without significant regulations, due to positive business case indicators. The global grid-connected energy storage sector is expected to expand from a total installed capacity of three GW at the end of 2016 to 28 GW by 2022, which is equivalent to the power used by 18.6 million households. By incorporating energy storage across the electric power network, Siemens will help utilities and communities around the world to optimize their infrastructure investments, increase network flexibility and resiliency, and accelerate cost-effective integration of renewable electricity generation (SDG 17).

CHALLENGE

To improve the operations of utility firms and help countries secure the reliability of their grid networks from power outages.

OPPORTUNITIES FOR SCALE

Outcomes of the adoption of smart grid technologies across the Australia and New Zealand region could deliver significant economy wide benefits in the order of AUD $9.5 to $28.5 billion over 20 years, and lower network prices. There is also potential for all customers to benefit from the introduction of a smart grid – even those customers who do not actively engage with the smart grid – by between AUD $156 and $2000 per year.

Sources and further information

- http://corporate.siemens.com.au/en/home/about-siemens.html
- http://corporate.siemens.com.au/content/dam/internet/siemens-com-au/root/siemens-in-aunz-2015.pdf
- http://corporate.siemens.com.au/content/dam/internet/siemens-com-au/root/about-us/siemens-company-presentation-au-nz-march-2017.pdf
- http://www.northeast-group.com/reports/Brochure-Oceania%20Smart%20Grid-Market%20Forecast%202017-2027%20-%20Northeast%20Group.pdf
- http://www.powerengineeringint.com/articles/2017/03/australia-and-new-zealand-to-invest-6-1bn-in-smart-grid-technologies.html
- www.smartgridobserver.com
- http://onlinelibrary.wiley.com/doi/10.1002/app5.95/full
- http://www.environment.gov.au/energy/programs/smartgridsmartcity

" SIEMENS' SMART GRID SOLUTIONS MAKE IT POSSIBLE TO MODERNIZE AND ADAPT EXISTING POWER GRIDS TO FUTURE EXPECTATIONS."

5. NEW TECHNOLOGIES: 3D PRINTING

3D printing (also known as 'Additive Manufacturing') will revolutionize the manufacturing industry and consumer access to customized products. It will create amazing opportunities for people in developed countries as well as unlocking incredible opportunities for people in developing countries. 3D Printing is a process that creates a physical object from a digital design. There are different 3D printing technologies and materials you can print with, but all are based on the same principle: a digital model is turned into a solid three-dimensional physical object by adding material layer by layer.

3D PRINTING TECHNOLOGY HAS THE POTENTIAL TO REVOLUTIONIZE MANUFAC-TURING, LOGISTICS, HEALTH CARE, AND EVEN FOOD PRODUCTION.

Although 3D printing is still in its beginning phases, experimenting with a variety of possibilities, this technology has the potential to revolutionize manufacturing, logistics, health care, and even food production to name only a few areas. Just imagine villages in the developing world printing parts for farm equipment or even printing artificial limbs for people who would otherwise not have the means to receive expensive - and most likely inaccessible - care. Imagine mobile production plants with the ability to quickly respond to disaster zones, printing out emergency provisions including anything from arm splints to tent stakes, to food even! 3D printers can now handle materials ranging from titanium to human cartilage to food nutrients.

The products that are replicated are fully functional. Batteries and body parts have already been printed, as have edible food products. Although this emerging technological advancement is in its experimental stages, it is very exciting, and fas-

cinating leaps are happening. As mobile phones were just starting to come on the market 20 years ago, but faced an exponential explosion with figures such as 750 million people owning a mobile phone in the year 2000, to reports that there are now more mobile phones that people in the world (over 7 billion!), one can easily imagine other technological advances such as 3D printing becoming mainstays, embedded in our everyday lives.

As Elkington stated in the *Breakthrough Forecast,* "It took the [3D] sector 20 years to reach a market value of US $1 billion. The second billion was attained only five years later, and analysts now believe that it could grow at least fourfold over the next ten years." Elkington also refers to a study by the McKinsey Global Institute that the 3D related activities could have an impact of up to US $550 billion a year by 2025. Startups are debuting all over the world already with applications to unlock new markets using 3D printing. For example, the company African Born 3D Printing (AB3D)[46] uses recycled materials to build affordable 3D printers and waste products as print filament. They are providing customized solutions to a variety of issues in Africa, such as shoes that are specially designed to tackle the issue of jiggers infestation in Kenya and shoes for people with deformities, and a 3D printed microscope providing medical equipment and laboratory analysis in areas where these facilities are otherwise limited or non-existent (See Case 19).

3D PRINTING MARKET FROM 2017 TO 2021; IT IS ESTIMATED THAT THIS INDUSTRY WILL BE SIZED AT AROUND US $26.5 BILLION IN 2021.[47]

"IT TOOK THE 3D SECTOR 20 YEARS TO REACH A MARKET VALUE OF US $1 BILLION. THE SECOND BILLION WAS ATTAINED ONLY FIVE YEARS LATER, AND ANALYSTS NOW BELIEVE THAT IT COULD GROW AT LEAST FOURFOLD OVER THE NEXT TEN YEARS."

JOHN ELKINGTON

CASE NO.

AFRICAN BORN 3D PRINTING (AB3D)

Locally Produced Products for Social Impact
3D Printing - Designing a better future and
making new technologies available to everyone

Case applied in: Africa, Kenya
Headquarters located in: Kenya
www.ab3d.co.ke

IMPACT SDGS

SDG 1
No Poverty
Focused on creating functional
products to improve the lives
of people living in poverty.

SDG 3
Good Health and Well-Being
Shoes specially made for
deformed feet and to protect
against jiggers.

SDG 4
Quality Education
Target market is diverse
schools, design architecture
firms, rapid prototyping and
manufacturing institutions.

SDG 11
Sustainable Cities and Communities
Provides autonomy of
production and access to
materials that are otherwise
too expensive. Uses plastic
and electronic waste.

SDG 12
Responsible Consumption and Production
Uses recycled electrical
materials and plastic waste;
buying a kilo of waste for
30ksh (less than $1) to build
printer motors.

BROADLY SPEAKING, WE WANT OUR PRINTERS TO PRINT SOLUTIONS
TO SOME OF THE PROBLEMS FACED BY KENYA AND THE GREATER DEVELOPING WORLD.
ROY OMBATTI FOUNDER AB3D

AB3D is one of the first companies bringing 3D Printing technology to Africa. They believe that the technology holds great potential to bring about positive change. They are focused on creating functional products that will improve the lives of people living in poverty (SDG 1). Based in Nairobi, Kenya, the company locally designs and manufactures quality and affordable 3D Printers and filament from recycled waste.

AB3D not only sells printers and filament, they sell components for the printers, rent the printers and provide training in how to use them, and provide repair services.

The printers are unique in that they are made out of waste material and the quality of the product rivals what is made using high-end machinery. AB3D printers are also locally produced and assembled using local materials, as opposed to importing foreign materials. The team is very focused on recycling and reusing waste and has developed a way to extrude the filament from recycled PET waste (SDG 12). To obtain filament, AB3D collaborates with waste collectors who collect and sort, then bring it to AB3D.

All AB3D's work is kept local, but the startup is open-sourcing all its designs. They aim to share knowledge with regard to 3D Printing and its future potential. Founder Roy Ombatti believes, "The gap between the haves and the have-nots is huge. We've got to continue trying to give others

a better life." Their goal is to get their printers into schools (all levels) since they see 3D printing as a powerful tool for education (SDG 4).

Partnering with local businesses, AB3D designs and produces custom products that help to solve local challenges (SDG 17), including access to shoes. In Nairobi there is a problem of jiggers which are fleas in the ground that burrow into the skin, ultimately causing foot deformities. This affects many children. Roy Ombatti, founder of AB3D created a project called "Happy Feet" to design custom-made 3D printed shoes for deformed feet (SDG 3).

AB3D's work centers around how it can contribute to the community (SDG 11) with their innovations. They offer unprecedented opportunities to the local population with their 3D printed microscope design which facilitates medical and educational independence. They have also produced other medical devices including a syringe extension which helps to solve the problem of imported syringes not being able to be used because of mismatched components.

Kenya has identified the issue of negative environmental impact from electronic waste and has recently made the need for solutions a national priority. Because AB3D uses electronic waste to build their 3D hardware, they are contributing towards turning the negative environmental impact of E-waste into positive impact for social advancement.

CHALLENGE

To produce affordable 3D printers so more people can have access to them, and bring this revolutionary technology to Africa, integrating local needs and challenges.

OPPORTUNITIES FOR SCALE

AB3D aim to get their printers to every school in Kenya to be used as a teaching aid and through this create jobs, alleviate poverty, and help clean the environment. E-waste dumps in Africa are a major issue, so reusing discarded electronic materials to bring communities the far-reaching benefits that 3D printing can offer, solves two significant challenges in that region. There are great opportunities in Africa for 3D printing. Countries that lack large-scale industrial manufacturing can be given the opportunity to level the playing field with the introduction of cutting-edge technology to an untapped market.

Sources and further information

- https://techpoint.ng/2015/09/30/ab3d-feature/
- https://www.3dhubs.com/what-is-3d-printing
- http://stisolutions4sdgs. globalinnovationexchange.org/innovations/ ab3d-african-born-3d-printing
- http://www.techfortrade.org/
- https://www.idin.org/blog-news-events/blog/ charity-roi-how-african-entrepreneurs-are- leading-way
- https://www.engineeringforchange.org/3d- printing-with-e-waste-five-questions-for-roy- ombatti/

" AB3D BELIEVES THAT 3D TECHNOLOGY HOLDS GREAT POTENTIAL TO BRING ABOUT POSITIVE CHANGE."

There is tremendous potential for 3D printing and as shown, it can impact many other sectors besides manufacturing, such as healthcare, logistics and food. 3D printing can have a huge impact on many of the SDGs. Take SDG 12 (Responsible Consumption and Production) for example, by printing components as needed, and at location, 3D printing contributes towards reduced waste and reduced pollution due to transport. Now the interesting challenge is to come up with environmentally responsible filaments for the printer to use. AB3D is doing that by using recycled E-waste and researchers at MIT have designed a way to use cellulose in 3D printing, potentially providing a renewable, biodegradable alternative to the polymers currently used as filaments. Because cellulose is so inexpensive, bio-renewable, biodegradable, and chemically versatile, it is used in a lot of products — from pharmaceuticals, medical devices, food additives, building materials, clothing, to many other items for consumer or commercial use.[48]

3D PRINTING, BY ITS VERY NATURE, AND WITH THE CURRENT EXPERIMENTS AND START- UPS, OPENS THE DOOR TO ACCELERATING MANY OF THE SDGs.

And even more phenomenally, the experiments that are already being made with 3D printing of food give way to a whole new perspective to achieving SDG 2 (No Hunger). And 3D printing of body parts, not only as prosthetics but using human tissue as filament and printing organs or real human limbs rather than the current artificial components can impact human beings in ways that are even hard to imagine. 3D printing, by its very nature, and with the current experiments and startups, opens the door to accelerating many of the SDGs.

The 3rd European edition of the 3D Food Printing Conference took place in June, 2017 in the Netherlands.[49] The event brought together over 300 attendees and speakers, who shared their opinions and views on the latest developments in 3D food printing, vertical farming, smart farming and healthy nutrition, and discussed the following questions: Which industries will be influenced by the technology? Which food components can be printed in the near future? And which aspects should be taken into account to ensure safety and maintainability of 3D printed food? As this technology is poised to explode in its applications, it is an interesting time to explore the possibilities and applications.

3D PRINTING OF FOOD CAN GO A LONG WAY TOWARDS FEEDING THE GROWING POPULATION, MEETING THE INCREASING DEMAND FOR FOOD, AND UTILIZING MORE NUTRITIOUS, SUSTAINABLE ALTERNATIVES.

Since 3D printers can utilize nutrients from a variety of sources to create food items, it can be used in developing countries and for other demographics to combat malnutrition. Already 3D food printing is being used to prevent malnutrition and hunger among the elderly in Germany as the German-based company, Biozoon Food Innovations use 3D printing to produce more enjoyable meals for the elderly who need to eat a pureed diet. Fresh ingredients, such as vegetables and chicken are broken down and printed into the same shape as the original ingredient, forming its three-dimensional shape. However, it has a softer texture, allowing for the food to be enjoyed as 'food' rather than a paste-type substance, but soft enough to meet pensioners' dietary needs.[50] And food scientists at IKEA's Space10 external innovation studio are exploring new ways of making a sustainable meat product. As meat production creates an enormous burden on the environment, many companies are experimenting with ways to use meat substitutes. By utilizing 3D printing, different ingredients can be used such as algae and even insects to create a meat-like taste, and shapes can be replicated to entice people to accept the meat substitute. This type of food production can go a long way towards feeding the growing population, meeting the increasing demand for food, and utilizing more nutritious, sustainable alternatives.

3D printing has the potential to be a disruptive technology on many fronts. Businesses in all sectors will likely be using this technology in some capacity in the future, and new markets will open up as a result.

6. NEW TECHNOLOGIES: ROBOTICS AND ARTIFICIAL INTELLIGENCE (AI)

Robotics is another technological development that will change the business landscape. Although we have had robotic automation for a while, it is developing along with artificial intelligence to become a phenomenon that will alter the job market significantly.

Firstly, robotics and AI technology will be implemented for jobs that the manufacturing world calls "the three Ds" – jobs that are dirty, dull and dangerous. In addition to the current use of robotics to do menial tasks faster, such as their use in industrial production, it is predicted that robots will be able to handle more complex matters and their use in other capacities will grow. The implementation of robotics and AI for jobs that are dangerous or extremely precise is already happening, robots are being used for firefighting[51] and for surgical procedures.[52] Robots will also quickly enter the high-tech service economy in legal analysis, medical diagnostics, and other areas of complex tasks and problem solving. According to the *Breakthrough Forecast* some 'sweet spots' in the development of robotic applications include the use of robots in the alternative energy sector as solar-panel cleaning robots. Robots will also be used more extensively in the health care sector to assist doctors and perform nursing duties such as delivering medicine throughout hospitals. There is also much talk about using robots in senior care

ROBOTICS TECHNOLOGY

- US $82.7 BILLION ESTIMATED MARKET SIZE IN 2020
- 20,000+ PATENT APPLICATIONS FILED ANNUALLY
- US $188 BILLION ESTIMATED SPENDING IN 2020.

BREAKTHROUGH.UNGLOBALCOMPACT.ORG

as the global population is living longer, and there is a severe shortage of nurses.

The estimated market for robotics in 2020 will be US $82.7 billion dollars, according to Allied Market Research and published in the article by Global Compact called *Next Generation Robotics* [53]. The article also shows some of the potential impact of robotics on the SDGs including SDG 14 (Life Below Water) by providing data relevant to pollution monitoring and supporting marine management through unmanned underwater vehicles. There are many opportunities for robots to help accelerate all of the SDGs and healthcare in particular is a hot spot now. In addition to the tasks mentioned above, robots can provide medical assistance in remote areas where few trained personnel are available, and because they can also perform dangerous tasks and thus relieve humans of the associated risks, they not only provide medical care but are technological preventers of health and safety dangers as well. This will certainly have an impact on SDG 3 (Providing Good Health and Well-being to All).

An example of robots 'doing our dirty work' can be found in the robotic "pig" from Thermo-System. This robot deals with sewage sludge to dry

CASE NO.

THERMO-SYSTEM

Pig Balthazar
Solar sludge-drying robotic system

Case applied in: Global
Headquarters located in: Germany
www.thermo-system.com

IMPACT SDGS

SDG 3
Good Health & Well-Being
Manage the 60 million tons of sewage sludge produced every year in Germany alone.

SDG 6
Clean Water & Sanitation
Containing mostly water, 90 to 95 % of wet sludge mass can be done away through the economically friendly drying process, saving energy and water resources.

SDG 7
Affordable and Clean Energy
In Luxemburg, the sludge is transformed to a valuable fuel – by using solar energy. The dried sludge is used in a local cement factory as a substitute for fossil fuels.

SDG 12
Responsible Consumption & Production
The processing of sludge is made more efficient through automation.

WHEN WE DEVELOPED THE PIG, WE THOUGHT: **HOW WOULD A MACHINE LOOK LIKE IF IT LIVED IN THE SLUDGE?**
DR. TILO CONRAD, FOUNDER & CEO THERMO-SYSTEM

Pig Balthazar is an electrical pig (also known as the Electric Mole) built by the German company Thermo-System to reduce sewer sludge disposal costs, make the process more efficient, and protect the environment from harmful substances during processing and use (SDG 3). Sewage sludge is traditionally deposited or is spread over farmland as fertilizer, but sludge may be full of harmful materials, such as germs, hormones or chemical substances. Therefore, Thermo-Systems developed a system to process the sludge in an environmentally safe way using automated robots to 'do the dirty work'.

The product was conceived with the idea that a manmade system should resemble nature and naturally breakdown matter. There are approximately 300 completes operating all over the world, each working day and night. The stainless steel pigs belong to a larger drying system patented by Thermo-System. In greenhouse-like sheds, the wet sewage sludge is spread for drying. The sludge absorbs the heat from the solar rays, and an innovative ventilation system based on sensors and microprocessors keeps the air inside the shed warm and dry.

The electrical pig is used as a fully automated robot. With its mixing tools, it turns over and aerates the microbiologically highly active sludge and thus accelerates the drying process and helps prevent rotting. The whole system works fully automatically, uses up very little energy, and can be easily maintained. It is highly efficient due to process control by the company's ClimaControl-System. Solar radiation is harvested by the greenhouse construction and utilized for water evaporation (greenhouse- effect). A sophisticated aeration system with oscillating fans (MoviVent) optimizes the air stream on the surface of the sludge. The air exchange with the ambient is controlled by wall-mounted fans. The sludge is then spread, turned and mixed by the fully automated Pig. All components are controlled by a central control unit, equipped with ClimaControl-Software. Therefore, the drying conditions are automatically optimized at every moment guaranteeing best drying performance (SDG 12).

After the drying process, the sludge has lost its strong odor, is virtually free of bacteria and the volume is significantly reduced (SDG 6). For example, 600 tons of sludge could be turned into 60 tons, which requires much less fossil fuel to transport and less fossil fuels to burn it when breaking it down. The sludge itself can also be used as a fuel source, as a cement factory in Luxemburg has done (SDG 7).

CHALLENGE

To solve waste disposal problems of sewage plants using renewable energy and robotics to do the dirty work.

OPPORTUNITIES FOR SCALE

The company has built more than 150 sewage-sludge drying plants worldwide. In 2016, the joint venture of Thermo-System and Waterleau was awarded the assignment to construct the largest solar sewage sludge drying plant worldwide in Marrakech, Morocco. In South America, Thermo-System's solar wood drying systems are becoming increasingly popular. Thermo-System expects more business from parts of Eastern Europe that are joining the European Union as they endeavor to meet environmental standards.

Sources and further information

- http://www.thermo-system.com/fileadmin/user_upload/PDF_Datei/en/eLeaflet_SolarBatch_2016.pdf
- http://www.upi.com/Business_News/Energy-Industry/2006/03/11/Robot-pig-drives-German-drying-plants/UPI-52961142091780/
- https://www.treehugger.com/solar-technology/robotic-pigs-help-dry-sewage.html
- http://www.thermo-system.com/produkte/solare-klaerschlammtrocknung/das-elektrische-schweinr/trocknen/

" THERMO-SYSTEMS DEVELOPED A SYSTEM TO PROCESS THE SLUDGE IN AN ENVIRONMENTALLY SAFE WAY USING AUTOMATED ROBOTS TO 'DO THE DIRTY WORK'. "

and aerate it so it can be transported more easily and efficiently to be used as fertilizer (See Case 20).

Artificial Intelligence can be, and is already being, implemented in a multitude of ways. Apple used AI to give us Siri – their virtual assistant. And Google recently announced that the company will be focusing heavily on AI both for its services and research. Google plans to not only use the developments of AI in its own products, but also use it to help medical researchers. CEO Sundar Pichai talked about using AI to help sequence DNA and help pathologists locate things like the spread of cancer. Pichai acknowledges that it's not completely perfect though: "There are important caveats, we do have higher false positives," Pichai said. "But already getting this into the hands of pathologists can improve diagnosis." [54] Google announced that it's already partnering with health care providers to put the technology into action to help improve care and prevent medical incidents.

COMPANIES AND DEVELOPERS SHOULD KEEP THE SDGs AND THE SPECIFIC ASSOCIATED TARGETS AND INDICATORS IN MIND AS THE GUIDELINES OF HOW WE WANT TO APPLY THIS TECHNOLOGY.

There are many opportunities for AI applications as companies such as ARM (See Case 20) understand. They are looking broadly at opportunities to utilize AI technology to facilitate and accelerate innovative projects from organizations involved in achieving the SDGs. As an example, widespread dissemination of information is often thwarted by illiteracy that prevails in poor areas of the world. By using voice activation, AI can be implemented to contribute to the spread of knowledge without needing to read. Voice activation and recognition – 'Chatbots' are becoming more commonplace. With the introduction of Siri in 2011 with the IPhone, artificial intelligence and a personal chatbot entered the homes of people worldwide.

While many applications of AI are fun, convenient and full of potential for positive impact of people's lives, scientists and leaders such as Elon Musk and Stephen Hawking are warning about not getting carried away with the development of AI. If we make artificial intelligence too intelligent, versatile and connected to other AI units, there is a risk that human beings can lose control of this technology. It can sound like the making of a science fiction movie, yet when the likes of people as Hawking and Musk speak out in warning, then it seems prudent to listen. That isn't to say though that there is limited opportunity in this field. On the contrary, there are many applications to explore and advances to make. But here again, it is the clarity of focus that is most relevant. Companies and developers should keep the SDGs and the specific associated Targets and Indicators in mind as the guidelines of how we want to apply this technology. Robotics and AI have the potential to create positive impact for humanity, but we should proceed with caution.

" WE MUST TAKE
ADVANTAGE OF THIS RAPID
TECHNOLOGICAL CHANGE
TO MAKE THE WORLD
MORE PROSPEROUS AND
INCLUSIVE."

JIM YONG KIM, PRESIDENT, THE WORLD BANK GROUP

21

CASE NO. ARM

Literacy Bridge, Simprints, Children for Health and Khushi Baby
Partnering for technology supported aid projects

Case applied in: Asia, Africa, Ghana
Headquarters located in: Cambridge, United Kingdom
www.arm.com

IMPACT SDGS

SDG 2

No Hunger

"Talking Book" provides education on health and agriculture to reduce maternal and child mortality, hunger and chronic malnutrition.

SDG 3

Good Health and Well-Being

Children for Health promotes good health, and vaccination monitoring to children who are tasked with caring for siblings.

SDG 4

Quality Education

Talking Book provided health, agriculture, and gender equality education to 175,000 people in under-served communities; Children for Health combined education and technology to provide information to children in impoverished areas.

SDG 10

Reduced Inequalities

Simprints made fingerprint scanners, providing 55,000 people a means of identification, to access essential services.

SDG 17

Partnerships for the Goals

Arm works with many partners to provide technological solutions to many global challenges.

I WANT ARM TO WORK WITH PARTNERS THAT CHALLENGE US TO THINK IN NEW WAYS, **ENABLING ARM AND THE ARM PARTNERSHIP TO CREATE SOLUTIONS** THAT ADDRESS LONG-STANDING CHALLENGES AND NEW OPPORTUNITIES.
SIMON SEGARS, CEO ARM

As the world's leading semiconductor IP company, Arm's technologies reach 80% of the world's population, and provides artificial intelligence solutions (AI) for a range of products. Arm is committed to contributing to the SDGs. CEO Simon Segars states: "As Arm develops innovative IoT solutions, we can both enable a high growth market and contribute to a sustainable future."

Arm partners with organizations such as Literacy Bridge who challenge Arm to think in new ways (SDG 17). Literacy Bridge is a charitable organization that uses Arm-based technology in their "Talking Book" to provide those living in extreme poverty with education on health, agriculture, and gender equality (SDG 2 & 4). Literacy Bridge developed and delivered more than 100 agriculture and health audio messages to every family in 49 villages in Ghana. Talking Book also included education using audio dramas that address how husbands and wives can re-examine gender roles to enable them to achieve more for themselves and their children. More than 140,000 hours of listening and learning were created. Talking Book can also be used as a recording device which enables people to share knowledge with each other.

Arm also collaborates with Simprints, a non-profit tech company, to scale-up its mission to reduce inequality (SDG 10) by simplifying fingerprinting technology. Fingerprint identification enables access to essential services, financing, and aid. Currently, 1.1 billion people worldwide lack formal identification, preventing them from accessing vital services, such as healthcare. Simprints manufactured the first fingerprint scanners, which were distributed in remote areas of Bangladesh and Nepal, reaching 55,000 mothers and children. Arm helped Simprints build low-cost, mobile biometric scanners and open-source software that digitally links a person's fingerprints to their health records. The tools are used by researchers, NGOs, and governments around the world.

Children for Health, another Arm partner focuses on engaging with children as ambassadors and communicators of critical health messages in their communities. Children in impoverished societies play a vital role in looking after their siblings, often without adult supervision. This initiative offer education and empowerment, giving more than 100,000 children information about tackling the threat of malaria, HIV/Aids and other life-threatening diseases (SDG 3).

Khushi Baby, a winner of the Arm, UNICEF and frog 'Wearables for Good' design challenge in 2015, is a wearable personal immunization record. The Khushi Baby digital necklace integrates Near Field Communication (NFC) technology with mobile health and cloud computing to make the wearer's medical history accessible to officials, providing a reliable, two-year immunization record for children – even those in remote and isolated areas. Khushi Baby is looking to expand its reach from 1,000 children in 100 villages in India, to children in Africa and the Middle East, and expand into broader maternal and child healthcare functions.

CHALLENGE

To utilize technology to provide education on health issues and to facilitate, and monitor, access to services and aid.

OPPORTUNITIES FOR SCALE

Arm is supporting the development of the next generation of Talking Book. The longer-term goal for Simprints is to reach between two to three million people in 2017. Children for Health is expecting to continue its work reaching hundreds of thousands of people. Arm continues to explore ways that its technology can be used to advance the SDGs, and work collaboratively with organizations to utilize Arm-based technology and expertise for a sustainable and connected future.

Sources and further information

- https://www.arm.com/company/corporate-responsibility
- https://www.arm.com/company/corporate-responsibility/read-our-reports
- https://www.bloomberg.com/research/stocks/private/snapshot.asp?privcapId=388030
- https://www.arm.com/innovation/products/talking-book.php
- https://www.simprints.com/
- http://wearablesforgood.com/
- https://2030vision.com/vision.html
- http://www.khushibaby.org/

" AS ARM DEVELOPS INNOVATIVE IoT SOLUTIONS, THE COMPANY CAN BOTH ENABLE A HIGH GROWTH MARKET AND CONTRIBUTE TO A SUSTAINABLE FUTURE."

7. NEW TECHNOLOGIES: DRIVERLESS VEHICLES

The autonomous road vehicle revolution has the potential to change the way we travel and interact with transportation. It is presenting new business opportunities and ownership models, with people buying mobility only when they need it.[55] In this sense, vehicles will be used more of the time which will not necessarily mean more cars on the road, but it will mean less cars parked. If vehicles are on the road and in use all the time, there will be less of a need for parking spaces and this could potentially free up roadside space for city planners to repurpose it (SDG 11).

Driverless cars are the best known examples of autonomous vehicles. Trials of driverless cars from large companies such as Tesla, Audi and Google have accelerated, with a number of other enterprises ramping up efforts to develop new solutions as well. Car manufacturers such as Toyota and Ford are already using this kind of technology to achieve their self-parking option, where drivers need only to press a button and sensors and software take over to park the car in the designated spot.

DRIVERLESS CARS PRESENT NEW BUSINESS OPPORTUNITIES AND OWNERSHIP MODELS.

The World Economic Forum predicts the tipping point to be when driverless cars equal 10 % of all cars on US roads. This occurrence is projected to be only a few years away, happening in 2026.[56] Autonomous vehicles are touted as having a number of benefits including: reduction of traffic and increase in safety as driverless vehicles communicate with each other and their surroundings. For passengers, it provides more free time and less stress due to the pressures of driving. And there are advantages to the environment too. It is predicted that the mass use of electric, driverless taxis could reduce CO_2 emissions by 87 to 94 % per mile by 2030.[57] Autonomous cars use less gas and energy when driving, compared to a vehicle driven by a human. Most gas is burned when driv-

> ## DRIVERLESS CARS ARE UNDOUBTEDLY A BOON FOR THE PLANET. NOT ONLY WILL THEY HELP CURB EMISSIONS, REDUCE FATALITIES OF HUMANS AND WILDLIFE, AND ALLOW CITY PLANNERS TO FOCUS ON GREEN SPACE MORE THAN ROADS, THEY'LL ALSO GIVE EVERY COMMUTER MORE TIME IN THEIR DAYS.[72]
>
> GREENER IDEAL

ing at high speeds, braking, and re-accelerating excessively. Self-driving vehicles cut these factors out of their driving style, meaning less gas is burned, or battery power consumed, resulting in less air pollution. Additionally, according to research from the US Department of Energy (DOE), automated vehicles could lead to better access to transportation and less road accidents.[58] Automated cars can safely travel significantly faster than human-driven vehicles— computers have much quicker reactions than human drivers— which matters of course on a safety level but also on an environmental level because fuel economy typically decreases at speeds over 50 miles per hour.[59]

Tesla is getting closer to having a fully self-driving car, which includes the Model S, Model X, and future Model 3. They are being built with new hardware that will enable them to be completely autonomous. The one caveat is that the feature won't be functional without further software validation and regulatory approval. These cars are being built with eight cameras that provide 360-degree visibility and 250 meters of range to better assist in driving themselves.

They come with one radar sensor, 12 ultrasonic sensors, and Nvidia's Titan GPU onboard comput-

Figure 21 **Key Numbers Autonomous vehicles**[63]

ing system to process all the information.[60] All of these additions also improve Tesla cars' Autopilot capabilities.

Driverless buses are also being developed in cities where there is a lot of constant transport. In 2016, Helsinki tried out an autonomous bus in one of the first tests of its kind.[61] Other cities such as Las Vegas and London have also been trialing this technology for their bus fleets. In Stockholm/Kista, Ericsson demonstrated – together with Nobina (a bus operator) and the city Stockholm/Kista Science City and a number of other supporting partners – solutions that show the future of bus transport and ticketing. Two other applications of the technology are freight platooning and waste

collection. Platooning, is when a number of vehicles are connected together and there is only a single lead driver, MAN and DB Schenker are planning European platooning trials in 2018,[62] which has the potential to be one of the first vehicles with partial autonomy on roads.

Autonomous vehicles could transform the efficiency and effectiveness of transport and logistics. Given the efficiency gains that autonomous vehicles could achieve, there would be a net positive environmental impact. The potential for this technology also lies in the self-driving sensors and software. It could be said that the true transformation isn't the car, but the underlying digital technology. To accommodate the enormous amount of data

Autonomous Car Sales Will Surge By 2035
The cars will represent 25 precent of the global market

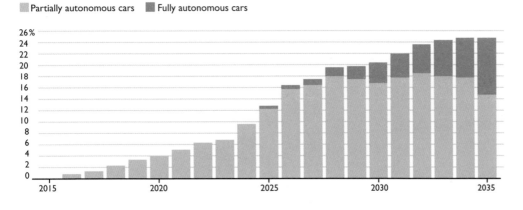

Figure 22

Autonomous Car Sales Will Surge by 2035[64]

needed for the sensors, edge computing is being used. The goal with edge computing is to act on data quickly without the delays incurred by transmitting across a wide area network. For an autonomous vehicle, the data that is transmitted needs to be acted upon immediately and processed at the source, such as responding to an approaching vehicle. A number of companies have been preparing for this technological breakthrough. Google, for example, already uses nearly a million servers in its daily operations. To manage this enormous complexity, the company created its own software known as 'Borg'. Systems such as this, improve the efficiency by dynamically allocating capability when needed, thus improving utilization. With this new technology rapidly coming online, and being used for autonomous vehicles, the number of self-driving vehicles on roads worldwide is expected to grow to 21 million by 2035.

8 NEW TECHNOLOGIES: DRONES

Also known as Unmanned Aerial Vehicles (UAVs) – are small flying devices used to photograph and to collect data. In addition, companies such as Amazon are exploring using drones for shipping and delivery, but this is still in its infant stage. Developments in drone technology include the use of artificial intelligence for more autonomous and safer flight, and better photographic technology is also being used. UAVs, or as they are popularly known, 'drones', are showing great potential for achieving sustainability. Drones are being implemented in the fields of scientific research, renewable energies, geology and agriculture, and they are already opening up a future full of possibilities.

DRONES ARE BEING IMPLEMENTED IN THE FIELDS OF SCIENTIFIC RESEARCH, RENEWABLE ENERGIES, GEOLOGY AND AGRICULTURE.

There are several benefits that drones have brought in the pursuit of supporting the SDGs.

First, UAVs with video cameras are very useful when flying over large areas of land to obtain images quickly. These include areas of agricultural crops, forest cover, fire control risks, and coastal regions. Two benefits of drone usage in these circumstances are 1) achieving a reduction in high polluting emissions that come along with traditional ground or air control vehicles and 2) getting critical information faster before an incident escalates. These unmanned devices are also being used to study air quality, pollen count or other characteristics of the atmosphere. Highly specific data collected by these drones are then used to launch alerts and develop scientific studies.

IN MANY CASES, DRONE DEPLOYMENTS CAN DELIVER A BETTER RETURN ON INVESTMENT THAN SATELLITE IMAGES OR AERIAL PHOTOGRAPHY FROM HELICOPTERS OR PLANES.

Drones are also being used to monitor solar power plants and wind farms. UAVs can fly over photovoltaic installations and wind turbines to check for technical failures, material loss or malfunctioning without taking up valuable labor time for workers or accumulating fuel costs for vehicle travel to sites. In many cases, drone deployments can deliver a better return on investment than satellite images or aerial photography from helicopters or planes. This is particularly true when detailed imagery of localized events is needed and in cases where specific imagery needs to be taken repeatedly for monitoring or record keeping.

Increasingly used in the aftermath of disasters, drones have proven to be helpful when reaching areas that are inaccessible or difficult to fly over with manned aircraft. For example, in 2013 after typhoon Haiyan hit the Philippines, a UAV was used to gather data, choose where to set up a base of operations, and verify if roads were passable.[65] The UAV was then flown up the coast to evaluate damage from storm surges and flooding and to identify the villages most affected. China has also been using drones for landslide and earthquake related damage and impact assessment. As an investment in furthering support for the use of drones in emergency response, the European Commission funded a €17.5 million research project to develop robotic tools that can assist human crisis intervention teams with search and rescue and emergency response.[66] In response to the wealth of data coming from new technological sources, including drones, a group of non-governmental organizations has formed the Digital Humanitarian Network.[67] This consortium aims to provide an interface between formal, professional humanitarian organizations and informal volunteer and technical networks.

Entrepreneurs such as Laurent Rivière, CEO of Sunbirds created a solar-powered drone with his eye on some of the challenges facing countries in Africa and elsewhere. For example, in Madagascar the farmers are plagued with an invasion of locusts with more than 100,000 tons of crops devastated every day. This is a tremendous loss to the farmers and the people depending on the food. The swarm covers dozen of kilometers destroying all the crops and creating a high-risk of starvation. Currently, there are only planes and helicopters for the preventive maintenance but the island lacks resources to finance the fuel and the pesticides. By using the solar-powered drone, they do not need a pilot, plane, or fuel. The drone is able to map thousands of hectares and immediately identify when new locust swarms are forming. Thereafter, instead of trying to destroy the swarm when it is already huge (up to 500 billion in 2014), they would be able to locate them early and treat them more easily with pesticides. In this way, the information collected by the drone plays a pivotal role in saving a country from starvation.

> **"WITH THESE [DRONE] APPLICATIONS WE CAN THEN HAVE A DIRECT IMPACT ON DEVELOPMENT ISSUES SUCH AS STARVATION AND DROUGHT."**
>
> LAURENT RIVIÈRE, CEO SUNBIRDS

22

CASE NO.

DJI

Phantom
Empowering vulnerable communities to prepare for challenges caused by climate change

Case applied in: Maldives
Headquarters located in: China
www.dji.com

IMPACT SDGS

SDG 13
Climate Action
Drones assist with the more than 200 inhabited islands spread over a vast area of the Maldives that require extensive mapping to study climate impacts for response preparedness.

SDG 17
Partnerships for the Goals
Partner with the United Nations Development Program (UNDP) to bring together disaster management practitioners to help face and solve climate change issues.

THE NEXT 5-10 YEARS WILL BE A VERY EXCITING PERIOD FOR UNMANNED AIRCRAFT AND **I AM LOOKING FORWARD TO THE FUTURE.**
FRANK WANG, CEO DJI

It is predicted that by 2050 most of the world's islands will be submerged due to rising sea levels and shifting weather patterns. Sophisticated mapping is needed to design actions to protect the island residents.

As 80% of the world's islands are at an elevation of one meter above sea level, they are at risk of rising sea levels due to climate change. This includes the coral atolls of the Maldives that are home to nearly 400,000 people. The Maldives is also one of the world's most geographically dispersed countries with over 200 inhabited islands spread over 90,000 square kilometers. This makes communication and transportation a serious logistical challenge. The local population is threatened by climate and weather conditions and significant areas have already been eroded by sea-level rise. To help people on these islands forecast and combat the dangers caused by climate change, DJI and UNDP have partnered to provide drones to local Maldives response teams.

Three-dimensional risk maps represent an important source of data as visual images of the same area taken over time, or before and after a disaster, can identify changes to the landscape thereby providing much needed evidence for decision-making. DJI drones collect data to show how the topography of the island is changing and to enhance the preparedness of the emergency response team.

The company has made the technology easier to use, more affordable, and better performing, which allows a larger sector of the population to gain access to the information drones provide.
In this case, technology is assisting in disaster risk reduction. Additionally, it is streamlining and simplifying the mapping process. Without the drones, it would take almost a year to map 11 islands; the drone was able to map the island of Maibadhoo in just one day (SDG 13).

The technology has and will continue to change the way disaster response is conducted, speeding up the times it takes to transmit an alert and significantly increasing mitigation abilities. DJI's more advanced, longer range communication that includes live streaming, changes the ways signals are sent and therefore enables a quicker response: saving time, money and lives. This technology is evolving and the government of Maldives and island communities are part of the innovation process. At least 20 islands in the Maldives will be equipped with DJI Phantom or DJI Mavic Pro drones, and local emergency officials will receive training from professional first responders in how to integrate drones into their disaster preparedness and response setups. At a national level, UNDP and DJI have been training the Maldives National Defense Force (MNDF) – a government agency responsible for disaster response – on how to integrate drones into operations involving firefighters, coast guards and other public safety forces (SDG 17).

CHALLENGE

To assist in the management of sea-level rise by mapping climate impact.

OPPORTUNITIES FOR SCALE

DJI is on the cutting edge of innovation and with the continuous evolution of technology, they see great promise for further innovations and applications of drones. DJI is exploring a variety of drone applications such as: emergency information gathering e.g. assessing fire progress with thermal sensors; inspecting power lines; precision spraying of pesticides; and powerful telephoto enabled drones for industrial applications.

Sources and further information
- http://www.dji.com
- https://www.fastcompany.com/company/dji
- http://www.asia-pacific.undp.org/content/rbap/en/home/blog/2017/1/26/using-drones-to-fight-risks-from-climate-change.html
- http://www.undp.org/content/undp/en/home/blog/2017/2/10/Using-drones-to-address-climate-change-risks-in-the-Maldives.html
- http://citizenship.dji.com/humanitarian/dji-and-undp-use-latest-drone-technology-to-protect-vulnerable-communities
- https://www.dronezon.com/drone-companies-news-interviews/dji-drone-company-ceo-frank-wang-interview-with-wsj

" DJI'S MORE ADVANCED, LONGER RANGE COMMUNICATION ENABLES A QUICKER RESPONSE: SAVING TIME, MONEY AND LIVES."

In another application of the use of drones for good, Amazon has begun development of an air-traffic control system to manage its fleet as the drones fly from warehouses to customers' doors. Amazon reports that about 85 % of the products on its website are light enough to be delivered by drones. To avoid other air traffic and birds when making a delivery, Amazon has proposed that the drones fly at heights between 200 feet and 400 feet, equivalent to being higher than an eight-story building.[68] The drones, which will operate autonomously without a pilot, will fly at speeds up to 50 miles per hour. The biggest benefits to drone deliveries would be the amount of savings in shipping costs and fuel for vehicle transport. According to the Deutsche Bank, delivery automation using drones presents the biggest cost reduction opportunity for Amazon, with an estimated 80 % cost savings in the shipment between the final storage hub and the customer's home.[69] "Robots and drones would reduce this to near-zero immediately and allow for much faster delivery times" said Deutsche Bank.

The following costs are samples for delivering a shoebox:

- Premium ground like UPS or FedEx: US $6 to US $6.50
- Mid-tier carriers like OnTrac: US $4 to US $5
- USPS for last mile alone: about US $2
- Robots/drones: less than US $0.05 per mile

AROUND THE UCLA CAMPUS ALONE, DRIVERS SEARCHING FOR PARKING DROVE 950,000 MILES, WASTED 47,000 GALLONS OF GASOLINE, AND CREATED 730 TONS OF GREENHOUSE GAS EMISSIONS.

YETI.CO

9. NEW TECHNOLOGIES: THE INTERNET OF THINGS (IoT)

The Internet of Things (IoT) links objects to the internet, enabling data, insights and machine capabilities never available before. The IoT represents a core set of emerging technologies, which have great potential to improve connectivity by linking smart devices, applications, services, and even people over the internet network. It can improve efficiencies, protect resources and influence our daily lives. The IoT extends to a wide range of machines, including vehicles, household appliances, wearable devices, health care monitors, energy consumption meters, and security systems. The IoT also facilitates the collection of small data.

ONE WAY THAT THE IoT CAN AFFECT THE SDGs IS IN THE INCREASINGLY COMMON PRACTICE OF BUILDING SUSTAINABLE AND SMART CITIES IN THE DEVELOPED WORLD.

When appliances are fitted with sensors that not only detect what we program them to, but also connect with the internet, then we get products such as thermostats in our home that can be controlled remotely using a smartphone. The IoT also allows smart grids to function by connecting energy producing and energy consuming devices and monitoring and managing them. The IoT is the technology behind 'wearables' that promises to be the next step in clothing, and devices designed to enhance people's health such as smart watches that monitor heart rate.

The IoT also provides opportunities to fulfill some of the expectations of the SDGs since the IoT spans multiple industries, including energy, automotive, consumer devices, healthcare and more. One way that the IoT can affect the SDGs is in the increasingly common practice of building sustainable and smart cities in the developed world, as is shown further in Chapter 5. For example, Barcelona has implemented IoT technologies to remotely sense and control park irrigation and

> **IoT TECHNOLOGY WILL BE RESPONSIBLE FOR UP TO US $15 TRILLION OF GLOBAL GDP IN THE NEXT 20 YEARS.** [72]
>
> YETI.CO

water levels in public fountains. Using sensors to monitor rain and humidity, park workers can determine how much irrigation is needed in each area. With this technological intervention, Barcelona estimates that IoT systems have helped save US $58 million on water. [70]

Other ways the IoT can help with the achievement of the SDGs include: water quality monitoring with contaminant sensors (SDG 6); drought crisis prevention by using soil sensors to measure water needs (SDG 11); reuse of technological devices to reduce E-waste by alerting users when repairs or maintenance is necessary and indicating to manufacturers which components can be reused(SDG 12); reduction of fuel waste and CO2 emissions by sensors in parking areas indicating

where parking is available, thus alleviating the practice of driving around parking lots looking for a space (SDG 13); and monitor logging activities to guard against illegal deforestation (SDG 15).

The IoT also has the potential to benefit populations in developing countries, as shown in the following case (See Case 23). Applications of IoT could facilitate impactful data collection in agricultural fields that help check soil conditions, monitor vaccine delivery and storage in real-time, measure levels of pollution in the air or water, and be integrated in other smart devices which can also provide remote diagnoses of diseases.

Ericsson reports that wireless broadband applications will continue to rise. And the IoT, in which billions of devices will be connected to wireless networks, will grow even more rapidly than devices and applications for human use. [71] There are already approximately 230 million cellular Machine-to-Machine (MTM) subscriptions for IoT applications, and it is projected to be up to 26 billion connected devices by 2020. McKinsey estimates that the IoT will add around US $11 trillion of market value globally by 2025, roughly divided equally between the high-income and developing economies. [73]

23

CASE NO. **ERICSSON**

Connected Mangroves
IoT - ICT and mobility used together to restore nature

Case applied in: Malaysia
Headquarters located in: Sweden
www.ericsson.com

IMPACT SDGS

SDG 6
Clean Water and Sanitation
Measures conditions for maximum 200 mangroves (covering roughly 2,500mts2), providing real-time data collection with sensors monitoring metrics including local water contamination levels.

SDG 13
Climate action
Increased survival of plants, addressed climate mitigation as more CO2e emissions are captured into the plants.

SDG 14
Life Below Water
The project ensures up to 50% better maturity rates for the mangrove saplings, which in itself assures that the community will increase its mangrove cover substantially in the next few years.

SDG 15
Life on Land
A typical mangrove hectare consists of 10,000 seedlings. 3.5 hectares of mangroves are capable of absorbing the carbon emissions of one typical passenger automobile per year. Increasing the yield of these hectares could help to increase carbon sequestration per hectare up to 75%.

THROUGH THIS INTERNET OF THINGS (IoT) SOLUTION, THE COMMUNITY HAS BEEN **EMPOWERED TO USE DATA TO MANAGE THEIR ENVIRONMENT** AND TAKE ACTION TO SUPPORT THE MANGROVES AND THEIR COMMUNITY.
TODD ASHTON, PRESIDENT OF ERICSSON MALAYSIA, SRI LANKA, AND BANGLADESH

In Ericsson's Connected Mangroves project, they worked with Luimewah, a local technology company, to place sensors in the plant site of the newly-planted mangrove saplings. The sensor system provides near real-time information about the mangrove plantation conditions, enabling ICT to play a key role in managing this important resource. Mangroves are vital for the local resilience hence addressing climate adaptation (SDG 13). Malaysia has a diverse array of mangrove species, with 36 out of the 69 species worldwide native to the country. Today, approximately 50% of Malaysian mangroves have been destroyed due to development, aquaculture farms, fire, wood harvesting and pollution. This has caused coastal areas to be unprotected from environment risks, especially the risks from flooding and tsunamis. Additionally, a recent study shows 35,594 acres of mangrove habitats can prevent the release into the atmosphere of about 13 million metric tons of carbon, which is equivalent to the carbon emissions of 344,000 cars. Phase 1 of this project involved a pilot of 200 seedlings and Phase 2 with 1,000 seedlings. The team's ambition is to plant a total of 10,000 seedlings. The project addresses the need to protect an important part of the ecosystem of the nearly 3,000 miles of coastline in Malaysia. Based on the initial pilot results, Ericsson expects an improvement rate of up to 50% on the mortality rate of seedlings. The main dashboard metrics set to measure the health of the mangrove plantations are: soil moisture, temperature, and electric conductivity; ambient humidity, temperature, and water level measurement (SDG 6). For each of these metrics, Ericsson, working with the NGO and the

community, defined thresholds that when surpassed triggers a message to a specified caretaker in the application. Through improving the quality and quantity of the data, the system is better able to cope with changing parameters. This is relevant when understanding trends about soil temperature, water level or soil acidity and could help researchers to better understand mechanisms to improve the life of seedlings via irrigation, fertilization or other methods (SDG 14).

The mangroves are important in rebuilding the ecosystem, as they serve as breeding grounds for crustaceans and fish which attract migratory birds. The communities that live near the mangrove plantations are among the most vulnerable socio-economic groups in the country. Access to this mobile application helps them to manage their mangrove plantations and is considered to be a big step forward in agriculture. In addition, these communities did not previously have resources to monitor the mangrove forest, and so were at risk of flooding. This risk has now been mitigated by the project. Being able to monitor large areas of forest to prevent fire, flooding and illegal logging can help local authorities to maintain protected forest areas in a better way (SDG 15). Leveraging on ICT technology can help them to find more sustainable and efficient ways to monitor and take actions regarding forest protection. Ericsson is using 3GPP technology for communications (2G/3G) which already has more than 6 billion subscriptions worldwide. This will ensure high level of coverage globally and will also help to find low-cost communication units for the sensor gateway.

CHALLENGE

To protect Mangroves which are a vital part of Malaysia's ecosystem.

OPPORTUNITIES FOR SCALE

Ericsson works with local technology providers and communities so that the development, installation, and support of sensors becomes sustainable. For instance in this case, the maintenance is supported by the community chief. The same real-time monitoring could be applied to other agriculture crops to tell farmers when it is best to plant, water and fertilize crops and how best to boost yields by studying how crops behave under different conditions. The solution can also be applied in specific areas like fisheries. A similar solution has also now been deployed in the Philippines, on an islet that is a proposed critical habitat and eco-tourism area. Aside from the sensors, near real-time images from cameras will also help the local government to monitor for intrusion as they keep the area safe for migratory birds and other wildlife.

Sources and further information

- https://www.ericsson.com/assets/local/news/2016/05/ict-sdg.pdf
- http://unfccc.int/secretariat/momentum_for_change/items/9937.php
- https://www.ericsson.com/en/about-us/sustainability-and-corporate-responsibility/sustainable-development-goals
- https://www.ericsson.com/thecompany/sustainability_corporateresponsibility/technology-for-good-blog/2015/11/18/connected-mangroves-bring-the-iot-to-life-in-malaysia/
- https://www.ericsson.com/en/news/2017/12/connected-mangroves-in-philippines

" ACCESS TO ERICSSON'S MOBILE APPLICATION HELPS COMMUNITIES MANAGE THEIR MANGROVE PLANTATIONS AND MITIGATE THE RISK OF FLOODING. THIS IS CONSIDERED TO BE A BIG STEP FORWARD IN AGRICULTURE. "

Figure 23

The Internet of Things offer a potential economic impact of 4 trillion to 11 trillion a year in 2025[74]

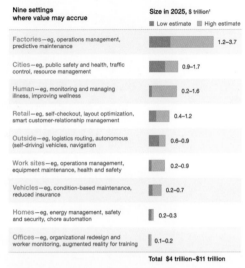

The Internet of Things offers a potential economic impact of $4 trillion to $11 trillion a year in 2025.

Nine settings where value may accrue	Size in 2025, $ trillion[1]
	■ Low estimate ■ High estimate
Factories—eg, operations management, predictive maintenance	1.2–3.7
Cities—eg, public safety and health, traffic control, resource management	0.9–1.7
Human—eg, monitoring and managing illness, improving wellness	0.2–1.6
Retail—eg, self-checkout, layout optimization, smart customer-relationship management	0.4–1.2
Outside—eg, logistics routing, autonomous (self-driving) vehicles, navigation	0.6–0.9
Work sites—eg, operations management, equipment maintenance, health and safety	0.2–0.9
Vehicles—eg, condition-based maintenance, reduced insurance	0.2–0.7
Homes—eg, energy management, safety and security, chore automation	0.2–0.3
Offices—eg, organizational redesign and worker monitoring, augmented reality for training	0.1–0.2

Total $4 trillion–$11 trillion

[1]Adjusted to 2015 dollars; for sized applications only; includes consumer surplus. Numbers do not sum to total, because of rounding.

10. NEW TECHNOLOGIES: BLOCKCHAIN AND CYBER-SECURITY

Blockchain is the revolutionary technology behind cryptocurrency Bitcoin and is essentially an ever-lengthening chain of blocks of data used for transactions such as financial payments. Each block contains a compact record of things that have happened in the process. The blockchain technology is to ensure trust and facilitate transparency among transactions as all transactions done in the blockchain are not changeable and will always be visible. The technology enables decentralized organizing, it is distributed and not centralized and therefore everyone can be a participant and there is no single entity in control.

Applications of blockchain technology are expanding and the reasons for its use are also becoming more convincing. The cost and inefficiency associated with making international payments across certain corridors present a barrier to economic development. Cross-border payments are inefficient, as there is no single global payment infrastructure through which they can travel. One consequence of the fragmented global payments system is the high cost of remittances, or payments, which are a critical source of development

financing. Roughly US $ 430 billion dollar of remittances were sent to developing countries in 2016, nearly three times as much as official aid.[75] The global average cost of sending remittances worth US $ 200 dollars is 7.4 % but varies greatly across corridors: for example, according to the World Bank, the average cost of sending US $ 200 dollars from a developed country to South Asia is 5.4 %, while the cost of sending the same value to Sub-Saharan Africa is 9.8 %. Over the past two years, these fees have remained at nearly 4.5 percentage points higher than the SDGs target of 3 %.

Blockchain technology for the financial sector has been seen as a potential solution to the high costs of client identification in banking transactions. In fact, financial institutions are embracing blockchain as a means to reduce fraud, costs, and delays. Large financial institutions are working together with some blockchain startups, such as KYC (Know Your Customer) Chain and Tradle, who have developed platforms that allow customers to record verifications in a "digital wallet" stored on a distributed ledger and then share that information with other financial institutions when requested. Financial institutions spend US $ 60 million to US $ 500 million per year to keep up with due diligence regulations and Know your Customer (KYC) practices according to a Thomson Reuters Survey.[76] This new approach could reduce duplication of effort by both the customer and the institutions, promoting efficiency while reducing time and costs.[77]

> **"THE BLOCKCHAIN IS AN EXCITING NEW TECHNOLOGY THAT CAN POTENTIALLY PRODUCE SOLUTIONS TO SEVERAL OF OUR PRESSING DEVELOPMENT CHALLENGES."**
>
> AANCHAL ANAND, WORLD BANK

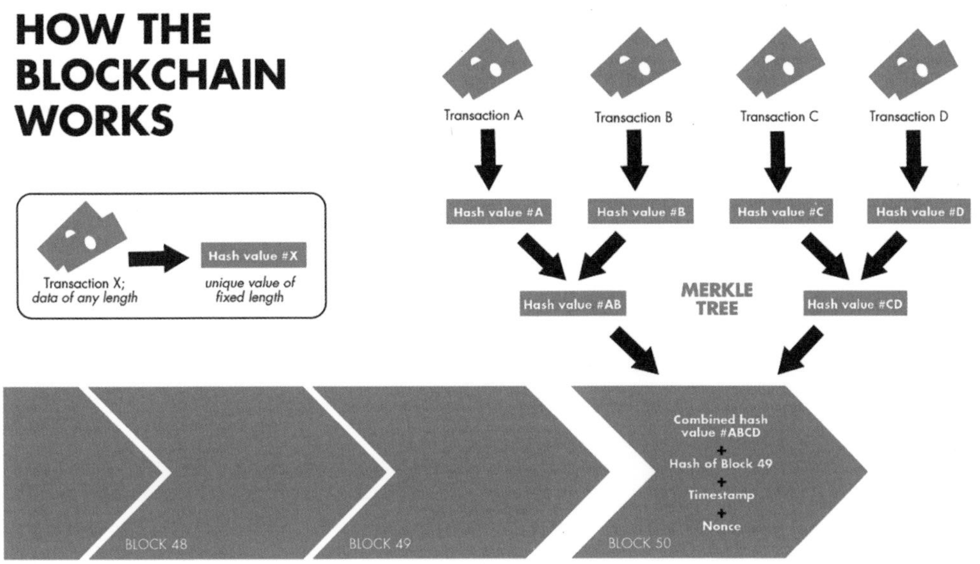

HOW THE BLOCKCHAIN WORKS

Figure 24
How a Blockchain Works[77]

In addition, blockchain can also be used in providing a secure digital infrastructure for verifying identity. Globally, 1.1 billion people, or roughly one in every seven, lack proof of their legal identity. This problem disproportionately affects children and women from rural areas in Africa and Asia. This is an even more severe issue for the world's more than 21 million refugees. In 2015, the World Bank estimated that "some fifty thousand Syrian refugee children have been born abroad and over 70 % of them have not been registered at birth, making it almost impossible for them to prove their citizenship later on."[78]

Without legal identification, it can be difficult accessing health and education services, open a bank account, get a loan, and even vote. Therefore, people who lack a legal ID struggle to fully integrate into society and achieve their economic potential. Due to this inequality in identification systems, blockchain developers are working towards implementing identity schemes that are crucial for development in a more transparent structure. This technological breakthrough can help meet the SDG Target 16.9 of "providing legal identity for all, including birth registration, by 2030."

Because of blockchain's transparency and lack of single-entity-control, people in developing countries where people either lack access to institutions or consider them expensive, unreliable or untrustworthy, gain a secure, affordable alternative. Researchers have identified the potential role blockchain can play in addressing four development challenges: (1) facilitating faster and cheaper international payments, (2) providing a secure digital infrastructure for verifying identity, (3) securing property rights, and (4) making aid disbursement more secure and transparent. There is consensus that, for blockchain-based solutions to reach their full potential, governments and development organizations first need to collaborate with developers and take steps towards facilitating the use of common reporting systems and creating reliable land registry systems.

Blockchain is also used for other transactions such as energy transactions facilitated by smart grids. In fact blockchain has the potential to transform transaction processes in a number of sectors such as logistics, retail, and stock trading. A research brief from CBINSITES[79] identified 30 industries that blockchain could transform. Blockchain is an

IN THE NEXT FIVE YEARS, THE CYBER-SECURITY MARKET SIZE WILL GROW FROM 137.85 BILLION DOLLARS IN 2017 TO 231.94 BILLION DOLLARS BY 2022.

MARKETSANDMARKETS.COM

exciting breakthrough in how we do business. Cyber-Security is a growing issue. Blockchain is helping to block fraud and hacking by its very design. Because transactions are followed and verified by multiple parties, there isn't one central computer system to hack. Companies such as Guardtime[80] and Remme[81] are bringing blockchain technology to companies and enhancing the security with better encryption and eliminating human error - caused for example by weak passwords.

As the world gets more connected and reliant on internet, cyber-security will become a vital piece of the puzzle to ensure safety. And we are not just talking about the safety of our money or documents, but physical safety as well. As driverless cars evolve, as well as the Internet of Things, we cannot tolerate infiltration and disablement. Therefore, cyber-security will grow as a market in the coming years. It is estimated that in the next five years, the cyber-security market size will grow from US $ 137.85 dollars in 2017 to US $ 231 dollars by 2022.[82]

WRAP UP

ICT and technology are rapidly advancing and can propel the solutions to the SDGs. The opportunities abound and are extremely exciting. But there are challenges facing this sector. The first predominant challenge that must be addressed in order to facilitate the burgeoning innovations as described in this chapter is: full worldwide saturation of internet connectivity.

The Ericsson report mentioned earlier projects that by 2021, over 90 % of the world's population will be covered by mobile broadband networks. This is promising but still needs to be achieved as according to the World Economic Forum[88], as of May 2016 more than half of the world's population did not have internet access. So if this projected 90 % coverage is going to be achieved in the next few years, internet companies must find ways to accelerate their efforts.

The second challenge is achieving sustainable energy production, storage and regeneration to fuel the technological products. This refers to the "greening of the ICT and Technology sector" that was mentioned earlier. Sustainable energy is of course vital to keep the technology running. With billions of devices running on electricity, electricity production has got to become clean and sustainable. In the section about energy, we will look into the challenges and opportunities for this sector. The third challenge is to partner with companies from all sectors, as well as governmental institutions to assist them in creating sustainable solutions within their domains. This refers to the "greening through ICT and Technology" discussed throughout this chapter.

THE FIRST PREDOMINANT CHALLENGE THAT MUST BE ADDRESSED IS: FULL WORLDWIDE SATURATION OF INTERNET CONNECTIVITY.

Other challenges at the moment for ICT and technology to make an impactful contribution to the SDGs are: big players in the technology industry must take a leading position, and the entire industry must focus on profitable sustainable solutions to the Global Goals. Given the enormous market that awaits ICT and technology now and in the near future, and the integral part this sector plays in all other sectors, if ICT and technology companies and innovators commit themselves to contributing to the achievement of the SDGs, then we will see a grand movement in the right direction.

ICT and technology can be a positive influence on our lives, our work and our environment. It can help people in developing countries gain education and break out of poverty. It can help to conserve our resources and provide information that can help us design sustainable solutions. But ICT and technological advances can also come with risks that we must not ignore. For example, while small and big data collection provides the information that can be used for people's benefit, it can also encroach on people's privacy. And with the importance and far-reaching benefits of universal internet connectivity and more connections with things and between them, we become more vulnerable to hacking and security breaches. And let's not forget the warnings mentioned earlier in the chapter about robotics and artificial intelligence getting out of our control. So make no

mistake, there are tremendous benefits awaiting us in this fourth industrial revolution, but as with any revolution, there are dangers as well.

ICT and technology have transformed the way we live. Technological applications transcend all sectors, and the technologies themselves work together such as IoT and smart grids, and drones and AI. There have been more rapid changes in technology than in anything we have ever experienced before. And further rapid changes await, with major tipping points happening within the next 10 years. But as stated in the beginning of this chapter, technology by itself does not assure us of positive impact on society and environment. It must be deployed as such and directed towards the Global Goals. ■

CAPITAL

Achieving the SDGs will require funding and cooperation on an unprecedented scale, with the private sector holding a pivotal position. The UN estimates the annual global cost to meet the SDGs is between US $5 and $7 trillion for the next 12 to 15 years. This enormous amount of capital investment will not be met by public funds alone, and it is therefore up to market participants to fill this financing gap. Although the movement towards "investing for good" is growing, it is still happening too slowly and continues to be a niche market that is not scaling up fast enough. Shared value thinking will become increasingly important and blended finance initiatives will be integral to success. This chapter explains the current gap in financing, the potential impact private capital can have on all SDGs, and the shared value investing opportunities. To demonstrate how we need all capital, we will explore some of the various parties and services in the capital spectrum, showing in what ways they can and must contribute in order to achieve progress on the SDGs.

4.1 THE CAPITAL CALL: THE GOALS NEED CAPITAL AS MUCH AS CAPITAL NEEDS THE GOALS

As much as capital needs to be directed toward the Goals, the Goals need to attract capital as well. There is a growing need for the world to mobilize capital in the direction of achieving the SDGs. The investment landscape now shows a large gap between the amount of capital it will take to achieve the SDGs by 2030, and the financial resources from government and development aid that are currently available. Therefore, private capital is urgently needed. By utilizing development finance and philanthropic funds strategically to mobilize and leverage private capital, we can propel business and create market opportunities for a more sustainable world.

FROM BILLIONS TO TRILLIONS

To meet the investment needs of the SDGs, the global community must change the discussion from billions to trillions. There needs to be a trillion dollar shift in investments of all kinds: public and private, national and global. The Goals need an innovative capital mobilization with a global change of mindset, approach and accountability to create the transformation needed in both developing and developed countries.

Traditionally, the majority of development spending comes from governments and public resources, yet the largest potential is from private sector investments.[1] This is precisely the trajectory from billions to trillions, which each country and the global community must support together to finance and achieve the vision of the SDGs. Private capital is becoming an increasingly important tool for global development as well as one of the biggest business opportunities.

> "WITH GLOBAL CHALLENGES SUCH AS CLIMATE CHANGE, POPULATION GROWTH AND RESOURCE SCARCITY ACCELERATING, THERE IS AN INCREASED URGENCY FOR THE FINANCE SECTOR BOTH TO ADAPT AND TO HELP BRING ABOUT THE NECESSARY CHANGES IN OUR ECONOMIC AND BUSINESS MODELS."
>
> SÉVERIN CABANNES, DEPUTY CEO OF SOCIÉTÉ GÉNÉRALE

The market opportunities in industries such as food and agriculture, cities, energy and materials, and health and well-being alone could create 380 million new jobs by 2030.[2] Although this presents unprecedented business potential, we still have a long way to go. The allocation of capital in some areas, like infrastructure investments, currently only garners about 10% of its money from the private sector proving that there is ample room for growth in private sector involvement.

TRADITIONALLY, THE MAJORITY OF DEVELOPMENT SPENDING COMES FROM GOVERNMENTS AND PUBLIC RESOURCES, YET THE LARGEST POTENTIAL IS FROM PRIVATE SECTOR INVESTMENTS.

"Billions to trillions" signifies the realization that achieving the SDGs will require more than what is available in public money, it will demand that the private sector step in to fill the gaps. The financial system consists of tens of thousands of institu-

tional participants – including regulators, banks, insurance companies, stock and bond exchanges – and billions of individual market participants – there is an immense opportunity to use this power of scale for profit and for good.

PRIVATE CAPITAL MUST FILL MOST OF THE GAP

Private capital is crucial to meeting the 2030 Goals, even more so since the relative impact of Official Development Assistance (ODA) funding has diminished. A significant amount of capital is needed to achieve the SDGs. With the necessary global investment of US $5 to $7 trillion, as reported by the United Nations Conference on Trade and Development (UNCTAD), to achieve the SDGs worldwide, we need all parties to participate. Of this total amount needed in state spending, investment and aid for infrastructure, such as water and sanitation, agriculture, clean energy, transportation, and telecommunications, as well as tens of billions each for such areas as health, food security, and education, it will take approximately US $3.9 trillion per year to achieve the SDGs in developing countries alone.[3] The funding available for this is estimated to fall

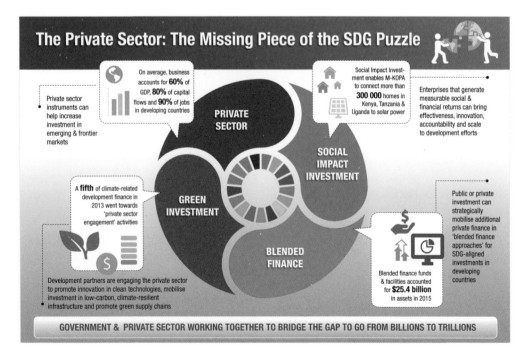

Figure 25
Funding Gap Chart[10]

Figure 26 **Funding Gap Chart**

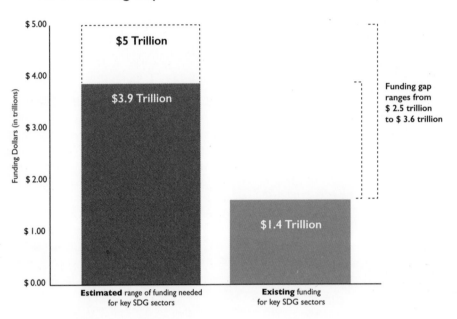

SDGs Funding Gap

Funding Dollars (in trillions)

$5.00 — **$5 Trillion**

$4.00 — **$3.9 Trillion**

$3.00

$2.00

$1.00 — **$1.4 Trillion**

$0.00

Estimated range of funding needed for key SDG sectors

Existing funding for key SDG sectors

Funding gap ranges from $ 2.5 trillion to $ 3.6 trillion

short. Current levels of both public and private funding cover only US $1.4 trillion. Taking the lower estimate of US $5 trillion needed annually, leaves a yearly investment gap of US $3.6 trillion worldwide (See Figure 26).[4] Although this amount may seem unreachable, it is small compared to the potential value that could be unlocked by investing in the SDGs. According to the Business and Sustainable Development Commission, there are opportunities worth US $20 trillion or more.[5]

SDGS FUNDING GAP

The UNCTAD report shows that in 2016, the total ODA reached a peak of US $142.6 billion, which is significantly smaller than the US $3.9 needed for developing countries.[6] Therefore, the estimated gap for key SDG sectors in developing regions is approximately US $2.5 trillion. A large part of this gap can be filled by private capital, as the amount of capital held by the private sector, both in business and finance, is larger than that of the public sector. Businesses and investors can seize this prime opportunity to shift course, reorienting themselves to invest in the SDGs.

Many of the leading attempts to reorient capital towards long-term value creation are motivated by concern about the world the next generations will live in. Aviva CEO Mark Wilson, for example, talks about "being a good ancestor."[7] But not all business leaders and investors think like this yet, although the momentum is in the right direction. A decade ago, the UN Principles for Responsible Investment (PRI) had just 200 signatories with US $5 trillion of assets under management. Today, it has 1,750 signatories with a collective portfolio worth over US $60 trillion.[8] The PRI's signatories represent around one third of global private capital. To meet the challenge of achieving the

NEW FLOWS OF PRIVATE SECTOR CAPITAL WILL BE CRUCIAL TO MEETING THE GLOBAL CHALLENGES PUT FORWARD BY THE SDGs.

PRI

> ## "WE'RE BASICALLY THROWING AWAY MONEY BY NOT ADDRESSING THE ISSUE [CLIMATE CHANGE]."
>
> MARSHALL BURKE, ASSISTANT PROFESSOR AT STANFORD UNIVERSITY. TIME.COM

SDGs, they would have to invest US $2 trillion annually in companies and other investments that directly link to positive SDG outcomes. By 2030, that should amount to cumulative 25% of assets under management having a direct positive contribution to the SDGs.[9] As the movement accelerates, we need all capital throughout the entire finance spectrum to make the necessary shift. The breadth of private capital opportunities is already acutely evident, especially in developing countries accounting for 60% of GDP, 80% of capital flows and 90% of jobs.[10] Due to the sheer size of the capital markets – estimated to hold more than US $200 trillion – they offer the ability to make the SDGs a reality in a way that public and philanthropic budgets simply cannot match.[11]

Private capital investments can be a source of comprehensive societal profit and employment. If we take green growth, for example, and invest in businesses that combat climate change, investments which influence 13 of the 17 SDGs, they will enjoy 18% higher returns on the investment than companies that do not address climate impacts.[12] Up until recently, climate action was seen as a cost rather than an opportunity. Today, we see the significant cost of taking no action. According to some sources, inaction to combat climate change could cost US $28 trillion globally by 2050.[13]

The more we wait to address the SDGs with private capital, the more it will cost us and the larger the gap will grow. Temperature rise due to climate change may also radically damage the global economy and hinder growth in the coming decades if nothing is done to manage it. According to new research, temperature change due to unmitigated global warming will leave global GDP per capita 23% lower in 2100 than it would be without any warming.[14]

So how much capital is out there to help cover these costs and fill the gaps? The International Finance Corporation recently compiled numbers to show the level of funding that is potentially available as opposed to what the gap is. In terms of assets held by the world's ten largest pension funds, there is approximately US $2 trillion; assets held by the world's largest insurance companies, US $4.5 trillion; assets held by the world's largest sovereign wealth funds, US $5 trillion; and Global bond market, $100 trillion.[15] Moreover, many multinationals' gross incomes outrank the national incomes of countries. There is clearly no shortage of capital in the global economy, so let's direct it in the most efficient way for our long-term Sustainable Development Goals and fill the financing gap.

According to the United Nations, it will cost approximately US $1.4 trillion to end extreme poverty for 700 million people and meet the associated Targets encompassed in SDG 1.[16] This amount must be devoted to low and lower middle-income countries. Further, to meet the other SDGs, investments will be required in all areas, including health, education, agriculture and food security, social protection systems, energy, infrastructure and ecosystem management. Infrastructure, particularly energy and transport, are considered the most important investment areas. Historically, many of the relevant infrastructure-type investments consistent with the SDGs would have been made through bank lending, but this has been curtailed post-financial crisis. As a result, attention has shifted toward identifying how other large pools of capital, including institutional investors like insurance companies, sovereign wealth funds and public pension funds, could be blended to help mobilize the necessary financing.[17]

Recent funding transactions have shown over US $1.7 trillion moved across the globe as foreign direct investment (FDI) in 2015. Developed econo-

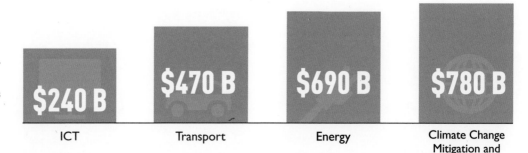

Figure 27 **Examples of annual investments needed**
Source: pubdocs.world-bank.org The Sustainable Development Goals and Private Sector Opportunities

mies received the most inflows of US $962 billion, while developing countries saw US $764 billion and transition economies US $35 billion.[18] While it is encouraging to see FDI inflows to developing countries, the developed markets continue to dominate as the preferred investment destinations.

Developing countries require more funds than they are currently receiving and will need different amounts in various sectors. Examples of annual investments can be seen in figure 27. When we consider the gap, it should be noted that 600 million jobs will be needed in the next 15 years to absorb the growing global workforce, mainly in Asia and sub-Saharan Africa.[19] In emerging markets, most formal jobs are generated by Small and Medium-sized Enterprises (SMEs), which also create 4 out of 5 new positions. However, access to finance is a key constraint to SME growth. Without access to capital, many SMEs either never get started or they stall. SMEs are less likely to be able to obtain bank loans than large firms; instead, they rely on internal funds, or cash from friends and family, to launch and initially run their enterprises.

PRIVATE INDIVIDUAL INVESTORS CONTROL ONE OF THE LARGEST POTS OF INVESTABLE CAPITAL IN THE WORLD—MORE THAN US $40 TRILLION.[20]

ROCKERFELLER FOUNDATION

About half of all formal SMEs do not have access to formal credit. The financing gap is even larger when micro and informal enterprises are taken into account. Overall, approximately 70% of all Micro, Small and Medium-sized Enterprises (MSMEs) in emerging markets lack access to credit. While the gap varies considerably region to region, it's particularly wide in Africa and Asia. The current credit gap for formal SMEs is estimated to be US $1.2 trillion; the total credit gap for both formal and informal SMEs is as high as US $2.6 trillion.

Bridging the gap in financing, and providing the credit and employment opportunities needed for a sustainable future, is a considerable challenge. There has been, and remains, commitment from governments which is crucial since governments have the power to direct funds, instigate and enforce regulations, and steer public institutions. In addition, they have the leverage and authority to collect and designate taxes. For example, Mexico collected US $1.3 billion in the first year of its tax on sugary drinks, which not only steered the society towards healthier habits, but created income for the government to use to benefit society. But government intervention can be fickle. In democracies, when new leaders or political parties step into power, governmental aid programs can be cut or reduced. In countries with differing political systems, or even worse, countries afflicted by political strife or corruption, governmental influence can also be unreliable. This is further confirmation of why private capital can be a steadying influence. If private capital institutions and investors set a determined path to fund endeavors that drive sustainability, then those endeavors will thrive and stay on course.

4.2 HOW PRIVATE CAPITAL CAN FILL THE SDG FUNDING GAP

There are many ways that private capital can be directed towards filling the funding gap and supporting the SDGs. In this section, we will explore some of these methods for sustainable investing, including: blended finance, collaboration and partnerships to promote SDG investment strategies, incorporating externalities in valuing investments, Environmental, Social and Governance (ESG) considerations, and impact investing.

BLENDED FINANCE: BLENDING PUBLIC AND PRIVATE CAPITAL TO FUND THE GOALS

Blended finance is essentially the act of blending public and private funds. More specifically, it is the strategic use of leveraging public development financing and grants, and philanthropic funding, to attract and mobilize private capital flows, with particular focus on emerging and frontier markets. Several countries and financial institutions started to experiment with public-private finance long before the SDGs, but the SDGs are becoming a way for both the public and private sector to communicate and set targets using a shared impact framework. Signatories to the Dutch SDG Investing Agenda have identified the systematic deployment of blended finance instruments as one of the avenues that will enable private investors to increase their involvement in sectors such as energy, infrastructure, water, agriculture and food and health care.[20]

Even with national commitments, the necessary funds continue to be lacking when implementing and sustaining the Goals. While public financing, including from ODA, will continue to be important, significant increases in private capital will be required if the SDGs are to be achieved. The good news is that along with this need comes unprecedented opportunity. Private capital has begun to take on a more prominent role and companies all over the world are beginning to see the business value in investing in the implementation of sustainability measures. Private capital flows to emerging and frontier markets are already growing. For example, Foreign Direct Investment (FDI) from private investors to these markets more than doubled between 2004 and 2014, from under US $400 billion to over US $1.1 trillion annually.[21]

Figure 28 **Blended Finance for the SDGs**

Private finance is "indispensable for sustainable development".[22] It is more abundant than public funding and operates independently of intergovernmental processes. Instead, it responds to market signals, guided by the need to maximize return within existing policy and regulatory frameworks. Directing private capital flows towards positive impact is one of the most important SDG challenges, and one of the greatest opportunities. There are five main challenges to maximizing private capital dissemination and scaling in the marketplace[23], according to the Principles for Responsible Investing.

1. Returns are seen as too low for the level of real or perceived risk

2. Local markets often do not function efficiently, with local financial markets in developing economies particularly weak

3. Private investors have knowledge and capability gaps, which impede their understanding of the investment opportunities in unfamiliar territories

4. Private investors have limited mandates and incentives to invest in sectors or markets with high development impact

5. Local and global investment climates are challenging, including poor regulatory and legal frameworks

In order to address these barriers, blended finance is being utilized. With blended finance, some of these challenges can be overcome, as the collaborative funding is characterized by a number of benefits for institutions, including:

1. Leverage, the use of public development finance and philanthropic funds to attract private capital, and mitigate perceived risk;

2. Impact, investments are identified that drive social, environmental and economic progress;

3. Returns, profitable returns are sought for private investors in line with market expectations based on perceived risk.

Blended finance investments are designed to yield a financial return while also contributing toward achieving social goals. A main component in blended finance is the use of public funds to de-risk investments. As Convergence's CEO Joan Larrea recently commented, the term *Blended Finance* refers to transactions that encourage more private investment by being strategic with the money already invested in official development assistance and philanthropic sources.[24] Blended finance represents an approach that has the potential to attract new sources of funding to the biggest global challenges. Public and/or philanthropic parties at the table are catalytic – making a deal happen that might otherwise attract little or no interest from the private sector. While it has been used in many forms in recent decades, blended finance is increasingly being discussed as a promising way to close the SDG funding gap. As a testament to this growing momentum, UN member countries reached consensus in June 2015 on the importance of deploying public funds to attract private investment through blended finance.[25]

By offering institutions a mechanism to address finance barriers and drive greater capital flows to projects and companies, blended finance delivers impact by shifting the investment risk-return profile to flexible capital with more favorable terms. This helps to overcome the problem of low returns relative to high, real and perceived risks that limits private investment. Further, implementing a blended finance structure can also have a positive impact through sharing local market knowledge and experience. Blended finance also helps to shape policy and regulatory reform to improve the local investment climate. Business leaders can strengthen the flow of capital into sustainable investments by pushing for the wider and more efficient use of blended finance. Recognizing that capital will need to be scaled, and private capital will need to play a critical role to narrow the SDG funding gap, the Blended Finance Taskforce was established by the Business and Sustainable Development Commission.[26] Working closely with other blended finance initiatives – notably the OECD and MDB/DFI efforts – and supported by a Steering Committee of 25 experienced practitioners and experts, as well as a broader informal advisory group, the Taskforce is focused on bringing the voice of the private sector into the agenda.

> **COMPANIES ALL OVER THE WORLD ARE BEGINNING TO SEE THE BUSINESS VALUE IN INVESTING IN THE IMPLEMENTATION OF SUSTAINABILITY MEASURES.**

The Taskforce focuses on capital mobilization in the private sector. Looking at how to allocate the largest flows of private investment with blended structures that use the least amount of public or philanthropic capital, the Taskforce employs a wide range of blending tools.[27] This initiative assists in lowering the cost of capital (concessional capital) and de-risking private capital entry (guarantees, insurance, technical assistance, etc.). Blended finance has an important role to play in financing the SDGs, and is a useful instrument in overcoming the investment gap.

CAPITAL FOR GOOD: INITIATIVES AND COLLABORATIONS THROUGHOUT THE WORLD

To fund the Global Goals, international and multi-party collaborations are absolutely necessary. To that end, many initiatives and partnerships are emerging. Around the time of the commencement of the SDGs, there was an agreement reached by all the UN member countries to support the SDGs financially. This agreement was defined at the third international Conference on Financing for Development, held in Addis Ababa, Ethiopia in 2015 where in a statement, the follow-

ing was put forth: "We, the Heads of State and Government and High Representatives, gathered in Addis Ababa from 13 to 16 July 2015, affirm our strong political commitment to address the challenge of financing and creating an enabling environment at all levels for sustainable development in the spirit of global partnership and solidarity."[28] Consequently, the focus of the conference was to mobilize financial and technical resources for development from various parties to support the implementation of the SDGs.

THE ADDIS ABABA ACTION AGENDA HIGHLIGHTS[30]

- The mobilization and effective use of domestic public resources are central to achieving the SDGs.
- Investment from domestic and international private business and finance in areas critical to sustainable development is important.
- The support of the SDGs requires scaled up and more effective international public finance to complement the efforts of countries to mobilize resources domestically.
- International trade is an engine for development and will contribute to achieving the SDGs.
- New financial instruments for developing countries experiencing debt distress should be further studied to manage debt sustainability.
- The UN leadership role in promoting development will continue to be strengthened.
- Increased investment in science, technology, innovation and country-driven capacity building will be integral to achieving the SDGs.
- A focus on increasing the use of high-quality disaggregated data will be an essential input for decision making in support of the SDGs, and can improve policy making and accountability.

Additional UN supported initiatives include the Sustainable Development Goals Fund (SDG Fund), created in 2014 to put in place and mobilize capital for the SDGs. It is an international multi-donor and multi-agency development mechanism to support sustainable development activities through integrated and multidimensional joint programs.[29] The Fund's main objective is to bring together UN agencies, national governments, academia, civil society and business to address the challenges of poverty, promote the 2030 Agenda for Sustainable Development and achieve the SDGs. Public-private partnerships for the SDGs form the core of the SDG Fund's actions.

MOBILIZING AND DIRECTING PRIVATE CAPITAL FLOWS IS ONE OF THE MOST IMPORTANT SDG CHALLENGES, AND ONE OF THE GREATEST OPPORTUNITIES.

All businesses, large and small, have the potential to make a significant contribution towards shared economic, social and environmental progress. This can be through core business operations and value chains, social investments, philanthropic contributions and advocacy efforts. The SDG Fund was conceived as a multi-partner facility open to public and private donors interested in advancing sustainable development through UN agency coordination. To promote business and create value for stakeholders, the Fund's programs focus on three key thematic areas including inclusive growth for poverty eradication, food security and nutrition, and water and sanitation and three cross-cutting themes: sustainability, gender equality and public-private partnerships.

In a panel discussion at the UN General Assembly in April 2017, moderator Rachel Kyte, CEO and Special Representative of the UN Secretary-General for Sustainable Energy for All, described the "gray area" where the public sector meets the private sector. This in between area presents challenges for accountability and incentives and she stressed the importance of "speed and scale" to achieve the SDGs.[31] Deputy Secretary-General Amina Mohammed also highlighted the role of leadership in financing the 2030 Agenda for Sustainable Development. There is a need for greater consistency in the dissemination of domestic resources and a big opportunity to activate local investor bases. Mohammed said pension funds, the insurance sector and other large pools of capital have the potential to provide "breakthrough opportunities" to implement the SDGs.

The UN Global Compact's Financial Innovation for the SDGs Action Platform brings together a multi-disciplinary group of finance practitioners and experts to develop innovative private financial instruments that have the potential to direct private finance towards critical sustainability solutions. Led in collaboration with the Principles for Responsible Investment (PRI) and the United Nations Environment Programme Finance Initiative (UNEP FI), the platform will develop guidance on impact investment strategies that support the Sustainable Development Goals (SDGs), map current and emerging financial instruments, and provide a laboratory for the development of new innovative instruments. Ultimately, the goal is to improve the risk/return profile of SDG investments to attract institutional investors.

PUBLIC CAPITAL MUST BE USED TO LEVERAGE OTHER TYPES OF FINANCING.

In addition to the aforementioned initiatives, many important activities are already underway to help promote sustainable finance and mobilize capital for the SDGs. The following list shows some of the prominent collaborative efforts working towards bringing together business and capital - both public and private - to support the SDGs. [32]

GLOBAL INITIATIVES

- The **Principles for Responsible Investment** advance Environment, Social and Governance (ESG) standards for investment processes across 1,500 corporate signatories with more than US $60 trillion in assets under management.
- The **U.N. Global Compact** has been helping companies, investors and stock exchanges to integrate ESG issues into their business practices, including through the launch of the Global Compact 100 index of responsible companies.
- The **G-20** discussed options developed by its Green Finance Study Group to create voluntary proposals for scaling up green finance at its 2015 leaders' summit in China.
- The **Financial Stability Board's Task Force on Climate-related Financial Disclosures,** chaired by Michael Bloomberg, is developing disclosure guidelines to provide a common reference point for companies, investors, lenders, insurers and other stakeholders.
- The **Global Reporting Initiative** promotes sustainability disclosures for companies around the world.
- The **Equator Principles** offer an approach for more than 80 financial institutions to manage and assess risk in project finance, corporate lending, and advisory services.
- The **Sustainable Stock Exchanges** initiative offers a peer learning platform for 48 exchanges from 52 countries to advance ESG reporting among listed companies.
- The **UNEP Finance Initiative** has partnered with the private sector since 1992; more recently the Inquiry into the Design of a Sustainable Financial System has mapped actions for accelerating the financial system's transition to support a green economy.
- A **European Union Directive on the Disclosure of Non-Financial and Diversity Information** requires ESG disclosures by large companies and groups, beginning in 2017.
- The **Sustainability Accounting Standards Board** has issued provisional sustainability accounting standards for 79 industries, aiming to inform the future work of the US Securities and Exchange Commission.
- The **International Integrated Reporting Council** is testing a framework to align capital allocation and corporate activities with broader objectives of financial stability and sustainable development.
- **CDP** (formerly Carbon Disclosure Project) works with more than 800 investors to help identify environmental risks embedded in their portfolios.
- The **Carbon Pricing Leadership Coalition** convenes more than 100 major companies and other stakeholders to advance global carbon pricing efforts.
- The **Portfolio Decarbonization Coalition** convenes 25 major investors overseeing the gradual decarbonization of US $600 billion in assets under management.
- The **Business and Sustainable Development Commission** has been launched with leadership from companies like Alibaba, Merck, Safaricom, Temasek, and Unilever to identify a business case for the SDGs.
- **Focusing Capital on the Long Term** has been launched to discourage market short-term strategy and instead encourage behaviors focused on longer-term economic progress across generations.
- The **International Development Finance Club** has established a set of guidelines for tracking the volume of climate mitigation and adaptation activities mobilized by long-term national and international financial institutions.
- The **International Standards Organization** has developed guidance on measuring an organization's contribution to sustainable development (ISO 26000) and has drafted guidance for public consultation on measuring the sustainability of corporate procurement (ISO 20400).

Source: Brookings

EXTERNALITIES: TRUE COSTS, TRUE VALUE

If the global need for finance and the unprecedented opportunity to leverage funds is not addressed, we run the risk of going "from billions to millions."[33] To address forced displacement, inequality, low growth, and demographic challenges, ODA will not be enough. Therefore, this public capital must be used to leverage other types of financing. There is great need for investments in human capital, skills and lifelong learning, infrastructure, and resilience. To fulfill this dire need to finance the SDGs, investors and businesses will be required to shift their focus to long-term results and start internalizing external costs.

Externalities are those external factors that are positively or negatively influenced by business practices or investment behaviors. It is further defined as the consequences of economic activities on unrelated third parties. This could include long-term pollution effects on the environment or people's health due to manufacturing. It could also be the benefits to the environment and society through circular use of resources, and zero-carbon manufacturing.

It is crucial to the transparent and real representation of an investment's value and the true value of a company to include and monetize externalities. It is important to do this because external factors have real costs and real financial opportunities. Resources and pollution, especially CO_2, comes with a price, both societally and economically. Not only is the impact on people's health from air pollution huge, bringing with it substantial costs, but the impact of climate change due to CO_2 emissions is also tremendously costly, and detrimental societally and environmentally. Furthermore, as we have come to understand, resources are not free, and we pay the price for imposed resource scarcity. While fossil fuels continue to be heavily subsidized throughout the world, pricing of renewable energy is not competing in a level playing field. Therefore, externalities simply must be priced if we want to support sustainable business and make sustainable investing financially attractive. It has been shown that the business case for market opportunities improves by 8% to 92%, with an average of almost 40%, when external costs are monetized (See figure 29).

IT IS CRUCIAL TO INCLUDE AND MONETIZE EXTERNALITIES.

In recent decades, investors have often sought market liquidity and short-term gains at the expense of sustainability efforts.[34] This investment strategy is linked to expediting payouts and maximizing returns, but fails to take into account the long-term costs or future detrimental effects of capital expenditures on things like resource exploitation or energy inefficiency. Because the full effects of paying prices that reflect these social and environmental externalities may not be immediately felt, many may still not consider the immense opportunity the SDGs offer and simply consider any large up front expense of switching to a more sustainable investment portfolio to be too costly. As financial performance is a primary signal that investors need to understand companies' relative performance on the Global Goals, taking into account the full prices and eventual costs and benefits of these investments across the economy is paramount to maximizing potential returns. Thus, considering how externalities will ultimately affect capital gains when making investment decisions will lead to more stability in financial performance while also supporting the SDGs.

> **SUSTAINABLE BUSINESS CAN UNLOCK AT LEAST US $12 TRILLION IN NEW MARKET VALUE, OR US $13 TRILLION IF EXTERNALITIES ARE INCLUDED.**[32]
>
> BUSINESS & SUSTAINABLE DEVELOPMENT COMMISSION

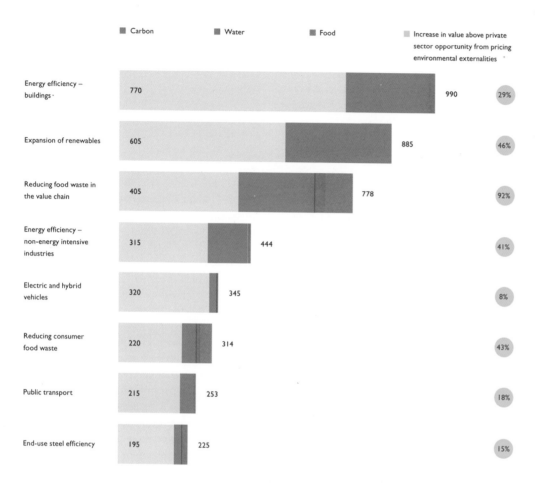

SDG opportunities — Size of incremental opportunity in 2030 with externalities priced US$ billions: 2015 values

Figure 29 **Pricing externalities into top market opportunities**[153]

Legend: ■ Carbon ■ Water ■ Food ■ Increase in value above private sector opportunity from pricing environmental externalities *

SDG opportunity	Private	With externalities	Increase
Energy efficiency – buildings ·	770	990	29%
Expansion of renewables	605	885	46%
Reducing food waste in the value chain	405	778	92%
Energy efficiency – non-energy intensive industries	315	444	41%
Electric and hybrid vehicles	320	345	8%
Reducing consumer food waste	220	314	43%
Public transport	215	253	18%
End-use steel efficiency	195	225	15%

* Based on estimated savings or projected market sizings in each area. Only the high case opportunity is shown here.
+ Externality sizing assumptions carbon price of US$50 tCO2e; average water price increased by US$0.08 for agricultural water and US$0.40 for industrial use (based on removal subsidies); food prices increased by US$44/t due to removal of subsidies. Rounded to nearest US$5 billion.
Source: Literature search; Alphabeta analysis

ENVIRONMENTAL, SOCIAL AND GOVERNANCE INVESTMENT CONSIDERATIONS

ESG considerations have been mentioned earlier with respect to the many collaborative initiatives that are helping to accelerate the sustainable investment movement. ESG criteria is a set of Environmental, Social and Governance standards for a company's operations that socially conscious investors use to screen investments. The criteria relate to the following three factors.[35]

- Environmental criteria is based on how a company performs on energy use, waste, pollution, natural resource conservation and animal treatment. It also takes into consideration which environmental risks might affect a company's income and how the company is managing those risks. For example, a company might face environmental risks related to its disposal of hazardous waste, its management of toxic emissions or its compliance with the government's environmental regulations.
- Social criteria examines the company's business relationships and how the company manages their relationships with employees, suppliers, customers and the communities where it operates.
- Governance deals with a company's leadership, executive pay, audits and internal controls, and shareholder rights. Investors also want to know that a company uses accurate and transparent accounting methods.

Nearly 75% of investment professionals worldwide take ESG factors into consideration in the investment process.[36] This is indicative of a trend in business to explore how to do business in a way that is actually aligned with people, planet and a sustainable economy. Because the world is experiencing problematic risks on multiple levels, we are being faced with hugely detrimental impacts in a dramatic way. For example, the onset of climate change brings with it severe weather events such as hurricanes, floods, droughts, and storms like never before with enormous financial consequences. Consider the economic losses the United States has recently suffered as a

NATURAL DISASTERS CAUSED A TOTAL OF US $1.5 TRILLION IN GLOBAL DAMAGE IN THE 10 YEARS BETWEEN 2003 AND 2013.

FAO

result of extreme climate events, totaling more than US $15 billion in just the first three-quarters of 2017.[37] Natural disasters caused a total of US $1.5 trillion in global damage in the 10 years between 2003 and 2013.[38]

These costly environmental effects of climate should be incorporated in valuing businesses and other investments. In addition, a recent analysis conducted by the World Bank suggests that in all of the 117 countries studied, the effect of floods, windstorms, earthquakes and tsunamis on well-being, measured in terms of lost consumption, is even larger than asset losses. It estimates the impact of disasters on well-being in these countries is equivalent to global annual consumption losses of US $520 billion, and forces 26 million people into poverty each year.[39] But resilience-building interventions, including universal early warning systems, improved access to personal banking, insurance policies and social protection systems could lessen climate shocks and in turn reduce the finance gap by reducing the needs. At the same time, the business opportunity presented in these measures has the potential to see a gain in well-being equivalent to a US $100 billion increase in annual global consumption, and a reduction of the overall impact of disasters on well-being by 20%.

Investments that support the achievement of the SDGs is critical. SDG investment (SDGI) is distinct in that it embodies two major shifts that are needed in markets today. First, SDGI represents a shift towards a world where all investments are reviewed for their societal impact, versus only 26%

or US $23 trillion of global assets under management today. Second, an allocation of capital geared towards the SDGs is a shift in movement. It signifies an ecosystem emerging where investors are triggered and equipped to maximize the positive contributions of each investment dollar while staying within their required risk and return expectations.

IMPACT INVESTING: OPENING THE DOOR TO OPPORTUNITIES

There is a loud and urgent call for capital to support positive impact on society and the environment. Impact investments are investments made into companies, organizations, and funds with the intention to generate positive social and environmental impact alongside a financial return.[40] Several leading financial firms have entered the impact investing market in recent years with the creation of platforms dedicated to this. The impact investing landscape has grown, with assets rising to US $114 billion, of which US $22.1 billion being committed in 2016 alone.[41] There is an expected impressive growth of 25.9% in capital commitment in 2017.[42]

Investing with the intention to create a positive impact is gaining ground. On September 14, 2016, the Global Impact Investing Network (GIIN) launched a campaign calling on asset owners and managers around the world to channel their capital into impact investments. Investing for positive impact opens the door to opportunities for

the explicit investment in businesses, funds and bonds that have a direct, positive impact on the SDGs. The growth of impact investing is currently demonstrated by the attention it is getting from investors as well as from stock exchanges. The door is being opened by business itself.

The strength of impact investing is threefold. First, innovative ideas are effectively linked to economies of scale and to financial power. This creates enormous potential leverage for business, especially if the multinational start-up or scale-up also provides access to the funds of their own global network and knowledge network. Second, this model helps large companies to realize their long-term strategic objectives. Third, impact investing steers capital towards the Goals.

As we have established, one of the critical success factors for achieving the SDGs is capital. In recent years, the realization that capital can be a main driver in sustainability has increasingly influenced the financial markets. In addition to positive impact investment strategies, exclusion criteria is becoming more ambitious and pervasive. There is also an unmistakable trend to divest from fossil fuels simply because the risk is now too high, and thus no longer in line with ESG strategies. Investors, banks and pension funds are consequently closing the door on unsustainable investments. Moving forward, capital will be mobilized as a force for good. In other words: investors must open the door, hold it open, and look towards our sustainable future.

Impact investment has become widespread across the globe. A 2017 GIIN Investor Impact Survey reported:

40% of investment was in U.S. & Canada	**14%** of investment was in WNS Europe	**10%** of investment was in Sub-Saharan Africa	**9%** of investment was in Latin America

4.3 CAPITAL IMPACT ON ALL SDGs

Capital flows are integral to the achievement of all of the SDGs. There are substantial public and charitable funds supporting SDG-related activities, but to speed up and scale up, more capital is needed.

> **TO ENSURE A SUSTAINABLE DROP IN HUNGER, "PRO-POOR" INVESTMENTS OF US $151 BILLION PER YEAR ARE NEEDED IN AREAS SUCH AS IRRIGATION, INFRASTRUCTURE AND CREDIT FACILITIES ON TOP OF CASH TRANSFERS.** [54]
>
> WEF

SDG 1: No Poverty; By providing low-income people with services they need to make investments and manage unexpected expenses, financial inclusion facilitates the alleviation of poverty and business growth. According to the World Bank, more than 700 million people live on or below US $1.90 a day.[43] A lack of access to basic financial services makes it difficult to take control of one's own economic life. Just 43% of adults in the poorest fifth of households have a bank account.[44] Financial services such as savings and capital management can have direct and indirect beneficial impacts on poverty. For example, giving poor people access to savings instruments can increase a country's net savings, which can lead to an increase in productive investment and consumption.[45] ODA remains a critical financing source for extreme pov-

erty eradication, especially in the LDCs. Estimates determine that annual spending needs for social protection, including health insurance, cash transfers, and pension systems, would require incremental public investments of between approximately US $40 and $60 billion per year in low- and lower-middle-income countries.[46] These estimates include costs accounting for the difficulty of targeting income transfers to the extreme poor. Lower poverty ratios are also linked to financial depth, which includes a robust stock market and active lending to businesses by banks. It was found that state-led bank expansion in India's rural unbanked locations significantly reduced those in rural poverty by 14 to 17 percentage points.[47]

SDG 2: No Hunger; Food expenses account for 50% to 70% of spending by people living under the US $1.25-a-day poverty line.[48] In addition to the money that already goes towards preventing people from starving, it will cost on average an extra US $11 billion per year of public spending from now to 2030 to end hunger.[49] US $4 billion of the additional spending needs to come from donors. The other US $7 billion will come from poor countries themselves. Donors currently spend US $8.6 billion per year on hunger programs, so the extra cost represents a 45% increase on current donor spending. The additional public spending will, on average, spur an extra US $5 billion in private investment per year. Farmers who have access to financial services often produce more bountiful harvests. A lack of access to credit and insurance prevents farmers from making investments that could increase crop yields and strengthen food security. Access to capital and agricultural insurance can embolden farmers to make more and riskier investments, which can lead to increased production and earnings. A study in Ghana found that farmers with rainfall-indexed insurance – in which insurance payouts are based on rainfall amounts – spent US $266 more on harvest expenditures compared with uninsured farmers. Insured farmers also earned US $285 more in revenue, while their post-harvest assets were US $531 higher.[50]

> **CURRENTLY, INVESTMENT IN EDUCATION IS ABOUT US $80 BILLION PER YEAR IN DEVELOPING COUNTRIES. MOVING TOWARDS SUSTAINABLE DEVELOPMENT IN THIS SECTOR WOULD REQUIRE A YEARLY INVESTMENT OF US $330 BILLION, IMPLYING AN ANNUAL GAP OF ABOUT US $250 BILLION.** [55]
>
> UNCTAD

 SDG 3: Health and Well-being; The World Health Organization predicts that low and middle-income countries will require an additional US $134 billion per year between now and 2025 to reach health-related targets under the SDGs, leading to universal health coverage. The ambitious scenario would require new investments increasing from an initial US $104 billion a year to $274 billion, or $41 per person, by 2030.[51] These investments would prevent about 71 million premature deaths and boost health spending as a proportion of GDP to an average of 6.5%. More than 14 million new health workers would be added, and nearly 378,000 new health facilities built, 93% of which would be primary health care centers. Engaging the private sector will be critical for the health care industry. Public-private collaboration on health can bring huge benefits to both sides. For instance, pooled procurement of medicine and other health commodities allows the public sector to leverage economies of scale, so it can then negotiate better prices with the private sector and pay less for the same items. Every year, about 100 million people fall below the poverty line as a result of out-of-pocket expenditures on health. Investments in pharmaceutical companies and retailers that are improving access to generic drugs for base-of-pyramid communities could help reduce household expenditure on health care, thus alleviating a key driver of poverty. Other strategies include investing in medical retailers, private clinics, ICT solutions, ambulance services and training providers in low income and rural communities.[52]

Financial services like medical insurance can provide a formal channel for mitigating the risks of health emergencies.[53]

 SDG 4: Quality Education; Human capital measured by education can be a stronger predictor of economic growth than initial per capita GDP. Early childhood programs, for example, produce very high returns on investment. For every US $1 spent on high-quality early childhood programs, US $8 to $16 is returned to society. As in the health sector, private household expenditure on education in developing countries accounts for a significant share of total investments and may be as high as 30%. In the United States, university tuition has skyrocketed in recent years and the average student debt upon graduation with a bachelor's degree is US $37,172, up 6% from 2016. Investment in education grows an economy. Global average social returns on education have been cited at 18.9% for primary education, 13.1% for secondary education, and 10.8% for tertiary education.[54] Further, returns to primary education tend to be considerably larger in less developed countries: average returns are 25.4% for sub-Saharan Africa compared to 8.5% in OECD countries. Rates of return to education have declined over time as per capita income and education levels increased, which suggests that education behaves like other investments in that diminishing returns apply. A noticeable exception is private returns to higher education, which have continued to increase, largely because of public subsidies for the tertiary education sector.

SDG 5: Gender Equality; The global income of women will grow from approximately US $13 trillion to $18 trillion in the next five years; that is more than the GDP growth of China and India combined during the same period.[55] By 2028, it is predicted that women will control 75% of discretionary spending around the world. Women in developing countries could be an estimated $9 trillion better off if their pay and access to paid work were equal to that of men. The additional output generated by decreasing the gap in employment between men and women could drive the wider economy, and US $12 trillion could be added to global GDP by 2025 by advancing women's equality.[56] It is further estimated that an US $28 trillion would be added by that date if women were to play an identical role to men in the labor markets. Recent studies looking at three critical financial measures show *Fortune 500* companies with the highest representation of women board directors attained significantly higher financial performance, on average, than those with the lowest representation of women board directors.[57] Measures include: 1) *return on equity* - companies with the highest percentages of women board directors outperformed those with the least by 53%; 2) *return on sales* - companies with the highest percentages of women board directors outperformed those with the least by 42%; and 3) *return on invested capital* - companies with the highest percentages of women board directors outperformed those with the least by 66%. In addition, there is also strong evidence that investing in women can improve financial performance. On average, there is a notably stronger-than-average performance at companies with three or more women board directors.

SDG 6: Clean Water and Sanitation; Businesses are major users of freshwater. For example, it takes around 150 liters of water to make one liter of beer, and 7,000 liters to grow the cotton to make one pair of blue jeans.[58] So it seems reasonable then to expect business and private investment to invest in clean water. Additionally, adequate sanitation is

> ## BY 2028, IT IS PREDICTED THAT WOMEN WILL CONTROL 75% OF DISCRETIONARY SPENDING AROUND THE WORLD.
>
> ERNST & YOUNG

necessary for employees to stay productive. Lost working days resulting from poor sanitation costs the global economy approximately US $4 billion annually. A 2016 analysis by the World Bank' estimates that US $114 billion per year of capital investments will be required to meet universal access to safely managed water and sanitation services by 2030, or about three times the current investment levels.[59] It should be emphasized that these expenditures include both capital and operation and maintenance. Globally, over US $11 billion in ODA grants and loans (US $7.4 billion), non-concessional loans/credits (US $3.4 billion), and other funds (over US $300 million) from high-income countries (bilateral aid, multilateral development banks, NGOs, and private foundations) was disbursed on water and sanitation in 2015. While external aid flows comprise a low proportion of global expenditures on WASH, in some countries, the amount of aid received from external sources is significant and may even be the largest source of WASH financing. Several major multilateral institutions, including the World Bank, the European Commission, and the African Development Bank reported large decreases in ODA commitments for water and sanitation in 2015, making it all the more urgent for private capital flows to fill the gap.

SDG 7: Affordable and Clean Energy; To address energy-related emissions, investments must be made in low carbon technologies and energy efficiency. To fully implement the 180 plus national action plans that were submitted to the UN in 2015, a cumulative investment of US $13.5 trillion in low carbon technologies and energy efficiency is needed.[60] It is a huge challenge that will require decarbonizing the global electricity supply. With at least 65% that must be generated from renewables by 2050, investment is also needed to improve the rate of energy efficiency gains.[61] Annual investments of US $45 billion will be needed to meet the expansion of grid electrification, and substantial development of mini-grid and off-grid solutions in remote areas where extension of the main grid would not be the most economically attractive approach.[62] A number of companies are taking part in public-private projects to improve energy access, one example being "Power Africa", where the governments of Ghana, Tanzania, Kenya, Nigeria, Ethiopia and Liberia and a group of private sector firms are taking part in an initiative to improve access to clean, reliable power in Africa, and ultimately deliver electricity to more than 20 million new households and companies by 2018.[63] The program known as the Renewable Energy Independent Power Producer Procurement Program (REIPPPP), has successfully channeled substantial private sector expertise and investment into grid-connected renewable energy in South Africa at competitive prices. Some of the ways in which capital is being mobilized for the energy sector include investing in the developing green bond market; using Development Finance Institutions' de-risking instruments to mobilize private capital; or exploring insurance products that focus on removing specific risks.

"TODAY, I CALL ON THE INVESTOR COMMUNITY TO BUILD ON THE STRONG MOMENTUM FROM PARIS AND SEIZE THE OPPORTUNITIES FOR CLEAN ENERGY GROWTH. I CHALLENGE INVESTORS TO DOUBLE – AT A MINIMUM – THEIR CLEAN ENERGY INVESTMENTS BY 2020." [157]

FORMER UN SECRETARY GENERAL BAN KI-MOON

This is important because significant investment is needed to mount an effective global response to energy challenges.

SDG 8: Decent Work and Economic Growth; Entrepreneurs and SME's are massive drivers of economic growth and development, especially in emerging countries. But with 50% of SME's lacking access to finance, this significantly hinders their growth. Financial products like microfinance and micro-insurance can play a pivotal role in empowering SMEs to sustain and grow. Over the past two decades, Swiss Investment Fund for Emerging Markets (SIFEM) has deployed around US $800 million toward economic growth, while earning strong financial returns and supporting more than 450,000 jobs.[64] Equally important, SIFEM's investments have supported numerous new fund managers in emerging economies, which are now starting to raise their second, third, or even fourth funds. The impact of this type of investment extends far beyond job creation and economic growth, it also embeds sustainability into all of its investments and supported businesses. Decent work.

FROM 2012 TO 2015, OVERALL DEVELOPMENT AID COMMITMENTS INCREASED OVER US$ 40 BILLION, WHILE AID COMMITMENTS FOR WATER AND SANITATION DECREASED BY US$ 2.2 BILLION. [156]

WHO

SDG 9: Industry, Innovation and Infrastructure; In 2014, investments in research and development stood at 1.7% of global GDP, up from 1.5% in 2000. Worldwide, there were 1,098 researchers per million inhabitants in 2014, ranging from 63 in the least developed countries to 3,500 in Europe and Northern America. ODA for economic infrastructure in developing countries reached US $57 billion in 2015, an increase of 32% since 2010. The main recipient sectors were transport and energy (US $19 billion each). Manufacturing is a principal driver of economic development, employment and social stability. Globally, manufacturing value added as a share of GDP increased from 15.3% in 2005 to 16.2% in 2016. In 2016, manufacturing value added per capita amounted to US $4,621 in Europe and Northern America, compared to about US $100 in the least developed countries. A large portion of transport infrastructure investments comes from traditional government sources. Attracting more revenues and unlocking public budgets to support investments in sustainable transport can include, among others: rationalizing inefficient fossil-fuel subsidies; expanding cost recovery through user charges; improving asset management of existing infrastructure; transfer-

ring commercial roles to the private sector; and prioritizing more cost-effective and sustainable transport modes and investments. There is opportunity for tapping into capital market financing for sustainable transport, for example in the form of national or municipal bonds. However, this is not feasible for many cities in developing countries. Currently, only 4% of the 500 largest cities in developing countries are rated creditworthy by international financial markets.[65] But this is slowly changing. For example, recently, the city of Lima, Peru, worked with international banks to enhance its credit rating, which enabled it to issue bonds to invest in low-carbon mass transit. Public-private partnerships (PPPs) also present the opportunity to leverage expertise, innovation, financial resources and policy mechanisms.

SDG 10: Reduced Inequalities; In many countries, there is a tradition of economically targeted investment where investors seek products that target specific underserved geographies or marginalized communities who may lack access to resources. Housing is a focus of, for instance, Legal & General Capital (LGC) and Dutch pension fund manager, PGGM, announced the launch of a Build to Rent partnership. The partnership initially invests £600m into building purpose built private rental housing across the UK, providing over 3000 homes to help mitigate the inequality-exacerbating rise in housing prices and support urban regeneration in strategic areas.[66] Globally, the rise of microfinance as an asset class has been specifically linked to the idea of "financial inclusion," increasing access to needed financial services and opportunities for economic development for poor communities in both developing and developed markets.[67] More generally, bottom-of-the-pyramid strategies, that focus on the delivery of goods and services to the poor, have been put forward as a means to mitigate poverty and so reduce inequality.

SDG 11: Sustainable Cities and Communities; From 2012 to 2016, the World Bank Group financed 79 core urban resilience projects in 41 countries. Over this five-year period, investment averaged a little over

> DUE TO FINANCIAL DIFFICULTIES, GLOBALLY, ABOUT 2.6 BILLION PEOPLE CANNOT ACCESS A RELIABLE ELECTRICITY SOURCE, WITH ANOTHER 2.6 BILLION WITHOUT BASIC SANITATION ACCESS. 1.5 BILLION DO NOT HAVE ACCESS TO RELIABLE PHONE SERVICES, AND OVER 4 BILLION ARE WITHOUT THE INTERNET.[158]
>
> PWC

US $1.8 billion per year. Over the next two decades, the Program aims to attract US $500 billion in private capital to finance resilient infrastructure and services that will contribute to the elimination of poverty and adaptation to climate change in 500 cities, benefitting one billion people. To achieve these ambitions of leveraging and impact, the World Bank Group would need to make more use of efficient financial instruments and double its current level of lending for urban resilience to approximately US $4 billion per year. Investment has primarily been in specific areas including, emergency recovery, technical assistance, adaptable programs, and financial intermediary lending. The World Bank Group has launched a Resilient Cities Program, which will serve as the structure within the Bank for any business or organization wishing to invest in urban resilience. Leveraging private investment enables the Program to scale up and achieve higher levels of climate resilience in urban areas. Many cities around the world have enough economic value that can be tapped to make investing in resilience a strategic choice. The low-to-negative interest rates currently experienced globally add incentive for private capital, institutional investors and sovereign wealth funds to invest in urban resilience.

SDG 12: Responsible Consumption and Production; The SDG Fund is collaborating with partners, including from the private sector, to invest in and promote more responsible consumption and outsourcing practices. Their particular focus is on ensuring that local farmers can obtain a fairer share of the value generated across the value chain. In Peru, the SDG Fund is contributing US $3.8 million, or 39% of total funding needed, to establish an inclusive value chain in the production of quinoa and other Andean grains.[68] This project is being implemented so that the increased demand in the international market can convert into economic and social improvements of currently vulnerable producers. The Fund is also promoting organic agriculture in Fiji with a US $2.4 million investment in a production system that sustains the health of soils, ecosystems and people. In Bolivia, the SDG Fund joint program is supporting

four municipalities to establish sustainable agricultural production systems, which will increase the incomes of the poorest families and improve nutrition. This investment is US $1.8 million amounting to 50% of project financing. Large corporations, some with economies bigger than many countries, also supply substantial capital.

SDG 13: Climate Action; Developed countries have committed to mobilizing US $100 billion in climate finance by 2020 and continuing at that level until 2025. Climate finance totaling US $81 billion was mobilized for projects funded by the world's six largest Multilateral Development Banks (MDBs) in 2015. Since 2011, MDBs have jointly committed more than US $131 billion in climate finance. Among the regions, non-European Union Europe and Central Asia received the largest share of total funding at 20%; with South Asia receiving 19%; Latin America and the Caribbean 15%; East Asia and the Pacific 14%; the EU 13%; Sub-Saharan Africa 9%; and the Middle East and North Africa 9%. Multi-regional commitments made up the other 2% of the total. On a sectoral basis, the largest recipient of adaptation funding was for water and wastewater systems (27%), followed by energy, transport and related infrastructure (24%), and crop and food production (18%). Renewable energy received the bulk of mitigation finance (30%), lower-carbon transport received 26%, and energy efficiency activities 14%. The World Bank Group is determined to increase annual funding for climate work to potentially US $29 billion annually in 2020, and they already have plans to provide more than US $1 billion to support India's ambitious initiatives to expand solar and have approved projects to help farmers in countries like Niger grow more to adapt to a changing climate.

SDG 14: Life Below Water; Ocean-related investments are growing and, as of 2016, there are commitments valued at over US $9.2 billion to protect marine life. The commitments focus on the key ocean issues of our time: marine protected areas, sustainable fisheries, marine pollution, and climate-related impacts on the ocean. At the 2016 International Union for Conservation of Nature (IUCN) World Conservation Congress, many NGOs and governments raised their support with the strong stance to protect at least 30% of the ocean by 2030 and philanthropic investments in ocean conservation were boosted by over US $5 billion.[69] Among them, the Nature Conservancy announced a commitment of over US $100 million, including private and public funding, to work with countries and communities to create ocean management plans, develop and implement innovative financing solutions to finance parks and protected areas, and to provide tools, case studies and scientific studies to manage and reduce local threats to coral reefs and reef fisheries. The Tiffany & Co. Foundation announced a three-year US $3.2 million commitment that supports the Nature Conservancy and well as the Bahamas National Trust and the Bahamas Reef Environmental Education Foundation to conserve 20% of the Bahamas marine and coastal environment by 2020, plus additional support for Oceans 5. Furthermore, the Global Environment Facility, Conservation International, and Rare announced the US $18 million Meloy Fund – an impact investment fund focused on community small-scale fisheries and providing financial incentives to fishing communities to conserve coral reef ecosystems in Indonesia and the Philippines.

SDG 15: Life on Land; In 2017, the World Bank embarked on its first-ever operation targeting greenhouse gas emissions from a landscape perspective with a US $18 million start-up grant for the Oromia Forested Landscape Program (OFLP) in Ethiopia.[70] Through its BioCarbon Fund (Initiative for Sustainable Forest Landscapes), the World Bank is supporting the Oromia Regional State in Ethiopia to establish community-centered activities that reduce deforestation and land-use based emissions. The grant will support participatory forest management and reforestation investments in deforestation hotspots, coupled with improvements to the institutional systems that underpin large-scale investments and emissions reduction purchases. If successful, this preliminary phase is ex-

pected to unlock a BioCarbon Fund commitment to purchase up to 10 million tons of carbon dioxide emission reductions. Also on landscapes, another World Bank-supported project will target rural poverty in Madagascar, while the Land Policy Initiative released an analysis of large-scale investments in Africa's land sector. In Madagascar, a Sustainable Landscape Management project of US $78.7 million, supported by the Global Environment Facility (GEF), the World Bank and the French Agency for Development (AFD), aims to contribute to improved livelihoods for more than 38,000 rural people by providing increased access to technical services, agricultural inputs and forestry services.[71] The project seeks to enhance the management of 10 protected areas and sustainably manage productive landscapes and forests covering more than 1.13 million hectares. It will also test and deploy innovative financing mechanisms such as payments for ecosystem services, REDD+ and carbon financing.

CONNECTING CORPORATE ACTIVITY TO POSITIVE SOCIETAL OUTCOMES IS A CRITICAL FUNCTION OF THE CAPITAL MARKETS.

SDG 16: Peace, Justice and Strong Institutions; Investors are increasingly seeking out companies that show positive leadership in improving impacts in areas that pertain directly to civil rights, conflict minerals, labor conditions, diversity and corruption. Calvert Investments, for example, is a global leader in responsible investing. Calvert is one of the largest responsible investment companies in the United States, operating from the foundational belief that investment performance is inextricably linked to responsible corporate behavior. As of the end of 2015, the company had US $12.2 billion in assets under management that were helping to address peace and justice throughout the world.[72] Connecting corporate activity to positive societal outcomes is a critical function of the capital markets. The strength of this connection should be priced into capital markets, and investors should have to take this into consideration. The BBVA MicroFinance Foundation actively works on the development of the microfinance sector through good corporate governance, human capital training, promoting appropriate regulations and social impact measurement. With regard to financial inclusion, the Foundation contributes to building effective, accountable institutions and peace, while strong institutions and peace also contribute to financial inclusion.[73]

 SDG 17: Partnerships for the Goals; The SDG Fund mobilizes and provides capital by bridging the efforts of different development partners such as UN agencies, national and local governments, businesses, civil society, and academia. All SDG Fund programs are cooperative or joint in nature, establishing integrated responses that address community-wide issues such as child nutrition, income generation for vulnerable populations, and gender parity at the institutional level. The SDG Fund has introduced the use of *matching funds* that are provided by national and local governments, international donors and the private sector. This increases sustainability, impact, national ownership and the potential to scale up. Another collaborative initiative is the Low Carbon Technology Partnerships initiative (LCTPi) which enables private sector action to help limit the rise in global temperatures to below 2°C.[74] Business-led LCTPi action plans were launched at COP21 in Paris in December 2015. This demonstrated that emission reduc-

> "IF WE DON'T GET THIS RIGHT OUR GLOBAL CAPITALIST SYSTEM CERTAINLY WON'T ACHIEVE ITS POTENTIAL, AND MOST WOULD SAY THAT THE SYSTEM ITSELF WILL BECOME UNSTABLE."[159]
>
> JOHN STREUR, PRESIDENT AND CEO, CALVERT INVESTMENTS INC.

tion across sectors can be rapidly scaled up by working together. Companies are engaged in LCTPi across 9 focus areas ranging from Renewables to Chemicals to Forest Products as Carbon Sinks. LCTPi has enabled businesses to develop strategies to unlock low-carbon development in each focus area. Through this collaboration, the LCTPi could get society 65% of the way to a 2°C ceiling for temperature rises. It could help channel US $5 to 10 trillion of investment toward low carbon sectors of the economy and support 5 to 10 million jobs per year around the world. Most importantly, the LCTPi provides a platform for all businesses to play a leading role in helping to achieve the UN Sustainable Development Goals while implementing sustainable technology practices.

4.4 SHARED VALUE OPPORTUNITIES

For the past several decades, investors have focused on short-term financial gains that were not necessarily aimed at what would provide the best outcome for the environment or society going into the future. Sustainable investing and SDG capital expenditure requires longer-term investments in initiatives that benefit multiple stakeholders. Growth-market private equity opportunities directed by the SDGs are longer-term investments, creating sustained value as compared to catering to shareholders' requests for immediate payouts.[75]

This longer-term Shared Value Investing (SVI) can be thought of as a type of change to accelerate change. The International Finance Corporation (IFC) itself, a part of the World Bank Group, is an example of how an institution can change from being a financier to a financial intermediary.[76] To help mobilize private capital and move from billions to trillions, it can be a "matchmaker" and provide more stability over time with guarantees. Financial institutions are in a unique position to provide capital for SDG implementation and create shared value opportunities.

> "WE FOUNDED SARONA TO PROVIDE SMART CAPITAL TO BUILD BETTER BUSINESSES ACROSS FRONTIER AND EMERGING MARKETS. IT IS EXCITING TO SEE THE SDGs PROVIDE A FRAMEWORK THAT THE WHOLE WORLD CAN SIGN UP TO."[160]
>
> VIVINA BERLA CO-MANAGING PARTNER AT SARONA ASSET MANAGEMENT

Impact investing with a social benefit and sustainable return is a logical way for capital to contribute to the SDGs. As is the integration and inclusion of ESG factors in financial analysis, which has been growing by 17% per year. ESG criteria are by their very nature shared value criteria. When examining an investment for its ESG values, an investor is in fact assessing the impact of the investment or company on the environment, and people. Used with nearly half of sustainable investments, this technique is now taking off with visible returns. The scale of the sustainable investing market, however, differs greatly from region to region. European asset managers have the highest proportion of sustainable investments (52.6% at the beginning of 2016), followed by Australia and New Zealand (50.6%) and Canada (37.8%).[77] Sustainable investing is less prevalent in the United States (21.6%), Japan (3.4%), and Asian countries other than Japan (0.8%), but the gap is narrowing.

There is a growing school of thought that the price of externalities should be integrated into the investment process. As mentioned earlier, incorporating externalities means taking into account the wider effects of investments by considering the impact on society, the environment, and future generations. In 2010, Trucost calculated the cost of global environmental damage and examined why this is important to the economy, capital markets, companies and institutional investors.[78] Annual environmental costs from global human activity were calculated at US $6.6 trillion in 2008, equivalent to 11% of GDP, with the top 3,000 public companies – i.e. those that make up large, diversified equity portfolios – responsible for a third of this (US $2.15 trillion). In a hypothetical investor equity portfolio, environmental externalities alone could equate to over 50% of the companies' combined earnings.

Therefore, sustainable performance and contributions to the SDGs is becoming an important value driver for investors when evaluating companies. Over the past decade, the way a company's value is defined has shifted from a purely tangible perspective to an integrated business approach. Up until the 1980's, tangible assets accounted for

IN 2015, RESEARCHERS FROM SHAREACTION INTERVIEWED
52 INSTITUTIONAL INVESTORS, BASED IN EVERY REGION OF THE
WORLD, ON THEIR ATTITUDES AND INTENTIONS IN RELATION TO
THE SDGs AND FOUND THAT:
- 95% OF RESPONDENTS PLAN TO ENGAGE WITH INVESTEE
  COMPANIES ABOUT ISSUES COVERED BY THE SDGs;
- 84% WILL ALLOCATE CAPITAL TO INVESTMENTS SUPPORTING
  THE SDGs;
- 89% WILL SUPPORT REGULATORY REFORMS THAT PROMOTE
  THE SDGs. [61]

80% of company value; the rest was made up by intangibles. Today it is the reverse, where 80% of a company's value is determined by looking at intangible aspects.[79] Integrating the SDGs in the core business and reporting cycle enables companies to focus on creating visible shared value. Returns on sustainability investments that create wealth, jobs, and employee development are being valued and monetized.

RESEARCH HAS SHOWN THAT "HIGH SUSTAINABILITY" COMPANIES SIGNIFICANTLY OUTPERFORMED "LOW SUSTAINABILITY."

Research has shown that "high sustainability" companies significantly outperformed "low sustainability" companies over the long term in both accounting and stock-price terms. A study of US companies that had adopted key sustainability policies by 1993 compared to those in the same industry that had adopted almost no key sustainability policies, tracking performance through 2010, showed value creation for both the business and stakeholders that were on the sustainability side. Over that time, US $1 invested in the stock of high sustainability firms grew to US $22.6 on a

value-weighted basis, compared with US $15.4 for low sustainability firms.[80] In accounting terms, the high sustainability firms outperformed the low sustainability firms as measured by growth in value of equity and return on assets.

As a result, sustainable investing is rapidly becoming part of the global investment mainstream. Many large institutional asset owners have embraced it, as have most of the world's largest asset managers. The world of business and finance is committing itself to incorporating sustainability issues into the investment processes. Evidenced by the UN-backed Principles for Responsible Investment which has more than 1,750 asset managers' signatories from over 50 countries, these sustainable investments represent approximately US $70 trillion.[81]

Large numbers of investors, particularly two groups that are becoming more prominent – women and millennials – consistently indicate they are highly interested in sustainable investing and its shared value components. It is estimated that these emerging investor groups could soon control upwards of $30 trillion in assets in the United States alone.[82]

National Australia Bank (NAB) has been a pioneer in promoting the shared value concept for SDG investments. The Bank set up the Fairtrade labeling system in Australia and New Zealand and implements shared value as a driver for sustainable social change. NAB believes that, while there are important roles for government, philanthropy and civil society in tackling complex challenges, the most effective way to unlock value at scale is through the power of business. NAB is working to develop shared value opportunities across a range of sectors locally – including the burgeoning market for renewable energy flowing from the Paris climate change agreement. NAB has been carbon neutral since 2010 and is the leading arranger of clean energy finance in Australia. In 2014 it issued the nation's first domestic green bond, raising AUD $300 million earmarked for funding solar and wind renewable energy projects (See Case 24).[83]

" **BUSINESSES ARE IN A GREAT POSITION TO CHANGE THE WORLD AND DO IT IN A WAY THAT STRENGTHENS THEIR PROFITABILITY.**"

MARK KRAMER AT SHARED VALUE FORUM EVENT. HOSTED BY
NATIONAL AUSTRALIA BANK

24

NATIONAL AUSTRALIA BANK (NAB)

Creating Shared Value for all Stakeholders
Supporting the transition to a low carbon
economy.

Case applied in: Australia, Global
Headquarters located in: Australia
www.nab.com.au

IMPACT SDGs

SDG 7

Affordable and Clean Energy
Committed to providing customers with AUD $55 billion in environmental financing by 2025; NAB has provided more than AUD $6 billion in project finance for renewable energy projects since 2003.

SDG 8

Decent work and economic growth
More than AUD $300 million in discounted equipment finance for energy efficient or renewable energy assets made available since June 2015; financier to Tilt Renewables, which is opening is Australasian headquarters in Melbourne, creating up to 35 jobs.

SDG 9

Industry, Innovation and Infrastructure
February 2017, NAB issued its second green bond, and the first offshore green bond by an Australian bank, raising €500 million for financing a portfolio of wind farms and solar energy facilities in the UK and Europe, plus electrified rail infrastructure in the UK and Australia.

> WE KNOW WE OWE OUR SUCCESS TO THE PEOPLE, BUSINESSES, AND COMMUNITIES WHO WE HAVE SUPPORTED AND PARTNERED WITH FOR ALMOST 160 YEARS. THAT SUCCESS BRINGS WITH IT A RESPONSIBILITY TO MAKE A SIGNIFICANT AND POSITIVE CONTRIBUTION.
>
> **ANDREW THORBURN, GROUP CEO AND MANAGING DIRECTOR**

NAB is one of the four largest financial institutions in Australia, with operations throughout Australia, New Zealand, Asia, United Kingdom and USA. It has been actively supporting the growth of the Australian impact investment market, and in particular supporting the transition to a low carbon economy. The Bank focuses its sustainable investments on shared value by ensuring its purpose drives both sustainable growth and financial business strategy.

Australian farmers and Agribusiness owners are some of its main targets for capital allocation, as these groups are good candidates for significantly reducing energy costs and further transforming their energy use.

The Clean Energy Finance Corporation (CEFC) is commited an additional AUD $ 180 million to the NAB Energy Efficient Bonus program (SDG 7) in June 2017, following its success in helping Australian businesses transform their energy use. The CEFC has now committed AUD $300 million to the program, which was launched in 2015 with an initial AUD $120 million commitment from the CEFC, in which 87% was used by NAB Agribusiness and rural customers. The Energy Efficient Bonus program provides customers with a 0.7% discount on NAB's standard equipment finance rate for loans for eligible clean energy investments, such as vehicles, energy efficient irrigation systems, solar PV, building upgrades, lighting upgrades, processing line improvements and refrigeration.
Recipients included businesses such as Austral-

ia-based GV Storage in Victoria, Australia that installed roof-top solar panels which generate enough power to meet more than 65% of the their energy needs. As farmers growing apples and pears, and currently processing 66,000 bins of fruit per year, GV required a massive amount of power, so they invested in a NAB-backed solar energy efficiency loan. It has not only reduced their energy costs, but has made the production process more sustainable.

Another NAB customer is the historic family owned winery Tahbilk that produces over 100,000 cases of wine each year, exporting to the US, UK, Canada, New Zealand, Switzerland and Scandinavian countries. Tahbilk installed a 100kw solar system (SDG 9). The installation of solar provided the ability to purchase fewer carbon credit offsets to maintain the winery's carbon neutral certification status with New Zealand's carboNZero program. And the new solar is expected to provide electricity for around 15 to 20% of Tahbilk's power supply needs.
Hundreds of Australia's agribusinesses have already transitioned to more sustainable business models. Out of 5,000 farmers surveyed by NAB for two consecutive years, 85% confirmed that they saw energy costs as a significant business risk (SDG 8). NAB is helping its customers transition to more sustainable business models and significantly reduce their energy and water bills. The Bank's Energy Efficient Bonus program had already provided finance for more than 1000 assets nationwide.

CHALLENGE

To provide products and services that enable customers to make long-term financial decisions that are good for the environment and their bottom line.

OPPORTUNITIIES FOR SCALE

The transition to a low carbon, resource-efficient economy in which our natural assets are valued and managed sustainably will require the scaling-up of private-sector investment in clean technology applications and systems for natural capital management around the world, both in developed and developing economies. NAB's goal is to provide AUD $18 billion in environmental financing activities over the next several years to 2025.

Sources and further information

- https://capital.nab.com.au/docs/170315-NAB-Social-Bond-Framework-and-External-Opinion.pdf
- https://news.nab.com.au/shared-value-and-banking-a-global-view/
- https://capital.nab.com.au/docs/2017-April-NAB-AUD-Climate-Bond-DNV-Verification-Statement.pdf
- http://news.nab.com.au/nab-and-cefc-announce-further-180m-for-energy-efficient-assets/
- https://www.cleanenergycouncil.org.au/policy-advocacy/reports/clean-energy-australia-report.html

" NATIONAL AUSTRALIA BANK HAS BEEN ACTIVELY SUPPORTING THE GROWTH OF THE AUSTRALIAN IMPACT INVESTMENT MARKET, AND IN PARTICULAR SUPPORTING THE TRANSITION TO A LOW CARBON ECONOMY."

Recent years have seen some of the world's largest institutional investors expand their sustainability efforts. In December 2015, the Dutch pension fund ABP, which is the second largest in Europe, declared two SDG-related goals: to reduce the carbon-emissions footprint of its equity portfolio by 25% from 2015 to 2020, and to invest €5 billion in renewable energy by 2020.[84] Japan's GPIF, the largest pension fund in the world with US $1.1 trillion in assets, announced in July 2017 that it had selected three ESG indexes for its passive investments in Japanese equities.[85]

Investment firms are also developing strategic partnerships with development finance institutions as a way to manage risk and mobilize the initial capital. One such investor, BlueOrange Capital, aims to bring US $10 in private capital for every US $1 in public investment.[86] In cooperation with the Inter-American Investment Corporation, a multilateral lender in Latin America, Blue-Orange mobilizes over US $1 billion of capital for Latin America and the Caribbean. Supporting high impact companies that deliver financial value and sustainable growth aligned to the SDGs, Blue-Orange's strategy is to complement development finance institution (DFI) deals and due diligence. In managing US $300 billion in global impact investments, DFIs have the most robust pipeline for social investing in the world.[87] BlueOrange relies on the DFI's investment and sustainability exper-

tise, local knowledge and relationships, and track record for preliminary due diligence on companies, impact assessment and data collection on social and financial performance. In cooperation with the Inter-American Investment Corporation, a multilateral lender in Latin America, Blue-Orange aims to mobilize over US $1 billion of capital for Latin America and the Caribbean. The innovative financing mechanism, and partnership, creates shared value and bridges capital gaps in two markets: small and mid-size business lending in Latin America and financing for sectors such as health care and agriculture that are aligned with the SDGs.

Investors have a wide range of reasons they pursue sustainable investing, but the most common include motivations tied to shared value returns. Three of the primary catalysts for sustainable investing are the following:

1. **Enhancing returns** Sustainable investing has been proven to have a positive effect on returns.[88] For many investors, the likelihood that sustainable investing produces market-rate returns as effectively as other investment approaches has provided a convincing incentive to pursue sustainable investment strategies.

2. **Strengthening risk management** Institutional investors increasingly observe that risks

> "LONG TERM INVESTING FOR US IS PROVIDING A VALUABLE FUTURE, PROVIDING A PENSION IN A SUSTAINABLE WORLD. IT'S WORKING FOR THE CURRENT GENERATION BUT NOT AT THE EXPENSE OF FUTURE GENERATIONS. A SUSTAINABLE AND VIABLE WORLD INCLUDES SAVING A GOOD PENSION AND CONTRIBUTING TO THE ECONOMIC AND FINANCIAL ENVIRONMENT IN WHICH WE OPERATE AND LIVE."
>
> RUULKE BAGIJN CIO OF PRIVATE MARKETS AT PGGM

related to environmental and sustainability issues can have a measurable effect on a company's market value, as well as its reputation. Companies have seen their revenues and profits decline, for instance, after worker safety incidents, waste or pollution spills, weather-related supply-chain disruptions, and other ESG-related incidents have happened.

3. **Aligning strategies with the priorities of beneficiaries and stakeholders** Demand from fund beneficiaries and other stakeholders has driven some institutional investors to develop sustainable investing strategies. This demand has followed greater public attention to the global sustainability agenda. Investors wish to "do good" for society by providing capital to companies with favorable ESG features (without compromising risk-adjusted returns).

> "SHARED VALUE IS CORPORATE POLICIES AND PRACTICES THAT ENHANCE THE COMPETITIVE ADVANTAGE AND PROFITABILITY OF THE COMPANY WHILE SIMULTANEOUSLY ADVANCING SOCIAL AND ECONOMIC CONDITIONS IN THE COMMUNITIES IN WHICH IT SELLS AND OPERATES. IT IS A NEW WAY TO ACHIEVE ECONOMIC SUCCESS." [62]
>
> MICHAEL PORTER

While companies have long been involved in promoting sustainability, corporate philanthropy, corporate governance and Corporate Social Responsibility (CSR). These approaches do not create the framework to create significant financial returns and have difficulties in reaching a global scale and impact.

Creating Shared Value (CSV) was discussed in Chapter 2, and the distinction was drawn between CSV and CSR. CSR is familiar by now to many people in business. And while CSR activities are good endeavors, with companies contributing to society, there is a big financial difference between the two approaches. Most CSR actions are financed from the company's profit margin, taking the form of donations. CSV, on the other hand, creates value for society and the environment within the core activities of the company. Creating shared value in a financial sense makes money for the company while also contributing to the betterment of society and the environment. Therefore, we need a shared value approach that sets the global development agenda and redirects both public and private capital flows towards the global developmental challenges. This will allow and trigger companies to advance sustainable development, both by minimizing possible negative impacts and maximizing positive impacts on society and planet.

4.5 WE NEED ALL FINANCE

The Council on Foreign Relations reports that a compilation of UN estimates of all investments needed to achieve the SDGs over the years leading to 2030, totals a cost between US $90 trillion and $120 trillion.[89] The financial services industry will undoubtedly have a role to play in funding the Goals. There are many opportunities for investors, banks and institutions to fund the SDGs, and banks and other companies have explored what these global goals mean to them and how they can help.

WE WILL NEED TO TAKE A MULTI-PARTY APPROACH TO SOLVING THE GLOBAL GOALS.

The financing needs for the SDGs are too vast to come from only one source, whether domestic or global. It must be a mixture.[90] We will need to take a multi-party approach to solving the Global Goals. We will need the private sector in many areas of infrastructure, as well as to promote economic development. But we will also need to look at the deeper financing needs, going Goal by Goal

and sector by sector. Neither public nor private finance are perfectly suited for implementation, yet business holds the key to a majority of the necessary capital mobilization.

The Principles for Positive Impact Finance – a set of criteria for investments to be considered sustainable – aim to provide financiers and investors with a global framework applicable across their different business lines, including retail and wholesale lending, corporate and investment lending and asset management.

Fostering foreign investment and supporting banks to invest in higher-risk, longer-term projects, many of which are concentrated in developing countries, will also be an important component to financing the Global Goals. There are also a number of opportunities presented to the international community to take advantage of the current, rare window of opportunity to catalyze change. This is mainly due to historically-low interest rates and the large pools of underperforming assets around the world.

More than US $11 trillion is currently invested in negative-yielding corporate and sovereign debt bonds – a figure which has been on the rise, and which is almost 100 times more than total global ODA.[91] In 2016, US $22.1 billion was committed to 8,000 investments by investors looking for financial returns that demonstrated societal improvement. In all, the emerging movement, which is less than a decade old, has at least US $114 billion in assets under management, according to Global Impact Investing Network, a nonprofit organization to increase the scale and effectiveness of impact investing.[92]

Because of the heterogeneous needs of countries and regions, financing solutions to the SDGs may often have to be context-specific. There is no one-size-fit-all strategy and we must call on all finance to help. All financial parties and services have an accelerating impact on the SDGs.

> "THE POSITIVE IMPACT PRINCIPLES ARE A GAME CHANGER, WHICH WILL HELP TO CHANNEL THE HUNDREDS OF TRILLIONS OF DOLLARS MANAGED BY BANKS AND INVESTORS TOWARDS CLEAN, LOW CARBON AND INCLUSIVE PROJECTS."[163]
>
> ERIC USHER, HEAD OF THE UN ENVIRONMENT FINANCE INITIATIVE

> **"WITH GLOBAL CHALLENGES SUCH AS CLIMATE CHANGE, POPULATION GROWTH, AND ACCELERATING RESOURCE SCARCITY, THERE IS AN INCREASED URGENCY FOR THE FINANCE SECTOR TO BOTH ADAPT AND TO HELP BRING ABOUT THE NECESSARY CHANGES IN OUR ECONOMIC AND BUSINESS MODELS."** [164]
>
> DEPUTY CHIEF EXECUTIVE OFFICER OF SOCIÉTÉ GÉNÉRALE, SÉVERIN CABANNES.

 1 Banks Existing national, regional and Multilateral Development Banks (MDBs) are taking action with commitments to provide hundreds of billions of dollars in resources over the course of the next several years. Banks are particularly active in infrastructure and small and medium enterprise financing. These come on top of the commitments made by developing and developed countries to set up new development banks.

 2 Institutional Funds More recently, traditional or mainstream investors – including pension funds, insurance companies and other institutional investors – have begun to demonstrate interest in the social impact investment market in developing countries. They are doing so despite the associated challenges, such as high risks and relatively costly investment environments. These investors tend to focus on investments with financial returns that are commensurate with higher risks.

 3 Bonds and Stocks Issuing bonds is one of the main mechanisms Multilateral Development Banks rely on. MDBs are able to issue a wide range of bonds to raise funds in the financial markets for development finance. As another financial instrument, stock exchanges can help build momentum in such areas as carbon pricing and the phasing out of fossil fuel subsidies. Sustainable stock ex-

changes can support the move towards renewable technologies, as they are able to mobilize partners with the necessary expertise, technology and financial resources.[93]

 4 Private Equity Private equity houses have started to see the unprecedented value that effective fund management in SDG-related investments can bring. The private equity industry is recognizing its vital role in a sustainable financial system that rewards robust governance allied to environmental and social responsibility as a fundamental part of economic success.[94]

 5 Corporate Venture Capital (CVC) Capital invested in positive impact enables business to provide the sought after financial returns while at the same time contributing to the strategic objectives and to the betterment of the world. This form of CVC is intended not only to realize the long-term strategic objectives of the investing company, but also to help solve the world's problems more quickly.

 6 MicroFinance and Crowd Funding Microfinance and crowdfunding can be viable mechanisms for mobilizing private sector resources in order to fill in the current aid and public sector funding gaps for financing SDGs and climate change initiatives. As it stands, crowdfunding has evolved into a US $16 billion market that is growing at approximately 300% per year.

7 Philanthropists Philanthropy is essential because of what it can bring to the SDGs – collaboration, engagement with grassroots leaders, a willingness to take risks and leverage resources – which are critical components of global development. Funders can bring this experience and expertise to bear as they align their domestic grants to a global development framework.

8 Data Providers Performance data is often the best determinant for SDG progress. When companies make tangible commitments to the SDGs, and progress and outcomes can be tracked using objective metrics, there is an opportunity for external observers to evaluate a company's actions and for business management to allocate resources.[96]

9 Asset Managers Global asset managers – with over US $80 trillion of assets under management – will have an increasingly important role to play to realize the SDGs.[97]

10 Accountants Accountants around the world are currently considering how the organizations they work for can meet the SDGs. As experts in measurement, data controls, analysis, reporting and monitoring, they have stake in the financial value of sustainability.

1. Banks

Banks are increasingly expected to embed consideration of environmental and social matters into core financial products and services. As this "mainstreaming" of sustainability risk assessment remains critical, greater emphasis is needed on the development of innovative investment solutions. A public policy and banking regulatory environment conducive to responsible business combined with stronger partnerships will be important to the SDGs.

Banks as financial intermediaries are in an ideal position to drive the integration of the SDGs into the products and services offered to clients, and to stimulate both supply and demand for sustainable approaches to business.[97] Nearly 20 leading global banks and investors, totaling US $6.6 trillion in assets, have launched a UN-backed global framework entitled the *Principals for Positive Impact Finance* aimed at channeling the money they manage towards clean, low carbon and inclusive projects.[98]

Providing people with access to banking services will have a huge impact on society and help to accelerate the SDGs. Bank accounts allow people to have greater security, privacy, and control over their money. In India, a government effort to open banks in rural areas helped cut poverty in those areas by up to 17%.[99] Women in Nepal who were offered a simple bank account increased their total assets by 16%.[100] Increasing bank account ownership also promotes gender equality (SDG 5). Evidence of this is that poor women account for 1.1 billion of unbanked adults, or most of the financially excluded. And when savings accounts were offered to female market vendors in Kenya, their daily expenditure increased by 37%.[101]

A well-regulated and transparent banking system can provide the debt finance that is a critical element to implementing the SDGs. Banks have the ability to provide "green" or "sustainable" lending – not just in the context of large infrastructure projects, but across the spectrum of all economic activity.

For example, Citi Bank's US $100 Billion Environmental Finance Goal is one of the initiatives in its Sustainable Progress Strategy. The strategy is organized into three pillars, 1. Environmental Finance, 2. Environmental and Social Risk Management, and 3. Operations and Supply Chain. Investment areas include renewable energy, energy efficiency projects, green buildings, sustainable transportation, and green bonds, Citi Bank is working together with clients in both the private and public sectors to address the challenges of

CURRENTLY, THE POSITIVE IMPACT WORKING GROUP INCLUDES:
AUSTRALIAN ETHICAL, BANCO ITAÚ, BNP PARIBAS, BMCE BANK
OF AFRICA, CAISSE DES DÉPÔTS GROUP, DESJARDINS GROUP,
FIRST RAND, HERMES INVESTMENT MANAGEMENT, ING, MIROVA,
NEDBANK, PAX WORLD, PIRAEUS BANK, SEB, SOCIÉTÉ GÉNÉRALE,
STANDARD BANK, TRIODOS BANK, WESTPAC AND YES BANK.

WWW.UN.ORG/SUSTAINABLEDEVELOPMENT/BLOG

climate change and the increasing global pressures on natural resources. Citi Bank's share of environmental financing activities totaled US $41.2 billion from 2014 through 2016.[102]

In an increasing number of emerging markets, banks are working collaboratively to establish guidelines and minimum standards of environmental risk management at the national level.[103] While these efforts are often voluntary, in a growing number of countries banking supervisors and regulators have started to engage in issuing clear requirements to assess risks. And they are adopting practices to mitigate the banking sector's exposure and contribution to environmentally unsustainable activities.

A WELL-REGULATED AND TRANSPARENT BANKING SYSTEM CAN PROVIDE THE DEBT FINANCE THAT IS A CRITICAL ELEMENT TO IMPLEMENTING THE SDGs.

In an effort to stimulate growth and economic activity, central banks have used their power to create new money to purchase unprecedented amounts of government debt. This process is known as Quantitative Easing (QE). The extent to which less advanced economies can implement their own type of QE programs to fund the SDGs is somewhat limited – due to limited reserve currency positions and less liquid or developed capital markets. However, many developing countries have managed to get around this issue when using the money creating powers of their central bank in a responsible, targeted fashion. Advanced economies that are currently implementing their own QE programs could re-direct their large-scale money creation programs to help finance the SDGs. In 2015, it was reported that European Investment Bank (EIB) was already investing 10% of its funding in developing countries.[104] The European Central Bank (ECB) is currently creating €80 billion a month to buy a number of financial assets. Some reports have shown that the ECB could simply allocate a small portion of this money to buy specially issued bonds designed to fund the SDGs from the EIB.[105] The European Investment Bank would then be able to finance investment for the SDGs.

Banks and similar financial institutions can also play an important role in promoting access to finance by providing financial services to micro entrepreneurs and small enterprises, who often find access to finance as a major barrier for growth. The development of the microfinance industry as well as initiatives such the Global Alliance for Banking on Values seek to develop the market of financial services for unserved people, communities and the environment. Banks also play a crucial role in providing financial services to businesses unable to access capital, like SMEs graduating from microfinance but unable to access the next stage of formal financing.

National Development Banks (NDBs) and Green Investment Banks (GIBs) are also important for mobilizing finance towards the implementing the Nationally Determined Contributions (NDCs) and the accomplishment of the SDGs. NDBs have a strong position in their local markets, solid knowledge of and long-standing relationships with the local private sector, a good understanding of local barriers to investment as well as opportunities, and vast experience in long-term investment financing.[106] In this context, a number of NDBs have been playing a key role. They have been scaling up private financing for climate change mitigation through the intermediation of international and national public finance in their respective local markets. Green investment banks are a more recent trend, having emerged in the past five to seven years. The green investment bank model has also been deployed in a number of areas around the world at the local level to fill financing gaps for clean energy projects. Although GIBs and GIB-like entities are not banks in a traditional sense, they work similarly to banks as investment struc-tures. They are publicly capitalized, domestically focused, specialist financial institutions which are specifically established to funnel private capital to investments in clean energy.[107] GIBs typically use the same tools and products that some national development banks use, including risk mitigation products, co-lending, co-investing, warehousing and securitization, and demonstration projects. They also provide various forms of technical and market development assistance (e.g., driving standardization of transaction formats).

FMO is an "entrepreneurial Investment bank" investing in growth and frontier markets. They look to simplify the manner in which capital is deployed and reduce complexity by delivering an innovative "whole-of-life" solution that provides a single financing source for each phase of a project's lifecycle. With their Climate Investor One approach, they focus on financing projects in renewable energy, in particular those in emerging markets (See Case 25).

DIRECTING PRIVATE CAPITAL TOWARDS POSITIVE IMPACT IS ONE OF THE MOST IMPORTANT SDG CHALLENGES, AND ONE OF THE GREATEST OPPORTUNITIES.

CASE NO. # FMO

Financing the energy crisis in emerging markets with clean energy
Climate Investor One aims to help fast-track renewable energy projects

Case applied in: Global
Headquarters located in: The Netherlands
www.fmo.nl

IMPACT SDGs

SDG 13
Climate Action
Invest in renewable energy in developing countries, mobilizing an estimated US $2 billion in finance and reducing 1.5 million tons of CO2 per annum.

SDG 17
Partnerships for the Goals
The Directorate-General for International Cooperation, Ministry of Foreign Affairs of the Netherlands, Atradius Dutch State Business, De Nederlandse Waterschapsbank N.V., Aegon Asset Management and FMO all work together with others to support financing.

FMO IS PROUD TO BE THE INITIATOR OF THIS GLOBAL CLIMATE FUND
WHICH INNOVATIVELY, THROUGH A BLENDED FINANCE APPROACH, CATALYSES INSTITUTIONAL INVESTORS FROM A BROAD SPECTRUM SEEKING COMMERCIAL, SOCIAL AND ENVIRONMENTAL RETURNS ON CLEAN ENERGY IN EMERGING MARKETS.
JURGEN RIGTERINK, CHIEF EXECUTIVE OFFICER

Climate Investor One (CIO) is an innovative approach to infrastructure financing, proposed by FMO, which is designed to accelerate the delivery of renewable energy projects in emerging markets.

CIO combines three investment funds into one facility to finance renewable energy projects at specific stages of the project lifecycle (SDG 13). At an early project stage, CIO provides financial, technical, environmental, social development and structuring support through a Development Fund. This way the fund reduces the complexity associated with multi-party negotiations by equity financing a large part of construction through a Construction Equity Fund. Once the project is operational, CIO then mobilizes long-term debt financing through a Refinancing Fund with the objective of optimizing the financing over the operational life of the project.

CIO is the inaugural financing facility launched by Climate Fund Managers (CFM). This is part of an intended series of climate finance initiatives designed to combat the detrimental effects of unmitigated climate change. CIO will provide expertise, technology and financing to renewable energy projects in developing and emerging markets by mobilizing private sector financing at scale supported by catalytic public sector donor funding. CIO builds on the significant energy infrastructure expertise and track record of its sponsors: FMO, the Dutch development bank, and Phoenix

InfraWorks, South African infrastructure development and fund management specialists, in association with Sanlam Investments Holdings.

CIO seeks to simplify the manner in which capital is deployed and reduces complexity by delivering an innovative "whole-of-life" solution that provides a single financing source for each of the respective development, construction and operational phases of a project's lifecycle. To this end, CIO provides early-stage project development services and financing, equity financing through construction and long-term debt once the project is operational. This approach will allow CIO to implement more projects and bring them to market more rapidly, delivering positive environmental and social impact sooner. Targeting Africa, Asia and Latin America, CIO will focus on Solar, Wind and Run-of-River Hydro renewable energy projects.

In the context of political commitment to prevent rising global temperatures from exceeding 2°C above pre-industrial levels, FMO has joined forces with several other organizations. Together with global partners from Norway (KLP), South Africa (Sanlam Investments Holdings) and the UK (Royal Borough of Windsor & Maidenhead Pension Fund), they collectively form the cornerstone support for CIO (SDG 17). This collaboration reaffirms a broad public and private sector commitment to innovative climate change solutions and to key overseas development and investment initiatives.

CHALLENGE

To accelerate the delivery of renewable energy in emerging markets by reducing the complexity of multi-party negotiations; to simplify how capital is deployed and deliver an innovative "whole-of-life" solution providing a single financing source for each phase of a project's lifecycle.

OPPORTUNITIIES FOR SCALE

Africa's energy landscape is largely characterized by a lack of available and readily deployable finance. CIO can be a "one-stop-shop" as a way continually to reduce transaction costs by providing easier access to partners, technical experts and investors, while at the same time investors benefit from lower risk profiles thanks to portfolio diversification.

Sources and further information

- https://www.fmo.nl/news-detail/d5cd9d98-884a-4dd6-bc6a-6c01b310037d/first-close-of-a-new-global-climate-fund-at-usd-412-million
- http://www.climatefundmanagers.com/home

" IN THE CONTEXT OF POLITICAL COMMITMENT TO PREVENT RISING GLOBAL TEMPERATURES FROM EXCEEDING 2°C ABOVE PRE-INDUSTRIAL LEVELS, FMO HAS JOINED FORCES WITH SEVERAL OTHER ORGANIZATIONS. "

2. Institutional funds

The sustainable investing market has grown significantly as demand for sustainable investment strategies has expanded and as evidence has accumulated about the benefits of investing with ESG factors in mind. Some of the world's leading institutional investors are at the forefront of adopting sustainable investing strategies. Most large funds are seeking to develop their sustainable strategies and investments, regardless of where they started. Institutional investors include asset owners and investment managers. Asset owners include pension funds, insurance companies, foundations and endowments, development finance institutions and sovereign wealth funds (SWFs).

Institutional investment funds are growing. The majority of institutional investors are based in high-income countries and tend to invest domestically, typically in listed equity and fixed income. Sustainable investing strategies will likely continue to grow as demand rises, driven by large institutional investors such as pension funds, endowments and foundations.[108]

Pension funds, insurance companies and similar institutional investors are driving this trend because they often have a long-term perspective. They are typically more inclined than other categories of investors to think about the long- term sustainability of financial markets and the economy, as they are expected to deliver long-term returns for their beneficiaries. Therefore, it is in their interest to consider global social and environmental factors, such as climate change, income disparity, unemployment, resource scarcity, energy risks and natural catastrophes in the investment decision-making process. Investors also have an interest in driving governance best practice as an enabler for sustainable development.

Over the past two decades, investors have been rethinking the ways company value is created and sustained over time. Many corporations no longer simply prioritize short-term profitability at the expense of longer-term growth. They are also becoming more likely to consider other stakeholders, including customers, suppliers and employees, as well as shareholders, in assessing a corporate's competitive advantage, sustainable growth potential and longer-term viability.

Corporations and investors have supplemented their new approach with public commitments. Investors managing over US $62 trillion have signed the UN-supported Principles for Responsible Investment (PRI) and over 12,000 companies have signed the United Nations Global Compact (UNGC).[109] One such example is Univest, Unilever's in-house central investment services company responsible for overseeing the €24 billion of assets of Unilever's more than 75 worldwide pension schemes in more than 40 countries.[110] With the support of Univest's CIO, Mark Walker, Univest recently became a PRI signatory. Unilever and Univest endorsed the benefits of taking a consistent approach to sustainability and responsible investment.

SUSTAINABLE INVESTING STRATEGIES WILL LIKELY CONTINUE TO GROW AS DEMAND RISES.

Several European funds are exploring ways to link their sustainable investing strategies to the SDGs. For example, Dutch financial institutions and policymakers have built an SDG investing agenda to integrate action across Dutch investment value chains.[111] Approaches involve prioritizing certain SDGs and planning investment strategies to improve corporate performance in those areas. In July 2017, Dutch pension funds APG and PGGM jointly published the *Sustainable Development Investments Taxonomies*, with an assessment of the investment possibilities associated with each of the SDGs.[112] APG manages €436 billion to US $465.8 billion on behalf of 4.5 million Dutch pension scheme members; PGGM manages pension assets worth €205.8 billion.[113]

Insurance agencies are important institutional investors as well. The UNEP FI Principles for Sustainable Insurance serve as a global framework

"AS INSTITUTIONAL INVESTORS, IT IS ESSENTIAL TO INVEST PENSION FUND ASSETS IN THESE GOALS, AND TO DO SO AT SCALE."[165]

INVESTORS STATEMENT, UN-BACKED PRINCIPLES FOR RESPONSIBLE INVESTMENT IN SINGAPORE

for the insurance industry to address ESG risks and opportunities. Insurance companies are increasingly incorporating ESG considerations alongside traditional risk factors in response to the changing landscape and the complex, changing and interconnected challenges facing the world. The insurer's liabilities, which can extend for 50 years or more, demand that governments and companies address long-term risks like climate change and extend prosperity to the world's poorest countries.[114] Insurance companies can provide risk transfer services and insurance solutions from the micro to macro level, protecting governments, companies, and individuals from unforeseen adverse events. In addition to providing protection, pricing risk also allows for more effective investment. And by reaching out to micro entrepreneurs and small companies through micro insurance products, the sector can also help drive growth and resilience for vulnerable populations.

As a good example of an institutional investor, insurance giant Aviva has more than US $500 billion invested globally. It is already working to strengthen the guidelines, benchmarks, and reporting criteria for investments so that they are either aligned with, or contribute to, the implementation of the SDGs (See Case 26).[115]

26

CASE NO.

AVIVA

A resilient, sustainable economy that
optimizes quality of life for all
Building capacity on sustainable finance; protect
what's important to 33 million customers
through market stability

Case applied in: Global
Headquarters located in: England
www.aviva.co.uk

IMPACT SDGs

SDG 8

Decent work and economic growth

Maintains record as the first carbon neutral insurer and their approach to carbon offsetting has directly improved the lives of over 800,000 people since 2011.

SDG 9

Industry, Innovation and Infrastructure

Investing over US $3.8 billion in low carbon infrastructure over 5 years, with an associated carbon savings target of 100,000 tons of CO2 annually.

SDG 12

Responsible Production and Consumption

Promotes good practice through the Corporate Human Rights benchmark, used to rank the top 500 globally listed companies on their human rights policy, process and performance.

SDG 16

Peace, Justice and Strong Institutions

Embeds responsible investment integration management system, which builds environmental, social and governance.

OUR IDEA IS SIMPLE. WE DRAW UP TRANSPARENT DATA ON SDG PERFORMANCE, AND RANK COMPANIES AS TO HOW WELL THEY ARE DOING. **THIS WILL MOTIVATE A RACE TO THE TOP**.

MARK WILSON, AVIVA CEO

Aviva's commitment to realizing the SDGs includes some simple calls for action. They look for initiatives that could make a real difference, promote dialogue among employees, and build on the work of Project Everyone founded in 2015 to bring the Goals to everyone across the world. Aviva benchmarks sustainability with a consistent, authoritative and simple set of measurements. They also help the UN engage with the investment community to harness the US $300 trillion of investment finance in global markets and secure a sustainable future. Aviva has a broad vision and ambition to shift the economy, and reorient capital markets. The company sees the primary failure of capital markets in relation to sustainable development as one of misallocation of capital. This, in turn, is a result of global governments' failure to properly internalize environmental and social costs into companies' profit and loss statements – the corporate cost of capital does not reflect the sustainability of the business. The global insurer endeavors to mitigate ramifications that could create a type of market failure where unsustainable companies have a lower cost of capital than they should and so are more likely to be financed than sustainable companies.

Aviva actively works to influence policy makers to both change the pricing signals within the market and improve the readiness of the supply chain of capital to integrate sustainability issues for a more "resilient, sustainable economy that optimizes quality of life for all" (SDG 8). The company calls on all governments to develop national capital-raising

plans covering how they intend to finance the delivery of a zero-carbon economy and the SDGs. These will include a view on the money that can be raised via infrastructure investment, project finance, corporate debt, foreign direct investment, equity investment and sovereign and Multilateral Development Banks debt (SDG 9).

Aviva's SDG capital-raising plans involve moving all participants towards a longer-term perspective when investing and exerting their influence as company owners. Aviva works with policymakers to equalize the market and improve the profitability of sustainable businesses relative to unsustainable ones. Within this context of establishing integrated incentives to promote business along the investment chain, Aviva's actions are fully aligned with long-term sustainable performance in terms of of sustainable consumption and production integration into all financial services (SDG 12). For instance, Aviva is divesting from fossil fuels and investing in renewables to help avoid financial risks over the long term.

By improving integrated corporate governance, Aviva believes "capital markets can become the primary facilitator of a global green and just economy" (SDG 16). The company helps governments to ensure all national corporate governance codes promote integrated sustainable development, and to establish a set of integrated investment legal duties for long-term sustainable development.

CHALLENGE

To promote capital markets that finance development that meets the need of the present, without compromising the ability of future generations to meet their own needs.

OPPORTUNITIIES FOR SCALE

Aviva launched a sustainable finance policy toolkit which sets out 13 practical solutions for changes that can help create a sustainable finance sector in Europe. The toolkit is a recent response to the European Commission's announcement that it will create an expert group to develop a sustainable finance strategy to make progress on the financing and implementation of the SDGs.

Sources and further information

- https://www.aviva.com/social-purpose/sustainable-finance-and-the-sdgs/
- https://www.aviva.co.uk/media-centre/story/17825/the-world-benchmarking-alliance-launches-global-co/
- https://www.aviva.com/content/dam/aviva-corporate/documents/socialpurpose/pdfs/thoughtleadership/Mobilising_Finance_Avivas_Calls_to_Action_2.pdf
- https://sustainabledevelopment.un.org/content/documents/10574avivabooklet.pdf
- https://www.aviva.com/newsroom/news-releases/2015/09/aviva-supports-global-goals-for-sustainable-development-17528/
- http://www.avivasustainablefinancetoolkit.com/

" **AVIVA HAS A BROAD VISION AND AMBITION TO SHIFT THE ECONOMY, AND REORIENT CAPITAL MARKETS.** "

3. Bonds and stocks

The market for green bonds has expanded rapidly in the past few years. What was in 2013 a US $9 billion niche market of bond offerings tied to environmental projects, surged to nearly US $80 billion of issuance by the end of 2016.[116] Green bonds represent the largest share of the Sustainable Development Bonds market with a value of US $41.8 billion, and saw a 42%-rise in the first quarter of 2017 compared to the previous years' first quarter.[117] The Climate Bond Initiative estimates that the total amount of green bonds issued in 2017 could reach $150 billion. This is a huge jump compared to 2016, when green bond issuances were $82 billion. Global green bond issuance will reach new heights as new players join this booming market. Investors and underwriters, such as Bank of America Merrill Lynch, Credit Agricole and HSBC, have seen a tremendous growth of issuers and issues, as numerous public and private entities joined or issued green bonds again in 2017.

Green bonds simultaneously achieve financial returns and have a positive impact on society. These bonds are typically fixed income measures with low to medium returns (around 2% to 3%). The proceeds are predominantly allocated to financing projects such as renewable energy, pollution prevention and conservation, among other things.

Both development and commercial organizations offer green bonds as they represent an opportunity to actively manage the environmental footprint of investors' portfolios. Two of the main characteristics of green bonds are transparency and reporting. They are also accountable financial instruments. The green bond market has rapidly become global, dynamic and well-known due to the number of financial players involved.

Municipal green bonds usually finance sustainable water management, pollution prevention, the diffusion of green buildings and aquatic biodiversity conservation at a local level. In the US, municipal green bonds were issued to help cities and local communities with the aim of reinforcing the fight against climate change and promoting a transition to renewable energy in line with international practices and standards. Globally, public and international institutions such as development banks reinforced their commitments to green finance by issuing multiple green bond programs to support local and international projects.

Furthermore, large corporations have also issued green bonds recently, including Apple, who announced in June 2017 that it is raising US $1 billion in debt in a green bond that will be used to fund environmentally focused initiatives. Iberdrola completed its sixth green bond issue worth €750

Figure 30 **Source: World Economic Forum**

Amount of green bonds issued since 2010

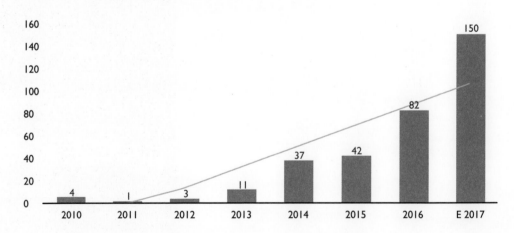

WORLD BANK-BNP PARIBAS[17]

The World Bank has launched the first bonds directly linked to the Sustainable Development Goals (SDGs). BNP Paribas arranged the bonds, which the World Bank will issue in order to raise financing to support projects that contribute to achieving the SDGs. The bonds directly link returns to the stock market performance of companies in the Solactive Sustainable Development Goals (SDGs) World Index. The Index includes 50 companies, being industry leaders on environmentally and socially sustainable issues, or that dedicate at least 20% of their activities to sustainable products. This initiative enables investors to financially support the SDGs, while raising awareness of the private sector for SDG investments. The bonds have raised €163 million from institutional investors in France and Italy.

million. QBE Insurance Group issued US $300 million in debt securities as part of a green investment program that aims to generate environmental benefits. TenneT added another €1 billion of green bonds bringing their total to €5 billion. And in November 2017, Danish wind developer Ørsted, formerly known as Dong Energy, issued €500 million in green hybrid capital securities with a 2.25% coupon to refinance 2013-issued securities. The company also issued €750 million of green senior bonds, maturing in 2029 with a 1.5% fixed coupon.[118]

GREEN BONDS SIMULTANEOUSLY ACHIEVE FINANCIAL RETURNS AND HAVE A POSITIVE IMPACT ON SOCIETY.

The number and variety of issuers has progressed further, with numerous issuances from emerging countries. Chinese and Indian players issued billions of green bonds to finance renewable energy, energy efficiency and sustainable projects in their territories. By doing that, emerging markets have shown their determination to finance a low-carbon future.

In the first quarter of 2017, the growing issuance of green bonds was recognized at the 2nd Annual Green Bond Awards hosted by Climate Bonds, in partnership with the City of London and the Green Finance Initiative. The event was held at the Guildhall in London to celebrate the stand outs and pioneers of the rapidly growing green bonds market.[119] Notably, China won first place in three categories: the "Largest Single Green Bond" – Bank of Communications; the "Largest Overall Issuer"– SPD Bank; and the most "Innovative Regulator" – People's Bank of China PboC.

Development Finance Institution (DFI) Bonds are bonds issued by DFIs to raise capital to support their initiatives that provide financial services in the public and private sector of developing countries and for investments that promote sustainable development. The World Bank is one of the DFIs that has issued bonds to support its activities. DFI Bonds are the second largest category of sustainable development bonds in terms of market size, representing more than US $23.5 billion.

Following the same approach, Microfinance Bonds and Charity Bonds are issued by microfinance institutions, social businesses, or charities to finance their business operations. Again, although these are similar to traditional bonds, the difference is that the organization is involved in activities related to microfinance and social or environmental improvements. Microfinance bonds tend to have higher returns (3-6%) compared to DFI Bonds. Symbiotics, a leading investment company specialized in emerging, sustainable and inclusive finance, issues such bonds via a platform to support microfinance institutions. Microfinance Bonds represent over US $500 million.[120]

> **"STOCK EXCHANGES ARE UNIQUELY POSITIONED AT THE INTERSECTION BETWEEN INVESTORS, COMPANIES, AND REGULATORS. AS SUCH THEY CAN PLAY A KEY ROLE IN PROMOTING RESPONSIBLE INVESTMENT AND SUSTAINABLE DEVELOPMENT."** [166]
>
> **JAMES ZHAN UNCTAD DIRECTOR, DIVISION ON INVESTMENT AND ENTERPRISE**

STOCK MARKETS

Stock markets can also play an important role in promoting good corporate practices and facilitating investment in sustainable development. Through activities such as sustainability reporting, mobilizing finance, gender equality and global partnerships, stock markets have considerable leverage. [121] Stock exchanges have helped build momentum for carbon pricing, and are moving away from fossil fuel subsidies towards renewable technologies. They are able to mobilize partners with the necessary expertise, technology and financial resources.

As an initiative to provide more guidance on, and deference towards, the SDGs, the Sustainable Stock Exchanges (SSE) was born (See Case 26). The SSE is a peer-to-peer learning platform for exploring how exchanges, in collaboration with investors, regulators, and companies, can promote responsible investment for sustainable development. Launched by UN Secretary-General Ban Ki-Moon in 2009, the SSE is a UN initiative, co-organized by UNCTAD (Investment and Enterprise Division), the UN Global Compact, the United Nations Environment Programs Finance Initiative, and the Principles for Responsible Investment.

The SSE initiative invites exchanges worldwide to become a Partner Stock Exchange within the SSE by making a voluntary public commitment to promote improved ESG disclosure and performance among listed companies. In addition, the SSE welcomes participation from securities regulators, investors, companies and other key stakeholders within its Consultative Group.

Stock exchanges are uniquely positioned to support the SDGs. Research by SSE revealed that there are four SDGs in particular that they can impact by mobilizing finance, namely SDG 5 Gender Equality; SDG 12 Responsible Consumption and Production; SDG 13 Climate Action; SDG 17 Partnerships for the Goals.

Further, a number of stock exchanges have established specialized green bond listings or dedicated segments to facilitate institutional investors in the discovery of investments addressing climate change. In 2016, and early 2017, many governments began developing of their country climate plans for achieving COP21 NDC targets. Subsequently, they incorporated into stock markets an increased green infrastructure, more sovereign green issuance, and the development of green bond markets to improve market liquidity, integrity and investor access to green finance opportunities. Exchanges are now a critical component to scaling up the green bond market. [122]

Some exchanges have created a separate listing section in their service offerings that allows direct access to green or sustainable products or companies. For example, the Mexican Stock Exchange developed MÉXICO2, its environmental markets platform, and the Luxembourg Stock Exchange utilizes the Luxembourg Green Exchange, exclusively for green, social or sustainable securities. [123] There is strong evidence of a positive correlation between ESG performance, which is a core component of achieving the SDGs, and strong financial performance. Stock exchanges play a critical role connecting investors and companies in their markets and as such are well positioned to play a direct role in achieving the SDGs.

ACHIEVING THE SUSTAINABLE DEVELOPMENT GOALS WILL REQUIRE FUNDING AND COOPERATION ON AN UNPRECEDENTED SCALE, WITH THE PRIVATE SECTOR HOLDING A PIVOTAL POSITION.

SUSTAINABLE STOCK EXCHANGES (SSE)

Green finance action plan
An international framework for contributing to the creation of sustainable markets

Case applied in: Global
Headquarters located in: United Nations, USA
www.sseinitiative.org

IMPACT SDGs

SDG 5
Gender Equality
Promotes gender equality to learn what can be done to support listed companies in their efforts to develop more gender diversity on boards and in management.

SDG 12
Responsible Production and Consumption
Encouraging corporate disclosure of ESG factors.

SDG 13
Climate Action
Luxembourg Stock Exchange (LuxSE) developed more than 110 listed green bonds.

SDG 17
Partnerships for the Goals
SSE now has 58 Partner Exchanges from 5 continents, listing over 30,000 companies and representing a market capitalization of over US $55 trillion.

> **WE ARE ENGAGING WITH STOCK EXCHANGES AND CAPITAL MARKET LEADERS TO ENCOURAGE THEM TO DEMONSTRATE LEADERSHIP**, SEIZE THE OPPORTUNITIES THAT GREEN FINANCE OFFERS, AND HELP US TRANSITION TO THE SUSTAINABLE ECONOMIES OF THE FUTURE.
>
> ISABELLE DURANT, DEPUTY SECRETARY GENERAL OF UNCTAD

The SSE green finance action plan identifies the main action areas that stock exchanges should work on. First, promoting green-labeled products and services. Second, support a green transition and ensure market resilience to the economic impacts of climate change with more systematic changes. Third, strengthen the quality and availability of environmental disclosure among issuers and investors. Fourth, contribute to dialogue with other capital market participants and consensus building on green finance. Like many UN initiatives, the SSE looks to the SDGs to help focus its activities. It focuses specifically on four SDG targets that are particularly relevant for stock exchanges.

Target 5.5 (SDG 5) is the focus of Ring the Bell events being held around International Women's day. In 2016, 34 exchanges participated, a more than threefold increase from the previous year.

Target 12.6 (SDG 12) was prominent in the Santiago Exchange strategy for 2015-2018 to promote a culture that integrates sustainability within the institution and broader capital market. As part of this strategy, the exchange is taking an approach to integrate sustainability and ESG issues into their reporting, investor relations and mobilize capital towards the achievement of the SDGs.

Oslo Børs contributed to Target 13a (SDG 13) with its sustainability strategy focused on climate, particularly the expansion of green bonds. This prompted it to become an SSE Partner Exchange in 2015 and increased its attention on green investment choices. Oslo Børs became the first stock exchange to offer a separate list for green bonds. Initially the list included five green bonds, and has since grown to 11 offered by eight issuers and valued at US $1.2 billion.

Lastly, Target 17.16 (SDG 17) encouraging multi-stakeholder partnerships to support the achievement of the Sustainable Development Goals in all countries, is advanced by the the World Federation of Exchanges (WFE) which represents over 100 exchanges and also offers stock exchanges the ability to form partnerships through its Sustainability Working Group (SWG). Established in 2014, the SWG seeks to define the most effective role of exchanges in supporting ESG disclosures and encouraging sustainable financial market development. In addition to partnering with the SSE initiative, stock exchanges are encouraged to become active in their mainstream arenas.

CHALLENGE

To guide stock exchanges in playing an important role in the growth of SDG financial products in their market, either by working on developing these products or promoting products where they already exist.

OPPORTUNITIES FOR SCALE

Significant growth opportunities for exchanges and other market actors exist, with potential concomitant revenue growth opportunities. For instance, exchanges have expressed intentions to increasingly list green bonds in the near future, and green finance experts foresee more growth in this area in the coming years. However, current number of exchanges listing green bonds is still low.

Sources and further information

- http://www.sseinitiative.org/greenfinance/
- https://www.world-exchanges.org/home/docs/studies-reports/SE&SD-Report17.pdf
- https://www.ifc.org/wps/wcm/connect/b96fcbb3-1bc2-4c53-8181-810ba8e2e9ac/Tiffany_Grabski.pdf?MOD=AJPERES
- http://www.corporateknights.com/reports/2017-world-stock-exchanges/
- http://unctad.org/en/PublicationsLibrary/unctad_sse_2016d1.pdf
- http://www.sseinitiative.org/home-slider/cop23-capital-market-leaders-gather-in-bonn-to-promote-green-finance/
- http://www.sseinitiative.org/wp-content/uploads/2017/11/SSE-Green-Finance-Guidance-.pdf

" LIKE MANY UN INITIATIVES, THE SSE LOOKS TO THE SDGs TO HELP FOCUS ITS ACTIVITIES."

4. Private equity private investors, angel investors and family offices

Bloomberg Businessweek has called private equity a rebranding of leveraged buyout firms after the 1980s. The most common investment strategies in private equity include leveraged buyouts, venture capital, growth capital, distressed investments, and mezzanine capital. According to the International Finance Corporation (IFC), a member of the World Bank Group, private equity investment in emerging markets stands at approximately US $320 billion today of the US $2.7 trillion global total.[124]

Private equity houses, or General Partners (GPs), are responding to demand from their Limited Partner (LP) investors, to greater societal concern about ESG factors, and to evidence that pro-active ESG management can deliver investment value.[125] A private equity investment will generally be made by a private equity firm, a venture capital firm or an angel investor.

Private equity firms are innovating for good, such as New Crop Capital, who invests in disrupters of animal agriculture. New Crop Capital argues that the meat, egg, and dairy sectors, representing a $700 billion global market, is ripe for innovation and large-scale disruption for sustainability purposes. Another private equity impact investor named LGT Impact, is targeting both attractive financial returns and measurable, positive impact. LGT Impact aims to improve the quality of life of underserved people and protect the environment through intentionally impactful and commercially attractive investments that consider SDG implementation. Focus sectors include health, education, financial inclusion, environmental services, energy, affordable housing and consumer goods. Headquartered in London and Zurich with local investment teams in Brazil, East Africa, India and the UK, LGT Impact manages a global portfolio of impact investments as well as the Impact Ventures UK fund.

The majority of this genre of investors, approximately 70%, has now made a public commitment to invest responsibly. And 96% currently has a formal responsible investment policy or will have shortly, with 83% also reporting to their investors on ESG activities.[126] Businesses are starting to quantify the benefits of adopting sustainable business practices. With an increasing focus on responsible investment, the private equity community is responding by building in new guidelines to reduce risk.

BUSINESSES ARE STARTING TO QUANTIFY THE BENEFITS OF ADOPTING SUSTAINABLE BUSINESS PRACTICES.

The International Finance Corporation's Asset Management Company (AMC) offers significant mobilization and scale-up opportunities. They use a strong governance structure and an innovative business model to match commercial capital with development finance. As of December 2014, AMC had approximately US $7.8 billion of assets under management in seven funds and had committed approximately US 4.5 billion in 58 emerging market companies and six private equity funds. With impressive results, AMC's global Infrastructure Fund has raised US $1.2 billion in equity commitments from commercial investors, which will support an estimated US $18 million of infrastructure projects in developing countries over the fund's five-year investment period.[127] AMC will continue to build out its portfolio of regional, sectoral and specialist funds, bringing additional capital to developing countries in an effective, efficient and sustainable manner.

Family offices have played a critical role in the development of social impact investment in parallel to their philanthropies. The Omidyar Network, a philanthropic investing group pioneered by eBay founder Pierre Omidyar has taken an approach where "In some cases — perhaps even most — a strong positive correlation does exist between financial return and social impact. In other cases, a company can generate significant social impact even if its financial return is modest."[128] To that end, Ford Foundation recently announced its commitment of US $1 billion towards more cause-aligned investments. Over the next decade, the company will focus its philanthropic endeavors on more mission-related investments, investments in projects that generate the return Ford needs, but also support things like affordable housing or better financial services for the poor.[129] The commitment makes Ford the largest private foundation acting in this area.

Another player in the private equity arena is Earth Capital Partners, a London-based firm focused on supporting, through investment, the Earth's resources (See Case 27). The figure shown maps the five dimensions of the Earth Dividend (ED) scorecard to their potential impact on individual SDGs. Some SDGs potentially span more than one ED dimension.

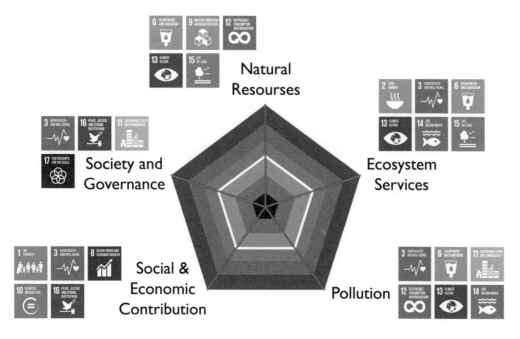

Figure 31 **Earth Dividend Scorecard: ECP Contribution to SDGs**[167]

CASE NO.

EARTH CAPITAL PARTNERS (ECP)

Investment in Sustainable Assets
Private equity addressing the Earth's challenges

Case applied in: **South America, Latin America, Europe, Africa, and Middle East**
Headquarters located in: **England**
www.earthcp.com

IMPACT SDGs

SDG 7

Affordable and Clean Energy

Invests in renewable energy markets that have experienced high growth with installed capacity forecasts to continue to grow significantly over the next decade with an estimated US $4.5 trillion of new investment capacity globally by 2035.

SDG 9

Industry, Innovation and Infrastructure

Invests in promising young technology companies, typically aims to invest from US $5 million to $15 million in each company.

SDG 15

Life on Land

Invests in the effort to develop 80 million hectares of new tree plantations by 2030.

MEETING THE NEEDS OF TODAY WITHOUT JEOPARDIZING THE ABILITY OF FUTURE GENERATIONS TO MEET THEIR NEEDS.
ECP

ECP is a private equity firm specializing in investments that address challenges such as climate change, water scarcity, food and energy security. The investment platform offers institutional products for clients wishing to invest in sustainable assets. The firm targets commercial returns alongside sustainability impact, which has proven to generate significantly higher demand for investments. Typically investing in sustainable and renewable asset classes through its existing funds, ECP provides advice on investments that deliver commercial risk adjusted return.

ECP implements sustainable development investments through five categories: Natural Resource Consumption, Ecosystem Services, Pollution Control, Social and Economic Contribution, and Society and Governance. The firm's Earth Dividend system provides an annual measure of sustainable development impact by tracking an ECP Fund's operating assets across these five categories of ESG issues comprising of 30 ESG indicators. ECP has identified a number of commercial benefits resulting from this approach, including the potential for higher financial returns through understanding that sustainability enables more effective investment decision-making.

ECP seeks to invest in growth companies with patented, substantially proven technology, but they may also consider earlier stage technology development on an exceptional basis. The firm has three primary investment focus areas: First, sustainable technology is often enabled and accelerated by digitalization, which is a strong focus as merging technologies offer industry disrupting opportunities and significant scale-up potential (SDG 9). Second, sustainable agriculture in new markets such as biomass for energy generation, advanced structural wood, and wood-fiber based bio-materials and bio-fuels, which are developing at a very fast pace and present an important investment opportunity in the development of new, sustainable sources of wood fiber around the world (SDG 15). Third, renewable energy which is paramount to the future of human prosperity and depends on how successfully the two central energy investment challenges facing the world today are addressed: securing the supply of reliable and affordable energy; and effecting a rapid transformation to a low-carbon, efficient and environmentally benign system of energy supply (SDG 7).

CHALLENGE

To respond to the long-term pressures arising from resource and energy constraints, waste, environmental and pollution concerns, and the need for a low carbon economy.

OPPORTUNITIES FOR SCALE

The private equity sector has a powerful and positive role to play in deploying capital toward a sustainable, inclusive economy. Sustainable investing will fuel innovation, growth, good business, and societal benefits. ECP will continue to protect against risk, enhance value, and improve sustainability while generating impressive returns for investors.

Sources and further information

- https://www.bloomberg.com/research/stocks/private/snapshot.asp?privcapId=51374180
- http://www.earthcp.com/investment-focus
- http://www.worldenergyoutlook.org/media/weowebsite/2009/WEO2009.pdf
- https://www.bsr.org/our-insights/blog-view/private-equity-esg-from-policies-and-efficiency-to-impact
- http://www.earthcp.com/sustainability/earth-dividend-tm
- https://issuu.com/aiglobalmedia/docs/w_f_fund_awards_2015

" EARTH CAPITAL PARTNERS TARGETS COMMERCIAL RETURNS ALONGSIDE SUSTAINABILITY IMPACT, WHICH HAS PROVEN TO GENERATE SIGNIFICANTLY HIGHER DEMAND FOR INVESTMENTS. "

5. Corporate Venture Capital (CVC)

The strength of the CVC model is twofold.[130] First, innovative ideas are effectively linked to economies of scale and financial power. Second, this model helps large companies to realize their long-term strategic objectives. The growth in CVC is fueled by numerous disruptive, transformative trends, which are greatly increasing the pace of innovation and business endeavours. Large companies are therefore looking for faster 'shortcuts' to enter new markets and accelerate growth. They are not only looking to innovate with a manageable risk and an assurance of a financial return, they are increasingly using Corporate Venture Capital to realize their long-term goals for 2020 and beyond based on the SDG agenda. Business for good is gaining ground, and capital.

The list of examples of CVC for good is getting longer every day, and moreover, the size and the funding is increasing as well. Examples include, Unilever Ventures which is investing US $200 million in promising young companies. These start-ups not only receive capital investment but also access to Unilever's global ecosystem as well as their assets and expertise. Hydra Ventures, the corporate venturing division of Adidas, invested nearly two million dollars in CRAiLAR Technologies Inc. CRAiLAR Technologies Inc. is a company that makes sustainable, environmentally friendly fibers and fabrics for textile, paper and composite use. And the listed publishing company Pearson poured US $15 million into the Pearson Affordable Learning Fund (PALF) for the development of low-cost private education systems in the developing world. The Body Shop International not only directly invested in Divine Chocolate Limited (a Fairtrade chocolate company owned by a cooperative of Ghanaian cocoa farmers), but also supported this cooperative through the purchase of raw cocoa products. And Morgan Stanley made a 5 million-dollar equity investment into Eleni LLC, a Nairobi-based company that designs, builds, and supports the commodity exchange eco-systems in frontier markets.

In a recent report by CB Insights, the impact of strategic investing is shown in the many activities and investments by CVC firms. These firms played a significant role by participating in 20% of the 3,113 venture-backed financing rounds in the first half of 2016. Since the end of 2014, there have been over 160 CVCs deals, with 2015 seeing an all-time high of 191 corporate venture capitals making an investment. Additionally, 53 new global CVCs made their first investment in the first half of 2016, including firms like General Mills Ventures and NBC Sports Ventures, and the number is expected to double by the end of this year.

Many investors are entering into the venture capital arena to help address the SDGs. The nature of venture capital is to look for one-of-a-kind business opportunities. They are often looking for businesses that can change the world, disrupt existing industries, and most importantly generate returns on investment. Investors ultimately invest in people, not just products.[131] As one of the most respected brands in the world, Virgin invests in the SDGs through a venture capital approach. Virgin CEO Richard Branson has stated that he needs to believe in an idea and its capabilities, as well as the people. The corporation's investment team focuses on the core consumer sectors of Travel & Leisure, Telecoms & Media, Music & Entertainment, Financial Services and Health & Wellness. Virgin aims to deliver long-term capital appreciation through investment in these sectors (See Case 29).

" AN ENTREPRENEUR IS AN INNOVATOR, A JOB CREATOR, A GAME-CHANGER, A BUSINESS LEADER, A DISRUPTOR, AND AN ADVENTURER."

RICHARD BRANSON, CEO VIRGIN

CASE NO.
VIRGIN GROUP

Corporate Venture Capital (CVC): investing in startups
Financing original products that make a positive difference to people's lives and supporting services that shake up markets

Case applied in: Global
Headquarters located in: England
www.virgin.com

IMPACT SDGs

SDG 8
Decent Work and Economic Growth
Over the next 15 years, Virgin intends to grow its purpose, assisting more businesses, entrepreneurs and individuals join in changing business for good.

SDG 9
Industry, Innovation and Infrastructure
Invested US $83 million in London fintech startup Transferwise, an innovative platform to transfer money between countries.

SDG 10
Reduced Inequalities
Virgin Group invests in peer-to-peer finance models where customers can save 90% on transfer fees compared to what traditional banks are offering.

SDG 17
Partnerships for the Goals
Virgin Pulse raised US $92 million in a deal led by Insight Venture Partners.

WHY DO I INVEST IN START-UPS? BECAUSE THEY ARE THE JOB CREATORS AND INNOVATORS OF THE FUTURE. I AM DELIGHTED TO SEE SO MANY ENTREPRENEURS TAKING THEIR START-UPS TO THE NEXT LEVEL AND TRANSFORMING THE WAY WE DO BUSINESS.
SIR RICHARD BRANSON, FOUNDER VIRGIN GROUP

Start-ups have the potential to become some of the world's largest and best companies. Virgin started off as a startup and it is part of the company's mission to continue to create the environment for startups to thrive while they embark on their new businesses.

Sir Richard Branson, founder of Virgin Group, backs many startups around the world. These businesses in which Virgin Group invests not only have the potential to become a vital source of employment, innovation and productivity to economies, they are a prime example to younger generations that "creativity, passion and hard work can change the world for the better."
Virgin is a brand that appreciates the benefits smart disruption can bring. The company endeavors to invest in products that make a positive difference to people's lives and services that move markets. Investing in new startups and giving them the funds they need to grow into companies that deliver on their disruptive potential is essential for business competition in the economy.

Virgin Group is a diversified grouping of more than 200 privately held companies. Virgin Group and recently opted to raise its first-ever round of outside funding and formed a company called Virgin Pulse. Virgin Pulse raised US $92 million in a deal led by Insight Venture Partners (SDG 17). Virgin Group also participated.

The finance industry is another area where Branson sees opportunities. Virgin Group has invested in several startups in the financial sector including Indiegogo, a crowdfunding platform, that allows entrepreneurs better and cheaper access to the seed financing they need to get their startups going. Similarly, Bitcoin is another company that Branson promotes and is a new payment form being accepted on Virgin Galactic. Square and Clinkle are other interesting start-ups in this sector in which Virgin Group invested. Transferwise is another US $83 million investment in a clever way to avoid hidden transfer costs when people send money abroad (SDG 9). By using a peer-to-peer model, customers can save 90% on transfer fees compared to what traditional banks are offering (SDG 10).

Virgin Group also encourages all of its people to live the company's purpose: to change business for good. In doing this, not only do the company's people benefit, but so do its customers and the communities in which they operate. Over the next 15 years, Virgin intends to grow its purpose, and looks forward to assisting more businesses, entrepreneurs and individuals join the movement to change business for good (SDG 8).

CHALLENGE

To prove that business can be a force for good, and support the creation of a thriving economy for people and the planet.

OPPORTUNITIES FOR SCALE

The Virgin Group's annual global revenue in 2016 was £19.5 billion with 71,000 employees, and these numbers are on the rise. As CVC funding is growing and more entrepreneurs are likely to attract potential corporate funders, Virgin is expanding its investments in startups with a disruptive product. The conglomerate is growing successful businesses in sectors ranging from mobile telephony, travel, financial services, leisure, music, holidays and health and wellness

Sources and further information

- http://www.businessinsider.com/18-tech-startups-backed-by-sir-richard-bransons-billions-2015-11/#500-million-329-million-in-internet-satellite-provider-oneweb-through-the-virgin-group-fund-4
- http://www.fundinguniverse.com/company-histories/virgin-group-history/
- http://www.businessinsider.com/18-tech-startups-backed-by-sir-richard-bransons-billions-2015-11/#8375-million-55-million-in-virtual-medical-care-provider-doctor-on-demand-1
- http://fortune.com/2015/05/27/virgin-pulse-raises-92-million-for-employee-well-being/
- https://www.virgin.com/richard-branson/why-i-invest-start-ups
- https://home.kpmg.com/xx/en/home/insights/2016/05/should-startups-pursue-corporate-venture-capital-funding.html

" VIRGIN GROUP ALSO ENCOURAGES ALL OF ITS PEOPLE TO LIVE THE COMPANY'S PURPOSE: TO CHANGE BUSINESS FOR GOOD."

6. Microfinance and crowdfunding

Microfinance and crowdfunding can be viable mechanisms for mobilizing private sector resources to fill the current funding gaps for financing the SDGs and climate change initiatives. Even though crowdfunding has experienced a slow adoption in developing economies, it has been estimated that the developing world will have a US $96 billion crowdfunding market by 2025.[132] Consequently, there have been calls to include microfinance and crowdfunding into the climate financing arena (e.g. through the introduction of a microfinance and crowdfunding window in the Green Climate Fund).

Crowdfunding for Climate Change (CF4CC) or integrating microfinance and crowdfunding for impact investing has various advantages over traditional financing models. For example, microfinance and crowdfunding can improve total volumes of funding for development projects. One way to do this is by providing micro and small entrepreneurs and community organizations improved access of finance, and enabling them to undertake sustainable small-scale climate actions. The speed of enablement can also be accelerated since mobilizing funding through crowdfunding and disbursing it through microfinance institutions (MFIs) can be a matter of days or weeks, considerably faster than ODA and with lower transaction costs.

The Crowd Investment Platform for Sustainable Development (CIP4SD) utilizes crowd-investment shares as an innovative and new approach to regulate the supply of funds/investments. This approach ensures that the volume of available funding does not exceed the demand of finance from credible recipients/loan applicants, thereby reducing investor's risks. The CIP4SD platform also provides guaranteed high returns at low risk to investors. The Platform provides loans to entrepreneurs, farmers, agribusinesses, inclusive businesses and social enterprises through a revolving fund thereby reducing risks to the investors. Investors pool their resources or invest in a revolving fund rather than investing in individual enterprises that possess a higher risk singularly.

The dissemination of microfinance resources has also made an impact in the mobilization of funding and services in a number of sectors. One area that positive impact can be felt the most is in health care. Digital platforms for monetary transactions have improved the delivery of government anti-poverty programs by reducing opportunities for corruption and ensuring funds reach their intended recipients.[133] By offering microfinance for providers and facilitating mobile payment to improve access to high quality care, businesses are leading the way in the access of capital through mobile technology and new payment platforms. This is shown in Chapter 8 Health and Well-Being, and particularly in the Medical Credit Fund case.

THE GLOBAL CROWDFUNDING INDUSTRY RAISED US $34 BILLION IN 2015.

Introducing crowdsourcing mechanisms into the development aid business would direct more funds to where they are most needed, wanted and effectively used. Such an approach could be inspired by popular sites such as GlobalGiving, Kickstarter and Indiegogo - the global crowdfunding industry raised US $34 billion in 2015.[134] Crowdfunding has established itself as a successful alternative way to raise capital. And as it has proved itself as a fundraising tool, the development community has begun to pay attention. Crowdfunding startup Homestrings recently partnered with USAid to channel investments into innovative projects on the African continent to support the SDGs.

7. Philanthropy

Philanthropic foundations play an important role in sustainable development – not only in mobilizing financial resources, but also as development actors on their own. Until recently, however, governments and foundations have often followed parallel paths without engaging in complementary partnerships. There is increasing recognition that including foundations more strategically in policy discussions at the global and the local levels will help optimize development results. This will require a shift in how governments approach foundations, embracing them as catalytic partners rather than solely considering them as financiers.

Philanthropy's financial contribution to development has nearly multiplied by ten over the past decade. Although the overall contribution of philanthropy to sustainable development is hard to quantify, OECD DAC statistics suggest that it has grown from around US $3 billion in 2003, to US $29.73 billion in 2013, including grants from NGOs.[135]

Philanthropic foundations' comparative advantages as development partners also include their unique potential to leverage funds and build multi-stakeholder partnerships around specific development issues. For instance, in some cases the closeness of corporate foundations to the private sector allowed them to access private flows at market rates; in 2013, these flows – including foreign direct investment – amounted to US $273.21 billion.

The SDG Philanthropy Platform is a vehicle specifically created for initiating and bringing together multi-stakeholder partnerships to advance the global sustainable development agenda. It is a project implemented jointly by UNDP, Foundation Center and Rockefeller Philanthropy Advisors.[30] Through fostering a multi-stakeholder approach at the country and global levels, and capturing philanthropic capital, the Platform aims to deepen collective, innovative and transformative solutions to achieving the SDGs. Global philanthropy perpetuates strong understanding of global chal-

lenges, networks and resources, whereas local philanthropy has regional insights and experience of what works at grassroots' levels. The Platform collected data on thriving local philanthropy, which has spearheaded innovative solutions in areas ranging from health and education to inclusive economic development.

FINANCIAL SERVICES

Financial service providers help to shift the capital toward sustainability and help to streamline fair reporting and facilitate access. The most crucial services in the financial supply chain are Data providers, Asset managers and Accountants. From a shared value perspective, they all – especially in collaboration - play an integral role in both enabling and accelerating the trillion dollar shift to SDG investing.

8. Data providers

Data serves many purposes including promoting transparency and helping to give a true analysis of SDG progress. Through tracked quantitative metrics and verifiable numbers, data is also an excellent way to have an honest dialogue on how businesses can realistically commit to the SDGs. The intersection of business needs, societal needs and far-sighted management can be navigated by data analysis enabling all parties to see concrete results and then shift course if necessary. Data providers are in a unique position to strengthen the capacity-building in the mobilization of capital through such actions as regional, interregional and global forums for knowledge-sharing, technical assistance and data-sharing.

Strong statistical systems that can measure and incentivize progress across the Global Goals will be crucial to success. It is estimated that a total of US $1 billion per annum will be required to enable 77 of the world's lower-income countries to put these systems in place.[136] Therefore, donors must maintain current contributions, and further leverage US $100 to $200 million more in ODA to support country efforts.[137] Recipient countries will also have the responsibility to fill the gap, mobilizing domestic resources behind clear

> ## ACCORDING TO JP MORGAN RESEARCH, DEMAND FOR IMPACT INVESTING STRATEGIES COULD REACH US $1 TRILLION BY 2020.[168]
>
> STANDARD LIFE INVESTMENTS

national strategies for the development of statistics (NSDSs). Data, and particularly open data, can improve decision-making and the lives of citizens around the world. This detailed information also has the potential to reduce spending through efficiency gains and innovation developments. For example, data analysis of sustainable and de-forestation-free practices in Brazil's beef industry found that the net benefits to ranchers ranged from US $18 million to $34 million (12% to 23% of revenues) in net present value projected over 10 years.[138] For slaughterhouses and retailers in Brazil, there were projected positive benefits: US $20 million to $120 million (0.01% to 0.1% of revenues) and US $13 million to $62 million (0.01% to 0.7% of revenues). Demonstrating that measuring the value of sustainable business can be done effectively.

Data helps sustainable business itself to be cost-effective. Such data analyses and projections could serve as powerful motivators to leaders' decision-making and bring sustainable business practices further into the mainstream. The most direct approach to data-driven management is to organize a project with well-defined objectives and measurable impact.[139] Let's consider the example of Southwest Airlines and its Evolve project. One of the key elements of the project was fuel efficiency, which combined two issues simultaneously: for Southwest, fuel is one of the primary drivers of cost and also has the largest environmental impact.[31] Therefore, reducing fuel consumption delivers shared value: it saves money for the airline and reduces emissions, thereby advancing SDG 13. Michael Thompson, general manager of Digital Solutions for GE Aviation said this of the data that would be provided, "A key component Southwest will receive is the flight efficiency analytics, enabling visibility of fuel savings and base line calculations to provide insight into true fuel usage across all stages of flight, and clear identification of fuel saving opportunities. Only accurate data enables good decision making ability."[140]

9. Asset Managers
The various actors in the investment value chain, including asset owners and asset managers, have been increasingly including Environmental, Social and Governance criteria, as well as sustainability information in their reporting processes. This has meant a strong boost for the Socially Responsible Investing market, which is now at US $22.89 trillion - up 25% since 2014.[141]

As an asset management firm, RobecoSAM contributes to the SDGs by integrating ESG factors into the investment decision-making process of various investment strategies. In addition, the firm encourages companies to take action on the SDGs through a constructive dialogue with them and by voting at over 4,000 shareholder meetings.[142] This asset management firm sees the SDGs as a business opportunity for listed and non-listed companies. Companies that align their business strategies with the SDGs will be more likely to anticipate future regulation and market developments. RebecoSAM sees this as a way for businesses to avoid the risk of losing their license to operate or facing future high costs of adjusting to necessary changes too late.

COMPANIES THAT ALIGN THEIR BUSINESS STRATEGIES WITH THE SDGs WILL BE MORE LIKELY TO ANTICIPATE FUTURE REGULATION AND MARKET DEVELOPMENTS.

RobecoSAM has a Governance & Active Ownership team that contributes to the achievement of the SDGs in two different ways. First, voting activities support environmental and social proposals that promote creation of long-term shareholder value. Second, the team encourages companies to take action on the SDGs through a constructive engagement. As an example, in the engagement theme Environmental Challenges in the European Electric Utilities Sector, electric utilities are encouraged to implement ambitious environmental strategies and focus on de-carbonization regardless of their historical energy mix: moving from coal to gas to renewables and using meaningful internal carbon prices in their planning. By encouraging 12

> **"IT'S VERY INSPIRING TO CONSTRUCT A PORTFOLIO WITH COMPANIES THAT COMMIT THEMSELVES TO IMPROVING THE WORLD BY ALIGNING WITH THE UN SDGs."** [169]
>
> **HUUB VAN DER RIET, LEAD PORTFOLIO MANAGER IMPACT INVESTING AT NN INVESTMENT PARTNERS**

utilities to shift from coal to gas to renewables, the asset management firm contributes to the realization of SDG 7 – Affordable and Clean Energy.

Sompo Japan Nipponkoa Asset Management Co., Ltd. also invests in companies that are highly evaluated both in terms of their environmental initiatives as well as on their value of investment. It sells *Sompo Japan Green Open*, which is an investment trust fund. Sampo was launched in September 1999 and has since been profitable in its sustainable investments, growing into one of the largest Socially Responsible Investment funds in Japan with a net asset value of approximately 23 billion yen (US $195 million) as of June 30, 2015.[143]

Investing in the SDGs can be a way for asset owners to meet the wishes of their participants and yield great financial value for shareholders too. Asset managers look to invest in firms that provide solutions for and contributions to the SDGs, which tend to be better prepared for the future, with lower chances of costly disruption. For example, a pension fund in the health care sector might prefer to invest in initiatives that support Goal 3, which strives for health and well-being. Eventually, this sort of alignment could become part of an asset manager's fiduciary duty. Assessment of the SDGs gives asset managers an opportunity to show added value in the form of conscious capital allocation. Firms that adopt responsible social and environmental practices are found to have lower financial volatility, higher sales growth, and higher chances of survival over a 15-year period.[144] Moreover, researchers did not find a cost in the sense of a difference in short-term profits.

10. Accountants

Implementing strategies to deliver the SDGs will engage the accountancy profession at many levels. Driving investment to build the infrastructure that will guide business, finance and government activity around the SDGs will require both the robust technical skills and in-depth knowledge that the accountancy profession is well equipped to deliver.[145] More effective use of data and reporting, and designing new business models that take advantage of opportunities that the SDGs present are some of the ways that professional accountants will be central to delivering this critical agenda that will help drive global growth.

Some accountancy firms have successfully led and partnered with other professionals to innovate sustainable business reporting such as the National Capital Protocol, Principles for Sustainable Insurance, Corporate EcoForum, Sustainable Investment Principles, The Nature Conservancy, WBCSD's Guide to Corporate Valuation, Sustainable Stock Exchanges, and Nigerian Sustainable Banking Principles (NSBPs).[146]

Accountants can build on existing tools and frameworks to identify the material climate adaptation risks and opportunities for the companies they represent. Major challenges for companies include estimating the costs and benefits associated with risks and opportunities, and understanding which of these are priorities for action and which can be re-evaluated over time. These actions may include investment in capital projects to increase resilience, low-carbon technologies to greenhouse gas emissions, forecasting and preparing for the re-cost of carbon when regulations are put in place, or preparing for the indirect cost of the price of carbon along supply chain. Accountants can have significant influence and will often persuade Boards and CEOs to guide their businesses to deliver economic returns to owners and investors.

Firms' reputations, legal responsibilities, regulatory obligations, financial reporting, operations and supply chains can be affected by the implementation of sustainability measures, all with direct bearing on strategic positioning. Having strong accounting systems in place can give businesses an edge to understanding how to manage and predict short- and long-term capital movement. There is increasing agreement that the interplay between business practice and taxation is of crucial importance to the SDGs. There are clear opportunities for businesses that engage in the policy debate and structure their accounting services accordingly. The opportunity to engage accountants and guide tax reform could be harnessed to help achieve the ambitions of the SDGs.[147] The issue of stranded assets, has also attracted ongoing discussion, with the Association of Chartered Certified Accountants concluding the risk of a "carbon bubble" due to excess fossil fuel reserves, and hence their over-valuation, is substantial.[148]

The big accounting and consulting firms are conducting the research others in the industry are looking to for guidance. PWC, for instance, is arguing for new approaches to the assurance of integrated reports. Deloitte partner Helena Barton chairs the Stakeholder Council of the Global Reporting Initiative, which sets globally recognized standards for sustainability accounting and reporting. KPMG has produced biannual reports following global trends in sustainability accounting and reporting. They have also strategically come up with a way to effectively demonstrate the problem of not valuing externalities, arguing that "the disconnect between corporate and societal value is disappearing."

THERE ARE CLEAR OPPORTUNITIES FOR BUSINESSES THAT ENGAGE IN THE POLICY DEBATE AND STRUCTURE THEIR ACCOUNTING SERVICES ACCORDINGLY.

They have consequently proposed an innovative approach to assessing a company's true value.[149] KPMG is convinced that "the value a company creates, and reduces, for society directly affects the company's earnings and their risk profile. In short, societal value is now inextricably linked with shareholder value."[150] The accountancy leader proffers taking the following steps to assess the true value of a company. First, identify the value that the company creates and reduces for society through its externalities and express this in financial terms. Second, assess how the internalization of externalities is likely to affect future earnings (through regulation, stakeholder action and market dynamics). And lastly, develop business cases that build and protect future value for shareholders by increasing the value created for society.[151] This is sound advice. The examples throughout this book of business cases doing exactly that shows how looking at value more broadly, creates profit for the financial bottom line while benefitting people and the planet. It can and should be done like this. Business for good and capital for good are interlinked and create true value.

> **"IT IS IN THE NAME OF NET PROFIT, BUDGET SURPLUS AND GROSS NATIONAL PRODUCT THAT THE NATURAL ENVIRONMENT IN WHICH WE ALL CO-EXIST IS BEING DESTROYED. THOSE WHO SPEAK THIS LANGUAGE HAVE MORE SOCIAL POWER TO INFLUENCE THINKING AND ACTIONS THAN THEY PERHAPS REALIZE, OR UTILIZE."**
>
> RUTH HINES, AUSTRALIAN ACCOUNTING ACADEMIC AT MACQUARIE UNIVERSITY

WRAP UP

Just like business, capital also needs the Goals as much as the Goals need capital. For business, and capital, there is a major role to play in achieving the SDGs. Capital invested in SDG themes will unlock markets and will bring revenues both direct and indirect. There are multiple avenues to use capital for good and there are many actors involved in the movement of capital all around the world. The speed, scale and scope of financing the SDGs must increase.

Investors worldwide are increasingly seeking investment opportunities that promise to bring environmental and social benefits, in addition to high rates of return. If this trend continues, it will strengthen the commitment to sustainability that is already gaining momentum among businesses around the world.

Public capital must be leveraged and blended to engage the trillions in private capital. Blended finance will be a key theme throughout the SDG implementation years, especially in the coming years. The SDGs should guide the way to impact investing. Furthermore, incorporating externalities

"INCLUDING THE VALUE OF NATURAL RESOURCES AND OUR SOCIAL CAPITAL IN NATIONAL ACCOUNTING IS A VITAL STEP TO ACHIEVE ECONOMIC GROWTH THAT IS EQUITABLE AND SUSTAINABLE."

ACHIM STEINER UNDP ADMINISTRATOR

will level the playing field and sustainable businesses, industries and investments will emerge on top.

On a macro-economic level, the costs to global GDP and society of not investing in the SDGs or investing too little, far exceeds the costs of the investments themselves. The trillion dollar shift to a better world is thus a shift for business, for capital and for good. ∎

PART 3 | THE TRILLION DOLLAR SHIFT IN SECTORS

INTRODUCTION

Sector and cross-sector approaches to achieving the SDGs are impactful. The dynamic capabilities and unique knowledge they bring are invaluable when addressing multilevel challenges. Food and Agriculture, Education and Learning, Cities and Transportation, Health and Well-Being, and Energy and Resources make up the sectors in the following chapters.

Because all sectors are interconnected and overlap in a number of business and capital areas, many of the initiatives mentioned can been seen as cross-sector or multi-sector approaches to addressing the Goals. Food and Agriculture, for example, is essential to everyday life and to basic survival. With hunger, malnutrition and obesity plaguing populations across the globe, there is an urgent need to act. Health and Well-Being is directly affected by food quality and nutrition levels, and addressing the health of society by solving food shortages, for example, has enormous benefits across sectors.

Capital expenditures in one sector will often enhance another, resulting in cross-sector and multi-sector benefits. For example, investments in Education and Learning are necessary to bring awareness about our global challenges to classrooms, workplaces, homes, and governments across the entire planet. Without the knowledge and skills to grow food, build energy infrastructure, provide health care or manage urban systems, we will be unable to adequately and efficiently perpetuate the required economic, social and environmental growth needed to reach our Goals. Business solutions mobilizing capital for Energy and Resources also present unparalleled potential. Never before have we experienced the growth potential for renewable energy and resource conservation. Investments in alternative power generation could have substantial returns in sectors such as Cities and Transport where there is a dire need for greater efficiencies.

Creating business solutions and mobilizing capital to address such important basic concepts offers endless opportunities in these five sectors and will positively affect all SDGs. We will need collaboration from all business and capital within and among sectors to sustainably prosper, and to achieve our common Goals.

CITIES AND TRANSPORTATION

Cities are at the heart of national and global growth. In an increasingly urbanized world, cities are both the source and the solution of many global problems. Not only do urban areas account for over half of the world's population, they also generate around 80% of global Gross Domestic Product.[1] They are further associated with around 70% of global energy consumption and energy-related greenhouse gas emissions.[2]

Urbanization is not a new phenomenon, but the world is now experiencing a new type of movement into cities. By 2030, around 60% of the global population will live in urban areas. Putting pressure on resources, services, and infrastructure, the growing populations of cities will also present new challenges for climate adaptation. This is significant in that cities and urban areas will be home to nearly all of the world's net population growth over the next two decades.

5.1 SDG 11: SUSTAINABLE CITIES AND COMMUNITIES

With the expectation that global urban population will grow by 2.5 billion by 2050, reaching 66% of the global population.[3] Cities in the developing world account for 90% of this urban transition, where there is urgent need for innovations in city planning and policy reforms. For instance, in 2030, China's cities will be home to close to 1 billion people or 70% of the population.[4]

Cities are often stricken with extreme poverty, unemployment and socio-economic disparities, unsustainable patterns of consumption and production, and they are primary contributors to climate change and environmental degradation. But cities also enable a significant portion of the world's businesses and informal enterprises, provide markets for industry and employment, foster technological innovations, and support high-density habitation and efficient land use.

The stakes for cities from the standpoint of growth, quality of life and carbon emissions are arguably at the highest ever. We are at a critical time to set the urban trajectory for the future. The infrastructure that is built now, including roads and buildings, and the ways in which business and financial systems are structured today could last

for a century or more. Yet growth today typically involves poorly managed, unstructured urbanization, where economic, social and environmental costs outweigh the benefits. Unmanaged urban sprawl alone costs the US economy, including residents and businesses, an estimated US $400 billion per year.[5]

THE SDGs CAN BE USED TO STRENGTHEN DEVELOPMENT OUTCOMES OF CITY PLANNING.

Although urbanization comes with its share of development challenges, it also has tremendous opportunities for advancing sustainable development. City officials, such as mayors and local leaders who are working to improve the quality of life in urban environments, look to the SDGs as a roadmap for structurally sound and environmentally conscious urban development. Aiming to increase prosperity, promote social inclusion, and enhance resilience and environmental sustainability, the SDGs help guide the existing political agenda in cities. The SDGs can be used to strengthen development outcomes of existing city planning frameworks, and provide additional resources for local governments. More relevantly, they also provide a set of guidelines for business to thrive within urban settings. The following Targets provide concrete areas of focus.

SDG 11: SUSTAINABLE CITIES AND COMMUNITIES
Make cities and human settlements inclusive, safe, resilient and sustainable

TARGETS

11.1 By 2030, ensure access for all to adequate, safe and affordable housing and basic services and upgrade slums

11.2 By 2030, provide access to safe, affordable, accessible and sustainable transport systems for all, improving road safety, notably by expanding public transport, with special attention to the needs of those in vulnerable situations, women, children, persons with disabilities and older persons

11.3 By 2030, enhance inclusive and sustainable urbanization and capacity for participatory, integrated and sustainable human settlement planning and management in all countries

11.4 Strengthen efforts to protect and safeguard the world's cultural and natural heritage

11.5 By 2030, significantly reduce the number of deaths and the number of people affected and substantially decrease the direct economic losses relative to global gross domestic product caused by disasters, including water-related disasters, with a focus on protecting the poor and people in vulnerable situations

11.6 By 2030, reduce the adverse per capita environmental impact of cities, including by paying special attention to air quality and municipal and other waste management

11.7 By 2030, provide universal access to safe, inclusive and accessible, green and public spaces, in particular for women and children, older persons and persons with disabilities

11.a Support positive economic, social and environmental links between urban, peri-urban and rural areas by strengthening national and regional development planning

11.b By 2020, substantially increase the number of cities and human settlements adopting and implementing integrated policies and plans towards inclusion, resource efficiency, mitigation and adaptation to climate change, resilience to disasters, and develop and implement, in line with the Sendai Framework for Disaster Risk Reduction 2015-2030, holistic disaster risk management at all levels

11.c Support least developed countries, including through financial and technical assistance, in building sustainable and resilient buildings utilizing local materials

SDG 11 calls for cities and human settlements to be inclusive, safe, resilient and sustainable.[6] It is a significant goal in that it responds to the growing number of people moving into cities. Currently, half of the global population - over 3.5 billion people – lives in cities. Because the world's cities occupy just 3% of the Earth's land, but account for 60 to 80% of energy consumption and 75% of carbon emissions, sustainable urban planning for transportation and other energy uses will become an even more pressing issue. The onset of rapid urbanization is putting pressure on fresh water supplies, sewage, the living environment, and public health. But the high density of cities also has the potential to bring beneficial efficiency gains and technological innovations while reducing resource use and energy consumption, which will be discussed in this chapter.

THE ONSET OF RAPID URBANIZATION IS PUTTING PRESSURE ON FRESH WATER SUPPLIES, SEWAGE, THE LIVING ENVIRONMENT, AND PUBLIC HEALTH.

The management of cities will shape public policy priorities and guide development finance flows for the next several years. SDG 11 presents a growth market with a tremendous opportunity for cities to build robust partnerships and gain additional resources for advancing sustainable urban development.[7] This potential is spurring interest and investment in twenty-first century urban development. As stated by the UN Deputy Secretary-General Amina J. Mohammed, "The battle for sustainability will be won or lost in cities."[8] With large-scale urbanization underway, government leaders, city planners and private consultants are pushing to meet the demands, including the development of sustainable megacities. The domains of smart cities, urban design, and transportation play a central role in building these densely populated and economically sound living areas.

> ## "THE BATTLE FOR SUSTAINABILITY WILL BE WON OR LOST IN CITIES"
> SECRETARY-GENERAL AMINA J. MOHAMMED, UN DEPUTY

Cities' importance for the world's global development calls mayors and local government leaders to the forefront of international politics. There are a number of serious actors making moves, both on the local and national fronts and on the business and government scales. As of May 2017, there were 149 countries developing national-level urban policies.[9] As a country surrounded by water, Denmark is a good example of a country vulnerable to the climate impacts of sea level rise. Copenhagen has garnered a lot of attention and attracted considerable investment for its sustainability initiatives by aiming to be the first capital city in the world to be carbon neutral. Danish city planners have the strong support of politicians and local residents for this climate change adaptation and are willing to commit the funds required. One of the city's main localized efforts is a sustainable climate change adaptation plan set to be completed by 2033.[10] Other cities are making similar commitments. In the wake of Hurricane Sandy, New York devised a record US $19.5 billion climate change adaptation plan, with 250 specific projects reaching into the 2050s.[11] Toronto, Rotterdam and Boston also have advanced plans with solutions from floating pavilions to terraced levees.

The global Compact of Mayors, with 507 cities as signatories, is also a pioneering force of city leaders addressing climate change by pledging to reduce their greenhouse gas emissions, tracking their progress and preparing for the impacts of climate change. The Compact is comprised of the C40 Cities Climate Leadership Group (C40), the International Council for Local Environmental Initiatives - Local Governments for Sustainability (ICLEI) and the United Cities and Local Govern-

> **"AS A GLOBAL MAYOR, AND ONE WHOSE CITY WILL FOREVER BE LINKED TO THE GLOBAL SUSTAINABLE DEVELOPMENT AGENDA, I CANNOT STRESS ENOUGH THE FACT THAT WITHOUT AN URBAN GOAL, THE SUSTAINABLE DEVELOPMENT GOALS WILL BE INCOMPLETE."**
>
> EDUARDO PAES, FORMER MAYOR OF RIO DE JANEIRO

their ability to withstand future impacts, including challenges like population growth and climate change. Building resilient cities requires a shift in thinking about city planning, community engagement, disaster prevention and recovery and public-private collaboration. Business has the potential to play a pivotal role in building better cities. The innovation, resources and experience of the private sector, in addition to the financial acumen of business, is needed in order to realize the full potential of SDG 11. After all, businesses themselves have a lot of stake in how cities are structured, and they want to be involved when it comes to urban and long-term planning. Conversely, and equally important, cities need business to thrive while shaping investment and capital markets to achieve the SDGs.

When local leaders implement extensive changes throughout the cities' system, it will lead to the emergence of a number of disruptive business opportunities. The largest opportunities include technological implementations, urban mobility solutions, circular economy models - such as the sharing economy, and durable and modular buildings. Improving energy efficiency in buildings could be worth more than US $3.7 trillion in 2030.[13]

ments (UCLG) –with support from UN-Habitat, the UN's lead agency on urban issues.[12] By establishing a common platform to capture the impact of cities' collective actions through standardized measurement of emissions and climate risk, it enables consistent, public reporting of their efforts. Having these types of common and standard metrics for urban areas and initiatives are extremely important and helpful in the long run for cities. Similarly, approaches from the private sector and business would benefit from a common, public good platform of shared information available to all cities.

Cities play a vital role in the global effort to achieve the SDGs. Whether it is local officials promoting business-friendly policies or businesses creating new avenues within urban regions, the ability for city initiatives to unlock new markets is far reaching. SDG 11 specifically demands governments to build cities in such a way that promotes our common sustainability objectives while also opening unprecedented business opportunities.

Thus, there is a pressing need for cities to go beyond merely adopting coping strategies and to focus on implementing SDG actions that strengthen

> **ANNUAL URBAN INFRASTRUCTURE AND BUILDING INVESTMENTS ARE EXPECTED TO RISE FROM US $10 TRILLION IN 2012 TO MORE THAN US $20 TRILLION IN 2025, WITH URBAN CENTERS IN EMERGING ECONOMIES ATTRACTING THE MAJORITY OF THE INVESTMENT.**
>
> SUSTAINABLEDEVELOPMENT.UN.ORG

Former UN Secretary-General Ban Ki-moon emphasized that the SDGs are the 'People's Agenda'.[14] That is, local governments, as the level of government closest to the people, are at the forefront of ensuring that no one is left behind. The Global Goals are therefore of significant importance in designing localization to be an inclusive and participatory process. Localization begins with raising awareness and understanding of the SDGs among all stakeholders, and continues with a dialogue on implementation that is participatory and partnership-based. The transformational change needed to achieve the SDGs requires broad-based public support and engagement, and a long-term shift in policy priorities towards sustainable development.

Achieving SDG 11 would mark a major step forward for urban development. In transforming the power structure to drive global change, the SDGs are giving city leaders the platform on which to act from the bottom up.[15] Moving away from a top down, command and control method, cities will begin to call on their mayors, business leaders and planning committees for support. But local administrations should not confine their role in the achievement of the SDGs to Goal 11. All of the SDGs have targets that are directly or indirectly related to the operations of local and regional actors. Instead of operating simply as facilitators or mechanisms for implementation, local governments can act as policymakers, as catalysts for change and as the level of leaders most equipped to link the Global Goals with urban communities.

Figure 32 **Cities' growth and carbon emissions**[15]

Emerging Cities will play a significant role in growth of the global economy and carbon emissions to 2030

URBAN GROUP	PROJECTED BASE GDP GROWTH FROM 2012-2030 USD TRILLIONS	PROJECTED BASE CASE EMISSIONS GROWTH FROM 2012-2030, MEGATONNES OF CO_2	PROJECTED POPULATION IN 2030, BNS	PER CAPITA IN 2030, TONNES OF CO_2 PER PERSON
Emerging Cities e.g. Bangalore, Kunming, Pune, Puebla	16	3230	~1.3	~7
Small Urban Areas Inc. villages, small Towns, peripheral industrial areas pop < 0,5 milion	16	1220	~2.2	~4.6
Established Cities e.g. Stuttgart, Minneapolis, Stockholm, Hiroshima	11	390	~0.4	~12.1
Global Megacities e.g. Beijing, New York, London, Rio Janeiro	10	1050	~0.6	~7.1
Total growth	~52	~5.890	Total population in 2030 ~4.5	
Share of world growth	~87%	~65%	Share of world pop, in 2030 ~55%	

5.2 SOLVING THE CHALLENGES: CITIES AS CATALYSTS FOR LINKING ALL THE GOALS

All of the SDGs touch the work of local authorities in one way or another. Goals such as ensuring clean water and sanitation (SDG 6), equitable education (SDG 4), and good health (SDG 3) all cannot be achieved without local-level leadership in cities. Further, Goals that focus on environmental, energy and climate management (SDGs 7 and 13) will play a major role in how cities move forward in a prosperous and equitable manner.

Yet local leaders also need the help of business transactions to support a financially sound and sustainable future. In Johannesburg, for example, the municipal Green Bond structure to fund the city's resource management is pioneering a system for both sustainable urban development and market-related financial security.[16] Unlocking markets by implementing innovative financing structures within the cities sector has unprecedented potential.

COOPERATION BETWEEN THE GOVERNMENT AND THE PRIVATE SECTOR NEEDS TO BE STRONG AND, WHEN THE GOVERNMENT COMMITS TO DEVELOPMENTS, THE WORK WILL BE PASSED DOWN TO THE PRIVATE SECTOR AS WELL.

Urban development will have a significant impact on national and local finance allocation, as well as on economic prosperity. How this Goal is addressed will have far-reaching effects on the rest of the 16 Goals. Although cities are efficient users of land, they have footprints that extend far beyond the city walls. For example, building better, more

productive and sustainable cities can boost economic prosperity and help tackle climate change all over the world (SDG 13). It is predicted that energy and greenhouse gas savings ranging from 13% to 26% are possible over the next ten years through investments, with payback periods of less than five years.[17]

City planning is becoming a business opportunity. As these growing, densely populated regions rely on the Goals to assist in easing conflicting national and local development policies, they also take part in bringing local populations out of poverty (SDG 1). As Johannesburg Mayor Mpho Parks Tau expressed, "The lack of systematic urban planning continues to urbanize poverty – with the poor located on the periphery of our cities and towns where basic services such as adequate shelter, water, sanitation, transport and energy remain limited."[18]

"THE LACK OF SYSTEMATIC URBAN PLANNING CONTINUES TO URBANIZE POVERTY."

MPHO PARKS TAU, FORMER MAYOR OF JOHANNESBURG

Besides participating more actively at the urban planning level, businesses can also help cities become more resilient by collaborating and creating opportunities for shared learning with local governments. A service and technology provider like Huawei is an example of a company that is heavily invested in supporting smart and sustainable cities and is poised to share its expertise as cities move towards being Internet of Things-enabled.[19] "The company has the potential to take on a more advisory role in terms of informing some of the decisions for infrastructure investment and planning, and digital enablement," said Kriv Naicker, Huawei's former general manager, strategy and business consulting.[20]

Another example of citywide public-private collaboration possibilities is how Singapore-based real estate developer City Developments Limited (CDL) has become a local leader in sustainability. When the Building and Construction Authority in Singapore first began implementing the Green Mark certification program for buildings, CDL offered invaluable expertise and knowledge.[21] The Singapore government has now pledged to have 80% of the city-state's buildings green-certified by 2030 up from the current 30%.[22] Cooperation between the government and the private sector needs to be strong and, when the government commits to developments, the work will be passed down to the private sector as well. The pursuit of resilient and sustainable cities is therefore a business opportunity for the private sector, as it can build a marketplace for resilience tools and services. And if it is profitable for the private sector to develop and sell resilience solutions, and valuable for governments to buy and implement them, then resilience thinking and planning can truly gain traction and become self-perpetuating.

5.3 IMPACT OF CITIES AND TRANSPORTATION ON ALL SDGs

With their large populations, bustling societies, commercial and non-commercial enterprises, what happens in cities can have an effect on all the SDGs. Cities and human settlements will be an integral part of achieving the SDGs.

> **"WHEN YOU GO DOWN TO [THE SDG] TARGETS AND INDICATORS, YOU WILL CLEARLY SEE THAT THERE ARE QUITE A NUMBER OF INDICATORS FOR WHICH THE UNIT OF MEASUREMENT IS THE CITY."**[23]
>
> ROBERT NDUGWA, HEAD OF U.N.-HABITAT'S GLOBAL URBAN OBSERVATORY UNIT.

 SDG 1: No Poverty; While poverty is an old issue, urban poverty is the new challenge for the international development agenda and it remains to be seen how these densely populated areas will manage an influx of residents. Disparity in urban growth is often exacerbated by inefficient, unequal land use and housing markets, lack of access to basic services and existing socio-economic traps. No matter how well a city's economy is doing, its budgetary bottom line is affected by financially insecure residents. The cost of residents' financial insecurity to city budgets in 10 American cities ranges from US $8 million to $18 million in New Orleans, to US $280 million to $646 million in New York City.[24] When considering these costs proportional to city budgets, it is found that residents' financial insecurity costs cities between 0.3% (San Francisco) and 4.6% (Seattle) of their total annual budgets.

The number of people living in urban poverty could be reduced by 25% or more though a combination of expense reductions for families, targeted job creation, and smarter public and private investments.

 SDG 2: Zero-hunger; Land available for farms is becoming an issue, as the open spaces on which many cities have been built are particularly fertile, and there is continual encroachment onto peri-urban land by development of housing, infrastructure, and industry.[25] The loss of precious farmland in and around cities has already had an impact on food access, price, and quality in many places. Addressing this issue, the Brazilian city of Curitiba, for example, is turning unused urban land into community gardens in order to improve food security and build social cohesion, while raising awareness about the environmental impacts of commercial food production. The Urban Agriculture program in Curitiba increases food security and can serve as an income generating activity for participants. Since its launch in 2011, the initiative has generated more than 750 tons of food and has benefited more than 83,000 people. By repurposing 67 million m^2 of land for cultivation under the program, the city is targeting urban food security.[26] Additionally, because this project is based in populated urban areas, it can also have a social impact element by providing a therapeutic group activity for a diverse group of participants, including children and the elderly and those afflicted by drug addiction and mental health issues. Food waste is another issue affecting cities. In some cities in the world, landfills are overflowing causing environmental hazards in the surrounding areas. Food waste is the largest component of municipal solid waste. If food waste is curtailed, cities could save money on landfills and mitigate the environmental damage.[27]

 SDG 3: Good Health and Well-Being; The health of city residents is essential to urban prosperity. In many countries, rates of health-related child mortality in cities due to air pollution or water contamination have not gone down even with prevention measu-

res. Only 12% of cities globally reach their pollution control targets.[28] Other health issues affecting cities include the spread of disease due to high density population and traffic deaths due to congestion. Local governments can address these challenges of course, but businesses can impact these issues in fundamental ways as well. For example, the advent of driverless cars promises to have a huge effect on traffic flows, and electric vehicles will reduce pollution due to fuel emissions. Other technological developments such as drones can be implemented to deliver life-saving medication especially in areas where road infrastructure is lacking or congested.

SDG 4: Education; On average, across OECD countries, students who attend schools in cities of more than 100,000 people perform better than students who attend schools in areas with fewer students.[29] This is the result of several factors including the wealth of cultural and social opportunities that big cities offer, the larger labor pool from which to employ teachers, and simply the greater number of schools to choose from. Because of high population density in cities, there are more building needs for schools. Businesses are helping to create social and environmental value by building learning conducive, environmentally efficient schools. Projects such as "School of the Future – Towards Zero Emission with High Performance Indoor Environment" are focusing on energy efficiency to promote sustainable learning environments. This European project renovated school buildings in Germany, Italy, Denmark and Norway. Local planning teams were supported by an advisory group consisting of researchers and building industry representatives who provided ideas to achieve reduction in energy by a factor of three. At the same time, the buildings' indoor comfort was improved resulting in better academic performance.[30] Continued education is also relevant to cites as studies show that lifelong learners – citizens who acquire new knowledge, skills and attitudes in a wide range of contexts – are better equipped to adapt to changes in their environments.[31] Lifelong learning facilities and a learning culture therefore have a vital role to play

in empowering citizens, and promoting social inclusion, economic development, cultural prosperity, and sustainable development.

> **IN 15 COUNTRIES ACROSS THE WORLD, STUDENTS WHO ATTEND SCHOOLS IN URBAN SETTINGS ARE MORE LIKELY TO BE ABLE TO CHOOSE AMONG A GREATER NUMBER AND WIDER RANGE OF EXTRACURRICULAR ACTIVITIES, IMPROVING FUTURE EMPLOYMENT POTENTIALS AND EARNINGS.[32]**
>
> OECD EDUCATION TODAY

SDG 5: Gender Equality; Local governments can act as a model for gender equality and the empowerment of women through non-discriminatory service provision to citizens and fair employment practices. Urban planning and local policing are both essential tools in managing violence against women and providing services to women affected by violence. Local governments also have a role to play in creating a platform to identify and tackle barriers to women's equal access to land control and business ownership. Getting more women into elected office at the local level is a priority in terms of empowering women.[33] Inadequate and inappropriate infrastructure and facilities in low-income urban communities contribute to violence against women and girls, thus compromising their livelihoods and financial opportunities.[34] The plight of a woman's life is also linked to urbanization, as countries with the lowest levels of urbanization also have the highest rates of girls forced into child marriages.[35]

SDG 6: Clean Water and Sanitation; The provision of clean water and sanitation in cities is an important aspect in lowering infant, child and maternal mortality. UN Water estimates that the world will need investments of US $50 billion annually to be able to provide water, sanitation and hygiene for all by 2030.[36] Some urban areas are experimenting with a closed-circuit water plan. The recycling of urban wastewater or rainwater collection is most developed in neighborhoods in China or Europe. And in countries like Israel that are under water stress, a solution to reuse 80% of their wastewater to provide for 25% of their needs is being explored.[37] Yet water provision in low-income settlements is still highly informal, particularly in sub-Saharan cities that have expanded rapidly without adequate planning.[38] In urban areas, the main challenges are often a lack of access to basic services, high prices and a lack of quality control.[39] Currently, 60 million new residents move to urban areas every year. One in four lives in slums, amounting to 1 billion people with inadequate housing and limited access to basic services. As a result, urban population growth dramatically outpaces gains in access to proper sanitation. Only 37% of urban excreta is safely managed globally. Evidence shows that even where piped water networks exist, many areas experience sewerage and septic tank connections that lag far behind.[40] Integrated water resource management requires increased access to safe drinking water and improved sanitation for large segments of the population, as well as proper waste disposal, pollution management and good hygiene.[41]

SDG 7: Clean Energy; Urbanization growth rates will significantly increase energy demand. City leaders and capital investors can contribute to energy efficiency by investing in energy efficient buildings and green energy sources. Introducing sustainability criteria into procurement practices, sustainable local transport and urban planning policies, as well as new 'smart city' technologies, can also have a significant impact on energy efficiency and carbon emissions.[42] Dense urban areas could take advantage of smaller microgrids, which can either connect to the larger grid or disconnect from it in extreme weather events or other grid emergencies. These can be powered by a variety of renewable sources, including solar and wind, combined with more consistent "baseload" power from geothermal power stations, gas turbines, or fuel cells.[43] Decentralized, peer-to-peer platforms and innovative energy storage technologies are disrupting the conventional concept of utility delivery and better preparing cities and residents for energy and climate resilience. This is responding to the emerging consumer movement on energy self-sufficiency, where consumers are also producers of energy. The microgrid industry generated US $4,083 million revenue in 2015 and is expected to generate US $12,315 million revenue by 2022.[44] Large urban metropolises emerging in Asia and Africa could embrace these new systems to power their homes and businesses, as well as generate income to boost local economies. In doing so, these cities would skip the older development models of the West and become the new model for sustainable and resilient development in the 21st century.[45] Cities will need to leverage financial resources through mechanisms to

> **THE INTERNATIONAL RENEWABLE ENERGY AGENCY (IRENA) ESTIMATES THE COST OF OUTDOOR AIR POLLUTION TO BE US $1.8 TO $6.0 TRILLION IN 2010, OR ABOUT 3% - 10% OF GLOBAL GDP. UNDER A BUSINESS-AS-USUAL SCENARIO, WITHOUT URBAN ENERGY UPGRADES, THIS WILL RISE TO US $2.4 TO $8.8 TRILLION PER YEAR BY 2030.**
>
> IRENA.ORG

de-risk investment in renewable energy technologies or projects and issue municipal green bonds and create funds to support municipal energy investments.[46]

 **SDG 8: Decent Work and Economic Growth;** Cities and metropolitan regions are dynamic centers of economic activity and vast resource flows. As such, cities and metropolitan regions comprise the world's most complex structure of social and economic systems. Local governments can generate growth and employment from the bottom up through economic development strategies that harness the unique resources and opportunities in communities. In addition, they can identify children at risk of child labor and work to ensure they attend school.[47] Local governments are well positioned to work with communities to assess the benefits and costs of business, such as tourism, and to develop strategic plans to ensure business activities are sustainable. Businesses are attracted to cities, and people are attracted to cities for the employment opportunities these businesses offer. Cities are inherently work and economic growth hubs, and therefore have a crucial role in the environmental footprint and social well-being of countries.

SDG 9: Industry, Innovation and Infrastructure; Regional and metropolitan governments are particularly important in developing and maintaining infrastructure to serve urban areas and to link them with their surrounding territories. Local governments can include the promotion of small-scale industry and start-ups in their local economic development strategies, taking into account local resources, needs and markets. Cities can also identify gaps in access to ICT and the Internet in their communities and take steps to bridge them, particularly through provision in public spaces such as libraries. A major investment opportunity exists for innovation in telematics, as a wide-range of innovative technologies are needed throughout cities for a number of public access purposes. Companies active in the development of IT solutions for transportation, for example, show a very high research

THE AMOUNT OF WASTE SENT TO LANDFILL IN THE ARGENTINE CAPITAL (BUENOS AIRES) INCREASED FROM 1.4 MILLION TONS IN 2002 TO 2.2 MILLION TONS IN 2010. FACED WITH THIS LOOMING CRISIS, A SCHEME TO FORMALIZE RECYCLERS IS HELPING THE CITY REACH ITS GOAL OF REDUCING WASTE TO LANDFILLS BY 83% BY 2017.

SUSTAINIA

and development intensity. Traffic demand management and Intelligent Transportation Systems (ITS) can enhance the operational efficiency of the entire transport sector and reduce energy consumption of all forms of motorized transport.

SDG 10: Reduced Inequalities; Local governments are essential to the reduction of inequality within countries. It will be vital to channel resources to local city governments in the most deprived areas, and to build capacities to identify and tackle poverty and exclusion. Local governments have a particular role to play in political inclusion at the local level. City officials can promote the participation of minority and traditionally underrepresented groups in public consultation processes, and encourage them to stand for elected office. Local governments can implement best practices in terms of equality and non-discrimination in institutions and operations, as well as foster business growth for equitable practices. Responding to inequalities will also draw more business to urban centers. Paris electric-vehicle car sharing service, Autolib, offers inexpensive access to electric vehicles for a broad segment of the urban population that do not own cars.[48] Autolib's car-sharing scheme reduces the total number of cars on the road and improves air quality in Paris by using exhaust-free electric vehicles.

 SDG 11: Sustainable Cities and Communities; Access to affordable housing is a pervasive issue even in many of the richest cities in the world. There is a need for local governments to regulate land and housing markets to guarantee the right to housing to their poorest residents.[49] In the context of rapid global urbanization, participatory urban planning is more important than ever to prevent urban sprawl, tackle segregation, and reduce carbon emissions in cities. Business opportunities abound in cities in a number of areas. Take smart cities for example, where millions of streetlights burn all night, even when there is no activity, and data collected on this inefficiency presents ample opportunity for both financial and energy savings. The Dutch company Tvilight estimates that the Netherlands alone pays over €300 million annually for street lighting electricity, with CO_2 emissions of 1.6 million tons.[50] Tvilight's intelligent streetlights reduce electricity consumption and maintenance costs by up to 80% and 50% respectively, without compromising public safety. In the buildings sector, opportunities include improved building design practices; insulation; more efficient heating/cooling, lighting technologies and appliances, and the adoption of small-scale renewables. For residential buildings in the Leeds City Region in the North of England, it was calculated that US $1.7 billion could be profitably invested in domestic energy efficiency measures, generating annual savings of US $626 million, paying back the investment in less than three years and reducing total emissions from the domestic sector by 16% relative to business-as-usual trends.[51] These investments could also achieve multiple other benefits, including reduced fuel poverty and improved public health.

 SDG 12: Responsible Consumption and Production; Local and regional governments can support short supply chains, thereby reducing transport and carbon emissions, through land management, infrastructure, urban planning, education and training, and public markets. Cities have a particular role to play in fostering the sustainable consumption and production of energy and water, which they can do using a wide variety of tools, from urban planning to the use of innovative pricing mechanisms. Cities can realize high returns on their investment in food waste reduction. In 2012, six West London boroughs implemented an initiative to reduce household food waste. The initiative resulted in a 15% reduction, with a benefit-cost ratio of 8 to 1 when considering just the financial savings to the borough councils.[52] In other words, for every GBP £1 invested in the effort, local governments saved GBP £8. The benefit-cost ratio was even higher, 92 to 1, when the financial benefits to households located in the boroughs were included. Sustainable waste management, with an emphasis on reuse and recycling, is also vital to the reduction of cities' environmental impact.

SDG 13: Climate Action; Local and regional governments, especially in cities, are often on the frontline of dealing with the effects of climate change. It is vital that cities' capacities to manage climate related hazards and natural disasters are strengthened so that communities are protected. Local leaders have the potential to lead from the bottom up in combatting climate change and raising awareness. It is essential that local governments, particularly in the most vulnerable cities, integrate climate change adaptation and mitigation into urban and regional planning to reduce the emissions and increase cities' resilience to environmental shocks.[53] Green bonds have grown in popularity over the past few years as a promising new source of funding for city initiatives. The City of Johannesburg, for example, experienced great interest from investors as the bond auction in 2014 was 150% oversubscribed. The South African metropolis has issued green bonds to finance investments in projects that help the city to mitigate and adapt to climate change. By issuing green bonds, Johannesburg is finding new funding sources for sustainable urban projects worth approximately

US $143 million.[54] The funding is used to implement and accelerate projects such as the Landfill Biogas to Energy Project, the Solar Geyser Initiative and the deployment of 152 hybrid buses.[55] Johannesburg is working with the C40 Sustainable Infrastructure Finance Network and the Climate Bonds Initiative to share the financing model with cities across the globe.

SDG 14: Life Below Water; Almost 80% of the pollution in the oceans comes from land-based activities, both in coastal areas and further inland.[56] Many of the world's largest cities are located on the coast and many coastal cities discharge sewage, industrial effluent and other wastewater directly into their surrounding seas. Worldwide, two-thirds of the sewage from urban areas is discharged untreated into lakes, rivers and coastal waters.[57] Urban sanitation and solid waste management are essential to reducing coastal zone pollution, as is collaboration between municipalities. The US tourism industry loses close to US $1 billion each year, mostly from losses in fishing and recreational activities because of nutrient-polluted bodies of water.

> EACH TIME COPENHAGEN SPENDS US $1 ON ITS CLIMATE PLAN, IT GENERATES $85 IN PRIVATE INVESTMENT ELSEWHERE IN THE CITY. THE CITY'S ECONOMIC STUDIES INDICATE THAT THE CLIMATE PLAN WILL GENERATE AN ECONOMIC SURPLUS OF ALMOST US $1 BILLION OVER ITS LIFETIME.
>
> ICLEI

SDG 15: Life on Land; Local governments' role as service providers (especially of water, sanitation, and solid waste management), coupled with cities' ability to incentivize behavioral change within urban communities, puts them in a unique position to protect natural resources and habitats. Coordinating partnerships with the private sector and communities, cities strive for cost effective integrated land management. Local and regional governments can work with surrounding businesses to ensure that biodiversity conservation is an integral part of urban planning and development strategy. Cities could also use local knowledge to help implement the "polluter pays" principle. Community-based participation and management, facilitated by local governments, is a powerful tool to halt biodiversity loss and prevent extinction. Conserving biodiversity often requires cooperation between municipalities and among businesses. Examples include the creation of trans-boundary, biodiversity and wildlife corridors; mainstreaming adaptation systems; and investing in green infrastructure. The city of Yokohama, Japan is a good example of a large metropolis protecting the nation's land through actions in response to climatic changes like increased downpours and extreme heat events. One such method is to install more than 1,000 infiltration inlet systems by 2018 to separate storm water and wastewater flows, thus improving flood response.[58] Other actions include hazard mapping and disaster mitigation; improving infrastructure around the city's rivers and sewerage system; and issuing public reminders about heat stroke prevention. Under the policy, the Yokohama Green Tax, which collects US $116 million yearly, enables protection of rivers, waterways, forests, parks, and farmlands.[59]

SDG 16: Peace, Justice and Strong Institutions; City governments are called on to become more accountable to their citizens. This requires cities to tackle corruption and increase the public's access to information. For decades, local governments have led the way in experimenting with new forms of participatory decision-making, such as participatory budgeting and planning.[60] Expanding

YOKOHAMA, JAPAN PLANS TO INVEST US $433 MILLION OVER THE NEXT FIVE YEARS TO INCREASE CONSERVED FOREST AREAS BY AN EXTRA 5 MILLION M², INCREASE RICE PADDIES BY 1.2 MILLION M², AND ESTABLISH A PUBLIC AGRICULTURE FARM WHICH WILL ALL ADD TO THE CLIMATE RESILIENCY OF THE CITY.

SUSTAINIA

these efforts and becoming even more responsive to communities, cities can make sure no group is excluded. In an increasingly urbanizing world, reducing violence in urban areas will become even more important in the quest for global peace and security. Building strong cities and addressing income inequality requires clusters of growing, healthy small businesses and capital markets that are willing to finance such growth and see significant economic and societal benefits in doing so. The Inner City Capital Connections (ICCC), an 11-year-old initiative now working in nine cities throughout the United States, including Boston and Worcester helps develop more equitable cities through a no-cost 40-hour program that teaches strategy, sales and marketing, finance and talent management to local entrepreneurs. During ICCC's first 10 years, more than 1,100 companies have participated. Collectively, they have received more than US $1.3 billion in capital and have created more than 11,000 good-paying jobs.[61] The initiative also indirectly reduces local violence and crime due to its relevance to the needs of inner city companies, 72% of which are minority-owned.

SDG 17: Partnerships for the Goals; Local governments are in the ideal position to encourage and facilitate partnerships among public bodies, the private sector and civil society in communities. Bringing these diverse groups together can be a difficult task, particularly when they have been working in isolation for so long. By working in concert with various actors, local leaders can implement effective public policies, promote the financing and delivery of sustainable infrastructure, goods, and services, support inclusiveness and enhance sound multi-level governance.[62] While New York City is learning from Copenhagen's experience with cloudburst management, Copenhagen is drawing on New York City's experience with coastal flooding. For example, New York City's Cloudburst Resilience Planning Study is based on Copenhagen's approach, seeking to use a combination of green and traditional infrastructure to manage extreme rain events. This approach brings added benefits of CO_2 sequestration, aesthetic improvements, and increased biodiversity. With full implementation of the Copenhagen cloudburst project, the avoided social and environmental costs are estimated at US $290 million in Copenhagen and US $603 million in NYC.[63]

5.4 SHARED VALUE OPPORTUNITIES

Urbanization will provide opportunities for business around the globe, but it will be most acutely felt as developing countries transition from "agri-centered" economies to product and service economies.[64] Putting pressure on quality living environments and employment, this urban influx requires a shared value approach that necessitates collaboration between business and government. Societies everywhere are facing significant social, environmental and economic development challenges. City governments and local NGOs lack sufficient resources and capabilities themselves to fully meet these challenges alone. It is business that can create wealth and prosperity.

URBAN INFLUX REQUIRES A SHARED VALUE APPROACH THAT NECESSITATES COLLABORATION BETWEEN BUSINESS AND GOVERNMENT.

Yet, recent financial crises around the world have raised many concerns about the current business system. Businesses and local governments are acknowledging that staying competitive and achieving sustainable development are going to be the major challenges, and realize they must work together to operate successfully. By continuing to leverage cross-stakeholder collaboration and refine strategic focus, businesses and governments are creating shared value.[65]

To achieve shared value within the cities landscape, businesses must also focus on important unmet needs where the organization can deliver unique results. Companies need to deliver an integrated set of activities to create value for cities and their residents, not just giving or making money. Michael Porter and Mark Kramer assert that while corporate philanthropy and corporate social responsibility programs have grown, the legitimacy of business has fallen. They therefore propose that businesses within cities can work toward their shared value goals by:[66]

- Selecting the best partners and helping improve their performance, integration and collaboration across entities and stakeholders.
- Finding leverage points that drive systems improvement, such as common measures of success.
- Advancing the state of knowledge and practice in the field.
- Making clear trade-offs, and choosing what not to do.

A business cannot thrive if it is not a part of a functioning ecosystem. Thus, shared value strategies, with the purpose to be financially successful while also enhancing communities, have the strength to drive the achievement of SDG 11. This goal encompasses every aspect of creating an ideal living and working environment. It promotes building strong communities, which provides a wide range of opportunities for business growth. It is essential to ensure that urban spaces are conducive to a better quality of life and reduce the harmful impact. Poverty is often concentrated in cities, and the rapid pace of urbanization is placing strain on integral systems such as water supply and sewage disposal. Businesses will only thrive in cities if the cities are adequately sustaining people's basic needs, and cities can only prosper of they are host to a robust business community.

Let's look at how city residents' access to water can affect urban economies and provide insight into the concept of shared value. It is undeniable that improved water efficiency promotes commercial viability and has large-scale social impact. Therefore, it is in the best interest of businesses and governments to create and sustain a well-functioning water system. In developing countries this can be particularly challenging. Water and Sanitation for the Urban Poor (WSUP) is an organization bringing together the private sector, research organizations and NGOs in a unique partnership focused on solutions to the global water challenge, and in particular the challenges faced in developing nations.[67] WSUP's aim is to bridge the capacity gap by supporting local institutions and private enterprises to provide sustainable water services. The company works closely with water utilities to provide a utility-managed water supply to people living in low-income areas. Water utilities in the developing world are typically mandated to serve the entire city - including these low-income areas - but may be overwhelmed by the pace of change and the scale of the task. WSUP develops business models that enable the private sector, especially entrepreneurs, to play a stronger role in water and sanitation (See Case 30).

CASE NO.

WATER & SANITATION FOR THE URBAN POOR (WSUP)

"Non-Revenue Water" (NRW) Reduction
Creates Financial Viability and more
Resilient Communities

Case applied in: Global
Headquarters located in: England
www.wsup.com

IMPACT SDGs

SDG 6
Clean Water & Sanitation
Improved access to water and sanitation services for 15 million people; unlocked an additional US $256 million investment since 2012.

SDG 8
Decent Work and Economic Growth
Redirected funds to assist low-income areas that were previously being lost due to NRW.

SDG 11
Sustainable Cities & Communities
Worked with municipal governments and utilities in 22 cities and major towns across Africa and Asia to improve services to low-income customers.

SDG 17
Partnerships for the Goals
Partnership-building approach with utilities has enabled these organisations to become much stronger institutions and more capable of addressing some of the negative impacts of urbanization.

WE ARE DETERMINED TO FIND NEW WAYS TO FINANCE AND DELIVER AFFORDABLE, **SAFE WATER AND SANITATION TO TENS OF MILLIONS OF PEOPLE.**
NEIL JEFFERY CEO WSUP

Shared value has been applied through WSUP's programs to address the specific issue of inadequate water supply for the world's rapidly expanding low-income urban population. One of the areas where WSUP has focused on is WSUP focused on "Non Revenue Water" (NRW) which is the amount of water a utility produces for which it receives no revenue, either because of physical losses through leaking pipes or commercial losses like unpaid bills and illegal connections. Lowering the levels of NRW can be very beneficial, as water loss is often more than 50%, creating massive operational inefficiencies and a needless waste of resources. Reducing that figure by just 10% generates substantial additional revenue for the utility that can be channeled into serving low-income areas. In 14 cities and major towns, a number of urban utilities have made material gains in NRW reduction as a result of ongoing partnerships with WSUP. This has led to huge decreases in water loss for customers and generated substantial revenues for utilities to invest in low-income areas (SDG 8). In 2008, WSUP signed a professional-services agreement with JIRAMA, the national water utility in Madagascar, relating to service improvements in the capital city Antananarivo. WSUP agreed to provide capacity-building assis-

tance, with a particular focus on reduced NRW, in return for a commitment to improve service delivery to the city's low-income areas (SDG 11).

WSUP brings together the private sector, research organizations and NGOs in a unique partnership focused on a specific and growing aspect of the global water challenge (SDG 17). The organization works closely with water utilities and starts with a guiding principle that appeals to the utility's bottom line: "people living in low-income areas are customers, too, and in most cases they can afford to pay for a utility-managed water supply." WSUP addresses the misconception that it does not make commercial sense for a utility to serve low-income areas. Low-income residents often already pay high prices for their water to an unregulated informal supplier; in many cases they pay more than the residents of a wealthier area with a piped utility supply. Improved water supply to low-income communities is a mutually beneficial endeavor, as low-income consumers benefit from a cheaper, more reliable utility supply and the utility generates additional revenue from all these new customers (SDG 6). This additional revenue can help to improve services to everyone in the city.

CHALLENGE

To develop services generating revenue while reaching the most vulnerable urban residents; and to advise regulators on how to create an environment that enables businesses to succeed.

OPPORTUNITIES FOR SCALE

WSUP aims to achieve scale through, firstly, policy change and increased investment in the public sector; and secondly, radically increased capacity from service providers to deliver effectively. Market thinking and institutional change are often viewed as alternative solutions; but WSUP believes that they are both essential activities.

Sources and further information

- http://wsupjobs.co.uk/Introduction.aspx
- http://sharedvalue.org/groups/shared-value-urban-water-supply-harnessing-improved-water-efficiency-extend-services-slum
- https://www.wsup.com/approach/
- https://www.wsup.com/impact/

" IN 14 CITIES AND MAJOR TOWNS, A NUMBER OF URBAN UTILITIES HAVE MADE MATERIAL GAINS IN NON REVENUE WATER REDUCTION AS A RESULT OF ONGOING PARTNERSHIPS WITH WSUP."

AkzoNobel's "Human Cities" initiative is another expression of a company's purpose to "create everyday essentials to make people's lives more livable and inspiring."[68] By combining its sense of care with people and products, leadership in innovation, and safety and sustainability, the company is creating shared value by helping cities to meet the many challenges they face, while still earning a profit. AkzoNobel uses its products and expertise to help cities deliver a stronger sense of community purpose, pride and happiness. Since the launch of Human Cities in 2014, many successful projects have been completed, bringing "essential ingredients, essential protection and essential color into the lives of people across the world." For example, historic landmarks such as Burkill Hall in Singapore and the Rijksmuseum in Amsterdam have been renovated and restored. During 2016, the company carried out 62 additional Human Cities projects benefitting over 5.2 million.

To understand where they can have the biggest potential impact throughout the value chain, AkzoNobel conducted a three-dimensional profit and loss (3D P&L) assessment across all business activities (See figure 33). By monetizing externalities and tracking data, the company is able to identify what generates the most substantial outcome in terms of minimizing negative impact and scaling up positive impact. It also helps companies to assess how investment decisions can contribute to generating more value in all three dimensions. Companies and communities both focus on areas that contribute to the achievement of Global Goal 11 within the cities. They are mak-

ing a commitment to the Shared Value approach that is aimed at strengthening urban citizens' and employees' progress toward achieving sustainable development. Globally, there is a need for around US \$5 to \$7 trillion annually to finance investments into sustainable infrastructure, transform production and consumption patterns, and optimize the sustainability of buildings, energy, water and sanitation systems in cities.[69] Although this is a large expenditure, there is ample business and economic opportunity regarding sustainable development in cities today. For businesses addressing urban challenges and responding to the SDGs, the largest opportunities have a potential value of US \$3.7 trillion.[70]

Another shared value initiative worth noting is a shopping mall that is driven by the circular economy and dedicated exclusively to selling repaired and up-cycled goods. Located in the Swedish city of Eskilstuna, 100 kilometers west of Stockholm, the mall hosts 14 shops, a restaurant, an exhibition area, conference facilities and even a training college for studying recycling.[71] The mall opened in 2015 and responds to the call made in the report Towards the *Circular Economy* by the World Economic Forum and the Ellen MacArthur Foundation which states that circularity could be a "tangible driver of industrial innovations and value creation" in tomorrow's economy. The report articulates that circular business models will gain a competitive edge in the years to come because they "create more value from each unit of resource than the traditional linear take-make-dispose model."[72]

Figure 33 **AkzoNobel 3D P&L assessment**[73]

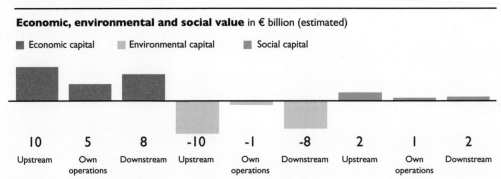

3d P&L assessment

Economic, environmental and social value in € billion (estimated)

■ Economic capital   ■ Environmental capital   ■ Social capital

| 10 | 5 | 8 | -10 | -1 | -8 | 2 | 1 | 2 |
| Upstream | Own operations | Downstream | Upstream | Own operations | Downstream | Upstream | Own operations | Downstream |

5.5 CAPITAL CONNECTIONS AND OPPORTUNITIES

The main challenges cities face include: inadequate housing, pollution, congestion, waste and energy use, and emissions. By 2025, up to 440 million urban households could be living in sub-standard housing.[74] Already, over 5.5 million premature deaths a year are attributable to household and outdoor air pollution.[75] Congestion is a costly urban problem as well, leading to 1.25 million deaths globally in 2013.[76] In cities, 10% to 15% of building material is wasted during construction, and cities account for 70% of global energy use and energy-related GHG emissions.[77]

To help solve some of these overarching challenges, the Business and Sustainable Development Commission (BSDC) cites 16 shared value opportunities in three categories to reach the US $3.7 trillion. The three categories that the BSDC identifies are the following:

Affordable housing: Providing affordable housing is a US $650 to $1,080 billion business potential within cities. Replacing today's inadequate housing and building the additional units needed by 2025 would take US $9 trillion to $11 trillion in construction spending alone. With land development added to that, the total cost could be US $16 trillion. Yet there is a wide gap of US $650 billion between income available for housing and the market price for housing.[78] Filling this gap requires innovations that will unlock new land and better use of space for development by cities offering shared value opportunities such as "density bonuses" to developers: in return for the right to build more units – substantially raising the value of the property – developers provide the city with land for affordable housing or finished units. In this way, the city captures the value and developers make money.

Energy efficiency: Implementing adequate and efficient energy solutions in urban buildings is a US $555 to $770 billion opportunity. The building sector accounts for around one-third of the total final energy consumption across the world and more than half of electricity demand.[79] Cities' energy demand could be minimized by taking such measures as retrofitting existing buildings with more efficient heating and cooling technology, and switching to more efficient lighting and other electrical appliances. Harnessing energy efficiency offers many opportunities to help rapidly growing cities achieve energy security, energy savings, and reduce costs and emissions.

Electric and hybrid vehicles: This clean transport solution represents a US $310 to 320 billion urban market. It is predicted that annual sales of battery-powered electric vehicles and hybrids will grow from about 2.3 million units in 2014 to 11.5 million by 2022, or 11% of the global market.[80] The total global passenger vehicle fleet is expected to turn over completely by 2030, presenting an opportunity for a huge increase in sales of electric vehicles and plug-in hybrid vehicles.[81] Electric and hybrid vehicles could comprise an estimated 62% of new light-duty vehicle sales in 2030, as battery costs continue to fall and investments in charging infrastructure grow.

Unexpected expenditures from storms, flooding, snow removal and drought can lead to major disruptions in business operations and city budgets.[82] But through collaboration, cities around the world have significant opportunities in the next five to ten years to boost resource productivity and reduce GHG emissions through economically attractive investments in the buildings, transport and waste sectors. However, without broader structural shifts in urban design and transport systems, the benefits of those measures would quickly be overwhelmed by the impacts of sustained economic and population expansion under business-as-usual patterns.

Innovative financing mechanisms, such as green bonds, can assist in managing the implementation and sustaining function of citywide climate mitigation measures. Utilizing this type of financial structure would allow for shared value as a potential source of finance for cities in developing countries looking to secure investment in low-carbon, climate-resilient infrastructure to meet the water, energy, housing and transportation needs of their expanding urban populations.

Since 2007, US $131 billion in green bonds have been sold to institutional and retail investors attracted by their link to green projects, goods and services. The last few years has seen an exponential increase in the value of annual bonds issued, from US $3.2 billion in 2012 to $75 billion in 2016. Most finance that flows to developing country city-based projects does so indirectly, with 94% from green bonds issued by Development Finance Institutions such as the World Bank and Asian Development Bank.[83] As of November 2016, the US $137 million bond from Johannesburg in South Africa is the only municipal green bond issued by a developing country city and has seen numerous shared value benefits. It helps the city in diversifying its funding instrument portfolio

and attracting new types of investors, providing potential a market for future issuances, and filling the gaps in needed development finance for city projects focused on climate change mitigation and adaptation. Activities targeted include reducing unaccounted for water (e.g. through smart meters), separation at source of waste, promotion of water harvesting and re-use, reducing congestions on public roads through better public transport, and energy conservation measures in low-income areas such as Solar water heaters, Solar PVs and insulated ceilings.

Shared value for cities is created when business and capital join the efforts of cities to achieve their goals. And by incorporating societal and environmental benefits, shared value is created for our planet and people. The economic gains are integral to this model, and with the multi-faceted opportunities that are paired with the challenges cities face, the gains are plentiful.

5.6 DOMAINS OF IMPACT

The three domains of SDG impact that we will explore in this chapter are: 1) Smart Cities; 2) Design; and 3) Transportation and Mobility. Through these three domains, cities can address the SDGs both from government and business standpoints. The first domain refers to the utilization of modern technologies to operate more effectively and efficiently, creating smarter cities. The second relates to the way cities are designed, from vertical architecture to green infrastructure, and the third encompasses how transport and mobility implementation lays the groundwork for urban living and business development.

1. SMART CITIES: THE DIGITAL SOLUTIONS

Smart cities use sensors, data collection, the Internet of Things, Smart grids and other technologies to make urban areas more efficient, more secure, and improve urban infrastructures while minimizing costs. Machine learning and Artificial Intelligence techniques are used to mine the vast amount of collected data to identify the sources of issues such as lead contaminated water or food poisoning. Drone technologies, such as hyper-spectral imaging, are used to identify important data that can be especially valuable in crisis situations. Mobile phones capture how people are moving around the city, which also offers beneficial information when determining market trends and consumer preferences.

Technology can advance urban areas by fostering innovation in a variety of industries, which improves the quality of life for citizens. Using smart systems that track data not only assists local governments in decision making, it also informs business trends. Sensors, data collection and storage enable real time observations of complex systems. Sensor networks employ a large number of sensors that can collaboratively collect and process data, and measure a wide range of information including temperature, sound, vibration, pressure, water quality, motion, pollutants, and many other things across different industries.[84]

Creating a system to effectively use the data generated by these sensors requires underlying systems that integrate computation, networking and physical processes. This includes sensor networks, monitoring/collecting equipment, data analytics – and humans. Many stakeholders – citizens, city authorities, government management, infrastructure and service delivery, local enterprises, and technology providers – must collaborate to make the smart city successful.

Business initiatives are contributing to the success of smart cities by developing technological operations, such as OpenTripPlanner, for example, which is an open source platform used to analyze urban transport networks. It was developed by a group of international development partners, private sector companies and academics, and it has already been used in places such as Lima, Nairobi and Buenos Aires. It allows cities to analyze and study how proposed changes affect how people access essential services.

> SIEMENS IDENTIFIED 30 MARKET-READY LOW-CARBON TECHNOLOGIES FOR 30 OF THE WORLD'S MEGACITIES, CREATING MORE THAN 2 MILLION JOBS AND AVOIDING 3 BILLION TONS OF CUMULATIVE GHG EMISSIONS AND 3 MILLION TONS OF LOCAL AIR POLLUTION BETWEEN 2014 AND 2025, WITH AN INVESTMENT VALUE OF US $2.5 TRILLION.[85]
>
> NEW CLIMATE ECONOMY

The rapid and pervasive development of digital technologies, along with an understanding of circular economy principles, will drastically change life for the average urban citizen much sooner than we think. The circular economy is a concept by which materials and products are utilized at their highest possible value at all times. Finite materials are not thrown into landfills and valuable assets such as cars, office space, and sporting equipment are not left idle. The rise of the Internet of Things (IoT) will help this to become a reality. Sensors and smart phones will be able to track materials and assets, letting people know when they are not being used, about to break, or where they are. This will unlock huge markets, create new business models, and will drastically change the way people and cities function. The digital circular city will not only save resources but will change citizens' experiences for the better.[86]

THE CIRCULAR ECONOMY IS A CONCEPT BY WHICH MATERIALS AND PRODUCTS ARE UTILIZED AT THEIR HIGHEST POSSIBLE VALUE AT ALL TIMES.

Imagine, in the not so distant future, when walking out the door of your home, smart thermostats will trigger the indoor heating to lower the temperature while you are away during the day, saving energy and money. Smart technologies could also make getting to work a far less stressful experience. Today the average city dweller spends 15% of driving time in congestion and 20% looking for a parking space.[87] In a digital-enabled city, real time traffic data streams, car sharing schemes and mobile parking apps will streamline the experience, decreasing road traffic, emissions, and time wasted. Transport apps use real time traffic and public transport data to offer commuters the quickest route to their destination by bike, train, self-driving car or bus. At bus stops, instead of waiting idly, you can do your food shopping by scanning the items shown on the poster at the bus shelter with your mobile phone, and have your food delivered to

your home after work. In some cities, like Seoul, these applications are already emerging.

As you walk into your workplace, you are likely to also experience more of what smart cities can offer. You may have a customized workspace based on who you're meeting with and your personal preferences. This is already the case in many buildings designed by OVG Real Estate. They have implemented an app for people to tailor the lighting and temperature in their workplaces using their smartphones (See Case 31). Then when you leave work at the end of the day, the office space around you could be converted into a social/networking event space. Developers will have planned out the space from its inception so that it is flexible enough to accommodate a variety of activities, not just desk-work, maximizing the value of urban space. Whole buildings could be designed as "resource banks" using solar panels to generate enough energy to supply the building as well as excess for the community. Tracking technologies and material passports could easily record exactly what materials were used to construct the building. All the assets in your office building could be effectively reused when the building is decommissioned or refurbished, saving time, money and resources.

SMART CITIES PROVIDE THE FOUNDATION TO CONSERVE RESOURCES, CREATE A HEALTHIER CITY-LIVING ENVIRONMENT, AND MAKE OUR DAILY LIVES MORE CONVENIENT AND EFFICIENT.

Smart cities provide the foundation to conserve resources, create a healthier city-living environment, and make our daily lives more convenient and efficient. Smart Cities also collect data, which provides information to city leaders in time to make appropriate decisions. Technological solutions have a variety of benefits, such as allowing leaders to learn about water and air contamination quickly, conserving energy with automated lights, controlling parking and traffic more effectively, and the list goes on.

> ## THE GLOBAL SMART CITIES MARKET COULD GROW IN JUST A COUPLE YEARS' TIME TO US $1.6 TRILLION BY 2020, COMPARED WITH US $1 TRILLION TODAY.[88]
>
> BANK OF AMERICA MERRILL LYNCH REPORT MARCH 2017. BIZTECH

Barcelona is an example of a smart city with smart leadership. Xavier Trias, Mayor of Barcelona from 2011 to 2015, ran on a platform of technological innovation in city services that harnessed technology to transform the city into a model of data-driven, sensing, smart urban systems. The forward-looking Mayor formed a new team, Smart City Barcelona, tasked with integrating existing projects and identifying new opportunities to enhance services for all of the city's people and businesses. Smart City Barcelona identified 12 areas for innovations that would simultaneously increase efficiencies and reduce costs. These areas included transportation, water, energy, waste, and open government, initiating 22 programs and encompassing 83 distinct projects across urban systems.[89] Examples of some of the smart systems include: solar paneled, USB enabled interactive bus shelters; 400 bike sharing stations; automated waste collection; and smart – motion activated - lighting which also gathers environmental information about temperature, pollution and noise.[90] These improvements have already saved the city money and reduced the consumption of valuable energy and water. Barcelona estimates that its smart systems have saved about US $58 million on water, increased parking revenues by US $50

million per year, and generated 47,000 new jobs. Through smart lighting, the city reports saving an addition US $37 million annually.[91] Barcelona is also host to the annual Smart City Expo World Congress where thousands of people from government, academic, and private organizations - large and small – come together to find partners, inspire, and be inspired about smart city opportunities.[92]

The rise of Smart Cities is inevitable as our technology facilitates the implementation of so many applications. But cyber-security and ethical guidance must rise alongside at the same pace. There has been a major shift in the way we handle, generate, store, process and leverage data. In fact, there is growing evidence that this data revolution, or big data, has fundamental ties to development.[93] Data is vital for designing efficient and effective development policy recommendations, supporting their implementation and evaluating the results in cities. All of this data collection can prove beneficial to human beings by saving us time, hassle, and wasted resources. But by its very nature, it infringes on our privacy and holds the risk of being misused. Data is emerging as a significant economic force across the globe, as the exchange of information becomes more critical to sustained global positioning across every sector, from economy to healthcare to government. Today, the global exchange of data, information, and digital flows generates more economic value than the global goods trade.[94] Although the access to data has some threatening elements, when used for good it has unprecedented potential to move the world toward a sustainable future.

As business facilitates the growth of smart cities, the collected data must be used wisely. Looking to the SDGs for guidance, a clear path can be set for technological advancement. Smart cities will undoubtedly accelerate the Global Goals, most notably with resource conservation and improved services to people. And while the world converts to smart city applications, the business opportunities are plentiful.

31

CASE NO. **OVG REAL ESTATE**

HQ Unilever – Sustainability the Dutch way

Case applied in: USA
Headquarters located in: The Netherlands
www.ovgrealestate.com

IMPACT SDGS

SDG 3

Good Health and Well Being

The new US Unilever HQ is designed to meet the strict guidelines of "LEED platinum" and "WELL New & Existing Building" certification criteria, to optimize a healthy work environment.

SDG 7

Clean Water and Sanitation

Design energy efficient buildings using mostly solar power and thermal storage (clean energy). Invests in renewable energy infrastructure and lean energy technology.

SDG 8

Decent Work and Economic Growth

Smart buildings attract employees, make the workplace more comfortable and enjoyable, and reduce operational costs and energy consumption substantially.

SDG 12

Responsible Consumption and Production

Rescues 'greywater' where possible and uses rainwater for toilets. The Unilever building reduces water demand via low flow plumbing, and diverts 75% of construction waste from landfill.

I AM PARTICULARLY LOOKING FORWARD TO SETTING A NEW BENCHMARK FOR SUSTAINABLE AND SMART BUILDING **WITH THE FOCUS ON A HEALTHY WORK ENVIRONMENT.**

COEN VAN OOSTROM, FOUNDER & CEO OVG

OVG takes a lead within the Netherlands in improving global resource efficiency in consumption and production, while decoupling their growth from environmental degradation. When reconstructing the Unilever headquarters in the US, OVG adhered to, and exceeded, the strict certification requirements of the Leadership in Energy and Environmental Design (LEED), and the International WELL Building Certification which is a framework for creating buildings that improve health and well-being for employees and visitors.

OVG Real Estate and Normandy Real Estate Partners created a joint venture to redevelop and expand Unilever's headquarters in the US. The large project involving a 300,000 sq.ft. corporate campus will be a sustainable retrofit of existing buildings. There will also be an addition of a central atrium resulting in a smart, energy efficient and highly advanced corporate facility. The renovated headquarters will deliver many sustainable benefits including reduced CO_2 emissions, reduced energy consumption, reduced water demand, and reduced landfill waste (SDG 12). Kees Kruythoff, President of Unilever North America, said: "This redevelopment is very much about improving the well-being of our people by providing them a healthy and productive work environment (SDG 3), while also reducing our environmental impact and helping increase the growth of our business."

Employees will be able to adjust their work environments, using a smartphone application, to modify the light level of their workspace, and find colleagues or an optimal workplace (SDG 8). The data is subsequently stored to promote the sensible use of energy, which at the same time significantly reduces costs. Through an "agile working" approach, OVG uses technology to allow an extra 600 people to comfortably and efficiently work at the Unilever headquarters, making it possible for 1,600 employees to use one building instead of two. In addition to the user application, other new technical solutions include an IP backbone, employee localization, integrated IoT systems in lighting, a grid of 3000 sensors (15,000 data points), integration of sensor data with the building management systems data, and integrated data analytics. The technologies are all centered around the common goal to support an unprecedented and optimally agile workplace at lower operational costs. Using this grid of sensors, it is possible to accurately monitor in real-time how the building is being used. The data is presented via a "heatmap-dashboard" on a smart device. This offers various possibilities for greater efficiencies like remote visibility on energy consumption in order to predict maintenance and inefficient energy consumption, focused cleaning of the property based on actual use, closing off office space in predicted times of low occupancy, and insight into spare building capacity to determine whether more employees can comfortably use the building. This results in lower operational costs and a decrease of the projected energy consumption by 43.8% (SDG 7).

CHALLENGE

To address and mitigate the negative impacts of buildings and the real estate industry on the environment and people's health, while improving energy performance.

OPPORTUNITIES FOR SCALE

OVG's dedication to reducing operational costs for building occupants ensures the attractiveness of investing in the reconstruction of older buildings to incorporate modern, sustainable design and technology. OVG's building endeavors are not limited to existing office buildings. Today, OVG is also focused on applying their know-how and innovative approach to new buildings, but as a consequence of smart technology, these new builds can have a smaller footprint, and occupants will need less volume than was needed before.

Sources and further information

- LEED report of Unilever HQ
- WELL report of Unilever HQ
- OVG Press Release: Sept. 14, 2016
- http://ovgrealestate.com/cases/unilever-na-headquarters

" OVG USES TECHNOLOGIES THAT ARE ALL CENTERED AROUND THE COMMON GOAL TO SUPPORT AN UNPRECEDENTED AND OPTIMALLY AGILE WORKPLACE AT LOWER OPERATIONAL COSTS."

2. REDESIGN: VERTICAL CITIES AND GREEN CITIES

As the population increases, so does the need for living space. Increasing the number of homes and neighborhoods often results in the destruction of forests and other habitats. This reduces natural resources, endangers wildlife, and threatens to disrupt ecosystems. Redesigning cities and rethinking practices to become more sustainable are becoming important themes in cities around the world.

VERTICAL CITIES

People are starting to look to the vertical city concept as a solution to house more people in a sustainable manner.[95] A vertical city is an entire human habitat contained in one or more massive skyscrapers. These proposed structures, which can be up to 400 floors, and could also be several buildings that are interconnected, contain all the components of a city, from housing and hospitals to universities and municipal departments. Advocates claim vertical cities will save energy, support a growing population, and preserve land for food production, nature, and recreation.[96]

In a vertical city, people would live, work, and go to school in a contained area. These tall structures would have mixed uses to meet essential needs for housing, employment, education, recreation, health care, and other services, optimizing the efficiency gains of centralized labor and consumption markets by doing away with long wasteful and polluting commutes between home and work. Specifically, vertical cities would "maximize density and compactness for optimum efficiency in clustered ultra-tall towers, while limiting the projected footprint to a 15-minute walk from one end to the other."[97]

With large-scale urbanization underway, government leaders, city planners, private consultants and businesses are pushing to meet the demands of growing cities. The vertical cities of tomorrow that will be required for high density areas are already being built. One building, 432 Park Avenue in New York City, was designed by Rafael Vinoly and rises to 1,396 feet. Another New York building 303–305 East 44th Street, designed by Eran Chen

at ODA Architecture, is just 47 feet wide and 600 feet tall. One more, 111 West 57th Street, is 1,428 feet tall. Designed by SHoP Architects, it is slim with a width to height ratio of 1 to 24.

According to the Council on Tall Building and Urban Habitats (CTBUH), we are actually entering a "megatall" era, as buildings taller than 1,969 feet are set to double by 2020. While only three megatall structures exist at present, in Dubai, Shanghai, and Mecca, three more will be completed in the coming years in Wuhan, Kuala Lumpur and Jeddah. In fact, the Jeddah Tower will be the tallest in the world, standing at an incredible 0.62 miles tall.

> A VERTICAL CITY IS AN ARRANGEMENT OF INTERCONNECTED MEGA TOWERS THAT ARE ENVIRONMENTALLY FRIENDLY, SELF-SUSTAINING AND CAPABLE OF PROVIDING A DIGNIFIED LIFE FOR 100s-OF-THOUSANDS OF PEOPLE.
>
> VERTICALCITY.ORG

Redesigning buildings to accommodate growing urban populations must include being able to withstand impacts such as earthquakes and fire. Modern techniques are changing the building process. For example, modular construction and pre-assembly strategies could significantly reduce both raw material use and construction time. The Broad Group in China recently built a 30-storey, earthquake-resistant hotel in only 15 days through modular construction – a process that typically takes two years – and it has managed in some cases to use 96% recycled steel.[98] Pre-manufacturing the components in a factory allows build-

Figure 34 **World's 10 Most Sustainable Cities**

1. **Frankfurt**
2. **London**
3. **Copenhagen**
4. **Amsterdam**
5. **Rotterdam**
6. **Berlin**
7. **Seoul**
8. **Hong Kong**
9. **Madrid**
10. **Singapore**

ers to optimize resource use during construction, achieving efficiencies similar to a manufacturing facility. Innovative approaches to construction that also include circular economy models contribute to providing the necessary safety while also delivering a sustainable solution.

The insulation company ROCKWOOL understands that safety and sustainability are paramount. The company takes a practical approach to linking the SDGs to its business purpose by connecting scientific research, business and civil society with its innovative construction design. They believe that investing in the redesign of healthy and safe buildings should be not be viewed as a cost, but as a contributor to primary processes of daily working life. While solving societal issues and bringing value to customers through fire safety and acoustic enhancement measures, the company thinks of its positive impacts in terms of monetizing shared value (See Case 32).

32 CASE NO. ROCKWOOL BENELUX

Building for Efficiency
Insulation as a driver for change: answering societal challenges by unlocking the potential of insulation

Case applied in: The Netherlands
Headquarters located in: Denmark
www.rockwool.com

IMPACT SDGs

SDG 3
Good Health and Well-being
Reduce indoor noise, enhance indoor climate quality, and fire safety for a healthy environment.

SDG 9
Industry, Innovation & Infrastructure
Develop durable and resilient infrastructure through resilient insulation.

SDG 11
Sustainable Cities and Communities
Prevent societal and governmental costs of over €17.4 million and business costs of 257.2 million while decreasing fire related deaths and injuries by 12%; Increase workers' productivity by providing first-rate acoustic insulation.

SDG 12
Responsible Consumption and Production
Increase circular production practices and reduce landfill waste by 85% by 2030.

SDG 17
Partnerships for the Goals
Partner with entire value chain to promote SDG legislation.

IF YOU CAN'T DEFINE YOUR POSITIVE IMPACT, THEN WHAT IS THE PURPOSE OF YOUR BUSINESS? **ROCKWOOL BELIEVES INSULATION CAN BE MORE THAN JUST ENERGY EFFICIENCY**; WE UNLOCK ITS POTENTIAL TO ENRICH SOCIETY.
HANNIE STAPPERS, DIRECTOR OF PUBLIC AFFAIRS ROCKWOOL

Taking a shared value and circular economy perspective has helped ROCKWOOL become an even stronger, more commercially successful business. The company incorporates this thinking into its production by recycling waste materials, using sustainable resources, and limiting its use of chemicals (SDG 12). As fire safety is one of the company's major differentiators, ROCKWOOL creates its insulation products by melting rock that does not need flame retardants - as this raw material does not burn - offering fire safety and contributing to a resilient society (SDG 9). Their selective insulation properties provide society with solutions for buildings that sustain for more than 50 years and can be recycled indefinitely.

The company focuses on the built environment (dwellings and public access buildings such as schools and hospitals) (SDG 11). Constructing buildings to be more fire-resistant and withstand disasters not only makes them more resilient, but enhances safety as well (SDG 3). In 2020, newly built houses will consist of over 50% (by volume) insulation material compared to 30% now. With this trend, the use of fire safe materials will become even more important. From a longevity standpoint, the closed-loop recycling quality of rock generates a product with a long life performance.

ROCKWOOL is also prompting extensive building renovation programs to respond to climate impacts and energy efficiency concerns. They reduced CO_2 from factories by 1.7% in 2016 with a target of 20% by 2030. In 2020, newly built houses will consist of over 50% (by volume) insulation material compared to 30% now. With this trend, the use of fire safe materials will become even more important.

Although the indirect costs of fire hazards are not completely monetized – including unemployment pay, business owners' expenses, psychological problems, etc. – ROCKWOOL cites an estimated 5 to 50 times cost increase from fire-related events. To monetize and reduce these external costs, ROCKWOOL looked at its market share and application areas and applied the World Health Organization's measurement of Disability Adapted Life Years (DALY). This metric helps in accounting costs to society, business and government. adding up to 17,4 million EUR prevented societal (governmental cost) per year. Furthermore, with the input of the association of insurers and large financial institutions, the company monetized their impact on business: yearly €90 million of prevented business costs (lower insurance premium and prevention of business disruption) and another €167 million of prevented business costs by increasing productivity in offices and schools.

CHALLENGE

To create value in the built environment through shaping a circular economy, enhancing resource efficiency, and nurturing the safety, health and well-being of society.

OPPORTUNITIES FOR SCALE

ROCKWOOL applies life cycle costing to calculate the total costs of ownership by adding the broader benefits from a different perspective on the business case, e.g. delivering business continuity by protecting human and business capital because of fire safe insulation, or contributing to a higher productivity because of acoustical insulation. By monetizing the social impact, they mobilized their value chain to partner up to urge governments to consider SDG impact areas when reviewing legislation. (SDG 17). The company also introduced a social impact tool, called AQSI, to Assess and Qualify the Social Impact of Buildings.

Sources and further information

- https://www.youtube.com/watch?v=wiuDnEqdJo4
- http://csr.rockwool.nl/docs/080716_MVO_EN_2015_spread.pdf
- http://www.who.int/quantifying_ehimpacts/about/en/
- https://www.rockwoolgroup.com/about-us/sustainability/
- http://newspublicator.com/e10/parker/pm/79413857d09dce43/mc1670594/download/dfe3e2_Sociale_impact_in_NL_cijfers_ROCKWOOL_bijdrage.pdf
- http://www.aqsi.eu/
- http://newspublicator.com/e10/parker/pm/79413857d09dce43/mc1670594/download/d7dbf8_23845_RW_POSTER_MANIFEST_2_1_.pdf

" ROCKWOOL IS PROMPTING EXTENSIVE BUILDING RENOVATION PROGRAMS TO RESPOND TO CLIMATE IMPACTS AND ENERGY EFFICIENCY CONCERNS. "

GREEN CITIES

Green Cities are emerging around the world as cities are helping their nations achieve their commitments to the Paris Agreement and the SDGs. Initiatives to encourage energy and fuel alternatives, investments in more parks and gardens, and recycling and waste management measures are accelerating. Frankfurt is the leading sustainable city with its many initiatives. Among these are the city's innovative green buildings and attention to preserving the 52% of the urban area that is green space marked as parks and woodlands.

To encourage energy and fuel alternatives, many cities are actively incentivizing or even mandating the implementation of solar panels on newly built structures. Solar energy benefits the city and the environment at large by decentralizing energy production and decreasing or eliminating the need for fossil fuels. Solar energy is becoming more widespread, according to a report by Zion Market Research,[99] and the solar panel market will nearly double in the next 5 years from US $30.8 billion in 2016 to $57.5 billion by 2022.

Nurturing the green areas in a city can be difficult to do as the city's population and infrastructure grows. Rooftop gardens are gaining popularity as designers, legislatures and citizens recognize the advantages they offer, including:

- regulating temperatures, working as heat insulators by keeping houses cool in the summer and warm in the winter;
- improving the air quality in cities by soaking up pollutants, which reduce respiratory diseases and can translate to a reduction in health expenditure;
- absorbing up to 80% of the rain, leading to improved capability to avoid potential floods;
- serving as urban vegetable gardens, promoting personal consumption in the community and reducing transport expenses and pollution.

The city of Rotterdam in the Netherlands has prioritized the construction of "green roofs" and already in 2012 achieved 100,000 m² of green roofs. In 2016, Rotterdam extended their mission to create a sensor controlled "smart roof" that has the capacity to buffer seven times the quantity of water that other green roofs offer. Additionally, rooftop farms in Rotterdam and other cities are growing significant food supplies for urban residents. For example, the New York-based company, Gotham Greens Farms LLC, sells more than 20 million heads of lettuce and leafy greens annually to restaurants, food service companies and retailers.

ROOFTOP FARMS IN ROTTERDAM AND OTHER CITIES ARE GROWING SIGNIFICANT FOOD SUPPLIES FOR URBAN RESIDENTS.

Waste management and recycling is another area where municipalities and businesses can work together to create positive impact. For example, San Francisco implemented a strict recycling program and was the first city in the US to ban plastic bags. The city committed in 2002 to zero waste by 2020 and it has taken tremendous political determination, in addition to a willingness by businesses such as restaurants, hotels, and the construction industry to achieve results. Today, San Francisco diverts 80% of its waste from landfills and is well on their way to achieving their goal. The city has also benefitted from partnering with the employee-owned, local waste management company Recology, which has helped by instituting bold moves to strengthen and accelerate the results. For example, Recology offers residents a 20% discount when they have zero waste to be collected on the waste collection days twice a month.

Cities across India suffer from overflows of waste. Urban India generates 72 million tons of garbage every year. In Mumbai, two out of three municipal dumps are shut due to over-capacity. Companies such as GPS (Green Power Systems) Renewables and Attero Recycling are tackling this issue not merely by aiming at mitigating the severity of the problem but by creating positive impact. GPS Renewables operates 25 projects in cities across

India and Bangladesh with another 20 planned in the US, Malaysia and Sri Lanka. Their "BioUrja" (a smart biogas plant) converts organic waste into energy. Founder Mainak Chakraborty says, "this is the first Internet of Things innovation in biogas." Attero Recycling focusses their attention on E-waste which accounts for 1.7 million tons of waste in India and is expected to increase by 21% in three years according to the United Nations. Already equating to 75% of India's total hazardous waste, finding a solution is critical. Attero Recycling is contributing to this solution by building India's largest E-waste recycling company and are planning to build plants in other countries as well, expecting to grow their business 10-fold in the next 3-5 years.[100]

While companies and municipalities are creating practical and effective solutions, they are experiencing hurdles as well. In India, the many business endeavors dealing with the dire waste situation come up against opposing cultural norms and a lack of legislative attention to waste management. In the case of San Francisco, the city is confident that they will reach 90% landfill diversion by continuing their current activities. To achieve the last 10%, however, the city is convinced that they will need state or national laws to require or incentivize more product manufacturers to agree to the program.[101] While the state of California is in favor of pursuing environmental legislation, the federal government of the United States is currently not supporting such legislation.

IT IS UP TO BUSINESS TO TAKE THE LEAD AND EMBRACE SUSTAINABILITY WITHOUT BEING FORCED TO DO SO.

In light of political fluctuations, and taking into consideration the need to do more to protect the environment, it is up to business to take the lead and embrace sustainability without being forced to do so. It is a matter of mindset and global consciousness, as well as a cultural shift. Business and public-private partnerships can and must do more to break through the obstacles and drive the change that is needed.

3. TRANSPORT AND MOBILITY

Of the 17 SDGs, seven of them include Targets that incorporate transport (including both rural and urban infrastructure). Sustainable transport is a key tool in reducing pollution, improving equity, and reducing poverty in cities. While some Targets name transport directly, many of the Targets incorporate transport by recognizing the importance of access in achieving advances in education, healthcare, and other critical needs. The most specific and relevant targets for transport belong to the SDGs shown in figure 35.

SUSTAINABLE TRANSPORT IS A KEY TOOL IN REDUCING POLLUTION, IMPROVING EQUITY, AND REDUCING POVERTY IN CITIES.

The transport sector, which is responsible for one quarter of energy-related GHG emissions worldwide, with its emissions increasing at a faster rate than any other sectors, will need to be included in any effective policy response to climate change in order to keep the global temperature increase below the two-degree Celsius danger level.[102] Specifically to manage transportation issues related to the SDGs, an expert panel appointed by former UN Secretary-General Ban Ki-moon was formed. In its report, titled *Mobilizing Sustainable Transport for Development*,[103] the group determined that the investments needed for transitioning to sustainable transport amount to the current business-as-usual spending but, unlike the current practices, would deliver savings up to US $70 trillion by 2050 and could produce a global gross domestic product increase of US $2.6 trillion.[104] The business case for following the SDGs' transport targets is clear, with the group providing ten recommendations on how governments, businesses and civil society should redirect resources

Figure 35 **SDG Targets relating to transport and mobility**

GOAL 2: ZERO HUNGER TARGETS

2a   Increase investment, including through enhanced international cooperation, in rural infrastructure, agricultural research and extension services, technology development, and plant and livestock gene banks to enhance agricultural productive capacity in developing countries, in particular in least developed countries

GOAL 3: GOOD HEALTH AND WELL-BEING TARGETS

3.6.   By 2030 halve global deaths from road traffic accidents

GOAL 7: AFFORDABLE AND CLEAN ENERGY TARGETS

7.a.   By 2030 enhance international cooperation to facilitate access to clean energy research and technologies, including renewable energy, energy efficiency, and advanced and cleaner fossil fuel technologies, and promote investment in energy infrastructure and clean energy technologies

GOAL 9: INDUSTRY, INNOVATION AND INFRASTRUCTURE TARGETS

9.1.   Develop quality, reliable, sustainable and resilient infrastructure, including regional and transborder infrastructure, to support economic development and human well-being, with a focus on affordable and equitable access for all

GOAL 11: SUSTAINABLE CITIES AND COMMUNITIES TARGETS

11.2. By 2030, provide access to safe, affordable, accessible and sustainable transport systems for all, improving road safety, notably by expanding public transport, with special attention to the needs of those in vulnerable situations, women, children, persons with disabilities and older persons

GOAL 12: RESPONSIBLE CONSUMPTION AND PRODUCTION TARGETS

12.c. Rationalize inefficient fossil fuel subsidies that encourage wasteful consumption by removing market distortions, in accordance with national circumstances, including by restructuring taxation and phasing out those harmful subsidies, where they exist, to reflect their environmental impacts, taking fully into account the specific needs and conditions of developing countries and minimizing the possible adverse impacts on their development in a manner that protects the poor and the affected communities

GOAL 13: CLIMATE ACTION TARGETS

13.2. Integrate climate change measures into national policies, strategies, and planning in the transport sector to advance sustainable development. The recommendations include:

- Make transport planning, policy and investment decisions based on the three dimensions of sustainable development (economic, social and environmental) and a full life cycle analysis.
- Integrate all sustainable transport planning vertically, among levels of government, and horizontally, across modes, territories and sectors; create supportive institutional, legal and regulatory government frameworks.
- Establish monitoring and evaluation frameworks for sustainable transport; and increase international development funding and climate funding for sustainable transport.

AUTOMOTIVE DEVELOPMENTS – THE DRIVE TO NOT DRIVE

In all parts of the world, transportation is a necessary factor to productive city living, and is a focal point for many cities Urban areas across the globe are looking for solutions that will facilitate the smooth transport of their citizens without contributing to pollution. Car sharing, electric cars, and driverless cars are some of the exciting developments in the automotive field. In addition, sustainable public transportation options remain a source of growth and attention. Companies like Tesla are pioneering many of these solutions. As a leader in electric vehicles, Tesla has made its mission "to accelerate the advent of sustainable transport by bringing compelling mass market

"DEVELOPED AND DEVELOPING ECONOMIES FACE DIFFERENT CHALLENGES WHEN IT COMES TO TRANSPORTATION. WHILE DEVELOPED ECONOMIES MOSTLY FACE CHALLENGES RELATED TO AIR POLLUTION, TRAFFIC CONGESTION AND THE EFFICIENCY OF THE TRANSPORTATION SYSTEM, DEVELOPING ECONOMIES NEED ROADS, INFRASTRUCTURE AND MECHANISMS FOR FINANCING THE DEVELOPMENT OF INFRASTRUCTURE."

PATRICK HO, CHINA ENERGY FUND COMMITTEE

electric cars to market as soon as possible."[105] And while pursuing this mission, they have continued to explore and prepare the foundations for the next technological breakthrough of driverless cars (See Case 33).

33

CASE NO. TESLA

Model 3
Designing electric vehicles to shift markets toward a sustainable future

Case applied in: Global
Headquarters located in: USA
www.tesla.com

IMPACT SDGs

SDG 7
Affordable and Clean Energy
The average battery electric vehicle in the US today emits 214g of carbon dioxide per mile—far less than the 356g to 409g of carbon dioxide per mile produced by conventional gasoline vehicles.

SDG 9
Industry, Innovation & Infrastructure
The number of public charging stations has grown rapidly in all countries and is projected to grow exponentially in the coming years. The global Electric Vehicle Charger (EVC) market is forecast to grow from more than 1 million units in 2014 to more than 12.7 million units in 2020.

SDG 17
Partnerships for the Goals
Panasonic supplies the batteries for Tesla's Model S, Model X and upcoming mass market Model 3, and will contribute US $1.6 billion to Tesla's $5 billion battery factory.

OUR GOAL WHEN WE CREATED TESLA A DECADE AGO WAS THE SAME AS IT IS TODAY: TO ACCELERATE THE ADVENT OF SUSTAINABLE TRANSPORT BY BRINGING COMPELLING MASS MARKET ELECTRIC CARS TO MARKET AS SOON AS POSSIBLE.
ELON MUSK, CO-FOUNDER & CEO TESLA

Tesla is a prime example of a business using its innovative power to design a product that can shift markets. Recognizing that electric vehicle market penetration is critical to efforts to address climate change, Tesla has capitalized on this opportunity with exceptional design and performance and catapulted the Model 3 into unprecedented high demand. At least 380,000 people put down US $1,000 deposits for the Model 3 before production started, generating US $380 million for the company.

With its US $35,000 base price, the Model 3 is a more consumer-friendly version of Tesla's luxury Model S. The new sedan is smaller but is expected to feature the same self-driving capabilities and will have a range of about 220 miles (354 kilometers) before needing to be recharged.

Tesla is not just an automaker, but also a technology and design company with a focus on energy innovation (SDG 7). The Model 3 was conceived in an effort to reduce the costs of lithium-ion battery packs, the fundamental component of an Electric Vehicle. Now Tesla and key strategic partners, including Panasonic, have begun construction of a gigafactory in Nevada that will facilitate the production of the mass-market affordable vehicle, and build enough batteries to equip 500,000 vehicles in 2018 (SDG 17). It will also produce battery packs for use in stationary storage, helping to improve robustness of the electrical grid, reduce

energy costs for businesses and residences, and provide a backup supply of power.

Tesla has initiated unique strategies to grow their business and disrupt the automotive, energy and fuel industries. By allowing technology patents to be used by anyone in good faith, they have unlocked a huge market for electric vehicles. This open access has given way to other car manufacturers producing electric vehicles, and as a result, there is higher demand for charging stations. This surge in demand for charging stations triggers needed changes to infrastructure, which ultimately drives demand for Tesla's products. This is clearly shown in their sales: in 2016, vehicle production increased 64%, as Tesla saw their revenue grow to US $7 billion that year, an increase compared to US $4 billion in revenue in 2015; gross profit in 2016 went up 73%, from US $924 million in 2015 to US $1.6 billion in 2016.

Market integration is also evident in recent price and infrastructure trends that have helped make Tesla's plug-in hybrid vehicles more affordable. As Tesla's total vehicle sales increased about 51% during 2016, the company aggressively expanded its Supercharger network to support its growing demand. Tesla ended 2016 with a total of 790 Supercharger locations and 5,043 Supercharger connections. This is up from 582 sites and 3,448 connections at the end of 2015 (SDG 9).

CHALLENGE

To create transportation options using a sustainable fuel source, and reduce healthcare costs, excessive emissions, lost productivity and other consequences of road pollution caused by the use of fossil fuels.

OPPORTUNITIES FOR SCALE

Electric Vehicles are expected to account for nearly 67% of new car sales in Europe by 2040, and for 58% of sales in the US and 51% in China by the same date. By 2040, Electric Vehicles will also be displacing 8 million barrels of transport fuel per day and adding 5% to global electricity consumption, scaling up market opportunities.

Sources and further information

- http://www.reuters.com/article/us-panasonic-tesla-idUSKBN1530UC
- http://ns.umich.edu/new/releases/24924-most-drivers-could-go-electric-within-10-years
- https://about.bnef.com/blog/electric-vehicles-accelerate-54-new-car-sales-2040/
- https://www.fool.com/investing/2017/03/22/9-key-metrics-from-tesla-incs-annual-report.aspx
- http://www.latimes.com/business/autos/la-fi-tn-elon-musk-model-3-20170708-story.html
- https://www.greenbiz.com/article/welcome-next-generation-sustainable-development
- https://www.dnvgl.com/feature/sdgs-business-action.html
- http://www.oecd-ilibrary.org/environment/the-cost-of-air-pollution_9789264210448-en

" BY ALLOWING TECHNOLOGY PATENTS TO BE USED BY ANYONE IN GOOD FAITH, THEY HAVE UNLOCKED A HUGE MARKET FOR ELECTRIC VEHICLES."

There is unprecedented potential for cost-effective investments in more efficient vehicles, cleaner fuels, and a range of public transport initiatives. To promote pollution free transportation, roughly 1000 cities have now invested in the implementation of bike-sharing schemes. Private enterprises have also tapped into "the sharing economy" by introducing car-sharing companies and platforms. Alongside the developments of electric vehicles, car-sharing, and sustainable public transportation alternatives, legislative decisions are also being made to push unsustainable, polluting practices out. London and Paris are among the cities to ban diesel cars by 2020, and cities such as Oslo and Amsterdam are actively discouraging car driving in the city center by redesigning roads to be more bike than car friendly and making parking difficult and expensive.

> **THE WORLD'S 724 LARGEST CITIES HAVE THE POTENTIAL TO REDUCE GREENHOUSE GAS EMISSIONS BY UP TO 1.5 BILLION TONS OF CARBON DIOXIDE EQUIVALENT ANNUALLY BY 2030, PRIMARILY THROUGH TRANSFORMATIVE CHANGE IN TRANSPORT SYSTEMS IN CITY SYSTEMS LIKE TRANSPORTATION.**[106]
>
> NEW CLIMATE ECONOMY

There is also a need to find ways to use market-based measures in a tailored way for sustainable transport and to bring together the supply chains in all sectors to work on common issues. Another interesting development in this regard is the electric bicycle. Delivery companies such as DHL are piloting electric cargo bikes which are not only cleaner than gasoline or diesel fueled trucks, but more maneuverable and practical in cities. DHL's "City Hub"[107] will enable increased use of cargo bicycles for inner-city deliveries. The City Hub is a customized trailer that can carry up to four containers for the DHL "Cubicycle," a customized cargo bicycle with a capacity of up to 125 kilograms. The solution significantly reduces emissions by minimizing the mileage and time spent on the road by standard delivery vehicles. Each City Hub can replace up to two standard delivery vehicles, with an equivalent CO_2 saving of over sixteen tons per year and a significant reduction in other emissions. Additionally, restaurants and other delivery services can utilize electric bikes to replace scooters and mopeds. This not only eliminates CO_2 emissions, but opens employment opportunities to youths without a driver's license, which could help to contribute to youth employment rates.

The Transportation Industry is, in fact, a major contributor to urban employment, accounting for millions of jobs globally. One in seven jobs in the US is transportation related, and it is estimated that for every one job created in Africa in the Transportation Industry, two or more indirect jobs are created in other sectors as a result. Furthermore, the efficient mobility of people, goods and materials is a vital enabler of sustainable social and economic development, connecting people to basic services, jobs, markets and each other.[108] Sustainable transport is an integrated, essential component in sustainable development strategies. Because transport infrastructure is put in place as a long-term system, the decisions that the local and national governments make today will have lasting impacts on urban development and form, as well as the climate and environment.

AIR TRAVEL

While aviation accounts for 12% of global CO_2 emissions compared to 74% from road transport, air travel and airports can also improve on sustainable practices. In 2016, at the Airports Going Green conference held at Schiphol Airport in the Netherlands, the Airports Sustainability Declaration was signed by over 25 airport representatives from around the world. In this declaration, the airports agreed to work together to take major steps forward in terms of sustainability. The joint ambition is to strengthen the system of sustainable and resilient airports worldwide, through collaboration, transparency, innovation, and engagement. It was noteworthy and commendable that these major global airports voluntarily joined forces to adapt their practices to create social, environmental and economic value. It signifies a commitment to a collaborative system change.

Gatwick, one of the signatories, is on track to becoming UK's most sustainable airport. Gatwick aims to cut emissions by 32.6% and energy by 16.6% by 2020, and they have already received the triple certification of the Carbon Trust Standard for achieving ongoing reductions in carbon emissions and water use, as well as improvements on waste management. Currently, 157 airports worldwide are certified at one of the four levels of the Airport Carbon Accreditation and 21 airport operators are carbon neutral.

AIRPORTS CAN BE INNOVATION BREEDING GROUNDS FOR TECHNOLOGICAL AND CIRCULAR SOLUTIONS.

Thus, there is already work in progress. But we need to raise the bar. Airports can do this through collaboration and with business initiatives that can help them achieve impact. If airports aim to move beyond carbon neutrality, and set their sights on becoming CO_2 positive, they could potentially become the renewable, power plants of the future.

As transportation hubs, airports do not only produce harmful emissions through air flight, but also through the congestion that tends to surround airports, and as nearly four billion people move through airports around the world each year, waste production is enormous. Airports are a great circular economy opportunity. Jos Nijhuis, CEO of Schiphol, explained at the 2016 conference how to build terminals with sustainable tech-

nologies and how temporary terminals could be recycled by literally folding them up.

Airports can be innovation breeding grounds for technological and circular solutions. Great examples around the world are appearing, such as the new Mexican airport which has brought together countless businesses collaborating to create the world's most sustainable airport, which will be equipped with solar panels providing enough power to supply a large portion of the airport's energy use, systems for re-utilization of rainwater and an intelligent ventilation system, among their many innovations. The coalition can share great innovations like these and use them to build new airports or renovate existing ones. In this way, airports can become truly circular hotspots, not only for themselves, but also with an impact on constructions for cities, factories and other facilities such as hospitals. The impact of airports extends to a much bigger system level; construction and architecture as a whole. In reverse, airports can learn from other constructing sectors to reach the highest possible circular rate, with the final destination being: carbon positive, energy efficient, and zero waste.

Furthermore, as electric vehicles advance, so too does the potential for electric aircrafts. And progress is already being made. Nasa has already started utilizing a new facility to test electric aircraft technologies for what will become the next revolution in aviation. And in a recent announcement, the low-cost airline EasyJet says it could be flying electric planes within a decade. The UK-based airline has linked up with the US firm Wright Electric to build battery-powered aircraft for flights under two hours.[109] Carolyn McCall, EasyJet's CEO stated, "It is now more a matter of when, not if, a short-haul electric plane will fly." As battery technology advances, so too do the opportunities of application. Just imagine the impact of eliminating all negative particles and the resulting CO_2 impact of air flight. And imagine from that moment on having silent airplanes during the day and, most significantly, at night. The impact on both nature and people would be tremendous and would contribute to many of the SDGs.

TRANSPORTATION IN DEVELOPING CITIES – A LONG ROAD AHEAD

Affordable and functional transport solutions in densely populated urban regions are very important for the poor to access economic opportunities and to conserve the little money they do have. For example, in Nairobi, Kenya the urban poor spend up to 30% of their household income on transport leaving less money to spend in the city economy.[110] Additionally, transport in cities is a major contributor to climate change but also to sustainable solutions. If approached in the right way, sustainable transportation options can contribute to Target 1.5, which is to "reduce exposure to, and the vulnerability of the poor, to climate-related extreme events." Resilient transportation systems also play a crucial role before, during and after a disaster. Yet despite this realization, adequate urban transport and infrastructure is unavailable or lacking for the world's poorest and most vulnerable people. Even though global transport investments are estimated at between US $1 and $2 trillion per year, less than 40% is in developing countries' cities, whose nations are home to more than 80% of the world's population.[111]

Technology can provide solutions to the inadequate infrastructure and investment in developing cities. As mentioned in Chapter 3, mobile phones bypassed improvements in land-line infrastructure in developing countries, connecting people in places where they had never had phone access before. Similar solutions can connect people to services and products where road transport is insufficient. In Rwanda, for example, this is already being done. Drones are being implemented to advance the transport in cities that lack road infrastructure. Companies such as Zipline are recognizing that a need which has existed for quite some time, can be solved with our technology today. Zipline, a Californian start-up improves access to medical supplies by flying their drones over impassable mountains and washed-out roads, delivering directly to remote clinics.[112] For example, when a woman who had just given birth in a mountainous region in the country started to lose a lot of blood, the doctors attending her called the national blood bank for more blood, but to travel the 25 miles by road would take up to four hours. The woman would not survive the wait. So, they called a Zipline distribution center who loaded the units of blood onto drones that were able to travel the distance in just 15 minutes. This innovative start-up has turned the delivery of emergency medical supplies into a routine business in Rwanda. Starting in October 2016, they have already made 1,400 deliveries. Zipline plans to expand their business to Tanzania to serve the nation's 55 million citizens.[113] This shared value solution represents a new business area that can be expanded and explored in many parts of the world.

WRAP UP

Local governments, business and capital will play key roles in achieving inclusive, safe, resilient and sustainable cities. Modern technological advancements will help to solve many of the challenges that we face today including pollution, energy efficiency, and transport. Smart cities are developing new systems all over the world, as cities and businesses recognize the endless opportunities technology holds. Megatall buildings and vertical cities are being built to accommodate growing urban populations. And attention to fundamental contributors to our environment and our health is leading cities to cultivate green areas, even taking us to the rooftops in congested areas. Developments in transportation, such as electric vehicles are also offering solutions to our climate and social goals. Because cities are both the source and the solution of many global problems, it is in cities that we will see the most significant developments in the coming years. Businesses thrive in cities and depend on urban infrastructure and prosperity. It is therefore in cities where sustainability must thrive too. ∎

BUSINESS HAS THE POTENTIAL TO PLAY A PIVOTAL ROLE IN BUILDING BETTER CITIES. **AFTER ALL, BUSINESSES THEMSELVES HAVE A LOT OF STAKE IN HOW CITIES ARE STRUCTURED.**

FOOD AND AGRICULTURE

Hunger, malnutrition, obesity, poverty, pollution, climate change and wasted resources are some of the many challenges related to the food and agriculture sector. In addition to these challenges, there are stark contrasts and vicious cycles affecting this industry. One such contrast is the fact that 795 million people go hungry every day while one-third of the food produced goes to waste. And the vicious cycles that are part of this industry include the fact that food production accounts for 30% of all global greenhouse gas emissions, while the industry suffers the most from climate change. Agriculture is extremely vulnerable as it is largely dependent on reliable weather patterns and conducive climate conditions. Furthermore, there is the deep-seated problem that food security directly influences the vicious cycle of poverty. When people do not have enough money to buy food, they suffer from hunger and chronic malnutrition, leading to stunted growth and other health conditions making it all the more difficult to break out of poverty because of their inability to work.

6.1 SDG 2: ZERO HUNGER

The challenges, contrasts and vicious cycles in the food and agriculture sector may seem insurmountable, but they are not. It is possible to accomplish the ultimate Goal of SDG 2, and it can be done with the resources we have right now. There is currently enough food being produced to feed everyone in the world. In fact, there is even enough potential production to feed the expected 25% to 30% population growth over the next 30 years. Yet, every day millions still go hungry. The two culprits standing in the way of accomplishing this Goal are: food waste and poverty. Food waste is tragic, not only in respect to the people who are dying of hunger, but also because of the terrible waste of resources that go into producing the food. It has been calculated that it takes 15,000 liters of water to produce just one kilogram of beef,[1] 2,500 liters for a kilogram of rice and 822 liters for a kilogram of apples.[2] Food waste should be stopped, and it can be stopped. Or at the very least severely curtailed. Just imagine it, one-third of all the food produced is wasted. One third! As if this wasn't outrageous enough, consider that food waste costs the global economy US $750 billion per year. [3]

It is compelling to focus on solving the issue of food waste and loss as major strides can be achieved. In addition, advances can be made related to another issue that affects this industry: sustainable food production. Improving food production practices would benefit the industry, people, and the environment. Farmers in developing countries could prosper from more information, and affordable, innovative solutions to help them not only produce more but get their produce to market. This chapter will take you through the issues of food waste and food production, presenting them as two interrelated domains within the industry and demonstrating both the challenges and the shared value opportunities.

> **THERE ARE SOME 500 MILLION SMALLHOLDER FARMS WORLDWIDE; MORE THAN 2 BILLION PEOPLE DEPEND ON THEM FOR THEIR LIVELIHOODS.**
>
> IFAD.ORG

2 ZERO HUNGER

SDG 2: ZERO HUNGER;
End hunger, achieve food security and improved nutrition, and promote sustainable agriculture.

TARGETS

2.1 by 2030 end hunger and ensure access by all people, in particular the poor and people in vulnerable situations, including infants, to safe, nutritious and sufficient food all year round

2.2 by 2030 end all forms of malnutrition, including achieving by 2025 the internationally agreed targets on stunting and wasting in children under five years of age, and address the nutritional needs of adolescent girls, pregnant and lactating women, and older persons

2.3 by 2030, double the agricultural productivity and the incomes of small-scale food producers, particularly women, indigenous peoples, family farmers, pastoralists and fishers, including through secure and equal access to land, other productive resources and inputs, knowledge, financial services, markets, and opportunities for value addition and non-farm employment

2.4 by 2030, ensure sustainable food production systems and implement resilient agricultural practices that increase productivity and production, that help maintain ecosystems, that strengthen capacity for adaptation to climate change, extreme weather, drought, flooding and other disasters, and that progressively improve land and soil quality

2.5 by 2020, maintain genetic diversity of seeds, cultivated plants, farmed and domesticated animals and their related wild species, including through soundly managed and diversified seed and plant banks at national, regional and international levels, and ensure access to and fair and equitable sharing of benefits arising from the utilization of genetic resources and associated traditional knowledge as internationally agreed

2.a increase investment, including through enhanced international cooperation, in rural infrastructure, agricultural research and extension services, technology development, and plant and livestock gene banks to enhance agricultural productive capacity in developing countries, in particular in least developed countries

2.b. correct and prevent trade restrictions and distortions in world agricultural markets including by the parallel elimination of all forms of agricultural export subsidies and all export measures with equivalent effect, in accordance with the mandate of the Doha Development Round

2.c. adopt measures to ensure the proper functioning of food commodity markets and their derivatives, and facilitate timely access to market information, including on food reserves, in order to help limit extreme food price volatility

Achieving an end to hunger, and improving food security, nutrition, and sustainable agriculture, as SDG 2 calls for, sounds like a lot to ask. But, as mentioned earlier, we do in fact have the necessary resources to end hunger. Ensuring food security, good nutrition, and sustainable agriculture will require innovation and collaboration. By zeroing in on the SDG Targets and Indicators as guidance, businesses in the food and agriculture sectors can have a tremendous positive impact. The Targets for SDG 2 are important to this in-

dustry and their achievement will benefit people around the world.

IMPACT OF SDG 12

Sustainable food production and consumption are areas to improve upon within this sector. As such, taking some of the Targets from SDG 12 into consideration can be helpful in transforming practices and initiating innovative approaches. Relevant Targets associated with SDG 12: Responsible Consumption and Production, are listed below.

---

12 RESPONSIBLE CONSUMPTION AND PRODUCTION

SDG 12: RESPONSIBLE CONSUMPTION AND PRODUCTION
Ensure sustainable consumption and production patterns.

TARGETS

12.2 By 2030, achieve the sustainable management and efficient use of natural resources.

12.3 By 2030, halve per capita global food waste at the retail and consumer levels and reduce food losses along production and supply chains, including post-harvest losses

12.5 By 2030, substantially reduce waste generation through prevention, reduction, recycling and reuse

12.8 By 2030, ensure that people everywhere have the relevant information and awareness for sustainable development and lifestyles in harmony with nature

12.a Support developing countries to strengthen their scientific and technological capacity to move towards more sustainable patterns of consumption and production

6.2 SOLVING THE CHALLENGES: FOOD AND AGRICULTURE AS THE COMMON THREAD THROUGH THE GOALS

The food and agriculture industry makes up an integral part of both society and the economy and has enormous business and shared value opportunities. This industry is of the utmost importance to both basic survival and economic prosperity and consequently a pivotal player in the achievement of the SDGs. The direct impact that the industry has on the SDGs is hugely influential. It is therefore critical that businesses within this sector keep this firmly in mind and shift their business strategies to include a positive impact on the SDGs. A report by Farming First called *The Story of Agriculture and the Sustainable Development Goals*[5] clearly shows how this industry impacts the SDGs and gives examples of companies integrating the Goals into their business practices. The Farming First framework proposes six interlinked imperatives for sustainable development. The six focal points not only emphasize the key role that smallholder farmers play in helping to feed the world, they succinctly state where business and regulators should put their attention so as to help these farmers achieve optimal production.

MORE THAN ANY OTHER SECTOR, AGRICULTURE IS THE COMMON THREAD WHICH HOLDS THE 17 SDGs TOGETHER.

FARMINGFIRST.ORG

As food constitutes a basic need for all people, this sector touches all of the Sustainable Development Goals with over half of them relating to global food security and nutrition. The figure on the next page, and a succinct video presentation[6] from the Stockholm Resilience Center shows how the SDGs all fit together and relate to the food and agriculture industry. As Professor Johan Rockström and Pavan Sukhdev say in their presentation, the biosphere needs resilience, society needs equity, and the economy needs efficiency. Rockström and Sukhdev talk about creating a "safe operating space", of a stable and resilient planet, and the role food plays in the transformation to a sustainable future.

To accelerate more sustainable practices in the industry, new business models should be developed. Cross-sector collaborations and innovations can accelerate these developments. As stated in

IMPERATIVES FOR SUSTAINABLE DEVELOPMENT

1. **SAFEGUARD NATURAL RESOURCES**
2. **SHARE KNOWLEDGE**
3. **BUILD LOCAL ACCESS AND CAPACITY**
4. **PROTECT HARVESTS**
5. **ENABLE ACCESS TO MARKETS**
6. **PRIORITIZE RESEARCH IMPERATIVES**

FARMING FIRST

reports by the International Food Policy Research Institute,[10] "The global food system needs to be reshaped to achieve a whole range of SDGs." An optimal food system should have six characteristics: "It should be efficient, inclusive, climate-smart, sustainable, nutrition - and health - driven, and business-friendly." The current system, however, falls short with respect to these characteristics. There is entirely too much food waste and loss, hunger, overuse of resources, and exploitation of people and the environment.

The industry must change its course. The transition needed to protect people and the environment creates social and ecological value as well as economic value. According to the Business Commission report: *Valuing the SDG Prize in Food and Agriculture,*[11] the largest business opportunities in the food and agriculture system could be worth US $2.3 trillion in 2030. The biggest opportunities

relate to opening new markets in low-income areas, creating technological solutions for farming, and reducing waste. Developing regions such as Africa and India also hold tremendous potential for growth and development within the food and agriculture sector. The promotion of gender equality and women's empowerment in these regions will contribute greatly to the growth and efficiency of smallholder farms.

> **"THE SDGS ARE A TREMEN-DOUS OPPORTUNITY AND A HUGE OBLIGATION FOR HUMANITY."**
>
> JOHAN ROCKSTRÖM

Figure 36 **Stockholm Resilience Centre; How food connects all the SDGs**

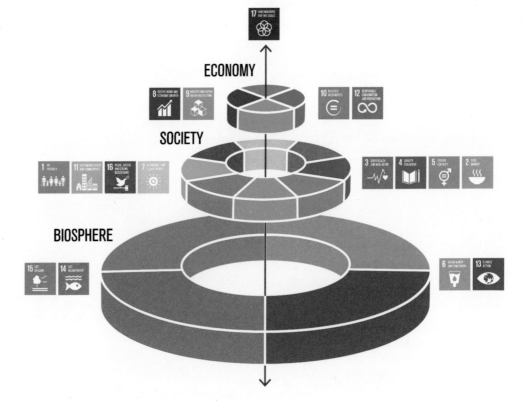

6.3 IMPACT OF FOOD AND AGRICULTURE ON ALL SDGs

The far-reaching impact of the food and agriculture sector makes it particularly important to achieving the SDGs. Sustaining the world's population with a sufficient supply of healthy food is vital. Attention to sustainable practices in the food and agriculture sector therefore plays a pivotal role.

 SDG 1: No Poverty; The vicious cycle of hunger, food insecurity, and poverty can be influenced by this sector. Poverty is the number one cause of world hunger. The World Bank estimates that 10.7% of the world's population, or 767 million people, lived on less than US $1.90 per day in 2013. People living in poverty spend much of the income they do have on food. In developed countries, living below the poverty line results in food insecurity and buying the cheapest food available which is often unhealthy junk food. In developing countries, up to 60% of agricultural workers live in poverty[12] and over 75% of the world's poorest people grow their own food. This causes widespread food insecurity in developing countries, as drought, climate change and natural disasters can easily cut off a family's food supply. [13]

795 MILLION PEOPLE GO HUNGRY EVERY DAY WHILE ONE-THIRD OF THE FOOD PRODUCED GOES TO WASTE.

 SDG 2: Zero Hunger; This sector can have a pivotal effect and essentially achieve the Goal of zero hunger if the issue of food waste can be eradicated. There are 795 million people starving in the world today, yet we annually lose and waste 1.3 billion tons of food – or enough to feed 3 billion people. As aptly stated in a report by Farming First,[14] "Tackling hunger is not only about boosting food production; it's also about increasing incomes and strengthening markets so that people can access food even if a crisis prevents them from growing enough themselves." Consequently, utilizing cross-sector opportunities with the ICT and finance sectors, and using the power of mobile networks to provide farmers with direct access to markets, mobile payments, financing, and crucial information such as weather conditions are also necessary measures in eliminating worldwide hunger and thus achieving SDG 2.

 SDG 3: Good Health and Well-Being; Health issues such as malnutrition and obesity are related to the provision of a stable, and nutritious, food supply. There are currently two billion people suffering from malnutrition and there are more than two billion overweight adults worldwide, including at least 300 million people who are clinically obese. This has everything to do with the types and availability of food. Therefore, developing fortified food products to address nutritional needs and malnutrition in developing regions is also part of this Goal. In underdeveloped countries such as India, malnutrition affects the lives of 40% of the children in the nation. In developed countries such as the United States, 20% of school age children are obese. With conscientious food production and innovation, these dramatic numbers can be reduced and this sector can have a major impact on promoting good health and well-being.

SDG 4: Quality Education; Sixty-six million primary school-age children across the developing world attend school hungry, with 23 million of these children living in Africa. Even in some developed countries like the US, children are not getting the nutrition they need to function properly at school, with 13 million children going to school hungry every day. Educating people about nutrition and teaching them about the importance of healthy diets, especially for infants and children, can lead to improved lives. People need to learn what foods to eat and what not to. For example, in Benin, The Hunger Project launched an educational campaign to teach people about the Moringa tree

that grows naturally in the area and is considered a "super food" because of its natural nourishment.[15] People in Benin learned about the tree's nutritional value and how to incorporate it into their diets. Education is also important when it comes to food handling and food safety. Poor food hygiene, and food poisoning from contaminated food causes diarrhea which is the second leading cause of death in children under five years old.

SDG 5: Gender Equality; As women comprise 43% of the agricultural labor force, providing female entrepreneurs with training, support and access to markets and supply chains can have a significant impact on gender equality. Promoting gender equality in this industry will also open new markets and new revenue streams. The empowerment of women in developing countries will advance gender equality while also affecting other Goals such as SDG 13: Climate Action. For example, to empower and teach women in India how to cope with climate change, the global food producer Kellogg has partnered with the non-governmental humanitarian organization CARE to train women in sustainable farming practices, and work to strengthen smallholder farmers' links with market actors.[16] Cross-sector collaborations are also providing support to women business owners. Financial service providers are collaborating to present women with access to finance for farms and equipment. Working with ICT companies to integrate technology into farming systems also enables women to participate in agricultural enterprises while fulfilling their family responsibilities at the same time. This is vitally relevant to addressing the challenges faced today, because if women are given equal access to resources, they would boost the agricultural output in developing countries by 2.5% – 4%, potentially resulting in the reduction of undernourished people in the world by 100 – 150 million.[17]

SDG 6: Clean Water and Sanitation; Groundwater contamination and fishery losses are two of the problems arising from industrial agriculture's use of chemicals. Pesticides pollute water causing approximately 4,500 children to die each day – that's one every 20 seconds – due to contaminated water. To ensure healthy food and clean water for all, ecological farming offers a more sustainable alternative. Furthermore, worldwide, intensive livestock production is the most significant contributor to water pollution because of the concentration of animals and manure located far away from where it could be used as a nutrient source. Fresh water is inextricably linked to food production. As many smallholder farmers rely on access to water, this Goal of "ensuring availability and sustainable management of water and sanitation for all" is a vital component to a sustainable food and agriculture industry. As it stands now, 844 million people in the world do not have access to clean water.[18]

SDG 7: Affordable and Clean Energy; Currently, food and agriculture production accounts for around 30% of the world's total energy consumption. Promoting and engaging in innovative product development that reduces energy consumption and improves energy efficiency benefits the planet and the industry. The global food manufacturer Arcor Group recognized this and began using an alternative fuel for their sugar mill in Argentina. They have been using available biomass fuel from sugar cane bagasse to generate the steam needed for their sugar mill, significantly offsetting the use of gas and oil. In 2014, Arcor was not only generating enough energy for its own sugar mill, it had a surplus allowing them to contribute to the energy needs of the province in which they operate. By exploring other energy resources and committing to consuming energy from renewable sources, the food and agriculture industry has the potential to greatly influence energy consumption. The industry's reach can scale even further if it not only adopts sustainable energy consumption itself but also demands it of its entire supply chain.

SDG 8: Decent Work and Economic Growth; About 40% of today's global population works in agriculture, making it the single largest employer in the world.[19] Women make up a major percentage of the people working in agriculture. Fair treatment, payment, and access to land ownership, training, finance and equipment is needed to enhance working conditions and opportunities for women. In many countries, child labor is associated with agricultural work. Worldwide, 60% of all child laborers in the age group 5 to 17 years old work in agriculture - including farming, fishing, aquaculture, forestry, and livestock – often performing hazardous duties.[20] This amounts to over 98 million girls and boys, with very early entry into work, sometimes between the ages of 5 and 7 years old.[21] Bear in mind that these statistics do not reflect the reasonable assistance by children in family farms, such as helping with light daily chores that are age appropriate and do not interfere with school. Child labor in the agriculture industry is defined as:"work that is inappropriate for a child's age, affects children's education, or is likely to harm their health, safety or morals."[22] Furthermore, agriculture is one of the three most dangerous sectors in terms of work-related fatalities, non-fatal accidents and occupational diseases. Agricultural workers are often one of the most disempowered groups within societies, often with poor labor conditions as well. Also in developing countries financial, managerial and technical constraints in harvesting techniques as well as the lack of storage and cooling facilities results in up to 40% of food losses at the early stages of the food value chain. This severely influences economic compensation. As economic growth is a key success factor in reducing undernourishment, this vicious cycle of poor conditions leading to poor yields which leads to food insecurity and diminished economic prosperity threatens the health and livelihoods of people in this sector.

SDG 9: Industry, Innovation and Infrastructure;

Strengthening the supply chain in developing countries through investments in infrastructure, transportation, as well as in an expansion of the food and packaging industry, could help to reduce the amount of food loss and waste. Food loss is considered the biggest contributor to hunger and food insecurity in developing countries. Especially in Africa, there is a dire need for infrastructure to adequately store, refrigerate and transport food from the farms to the markets. Innovations are needed to overcome these obstacles. Sustainable industry and infrastructure is necessary for this sector as it meets the responsibility of feeding the world's growing population. Support of smallholder farmers who feed 70% of the world's population is important not only for the industry but also for the people and the planet. In contrast, the large industrial agricultural model is likely to have devastating ecological effects and often includes exploitive environmental and social practices. Large-scale, chemical-based monoculture farming is widely recognized as a major contributor to both climate change and biodiversity loss, problems that pose significant threats to long-term food security.

SDG 10: Reduced Inequalities;

Poor and vulnerable people, especially women living in rural areas, continue to have limited access to land and natural resources. Rights of land ownership and use for those who farm, keep livestock, fish, and manage forests is a major factor in addressing inequalities over the long term. Almost 70% of the world's population does not have access to land registration systems. In Kosovo, for example, World Bank development experts are working in a village that is populated largely by war widows, yet less than 8% have title to property.[23] To claim title, the time, cost, and complexity of surveying and registering land presents huge obstacles for women, leaving them without information or legal protection for their property. To break the impasse, the World Bank turned to technology; surveying property with small, unmanned aerial drones that involve the whole community in the mapping process and help the government produce a national land registration system. The drones offer mapping services in a matter of days or weeks, at a fraction of the cost and time of conventional surveying using manned aircraft.[24] Malnourishment, hunger and food security are pressing issues in developing countries, but these issues also afflict developed nations as well, with food security undermining equality. Food insecurity impedes productivity, causes stress and affects overall health. A lack of food security creates unequal starting points and positions. To address systemic international inequality, fair wages and sustainable resource management must be cultivated in order to reduce inequalities.

SDG 11: Sustainable Cities and Communities;

Rooftop farms are becoming a viable alternative for local food production for city dwellers. Rooftop farms effectively utilize unused space to grow food and provide ecological benefits related to air quality and water runoff in addition to providing locally produced food requiring very little transportation to markets. Sustainable farming contributes to sustainable communities. Raising awareness about how climate change impacts farming practices, and proposing relevant modifications to maximize labor efficiencies, can help increase food production within communities of all sizes. Technological innovations such as mobile apps that inform farmers of best practices when it comes to climate resilience are helping to disseminate current knowledge. Additionally, increasing inclusion of women in farming control helps to improve communities. Women already make up the majority of agricultural workers in some countries, producing 80% of Africa's food, however they enjoy few of the associated rights. Projects that give women more rights and control have proven to lift communities by improving food supply, and decreasing poverty. In 2011, for example, a project funded by the Bill and Melinda Gates Foundation supported 22 rural women's groups working on sustainable agriculture and women's rights in Burkina Faso, Kenya, and Uganda. Training was given to women on literacy, business, and sustainable agricultural practices. The results included 5 to 50% increase in crop yields, 30% increase in women's income, and the majority of households eating three meals a day.[25]

SDG 12: Responsible Consumption and Production;

Excessive resource use by the food and agriculture sector contributes to the depletion of the planet's resource security, using 70% of all the water consumed by human beings,[26] and 30% of the world's energy. Responsible production is necessary on many fronts. Food production must find ways to conserve resources and produce less greenhouse gases. To save water, for instance, utilizing sophisticated water measuring systems with data collecting sensors can be useful to monitor and reduce consumption. Additionally, using wastewater can also have a big impact. General Electric (GE) Water noticed that "failure to reuse wastewater streams is the biggest area of inefficient water use, and if treated properly, wastewater streams can be reused within food and beverage plants to increase efficiency while reducing costs."[27] Resource conservation also includes using the soil responsibly. Large-scale, chemical-based monoculture farming leads to biodiversity loss, posing significant threats to the environment, and long-term food security. The use of pesticides also poses danger to people's lives and health. There have been cases proven in the past that pesticides led to disease and death for people living close to the areas using the heavy pesticides. Each year, 200,000 people die from pesticide poisoning.[28] So responsible production is vital to our collective health and the health of our planet, and responsible consumption is critical as well. By changing our wasteful behaviors related to food, we can save an enormous amount of resources and help feed the global population. Since every single person on the planet is a consumer of food, we all have a responsibility to be more sustainable and responsible consumers.

SDG 13: Climate Action;

Agriculture and fisheries are highly dependent on the climate. Rainfall is also vital to the health of crops. Droughts and storms affect agricultural areas dramatically, sometimes wreaking devastating effects on farmland. Additionally, warmer water temperatures and high levels of CO2 affect the pH balance in the water. This is likely to cause the habitat ranges of many fish and shellfish species to shift, potentially disrupting ecosystems. Increased ocean acidification also negatively affects the ability of shellfish and coral to produce their skeletons. Curbing climate change is crucial to this industry, as it is already predicted that total food production will decrease by 2% in the next 10 years due to climate changes. The industry itself can work towards decreasing its own carbon footprint. Food production generates nearly one-third of all greenhouse gas emissions with animal agriculture accounting for 14% to 18% of the greenhouse gasses. Resource use is also an issue in this industry as farming is responsible for two-thirds of all water withdrawals and 85% of total water consumption.

 SDG 14: Life Below Water; Overfishing and polluted waters undermine food security, which depends on sustaining a steady food supply from the oceans. Climate change can potentially lead to fewer fish due to higher water temperatures causing the disease or demise of underwater life. With over 100 million tons of fish eaten worldwide each year, providing 2.5 billion people with at least 20% of their average per capita animal protein intake, less fish could therefore cause a food crisis. Sustainable fish stocks are needed as a significant and renewable source of healthy food for large parts of the world's population. Continued sustainable ocean use provides increased food security on a global basis. However, there is the significant challenge of overfishing. The global fishing fleet is two to three times larger than the oceans can sustainably support with much of the fish being used in the livestock and fish feed market. Initiatives to grow insect proteins from food waste to create livestock and fish feed can replace a significant portion of the proteins currently sourced for the same purpose from trawling the world's oceans.

FISH PRODUCTION AND CONSUMPTION AFFECTS 560 MILLION PEOPLE GLOBALLY.

 SDG 15: Life on Land; Worldwide, farming uses around 40% of total land area; 26% is used for cattle; 13% for growing crops; and 3% for growing livestock feed, totaling 42% of land currently used one way or another for food. This is destined to grow to an estimated 70% if we continue business as usual. Deforestation has a significant impact on food production. Often deforestation is done in the name of claiming land for farming, however, deforestation increases global warming which in turn increases unfavorable weather conditions for animals and crops. Since 2000, approximately 1.5 million square miles of land around the globe has been depleted by deforestation.

 SDG 16: Peace, Justice and Strong Institutions; Food security and food waste is affected when there are regional or national conflicts. For people forced to flee or living in makeshift refugee camps, food access and flows are interrupted, leading to hunger and malnourishment. In areas afflicted by war, vulnerable people, especially children and the elderly, are subjected to potentially fatal disruptions of food supplies. Peace and trade agreements among countries is crucial to stable food supplies. Additionally, strong governmental enforcement of legislation against detrimental environmental practices is necessary. Controlling deforestation is essential to sustaining the environment, and has proven effective. For example, China, the Philippines and Thailand have significantly reduced deforestation rates in response to experiencing severe environmental and public health consequences of forest loss and degradation. In India, the Joint Forest Management program has successfully partnered with communities to reduce forest degradation. These examples indicate that strong, motivated government institutions and public support are key factors in implementing effective forest policies.[29]

 SDG 17: Partnerships for the Goals; The Food and Agriculture Organization of the United Nations (FAO) has multiple international alliances to address the issues of the food and agriculture industry and improve its sustainability. Partnerships include: Energy-Smart Food for People and Climate (ESF), CSA Alliance (Climate-Smart Agriculture), and many others. The FAO is an international organization established in 2014 to propel the mission to "Make agriculture, forestry and fisheries more

productive and more sustainable."[30] There are also other partnerships that have been successful. In Denmark, for example, the initiative called Stop Wasting Food[31] partners with the UN, FAO/UNEP, and the EU Fusions project to develop over 200 initiatives, activities and campaigns against food waste. They also collaborate with the Danish government, and many retail chains. Another partnership organization working towards finding solutions for the Goals is the consortium, SUSFOOD2 ERA-Net Cofund, which involves 25 partners from 15 countries working together to strengthen efforts to support research in the field of sustainable food systems from production to consumption.[32] SUSFOOD aims to contribute to a better coordination between partners' research programs by monitoring participating countries' research programs; identifying complementary areas, research gaps and synergies; redesigning research programs in order to eliminate duplication of overlapping initiatives; and addressing priority research topics and knowledge gaps.

6.4 SHARED VALUE OPPORTUNITIES

Looking at the potential for shared value in this sector, we see there is ample opportunity for businesses to prosper. As identified in KPMG's *SDG Industry Matrix,*[33]some of the most significant shared value opportunities, initiatives and collaborations are aligned with one or more of the following four themes: Enterprise Development, Sustainable Supply, Healthy and Sustainable Living, and Product Innovation.

Enterprise Development includes the following six aspects: 1. increasing the participation of small and medium sized enterprises (SMEs) in developing economies; 2. providing training and information access to small scale and women-owned producers and retailers to improve their productivity, capacity, logistics and market efficiency; 3. connecting small businesses to capital; 4. creating new markets through innovation and mobile technology; 5. pursuing investments and cross-sector partnerships to develop infrastructure; and 6. enacting supplier diversity programs. An example of a company involved in enterprise development can be seen later in this chapter in the featured business Case 36 showing how GSMA uses mobile internet technology to provide information access to smallholder farmers to improve their productivity and profit.

Sustainable Supply involves reducing negative climate impact by working with the supply chain to ensure sustainable practices. This not only benefits the suppliers and the buyers, it benefits the environment and positively impacts multiple SDGs. Developing a sustainable supply includes the following measures: embedding sustainability criteria in procurement processes and project evaluation; increasing the share of energy from renewable sources; and enhancing climate resilience across the supply chain. The Nestlé case shown in Chapter 2 is a good example of a company that has embedded sustainability criteria in their procurement and is actively creating shared value by im-proving the sustainable practices of the farmers who supply their coffee beans.

Healthy and Sustainable Living is mainly about consumer behavior and policy change. Sustainable consumption is a huge challenge within this industry as is sustainable food production. Developing consumer awareness of sustainable food consumption and production including buying behavior, packaging and storage, nutrition, and healthy lifestyles is an important way to involve consumers in the challenges and processes this industry contends with. Consumers are integral to a shared value proposition, and benefit not only from food security and healthy food choices, but also from affordable food options.

CONSUMERS ARE INTEGRAL TO A SHARED VALUE PROPOSITION.

Big players in this industry and governments can also set the stage for shared value and create the foundation on which smaller companies can build. As illustrated in Chapter 1, Unilever, one of the biggest food product companies worldwide, has made sustainable practices a high priority and is vocal within the industry and beyond on the importance of adopting sustainable practices. Governments in Europe, Asia and elsewhere are creating policies to curb food waste, encourage recycling of packaging, and campaign for healthier lifestyles. For example, countries around the world are taxing or banning the use of plastic grocery bags, encouraging – or requiring – people to recycle bags and reduce the eight million tons of plastic bags that make their way into the world's oceans. This kind of regulation works wonders. The United Kingdom saw an 85% decrease in the amount of plastic bag waste after it introduced a five-pence charge.[34] Other examples of successful regulations include taxes on unhealthy food products and food labelling requirements. There are also many public-private partnerships working towards promoting healthy and sustainable living, such as the EAT Initiative founded by the Stockholm Resilience Centre, and the Norwegian-based Stordalen Foundation. EAT is an international consortium involving governments, world leading universities and research institutions, philanthropic foundations, non-government actors and organizations, and companies. They all share the common understanding that it is essential to collectively address the issues of food, health and sustainability across the fields of academia, business, politics and civil society to ultimately be able to feed nine billion people sustainably.[35]

Product Innovation represents endless opportunities for businesses of all sorts to invent innovative products that can be used in the food and agriculture industry. Considering the scale, reach and fundamental necessity of food production and consumption, clever innovations can have tremendous potential for profit. And if the SDGs are kept in mind, the products' use can go a long way towards achieving the Goals. Innovations targeting developing countries and especially smallholder

farmers are particularly relevant. These products create, enter and develop whole new markets. We will explore some innovations related to this sector later in the chapter with the featured business cases.

Shared value solutions create value for society, the environment, the food industry, and innovative companies from other sectors as well. By incorporating the SDGs in business propositions, the shared value that is created moves the global agenda forward. The food and agriculture industry, together with businesses that contribute to this sector have the potential to generate tremendous shared value when implementing each SDG. To start up, scale, and steer your company, it is the SDGs, shared value and a clear focus on the four themes mentioned above: Enterprise Development, Sustainable Supply, Healthy Sustainable Living, and Product Innovation, that give rise to inspiration for profitable and valuable business cases.

COMPANIES WILL NEED TO OPERATIONALIZE SUSTAINABILITY ACROSS THEIR SUPPLY CHAINS **AND INTERNALIZE SOCIAL AND ENVIRONMENTAL COSTS.**

US $320 BILLION A YEAR
IS NEEDED TO BUILD MORE
SUSTAINABILITY INTO THIS
SECTOR.

**CREATING A MORE
SUSTAINABLE SECTOR
UNLOCKS NEW MARKETS AND
NEW OPPORTUNITIES WORTH
US $2.3 TRILLION A YEAR.**

6.5 CAPITAL INVESTMENT REAPS MORE THAN IT SOWS

Capital investments are needed to facilitate transformation within this industry. It is estimated that US $320 billion a year is needed to build more sustainability into this sector.[36] Bearing in mind that creating a more sustainable sector unlocks new markets and new opportunities worth US $2.3 trillion a year, this gives a seven-fold return on investment. The investment could also lead to more than 80 million jobs. However, the current capital base in 31 leading agriculture funds is just under US $4 billion a year – less than 1.5% of the annual investment needed.

Companies will need to operationalize sustainability across their supply chains and internalize social and environmental costs. Unlocking social and economic rewards in food and agriculture will require closer collaboration among business, government and society. And new ways of working together will have to be forged in order to advance common social, economic and environmental objectives. Investment in agricultural research, crop yield improvement, infrastructure and cold storage would improve sustainable practices, draw higher revenues, and decrease food waste and loss.

> **WFP CALCULATES THAT US $3.2 BILLION IS NEEDED PER YEAR TO REACH ALL 66 MILLION HUNGRY SCHOOL-AGE CHILDREN.**[37]
>
> WFP.ORG

Research shows that developing countries have the most to gain from SDG-aligned business opportunities, capturing more than two-thirds of the estimated economic value due to their large shares of arable land, high future consumption, and large potential gains resulting from improved efficiency. The biggest business opportunity in developing Asia and Africa is in cutting food loss across the supply chain; in India, low-income food markets are the strongest opportunity for businesses; and in Latin America and Africa as well, the conservation of forest ecosystems present opportunities for business to collaborate with government. In developed countries in Asia, Europe and North America, the opportunities in this sector are greatest in finding ways to curtail consumer waste.

PUBLIC-PRIVATE PARTNERSHIPS ARE CRITICAL.

Public-private partnerships are critical in order to put in place appropriate policies and the right regulatory frameworks to advance research for facilitating product innovation. For example, the US Agency for International Development (USAID) partners with companies to support advisory services to governments to improve policies and regulations; invests in research to improve seeds and other inputs and agricultural practices; helps small farmers and cooperatives to reduce waste and adapt new technology; and works with US and local companies on specific investment projects. Through Feed the Future and the New Alliance for Food Security and Nutrition, the USAID has engaged with over 200 global and domestic companies and secured more than US $10 billion in investment commitments. The Coffee Farmer Resilience Initiative has brought the agency together with private companies to limit their risk in extending support to coffee farmers in Latin America. The agency has also partnered with a local company and the Cold Chain Bangladesh Alliance to build a "cold chain" that makes it possible for small farmers to get their produce to market through temperature-regulated shipping.[38] Public-private partnerships such as these are needed worldwide. It is estimated that the demand for food will increase by 70% by 2050, and at least US $80 billion in investments will be needed annually to meet this demand, most of which is expected to come from the private sector.[39]

6.6 DOMAINS OF IMPACT

There are many challenges that touch the food and agriculture industry as mentioned in the introduction of this section. Some of those challenges relate to other sectors as well, and will be discussed in subsequent sections of this book, such as nutrition, malnutrition and obesity which will be approached in the chapter on Health and Well-Being. Food security, waste, loss and production are the main issues that will be addressed in this chapter, while focusing on the following two points of attention:

1. **Food waste:** solving and reducing food waste and loss, along the entire supply chain for greater food retention.
2. **Food production:** boosting sustainable production, i.e. making production and distribution more sustainable in qualitative terms, and making production more efficient and effective to obtain more food.

> **THE LAND DEVOTED TO PRODUCING WASTED FOOD WOULD BE THE SECOND-LARGEST COUNTRY IN THE WORLD, AND THIS WASTED FOOD ACCOUNTS FOR 8% OF ALL HARMFUL EMISSIONS.**
>
> 2013 ANALYSIS: UNITED NATIONS' FOOD AND AGRICULTURE ORGANIZATION

1. FOOD WASTE AND LOSS

When talking about food waste, most people think about the leftovers in the refrigerator that never gets eaten, or the bruised apples that aren't accepted by the supermarkets for sale. But think about all the resources that go into food production in the first place, and the pollution it produces in the process. As mentioned earlier, food production uses 70% of all human water consumption, 30% of all energy, and produces 20% to35% of all greenhouse emissions.

When food is wasted, resources are wasted too, and more pollution is created in the process. According to a 2013 analysis by the United Nations' Food and Agriculture Organization, the land devoted to producing the 1.3 billion tons of wasted food would be the second-largest country in the world, and this wasted food accounts for 8% of all harmful emissions.[40] So, all these harmful emissions and wasted resources result from the production of a product that just gets thrown away. It is clear that if solutions are found to prevent waste, significant headway can be made towards eliminating hunger worldwide, preserving our resources, and reducing pollution. With focus and willingness to deal with this pressing issue, business opportunities abound and pivotal impact can be made.

GETTING THE HARVEST TO MARKET

Waste is generated all along the supply chain. In developing countries, food waste happens at the beginning of the food chain with 40% of losses occurring post-harvest and during processing and transportation. As much as half the food produced in developing countries never makes it to the market.[41] Moreover, 630 million tons of food equaling US $310 billion is lost or wasted in developing countries. Of the world's annual food production, statistics show that 30% to 50% is wasted. China, for example, produces 60 million tons of food waste every year, equivalent to the food requirements of 200 million people.

Smallholder farmers in poor rural areas make up the bulk of the food producers in Africa and Asia, and in countries like Guatemala, for example, smallholder farmers represent approximately one-third of the country's entire population. These farmers often do not have access to, or education about, modern harvesting techniques, storage facilities and transport options. Through education and minor investments, increases in product yield, more efficient production, and better storage and transport can be achieved, and higher incomes for these farmers can result. The Food and Agriculture Organization of the United Nations has already predicted that hunger levels are likely to decrease by hundreds of millions of people by 2030, but notes that sub-Saharan Africa as a region, and rural women as a demographic group, may still be most at risk. Smallholder farmers, women, and youths have important roles in ending hunger and malnutrition. However, these groups often lack access to assets and markets and are at risk of exclusion from increasingly complex food value chains. Maximizing the potential of commercially viable smallholder farms, empowering women, and making agriculture more attractive to young people can enhance their contribution to global food security and nutrition. This is also central to achieving other SDGs, such as reducing inequalities (SDG 10).

Businesses such as software developers and consultants can play an important role in providing information to farmers. Apps such as Kuza Doctor and Kilimo Salama[42] provide information and tips to smallholder farmers about weather conditions, planting and harvesting. Because these apps are also modern in their approach, they help engage tech savvy young people to become more involved in farming by simply using this method of information dissemination.

Tips can also be shared easily with other farmers and nearby communities, thus supporting smallholder farmers to gain more interaction and better networks. Dairy hubs, for instance, have had huge success in Bangladesh and Pakistan, connecting smallholder farmers to dairy processors, cutting costs and putting money back into local communities. By using technology and data exchange, farmers can improve their yields, their incomes and their processes. But there is also a lot that can be done low-tech. Simple solutions, like using crates instead of bags to transport vulnerable vegetables such as tomatoes can be encouraged by providing low-cost options and training. Improved processes and better education leads to less waste. Refrigerated storage and transport is another difficulty smallholder farmers face in warm regions of Africa, India and other parts of the world. This is a rather dire issue related to poverty and the lack of access to energy. An innovative low-tech, but brilliant solution to the lack of refrigeration plaguing these areas was thought of by MIT students as part of an assignment. Now they are making a business out of their idea, called Evaptainers, and are in the process of launching their product on the market. Evaptainers uses the highly efficient cooling effect of evaporation in their cool-box design which uses only sand and water. The water doesn't even need to be pure. It can come from a river, a pond, or anywhere else. And what makes it most accessible to poor farmers is the sustainability of it, as it uses zero energy. (See Case 34). Innovations in refrigeration and energy supply is important in developing countries as approximately 25% of food waste in the developing world could be eliminated with better refrigeration equipment.[43]

> ## THE UK REMAINS ONE OF THE MOST WASTEFUL OF THE EU'S 27 MEMBER STATES, THROWING AWAY 14.3 MILLION TONS (MT) A YEAR. [44]
>
> EDIE.NET

As fruits and vegetables have the highest wastage rates of any foods, packaging and storage is a business solution area needing attention. Companies such as PerfoTec have created innovative solutions to this issue. PerfoTec[45] is a scientific and technological approach to packaging that allows for the right amount of oxygen to reach the perishable food items. PerfoTec supplies the equipment to quickly measure the respiration rate of fresh fruits and vegetables and the supplied software calculates the required film permeability. The PerfoTec laser systems then uses this information to adapt the film permeability through micro perforations. This helps to extend the food's shelf life considerably.

34 CASE NO. EVAPTAINERS

EV-8
Zero - energy refrigeration

Case applied in: Africa
Headquarters located in: USA
www.evaptainers.com

IMPACT SDGs

SDG 2

Zero Hunger

Approximately 40% of food produced in African developing countries rots before it reaches the end consumer.

SDG 7

Affordable and Clean Energy

The Evaptainer is a "zero-energy" refrigeration device, ideal for low-income, off-grid areas.

SDG 10

Reduced Inequalities

The US $10 to $20 units are an improvement on a traditional cooling method used throughout much of Africa and the Middle East; up to 10% of total household income is saved.

SDG 12

Responsible Consumption and Production

About 470 million small farms lose an average of 15% of their income to food spoilage due to a lack of refrigeration.

WE'VE CREATED A MORE EFFECTIVE AND SCALABLE CLEAN ENERGY REFRIGERATION SOLUTION, ENABLING THE COLD CHAIN TO REACH FARTHER THAN EVER BEFORE. BUT WE'VE DONE MORE THAN SIMPLY INVENT THIS DEVICE; WE'VE USED IT TO CHANGE PEOPLE'S LIVES.

QUANG TRUONG AND SPENCER TAYLOR, CO-FOUNDERS

Evaptainers present a solution to the problem of food spoilage in developing countries and impoverished regions (SDG 2). This spoilage is in large part due to refrigeration being both expensive and inaccessible in developing areas. Conventional refrigerators consume a lot of electricity and leak greenhouse gasses into the air. Because of this, there is a critical need for eco-friendly alternatives. Creating opportunities for consumers and farmers so they are not so dependent on conventional refrigeration, Evaptainers is harnessing the power of evaporative cooling to keep food fresh.

The business tackles the problem of spoilage in developing countries, where nearly half of the food goes to waste before ever even reaching the consumer (SDG 12). It addresses the problem through a new invention: a low-cost fridge that runs only on water and sand. This innovative product is called the EV-8 and addresses both prosperity and the planet by providing low-income off-grid families, and poor smallholder farmers, with access to refrigeration (SDG 10). It is an environmentally sound alternative to conventional refrigerators that consume electricity and emit hydrofluorocarbons into the atmosphere as a byproduct (SDG 7). As the world's first commercialized "zero-energy" (requiring absolutely no external electricity) refrigeration device, it is a lightweight and collapsible evaporative cooler.

The need for food preservation is essential to the survival of many communities, as global demand for food is expected to rise significantly. Although there is development of other such refrigeration devices, Evaptainers uses state-of-the art materials and an improved design resulting in a more effective and scalable clean energy refrigeration solution. The technology has the potential for a wide range of benefits. Most importantly, low-income families would have a reliable device where they can store food, allowing them to save money and eat more nutritious meals. Farmers and outdoor venders would also have access to a shelf-life enhancing device that would keep harvested produce and fresh goods cool during the hottest months, and during transport.

Evaptainers is collaborating with USAID on a larger pilot program that will distribute the product to 300 families in Southern Morocco.

The Technical specifications of the EV-8 are:

- Storage Capacity: 60 liter (2.1 cu. ft.) internal capacity for storage of fruits, vegetables, and other perishable products.
- Water Reservoir: 1.5 liter water capacity. Average water consumption is 1 liter per day.
- Cooling Capacity: 15-20°C drop from ambient temperature.
- The temperature decrease will be greater in dry, arid conditions and less in humid conditions
- Insulation Type: Expanded Polypropylene
- Electricity Consumption: 0 watts

CHALLENGE

To help manage food spoilage rates, which the UN estimates to account for a total annual loss of US $4 billion in Africa.

OPPORTUNITIES FOR SCALE

There is a high growth potential in Africa and elsewhere for the implementation of this innovative new product. Therefore, the company hopes to launch the product worldwide and help the over 2 billion people globally that still lack access to refrigeration. In addition to food refrigeration, this product can also be used to refrigerate medicines when needed – thus opening another potential market for the EV-8.

Sources and further information

- https://challenges.openideo.com/challenge/bridgebuilder/ideas/evaptainers
- http://www.evaptainers.com/
- https://www.unido.org/news/press/winners-of-the-in.html
- http://money.cnn.com/2015/04/07/smallbusiness/evaptainer-cooler/index.html?iid=HP_LN

" EVAPTAINERS HAS CREATED THE FIRST COMMERCIALIZED ZERO-ENERGY REFRIGERATION DEVICE."

FRESH SOLUTIONS FOR FISHERMEN

Fishing is another area of this sector where there is too much waste at the beginning of the chain. Considering that global fish production is worth US $150 billion annually, this is an area where innovative efficiency solutions can scale rapidly. With over 44 million people employed in the fishing industry, one billion people depending on fish as their main source of protein, and fish production and consumption affecting 560 million people globally, a sustainable fishing industry is essential for food security, hunger mitigation and nutrition.

OVER 44 MILLION PEOPLE ARE EMPLOYED IN THE FISHING INDUSTRY.GLOBAL FISH PRODUCTION IS WORTH US $150 BILLION ANNUALLY.

In developing countries, 35% of the fish is lost because it is not processed in a timely manner. Low and medium income countries in Africa, Asia and Latin America suffer severe fish shortages due to climate change, overfishing, environmental pollution, poor management and post-harvest losses.

Companies and organizations are coming up with solutions for this as well. For example, the EU-project Securefish[46] is a collaborative endeavor led by entrepreneurs, European researchers and institutions, and local companies in Africa, Asia and Latin America all working together to come up with viable solutions to counteract waste and loss. The overall objective of Securefish is to reduce post-harvest losses by strengthening the local capacity in processing, preservation and quality control of fish and fish products. Securefish sets out, among other things, to utilize fish byproducts and waste to make value added products.

Innovations in packaging specifically for fish have been created in Europe as well. Norwiegian research institute Nofima designed a form of packaging called Superfresh[47] that not only keeps fish fresh for longer, but also has benefits for trans-

porting the fish. The packaging requires less volume and allows the fish to be transported together with other foods as well.

Using the bycatch fish that are often caught unintentionally is another development that can contribute to the reduction of wasted resources. This was recently initiated by several supermarket chains in the Netherlands,[48] and holds the potential to open up a brand new market.

Other ways to create shared value in the fishing industry include the innovative solution by Interface. As shown in Case 6 in Chapter 2, the carpet manufacturer helps fishermen create extra income and eliminates pollution of the seas at the same time. Interface created a new revenue source for fishermen by buying old fishing nets to be used for thread in their carpets.

Business area solutions for the fishing industry can be found in many facets of the industry including the streamlining of processing, technological and logistic solutions, innovations to eliminate, reverse and prevent pollution, and changes in business practices for overfishing.

A CULTURE OF WASTE

While most food loss happens at the beginning of the supply chain in developing countries, the dominant cause of food waste and loss in developed countries happens at the end of the supply chain. Consumers and retail businesses are the main culprits with more than 40% of all waste happening at consumer and retail levels. The numbers are actually staggering. 670 million tons of food equaling US $680 billion is wasted every year in developed countries. France wastes 7.1 million tons of food annually with 67% being thrown away by consumers, 15% by restaurants, and 11% by retail stores. And the USA wastes a whopping 50% of all their food amounting to 60 million tons of food thrown in the garbage while in some areas of the country people do not have a steady supply of food, like in Mississippi where one in four people have reported not having enough money to consistently provide food for their families. Consumers account for 43% of this waste, with the average family of four wasting about US $1,500 per year on food they don't eat, simply due to buying too much and consequently throwing it away, making too much and not eating leftovers, or putting too much on a plate and discarding the remainder.

670 MILLION TONS OF FOOD EQUALING US $680 BILLION IS WASTED EVERY YEAR IN DEVELOPED COUNTRIES.

Solutions to the problem of consumer waste can be found in raising awareness and knowledge. Standardized labelling of when foods expire would also help, since there are many different labelling techniques and requirements at the moment, potentially causing confusion. Consumers can also participate in helping each other find ways to reduce waste by using social media to exchange inspirational recipe ideas for leftovers, or sharing information on how best to store food at home. Technological solutions such as IoT and apps alerting consumers when items in their refrigerators or pantries are about to go bad, such as the app Green Egg Shopper,[49] are also useful to help consumers plan and track their food purchasing, and eat the food they have in time. The advent of internet shopping may also have a positive influence as this different buying behavior may reduce impulse buying at the supermarket. Meal planning apps with automatic links to order the items needed could also reduce over-buying. Tristram Stuart, a UK based anti food-waste campaigner, talks about this issue and offers useful advice and inspiration in his video[50] and his book titled, *Waste: Uncovering the Global Food Scandal.* Stuart has dedicated his career to making people aware of the pressure that the production of this wasted food puts on the environment, and consequently showing how relatively simple changes can significantly reduce food waste. There is quite a lot that consumers can do towards reducing food waste. There are also other behavior modifications that individuals can implement in order

to help achieve the SDGs. The UN provides some suggestions of what people could do fairly easily in their tips called, "The Lazy Person's Guide to Saving the World" shown on their website page dedicated to how to take action.[51] One of the actions they encourage people to do is compost their food scraps. Composting can help to reduce climate impact while also recycling nutrients. It is an environmentally useful process which also serves to tackle food waste by putting the nutrients back in the soil.

COMPOSTING ORGANIC WASTE – THE CIRCULAR SOLUTION

Even if food waste is reduced significantly there will still remain some food scraps that are inedible. If these scraps can be given to animals as food, that can be a good option. Another option is composting this waste to ultimately be used as fertilizer. In this way, a circular solution is created. Composting is beneficial in many ways. It can eliminate the need for chemical fertilizers, promote higher yields of agricultural crops, aid reforestation, wetlands restoration, and habitat revitalization efforts by improving contaminated, compacted, and marginal soils. Compost can be used to remediate soils contaminated by hazardous waste in a cost effective manner, and it can even capture and destroy 99.6% of industrial volatile organic chemicals (VOCs) in contaminated air. Compost also enhances water retention in soils, and provides carbon sequestration,[52] which is a process of capturing and storing carbon dioxide with the purpose of slowing the accumulation of greenhouse gases and thus mitigating global warming.[53]

THERE IS QUITE A LOT THAT CONSUMERS CAN DO TOWARDS REDUCING FOOD WASTE.

Composting produces organic fertilizer. Additionally, it can also be used to grow larvae which can be used as high-protein animal feed, presenting an alternative to using fish, crops, or other animals

20-35% OF THE TOTAL GREENHOUSE EMISSIONS IN THE WORLD COME FROM PRODUCTION AND CONSUMPTION OF FOOD WITH NEARLY 7% OF GREENHOUSE GAS EMISSIONS COMING FROM FOOD WASTE WORLDWIDE.

for feed – which only increases the burden to the environment. The consortium, EVO Conversion Systems X JM Green[54] developed a way to use black soldier fly larvae to transform waste into insect biomass as a sustainable animal feed ingredient, and crop fertilizer. They can convert 100 tons of organic waste into 20 tons of larvae and 40 tons of fertilizer. In 2016, JM Green processed 150 tons of organic waste per day.[55] Whether individuals use their own compost to enrich the soil in their gardens, or they contribute it to the municipal collection, using food scraps for compost is the best way to dispose of food waste.

HOSPITALITY AND RETAIL SHARE THE RESPONSIBILITY

Supermarkets, restaurants and other food vendors play a significant role in wasting food as well. In the United Kingdom, for example, 920,000 tons of food is thrown away by the hospitality industry every year amounting to GB £2.5 billion. Three-quarters of this food is still perfectly good and could create 1.3 billion meals. Yet it is just tossed away. Technological solutions can help make a difference here too. Q-Point, a Dutch consultancy specializing in consultancy projects for agro-food businesses, developed a data collection and estimation solution to food purchasing and planning to help companies in the catering and hospitality industries to accurately estimate the amount of food needed. By using concrete data, vendors can avoid over-surplus resulting in

waste. Initially, Q-Point's business activities were only in the Netherlands, but they are currently scaling their endeavors to Asia, Eastern Africa and the Middle East.[56]

Another solution that is rapidly scaling from one country to many others is an app developed by Unilever in 2013 called the Wise Up on Waste app.[57] It was specifically created to help chefs and caterers cut their food waste and see how much money they could save in the process. This was an industry-first mobile app that allows chefs to track food waste. The app highlights the average volume of each type of waste (spoilage, preparation or customer plate waste) generated during a given part of the day (i.e. breakfast, lunch or dinner). It gives week-by-week comparisons to help identify the cost savings for a business. It also contains case study videos, waste action tips, recipes and spoilage prevention advice. By the end of 2015, the Unilever Food Solutions team supported the reduction of waste by over 10% and cut over 16 tons of food waste. In 2015, the app was rolled out in Belgium, France, the Netherlands, UK, Spain and Australia.

Food vendors can also take note for themselves where food waste and excess costs are occurring. This is what the cafeteria at the University of California Santa Barbara did when they noticed that people were piling food onto their trays and much of it ended up uneaten in the disposal area. They simply decided to eliminate the food tray and adjust the food proportions according to the waste they had noticed; the overall food waste went down by 50%.

FOR EVERY US $1 INVESTED IN TRAINING STAFF HOW TO WASTE LESS FOOD IN PRODUCTION, US $14 OR MORE WERE SAVED.[58]

WRI AND WRAP RESEARCH

In a study to evaluate measures taken by businesses to reduce food waste, Craig Hanson, Global Director of Food, Forests, and Water at the World Resource Institute (WRI), and Peter Mitchell, Head of Economics at Waste and Resources Action Programme (WRAP), created a report named *The Business Case for Reducing Food Loss and Waste*. This report was released on behalf of Champions 12.3, a coalition of nearly 40 leaders across business, government and civil society who are dedicated to achieving the SDG Target 12.3: To halve food waste and cut food loss by 2030. After evaluating cost and benefit data for 1,200 business sites across 700 companies in 17 countries, researchers from WRI and WRAP found that nearly every company had a positive return on their investments to curb food loss and waste in operations. Half realized a 14-fold or greater return. Simply put, for every US $1 invested in training staff how to waste less food in production, US $14 or more were saved. However,

even with training and helpful technology, sometimes surplus is unavoidable. Catering companies run into this issue, for example, when a certain amount of food is ordered for a number of people, but in the end, it is not all eaten. What can be done about this?

SUPERMARKETS, RESTAURANTS AND OTHER FOOD VENDORS PLAY A SIGNIFICANT ROLE IN FOOD WASTE AS WELL.

An innovative start-up in California called Copia came up with a business idea to collect the food that is left-over at events and deliver it to people in need. Companies pay a nominal price to Copia equivalent to composting fees and get a charity tax deduction for every pound donated. (See Case 35).

CASE NO. 35

COPIA

Food Recovery App
Connecting food waste with food use

Case applied in: USA
Headquarters located in: USA
www.gocopia.com

IMPACT SDGs

SDG 1

No poverty

Alleviating the affects of poverty by providing people in need with nourishment.

SDG 2

Zero Hunger

Mitigating hunger in the US, as almost 50 million Americans live in food insecure households today.

SDG 10

Reduced Inequalities

Creating a solution to the imbalance of a system of waste by those who have excess, and need by those with limited means.

SDG 11

Sustainable Cities and Communities

Providing more than 10,000 meals per week to those in need, while saving businesses thousands of dollars through reduced waste and enhanced tax deductions.

SDG 12

Responsible Consumption and Production

Wasted food costs approximately US $680 billion in industrialized countries and US $310 billion in developing countries.

> HUNGER IS THE WORLD'S DUMBEST PROBLEM, ESPECIALLY IN THE WORLD'S WEALTHIEST COUNTRY. IT'S A DISTRIBUTION PROBLEM. **WE GET FOOD FROM THOSE WHO HAVE IT TO THOSE WHO NEED IT**.
> KOMAL AHMAD, FOUNDER & CEO COPIA

There are billions of kilograms of food being wasted every year, yet people still go hungry. In wealthy countries alone, 222 million tons of food is wasted, which is almost as much as the entire net food production of sub-Saharan Africa (SDG 10). Copia's mission is to reduce waste by connecting businesses with excess food to those who need it most. Food waste is a significant issue in the United States, as one in six people live in food insecure households.

Established at the beginning of 2016, Copia is on a mission to reduce waste by connecting businesses with excess food to those who need it most. With hunger being a problem in not only the poorest countries in the world but also in the wealthiest, Copia has recognized that technology can instantly connect those who need food with those who have it (SDG 2). Developing a new app to help end hunger and reduce food waste, Copia harnesses technology to reach the larger community (SDG 11). As a for-profit company, Copia requires businesses to pay volume-based fees for access to Copia's waste reduction dashboard and to have Copia drivers pick up and deliver food to local shelters, after-school programs, and other non-profit organizations. Customers can use Copia's analytics to reduce waste at the source and access enhanced tax deductions. This facilitates full transparency into their environmental and com-

munity impact. So far Copia has collected more than 800,000 pounds of food, connecting it to 700,000 hungry people. Using an algorithm-based smartphone app, Copia facilitates donations and deliveries of excess food in six cities across the San Francisco Bay Area in California (SDG 1). Those with food to donate post their information via the app, and a driver will come pick it up. Similarly, someone looking for food can post their request online and wait for a match.

Customers with excess food benefit in three ways from Copia's services: real-time sustainability and environmental metrics, itemized surplus analytics to help reduce waste at the source, and fully automated tax receipts and reporting. Another innovative aspect of the platform is that it can track food throughout the system, which means optimized routing of food (SDG 12). This technology further minimizes waste and maximizes savings.

The company's innovative service is a unique approach to exploring an untapped market that has shared value potential with both the hungry and businesses benefitting. It is the only end-to-end food waste reduction and recovery solution on the market. Copia provides thousands of meals per week to those in need while saving businesses thousands of dollars through reduced waste and enhanced tax deductions.

CHALLENGE

To help alleviate food waste and provide food to people in need.

OPPORTUNITIES FOR SCALE

With plans to expand to other cities, the platform has the potential to use the technology to distribute other much-needed items, like medicine for example. Copia wants to first expand to use the platform to redistribute food to Syrian migrants in in the United States.

Sources and further information

- http://www.huffingtonpost.com/ entry/app-copia-food-for-hungry_ us_57068b32e4b0a506064e6bcf
- http://enb.iisd.org/sdgs/sti/forum1/brief/sti1_ brief.pdf
- https://foodtank.com/news/2017/01/technology- is-reducing-food-waste-an-interview-with- copias-mike-goldblatt/
- https://foodtank.com/news/2016/07/fighting- food-loss-and-waste/

" COPIA HAS RECOGNIZED THAT TECHNOLOGY CAN INSTANTLY CONNECT THOSE WHO NEED FOOD WITH THOSE WHO HAVE IT."

THE TIME IS RIPE FOR A SHIFT

You have just read some of the innovative, and sometimes simple business solutions for the problem of food waste and loss. And there are many other cost-saving and resource-saving initiatives that can be implemented at the beginning and the end of the supply chain to solve this problem.

In developing countries, the focus should be on uplifting small farmers. This is a major focal point for shared value solutions at the beginning of the food chain, and a source of opportunities to develop and open markets. Increasing incomes of smallholder farmers, who make up a significant portion of society in most developing countries, will make great strides towards reducing poverty and bringing us closer to reaching the first Sustainable Development Goal of No Poverty. Half of those who are hungry in the world are, in fact, smallholder farmers.[59] The goal must be to help these farmers, who are not even producing enough for their own families, become profitable businesses.

IN DEVELOPING COUNTRIES, THE FOCUS SHOULD BE ON UPLIFTING SMALL FARMERS.

In developed countries, consumers at the end of the chain can create massive impact on food waste with a change of mindset and habits. We have seen this already with attitudes and behavior regarding recycling, and healthier choices, but attention to consumers' buying behavior, and balancing supply and demand within retail and hospitality can be improved greatly. Innovations, regulations, and sustainable business and behavioral patterns are needed. The time is ripe for a shift. If the amount of food wasted around the world were reduced by just 25% there would be enough food to feed all the people who are malnourished, according to the UN. [60] Reducing food waste could save between US $120 and $300 billion per year by 2030 and reduce greenhouse gas emissions by one billion tons of CO_2 per year.[61] This would make a major positive impact on the SDGs and their Targets. It is good business, responsible

> ## REDUCING FOOD WASTE COULD LEAD TO ELIMINATING ONE BILLION TONS OF CO2 EMISSIONS PER YEAR.
>
> UNILEVER

consumption, and good for the world. Governments and regulators can also support, or set, certain directions. In the past few years, there have been some governmental regulations targeting the food industry in an effort to combat food waste. For example, the EU is currently exploring modification of the terminology used to indicate when a food item expires. As this is often confusing for customers, and food vendors, leading to unnecessary waste. Also to address food waste, in February 2016, France became the first country in the world to ban supermarkets from throwing away or destroying unsold food. Instead they must donate it to charities and food banks. The law follows a grassroots campaign in France by shoppers, anti-poverty campaigners and those opposed to food waste, showing the influence consumers can have on government regulation.

CONSUMERS AT THE END OF THE CHAIN CAN CREATE MASSIVE IMPACT ON FOOD WASTE WITH A CHANGE OF MINDSET AND HABITS.

Businesses, consumers, and governing bodies all play important roles in solving the problem of food waste. Creating solutions with shared value, the various players as well as the environment can all benefit. Food retention is vital. With the growing population, we cannot afford to waste food as we have been doing up to now. We must change our habits, develop more efficient and effective processes to get the food from the farms to our plates, and encourage regulations that protect the environment and promote healthy lifestyles.

2. IMPROVING PRODUCTIVITY

Food production is the second major issue facing this industry and threatening food security, and must be examined if the industry is to meet the increasing demand. Food production must be boosted to provide enough food for the exponentially growing population. By 2050, a global population of 9.7 billion will demand 70% more food than is consumed today.[62] How will it be feasible to increase production to the levels needed? The shared value model offers the framework to find innovative solutions. The specific challenges in food production include adequate input – namely land, fertile soil, water, and plant genetic resources. Appropriate and dependable environmental conditions are also a big challenge as climate change wreaks havoc and causes natural disasters, drought and floods. And lastly, production processes can and must be improved to include more effective smallholder farmers and better multi-stakeholder systems. Increased productivity, when coupled with better access to markets, can help address hunger directly at the farm level or provide sufficient additional income to buy food at the market.

SCIENCE AND TECHNOLOGY DRIVE INNOVATIVE SOLUTIONS

Technological solutions are being developed to cultivate the agricultural input, assess the environmental conditions, and improve the production processes. Many companies in the food and agriculture industry are investigating the role that technology and specifically big data can play in managing the supply chain.

> **BY 2050, A GLOBAL POPULATION OF 9.7 BILLION WILL DEMAND 70% MORE FOOD THAN IS CONSUMED TODAY.**[63]
>
> WEFORUM.ORG

An example of an application of big data technology helping smallholder farmers in developing countries is an acclaimed innovation aimed at helping farmers in India. In December 2014, the Indian financial newspaper *The Economic Times* presented the big data GSMA Airtel Green SIM project with an award for the Best Use of Telecom for Social Good – For Profit Company. The technological solution was aimed at helping small farmers deal with the three challenges: agricultural input, environmental conditions, and production processes. It created shared value for the farmers, the companies involved, and the environment (See Case 36).

BIG AND SMALL DATA APPLICATIONS INCLUDE:

- Mapping of fields to provide more tailored watering, sowing, harvesting and other agricultural interventions.
- Using technologies such as drones to investigate the fields, collect data and analyze the overall progression of crops throughout the season.
- Placing sensors onto existing farming equipment, such as tractors, harvesters, etc. that transmit data for analysis in order to improve crop yields.
- Combining the above data with weather information, detailed field topography and previous crop performance.

Source: World Economic Forum

36

CASE NO. **GSMA**

Airtel Green SIM
Voice-based agricultural information - helping
rural farmers improve farming practices

Case applied in: India
Headquarters located in: England
www.gsma.com

IMPACT SDGs

SDG 1

No poverty

Improved crop yield and
increased income; accurate
market prices to earn more
from crop yields.

SDG 8

Decent Work and Economic Growth

Catalyzes scalable,
commercial mobile services
that improve the productivity
and incomes of smallholder
farmers and benefit the
agriculture sector in emerging
markets.

SDG 10

Reduced Inequalities

Reach the poorest populations
and provide information
to them that they would
otherwise not have access to.

SDG 12

Responsible Consumption and Production

Technological facilitation
of improved information
to provide information
dissemination and knowledge
sharing in rural villages about
planting to prevent low crop
yields.

OUR PURPOSE IS THE DRIVING FORCE BEHIND OUR INDUSTRY'S COMMITMENT TO PLAYING THE LEADING ROLE IN CONNECTING THE WORLD AND ACHIEVING THE SDGs. **ACCESS TO THE MOBILE INTERNET IS A DEFINING MOMENT IN A COMMUNITY'S ECONOMIC, SOCIAL AND POLITICAL DEVELOPMENT.**

GSMA

The Green SIM card provides subscribers with regular network services, just like any other Airtel SIM card, but in addition it provides free voice and SMS messages with agricultural content. Customers also have access to a helpline where they can speak directly with agricultural experts to ask questions. Agricultural content is a mix of state-level, district-level and also more localized information for maximum impact. Airtel Green SIM users receive four voice SMS and one text SMS daily on agricultural news. Green SIM cards are affordable and cost the same as a regular SIM card, approximately US $1.

Relationships with other businesses and information about other ecosystems are critical to farmers' business success. This platform facilitates vital information dissemination to the user communities of partner organizations, leveraging partner content and farmer networks to provide valuable information-sharing services and increase acquisitions.

The Airtel Green Sim is helping smallholder farmers connect to markets and achieve higher profits. Some of the success stories of farmers who used the app include: 1) Improved Crop Yield and Increased Income: after being advised to spray a chemical that would eliminate pests at a low cost, farmers were able to successfully farm approximately eight additional acres and increase net income from the harvest by 8,600 INR per

acre (SDG 12); 2) Accurate Market Prices to Earn More From Crop Sale: obtaining the price for which soybeans were being sold at a near-by market from the service instead of relying on a middleman, famers earned 150 INR more per quintal (equal to 100 kg) sold of the crop (SDG 8); 3) Weather Information to Prevent Costly Wastage: listening to messages on weather forecasting that suggested they should delay spraying crops due to impending rains, farmers were able to avert spraying unnecessarily before the rains and avoided a loss of 350 INR for each 15 acres (SDG 10). 4) Informed Planting to Prevent Lost Crop Yields (SDG 1): calling the Green SIM helpline to get assistance selecting wheat varieties that should be planted to boost production, farmers spend 500 INR for this information yet experience an income increase of approximately 21,000 INR, achieving a profit of 20,500 INR.

GSMA has also recently launched the mNutrition initiative. It is designed to improve nutrition for underserved populations through mobile-based services that aim to change behaviors. GSMA released an impact report on the initiative and reported 5.1 million agricultural value-added service users (Agri VAS) as a result of the efforts conducted in 6 countries. Out of these, 760,000 are from Bangladesh using Grameenphone's Krishi Sheba service and 2.9 million are active users of Khushhaal Zamindar service, created by Telenor Pakistan.

CHALLENGE

To provide rural Indian farmers access to agricultural information to be able to better anticipate weather patterns and shifts in the marketplace.

OPPORTUNITIES FOR SCALE

Airtel estimates that 50% of the current user base have data-enabled handsets, and of these users, approximately 20% use data on their phones. GSMA is committed to expanding connectivity and exploring ways in which mobile technology can help achieve the SDGs.

Sources and further information

- http://businesscommission.org/our-work/spotlight-mobile-phones-prove-to-be-a-lifeline-for-rural-farmers-in-india
- http://www.ict4ag.org/en/emerging-innovations/day-3/ictsmobile-apps-for-access-to-financial-services-and-insurance.html
- https://www.ericsson.com/assets/local/networked-society/reports/ict-and-the-future-of-food-and-agriculture_ericsson.pdf
- http://www.ifpri.org/blog/new-global-food-system-achieving-sustainable-development-goals
- http://www.trai.gov.in/sites/default/files/Consultation_Paper_16_jan_2017_0.pdf
- https://www.gsmaintelligence.com/
- https://www.gsma.com/mobilefordevelopment/wp-content/uploads/2015/03/GSMA_Case_IKSL_web2.pdf
- http://measict.weebly.com/uploads/3/2/4/3/3243215/iksls_green_sim_card-ag_info-mobilephone-india.pdf
- https://www.gsma.com/mobilefordevelopment/wp-content/uploads/2017/07/Khushaal-Zamindar-A-mob

" ONE OF THE SUCCESS STORIES OF FARMERS WHO USED THE APP INCLUDE: IMPROVED CROP YIELD AND INCREASED INCOME."

In addition to big data, other new technology is likely to become relevant for this sector in the future such as technologically assisted development of high yield crops, 3D printing of food, sensors to detect crop disease, and communication methods to connect information to broader farm communities. Also, digital connectedness between producers and consumers is inclined to develop to better coordinate supply and demand. Watching, or being involved in, technological advances, (some of which were discussed in the chapter on ICT and Technology) and honing in on how they can be applied to this sector can be very interesting for innovative businesses looking to improve the efficiency and sustainability of food production.

IN ADDITION TO BIG DATA, OTHER NEW TECHNOLOGY IS LIKELY TO BECOME RELEVANT FOR THIS SECTOR IN THE FUTURE SUCH AS TECHNOLOGICALLY ASSISTED DEVELOPMENT OF HIGH YIELD CROPS, 3D PRINTING OF FOOD, SENSORS TO DETECT CROP DISEASE, AND COMMUNICATION METHODS TO CONNECT INFORMATION TO BROADER FARM COMMUNITIES.

Scientific drivers are also helping to improve and increase food production, enhance adequate input, cope with environmental impacts, and streamline production activities. Let's consider global cereal yields, for example, which are projected to fall by 20% by 2050 due to climate change. Since cereals are leading staple foods in the human diet, this projected shortfall requires innovation and an environmentally sustainable global food system. Climate-ready crop varieties such as C4 rice can help meet these goals.[64]

RESEARCHERS CALCULATE THAT ENGINEERING C4 PHOTOSYNTHESIS INTO RICE AND WHEAT COULD INCREASE YIELDS PER HECTARE BY ROUGHLY 50%.

TECHNOLOGYREVIEW.COM

The C4 Rice Project is one of the scientific Grand Challenges of the 21st Century. Researchers from 12 institutions in 8 countries are working together to apply innovative scientific approaches to the development of high yielding rice varieties for smallholder farmers.[65] Farmers are struggling to meet growing demand for rice, which is a staple food for half of the world's population – it provides approximately 20% of global dietary energy. In 2050, the expected demand for rice is 1,309 million tons, leaving a shortfall of 394 million tons. The innovative process, called C4 photosynthesis, boosts plants' growth by capturing carbon dioxide and concentrating it in specialized cells in the leaves. Allowing the photosynthetic process to operate much more efficiently, the C4 process is the reason corn and sugarcane grow so productively. Researchers calculate that engineering C4 photosynthesis into rice and wheat could increase yields per hectare by roughly 50%.[66]

By using scientific methods to enhance foods and yields, production can be boosted significantly. Scientific and knowledge organizations are joining forces with businesses around the world to explore the possibilities to expand and increase food production.

Utilizing underused sources, such as algae and insects, to supplement the demand for protein represents other avenues that are being explored by businesses and knowledge organizations. There are many platforms and partnership organizations designed to move this agenda forward. One such organization is TNO,[67] a knowledge organization headquartered in the Netherlands, that offers information and collaboration with small and large businesses as well as governing bodies to develop scientific solutions for many of the world's challenges including food and nutrition.

Innovative businesses are also coming up with ways to make better use of the resources we do have. An example is the company Coffee Flour who realized the market potential of utilizing commonly discarded parts of crops. They focused their attention on the coffee plant and found that the berries are habitually discarded when extracting the coffee bean. Coffee Flour has used a shared value approach to create a unique product while finding a productive and healthy use for the fruit in order to more fully utilize the plant. It is at the same time both creating a new revenue stream for farmers and decreasing botanical waste for environmental good (See Case 37).

37 CASE NO.

COFFEE FLOUR

Coffee as Food
Agricultural innovation and waste reduction

Case applied in: Nicaragua, Guatemala, Brazil, El Salvador, Papua New Guinea, Vietnam, Mexico
Headquarters located in: USA
www.coffeeflour.com

IMPACT SDGs

SDG 1
No poverty
By producing coffee flour, coffee-farming communities earn income from fruit for which they have not previously been compensated.

SDG 2
Zero Hunger
One in nine people in the world are malnourished. By harvesting the cherries, coffee-farming communities can create a new, nutrient-dense food source with minimal additional labor.

SDG 12
Responsible Consumption and Production
Using parts of the coffee plant that is usually discarded, turns a byproduct into a source to produce a new product for consumption.

SDG 13
Climate Action
Each pound of decomposing food in landfills emits 0.36 kg of CO2e. Based on the global consumption of coffee in 2015, an estimated 16 MTs of CO2e or 0.2% of the world's carbon emissions would be attributable to coffee pulp waste alone. (USDA)

OUR PRIORITY AT COFFEE FLOUR IS ENSURING THAT WE CAN CONTINUE TO MAKE A SIGNIFICANT IMPACT ON WASTE REDUCTION IN THIS INDUSTRY **SO THAT THE ENVIRONMENTAL, SOCIAL, AND ECONOMIC BENEFITS OF COFFEE FLOUR ARE AS WIDESPREAD AS POSSIBLE**.
DAN BELLIVEAU, FOUNDER AND CEO COFFEE FLOUR

Coffee Flour is a new global impact food made from the discarded pulp and skin of the coffee cherry. The pulp is sometimes composted, but still billions of kilograms of pulp is dumped in landfills or thrown into waterways, threatening ecosystems and contributing to global warming by releasing significant amounts of methane into the atmosphere as well as affecting local water supplies.

Coffee Flour's business model also provides supplemental income for smallholder farmers (SDG 1) and creates additional jobs, many of which are accessible to women for the first time, turning what was once a pollutant into an economic boost to coffee-growing communities around the globe.

The company pioneered a process that converts this coffee byproduct into a nutrient-dense new super-ingredient for cooking and drinking. By repurposing waste from coffee production and turning the byproduct into a sustainable source of revenue and nutrition, Coffee Flour has structured the business to reap economic benefits both at the source and all the way up the value chain. In 2015, they harvested 47 billion kilograms of coffee cherry, providing the potential to make 3 billion kilograms of flour. Thus, this "found food" has the potential for a market value equivalent to that of the cocoa industry. Taking the leftover coffee cherry pulp and converting it into flour significantly reduces waste and is also a benefit to coffee growers as an additional income stream. "Instead of throwing it away, they have something else to work with and to sell. We want the communities that harvest coffee to see economic gains," explains CEO Dan Belliveau.

When dried and milled, coffee cherry pulp becomes a nutritionally-dense powder that is high in fiber, antioxidants, protein, potassium, calcium, and iron. Its subtle sweet flavor is now being incorporated into chocolate, baked goods, and beverage products worldwide to combat global hunger issues (SDG 2). Belliveau emphasizes that "This is an ethical, sustainable new product that can feed people."

Environmentally, the company has reduced the pulp waste pile by 75% to 80% in some areas and has dried approximately two million pounds of coffee cherry pulp, equating to nearly 14.5 million pounds of wet waste to date (SDG 12). Coffee Flour's commitment to address the long-standing, environmental issues associated with coffee pulp waste has led to it being a pioneer in transforming coffee-growing communities. The company was awarded the Global Sourcing Council's GSC 3S 2017 Climate Change Award for its outstanding commitment and business model for impacting climate change (SDG 13).

CHALLENGE

To reduce the waste of coffee cherry pulp, to present another revenue stream to farmers, and to provide a new food source.

OPPORTUNITIES FOR SCALE

Coffee Flour has grown from its foundation in 2013 to a thriving company. Their flour is in production in three continents and their business is growing quickly. The company's mission is a global one - to achieve the greatest sustainable impact possible and strive to create a system where all coffee production in the world is repurposing its waste into Coffee Flour.

Sources and further information

- http://bakerpedia.com/coffee-flour-waste-product-super-food/
- http://www.snackandbakery.com/articles/90201-coffee-flour-wins-multiple-industry-awards
- http://solutions.sustainia.me/solutions/from-coffee-waste-to-superfood/
- https://www.bloomberg.com/news/articles/2014-04-09/introducing-coffee-flour
- https://livingcircular.veolia.com/en/lifestyle/making-flour-coffee
- https://issuu.com/sustainia/docs/sustainia100_2016
- http://www.foodnavigator-usa.com/Suppliers2/CoffeeFlour-expands-as-demand-increases-for-novelty-sustainability
- http://www.huffingtonpost.com/entry/coffee-waste-flour-environment-cookies-environment_us_5783a161e4b01edea78e9377

" INSTEAD OF THROWING IT AWAY, THEY HAVE SOMETHING ELSE TO WORK WITH AND TO SELL. WE WANT THE COMMUNITIES THAT HARVEST COFFEE TO SEE ECONOMIC GAINS, EXPLAINS DAN BELLIVEAU, CEO."

COPING WITH CLIMATE CHANGE

Millions of people around the world are affected every year by climate change and weather extremes. To mitigate the impact of climate change, the food and agriculture industry needs to transition to a low-carbon system. As mentioned earlier, the fact that this industry accounts for 30% of all global greenhouse gas emissions, while it is also the most vulnerable sector to climate change, is an issue that must be faced and solved. Some businesses are taking active steps towards developing sustainable practices and changing the way they produce in order to reduce their carbon footprint. Adnams is one such company. The brewery based in England, took a look at their product lifecycle from farm to delivery and was able to target the key parts of the process where emissions could be cut. From this, they developed their carbon neutral beer, East Green. It is made in a brewery with an Energy Recovery System which recycles 100% of the steam produced during the process to be used to heat 90% of the following brew.[68]

SUSTAINABLE AGRICULTURAL PRACTICES SHOULD NOT ONLY PRODUCE ADEQUATE SUPPLIES, BUT THEY MUST ALSO MINIMIZE NEGATIVE IMPACTS TO OUR PLANET.

Climate change threatens food security. Deforestation, depletion of soil fertility and water scarcity are all pressing issues. As stated by the UN's Sustainable Development Knowledge Platform, "given the expected changes in temperatures, precipitation and pests associated with climate change, the global community, but business specifically, is being called upon to increase investment in research, development and implementation and of course scaling up of technologies to improve the sustainability of food systems everywhere and to enhance production of healthy food. Building resilience of local food systems will be critical to averting large-scale future shortages and to ensuring food security and good nutrition for all." [69]

Sustainable agricultural practices should not only produce adequate supplies, but they must also minimize negative impacts to our planet, such as land degradation, and contribute to leading the world in mitigating climate impacts. Integrated agricultural development, climate action, and biodiversity conservation could greatly contribute to agro-ecological resilience.

NEW SOLUTIONS TO AN OLD PROBLEM

Production processes can be made more efficient and more prolific. Many innovations in this area have already been mentioned, such as the GSMA Airtel Green SIM project profiled in Case 36, which helps smallholder farmers efficiently approach their crop cultivation. But there remains a stumbling block for smallholder farmers that has posed challenges for many years. The infrastructure in developing countries is inadequate. And while technology is making a valuable contribution to disseminating vital information, there also needs to be a way to physically deliver farming necessities such as seeds to the farmers in remote rural areas. Drones may offer a technological solution to the infrastructure problem. The World Economic Forum estimates that "drones could account for 10% to 15% of Africa's transport sector in the next decade." As the world experiences changes in climate conditions and at the same time sees rapid advancements in technology and knowledge, production processes can and should be transformed. There are many emerging opportunities and markets opening up or waiting to be opened. Utilizing new means and new knowledge to address old problems makes good sense and holds great potential. In keeping with the evolution of drones, you could say "the sky is the limit."

Developing effective, sustainable and improved food productivity requires attention to resources, environmental influences, and production processes. Technology is being integrated into the solutions creating shared societal and environmental value. We have discussed some of the many ideas in this chapter and there are also numerous organizations involved in the global food and agriculture arena. By forming partnerships such as those created by the World Economic Forum, companies and institutions can join forces to achieve the goal of more food production while ensuring sustainability in the process.

UTILIZING NEW MEANS AND NEW KNOWLEDGE TO ADDRESS OLD PROBLEMS MAKES GOOD SENSE AND HOLDS GREAT POTENTIAL.

There are many governmental and non-governmental organizations that offer or promote partnerships to further the sustainability of this industry and support food security. The World Economic Forum, for instance, created a System Initiative on Shaping the Future of Food Security and Agriculture. With this initiative, they seek to develop a long-term strategy to work across the public, private and social sectors to achieve a 20% improvement each decade in food security, environmental sustainability and economic opportunity. This will be achieved through a market-based and multi-stakeholder approach, in line with the New Vision for Agriculture (NVA). They have initiated specific partnerships for the development of Africa and Asia. Developing agricultural productivity is particularly important in these regions as the agricultural sector accounts for one-third of GDP and three-quarters of employment in sub-Saharan Africa.

Their Grow Africa Partnership was founded jointly by the African Union (AU), The New Partnership for Africa's Development (NEPAD) and the World Economic Forum in 2011. Grow Africa works to increase private sector investment in agriculture, and accelerate the execution and impact of investment commitments. The aim is to enable countries to realize the potential of the agriculture sector for economic growth and job creation, particularly among farmers, women and youth. Grow Africa brokers collaboration between governments, agriculture companies, and smallholder farmers in order to lower the risk and cost of investing in agriculture, and improve the speed of

return to all stakeholders.

Grow Asia is a multi-stakeholder partnership that aims to reach 10 million smallholder farmers by 2020, helping them access knowledge, technology, finance, and markets to increase their productivity, profitability, and environmental sustainability by 20%. Grow Asia brings together South East Asia's smallholders, governments, companies, NGOs, and other stakeholders, to develop inclusive and sustainable value chains that benefit farmers. Today, Grow Asia collaborates with 261 partners across five Country Partnerships, reaching nearly half a million smallholder farmers.

WRAP UP

Food sustains humanity and all other animals. It is at the essence of survival for all living beings. Food security is one of the most crucial achievements that we need to reach and sustain. It can be achieved by eradicating waste and increasing production, along with ensuring adequate social and economic frameworks to facilitate food access to all. To eradicate waste, there are several key focal points, including developing technological and low-tech innovations to help producers retain and transport their harvest, and changing business and consumer practices. To increase production, information dissemination plays an important role, as well as partnerships to collectively address climate issues.

FOOD SECURITY IS ONE OF THE MOST CRUCIAL ACHIEVEMENTS THAT WE NEED TO REACH AND SUSTAIN.

Shared value is inherent in solutions to creating food security, as food production and consumption transcends borders and socio-demographics. It is an industry involving multi-stakeholders, and societal and environmental factors are integral in food production and consumption. Therefore, shared value models should form the foundation of solutions to the issue of food security. The food and agriculture sector is already a trillion dollar industry, and the potential for shared value with other sectors, such as ICT, is tremendous.

All of the Sustainable Development Goals are relevant to food security. The biggest opportunities relate to opening new markets in low-income areas, creating technological solutions for farming, and reducing waste. By focusing on achieving the Sustainable Development Goals, and preparing to meet the demands of a rapidly growing population while embedding sustainable practices, the sector can change its course and consequently gain new business opportunities. Dr. Fraser Thompson, Director of AlphaBeta, which conducted the research for the Business Com-

mission, addressed hesitation to engage with the SDGs when he said, "Many commentators have incorrectly perceived the SDGs to represent an additional headwind to growth and profitability. The reality is that in many cases the SDGs offer a new and higher quality channel for economic growth and business profitability." While there are considerable challenges facing this sector, with a clear focus and concerted efforts by businesses, consumers and consortiums, significant strides in creating a sustainable food and agriculture system to feed the world can be achieved, and the food and agriculture sector can make a considerable contribution towards reaching all of the Sustainable Development Goals. ■

> "MANY COMMENTATORS HAVE INCORRECTLY PERCEIVED THE SDGs TO REPRESENT AN ADDITIONAL HEADWIND TO GROWTH AND PROFITABILITY. THE REALITY IS THAT IN MANY CASES THE SDGs OFFER A NEW AND HIGHER QUALITY CHANNEL FOR ECONOMIC GROWTH AND BUSINESS PROFITABILITY."
>
> DR. FRASER THOMPSON, DIRECTOR OF ALPHABETA

DEVELOPING EFFECTIVE, SUSTAINABLE AND IMPROVED FOOD PRODUCTIVITY REQUIRES ATTENTION TO: RESOURCES, ENVIRONMENTAL INFLUENCES, AND PRODUCTION PROCESSES.

EDUCATION AND LEARNING

We are in a global learning crisis. Quality education has been pushed to the side and is not a priority in many areas of the world, leaving millions without the basic tools for full participation in the global economy. In developing countries, the population of 15 to 24-year-olds totals over one billion - roughly one-sixth of the world's population. In many of these regions, there are limited investments in quality education. The inevitable result of a lack of educational opportunities is a huge population without the skills, knowledge or attitudes to engage positively in society. Therefore, if we fail to act, we face deepening inequalities and the untapped potential of millions to drive our collective future. Education must continue to evolve and stay up-to-date. In countries where education is readily available, there is a continuous need for improvement. As education is the key to personal development, there is a need to continue to enrich the quality, and expand the quantity of educational opportunities.

7.1 SDG 4: QUALITY EDUCATION

Education is a sector, it is a fundamental process, and it is the fourth Goal among the 17 SDGs. It is also the basis for a sustainable society, as it enables populations to address shared challenges through collaboration, skills training, and empowerment. Education is the key to improving people's lives all over the world and is essential to the success of sustainable development as a whole. Making quality education affordable and accessible will assist in creating collaborative platforms and promoting entrepreneurship. Education can in fact "catalyze a shift towards a greener, brighter future."[1] With this in mind, the Sustainable Development Goals include Goal number four dedicated to ensuring inclusive and equitable quality education and promoting lifelong learning opportunities for all. The following Targets are associated with SDG 4 and are useful to keep in mind.

Ensuring inclusive and equitable quality education for all is not easy. The current education disparity is worse in conflict-affected countries. Many children have had their education interrupted and the quality and prevalence of education have decreased in many of these areas. In some countries, progress has stalled or even reversed. Natural disasters also cause crises, which can interrupt educational progress. These interruptions put children at a disadvantage, needing to find ways to overcome the gaps in their education. There are also chronic inequalities in educational opportunities in parts of the world as children, youths and adults - and especially women and girls - still face difficulties or discrimination accessing quality learning opportunities, despite international affirmation of the right to education.

IF WE FAIL TO ACT, WE FACE DEEPENING INEQUALITIES AND THE UNTAPPED POTENTIAL OF MILLIONS TO DRIVE OUR COLLECTIVE FUTURE.

Once access is attained, there are still significant failings in the quality of education, with children and youths often not learning the skills they need even when they are given schooling. There are 274 million children of primary school age around the globe who are not learning the basic foundational skills to lead productive and healthy lives.[2] The issue is further exacerbated by the fact that still today more than 750 million adults, nearly two-thirds of whom are women, also cannot read or write.[3] While progress for youth literacy has improved in recent years, there continues to be a persistent discrepancy in literacy levels between men and women.

SDG 4: QUALITY EDUCATION
Ensure inclusive and equitable quality education and promote lifelong learning opportunities for all

TARGETS

4.1 By 2030, ensure that all girls and boys complete free, equitable and quality primary and secondary education leading to relevant and effective learning outcomes

4.2 By 2030, ensure that all girls and boys have access to quality early childhood development, care and pre-primary education so that they are ready for primary education

4.3 By 2030, ensure equal access for all women and men to affordable quality technical, vocational and tertiary education, including university

4.4 By 2030, substantially increase the number of youth and adults who have relevant skills, including technical and vocational skills, for employment, decent jobs and entrepreneurship

4.5 By 2030, eliminate gender disparities in education and ensure equal access to all levels of education and vocational training for the vulnerable, including persons with disabilities, indigenous peoples, and children in vulnerable situations

4.6 By 2030, ensure that all youth and a substantial proportion of adults, both men and women, achieve literacy and numeracy

4.7 By 2030, ensure all learners acquire knowledge and skills needed to promote sustainable development, including, among others, through education for sustainable development and sustainable lifestyles, human rights, gender equality, promotion of a culture of peace and non-violence, global citizenship, and appreciation of cultural diversity and of culture's contribution to sustainable development

4.a Build and upgrade education facilities that are child, disability and gender sensitive and provide safe, non-violent, inclusive and effective learning environments for all

4.b By 2020, substantially expand globally the number of scholarships for developing countries in particular least developed countries, small island developing States and African countries for enrolment in higher education, including vocational training, and information and communications technology, technical, engineering and scientific programs in developed countries and other developing countries

4.c By 2030, substantially increase the supply of qualified teachers, including through international cooperation for teacher training in developing countries, especially least developed countries and small island developing States

7.2 SOLVING THE CHALLENGES: EDUCATION AS A FUNDAMENTAL BUILDING BLOCK FOR THE GOALS

Education is the cornerstone of thriving societies worldwide, and is directly linked to prosperity. Consequently, basic education is provided as a right in many developed countries as governments recognize that education provides the foundation for democratic participation and economic success. For this reason, education is the great global equalizer, and developing countries will benefit from improving the quality of education.

Learning and education are broad concepts, but mostly when we think of education, we think of primary and secondary school for children, higher education in the form of vocational schools or universities, and business training and other courses to learn a specific skill or expand knowledge. In recent years, "life-long learning" has become a common theme for adults continuing to seek training and educational opportunities throughout their lives. Businesses have been recognizing the need to offer their employees training courses, coaching and skill development in an effort to nurture their growth and keep their resource pool relevant.

A LACK OF QUALITY EDUCATION CONTRIBUTES TO HIGHER UNEMPLOYMENT AND WEAKER ECONOMIES.

While some people in the world have access to quality education their whole lives through, others are denied access to even the most basic educational skills. This educational disparity is a global challenge, and the consequences of educational inequity affect individuals, communities, and society at large. A lack of quality education contributes to higher unemployment and weaker economies. Achieving quality education for all involves identi-

fying the needs in different areas and looking for solutions that provide shared value. As a foundational building block, education impacts all the Goals. But the challenges related to education vary depending on regions in the world and the circumstances that prevail.

> **THERE ARE 274 MILLION CHILDREN OF PRIMARY SCHOOL AGE AROUND THE GLOBE WHO ARE NOT LEARNING THE BASIC FOUNDATIONAL SKILLS TO LEAD PRODUCTIVE AND HEALTHY LIVES.**
>
> GLOBALPARTNERSHIP.ORG

In developing countries, education is not always provided as a right, and educational opportunities that are available are often lacking. Issues facing developing countries regarding educational attainment include access to basic schooling, reducing - or preferably eliminating - illiteracy, and specific work training. Especially relevant in developing countries is access to education for women and girls.

In developed countries, even though most children have access to basic education, quality education is sometimes lacking. There are millions of students who leave school every day without the skills they need to attain financial security and be informed citizens with real prospects for the future. This type of educational inequity sustains unemployment, crime, and violence. In the United States, for example, a male high school dropout is 47 times more likely to be incarcerated than a college graduate.[5] Furthermore, the need for continued training is more relevant now than ever before. The business landscape is changing rapidly, and companies are wise to provide educational opportunities to their workforces for optimal adaptability.

> ## GLOBAL EDUCATION FACES AN ESTIMATED ANNUAL BUDGETARY SHORTFALL OF US $26 BILLION.
>
> UNESCO

All over the world, there are improvements to be made to education. However, global education faces an estimated annual budgetary shortfall of US $26 billion.[6] Governments, foundations, and nonprofits can help with various aspects of this problem to a certain extent, yet education spending is undoubtedly also a business issue, and businesses can contribute to developing solutions. Without money allocated to education both for and from the public and private sectors, there will be a shortfall of knowledge and skills to drive business forward and address all the Goals. Educated workers, for example, are better equipped to become gainful employees as well as profitable consumers. And businesses that have an educated workforce are more productive and profitable, giving them the ability to strengthen the economy.

WITHOUT MONEY ALLOCATED TO EDUCATION BOTH FOR AND FROM THE PUBLIC AND PRIVATE SECTORS, THERE WILL BE A SHORTFALL OF KNOWLEDGE AND SKILLS TO DRIVE BUSINESS FORWARD AND ADDRESS ALL THE GOALS.

A world of expanding educational opportunities and decreasing disparities is likely to be a more prosperous, peaceful, and sustainable world where more children and communities thrive. Be-cause education is a shared global value, one that intersects with most of the SDGs, the sector can be improved by working together across industries and incorporating learning into core businesses strategies.

COMPANIES ARE WISE TO PROVIDE EDUCATIONAL OPPORTUNITIES TO THEIR WORKFORCES FOR OPTIMAL ADAPTABILITY.

Solutions to the education challenges can involve the use of ICT and other technology, which can be implemented to facilitate access and improved quality of education. All over the planet, there are rural, hard to reach areas where people live. In many of these areas, access to schools is limited, if not altogether unavailable. Imagine smallholder farmers in Africa that cannot be reached easily but could benefit from up-to-date information on market trends, weather pattern shifts, and sustainable business practices. They can now access that knowledge using their mobile phones. And people who live too far from higher education institutions, or cannot attend classes because of other circumstances, now have the opportunity to follow educational courses online. The application of technological solutions to learning opens new business markets in this sector that could be beneficial to all.

Education is crucial to accelerating the achievement of nearly all the Goals. For instance, climate action (SDG 13): we can install systems such as windmills and solar panels to reduce carbon emissions and slow climate impacts, but if we don't educate engineers and maintenance workers on how to work with these systems, we simply will not have enough professionals with the know-how to maintain them.

7.3 IMPACT OF EDUCATION AND LEARNING ON ALL SDGs

Addressing this Goal is fundamental to the achievement of all the Goals, as progress in education is also linked to solutions for many of the world's most pressing challenges. And the reverse is also true; impact on the other Goals affects education.

SDG 1: No Poverty; Education has proven to promote economic growth and be one of the most effective ways to reduce poverty. Illiteracy cost the global economy an estimated US $1.2 trillion in 2015.[7] More than 790 million people are either completely illiterate or functionally illiterate. Without quality and accessible education, people in both rich and poor countries can become trapped in a cycle of poverty with limited opportunities for employment or income generation. This cycle is often perpetuated with children needing to leave school due to the obligation to work and provide support for the family. Research shows that for every US $1 invested in early childhood education, it is estimated to lead to a return as high as US $17 for the most disadvantaged and impoverished children.[8] Many of the poor work as daily laborers or run microenterprises. The more educated they are, the more likely it is that they will start a business and that their businesses will be profitable. In impoverished areas of Uganda, for example, owners of household enterprises who had completed primary education earned 36% more than those with no education, and those who had completed lower secondary education earned 56% more.[9] It is estimated that 171 million people could be lifted out of poverty - a 12% drop in people living on less than US $1.25 a day - if all students in low-income countries attained basic reading skills.[10] One extra year of schooling increases an individual's earnings by up to 10%, and each additional year of schooling raises average annual gross domestic product by 0.37%.[11]

SDG 2: Zero Hunger; There is strong evidence that a mother's education improves her children's nutrition, especially as she seeks higher levels of schooling. It is estimated that 1.7 million more children can reach full growth potential if all women complete primary education, rising to 12.2 million more if secondary schooling is complete.[12] There are approximately 47 million children in low-income countries that are stunted as a result of malnutrition in early childhood.[13] Without proper nutrition in the first 1000 days of life, children may suffer from physical and psychological ailments disrupting their ability to learn over their lifetimes. Furthermore, investments in agriculture education yield 80% annual rates of return and can help farmers double their crop yields.[14] Food production education programs should be farmer-centered and knowledge-based so that the full potential of farmers can be harnessed in making food security and sustainable development a reality.

> **ILLITERACY COST THE GLOBAL ECONOMY AN ESTIMATED US $1.2 TRILLION IN 2015.**
>
> UNGLOBALCOMPACT

SDG 3: Good Health and Well-Being; Good health is often a requisite to non-interrupted education. Many children from disadvantaged backgrounds are forced to abandon their education due to health problems related to malnutrition. This is an unfortunate vicious cycle because better educated people are much less vulnerable to health risks. Furthermore, behavior-change based education programs are effective in addressing the risks associated with nutrition and disease. When mothers in particular are educated, even at the most primary level, they are more likely to be well informed about various diseases and take steps to prevent them.[15] Four million child deaths have been prevented over the past four decades

MILLIONS OF CHILDREN IN THE DEVELOPING WORLD GO TO SCHOOLS WHICH HAVE NO DRINKING WATER OR CLEAN LATRINES – BASIC THINGS THAT MANY OF US TAKE FOR GRANTED.[18]

UNICEF

thanks to the global increase in women's education.[16] Each extra year of a mother's schooling reduces the probability of infant mortality by as much as 10% and a child whose mother can read is 50% more likely to live past age five.[17] Increasing investment in family planning and other maternal and child-health programs can empower families to lead healthier lifestyles. Sanitation and hygiene are critical to survival in many areas of the world, and there have been community mobilization efforts to teach citizens how to access credit and materials to build sanitation facilities. Employing and training marginalized people as masons and bricklayers, for example, helps build safe and hygienic toilets while promoting economic growth. And education and training of medical professionals are also essential for building effective health systems.

SDG 4: Quality Education; Education builds on itself, creating greater capacity to educate others and nurture a culture that values learning. Investing in and strengthening a country's education sector is key to the development of any country and its people. Research shows that for every US $1 invested in a child's education, there is a US $53 return to a company at the start of employment.[19] Getting all children into primary education, while raising learning standards, could boost economic growth by 2% annually in low-income countries. Without investment in quality education, progress on all other development indicators will not be as strong. Globally, around 250 million children are

not learning basic skills, even though half of them have spent at least four years in school. The annual cost of this failure to society is estimated to be US $129 billion.[20] Education is expanding business opportunities within societies. Investment in education leads business to new market opportunities and customer bases. From a brand perspective, knowledgeable consumers indicate a greater willingness to buy – and reward – socially conscious brands. Additionally, informed shareholders of companies are more likely to have expectations for business to manage its social impact.

SDG 5: Gender Equality; Education enables girls and women to reach their full potential in their homes, communities, workplaces, and institutions of influence. According to World Bank studies, one additional school year can increase a woman's earnings by up to 20%. Some countries lose more than US $1 billion a year by failing to educate girls at the same level as boys. As the gap between girls' and boys' education narrows, gender disparities in wages and employment decrease as well,[21] yet there is still a long way to go to equalize this entirely. Women in developing countries could be an estimated US $9 trillion better off if their pay and access to paid work were equal to that of men.[22] Firms with greater upper-level diversity report performing better throughout the business, out-performing others by 53% return on equity and 66% return on invested capital. This closing

IF WOMEN PARTICIPATE IN THE ECONOMY IDENTICALLY TO MEN, IT COULD CREATE INCREMENTAL ANNUAL GDP IMPACT OF US $28 TRILLION IN 2025 COMPARED WITH A BUSINESS-AS-USUAL SCENARIO.[24]

VALUING THE SDG PRIZE

of the higher education gender gap creates societies with more disposable income for goods and services, while strengthening women's empowerment in families and communities. Increased educational attainment accounts for approximately 50% of the economic growth in OECD countries over the past 50 years, over half of which is due to girls experiencing greater access to education.[23]

SDG 6: Clean Water and Sanitation; As societies become more economically prosperous and formally educated, they will be better able to create modern water and sanitation facilities and systems. In many societies, girls can spend as many as 15 hours per week fetching water for their families, leaving little or no time for school.[25] Similarly, without knowledge of access to safe sanitation, there are many more sick children who will miss school. Educated households are also more likely to use different methods of water purification through filtering or boiling. In urban India, the probability of purification increased by 9% when the most educated adult had completed primary education and by 22% when the most educated adult had completed secondary education.[26] Many schools in poorer countries lack adequate water and sanitation facilities, affecting children's educations and even claiming lives as 1.5 million children under the age of five die every year of diarrhea due to unsafe water, inadequate sanitation and lack of hygiene.[27] With nearly 300 million school days missed worldwide due to diarrhea, better water, sanitation, and hygiene is needed to reverse the trend.[28] Improved hygiene will lead to less risk of disease, which in turn will result in more consistent school attendance and ultimately a nation's economic growth. In Ethiopia, 6.8 million people learned about and gained access to improved sanitation from 1990 to 2006.[29]

SDG 7: Affordable and Clean Energy; Adequate energy supply is necessary for well-lit, well-heated, and well-cooled schools and households which are essential for creating conducive learning spaces for children and adults. It is also needed for information and communication technologies that facilitate modern learning. Ensuring energy access in countries where reliable energy services may be lacking can therefore reinforce education methods. Science and technical education is needed now more than ever. To design, maintain and understand the need for sustainable and clean energy, high-level education is needed. Additionally, since renewable energy is the necessary path for sustainable energy production, and a growing domain, people in polluting energy industries, like coal, will need retraining to adapt to the changing employment opportunities. Within the decade between 2000 and 2010, 30,000 jobs were lost in the coal industry in the US, leaving approximately 86,000 coal miners still employed in the country in 2010.[30] In contrast, in that same year, renewable energy accounted for about 175,000 US jobs. According to a recent US Department of Energy report, as of January 2017, that figure had grown to almost 800,000 workers employed in low carbon electricity generation,[31] while the number of coal miners decreased further to 50,000. Therefore, it is evident that appropriate education and training is needed to meet the needs of growing energy industries such as solar and wind. So, while education is needed to achieve and maintain affordable clean energy, sustainable energy is required for the growing needs of education especially in the current technology-dependent society.

SDG 8: Decent Work and Economic Growth; Education is fundamental to the development of future workforces. It supports higher levels of productivity, adaptability, and innovation. Education also fosters more stable and prosperous societies, such as larger and more sustainable markets for products and services. It can also develop capacities of the future workforce. An increase of one year in the average educational attainment of a country's population increases annual per capita GDP growth from 2% to 2.5%,[32] and leads to a 10% increase in income across 139 countries. Businesses should identify current and future competencies needed for the labor market, and make sure to design and implement appropriate training programs for their workforce. Also, businesses can invest in basic education in develop-

IF WE CONTINUE TO PROGRESS AT OUR CURRENT PACE, BY 2030 HALF OF ALL THE YOUTH—OVER 800 MILLION YOUNG PEOPLE—WILL NOT HAVE BASIC SECONDARY EDUCATION LEVEL SKILLS NEEDED TO KEEP UP IN A NEW ECONOMY. [33]

BROOKINGS.EDU

ing markets in order to improve the future talent pool. In addition, businesses will need to consider that the aging population provides significant opportunities for sustainable development through the active participation of older generations in the economy, labor market and society at large (e.g. by unpaid care work, political participation and by continued work after retirement). Education and skills development equip people for productive and sustained employment and entrepreneurship. Furthermore, in the rapidly changing environment of technological advances, technical education and training are becoming necessary to function and excel in many sectors. It is expected that many jobs will be lost due to automation and other technological disruptions. Knowledge workers and highly skilled workforces are, and will continue to be, necessary for economic growth.

 SDG 9: Industry, Innovation and Infrastructure; Adequate infrastructure makes it possible for children to get to school conveniently and quickly. In some parts of the world, this infrastructure is lacking. With the development of wireless telecommunications, education has been able to reach people in remote areas enabling countries lagging behind others to leapfrog over the expensive investment in infrastructure that would otherwise be necessary.[34] Nonetheless, improvements in infrastructure help immensely in the pursuit of

formal education. Innovation and education often go hand-in-hand. Education inspires and provides the tools for innovators to thrive. Industry can provide cost-effective educational products and services, and eliminate barriers to access, such as cost, distance, and infrastructure inadequacies. Innovative businesses can also improve the quality of learning through an array of learning and measurement tools.[35] By taking a long-term perspective, business has a lasting effect on education by investing in educational innovation, infrastructure, and workforce training.

 SDG 10: Reduced Inequalities; As more children from across the demographic, geographic and cultural spectrum become educated, improvements in a country's income inequality are likely. Numerous studies confirm that a more equitable distribution of education opportunities reduces income inequality. One study showed that a 0.1% improvement in a country's education equality could, over forty years, raise its per capita income by 23%.[36] As an example, research demonstrated that with more education equality, Vietnam's economic performance improved and, in 2005, its GDP surpassed Pakistan's, where education equality levels are half those of Vietnam's.[37] And, with quality education, people from traditionally disadvantaged communities are better positioned to advocate for their own rights and needs, gain entry into higher echelons of economic, social and civic life and help narrow gaps of inequality across their societies.

 SDG 11: Sustainable Cities and Communities; With education, people are more likely to understand, support and craft creative solutions for the development of sustainable cities and communities. Good urban planning, efficient energy use, good water and sanitation management, social inclusion and other elements of well-working communities require people with knowledge and skills. Only with quality education can these skills be developed. At the core of a World Bank Sustainable Cities Initiative, for example, are awareness-building programs, development and implementation of local

diagnostic tools, the creation of policy reforms and other tasks that require not just primary but advanced education. Specific educational training is also needed to achieve solutions for issues facing cities and communities to make them more sustainable. One such issue is the projection that world cities are expected to generate 2.4 billion tons of solid waste per year by 2025. Some innovative businesses, such as Wongpanit, have developed training programs for communities on how to start recycling businesses.[38]

 SDG 12: Responsible Consumption and Production; Digital connectivity plays a critical role in bettering lives, and it provides unprecedented access to knowledge for billions of people worldwide. As a result, people increasingly have access to free education online. Technology companies from Silicon Valley and other regions have begun providing solutions to problems ranging from adaptive learning to global access of high-quality education. This type of education technology, also known as edtech[39] or E-learning, is growing more important with regard to learning across the globe and in the last few years, there has been a surge in investment from schools and investors in this industry. Massive Open Online Courses (MOOC) are also becoming more popular and have the potential to reach people around the world with quality higher education courses. Universities in the US, UK and elsewhere have made classes available to millions of people. The education market is constantly growing, and it is forecasted that edtech investment alone will reach US $252 billion by 2020.[40] Some examples of current top edtech companies are Duolingo,[41] Noodle[42] and Knewton.[43] And MOOC platforms include Coursera and FutureLearn. Digital learning is also teaching people to be sustainable producers, for example, mobile teaching is being made available to smallholder farmers, teaching them how to produce their crops more sustainably. And educational apps are also being used to educate people about sustainable consumption patterns. For example, apps have been developed to teach people in hospitality industries how to eliminate food waste.

 SDG 13: Climate Action; In 29 countries, 25% of people with less than a secondary education expressed concern for the environment compared to 37% of people with secondary education and 46% of people with tertiary education, research shows.[44] With higher levels of education, people across many different societies show greater concern about the well-being of the environment. Scientific education also helps people to understand the effects of climate change and inspires solutions to help curb these effects. Specific climate change education is beginning to find its way into the curriculum of current and future business leaders. Strategies to limit the magnitude of climate change, adapt to the impacts, and develop effective responses to climate change include business schools preparing their students to be environmental and social stewards and ethical actors in the workplace. In doing so, faculty are drawing on interdisciplinary resources to teach sustainability and instill habits and mindsets that will serve students well in their careers. This education-based response to climate change also includes social enterprises that create sustainable livelihoods by training entrepreneurs to provide customers with sustainable life-improving and affordable products. Educating people in climate sensitive areas and lines of work, such as people living on islands and people working in agriculture, teaches them how to respond to natural disasters, prevent them, preserve the environment and protect the people and the planet.

> **IN 2016, YALE UNIVERSITY RESEARCHERS FOUND THAT 40% OF ADULTS WORLDWIDE HAD NEVER HEARD OF CLIMATE CHANGE. IN SOME DEVELOPING COUNTRIES, SUCH AS INDIA, THAT FIGURE CLIMBED TO 65%.**[45]
>
> PROJECT-SYNDICATE.ORG

IN SYRIA, ONE IN THREE SCHOOLS IS NOW OUT OF USE BECAUSE THEY HAVE BEEN BOMBED, TAKEN OVER BY ARMED GROUPS OR TURNED INTO SHELTERS. OVER 1.75 MILLION CHILDREN ARE OUT OF SCHOOL AND, AFTER SIX AND A HALF YEARS OF WAR, MANY YOUNG CHILDREN HAVE NEVER ATTENDED SCHOOL.[50]

RELIEFWEB.INT

 SDG 14: Life Below Water; The market value of marine and coastal resources and industries is estimated at US $3 trillion per year, or about 5% of global GDP.[46] Yet, as much as 40% of the oceans are suffering negative effects from human activities, including pollution, depleted fisheries, and loss of coastal habitats because of poor management. Providing education on sustainable practices to fishing communities in developing regions can help to enhance economic returns and manage ocean degradation. For example, teaching people how to reduce the number of abandoned nets in ocean environments protects aquatic life from the dangers of lost or discarded nets that damage coral reefs and trap and entangle fish, marine mammals and birds. Education is necessary for people to learn how to conserve and sustainably use the oceans, seas and marine resources for sustainable development. Environmental education programs have facilitated important advances in national and regional efforts to fight climate change and protect marine life and ecosystems. But for these programs to reach their full potential, it is important that a country's or region's inhabitants have a strong primary and secondary educational base.

 SDG 15: Life on Land; People with more education are more likely to engage in actions in relation to protecting the environment. In Germany, while 12% of people with less than secondary education took a stance on the environment and engaged in political action, the share rose to 26% of those with secondary education and 46% of those with ter-

tiary education.[47] Around the world, smallholder farmers can increase efficient food production and harvest by making better use of available arable lands. Increasing smallholder food production through education and training programs can make low-income rural communities self-sufficient and reduce hunger. Teaching people to participate in more sustainable and resilient agriculture practices aligned to ecosystems' management can reinforce protection, restoration and sustainable use of terrestrial ecosystems. Better educated citizens are more likely to participate in sustainable forestry and help stop deforestation, while also contributing to the restoration of degraded land and soils as well as combating desertification.[48]

SDG 16: Peace, Justice and Strong Institutions; Education is an essential precursor to peace, tolerance and a healthy civil society. People with secondary educations are more likely than those with only primary education to show tolerance for others and behave less violently. Juvenile crime is often associated with local unemployment and poverty. Literate people are also more likely to participate in the democratic process and exercise their civil rights. In Colombia, for example, it was estimated that if all school children completed primary school, they would be 1.5 times more likely to vote for their own economic interests; and their propensity to vote in the next presidential election would increase from 31 to 47%.[49] Furthermore, this Goal of Peace, Justice and Strong Institutions promotes transparency and public access to information – education is a crucial precursor to understanding the information made available by governing institutions. Education not only influences this SDG, but education is also influenced by it. There are 24 million children living in 22 countries who are affected by national or regional conflicts. In war-torn areas, education opportunities are interrupted. That leaves millions of children with significant gaps in their development.

SDG 17: Partnerships for the Goals; The Global Partnership for Education (GPE) is a prominent example of how working in a collaborative partnership can enhance progress in education and in the other development sectors. The GPE brings together developing countries, donors, international organizations, civil society, teacher organizations, the private sector, and foundations.[51] The partnership model of the GPE mobilizes and aligns donor financing behind national education plans that are based on needs assessments and evidence-based policy-making. Businesses have the opportunity to engage in global education initiatives, offering a diverse variety of partnerships with governments and education organizations across the globe. Some examples of educational partnerships that could be engaged in are One Eleuthera (center for Training and Innovation), Nations play (a global learning program) and the ILead Program (center to promote a reading culture among children living in rural areas).[52] The GPE is enabling marginalized children to have quality education and shows how collaboration can bring better results.[53]

Figuur 37 **Education and the Global Goals** Source: **sendmyfriend.org**

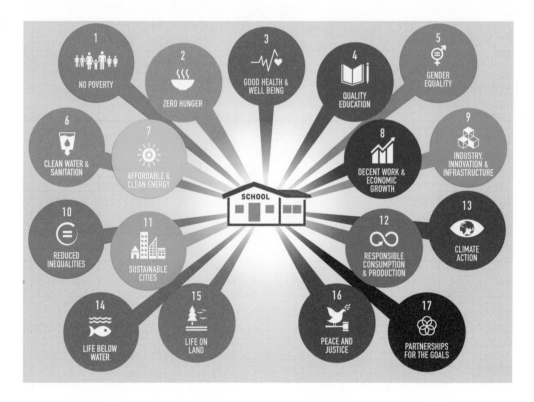

7.4 SHARED VALUE OPPORTUNITIES

Shared value "is a business approach that increases profits by improving the effectiveness of education systems at scale," explains John Elkington, a world expert on sustainability.[54] While governments are often tasked with providing education to their citizens, there is tremendous potential for the private sector to contribute to improving education around the world. Business has been able to drive progress in areas such as health, and business can drive progress in education as well. Experience shows that business has the potential for transformational impact in education and can be an effective partner in improving education systems and learning worldwide. While some businesses already lead the way in effective engagement, the shared value framework can help other companies advance global education goals. Business must align its core economic and social objectives. As the former UN Secretary-General Ban Ki-moon so aptly stated to business leaders, "You understand investment. You focus on the bottom-line. You know the dividends of education for all." Business, the economy, and society at large reap the benefits of an educated population.

Global education shortfalls are challenging social stability and economic progress. This is evident when you look at the 200 million people who are unemployed, while nearly 60% of CEOs report that a shortage of skilled labor is holding back their company's growth.[55] Schools are failing to provide students with the skills they need in the workforce today. The education system must adapt to societal transformations. At the moment, scholastic education as a whole is not keeping up with technological advances and the changing habits, attitudes, and abilities of students.

To help solve this issue, technology companies such as Cisco, the leading provider of networking equipment, are creating their own educational academies. Cisco, for example, created 10,000 networking academies in 165 countries that have graduated 4.75 million trained network administrators, improving students' employment prospects and increasing the demand for Cisco's equipment.[56] Cisco's Networking Academy equips students with the necessary knowledge and skills to fill an estimated eight million networking jobs around the world. When companies take it upon themselves to create educational opportunities, training people in the skills necessary for jobs in their industry, they help to increase their own labor market and that of the rest of the industry — fueling economic growth, and creating shared value.

SHARED VALUE DEFINES A NEW ROLE FOR BUSINESS IN HELPING TO OVERCOME THE GLOBAL EDUCATION AND UNEMPLOYMENT CRISIS.

Shared value defines a new role for business in helping to overcome the global education and unemployment crisis. By aligning profit with purpose, companies can become instrumental partners for schools, nonprofits, and governments. This alignment is mutually beneficial as their involvement can simultaneously help businesses discover new

> **THERE ARE 200 MILLION PEOPLE WHO ARE UNEMPLOYED, WHILE NEARLY 60% OF CEOs REPORT THAT A SHORTAGE OF SKILLED LABOR IS HOLDING BACK THEIR COMPANY'S GROWTH.**
>
> SHAREDVALUE.ORG

ways to increase their productivity, strengthen industry clusters, and expand their markets. By using a shared value approach, businesses create the power to scale solutions to our world's greatest education challenges far beyond what they could do with philanthropy alone.

Companies in the technology sector have additional opportunities to create shared value in learning outcomes. And the technology sector has even more motivation than other sectors to do so, as there is tremendous and increasing demand for skilled technical workers. Technology can play a big role in delivering quality education and training to people all over the world. E-learning is supporting education initiatives across a wide range of demographic needs. From overcoming illiteracy at the most fundamental level to bringing better teachers to remote areas that need more extensive and accessible learning offerings, and making technology and E-learning at universities available to people who otherwise could not afford it, technological advancement in education is helping to reduce inequality and raise people out of poverty.

All companies can create shared value in education, but their opportunities to do so depend on their specific needs and capabilities. For companies that sell products and services to educators, shared value opportunities are driven by a rapidly expanding global market. A growing global middle class is expanding the overall market for educational products and services by nearly 50% from US $4.4 trillion in 2012 to $6.2 trillion by 2017.[58] Competition in educational products and servic

es is favoring companies that create the greatest value for society. By developing new materials and trainings that enhance educational outcomes, companies are also able to gain market share and shift the underlying basis of business competition to student success.

Verizon Wireless has paved a road to shared value, reflecting a fundamental organizational commitment to linking innovation and financial growth with social outcomes (See Case 38). The company recognizes that it can best deliver on outcomes when their own incentives and processes are closely aligned with student success. In doing so, Verizon moves beyond good intentions for creating student achievement to embedding that objective into their business model. The company launched Verizon Innovative Learning Schools (VILS) as the base for its corporate citizenship education programming. VILS is Verizon's innovative approach to pioneering shared value and rethinking the role of its various functional units in creating shared value. While choosing its education strategy based on the ability to leverage its core competencies—mobile devices and wireless technology—Verizon addresses the central barriers and enhances student outcomes in the STEM field. Verizon has transformed its purpose from philanthropic endeavors to an effective platform for testing educational technology approaches and accelerating potential shared value products and services within the business.[59] This shift in implementation allows Verizon to more directly assess the impact of its own technology and mobile services on educational outcomes.

ACTIVITIES THAT HELP DELIVER SOCIAL AND BUSINESS VALUE:[57]

- PILOT NEW, OPEN SOURCE TECHNOLOGY TO IMPROVE THE DELIVERY OF EDUCATION FOR HARD-TO-REACH COMMUNITIES.
- APPLY DESIGN-THINKING TO DEVELOP LOW-COST LEARNING MATERIALS FOR UNDER-RESOURCED SCHOOLS AND BOTTOM OF THE PYRAMID COMMUNITIES.
- IDENTIFY INNOVATIVE PRODUCTS BY SPONSORING COMPETITIONS FOR EDUCATION ENTREPRENEURS AND COMMERCIALIZING SUCCESSFUL IDEAS.
- UTILIZE CORPORATE TRAINING CURRICULA TO DEVELOP SKILL CERTIFICATION OPPORTUNITIES IN COOPERATION WITH EXISTING PROVIDERS AND GOVERNMENT.
- LEVERAGE ANALYTICAL EXPERTISE TO DEVELOP TOOLS TO MEASURE THE IMPACT OF EDUCATION PROGRAMS.
- SUPPORT INNOVATIVE TEACHING METHODS AND TOOLS THAT FOSTER CREATIVE AND ENTREPRENEURIAL THINKING.

UN GLOBAL COMPACT

38
CASE NO. **VERIZON**

Verizon Innovative Learning Schools
Investing in STEM related education to
build a better future

Case applied in: USA
Office located in: USA
www.verizon.com

IMPACT SDGS

SDG 4
Education for All

Impact with a commitment
of US $160 million for over
300,000 students, 7,400
teachers, and 1,900 schools
and clubs.

SDG 5
Gender Equality

Launching a dynamic,
experiential summer program
for middle school girls at
community colleges in rural
areas, where they will learn
coding, design thinking, social
entrepreneurship, storytelling
and augmented reality.

SDG 9
**Industry, Innovation and
Infrastructure**

More than 1 in 3 students
improved in academic
achievement, 4 in 10 exhibited
more sophisticated projects,
and 60% strengthened their
technology skills.

SDG 10
Reduced Inequalities

Target underserved
populations, thereby achieving
significant diversity in
demographics, location, and
socio-economic status.

> WE WANTED TO MOVE AWAY FROM BEING A GRANT-MAKING ORGANIZATION TO BECOMING AN INCUBATOR FOR SOLUTIONS THAT CAN ASSIST THE BUSINESS AS IT IS CONTEMPLATING ITS FUTURE STRATEGY. **THAT HAS BEEN A VERY CONSCIOUS CHANGE.**
>
> ROSE STUCKEY KIRK, PRESIDENT, VERIZON FOUNDATION

As Verizon embraces a shared value approach, it is pioneering technology products and solutions that provide "powerful answers" to pressing problems facing society. The company has coined its own philosophy: Verizon "Shared Success."

Verizon believes that to compete for the jobs of the future, it is essential for every child to have access to technology and STEM (science, technology, engineering and math) education. Therefore, Verizon developed the Verizon Innovative Learning Schools (VILS) program, committing US $160 million in free tech, free access and hands-on immersive learning in STEM for students in need. Verizon does not simply fund these programs, it also creates and administers them. The company also has a diligent measurement system to test the impact of its work and to refine programs.

Many schools across America lack the technology and resources to prepare students for a future in the digital world. To maximize its impact and make a real difference, Verizon focusses on more than just technology. Through its partnership with Digital Promise, it has not only made it possible for every child and teacher at middle schools across America to be equipped with a tablet and two-year data plan, but has also developed a unique, immersive curriculum that engages students beyond just using the technology (SDG 10).

VILS provides teachers with the tools to unlock the potential of classroom technology. By part-

nering with the International Society for Technology in Education (ISTE), starting in 2012, Verizon supported technology-specific professional development and in-school coaches that enabled teachers and students to better leverage mobile devices as learning enhancements, ultimately improving student outcomes on STEM subjects (SDG 4).

By 2014, the 24 VILS trial sites had seen a significant positive shift in student outcomes and equality (SDG 5 & 10). In the first year, math scores for VILS students at the 6 schools improved by more than 4%, while their peers at non-VILS schools experienced an average decrease of more than 4%. In the second year, math scores for VILS students at the 7 schools increased by 6.97%, while peers at non-VILS schools improved by an average of only 4.23%. Additionally, 99% of the teachers in the program reported some positive effects on student behavior and attitudes. Integrating technology into the classroom proved to work best when paired with focused professional development. VILS demonstrates that applying technology solutions to social challenges can uncover new opportunities for the business to achieve greater social and business impact (SDG 9). Verizon's strategy is at the forefront of a unique path to shared value. Specifically, by investing in innovation through deployment of its technology in underserved communities, Verizon has set the groundwork for a long-term shared value strategy for one of its main business lines.

CHALLENGE

To address the educational need for science and technology to fill the 9 million available jobs requiring this knowledge.

OPPORTUNITIES FOR SCALE

Verizon endeavors to enhance its capacity to provide solid data on social impact and to discover technologies, supports, and other resources that can create lasting results for students and schools across the country. Verizon plans to learn from these insights and determine how it can potentially contribute to student achievement through its product and service lines. While Verizon progresses on its shared value journey, its evolution is laying the foundation for years to come.

Sources and further information

* http://www.verizon.com/about/responsibility/verizon-innovative-learning
* http://www.verizon.com/about/responsibility/schools
* https://sharedvalue.org/sites/default/files/resource-files/FSG%20Verizon%20Case%20Study.pdf

" VERIZON BELIEVES THAT TO COMPETE FOR THE JOBS OF THE FUTURE, IT IS ESSENTIAL FOR EVERY CHILD TO HAVE ACCESS TO TECHNOLOGY AND STEM (SCIENCE, TECHNOLOGY, ENGINEERING AND MATH) EDUCATION."

7.5 CAPITAL AND THE SKILLS GAP

Strong leadership from more companies that connect their financial success and the success of their surrounding education ecosystem is needed. Companies that do this can create unique positioning in the market and differentiate themselves from their competitors.

Many companies are already responding: education is the issue most commonly addressed by companies working towards the SDGs, demonstrating that the business community views education as a top global development priority. Businesses with a strong commitment to changing the education landscape are expanding their work with partners to maximize the impact of their investments. Taking a proactive role in improving educational outcomes has the potential to be an increasingly profitable endeavor for companies. Businesses are creating shared value by filling unmet educational needs, improving student outcomes, and overcoming workforce constraints in ways that bring economic benefits to whole communities as well as the company. Companies can play an integral role in tackling skills shortages at scale. Forward-thinking businesses that transform themselves from passive consumers of talent to catalysts for developing a skilled workforce create a long-term competitive advantage. By contributing their substantial resources and providing insights to help increase employability and economic mobility in their communities, they create shared value.

> **FORWARD-THINKING BUSINESSES THAT TRANSFORM THEMSELVES FROM PASSIVE CONSUMERS OF TALENT TO CATALYSTS FOR DEVELOPING A SKILLED WORKFORCE CREATE A LONG-TERM COMPETITIVE ADVANTAGE.**

Consider the Godrej Group, for example. The major Indian conglomerate with diverse holdings across real estate, consumer goods, appliances, and agricultural products is unable to meet its annual growth target of 15 to 20% because of widespread skill shortages throughout its potential workforce. Young Indians between ages 15 and 24 make up the fastest growing segment of the population, representing 30% of the labor force. Yet this demographic is three times more likely to be unemployed, often because they lack marketable skills. These issues are a problem not only for Godrej companies, but also for their suppliers and distributors. In response to this dilemma, the company set a goal of training one million urban and rural youths in employable skills by 2020.[60] Adi Godrej, Chairman of the Godrej Group stated his, and other company's commitment to continued educational opportunities for their employees, when he said, "Many Indian companies have increased their emphasis on training tremendously. I think it is absolutely essential to spend a lot of money on training and continuous improvement. In our group every employee has to undergo at least five days of training a year."

> **IN 2012 THE GLOBAL SKILLS GAP COMPRISED: 40 MILLION TOO FEW COLLEGE-EDUCATED WORKERS; A 45 MILLION SHORTFALL OF WORKERS WITH SECONDARY AND VOCATIONAL EDUCATION IN DEVELOPING COUNTRIES; AND UP TO 95 MILLION WORKERS LACKING THE SKILLS NEEDED FOR EMPLOYMENT IN ADVANCED ECONOMIES.**
>
> PWC.COM

61%

Undereducated in Sub Saharan Africa

$586BN

This smart education and learning market size is expected to grow from $ 193.24 Billion in 2016 to $586,04 Billion by 2021

24%

The smart education and learning market size is expected to grow at a CAGR of 24.84% between 2016 and 2021

Figure 38 **Market key numbers. Based on Sustainia**

Taking a more flexible attitude towards education can help bridge the skills gap. Education for a changing labor market needs to be adaptable and have opportunities outside of the traditional scholastic setting. This strategy gives youths the ability both to learn new skills and learn *how* to learn new skills when needed. To create a more agile education system, we need to foster closer relationships between employers, education providers, and students to close the skills gap. Enhancing the links between business and formal education can enrich the business ecosystem and bring more innovative ideas to fruition, launch more job-creating start-ups, and help more companies find skilled labor and innovations.[61]

The skills gap is present with each shift we encounter in the labor market. As mentioned earlier, the transition from fossil fuels to renewable energy sources requires people who are trained to work in these new industries. Additionally, with the advent and expected surge in robotics, and other technological innovations such as driverless cars, more industries will shift. Taxi drivers, truckers, and bus drivers will probably find that they need reschooling to find jobs in growing industries, as the need for humans to do this kind of driving diminishes. Other areas where automation is likely to prevail include low-skilled jobs, but also some traditionally higher skilled jobs such as doctors and accountants. Not only will some of these jobs disappear, but the

skills needed for the jobs that remain will evolve and necessitate a better command of technology. Surgeons, for example, are working together with robots to perform intricate surgeries that require high-level technical skills. Other jobs that used to require high school diplomas are now evolving to require specialized training of advanced skill-sets. The reality is that we are facing change in the employment landscape and education offerings must keep up with these changes.

Keeping up with the changing employment needs requires funding. But even with the progress that is being made in the education field, there is a large gap between the funding for education that's currently available and what's needed to achieve the sustainable education goal. Worldwide development assistance for basic education dropped by almost 7% between 2010 and 2013, while overall global development aid increased by more than 9%. In addition, there is declining support for fragile and conflict-affected countries. Globally, there is a significant gap in the amount of capital that will need to be allocated to education. Ensuring that every child and adolescent in low and lower middle-income countries has access to good quality education from the pre-primary to upper secondary level requires an influx of billions of dollars. Closing the gap and raising the necessary capital will not be easy without help from the business community.

7.6 DOMAINS OF IMPACT

The three domains of education that we will explore are:

1. Access to Education;
2. Education for Business Development;
3. Lifelong Learning.

Through these three domains, the SDGs can be influenced. Moreover, they represent the greatest points of impact for achieving quality education for all. Providing equal access to education brings everyone along together at the same pace, and levels the playing field. Education for business development improves economic prosperity across societies, and life-long learning provides the fertile ground for people to continue to grow and prosper.

1. ACCESS TO EDUCATION (ESPECIALLY FOR WOMEN AND CHILDREN)

Education systems are failing to deliver access to high-quality schooling to match the demands of the workforce. Without urgent action, the prospects for more than 263 million children and young people out-of-school and a further 274 million not learning the basic primary-level skills are severely diminished. If solutions are not found immediately, it is predicted that by 2030 there will be 435 million children lacking basic education.[63] Furthermore, education and health outcomes are inextricably linked. With adequate education, overall health prospects improve. As mentioned earlier, a child's nutrition levels affect learning outcomes and there is strong evidence that a moth-

er's education improves her children's nutrition. Poor nutrition can affect brain development and the ability to learn. Unhealthy women and children without access to quality education cannot participate fully in the global economy, threaten-

> **WELL OVER 20 NATIONS DISCRIMINATE AGAINST FEMALES BY PREVENTING THEM FROM LEARNING.**[64]
>
> TOURDESTFU.COM

ing business and economic growth. This type of health issue not only threatens the achievement of SDG 3, Good Health and Well-Being, but it also diminishes the chances of reaching the education for all Goal of SDG 4.

Universal provision of basic education would ensure an additional 59 million children of primary school age and 65 million young adolescents are in school. The largest of these estimated impacts is related to gender equality. Despite major progress in advancing gender equality in education, girls are still more likely than boys to never attend primary school.[65] This is the case despite the fact that an educated female population with equal paid employment rates could increase a country's productivity and fuel economic growth by as much as 14% per capita income by 2020 in 15 major developing economies. Empowering women and girls with quality education can improve their lives and the lives of their families, communities and society as a whole. Education prevents the

> **"WE KNOW LEARNING UNLOCKS HOPE, DEVELOPS TALENT, AND UNLEASHES POTENTIAL. NOW WE MUST REAFFIRM EDUCATION'S STATUS AS A HUMAN RIGHT, A CIVIL RIGHT, AND AN ECONOMIC IMPERATIVE."**[67]
>
> RT HON GORDON BROWN

transmission of poverty over generations, which is why education is a major influencer in achieving SDG 1 to end poverty. In Guatemala, higher levels of education among women increased the number of years their children spent in school. In turn, each grade completed raised the wages of these children once they became adults by 10%, while an increase in the reading comprehension test score from 14 points to 36 points raised their wages by 35%.[66]

Many developing countries lack the resources to provide quality education, especially to women and children. This is where digital solutions are having an impact. In many parts of the developing world, infrastructure is lacking, children have to help their parents work, leaving less time to pursue school, and military conflict stands in the way of children accessing school. In areas like these, it is remarkable but true that many people have access to mobile communication and the internet. As explained in the chapter on ICT and technology, people all over the world are making it

MORE THAN 35 MILLION PEOPLE HAVE ENROLLED IN ONLINE COURSES IN THE LAST FOUR YEARS.[68]

FORBES.COM

a priority to have access to internet connection. And with this connection, people have access to information and education.

Nafham is one of the many companies tapping into this opening to reach children in areas where they need educational support. In doing so, the company helps achieve Target 4.5 which calls for ensuring access to education for children in vulnerable situations (See Case 39). Businesses like Nafham are using technology to develop solutions that close the education divide and meet the Goals.[67]

39 CASE NO. **NAFHAM**

Nafham ("we understand" in Arabic)
Online Educational Platform
Online video lessons following K - 12 curricula to support learning in Egypt, Syria, and more countries

Case applied in: Egypt, Algeria, Saudi Arabia, Kuwait and Syria
Headquarters located in: Egypt
www.nafham.com

IMPACT SDGS

SDG 4
Quality Education
The platform currently has more than 23,000 videos covering Egyptian, Saudi, Kuwaiti, Algerian, and Syrian curricula and is available online through the website, mobile apps (Android/iOS) and the smart TV app. To date more than 5,000 videos have been crowd-sourced.

SDG 17
Partnerships for the Goals
A Cairo tech-focused accelerator Flat6Labs, four entrepreneurs, including Ahmad El Alfi, the head of parent fund Sawari Ventures, have partnered to support and improve education systems.

AT NAFHAM, WE FIRMLY BELIEVE THAT ENGAGING YOUNG AND CURIOUS MINDS IS THE MOST CREATIVE AND **EFFECTIVE APPROACH TO A BETTER UNDERSTANDING**.
MOSTAFA FARAHAT, CEO AND CO-FOUNDER NAFHAM

The Egyptian educational system is overwhelmed by 1.1 million students yearly. A class initially designed for 40 students now hosts 60 or 70. Additionally, households in the region spend up to 17% of their budget on private tutoring as a supplement to public school.

Nafham's online educational platform was launched in 2012 to help solve these issues. The founders: Ahmed Alfi and Mostafa Farahat were inspired by Egypt's national educational crisis to search for solutions. They created the platform with the aim to instill in students a love for education and a deeper understanding of the learning process, while reducing cultural obstacles to educational success that exist in some environments, and diminishing the need for families to have to resort to private tutoring to supplement an inadequate educational system. Nafham aims to compensate for current shortcomings in the traditional school system and support reform of current educational systems in Egypt and other countries in the region that do not adequately provide education to all (SDG 4). Nafham hosts and produces video lessons covering the curricula in several Arab countries. This free online K-12 crowd-sourced educational platform is linked to the mandated public curriculum and provides 5 to 20 minute videos that are checked and revised by professionals. The videos explain concepts usually studied in class using different approaches and are categorized by grade, subject, term and academic schedule.

The platform also allows parents to follow their children's progress through regular reports, and provides a social environment like that of Facebook, to attract students and increase their participation and commitment. It also helps students follow-up with teachers through an interactive electronic environment, while allowing teachers to supplement their teaching by posting films or other creative media. Nafham also encourages crowd-teaching among students.

Nafham's performance reflects two concepts that have become evident in today's digital culture in Egypt. The first is the importance of the internet in Egypt after the 'January 25 revolution' in 2011; increased internet uptake and social media use has allowed avenues for web platforms' potential success. The second is that the internet is now considered an essential learning tool in all successful educational systems. Nafham recently expanded its content and entered into a partnership with Trend Micro, offering students the chance to win EGP 40,000 worth of prizes through the "What's Your Story" online video competition in an effort to raise the awareness about internet safety among the community (SDG 17).

CHALLENGE

To enhance school systems in regions where there is inadequate educational facilities or lack of access to schools.

OPPORTUNITIES FOR SCALE

Nafham's strategy involves expanding access to other technological devices as well as other student populations. In partnership with Samsung, Nafham recently released a smart TV app, and is working to promote similar forms of delivery, such as a mobile app. Nafham plans to provide various sponsorship and advertising packages to match different needs, including those of schools and technology companies. Nafham believes that once its platform is given to a larger crowd, it could have the power to transform education in ways beyond what its founders have initially envisioned.

Sources and further information

- http://www.educationinnovations.org/program/nafham
- https://www.wamda.com/2012/04/nafham-a-learning-management-platform-to-enhance-education-in-egypt
- https://www.nafham.com/about_us?ref=hp
- https://egyptianstreets.com/2017/03/19/press-release-nafham-partners-with-trend-micro-in-whats-your-story-video-contest/
- http://www.wise-qatar.org/nafham-egypt
- https://www.youtube.com/watch?v=GlLnzsXQuP8

" **NAFHAM AIMS TO COMPENSATE FOR CURRENT SHORTCOMINGS IN THE TRADITIONAL SCHOOL SYSTEM** AND SUPPORT REFORM OF CURRENT EDUCATIONAL SYSTEMS. "

2. EDUCATION FOR BUSINESS DEVELOPMENT

Employers know the importance of hiring skilled, educated people to fill positions in their companies. What is the point, after all, of reviewing résumés, interviewing people and paying agencies to pre-select if employers just need bodies to fill their vacancies? The point is, employers don't need bodies, they need minds. Knowledge, competence, and ability to learn are necessary components to most, if not all, of the jobs in the world. Because employers recognize this and because it is a costly factor to fill jobs and even more costly to have vacancies go for extended periods unfilled, it is a cost-benefit for companies to do what they can to ensure that there is a continued flow of employable people for their companies to thrive and grow. A recent study in the US conducted by Harris Poll on behalf of CareerBuilder, found that nearly 60% percent of US employers have job openings that stay vacant for 12 weeks or longer. The average cost companies say they incur for having extended job vacancies is more than US $800,000 annually.[69]

> ## THE COST OF THE SKILLS GAP: THE AVERAGE REPORTED COST THAT US COMPANIES INCUR FOR HAVING EXTENDED JOB VACANCIES IS MORE THAN US $800,000 ANNUALLY.
>
> WORKFORCE.COM

While each company will have its own needs for employee development to enhance output and brand value, there are benefits to considering a broader view of employees' educational needs and professional potential. Doing so contributes beyond the skills needed for the job right now and considers the future needs of the business as well as opportunities for employees' personal and professional growth. Therefore, companies are investing in their people by offering training throughout employees' careers and in this way contributing to Target 4.4, which recognizes the value of this kind of education in increasing the number of people with relevant skills. Some training may be job specific, such as financial service providers giving their representatives periodic training to update their knowledge of financial products and regulations. And other business-oriented training can be broader in scope, like communication, leadership, and sustainability training. Enhancing agility and performance outcomes, these kinds of programs offer comprehensive skill development that support workforce growth and improve individual competencies. Businesses recognize that agile, competent people who know how to learn and develop good communication, leadership, and other intangible skills are valuable assets. In a business sense, companies know the investment in training programs for their employees pays off in the short and long run. And training employees in sustainability, in particular, creates partners and ambassadors for helping the company and their communities reach the SDGs.

Business partnerships are also an important component to addressing skill gaps at scale within a sector and to strengthening cross-sector skills within key markets. In addition to these industry-partnerships, businesses that engage with governments and education institutions to develop education policies, curricula, and standards aligned with workforce needs can further drive business growth. These partnerships and initiatives can also help to further sustainability and the Goals.

To accelerate innovation, there are a number of pioneers who are leading in education for business development. Fab Labs, for example, is an international network of innovation hubs that invites members to imagine and prototype their inventions using openly available equipment and software.[70] Fab Labs are open spaces for innovation and prototype development that are increasing access to modern tools and technology, as well as stimulating local entrepreneurship. The initiative, which started as an outreach project at the Massachusetts Institute of Technology's Center for Bits and Atoms, has expanded to more than 1,000

Fab Labs in operation in 78 countries. Empowering talented individuals with access to the tools they need to design new products, the initiative generates valuable educational opportunities and accelerates the discovery of new sustainable technologies.

BUSINESSES RECOGNIZE THAT AGILE, COMPETENT PEOPLE WHO KNOW HOW TO LEARN AND DEVELOP GOOD COMMUNICATION, LEADERSHIP, AND OTHER INTANGIBLE SKILLS ARE VALUABLE ASSETS.

LEGO is another innovator laying the building blocks for education for business development. Derived from the Danish phrase *leg godt*, which means "play well", LEGO promotes universal design for learning (e.g., using pictures rather than words in its building instructions) that does not differentiate between learning abilities and intended learning outcomes. Its products are therefore accessible and usable to everyone. Throughout its growth as an education company, LEGO Education has partnered with education experts, such as academic institutions and teachers, to fill gaps where it lacks its own internal knowledge and capacities.[71] This approach enables LEGO Education to develop its business by creating products that are valued by educators as quality learning tools. Being a profit-driven company requires LEGO Education to be outcome-oriented. As a commitment to its efforts to enable its customers to continue to "play well", the toy company promotes

and invests in Science, Technology, Engineering, and Mathematics (STEM) education to secure access to employees with skillsets that meet LEGO's future needs in the countries in which it operates.

As a part of LEGO Education, the company has developed LEGO Serious Play (LSP) specifically designed to enhance innovation and business performance (See Case 40). Tapping into the hidden expertise of an organization's employee pool, LSP educational program helps "transform insight and awareness into commitment and shared goals."[72] The methodology is based on research showing that a "hands-on, minds-on" learning technique produces a deeper, more meaningful understanding of the world and its possibilities. It is an innovative, experimental process designed to enhance innovation and business performance.

"THE SKILLS WE'RE TEACHING HAVE TO INCLUDE EMPATHY AND WORKING IN TEAMS AND ADAPTABILITY. IF THE TRAINING IS TOO NARROW AND [WORKERS ARE] NOT PICKING UP ON SKILLS TO ADJUST TO THE NEXT JOB, WE'RE GOING TO HOLD PEOPLE UP."

DONNA SHALALA, FORMER PRESIDENT OF THE CLINTON FOUNDATION

CASE NO. LEGO

LEGO Serious Play (LSP)
Build your way to a better business

Case applied in: Global
Headquarters located in: Denmark
www.lego.com

IMPACT SDGS

SDG 4
Quality Education

Develops an understanding of the value of employees and the concept of an evolving, adaptive strategy that includes using LEGO elements as three-dimensional models of business issues and challenges.

SDG 9
Industry, Innovation & Infrastructure

Solves complex issues by building models using LEGO bricks, while metaphors in the models serve as the basis for group discussion, knowledge sharing and problem solving and help foster creative thinking and finding unique solutions.

SDG 17
Partnerships for Goals

Partners with companies to offer practical workshops exploring how LEGO can develop 21st Century skills for business through helping participants gain skills to communicate more effectively, to engage their imagination more readily, and to approach their work with increased confidence, commitment and insight.

IT IS THE [LSP] FACILITATOR WHO ASKS A QUESTION, **THEN THE PARTICIPANTS BUILD THE ANSWER TO THAT QUESTION USING LEGO BRICKS**, USING THEM METAPHORICALLY TO ADD MEANING.
ROBERT RASSUMSEN, LEGO PROFESSOR OF PLAY, EDUCATION, AND LEARNING

LEGO Serious Play (LSP) was specifically designed to explore how LEGO bricks could help a company improve its strategic planning, communication, and creative thinking. The LSP methodology was developed in summer of 2015 when Cambridge University announced a search for a "LEGO Professor of Play, Education, and Learning." With the support of US $6.1 million from the LEGO Foundation, the new professor would lead an entire research department dedicated to examining play. Sessions vary in scope and content. They can, for example, start off with a task such as, "Name one challenge that is preventing growth in your company and build your answer with LEGOs. You have four minutes. Go." Facilitators support this process by anticipating appropriate questions to ask and helping participants draw out the meaning from their answers through the building of bricks. Through this education model, LEGO is unlocking the knowledge from the people they feel are the most qualified to offer solutions: the employees themselves.

LEGO recognizes that the fast pace of technology calls for innovative, "out-of-the-box" thinking. The company has turned its attention to how corporations are looking for more unusual teaching styles to meet the challenges they face, often with "hands-on" or "unplugged" approaches. Just as LEGO bricks can be used to build a representation of virtually anything, the LSP method can be applied to any company objective. It is used to

address important issues like solving a media crisis or brainstorming ways to transform a current business model. The LEGO Professor of Play is invited to guide companies that are looking to solve a problem. Such companies that partner with LSP operate in a variety of industries from all over the world including Google, NASA, Coca-Cola, Toyota, and Unilever (SDG 17).

LSP is often brought into companies to apply the 80-20 principle to meetings. This is where 20% percent of the group will talk 80% percent of the time, with the same people doing all the talking. LSP helps change these workplace dynamics through its education initiative, empowering the 80% to participate. For instance, when firms want to help managers further develop their skills with LSP seminars, they have the opportunity to foster different mindsets and new innovative ideas throughout the company - from call center agents to C-level employees (SDG 4).

To fully take advantage of employee insight, ideas and imagination available, the LSP methodology taps into the human ability to imagine – "to describe and make sense of the business at hand, to initiate change and improvement, and even to create something radically new" (SDG 9). By building the models with their hands, the participants use their knowledge and imagination much faster than traditional rational brainstorming techniques will do.

CHALLENGE

To facilitate a method for strategic decision-making and problem resolution in business environments through workshops directly aligned to business goals.

OPPORTUNITIES FOR SCALE

The LSP method is expanding and moving into the public sector. Several public organizations are taking steps to increase their internal knowledge of this tool by having key leaders and HR employees attend facilitator courses. In this regard, providing courses that combine a solid theoretical knowledge with practical hands-on experience is a growing market.

Sources and further information

- https://sustainabledevelopment.un.org/content/documents/9786CRT046599%20SDG_Food_Bev_24Feb_WEB_FINAL.pdf
- https://biglearningcompany.com/linking-lego-with-learning
- https://qz.com/503512/how-companies-are-using-legos-to-unlock-talent-employees-didnt-know-they-had/
- http://www.admin.cam.ac.uk/reporter/2014-15/weekly/6390/section5.shtml#heading2-17
- https://www.lego.com/en-us/seriousplay
- http://www.plays-in-business.com/why-are-lego-serious-play-workshops-successful/#Why_LEGO_Serious_PlayWorks
- http://seriousplaypro.com/2017/08/16/lego-serious-play-methodology-powerful-widespread-tool-public-sector/

"LEGO RECOGNIZES THAT THE FAST PACE OF TECHNOLOGY CALLS FOR INNOVATIVE, "OUT-OF-THE-BOX" THINKING."

3. HIGHER EDUCATION AND LIFELONG LEARNING

Businesses and business schools are collaborating to co-create solutions for sustainability challenges. For business, these are win-win partnerships that yield fresh and innovative input on a company's most pressing challenges and also create a pipeline to recruit the top talent. Simultaneously, partnerships enable higher education institutions to train students and future leaders effectively in a way that they are prepared to tackle real-world challenges. Business support inspires real-time curriculum adaption to reflect the issues that companies are faced with now and in the future. Talent development is a running theme at many companies, and businesses recognize that it is in their best interest to continue to invest in the personal and professional growth of their employees, as mentioned in the previous section. But businesses also recognize that by working with universities and other institutes of higher education, they can increase the talent pool for new recruits. Businesses are redesigning work at such high speeds that educational institutions are finding it difficult to adapt accordingly. This opens an opportunity for those who can facilitate closer collaboration between business and higher educational institutions on how to manage ongoing adaptation of curricula in response to the shifting competences demanded by businesses. Developing five-year skills forecasts at the level of businesses, for example, can help guide both educational institutions and students in the shifting demands in the labor market. For example, businesses around the world have a shortage of engineers and technical personnel to meet the current demands and estimate that the need for people with a technical education background will increase considerably. Companies that connect specific job needs to education and partner with educators to develop and deliver relevant curricula can extend their reach far beyond workforce development programs. For example, Intel created higher education curricula in high-demand areas like microelectronics, nanotechnology, security systems, and entrepreneurship. Intel, faced with business growth constrained by a chronic shortage of talent in STEM disciplines across the United States, has invested heavily in these subjects and benefitted millions of higher education students and company employees (See Case 41). This action is fueling the company's talent pipeline and continuing education for employees, all while increasing its revenue stream.[74]

> **"LEADERS IN BUSINESS, EDUCATION, AND GOVERNMENT MUST TAKE ACTION TO FOSTER A NEW GENERATION OF TALENT WITH THE TECHNICAL EXPERTISE AND UNIQUE IDEAS TO MAKE THE MOST OF THIS TSUNAMI OF BIG DATA."[73]**
>
> RICHARD RODTS, MANAGER OF GLOBAL ACADEMIC PROGRAMS, IBM

" 65% OF TODAY'S SCHOOL KIDS WILL END UP DOING JOBS THAT HAVEN'T EVEN BEEN INVENTED YET. "

ALEXIS RINGWALD, CO-FOUNDER AND CEO LEARNUP

CASE NO. 41

INTEL

Intel Teach Program
Transforming today's students into
tomorrow's innovators

Case applied in: USA
Office located in: USA
www.intel.com

IMPACT SDGS

SDG 4
Quality Education

Reached more than 10 million teachers in 70 countries to help them with higher education instruction and preparing students for relevant job placement opportunities.

SDG 8
Decent Work & Economic Growth

Sends researchers and anthropologists to observe students using technology in school in order to develop more culturally adaptive products and programs.

SDG 9
Industry, Innovation & Infrastructure

Invests more than US $100 million annually in STEM education, impacting millions of students across the U.S. and fueling the company's talent pipeline, while increasing revenue.

SDG 17
Partnerships for the Goals

Works with countries, communities, and schools worldwide to advocate and support technology use in learning and discovery.

WE INVEST IN TEACHERS SO THAT THEY WILL INSPIRE OUR STUDENTS TO BE INNOVATIVE, CREATIVE AND PREPARED WITH THE CRITICAL THINKING AND PROBLEM-SOLVING SKILLS THAT ARE IMPERATIVE TO OUR FUTURE.

PAUL OTELLINI, FORMER PRESIDENT AND CEO INTEL

For over 40 years, Intel has created technologies that transform the way people live, work and learn. The company is committed to connecting people to their potential and empowering them to seize the opportunities that technology makes possible. From teaching resources and student courseware to world-class research collaborations and technology competitions, Intel has invested over US $1 billion in higher education programs since their founding. Collaborating with others, it initiates programs that utilize the power of technology to create value for society, expand access, and foster economic empowerment.

Intel has embarked on a company-wide effort to transform STEM education nationwide. Through programs like Intel Teach, the company has delivered instructional materials, online resources, and professional development tools for hundreds of thousands of educators across the United States to enhance students' STEM and other 21st century skills, including critical thinking with data and scientific inquiry (SDG 4). By analyzing its own workforce needs, Intel uncovered specific skill gaps in areas like technology and engineering, and the company has focused its investments accordingly. For example, it created higher education curricula in high-demand areas like microelectronics, nanotechnology, security systems, and entrepreneurship (SDG 8). Outside the classroom, Intel has developed a STEM policy toolkit and leverages its lobbying capabilities to encourage policies that

promote a more globally competitive and sustainable education system in the in the United States. Together, these efforts have affected millions of students across the country and are fueling Intel's talent pipeline and innovations in science, while simultaneously increasing the company's revenue (SDG 9).

Intel Teach empowers teachers to engage students with digital learning and STEM-related content, including Web 2.0, social networking, and online tools and resources. Teachers gain the knowledge they need to integrate technology effectively into their existing curricula and focus on their students' problem-solving, critical-thinking, and collaboration skills – precisely the ones required in today's high-tech, networked society. With 49 hours of professional development, teachers can boost student results by up to 20%. By investing in STEM development and curricula for higher education, Intel Teach partners with schools and other educational institutions to transform the lives of millions and cultivate the innovators and visionaries who will lead technology into the future (SDG 17).

Accelerating access to innovative technology and ideas brings quality education to more people everywhere – Intel inspires a new generation of thinking and doing that creates more possibilities now and into the future.

CHALLENGE

To serve as a competitive differentiator that complements Intel's other education assets by training teachers to use technology in the classroom to develop 21st century skills.

OPPORTUNITIES FOR SCALE

Emerging computer science and other engineering disciplines for higher and continuing education are opening new paths to innovation. From autonomous machines to embedded design to big data analytics, engineering and computer science is changing faster than ever — and education is evolving to keep pace.

Sources and further information

- https://www.intel.com/content/www/us/en/corporate-responsibility/sdgictplaybook.html
- https://www.intel.com/content/dam/www/program/education/us/en/documents/stem-resources-k12-educators.pdf
- http://www.efe.org/media/1282/the-new-role-of-business-in-global-education.pdf
- https://www.intel.com/content/www/us/en/education/k12/intel-teach.html
- https://www.intel.com/content/www/us/en/education/highered/higher-ed-overview.html
- https://newsroom.intel.com/news-releases/intel-celebrates-10-million-teachers-trained/

" THE COMPANY IS COMMITTED TO CONNECTING PEOPLE TO THEIR POTENTIAL AND EMPOWERING THEM TO SEIZE THE OPPORTUNITIES THAT TECHNOLOGY MAKES POSSIBLE. "

There are many businesses endeavoring to provide access to higher education and lifelong learning initiatives. NAF, for example, is an American organization that endeavors to solve some of the biggest challenges facing education and the economy by bringing education, business, and community leaders together to transform the high school experience to prepare students for their next educational steps. NAF's educational design is intended to foster students' passion for learning and give businesses the opportunity to shape the future workforce. NAF is transforming the learning environment to include STEM infused industry-specific curricula and work-based learning experiences, including internships. It has grown from one NAF Academy of Finance in New York City to hundreds of academies across the United States focusing on growing industries including finance, hospitality and tourism, information technology, engineering, and health sciences.

Higher education and opportunities for lifelong learning are being made available to people all over the world regardless of proximity to educational facilities and income level. Massive Open Online Courses (MOOC) are online lectures on a broad range of subjects. They are often presented by university professors, giving people access to knowledge that they might otherwise not be able to get. Universities of such caliber as Harvard, Oxford and Yale are now providing free courses online. There are now 700 universities around the world that have launched free online courses. By the end of 2016, around 58 million students had signed up for at least one MOOC.[75] Opening up higher education in this way takes it from a once exclusive realm into the realm of equitable quality education for all. Creating and maintaining platforms for education of this sort is becoming an industry itself, as companies such as Coursera, Futurelearn, and XuetangX recognize. XuetangX of China, for example, has grown to be the number one education platform in the country, and in the top five MOOC platforms in the world. Courses are offered in all subjects to their five million registered students. It is interesting to note the popularity of certain courses and confirms that not only hard skills such as Basic C++ computer programing are sought after, but also 'softer' skills such as psychology and the English language. English language courses are by far the most popular of all the courses, as English is the global common language of commerce, and mastering English allows people all over the world to participate in the global economy (See Figure 39). MOOC not only offers access to education, but offers access to higher education and continued development in the form of lifelong learning, as students can tap into MOOC courses at any time in their lives.

Figure 39 **MOOC - popular courses in China**[76]

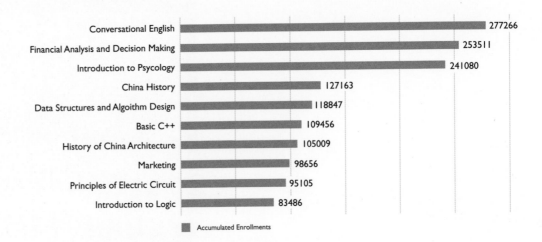

Lifelong learning is desired by people all over the world. In developed countries, employees and job applicants are interested in companies that offer training and development opportunities. And people are seeking ways to grow and stay up-to-date. Continued learning, and certainly continued skill development is needed to compete with the changing landscape of employment. Employees and employers are acutely aware of the need to stay agile. That is to develop a workforce that is able to perform with flexibility and capability.

In developing countries, lifelong learning can help adults who perhaps missed out on educational opportunities in their youth. It can also present new information and introduce new skills to people, thus lifting whole societies. Internet connections will play a pivotal role in bringing continued educational opportunities to people in the developing world.

TO ENSURE PROGRESS TOWARDS THE SDGs AND GLOBAL SUSTAINABILITY, BUSINESS SCHOOLS MUST TEACH SUSTAINABLE BUSINESS MODELS THAT INCLUDE THE FRAMEWORK OF CREATING SHARED VALUE.

Updated business education is also necessary to teach future leaders about sustainable practices. While most business schools today are still teaching business as usual, many of these traditional models are becoming outdated economic growth models that we want to move away from as soon as possible. To ensure progress towards the SDGs and global sustainability, business schools must teach sustainable business models that include the framework of creating shared value. Fortunately, in July 2017, a great number of business schools declared they would commit to teaching sustainable development across all disciplines of study. They are increasingly encouraging research and dissemination of sustainable development knowledge. Business schools and universities are also making their campuses more sustainable, supporting local sustainability efforts, and sharing information with international networks.[77]

IF YOU GIVE A MAN A FISH, HE WILL EAT FOR ONE DAY. IF YOU TEACH HIM TO FISH, HE WILL EAT FOR A LIFETIME. (AGE-OLD PROVERB).

Since educating current and future decision-makers is key to a sustainable future, schools play an important role in building more sustainable societies and creating new business paradigms. As educational institutions, they have the mission to promote development using a variety of means, such as: research, teaching, sharing new knowledge and insights, and building students' capabilities. But schools are not the only faculty of influence. Alternatives to formal schooling can also develop people's knowledge and skills, and serve to build a more sustainable world. Upskilling, re-skilling, apprenticeships, E-learning and vocational training also facilitate people with the improvement of their skills and capabilities.[78] These opportunities have the potential to benefit people, business, and society simultaneously and address any mismatch in the school-to-work pipeline. Businesses helping to cultivate the next generation of workers through more collaboration with education serves to foster a prosperous society. Bringing business into discussions about education ensures a more precise match between skill supply and demand.

Many companies rely on research and thought leadership from academic institutions to explore new thinking on the SDGs or help them understand the social impact of their business models. For example, organizations such as Climate-KIC is Europe's largest public-private innovation partnership focused on climate change. It joins dynamic companies, academic institutions and the public sector together to create a forum for accelerating education, innovation, and entrepreneurship to mitigate climate change. Climate-KIC Education provides knowledge and skills development opportunities for students, professionals and innovators to collaborate on business climate change challenges. Many businesses have formulated these kinds of partnerships to move beyond traditional frameworks and tools, and are looking to academic partners to create tailored educational products that respond to their specific interests. Mars and Şekerbank are examples of companies that have partnered with business schools to engage more deeply in subjects most important to their companies.[79] Şekerbank's partnership with local universities was forged to help move them beyond just measuring greenhouse gas and water impacts.[80] The company's partner universities look at the long-term outcomes of their financial products on community livelihoods and development.

Mars takes a similar approach as the company's internal think tank (Catalyst) is working in collaboration with the Saïd Business School of Oxford University to examine "mutuality" (shared value) as a business model. This is with a view to advancing understanding of how to drive mutuality in business, to develop the business education curriculum and to generate new thinking on how business can benefit society.

WRAP UP

Solving the challenge of providing equitable quality education will take concerted efforts and innovative solutions. To connect educators with students and provide broader educational offerings to people in developing and developed countries, technology can play an important role. It can serve as integral parts of innovations that give access to education. Technology can also help people to improve their skill and knowledge levels to close the gap between schooling and employment opportunities. In developing countries, the greatest problem is access to education. But other problems that engulf these areas, such as poverty, poor health, conflict, and gender discrimination, influence the achievement of this goal. And this is exactly why no one Goal functions in isolation and why shared value solutions are the best model. Businesses are already finding ways to break through the vicious circles that plague some areas in developing and less developed countries. In developed countries, the main challenges are the skills gap and personal, professional development to meet the changing business needs. With consideration towards solving the issues faced in all parts of the world, business can transcend borders and create shared value. Education is fundamental in life, let's make it fundamental in business as well. ■

"HIGHER EDUCATION IS THE STRONGEST, STURDIEST LADDER TO INCREASED SOCIO-ECONOMIC MOBILITY."

DREW FAUST, PRESIDENT HARVARD UNIVERSITY

8

HEALTH AND WELL-BEING

Health and well-being are essential starting points for achieving many of the aspirations people have. The prosperity of individuals, communities, companies, and countries depends on healthy people. Of course, not everyone can be healthy all the time, so prosperity also depends on access to health care. Achieving SDG 3: "Ensuring healthy lives and promoting well-being for all at all ages" is one of the most crucial SDGs. As Sir Andy Haines, Professor of Public Health Policy at the London School of Hygiene and Tropical Medicine, puts it: "Health and sustainability are indivisible at a global level, as improvements in health cannot be maintained without safeguarding the underlying systems on which human health and development depend."[1]
However, SDG 3 is also one of the most complex Goals to achieve, as health and well-being are directly affected by environmental and social factors. The environment, living conditions, and lifestyles influence health and well-being. Therefore, the achievement of SDG 3 relies in part on the achievement of all the SDGs.

8.1 SDG 3: GOOD HEALTH AND WELL-BEING

A large part of the world's population is healthier than ever before in history. On average, we are living longer, healthier lives, and the global population is thus aging at an unprecedented rate. Over the past century, the average global life expectancy has risen by more than 30 years. This trend shows no sign of stopping. Already, 600 million people are over 65 years old. By 2050, this number will almost triple to 1.5 billion. Most of this growth will come from the developing world, where the population over 65 is expected to increase by at least 250%.[2]

OVER THE PAST CENTURY, THE AVERAGE GLOBAL LIFE EXPECTANCY HAS RISEN BY MORE THAN 30 YEARS.

At the same time, we are facing a fast-growing category of new diseases, partly as a result of our increasing life expectancy, and partly as a result of our lifestyles. Non-Communicable Diseases (NCDs) were the number one killers during the first decade of the new millennium, accounting for almost two-thirds of deaths worldwide.[3]

The most prominent NCDs include: cardiovascular diseases (heart attacks and strokes), cancers, chronic respiratory diseases and type 2 diabetes. Obesity is also increasing in developed countries with numbers tripling since 1975.

IT WILL BECOME PARAMOUNT FOR THE HEALTH CARE MARKET TO DEVELOP INNOVATIVE NEW BUSINESS MODELS AND MENTAL HEALTH TREATMENTS THAT WILL KEEP BOTH OUR MINDS AND OUR BODIES VIBRANT.

Mental well-being is an area that has seen degeneration in recent years. We are rapidly approaching a time when the costs of psychological and neurological disorders will surpass those of physical ailments. It is estimated that one in four people will face mental health issues in their lifetimes. Depressive disorders already rank fourth place in the global disease burden and are on track to claim second place as early as 2020, according to reports from the World Health Organization (WHO).[4] It will become paramount for the health care market to develop innovative new business models and mental health treatments that will keep both our minds and our bodies vibrant.

SDG 3: GOOD HEALTH AND WELL-BEING;
End hunger, achieve food security and improved nutrition, and promote sustainable agriculture.

TARGETS

3.1 By 2030, reduce the global maternal mortality ratio to less than 70 per 100,000 live births.

3.2 By 2030, end preventable deaths of newborns and children under 5 years of age, with all countries aiming to reduce neonatal mortality to at least as low as 12 per 1000 live births and under-5 mortality to at least as low as 25 per 1000 live births.

3.3 By 2030, end the epidemics of AIDS, tuberculosis, malaria and neglected tropical diseases and combat hepatitis, water-borne diseases and other communicable diseases.

3.4 By 2030, reduce by one third premature mortality from non-communicable diseases through prevention and treatment and promote mental health and well-being.

3.5 Strengthen the prevention and treatment of substance abuse, including narcotic drug abuse and harmful use of alcohol.

3.6 By 2020, halve the number of global deaths and injuries from road traffic accidents.

3.7 By 2030, ensure universal access to sexual and reproductive health care services, including for family planning, information and education, and the integration of reproductive health into national strategies and programs.

3.8 Achieve universal health coverage, including financial risk protection, access to quality essential health care services and access to safe, effective, quality and affordable essential medicines and vaccines for all.

3.9 By 2030, substantially reduce the number of deaths and illnesses from hazardous chemicals and air, water and soil pollution and contamination.

3.a Strengthen the implementation of the WHO Framework Convention on Tobacco Control in all countries, as appropriate.

3.b Support the research and development of vaccines and medicines for the communicable and non-communicable diseases that primarily affect developing countries, provide access to affordable essential medicines and vaccines, in accordance with the Doha Declaration on the TRIPS Agreement and Public Health, which affirms the right of developing countries to use to the full the provisions in the Agreement on Trade-Related Aspects of Intellectual Property Rights regarding flexibilities to protect public health, and, in particular, provide access to medicines for all.

3.c Substantially increase health financing and the recruitment, development, training and retention of the health workforce in developing countries, especially in least developed countries and small island developing States.

3.d Strengthen the capacity of all countries, in particular developing countries, for early warning, risk reduction and management of national and global health risks.

Innovation in mental health services, NCDs, and elderly care are some of the markets that could lead to interesting opportunities for business solutions. Achieving good health and well-being for all will require different focal points for developed and developing countries. The issues mentioned above tend to affect more people in developed countries. Health issues affecting people in developing countries mostly revolve around lack of access to health care and deficiencies in nutrition, clean drinking water, and hygienic conditions. This leads to infant mortality and regular outbreaks of infectious diseases.

The global challenges related to this SDG are therefore numerous. In this chapter, we explore some of the challenges as well as the business opportunities when striving to solve them. The Targets associated with SDG 3 are useful to keep in mind.

8.2. SOLVING THE CHALLENGES: HEALTH AND WELL-BEING AS THE PREREQUISITE FOR ACHIEVING THE GOALS

SDG 3 is deeply interconnected with other SDGs as shown in figure 40. With improved health and well-being, people are in a better position to work on the achievement of other goals. Health, like food, is a primary need that takes precedence over all else. Consequently, a good foundational state of health and well-being is a prerequisite to achieving all of the Goals. Developing a solid foundation by improving health and well-being can contribute to all of the Global Goals; in particular to reducing poverty (SDG 1); balancing inequalities (SDG 10); improving work opportunities and economic growth (SDG 8); and protecting the environment (SDGs 13, 14 and 15). SDG 3 will be furthered by achieving other Goals including ending hunger (SDG 2); improving access to clean water and sanitation (SDG 6); attaining gender equality (SDG 5), as women often bear primary responsibility for health in families; promoting decent work (SDG 8), as work opportunities and work conditions play an important role in well-being; and expanding quality education (SDG 4). When people are empowered, paid a living wage, nourished, educated, and live in safe environments they have the foundations to lead healthier lives.[5]

WHEN PEOPLE ARE EMPOWERED, PAID A LIVING WAGE, NOURISHED, EDUCATED, AND LIVE IN SAFE ENVIRONMENTS THEY HAVE THE FOUNDATIONS TO LEAD HEALTHIER LIVES.

Within the process of making these improvements there are many business opportunities.

However, in the short run, there may be some companies that experience a downturn as they adjust their strategies to develop sustainable products. For example, progress on SDG 3 will require improvements in nutrition with a reduction in the consumption of sugars, smoking tobacco, and the use of other substances that have been shown to be detrimental to health. This could lead to adjustments in agriculture and food processing that could offset profit. Expanding access to health care services is generally a positive measure, but it could entail increased consumption of disposable products to assure hygiene and safety, which could influence progress on responsible consumption and production (SDG 12). There are also risks of negative impacts on SDG 3 associated with advancing other Goals if these advancements are not done conscientiously. For example, SDG 2: Zero Hunger can compromise health if the effect of toxic inputs is not considered, such as how use of antibiotics in animal feed could lead to the emergence of antimicrobial drug resistance.

WHEN MAKING A SHIFT TOWARDS SUSTAINABLE PRACTICES IN ONE FIELD, ALL OTHER SDGs SHOULD BE CONSIDERED.

Consequently, when making a shift towards sustainable practices in one field, all other SDGs should be considered. That is not to say that if the move towards sustainability in your company has a negative influence on another SDG, you should give up the idea of making that shift. It means that your innovative ideas should be expanded to include the other SDGs in the picture. By doing this, you may just unlock unlikely and unexpected new markets for your business to engage in. This is the story behind DSM. Founded in 1902 in the Netherlands as a coal mining company, DSM has transformed over the years in their drive towards sustainability from coal miners to a global science-based company active in health, nutrition and materials, generating a yearly revenue of nearly €8 billion euros.

According to the World Economic Forum, "In the next 15 years many of the major challenges to human health will originate outside of the health sector. These range from emerging zoonotic diseases to pollution, climate change and the growing epidemic of obesity.

Tackling these challenges effectively will require health experts to better understand and inter- vene in the health system. But they will also have to consider and effect change in broader social systems that encompass health – such as housing, transport, animal health, urban land use and agriculture."[6] The wide-sweeping reach of health and well-being places it at the very core of the cycle that contributes to the delivery of the Global Goals.

Figure 40 **Health in the SDG Era** [7]

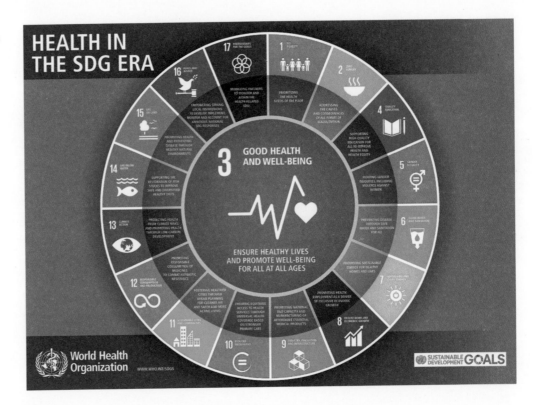

8.3 IMPACT OF HEALTH AND WELL-BEING ON ALL SDGs

The fundamental nature of SDG 3 makes it compelling to relate all of the other SDGs to how it will affect our health. The well-being of people all over the world will be improved as a result of achieving all of the SDGs.

SDG 1: No Poverty; Poverty reduction leads to improved health and well-being, while good health is a strong enabling factor for effective poverty reduction. In fact, a healthy population is the power behind development, constituting an engine for economic growth. Conversely, it is very difficult to ensure health without addressing poverty. At low income levels, rising incomes lead to health gains as basic needs are fulfilled such as nutrition, health care, and shelter. Increased income is likely to enable positive effects, yet beyond a certain threshold, further increases may not lead to further positive health effects. Poverty reduction also affects health in regards to illness and diseases associated with poverty, including diarrheal and respiratory diseases, and the consequences of malnutrition. Additionally, overcrowded living situations in which many impoverished people reside, often result in the spread of disease. Where poverty reduction is most needed, great health challenges usually exist. Reducing poverty will generally result in immediate and long-term improvements in health. Ill health can also constitute an inescapable poverty trap. As poverty is the main cause of malnutrition, it creates a vicious cycle. Chronic poor health can stop people from accessing work, thus trapping them in poverty.

SDG 2: Zero Hunger; Malnutrition is one of the main contributors to high child and maternal mortality rates in developing countries. There are 795 million undernourished people in the world today. That means one in nine people do not get enough food to be healthy and lead an active life.[9] Malnutrition is also a leading cause of death among children, with 45% of all child deaths attributed to malnutrition.[10] Food security is crucial to healthy development and well-being. Interruptions in food supply, intake and quality, whether short or long term, can have lasting impacts. Lack of adequate nutrition that begins during prenatal growth and continues throughout childhood can negatively affect mental and physical development. Mothers who lack access to proper nutrients bear malnourished children. These children face greater challenges in their ability to learn and thrive.

Good health also depends on lifelong consumption of sufficient micronutrients. Reducing hunger will result in immediate improvements in health, and carries long-term benefits for physical, psychological and neurological development. Increasing agricultural production may improve food security and reduce hunger; however, it also impacts the environment, with potential implications for infectious disease transmission, and can negatively affect health through contamination of local environments with pesticide residues.[11]

> **7.3 BILLION PEOPLE IN THE WORLD, OR ONE IN NINE, WERE SUFFERING FROM CHRONIC UNDERNOURISHMENT IN 2014-2016.**
>
> WORLD HUNGER EDUCATION SERVICE

SDG 3: Good Health and Well-Being; When people are in a state of good health and well-being, it tends to perpetuate. However, it is remarkable how people do engage in activities that they know put their health at risk. For example, although the number of cigarette smokers has decreased considerably in many countries, there are still millions of people who smoke despite evidence that this is detrimental to one's health. Personal choice is still a main influencer when it comes to health and well-being.

> **GLOBALLY THERE ARE OVER 180,000 FITNESS CLUBS, ESTIMATED TO HAVE EARNED US $84 BILLION FROM THEIR 145 MILLION MEMBERS. IN THE US ALONE, MEMBERSHIP GREW 18.6% BETWEEN 2008 AND 2014.** [12]
>
> FITNESS INDUSTRY ANALYSIS 2017

Even so, there are some unhealthy behaviors that expose others to risk, giving reason for regulatory intervention, such as limiting smoking in public areas, and banning the use of certain pesticides for agriculture. As science raises awareness of unhealthy and healthy behaviors, and as cultural habits begin to change, and healthier habits emerge, there will be a surge in demand for foods and products that support a healthy lifestyle. As an example, Tesco, one of the largest UK food retailers reported year on year growth of 5% in sales of organic food, with a 15% surge in 2016.

SDG 4: Quality Education; Access to education is associated with better health and well-being. Higher levels of education tend to lead to better options for employment which benefits well-being. Education can affect long-term health through increased income, opportunity, self-reliance and empowerment. It can affect health immediately through changed behavior and increased control over one's own health care and decisions. Educated individuals can better understand information they receive from health care professionals, and can potentially conduct research themselves to assess health concerns. Health benefits from education are not limited to early schooling. Lifelong learning offers important opportunities in contexts of rapid change. New technologies, such as health promotion using ICT and the IoT, may increase the efficiency of health interventions and spread knowledge to more people. Also, basic reproductive education is also a key factor to improving health and well-being. According to UNESCO research, "The evidence is clear. Comprehensive Sexuality Education (CSE) leads to improved sexual and reproductive health, resulting in the reduction of sexually transmitted infections, HIV, and unintended pregnancy." [13]

SDG 5: Gender Equality; Improving gender equality generally enables the achievement of better health. Women's health issues are in some contexts underprioritized and underfunded, and promoting gender equality in these cases leads to noticeable health gains. Ensuring universal access to sexual and reproductive health and reproductive rights is one of the Targets for SDG 5. Access to quality health care related to reproduction, from prevention to early maternal care, care throughout pregnancy, birth and after care for mothers is vital for good health and well-being as well as gender equality. [14] Gender equality also includes equal rights for women, which gives them greater freedom of movement, employment, education and land ownership. With these rights, women gain more control over their own bodies, and external circumstances, thus increasing well-being. SDG 5 also calls for the elimination of violence against women. This too is a matter of health and well-being.

SDG 6: Clean Water and Sanitation; Improving water quality and access leads to improved health. Without clean water and adequate sanitation, health is at risk. Water-borne infections leading to acute diarrheal infections and viral hepatitis can be eliminated with adequate sanitation. Clean drinking water is necessary for good health. Therefore, improving water quality and sanitation leads to long-term developmental gains. The interaction between this Goal and SDG 3 is strongest in parts of the developing world where water-borne infectious disease is still prevalent, yet water quality and environmental pollution issues are also prevalent in many high-income regions. Contaminants in drinking water can be detrimental to people's health and sometimes even fatal. Regulation, self-constraint by businesses, and monitoring using state-of-the-art technology is crucial to ensure clean water and good health.

> **"MORE PEOPLE DIE FROM UNSAFE WATER THAN FROM ALL FORMS OF VIOLENCE, INCLUDING WAR. THESE DEATHS ARE AN AFFRONT TO OUR COMMON HUMANITY, AND UNDERMINE THE EFFORTS OF MANY COUNTRIES TO ACHIEVE THEIR DEVELOPMENT POTENTIAL."** [15]
>
> BAN KI-MOON, FORMER SECRETARY-GENERAL, UNITED NATIONS

SDG 7: Affordable and Clean Energy; The use of various energy sources can influence health in a variety of ways. "Dirty" fuels such as coal and diesel are known for their negative health effects. It has long been established that coal miners suffer from respiratory ailments as a result of working in the harsh environment of a mine. And diesel fueled vehicles are set to be banned in several cities in Europe, including Paris, Copenhagen and Oxford in the next few years because of their harmful emissions. Nuclear energy poses unique risks in terms of waste storage and accidental release. In developing countries, the use of kerosene for indoor energy is hazardous, accounting for 173,000 yearly instances in Bangladesh of children being burned accidentally. In South Africa, an estimated US $26 million is spent annually on burn care for victims of accidents involving kerosene. According to WHO, air pollution caused by fossil fuel emissions has become the world's single biggest environmental health risk, linked to around 7 million deaths in 2012.[16] The widespread pollution, the

negative impact on the environment and the ozone layer, and the many preventable accidents are some of the reasons that the achievement of SDG 7 is so urgent and necessary. With the increasing affordability and sophistication in solar and wind power, renewable, clean, and safe energy is becoming more accessible for people.

SDG 8: Decent Work and Economic Growth; Decent work conditions play an important role in a person's well-being. Firstly, being paid a living wage is a key to reducing stress, and assuring food security. Secondly, non-hazardous conditions reduce the risk of accidents and illness. On the whole, working conditions have improved in developed countries since the industrial revolution. In developing countries, some conditions have improved, but certainly not everywhere. Fortunately, there has been public outcry for businesses patrons to improve all work conditions for employees and the employees of suppliers. There is much that businesses can do to ensure that people are not exploited in their primary offices or factories and in their extended supply chain. Adhering to strict compliance guidelines and enforcing these guidelines is one assurance. Also, creating a culture of respect and decency within the company is another. Considering that over 600 million new jobs need to be created by 2030, just to keep pace with the growth of the working-age population, equaling around 40 million per year, [17] it is crucial to take the Targets and Indicators into consideration when creating these jobs, so employment conditions can get off to the right start, and healthy workforces can be built and sustained.

> **OVER 600 MILLION NEW JOBS NEED TO BE CREATED BY 2030, JUST TO KEEP PACE WITH THE GROWTH OF THE WORKING-AGE POPULATION.**
>
> INTERNATIONAL LABOUR ORGANIZATION

SDG 9: Industry, Innovation and Infrastructure; Industrial development can be hazardous to people's health if factories and plants produce air or water pollutants. However, appropriate planning and regulations, especially in cities, can minimize adverse impacts. Improved health can even be achieved when industrial growth is paired with conscientious health promotion, such as through promotion of active transport, or green belts and parks. Health effects can be immediate to long-term, both positively and negatively. Companies are creating industrial ecosystems to counteract potential negative impacts. This system involves using by-products and waste from one industry that are resources for another. For example, Blue Marble uses coffee grounds, sawdust, brewer's waste, and other organic waste to create "green fuel," as well as other ingredients that can be used as "green chemicals" for cosmetics and other products instead of petroleum based chemicals.[18] Blue Marble recently came to an agreement with Anheuser-Busch to work together to convert the brewery's waste into biogas and green chemicals.[19] This kind of arrangement has many benefits. It reduces the need for non-renewable raw materials, reduces toxicity and pollution, and reduces emissions and waste. Innovative ecosystem frameworks are examples of innovative thinking that can help improve health conditions for all. Additionally, scientific and technological innovations such as the use of sensors can help diagnose disease. Currently, the University of Illinois is working on a sensor that can be used to detect diseases such as an early indicator of kidney failure.[20] Infrastructure is also an important factor in sustaining good health. Care facilities must be prevalent enough to sufficiently serve communities and they must be able to be reached in a timely manner in order to ensure access to health care.

SDG 10: Reduced Inequalities; Disparities in socio-economic status among people and societies directly influence health outcomes. Some statistics collected by WHO show how the health of people who live in poverty, or in poor countries, suffer as a result of a lack of access to quality medical care. The conditions that poor people live in around the world also negatively influence people's health. Some examples include: maternal mortality accounts for 1 in 16 deaths in Chad while the risk is 1 in 10,000 in Sweden; 95% of deaths caused by Tuberculosis is in developing countries; and life expectancy varies by 34 years between developed and developing countries.[21] Finding ways to provide health care, a decent living wage, and a way out of living in overcrowded, unhygienic circumstances like slums, would go a long way in solving some of these disparities. Government policies and tax systems directed at a more equal distribution of resources, wealth, and opportunities are needed to overcome these, and other problems attributed to lower socio-economic status.[22]

Of course, changes in governmental approach can be unreliable with the changes in leadership taking sometimes contrary positions to predecessors. Therefore, if business steps in and builds sustainable momentum towards creating equal opportunities, a wave can develop in the right direction. According to the UN, "Income inequality cannot be effectively tackled unless the underlying inequality of opportunities is addressed."[23] Business endeavors can help to level the playing field of opportunity with initiatives such as developing systems using current technology to help people in poor circumstances access finance. For instance, there are 2 billion "unbanked" people in the world and this has a big influence on inequality as people without bank accounts lack the possibility of attaining loans, transferring money and building up credit.[24] Kenya's largest cell phone companies, Safaricom and Vodacom, decided to do something about this and created M-Pesa, launched in 2007 by Vodafone. M-Pesa allows users to deposit money into an account stored on their cell phone and transfer money using text messages. By 2012, there were 17 million users of this system. M-Pesa is now available in other countries as well.[25]

SDG 11: Sustainable Cities and Communities; The impact of cities on health is well recognized. Poorly designed cities create unhealthy environments, discouraging physical activity, exposing people to

> **AIR POLLUTION HAS BECOME THE WORLD'S SINGLE BIGGEST ENVIRONMENTAL HEALTH RISK, LINKED TO AROUND 7 MILLION – OR NEARLY ONE IN EIGHT DEATHS IN 2012.**[28]
>
> WORLD HEALTH ORGANIZATION

hazards such as air pollution and dangerous traffic, and contributing to mental illness and non-communicable diseases. While well-designed cities promote health and support the achievement of SDG 3. Housing which is free of pollutants and hazards, and provides adequate temperatures and space, supports health. In addition, transportation infrastructure promotes health immediately and directly by improving access to health care, work and education. Reducing air pollution in cities will significantly improve human health; it is a significant causal factor in stroke, heart disease, lung cancer, and both chronic and acute respiratory diseases, including asthma.[26] According to WHO, "South-east Asia is now the most polluted region in the world, with 3.3 million deaths linked to indoor air pollution and 2.6 million deaths related to outdoor air pollution in that area. This reflects the explosive growth of cities and industrial development in China and India, as well as continuing deep poverty in rural areas."[27] Innovations in energy sources, alternatives to fossil fuel driven vehicles, and the commitment by companies to eliminate polluting practices all contribute greatly to the reduction of pollution in cities resulting in healthier communities.

 **SDG 12: Responsible Consumption and Production;** Responsible production has health benefits as it invariably leads to the elimination of toxic ingredients and processing methods. This goal encompasses the objective to reduce pollution and negative impacts on the environment. Achieving these objectives is beneficial for people's health. The production of food can also be beneficial or detrimental to health. The use of certain chemicals or high amounts of sugar can lead to health problems. On the other hand, food production can be enhanced using "biofortification" to add micronutrients to food as it is growing in order to improve the nutritional value. WHO estimates that biofortification could help cure the two billion people suffering from iron deficiency-induced anemia, and the 190 million school children suffering from vitamin A deficiency. Biofortified foods can also help the 17% of the global population that has a zinc deficiency, preventing the deaths of 116,000 children who die each year as a result of this deficiency.[29] On the consumption side, individuals can potentially hurt their own health by consuming certain substances such as tobacco. Even the positive health measures of expanding access to health care services can affect this goal as it entails increased consumption of disposable products (to assure hygiene and safety), which could hinder progress on responsible consumption and production.[30]

SDG 13: Climate Action; Climate change disproportionately affects people in poor countries. People suffer from food insecurity as a result of droughts or floods, and have less external defenses (like adequate housing) against extreme cold or heat. For example, in 2016, temperatures soared in India to a record breaking 51°C (123.8°F). India has been increasingly suffering from heat waves recently and statistics reveal that at least 4,620 people have died in the last four years due to extreme heat causing dehydration and heat stroke.[31] There are many business opportunities in developing low-cost heating and cooling systems to be made available to millions of people. Indirect effects from climate change include the spread of disease. For example, the Zika epidemic was made worse by climatic conditions speeding up the incubation and reproduction processes of the Zika carrying mosquito. Warmer temperatures also make the mosquito hungrier, rendering them

more prolific in spreading the disease.[32] Climate change will most likely lead to greater spread of many vector- and water-borne diseases, including malaria and cholera.

 SDG 14: Life Below Water; Healthy marine life is connected to human health as millions of people depend on fish as a food source, and depend on fishing and coastal tourism as a source of employment and income. As a food source, fish is an extremely nutritious source of protein and essential nutrients, which is especially important as a dietary staple in many poorer communities. Pollution of oceans, seas, rivers and streams diminishes the survival of marine life, thus decreasing food supplies and affecting marine biodiversity. As a source of income, you could say that life below water supports life above water. Pollution and climate change are threatening marine life, and this has a direct affect on people's health. Finding solutions to the problem of plastics ending up in the world's oceans is one way to help preserve marine life.

According to a study from Plymouth University, plastic pollution affects at least 700 marine species, while some estimates suggest that at least 100 million marine mammals are killed each year from plastic pollution. In particular, sea turtles, seals, seabirds, fish, whales and dolphins are affected by plastic pollution.[33] In addition to this being detrimental or fatal for marine animals, many fish that bring contaminated water into their systems through their gills, including microscopic plastic debris, are consumed by people which means that people are ingesting the plastic pollution. Plastic contains toxins that are bad for human and animal health. To combat the increasing contamination of the water with plastic debris, people can have an impact by decreasing their use of plastics and recycling plastic waste properly.

 SDG 15: Life on Land; Human health and the survival of animal and plant species all over the world depend on environmental preservation. Biodiversity is the foundation of functioning ecosystems, which we depend on for our health and well-being. Terrestrial ecosystems also regulate the atmosphere, reducing the effects of pollution. Deforestation, desertification, pollution and contamination are all associated with decreased or lost biodiversity. Monoculture farming also results in the loss of biodiversity and negatively affects life on land in several ways, including soil degradation, which is due in part to the depletion of ground cover plants. Without ground cover plants, the soil lacks protection and moisture, leading to the less fertile soil and the necessity to use more water to irrigate monoculture crops.[34] Organic farming, commitments by companies to curtail deforestation, business support for environmental protections, and innovations to conserve natural resources are some of the ways the business world can help to preserve life on land. Capital investments in the form of impact and green investments concentrating on organizations, products and business endeavors that promote a healthier environment for humans, plants and animals are also constructive methods to support the preservation of a healthy planet.

 SDG 16: Peace, Justice and Strong Institutions; The three pillars of this Goal are strong enablers of improvements in health and well-being. Conversely, the absence of peace, justice and strong institutions can have negative effects. The impact of war is quite obviously bad for people's health and well-being. The current crisis in Syria for example has given way to mass migration in difficult conditions. Fleeing one's home in urgent circumstances, living in refugee camps, or worse, having no place to settle even temporarily puts a high burden on health. Migration dangers, such as piling into overcrowded inflatable boats, introduce grave hazards. Peace, stability, and equal inclusion in economic life and governance are circumstances that allow people to pay attention to their health and well-being.

SDG 17: Partnerships for the Goals; Effective partnerships are critical for achieving healthy populations. Cross-sectoral, cross-spatial and multiregional partnerships and exchanges of information groun-

ded in systems thinking are needed. Disease control is a global issue, as are illnesses such as cancer. Therefore, research and information exchange are vital. In 2005, The Paris Declaration of Aid Effectiveness was signed by 125 countries and over 50 donors and international organizations. In the declaration, signatories approved the following principles: Ownership, Harmonization, Alignment, Results and Mutual Accountability.[35] Unfortunately, by many accounts, the effectiveness of this declaration is falling short, due to coordination failings.[36] But smaller partnerships, however, do seem to be successful for instance when universities partner with schools in other countries to share research. There is an urgent need for more international, well-coordinated, partnerships. One of the global concerns today is the development of antimicrobial resistance (resistance to antibiotics). According to the 2016 Review on Antimicrobial Resistance "If left unchecked, it's thought that by 2050 the global number of deaths from antimicrobial resistance may be as high as 10 million per year - costing US $100 trillion annually just to

manage the effects."[37] This particular concern is demonstrative of the need for not only international collaboration for research and innovation for fighting disease and illness, but also international coordination on health care practices, and cross-sector incorporation as well, as the use of antibiotics in meat could lead to increased antimicrobial resistance in humans.

> **"STRONG, SUSTAINED ACTION ACROSS ALL SECTORS IS VITAL IF WE ARE TO TURN BACK THE TIDE OF ANTIMICROBIAL RESISTANCE AND KEEP THE WORLD SAFE."**[38]
>
> DR TEDROS ADHANOM GHEBREYESUS, DIRECTOR-GENERAL OF WHO

8.4 SHARED VALUE OPPORTUNITIES

Advances in health and well-being directly improve people's lives. For companies, creating shared value by producing products and developing innovations that bring financial profit to the business and health benefits to individuals and communities is a win-win situation. Examples include GE's invention of low-cost, portable medical devices such as a hand-held ultrasound machine that can be used in remote rural communities and transmit pictures to clinics in faraway towns.[39] Incorporating value for the environment, as well as social and financial value, perpetuates the SDGs even further. Companies such as DSM are doing just that. DSM has embedded the SDGs into their business strategy and has been creating shared value with their many endeavors for years (See Case 42). DSM's innovations to help alleviate malnutrition are paired with their attention to renewable energy sourcing and the reduction of their carbon footprint. This multi-faceted approach leads the company to broader innovations for sustainable life-styles.

FOR COMPANIES, CREATING SHARED VALUE BY PRODUCING PRODUCTS THAT BRING FINANCIAL BUSINESS PROFIT AND HEALTH BENEFITS IS A WIN-WIN SITUATION.

Health care providers can also increase their shared value by following the advice from author Leith Greenslade in the report *Competing by Saving Lives*, released in 2012,[40] just one year after Michael Porter and Mark Kramer published *Creating Shared Value*. According to Greenslade, health care companies create shared value when they compete on the basis of improving health outcomes for the underserved; in other words, by saving the most lives in low and middle-income countries.

To succeed in creating shared value, Greenslade advises health care companies to cultivate five things:

1. A deeply committed CEO
2. A culture of innovation
3. Performance indicators that include how many lives the company is saving
4. Staff with cross-sector skills
5. Partners from beyond the business community

Cross-sector collaborations and public-private partnerships addressing health issues are also extremely useful in creating broad shared value. For example, the food and agriculture industry, the energy industry, and many other sectors have direct influences on people's health and well-being. Health and well-being can also be advanced by governments putting regulations in place such as limiting pollutants or harmful food additives. Furthermore, technology companies are also instrumental in creating new solutions for patient monitoring and diagnostics, access to medical information and supplies, and support of health care initiatives.

Achieving the SDGs by accomplishing Targets such as stopping the spread of AIDS, TB, and malaria; reducing maternal mortality; and eliminating preventable deaths of newborns, requires the scaling up of shared value strategies in health care. In the *shared value competition* that Greenslade proposes, the winners, he claims, will be those companies that achieve a competitive advantage across five areas:

1. Data quantity and quality
2. Application of new and emerging technologies (e.g. AI/machine learning, DNA sequencing, CRISPR, nanotechnology, drones, 3D printing)
3. Network reach and quality
4. Partner quality (government, NGO, academic, business)
5. Leadership quality

" WHILE THERE HAS ALWAYS BEEN A HEATED DEBATE ABOUT THE VALUE ADDITION OF THE PRIVATE SECTOR IN HEALTH, **FROM MY POINT OF VIEW IT'S THE BEST WAY FORWARD."** [41]

DR. SUSANN ROTH, SENIOR SOCIAL DEVELOPMENT SPECIALIST AT THE ASIAN DEVELOPMENT BANK

CASE NO.

DSM

Nutrition Improvement Program
Fighting malnutrition around the world

Case applied in: Global
Headquarters located in: The Netherlands
www.dsm.com

IMPACT SDGs

SDG 3
Good Health and Well-Being

Reach more than 28 million people per year with improved nutrition through biomedical, health and nutrition product portfolios geared toward maintaining, protecting or regenerating health.

SDG 7
Affordable and Clean Energy

Enable energy solutions such as advanced biofuels and materials for solar panels, and support clean energy efforts via the Bright Minds Challenge, while increasing use of renewable energy.

SDG 12
Responsible Consumption and Production

Reduce food waste through solutions such as Pack- Age; replace fossil fuel based alternatives with advanced biofuels and bio-succinic acid.

SDG 13
Climate Action

Focus on reducing the company's carbon footprint and enabling the low-carbon economy.

THE RIGHT NUTRITION IN THE CRITICAL FIRST 1,000 DAYS OF LIFE **PROVIDES THE FOUNDATION FOR CHILDREN TO THRIVE AND NATIONS TO PROSPER.**
FEIKE SIJBESMA, CEO/CHAIRMAN MANAGING BOARD DSM

With decades of experience in vitamin and mineral fortification of foods, beverages, supplements, etc., DSM has unique expertise to develop products that can positively impact global nutrition, health and development. DSM has prioritized the issue of malnutrition and advocates for improved nutrition all over the world. As a leading micronutrient provider, DSM develops innovative solutions to fight both overt and hidden hunger, defined as the micronutrient (vitamin and mineral) deficiency in a person's diet.

DSM works to improve nutrition via initiatives such as the Nutrition Improvement Program and Africa Improved Foods, providing fortified food solutions and micronutrient products, as well as through partnerships such as with WFP. DSM supports the base of the pyramid sector of the population with fortified food solutions and programs, providing micronutrients through products such as MixMe sachets.

DSM's health, nutrition, biomedical and high-performance materials portfolios endeavor to maintain, protect or regenerate health in all age groups - for example, by reducing salt and sugar levels in processed foods, or by reducing emissions associated with chemical manufacturing processes. The company's First 1,000 Days Program supports mother and child health. It also employs the DSM Life Saving Rules to protect employees from harm

and the DSM Vitality Program to promote awareness of good health and healthy living options among their employees (SDG 3).

In addition to their commitment to improving health, in partnership with RE100, DSM is also increasing the use of renewables in its own energy mix and reducing its carbon footprint. DSM enables solar and bio-based energy solutions and supports a low-carbon economy through solutions such as POET-DSM advanced biofuels and high-performance materials for solar panels (SDG 7). The company's Bright Minds Challenge is also identifying innovative solutions and new materials that will accelerate the global movement toward 100% renewable energy. Further, DSM strongly advocates for responsible action on climate change in combination with all its stakeholders (SDG 13).

DSM contributes to a bio-based, circular and low-carbon economy with products such as DSM-Niaga, which enables the manufacture of carpets that can be recycled over and over again. Food waste is also reduced through DSM food solutions like Pack-Age, while bio-based chemicals such as bio-succinic acid replace fossil fuel based alternatives in applications for packaging. Through the Brighter Living Solutions program, DSM considers the impact of their products throughout the value chain (SDG 12).

CHALLENGE

To address malnutrition issues affecting 2 billion people living on US $2 a day or less.

OPPORTUNITIES FOR SCALE

DSM aims to end all forms of malnutrition by 2030 by working together with cross-sector partners to make good nutrition aspirational, affordable and available to all. An investment of US $60 million dollars a year in micronutrient provision going forward could yield benefits in terms of improved health, lower mortality and increased income opportunities worth US $1 billion dollars; an annual investment of US $19 million dollars in fortification could bring US $570 million dollars in benefits globally.

Sources and further information

- http://annualreport.dsm.com/content/dam/annualreport/ar2016/en_US/documents/DSM-Annual-Report-2016.pdf
- http://annualreport.dsm.com/ar2015/en_US/section-557009.html
- https://www.dsm.com/content/dam/dsm/cworld/en_US/documents/factbook-2017.pdf
- https://www.dsm.com/products/nip/en_US/home.html
- https://www.dsm.com/content/dam/dsm/nip/en_US/documents/unlocking-human-potential.pdf

" DSM HAS PRIORITIZED THE ISSUE OF MALNUTRITION AND ADVOCATES FOR IMPROVED NUTRITION ALL OVER THE WORLD. "

8.5 CAPITAL SUPPORTS IMPROVED HEALTH AND WELL-BEING

Affordable medication and services are inextricably linked to a well-functioning medical provision. Universal or free health care is provided in many countries already, but there are also nations that do not offer this. For individuals living in these countries, getting ill can lead to financial strain and in some cases, push people to sell off property or assets or cause people to fall into extreme debt or even become impoverished.

GETTING ILL CAN LEAD TO FINANCIAL STRAIN.

In some developing countries, health care providers do not have the financial means to do their work sufficiently. Already in 2001, the Dutch physician Joep Lange recognized the need for making health care finance and delivery more effective and more inclusive. He therefore started PharmAccess, which is still today a frontrunner in digital innovation for health care. The firm develops methods to explore new directions and provide real world solutions in order to reverse the vicious cycle that stifles progress. It's goal is to mobilize public and private resources for the benefit of doctors and patients through a combination of health insurance, loans for health care providers, quality standards, provider services, health analytics and mHealth innovations. One such innovation that they are involved in is the M-TIBA mobile health wallet, a digital wallet on the mobile phone that contains funds and benefits that can only be used for health care. PharmAccess also created the Medical Credit Fund (MCF) to provide much-needed financial assets to health care facilities in Africa (See Case 43). The Medical Credit Fund works with African banks to help private health care facilities access loans. They also give support and guidance to heath care provid-

ers to develop their growth strategy and identify the most effective areas of investment.[42]

Health care providers in low and middle-income countries need to develop innovative low-cost preventive and curative treatments for communicable and non-communicable diseases. To do this, they could actively adopt low price, high volume pricing models to expand access to vaccines, diagnostic tests, pharmaceuticals, supplements and family planning and invest in the development of low-cost medical devices, which are easy to operate and maintain. Novartis International AG acted in the spirit of this call when it launched Novartis Access in 2015, a portfolio of 15 medicines to treat chronic diseases in low and lower middle-income countries. The portfolio addresses cardiovascular diseases, diabetes, respiratory illnesses, and breast cancer and is offered to governments, non- governmental organizations and other public-sector health care providers for US $1 per treatment, per month. The Novartis Access portfolio includes patented and generic Novartis medicines. Being first launched in Kenya, Ethiopia and Vietnam, Novartis now plans to roll out this program to 30 countries, depending on demand. The products included in the product portfolio have been selected primarily based WHO's Essential Medicines List and are among the most commonly prescribed medicines in these countries. Novartis expects this approach to eventually reach a scale where it will be profitable, making it sustainable over the long term and enabling continuous support in those regions.[43]

INVESTMENT IN SUSTAINABLE AND INNOVATIVE HEALTH CARE SOLUTIONS IS NEEDED.

Investment in sustainable and innovative health care solutions is needed and social impact funds are helping to fill that need. The Global Health Investment Fund (GHIF) is a US $108 million social impact investment fund designed to provide financing to advance the development of drugs, vaccines, diagnostics and other interventions against diseases that disproportionately burden low and middle-income countries.[44] LeapFrog Investments is another example of private equity firms that concentrate on heath care. Founded in 2007, LeapFrog launched a US $135 million social-impact investing fund aimed at emerging markets in Asia and Africa. Among the LeapFrog stars: South Africa's AllLife, the first company to offer life insurance coverage to HIV-positive individuals, and Petra, the largest independent pension trustee in Ghana.[45] LeapFrog also recently announced a US $22 million majority stake in Goodlife Pharmacy – the largest direct investment in the East African retail pharmacy sector to date.[46] LeapFrog has backed 17 companies across finance and health that operate in 23 countries, employing more than 100,000 people and providing insurance and other services for 91 million people.[47]

Health insurance needs and offerings vary greatly from country to country. In some developing countries, microinsurance is offered to meet the needs of people living on US $1 to $4 a day. Microinsurance is aimed at protecting low-income people against specific health risks. As a provider of microinsurance, the Swedish insurer BIMA built a life and health insurance proposition in developing markets that differentiates itself from other microinsurance providers through a simple and yet customizable mobile phone ICT platform. Clients use their mobile numbers as ID and pay their premium via mobile top-up cards. BIMA's sales force also focuses on developing insurance literacy among their clients. Within only seven years, BIMA has grown to serve 30 million customers, 90% of whom had no prior insurance. In some markets, as many as 85% of BIMA's clients purchase at least a second BIMA product, which is a first indicator of perceived customer value. At present, BIMA has achieved profitability in 4 of its 15 markets, and aims for 8 by the end of 2017.[48] BIMA health services also offers a hotline for people to get free, unlimited consultations with a doctor.

CASE NO.

MEDICAL CREDIT FUND

Initiated by the PharmAccess Group
Investing in quality health care in private
SME facilities

Case applied in: Sub-Saharan Africa
Headquarters located in: The Netherlands,
Ghana, Kenya, Nigeria and Tanzania
www.medicalcreditfund.org

IMPACT SDGs

SDG 3
Good Health and Well-Being

Improved the quality of services (measured by SafeCare standards) for health SMEs with an MCF loan. Patient visits have increased to over 700,000 monthly.

SDG 8
Decent Work and Economic Growth

Since 2011, over 1,400 loans totaling over US $26 million have been disbursed to more than 850 health SMEs. At 97%, the historical repayment rate is excellent. Over 1,600 health care staff and 1,800 bank staff have been trained.

SDG 10
Reduced Inequalities

People at the base of the pyramid benefit from improved services, with 35% of patients classified as low-income and 22% as very low income.

SDG 17
Partnerships for the Goals

Disbursed loans through 13 African financial institutions, with 3 partner banks marketing the program as their own health sector products.

POOR PEOPLE RELY ON PRIVATE HEALTH MARKETS BY DEFAULT, AND SUFFER DISPROPORTIONATELY FROM HIGH OUT-OF-POCKET EXPENSES. WE NEED TO ACKNOWLEDGE THIS REALITY AND MAKE HEALTH MARKETS WORK FOR THE POOR.
ONNO SCHELLEKENS, CEO PHARMACCESS GROUP

As populations continue to rise, the demand for affordable, quality health care has never been greater. Low-income groups in Sub-Saharan Africa generally look to the private sector for health care, usually because of the better care and customer service (SDG 3), as well as a low level of trust in government services. However, the segment of the private sector that serves low-income groups faces many challenges as well, such as below-standard infrastructure and equipment, lack of skilled medical staff and poor quality of the services provided. In 2009, PharmAccess endeavored to solve this dilemma and set up the first and only dedicated fund providing loans to small and medium- sized health enterprises (SMEs) in Africa: the Medical Credit Fund (MCF).

Medical Credit Fund makes investment capital available for health care providers and combines this with technical assistance, enabling health care providers to strengthen their business case, increase capacity, and improve the quality of their health care services (SDG 8). MCF helps these clinics build a financial track record and become bankable. Because health SMEs often lack a credit history, adequate bookkeeping and accounting systems, financial performance records and sufficient assets to serve as collateral, MCF mitigates risks for African banks in order to bridge this gap (SDG 10).

The Fund's capital base comprises grants from public and private parties, which serve as a risk cushion for investors. MCF's strong partnerships have led to integrated loan products such as Sidian Bank's Tabibu loan in Kenya, Fidelity Bank's MediLoan and uniBank's uniHealth loan in Ghana, and Diamond Bank's Mediloan in Nigeria (SDG 17). MCF has shown a strong repayment performance that is prompting banks to take an increasingly large share of the funding and repayment risk.

Over the years, MCF has seen a growing demand for larger and more flexible loans. In 2015, the Dutch Good Growth Fund and Pfizer Foundation provided support for MCF to prepare an expansion of its mandate. This, in combination with a loan from the Calvert Foundation, allowed a reduction in the investment risk for follow-on investors and brought about more impact investments. In 2016, MCF raised an additional US $17 million from OPIC, the Calvert Foundation and two private investors. In 2017, a number of development banks also joined, bringing the fund size to US $45 million. This expansion allowed for loans of up to US $2.5 million – a significant rise from the previous US $350,000 – and for partnerships with non-bank financial institutions.

CHALLENGE

To secure formal bank loans for healthcare SMEs that struggle to purchase modern equipment, maintain adequate stock of medicines or even pay for basic repairs.

OPPORTUNITIES FOR SCALE

Mobilizing capital into the private health sector will remain a primary focus. MCF will continue to lower investment risks for banks, through transparency delivered by SafeCare standards and by shouldering some of their partner banks' financial exposure. Since expanding its mandate, MCF can now serve other players in the health sector, explore new markets, and work with non-bank financing institutions. MCF will also continue developing (digital) financial innovations, tackling sector-specific obstacles like collateralization requirements, receivable financing and working-capital shortages.

Sources and further information

- https://www.medicalcreditfund.org/update/new-financing-round-brings-medical-credit-fund-usd-40m-catalyzing-access-capital-health-smes-africa/
- https://nextbillion.net/two-sided-mobile-platform-creates-network-effect-to-help-patients-health-clinics/
- https://www.pharmaccess.org/update/pharmaccess-progress-report-2016/
- http://hmpi.org/2017/09/06/strengthening-the-private-health-sector-in-africa-the-pharmaccess-solution/
- http://fairpolitics.nl/doc/Ready%20for%20Change%20report%20May%202016.pdf

" MEDICAL CREDIT FUND MAKES INVESTMENT CAPITAL AVAILABLE FOR HEALTH CARE PROVIDERS AND COMBINES THIS WITH TECHNICAL ASSISTANCE."

8.6 DOMAINS OF IMPACT

The three domains of impact for health and well-being that we will explore are:

1. Access to basic health care
2. Innovations in health care
3. Promoting healthy lifestyles and well-being

1. ACCESS TO BASIC HEALTH CARE

SDG 3, and specifically Target 3.8 aims to: "achieve universal health coverage, including financial risk protection, access to quality essential health care services and access to safe, effective, quality and affordable essential medicines and vaccines for all." In 2015, the WHO and World Bank Group measured global health service coverage and financial protection, showing their finding in their report, *Tracking Universal Health Coverage*. The report looked at access to health including: family planning, antenatal care, skilled birth attendance, child immunization, antiretroviral therapy, tuberculosis treatment, and access to clean water and sanitation – and found that at least 400 million people lacked access to at least one of these services.[49] The report also found that, across 37 countries, 6% of the global population fell into extreme poverty (US $1.25/day) because they had to pay for health services out of their own pockets.

THE LACK OF SAFE WATER, SANITATION AND HYGIENE SERVICES IN MANY PARTS OF DEVELOPING NATIONS CREATE MAJOR RISK FACTORS FOR COLLECTIVE HUMAN HEALTH.

Considering that at least three of the thirteen Targets associated with SDG 3 are aimed at specifically improving access to health services to women and children, it is an important focal point. Target 3.1 calls for the reduction of global maternal mortality; Target 3.2 specifies the elimination of preventable deaths of newborns and children under 5 years of age; and Target 3.7 places attention on the inclusion of sexual and reproductive health care services in the general Target of 3.8 which aims for universal health care for all. In 2015, global maternal mortality was 216 maternal deaths per 100,000 live births. This is a decrease from 1990, which counted 385 maternal deaths per 100,000, but further reduction should still be sought.[50] In many countries, most maternal death is due to a lack of basic medical facilities and skilled care during delivery.[51] The lack of access to sexual and reproductive education and medical services also has an impact on unintended and adolescent pregnancies. Universal access to sexual, reproductive and maternal health care is crucial to the health and well-being of women, children and adolescents.

ACCESS TO HEALTH CARE IS CRUCIAL TO BOTH INDIVIDUALS AND COMMUNITIES.

Supporting good health for children is the focus of numerous initiatives as it is critical to specifically aid this vulnerable group. Access Afya, for instance, is a social enterprise that created a model for integrated community health. It runs a chain of micro-clinics in Nairobi's informal settlements and a "Healthy Schools" program that delivers check-ups, treatments, and training to children in their schools. Access Afya makes a difference by getting essential health products and services to a population that is under-served by the current health system.[52] There are many philanthropic, NGO, governmental, and business initiatives that endeavor to increase access to health care for people who currently do not have it. More still needs to be done. Furthermore, the initiatives, like Access Afya, that are working, need to be scaled up. As discussed elsewhere in this book, partnerships between large companies and small start-ups, together with capital investments, can turn local small-scale initiatives into large-scale shifts. In a recent blog, Access Afya reported a new corporate partnership with the Heineken

Africa Foundation to "launch a mobile maternal and child health clinic, sharing essential devices such as ultrasound with multiple communities." [53] This kind of partnership helps to grow the impact of social enterprises such as Access Afya.

Infectious diseases are a growing concern. Global warming is presenting conditions that support the proliferation of disease carrying mosquitos. Additionally, in many parts of the world, people are building up antimicrobial resistance due to overuse of antibiotics. Antibiotics use in agriculture also leads to new strains of resistant bacteria, which is then spread to humans upon consumption. The lack of safe water, sanitation and hygiene services in many parts of developing nations create major risk factors for collective human health. The lack of access to quality medical facilities contributes to the spread of infectious diseases, and mortality due to illnesses caused by unclean water and lack of sanitation.

Premature deaths (before 70 years of age) from cardiovascular disease, cancer, chronic respiratory disease or diabetes totaled about 13 million in 2015, accounting for 43% of all premature deaths globally. Although cures for these illnesses are out of reach, good medical care can help to partially detect and prevent them at an early stage, managing the progression to extend people's quality of life.

Access to health care is not only important for individuals, it is important to communities as well. Infectious diseases that spread because individuals cannot access or afford health care threaten entire communities and can potentially reach an epidemic level with a possibility of affecting people in other countries as well.

As the global population ages, access to care for the elderly is becoming a concern. By 2050, there will be more old people than children under the age of 15 for the first time in history.[54] In many countries, elderly people suffer from loneliness and do not have sufficient help to carry on living independently, nor are there sufficient care homes for them. In Japan, where in 2016 the annual birth rate dropped below a million for the first time since 1899 and a quarter of the population is already greying, they are looking to technological innovations for support for their aging population.

2. INNOVATIONS IN HEALTH CARE

Technological innovations are bringing exciting opportunities to health care. 3D printing, for example, is making prosthetics more widely available. Robotics and artificial intelligence are changing the way surgery is being performed and bringing other far-reaching opportunities. Drones are delivering medical supplies in hard to reach areas, and the Internet of Things is helping people and medical practitioners monitor overall well-being. In the near future, we will see an explosion of technology assisted solutions.

Many experts and companies also see a great future for eHealth applications. MediAngels, a Mumbai based innovative global eHospital, aims to remove geographical barriers between health care consumers and medical specialists from around the world. As health care is human capital intensive, the best doctor for a particular disease may not be within a reasonable traveling distance. At MediAngels, patients can potentially access doctors regardless of physical location. MediAngels makes it possible to consult a specialist who is unavailable locally for any ailment, at any given time, directly from home.[55]

IN THE NEAR FUTURE, WE WILL SEE AN EXPLOSION OF TECHNOLOGY ASSISTED SOLUTIONS.

As the population ages, solutions for elderly care will need to be developed. Management consulting firm Accenture foresees that digital health innovations and advances in robotics will lead to improvements in self-management. The consulting firm has identified technological influences on health care as "Trend 5: The Uncharted." Accenture explains that we are entering an "uncharted"

TECHNOLOGY IN ITS MANY FORMS WILL TRANSFORM MEDICAL CARE, **BRINGING TREATMENT TO MORE PEOPLE AND IN A MORE CUSTOMIZED MANNER.**

time when we are inventing things that no one has ever thought of or heard of. Technological advances are being made rapidly and technology companies need to therefore take a more active role in creating conscientious solutions. Together, technology companies and health care providers must ensure trust and recognize that technologies will have far-reaching implications.[56] Additionally, ethical frameworks, and government regulations must evolve alongside the science and technological developments. Technological innovations will also contribute to closing the care gap, as many countries struggle with a shortage of caregivers for the elderly.[57]

Another new product on the market is taking Japan by storm. To help alleviate loneliness and care issues for the large amount of elderly in the country, Japan is piloting "Support Robots" to keep retirees physically, socially, emotionally, and mentally engaged. Japan's Ministry of Economy, Trade and Industry expects a boom in the robotic service industry to nearly US $4 billion annually by 2035 – 25 times its current level. With the current pace of technological advances, we can expect to see robots develop in sophistication and nuance. For now, other countries too, such as Germany, are implementing the robots to help out in assisted living facilities by ferrying food and drinks to residents from the kitchen as well as keeping them entertained by playing memory games to help keep their minds sharp. Other Robotic versions are currently available to suit different needs such as keeping track of medication, connecting through video to family and friends, monitoring health and robots with integrated AI learning ca-

pabilities to interact and adjust to the person they are serving. Although this may seem to be a solution to issues of care for many people, there are some concerns at the broad, big picture level. Advances in robots and artificial intelligence must be controlled carefully. Additionally, although robots can provide companionship at times, ultimately, "humans need humans," as aptly said by Susan Madlung, gerontologist and Clinical Educator for Regional Programs and Home Health Re-Design at Vancouver Coastal Health when speaking about the use of robots in care of the elderly.[58]

The use of robots for dangerous activities or unsafe jobs is another way this technology can help humans and reduce health risks. Robots are being employed as firefighters, assisting fire departments in situations where it is just too hazardous to send someone into a burning building or area. In this way, robots can play an important role in preventing harm or death to human beings.

> JAPAN'S MINISTRY OF ECONOMY, TRADE AND INDUSTRY EXPECTS A BOOM IN THE ROBOTIC SERVICE INDUSTRY TO NEARLY US $4 BILLION ANNUALLY BY 2035 – 25 TIMES ITS CURRENT LEVEL.
>
> ENGADGET

3D printing will also play an increasingly important role in the coming years. Already 3D printing is creating exciting new opportunities for health care, especially as the cost of 3D printing decreases and the technology becomes more accessible. For example, 3D-printed skin for burn victims is already available, as are 3D printed prosthetics. Experts have even printed airway splints for babies with tracheobronchomalacia, which makes the airways around the lungs prone to collapsing. The 3D printed airway splints are a breakthrough, as they are the first 3D implant that is able to grow with the patient. The splints can be produced in a matter of hours, and they only cost about US $10.[59] 3D printing makes it easier to customize medical supplies and also presents the opportunity of more mobility for medical assistance. Technology in its many forms will transform medical care, bringing treatment to more people and in a more customized manner.

3. PROMOTING HEALTHY LIFESTYLES AND WELL-BEING

Nutrition is a vital factor in health and well-being. As mentioned earlier, The United Nations Food and Agriculture Organization estimates that about 795 million people of the 7.3 billion people in the world, or one in nine, were suffering from chronic undernourishment from 2014 to 2016.[60] As a business initiative to tackle the pervasive problem of malnutrition in communities in India, Cargill has created the "Nourishing India" platform that provides 25 million people with vitamin-fortified cooking oil. With 25% of the world's malnourished people living in India, and an annual per capita consumption of 15.4 liters of oil, this initiative has the potential to make a considerable impact.

Understanding which foods to eat can also influence malnutrition significantly. Sweet potatoes, for instance, are naturally high in vitamin A and sweet

Figure 41 **Nutrition and SDGs**[63]

17 Aid allocated to nutrition has high returns a $1 investment in nutirtion has demonstrated a $16 return in economic growth

01 Being poor limits the ability of individuals to access adequate food

16 War and conflict are major underlying factors of nutrition insecurity

02 Agriculture and food security are cornerstones of nutrition

15 Soil degradation threaten our ability to grow food

03 Up to 45% of deaths in children under 5 are caused by undernutrition

Achieving the SDGs

13 Climate change may reduce food production and cause water scarity

04 Learning and focusing in school is difficult without a sufficient diet

12 Tackling resource use and degradation is key for sharing resources and improving access to quality food

05 When women control the family income, children's health and nutrition improve at a greater rate

08 High levels of malnutrition in some countries may result in an 11% loss to GDP

06 Access to safe water and sanitation is an absolute prerequisite for nutrition

FACTS ABOUT OBESITY AND OVERWEIGHT IN USA

- **MORE THAN TWO-THIRDS (68.8%) OF ADULTS ARE CONSIDERED TO BE OVERWEIGHT OR OBESE.**

- **MORE THAN ONE-THIRD (35.7%) OF ADULTS ARE CONSIDERED TO BE OBESE.**

- **MORE THAN 1 IN 20 (6.3%) HAVE EXTREME OBESITY**

- **AMONG CHILDREN AND ADOLESCENTS AGES 6 TO 19: ALMOST 1 IN 3 (33.2%) ARE CONSIDERED TO BE OVERWEIGHT OR OBESE, AND 18.2% ARE CONSIDERED TO BE OBESE.**

WRI AND WRAP RESEARCH

potatoes can also be bred to have higher amounts of micronutrients as well. The 2013 Lancet report on Maternal and Child Undernutrition and Overweight attributed 157,000 childhood deaths in 2011 to vitamin A deficiency.[62] Nutrition is such an important part of good health and so essential to our well-being that it is in fact a part of all of the SDGs, as shown in figure 41.

Obesity and overweight are also a health concerns. There are 1.9 billion overweight people worldwide, and of these over 650 million are obese. Obesity has nearly tripled since 1975 all over the world.[64] While obesity can be a disease that could potentially only be treated medically, overweight is often caused by food choices. For example, the impact of sugary soft drinks has been studied and findings show a significant link between sugary drink consumption and weight gain, especially in children. These kinds of drinks have become cheaper than healthy drinks in many countries and are available in larger sized containers. To combat this, France became one of the first countries to introduce a targeted sugar tax on soft drinks in 2012. Following this groundbreaking move, similar measures were announced

in Mexico in 2013 and in the UK in 2016. Considering that nearly two-thirds of adults in the UK are overweight or obese, this is a very relevant measure. And in the United States, in November 2014, Berkeley, California was the first community to pass a targeted tax on soda.

3.1 MILLION CHILD DEATHS DUE TO MALNUTRITION EACH YEAR. [61]

FARMING FIRST

Well-being is not only defined as good physical health, but good mental health as well. Stress can cause people to not feel well. Contributors to stress include unemployment and money concerns. To address this societal issue, Vebego set out to employ people who would otherwise have difficulty finding a job, and also offers financial coaching to help them gain control of their finances (See Case 44).

CASE NO.

VEBEGO INTERNATIONAL

Financial Vitality and Meaningful Work
Healthier and Happier Communities and
Employees

Case applied in: **The Netherlands,
Switzerland, Belgium, and Germany**
Headquarters located in: **The Netherlands**
www.vebego.com

IMPACT SDGs

SDG 3
**Good Health and
Well-Being**

Provides €700 per person in
debt relief through its positive
impact programs; societal
total of €11 billion in debt
relief.

SDG 4
Quality Education

Offers a budget coach program
for employees, for every €1
invested by the company, the
program reduces societal
costs by €3.50 per person.

SDG 8
**Decent Work and Economic
Growth**

Placed 660 unemployed people
back into jobs during 2012 to
2016 time period.

SDG 10
Reduced Inequalities

In sheltered workplaces there
are over 6000 employees with
a distance to the labor market
working in a normal working
environment.

**OUR MISSION IS TO VITALIZE WORK AND HEALTH CARE. I SEE IT AS
A DUTY.** WE ARE ALWAYS TRYING TO PENETRATE NEW MARKETS SO THAT WE
CAN OFFER EVERYONE PROSPECTS FOR THE FUTURE.
RONALD GOEDMAKERS, CEO AND OWNER VEBEGO

Vebego believes that it cannot prosper if it does not also help the world to prosper. The company's social value creation model is to use the shared value methodology to measure the social and economic impact of the sustainable activities on the macro- meso- and micro levels. The social costs Vebego identifies consist of depreciation, relief, health expenses, lost working hours, benefits and home expenses. The company endeavors to help the 1 out of 4 employees who have problematic debt by developing a debt assistance program and reduce societal debt at large while giving people work they enjoy. It is the company's mission to offer good jobs, to ensure healthy lives, and promote well-being among community members.

Through the Financial Vitality program, which was launched in 2016, Vebego's subsidiaries can offer employees assistance to reorganize their personal finances, get out of debt faster, and receive financial education (SDG 4). This supports more than 30,000 people across the company. The program assists employee households that suffer from debts that create a feeling of being excluded from society and financial problems that cause strain on individuals, the company, and the community. Employees are not only more productive when they have less financial stress, they are likely to take approximately 9 to 14 fewer sick days per year (SDG 3). When employees miss work, this

costs Vebego money and time and conversely, when people really like their work, they are able to work more. Further, debt-free families are more likely to indirectly contribute beneficially to society.

Meaningful work is also an important value for Vebego, as they not only focus on being client-oriented and innovative, but also on building internal bonds. The company believes that it is through this value of employee well-being that they can distinguish themselves and create the most value for the business. Not only do people often stay with the company throughout their entire career, Vebego also hires those who otherwise may not be able to work, and places them in good jobs (SDG 8 & SDG 10). Since 2012, Vebego has had a program where it is working together with social services to get the unemployed back to work. As one of the largest employers in Europe of people with poor job prospects, the company promotes work and economic growth for all. Vebego typically hires these workers for its landscaping and cleaning businesses, currently employing approximately 6,000 people. As those employees enjoy this meaningful job, they in turn have an improved quality of life and it becomes beneficial for everyone (SDG 10). Since Financial Vitality began, unemployment benefits amounting to €7,500 have been avoided, saving a total of €4 million for society as a whole.

CHALLENGE

To foster employees who deliver the best performance to clients while also increasing brand value through increased profits and stakeholder satisfaction.

OPPORTUNITIES FOR SCALE

As one of the largest employers in the Netherlands of people with poor job prospects, Vebego has the potential to scale the program and form long-term partnerships that create significant social impact and economic growth. While continuing to promote good employability through meaningful work programs and debt relief, the business can foster employees who deliver the best performance to clients while also increasing brand value through increased profits and stakeholder satisfaction.

Sources and further information

- http://www.magazine.about.pwc.nl/december2016#!/interview-ronald-goedmakers
- www.vebego.com
- www.vebegofoundation.nl
- http://wbcsdpublications.org/wp-content/uploads/2015/11/Social_Capital_in_Decision-Making_How_social_information_drives-_value_creation_print.pdf
- Vebego Program Update and Next Steps, RvB and RvE Slide Deck, April 2017
- https://translate.google.com/#auto/en/Financi%C3%ABle%20vitaliteit%20voor%20medewerkers
- More information: drs A.I.H. van Waning – Head of Sustainaility & Impact – annette.vanwaning@vebego.com

" IT IS THE COMPANY'S MISSION TO OFFER GOOD JOBS, TO ENSURE HEALTHY LIVES, AND PROMOTE WELL-BEING AMONG COMMUNITY MEMBERS. "

WRAP UP

Access to health care is an important element in this SDG. To reduce mortality and disease, people need to be able to get medical treatment when they need it. In most developed countries, access is guaranteed. In developing countries, there are major improvements needed in availability and affordability. Innovations in health care can help tremendously with overcoming the shortcomings. Technological innovations such as 3D printing, drone medicine delivery where road infrastructure is lacking, and mobile phone access to medical consultations regardless of distance to the nearest clinic, are helping more people gain access to health care.

To sustainably achieve the SDG 3 to ensure good health and well-being for all, healthy lifestyles must be promoted and supported. There are numerous business opportunities here. Trends have already shown that people are cutting down on smoking, increasing physical exercise and eating healthier foods. So businesses that capitalize on these trends and look to business practices and strategies that support healthier lifestyles are growing profit and creating value. Organizing work conditions and employment benefits to promote this trend will also help to accelerate and embed healthier habits. Businesses can look to their in-house canteens to ensure that the foods they provide are healthy. They can also keep an eye on stress building activities and long hours to be sure this does not cause unhealthy stress levels. When people are stressed, they can experience burn-out which results in little or no productivity. Therefore, it is good business sense to prevent overstress.

It is to everyone's benefit to have healthy individuals, communities and employees. To truly conduct business for good, the health and well-being of a company's stakeholders should always be considered and supported. ∎

" THE KEY IS TO ARTICULATE A STRONG VISION AND SHARE IT AS WIDELY AS POSSIBLE, SO THAT IT IS TRANSLATED CONCRETELY INTO MANAGEMENT AND DECISION MAKING."

GÉRARD MESTRALLET, CHAIRMAN OF THE BOARD OF DIRECTORS ENGIE

9

ENERGY & RESOURCES

Hurricanes Harvey, Irma and Maria and the massive floods in South Asia are just the most recent demonstration of the urgency of tackling climate change. The number of such events has nearly quadrupled since 1970. It is predicted that such events will only become more frequent, so we need emissions to peak and resilience to build. In 2016, more than 24 million people were displaced by weather-related disasters, affecting the economy, business and society at large.[1] As climate change is challenging the security of many regions around the world, we need to transform our economies. If we want to meet the Targets of the Paris Agreement of 2015, there is a turning point right here, right now. The world has barely come to the realization that this implies that the world's carbon budget is practically used up. "Climate change is not only a societal disaster but also an economic catastrophe," business leaders like Gérard Mestrallet point out regularly. The energy and resources sector is an integral part of both society and the economy. This sector plays a key role in climate action and achieving economic prosperity sustainably, and consequently a pivotal player in the achievement of the SDGs.

9.1 SDG 13: CLIMATE ACTION

Climate change is threatening both society and the economy on an unprecedented scale. The Intergovernmental Panel on Climate Change (IPCC) reports that global warming is unequivocal, and is in large part due to an increase in greenhouse gas (GHG) emissions from human activities.[2] It is clear that climate action must be taken. Substantial and sustained reductions of GHG emissions are needed to limit warming to 2°C, the threshold recognized by governments as limiting the worst impacts of climate change. At COP21 in 2015 all 193 member nations agreed to the urgency of reducing CO2 emissions and taking action on climate change.

MULTIPLE STUDIES SHOW THAT 97% OR MORE OF ACTIVELY PUBLISHING CLIMATE SCIENTISTS AGREE: CLIMATE-WARMING TRENDS OVER THE PAST CENTURY ARE EXTREMELY LIKELY DUE TO HUMAN ACTIVITIES.[3]

NASA

As the world becomes more populated, urbanized and prosperous, the demand for energy and other resources will continue to rise exponentially, further exacerbating climate change. In light of the growing demand for energy in emerging economies, this challenge presents a dire need to achieve substantial and rapid GHG emissions reductions. Yet the scale, cost and immobility of much of the world's existing energy infrastructure, and precedent for inefficient use of finite resources, could slow down the transition to a lower-carbon future.

IF WE WANT TO MEET THE TARGETS OF THE PARIS AGREEMENT OF 2015, THERE IS A TURNING POINT RIGHT HERE, RIGHT NOW.

Climate change has detrimental consequences, creating energy inequality and resource scarcity that are intertwined: a negative impact on one has a negative impact on the other. Poverty is closely related to these negative climate impacts as well. Climate impacts affect the poor more prominently. Many millions have no access to basic energy services, fresh water or sanitary provisions. Even though the global economic output has increased approximately one hundred times since the beginning of the industrial revolution, there continue to be some 1.5 billion people living without access to electricity.[4] A lack of access means that development is slowed leading to approximately 1.3 billion people living in abject poverty. This lack of access to electricity affects people's ability to protect themselves against extreme weather conditions due to a lack of cooling or heating.

A UN International Resource Panel Report says that material resource use is expected to reach nearly 90 billion tons in 2017, and may more than double from 2015 to 2050. This means that without greater resource efficiency, the SDGs will not succeed.[1] Growing material and resource use is driven by expanding populations, consumption trends, mainly in developed economies, and the transformation of developing economies. Demand for resources has shifted from traditionally agriculture-based economies to modern urban and industrial economies. This creates new waste flows, thereby increasing emissions and pollution and increasing global warming. For example, data

shows that the steep increases in demand for ores, like iron, have contributed to sharp rises in greenhouse gas emissions, acidification, aquatic eco-toxicity and emissions of smog-forming substances.[5]

DEMAND FOR RESOURCES HAS SHIFTED FROM TRADITIONALLY AGRICULTURE-BASED ECONOMIES TO MODERN URBAN AND INDUSTRIAL ECONOMIES.

Climate change adversely affects important aspects of everyday life. For example, agricultural productivity is reduced while demand for water and energy will increase by an estimated 40% and 50%, respectively, by 2030.[6] In addition to resource stress, global warming puts stress on the economy and business growth. A 2015 report from the Economist Intelligence Unit stated that the world's stock of manageable assets

Roughly **60%** of global final energy is used by the richest **20%**

With only **5%** going to the poorest **20%**

half of the global population living in cities accounts for **60% to 80%** of total energy and resource needs.

As urbanization progresses, there is expected to be a **doubling** of these needs.

Figure 42 **Global final energy**

was about US $143 trillion.[7] Expected losses from climate change are valued at US $4.2 trillion in 2100 in today's value. That's roughly equivalent to the total value of all the world's oil and gas companies, or the entire GDP of Japan. Addressing climate change will require energy and resource usage to become more efficient and sustainable. Meeting the climate challenge requires new business models that conserve and manage these vital societal necessities, opening markets that will foster the circular economy. Access to energy and resources is increasingly seen as an intrinsic catalyst to wider social and economic development, enabling education, health and sustainable agriculture, and creating jobs. These global challenges related to SDG 13 are therefore complex. In this chapter, we explore some of the challenges as well as the business opportunities when striving to solve them. The following Targets associated with SDG 13 are useful to keep in mind.

SDG 13: CLIMATE ACTION;
Take urgent action to combat climate change and its impacts

TARGETS

13.1   Strengthen resilience and adaptive capacity to climate-related hazards and natural disasters in all countries

13.2   Integrate climate change measures into national policies, strategies and planning

13.3   Improve education, awareness-raising and human and institutional capacity on climate change mitigation, adaptation, impact reduction and early warning

13.a   Implement the commitment undertaken by developed-country parties to the United Nations Framework Convention on Climate Change to a goal of mobilizing jointly $100 billion annually by 2020 from all sources to address the needs of developing countries in the context of meaningful mitigation actions and transparency on implementation and fully operationalize the Green Climate Fund through its capitalization as soon as possible

13.b   Promote mechanisms for raising capacity for effective climate change-related planning and management in least developed countries and small island developing States, including focusing on women, youth and local and marginalized communities

9.2 SOLVING THE CHALLENGES: ENERGY AND RESOURCES AS THE FUEL FOR CLIMATE ACTION

While climate change is complex, it is clear that our collective energy choices and use of resources have a direct influence on the climate, the economy and the marketplace. As we discuss SDG 13, we will begin to discover how it is interconnected with several other Goals. First, developing a system for clean and affordable energy production (SDG 7) can be an integral factor in climate action. Not only are fossil fuels polluting the environment, but they are finite resources putting strain on the economy as prices rise. Other finite resources are also being used at an accelerated rate and more responsible consumption and production patterns must be adopted (SDG 6 & 12). As developing countries prosper and technology expands over the next 25 years, world energy consumption will increase by about one-third, placing strain on the planet and the economy.[8] The use of energy and resources are integral parts of production processes such as manufacturing. Therefore, we must explore innovative, sustainable processes while simultaneously pursuing a circular economic approach that promotes sus-

tainable business and growth (SDG 8 & 9). That is, a circular economy will "provide a profitable opportunity to move away from resource-intensive processes, while maximizing the use of existing assets and creating new revenue streams."[9] Only then will we be able to save our one and only planet and slow climate change.

> **57% OF BUSINESS LEADERS BELIEVE INVESTMENT IN CLIMATE SOLUTIONS IS ESSENTIAL TO COMPETITIVE ADVANTAGE, BUT JUST 29% OF COMPANIES SURVEYED ALLOCATE A SIGNIFICANT PORTION OF THEIR R&D BUDGET TO THIS INITIATIVE.[10]**
>
> ACCENTURE

The direct impact that climate has on the SDGs is hugely influential. It is therefore critical that businesses within this sector keep this firmly in mind and shift their business strategies to include a positive impact on both the climate and the SDGs. Businesses will need to take into account the potential rise in energy and resource consumption. Energy use in OECD countries will continue to grow another 35% by 2020.[11] Commercial and residential energy use is the second most rapidly growing area of global energy use after transport.

In the UK, for example, although household CO2 emissions have reduced since 1990, still 40% of UK emissions come from households. Consequently, there is much more that can be done to further curb the average household's carbon footprint. The Committee on Climate Change put together some suggestions and statistics on what people could do to reduce emissions.(see figure 43).

> **"CO2 IS THE EXHALING BREATH OF OUR CIVILIZATION, LITERALLY... CHANGING THAT PATTERN REQUIRES A SCOPE, A SCALE, A SPEED OF CHANGE THAT IS BEYOND WHAT WE HAVE DONE IN THE PAST."**
>
> AL GORE

Figure 43 **UK Emisions Saving Measures Based on: Committee on Climate Change**

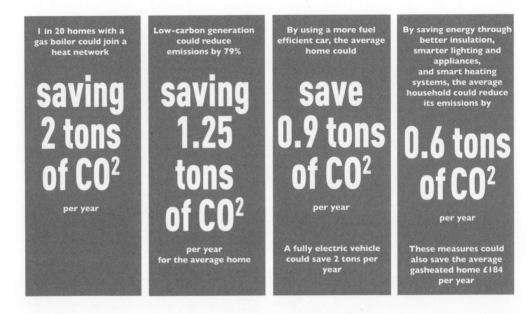

I in 20 homes with a gas boiler could join a heat network

saving 2 tons of CO^2

per year

Low-carbon generation could reduce emissions by 79%

saving 1.25 tons of CO^2

per year for the average home

By using a more fuel efficient car, the average home could

save 0.9 tons of CO^2

per year

A fully electric vehicle could save 2 tons per year

By saving energy through better insulation, smarter lighting and appliances, and smart heating systems, the average household could reduce its emissions by

0.6 tons of CO^2

per year

These measures could also save the average gasheated home £184 per year

Many of the world's largest companies recognize the potential value of investing in sustainable technologies and approaches to combat climate change. Disruptive circular business models, which foster the reuse or reduced use of resources and materials, can generate additional revenue and help fuel the development of new markets. Yet, less than a third of companies are seizing the strategic opportunity and dedicating the funds needed to adopt low-carbon solutions underpinned by innovative new technologies.[12]

More frequent droughts and severe storms, like our recent severe hurricanes, causing domestic and international supply chain interruptions, increased insurance costs, and long-term valuation risk for companies not addressing climate change, are detrimental economic factors. Therefore, recognizing the many ways that climate change will impact business creates a competitive advantage. The businesses that support acting on climate change are the ones that think strategically over the long term and turn their energy and resource efficiencies into a profitable business model both over the short and long terms.

One of the significant roles of business leaders is to manage risk to their business. At a minimum, climate change creates uncertainty, since it is difficult to predict the exact impacts on any individual business. Uncertainty makes it difficult to plan and is something all good business people try to reduce. Businesses that take action against climate impacts are less likely to be at risk, as managing energy and resource spending and guarding against market volatility of things like fossil fuel prices can promote financial stability and stakeholder confidence.

WHAT MOTIVATES CEOs TO DRIVE BUSINESS ACTION ON CLIMATE CHANGE: [13]

1. FUTURE GENERATIONS 81%
2. REPUTATION 63%
3. SHAREHOLDER VALUE 53%
4. BUILDING TRUST 52%
5. CONSUMER DEMAND 50%
6. RESILIENCE 44%
7. TALENT 40%

CEOWORLD.COM

Carbon Tracker is an independent financial think tank that analyzes the impact of the energy transition on capital markets, and the investment in fossil fuels. Their new report, *Margin call: Refining Capacity in a 2°C world*, looks at how a scenario for oil demand that is compliant with limiting the rise in global warming to 2°C might affect the oil industry's refining assets. It can be safely said that far less than the full levels of reserves will be used as we move towards other energy sources. Therefore, huge stranded assets are to be expected, which substantiates the massive divestment move that is underway.

Many large companies including ENGIE, DSM, and Tesla support acting on climate change.[14] They all recognize the serious risks associated with delaying action and the need to create more predictable business actions. Many also recognize the opportunities for innovation and growth associated with the changes that are necessary within their energy and resource portfolios.

Energy as a production enabler is especially important to allow local business innovation and create a more vibrant economy while also providing societal benefits. Some potentially important lower-carbon technologies, including carbon capture and storage, electric vehicles and wind energy, face significant political, infrastructure, logistical or cost challenges. The costs for some technologies, like solar, have fallen and perpetuated market growth, while others have remained high, mainly due to a lack of industry maturity. As a result, some governments have reduced their levels of support if not required or too costly. Businesses can step in to spur innovation, develop the industry, and lead climate action to a low carbon future.

We are seeing industries do just this as businesses continue to mobilize around climate solutions.[15] Placing an economy-wide price on carbon — either through carbon taxes or a cap-and-trade system — is a potential solution that has been employed. This allows companies to provide energy competitively while taking steps to limit GHG emissions and resource use.

Today, over half of all new power generation capacity comes from renewable energy. In Europe, it is 90%.[16] Off-grid energy solutions are also becoming simpler and cheaper. In the US, Tesla solar roof tiles are stronger and 20% cheaper, when you factor in energy savings and tax credits. And jobs are being created in the renewable energy sector as well. Last year, the renewable energy sector employed 9.8 million people, and such jobs are projected to rise to 26 million by 2050. But even though this progress looks promising, we still have a long way to go. The World Resource Institute notes that "Energy and material consumption raises a striking paradox: current environmental impacts due to energy production and waste are enormous, but 1.2 billion people still lack access to electricity, and supply must increase to fill this gap."[17]

> **ONLY ONE-FIFTH OF THE WORLD'S FINAL ENERGY CONSUMPTION IN 2013 WAS FROM RENEWABLES.**
>
> UN

The amount of natural resources used is closely linked to the amount of final waste and emissions generated through their use. Therefore, effective pollution control must also look to minimize raw material use, thereby decreasing final waste and emissions. Some numbers to consider as we think about how business opportunities can be created in the energy and resources sector include: More than 1.5 billion anticipated additional high-energy consumers by 2030; US $4.3 trillion and 86 million jobs as the potential payoff of circular models, renewable energy, energy efficiency and energy access; and US $780 to $1135 billion potential for collecting and repurposing cars and appliances (currently, cars are generally recycled into scrap metal, whereas appliances are rarely collected at all).[18]

9.3 IMPACT OF ENERGY AND RESOURCES ON ALL SDGs.

Everyone depends on energy and resources to varying degrees. Just as many resources such as water are necessary to sustain life itself, energy is required to sustain and improve quality of life. Therefore, energy and resources have impacts on all of the SDGs.

 SDG 1: No Poverty; Energy poverty is the lack of access to modern energy services, affecting many people in developing countries and some in developed countries as well. Worldwide, it is estimated that 16% of the global population, about 1.4 billion people, have little or no access to electricity. Without basic amenities like adequate light, clean water, cooking fuels, heating and cooling systems, people's well-being is negatively affected, and they are more likely to remain trapped in poverty. Additionally, when forced to seek and use resource intensive forms of fuel, including those that are polluting or dangerous, people spend time collecting or arranging these sources to meet their basic needs instead of engaging in employment. Eradicating poverty requires capital for access, maintenance and repairs of energy and resource infrastructure. One solution to alleviate energy poverty is the creation of a sustainable business model that supplies clean power at a fair price, allowing utilities to efficiently operate and scale up.

 SDG 2: Zero Hunger; Resource scarcity influences food security. Nutrient poor soil prevents people from producing enough to eat, and when they do manage, the foods are not rich enough to provide adequate nutrition. Energy poverty in many regions is a fundamental barrier to reducing hunger and ensuring that the world can produce enough food to meet future demand. Rethinking how we grow, process and consume our food is important to eliminating hunger. Much of the food production today is rapidly degrading soils, freshwater, oceans, forests and biodiversity. Climate change is also

putting even more pressure on the resources farmers depend on. Increased risks associated with disasters such as droughts and floods, in addition to episodes of heat stress, are putting pressure on land and reducing crop yields considerably which in turn causes low resource use efficiency. Further, the use of resource intensive irrigation is common in industrial crop production. For example, agriculture accounts for 80% to 90% of US consumptive water use. In much of the world, water resources for agricultural irrigation are taken from ground water supplies that do not replenish themselves. Intensive irrigation can also lead to salinization deposits of salt in soil, eventually leading to declines in yield.

 SDG 3: Good Health and Well-Being; Non-renewable energy and hydrocarbons that emit toxic pollutants can lead to severe health issues. Household air pollution as a result of cooking with unclean fuels or using inefficient technologies caused an estimated 4.3 million deaths in 2014. That same year, approximately 3.1 billion people across the world relied primarily on polluting fuels (e.g. coal and kerosene) for cooking. Often used in enclosed dwellings with poor ventilation, the smoke arising from this inefficient energy is laden with health-damaging pollutants. On a societal level, costs arising from energy and resource inefficiencies within healthcare facilities has also risen. Construction and operation of hospitals uses 5% of all energy consumed in the US, including buildings, transportation, and industry. There is a huge opportunity for hospitals and healthcare institutions to save money by achieving high standards of energy and resource conservation and efficiency. Savings would lead to operational cost reductions, which directly affect a hospital's bottom line and allow more funds to being allocated toward patients' well-being.

 SDG 4: Quality Education; Education services are directly impacted by energy and resources. Without light, controlled temperate conditions, or sufficient infrastructure, it is more difficult to facilitate an adequate educational environment. Additionally,

since the extension to the internet provides infinite access to education, those without electricity are barred from modern educational opportunities. Furthermore, it is important to educate people in the skills necessary for participation in emerging energy industries and in new ways to conserve resources. Educated citizens will likely be more inclined to recognize and adopt new practices and technologies that will help them and their communities prosper. And, with education, businesses and their employees better able to build and maintain energy infrastructures that will sustain their companies, promoting growth and limiting financial and regulatory risk. For example, DuPont provides training to local suppliers and service providers to increase the quality and sustainability of their operations. Each year DuPont awards funding to a promising new university faculty to address global challenges in energy and resources. The overarching goal of this program is to help research faculty students begin their research careers, while also establishing mutually beneficial relationships, including future research partnerships.

 SDG 5: Gender Equality; Considering gender equality and clean energy together as one issue is critical to sustainable development. The topic of gender equality in clean energy is unique in that the challenge is shared across developed and developing countries, and throughout all levels of the energy sector. Providing female entrepreneurs and small business owners with training and support, and including them in supply chains, can help meet the global energy and resource efficiency goals more quickly. In order to attract more women to employment in the energy industry by creating a gender-sensitive work environment, companies have been investing in gender awareness training, accommodating women's needs on extraction and production sites (e.g. different sizes of protective equipment, gender sensitive changing areas, etc.) and providing flexible work hours and/or childcare facilities. Not only does this provide women with more employment opportunities, it also includes them more directly in the energy and resource industry. In three African countries,

Solar Sister is addressing energy poverty and women's empowerment simultaneously through providing a social enterprise opportunity for women entrepreneurs to buy and sell solar lights at a profit.

 SDG 6: Clean Water and Sanitation; Smart water products and services – that is, data and sensor-driven products to help cities manage their water distribution networks and infrastructure – have been identified as a significant source of energy and resource savings. By automatically reducing water loss and minimizing water consumption, this technology can help cities and communities cope with climate impacts such as droughts or growing population pressure on water resources. The global market for smart water management technology is estimated to grow from US $8.46 billion in 2016 to US $20.1 billion by 2021, with climate change and the need to replace ageing water infrastructure as the key drivers for demand. The United States and Europe are currently major markets for the sector, but there is a strong business potential for these products emerging in India and China as well.

ANTICIPATED ADDITIONAL HIGH-ENERGY CONSUMERS BY 2030 COMES TO MORE THAN 1.5 BILLION.

SDG 7: Affordable and Clean Energy; To attain our energy objectives, such as SDG Target 7.3 (which aims to double the global rate of improvement in energy efficiency by 2030), manufacturing and production leaders will need to bring their expertise to others in the industry and to government bodies. The true leaders in increasing energy efficiency, and those who will gain the most financial value, will be those who incorporate a holistic mindset paired with integrated technologies, people and processes. An example of new fuel alternatives that CEMEX UK launched is a new facility to turn waste into fuel. The new Solid Recovered Fuel (SRF) facility will supply the CEMEX Rugby Cement Plant with a sustainable alternative to fossil fuels for the next 25 years, using nothing but regionally sourced household and commercial waste from the English Midlands Area. The fuel, known as Climafuel®, replaces traditional coal as an energy supply.

SDG 8: Decent Work and Economic Growth;

The basis of a modern, competitive, and productive econo-my is a secure and reliable energy supply. Bioenergy – which uses readily available non-food biomass resources – has significant potential to serve as a vehicle for job creation and economic opportunity for communities throughout the nation. Biobased activities in the current economy are estimated to have already generated more than US $48 billion in revenue and 285,000 jobs in 2014. Estimates show that continuing to develop our domestic biomass resources could contribute nearly US $259 billion and 1.1 million jobs to the US economy by 2030. These are jobs covering a broad range of fields, from scientific research to plant operations, business, farming, and manufacturing. Having a company-wide method to engage employees in energy efficiency efforts is a critical part of an effective strategy. When people believe that their personal actions can make a difference, they are more apt to repeat these actions out of personal desire, not because of a business mandate. Empowering employees to recognize that their small steps make a difference is a key factor in reaching energy objectives because of the cumulative effect of all those small actions.

SDG 9: Industry, Innovation and Infrastructure;

Many countries face growing resource stress. Businesses will be increasingly called on to balance sustainable supply and use, reduce water loss, improve water retention, and lower pollution. A consequence of the growing demand for primary commodities and stresses on the world's food supplies is the recent sharp rise in the market values of land, minerals, hydrocarbons, freshwater,

and other primary resources. Meeting the challenges of providing universal energy access while also reducing carbon intensity will require innovations in the energy system. Creating a disciplined, systems-level approach that views technical solutions as an investment designed to achieve organization goals, requires businesses to look at the root of energy inefficiencies and lack of access. Eskom, the national electricity utility of South Africa, has done this and helped to provide electricity to four million homes since the 1990s. From 1994 to 2011, the number of South African households with electricity has increased from 36% to 83%. A key element to Eskom's activities has been innovative program management and technological developments that have increased efficiency, effectiveness and the financial performance of the program. As a direct result of innovation measures, Eskom was able to electrify 1.5 million homes over five years while halving the average cost per connection.

SDG 10: Reduced Inequalities;

Energy efficiency upgrades reduce buildings' energy consumption; reducing energy consumption in turn reduces carbon emissions. Money saved from energy retrofits can be reinvested in the communities, helping them improve services and standards of living. In low-income communities in New York City, people often spend 30% of their income on energy costs. Also, these communities face 30% to 50% unemployment rates.[19] By providing an option for low-income communities to affordably retrofit their buildings, BlocPower helps reduce carbon emissions, save building owners money, and create jobs. The company, basing its business model on using IoT, machine learning, and structured finance to build a platform that will scale clean energy, organizes micro-portfolios of all sorts of buildings in low-income communities in need of retrofitting, aiming to cut energy costs by an average of 25%. The portfolios of clean energy projects are connected to investors seeking social, environmental, and financial returns via an online platform. Investors financing micro-portfolios are repaid by the energy savings generated by the project. BlocPower creates jobs by sending disadvantaged youths to training courses and subsequently employing them. By creating equality through jobs for local youth, BlocPower helps increase urban tax bases, improve quality of life, and provides stability for low-income families.

SDG 11: Sustainable Cities and Communities; Shared energy solutions offer opportunities to fully utilize alternative energy options. Smart technology present smart solutions to cities and communities. For example, by deploying residential battery storage systems to store energy from the sun in urban regions, the sonnenBatterie and the sonnen-Community are paving the way for a transition from centralized power plants running on fossil fuels to cheap renewable energy. The sonnenBatterie, a lithium energy storage system, is charged using electricity from solar panels, enabling a household to cover the biggest part of its electricity needs with emissions-free solar energy. The battery works with the online network of sonnenBatterie owners connected by centralized software that links and monitors all members. Members can share their surplus self-produced electricity with others in the community who cannot produce enough electricity due to bad weather, making the community independent from conventional energy suppliers and less vulnerable to rising energy prices. With more than 10,000 customers, sonnen saves hundreds of thousands of megawatt hours of fossil fuel-based emissions by using clean, emissions-free electricity. After acquisition costs, sonnen claims the solution can cut electricity expenses of a typical household by up to 75% within a year.[20]

SDG 12: Responsible Consumption and Production; Developing a strategy for energy and resource efficiency that is rigorously implemented and maintained throughout industries will help address business challenges. Implementing energy and resource management should follow a similar framework as any other investment opportunity under consideration; including a mission, vision, objectives and key performance indicators fo-

cused on financial results. Since launching its "Shwopping" initiative, multinational retailer Marks & Spencer (M&S) has prevented over 27.8 million items of clothing materials from ending up in landfill and generated over £7 million for Oxfam since April 2012.[21] Working with the University of Cambridge Institute for Manufacturing, the company investigated opportunities to increase the volume and value of textile recovery via a product-to-service approach by leasing or even sharing clothing. These successful initiatives have the power to move public awareness and perceptions, paving the way for the next innovative offering to be more mainstream.

ANTICIPATED ADDITIONAL HIGH-ENERGY CONSUMERS BY 2030 COMES TO MORE THAN 1.5 BILLION.

SDG 13: Climate Action; The manufacturing industry is making strides on climate change mitigation, creating solutions through cleaner energy sources and strategies that use energy more efficiently. However, to create the macro-level change needed to limit rising temperatures to below 2°C, we need global strategies that unite energy efficiency efforts across industries and tie incremental advances to climate improvements at the international level. Siemens announced plans to cut its carbon emissions in half by 2020, and become carbon neutral by 2030. In the quest to become carbon neutral, companies are identifying their emissions, investing in projects to reduce them, and signing on to external projects that offset any emissions the company cannot eliminate. To achieve its goals, Siemens, plans to make its company vehicles greener, and invest in new energy efficient manufacturing technologies. Dell has focused on using more recycled materials for its packing and computers. It uses for example wheat straw, a by-product of wheat harvesting - the wheat straw packaging uses 40% less energy to produce, 90% less water, and costs less to make than traditional packaging.

SDG 14: Life Below Water; Harmful algal growth, known as algae blooms, is increasingly prevalent.[22] At the same time, the world's plastic consumption continues to increase; the deployment of 3D printers alone is forecast to exceed 5.6 million units by 2019.[23] By creating an algae-infused biodegradable filament for the rapidly growing 3D printing industry, the solution uses the vast potential of algae in the creation of filament without putting stress on the environment. Bringing algae from pond to production, ALGIX utilizes algae blooms to produce biodegradable 3D-printing feedstock, which requires less energy during the printing process. ALGIX harvests microalgae blooms to create various products, including 3D filaments and plastic foam. The company removes algae blooms from ponds and lakes without causing harm or disturbance to fish and plant life. The algae are dried and processed before being combined with plastic resins for filament production. The filament for 3D printing has an algae content of 20%, while the remaining 80% is made from PLA, a nontoxic resin made of lactic acid derived from plant sugars. In 3D printing, using algae-based filament compared to traditional filament requires less energy because algae filament prints at a lower temperature. The solution reduces the environmental impacts of global plastic production, which has increased twenty-fold in a 50-year period, reaching 311 million tons in 2014.[24] Together with local volunteers, ALGIX cleans up toxic algae blooms, providing clean waterways and reestablishing sustainable fisheries, where the company operates. The market for thermoplastic filament is expected to reach over $1 billion by 2025, despite the falling price per kilogram.

SDG 15: Life on Land; Around 1.6 billion people directly depend on forests for their livelihood, and forests are home to more than 80% of all terrestrial species of animals, plants and insects. Every business has an impact on land, ecosystems and habitats. Some sectors, like the extractive industry sector, have a direct and visible impact, while others, like the manufacturing sector, have an indirect and less visible impact, with the services sector even further removed from direct impact. Across industry sectors, different businesses have different impacts on biodiversity, but all business has an impact. It is this commonality that should compel all businesses, not just those with direct impacts, to consider their land use impacts, their communities and their opportunities to protect the earth. Between 10% and 20% of drylands and 24% of usable land globally are degraded. Land degradation represents an estimated economic loss of $40 billion per year. Additionally, land degradation leads to food insecurity, increased pests, biodiversity loss, reduced availability of clean water and increased vulnerability of affected areas and their populations to climate change and other environmental changes. Investment in land restoration can help secure access to raw materials and expand production of forest and agriculture commodities. It can help avoid deforestation, scale up low carbon agriculture and contribute to a net-positive forest and carbon footprint. By supporting highly impactful carbon finance projects, businesses can deliver essential emissions reductions and support low carbon sustainable development in landscapes most in need.

CURRENTLY, CARS ARE GENERALLY RECYCLED INTO SCRAP METAL, WHEREAS APPLIANCES ARE RARELY COLLECTED AT ALL.

SDG 16: Peace, Justice and Strong Institutions; In the current economic situation, investment in energy efficiency offers governments a much-needed tool to avoid economic stagnation. Countries preoccupied with job creation are looking at green jobs as an environmentally and economically sustainable solution – as some green jobs cannot be exported. Investment in energy efficiency that redirects money otherwise spent on energy costs, reduces emissions and uncertainty, and creates jobs. We have already seen energy efficiency programs deployed as an important part of stimulus

packages in Europe and the United States. The investment in energy efficiency, especially, has immense positive and immediate economic implications. Programs such as building retrofitting and weatherization are labor intensive and require onsite work that does not compete with cheaper overseas labor. Efficiency programs can create net employment that would otherwise not be offered during economic downturns.

SDG 17: Partnerships for the Goals; As national borders do not contain air pollution, partnerships and international agreements must be pursued to ensure that clean energy options have a level playing field. The Carbon Pricing Leadership Coalition, a voluntary partnership of national and sub-national governments, businesses, and civil society organizations have agreed to expand the use of effective carbon pricing policies. By implementing carbon pricing, companies are further incentivized to seek cleaner alternatives to fossil fuels, making competition fairer for renewable energy production. To track carbon emissions, the Long-Range Energy Alternatives Planning (LEAP) tool enables governments and other organizations to assess pollutant emissions and build mitigation scenarios. The tool is currently being used by 35,000 users in 195 countries.[25] Coalitions and shared tools help create global solutions.

> **"SCIENCE TELLS US CURRENT EFFORTS ARE NOT ENOUGH TO STAY ON THE WELL BELOW 2°C PATHWAY. WE MUST SCALE UP OUR COLLECTIVE ACTION, AND FAST."**
>
> LISE KINGO EXECUTIVE DIRECTOR OF THE UNITED NATIONS GLOBAL COMPACT

9.4 SHARED VALUE OPPORTUNITIES

Saving the planet from pollution, resource scarcity, and the other disasters associated with climate change is no longer seen as merely an economic burden for humanity. In fact, evidence for the opposite is actually growing and companies and investors are already gaining a competitive advantage by being more sustainable than their peers. They are "doing great by doing good" and, as the business case for sustainable investments grows stronger, the shared value benefits are becoming clear.[26]

Achieving energy and resource efficiencies requires a scaling up of shared value in business strategies. Protecting the environment, and the resources in it, while delivering benefits to people is facilitated by a circular economy approach. As an extension of this approach, measuring results and using insights to unlock new value can help to guide sustainable production models. Transforming production in the value chain to be more sustainable, focuses on improvements in internal operations that improve cost, input access, quality, and production through environmental improvements, better resource utilization, supplier capability, and other areas. More than simply raw materials as a means for operation, incorporating energy and resources into a business's shared value approach can pay dividends while saving money and also addressing climate change. Creating shared value as a business model that generates financial profits through energy and resource efficiency measures will enhance both the company's bottom line and shareholder trust.

Driving progress towards universal access to affordable, reliable and sustainable energy is a key enabler for multiple SDGs.[27] Examples such as providing off-grid communities with access to affordable renewable energy (e.g. through low-carbon micro-grids or low-cost community solar systems) create shared value solutions that generate profits for companies as well help local communities prosper. As a Spanish public multinational electric utility, Iberdrola aims to provide an additional four million people with access to energy by 2020 through its Luz para Todos (Electricity for All) initiative. This project focuses on economically sustainable electrification scheme which has already brought electricity to over 1.4 million, including to the beneficiaries of the scheme in Brazil's most disadvantaged areas. Iberdrola's activity is a clear engine for wealth and economic and social development as it creates stable, quality employment and generates €11.1 in the GDP within the countries in which it operates for every euro of profit it earns.[28] The shared value model is truly evident when considering how the company adds positive economic impact through a large societal tax contribution, which exceeded €5.7 million in 2016, and provides an increasing remuneration for its almost 600,000 shareholders, who have seen overall returns of 55% in the period 2014 to 2016.[29]

Developing and sharing scalable systems to improve the resource efficiency and sustainability of production across the value chain in order to reduce the environmental footprint of oper-

> **ACCORDING TO THE IEA (2014) AND THE SE4ALL FINANCE COMMITTEE REPORT (2015), ANNUAL INVESTMENTS OF US $45 BILLION WILL BE NEEDED FOR THE EXPANSION OF GRID ELECTRIFICATION, THUS WE NEED BUSINESS TO PARTICIPATE IN CREATING A SHARED VALUED APPROACH.**
>
> WORLD BANK

ations, while reducing cost, will drive SDG initiatives even further. By implementing improved processes to reduce inputs such as raw materials, water and nonrenewable minerals, businesses can incorporate value for the environment, as well as social and financial value. Companies such as premium Italian tire manufacturer Pirelli are looking to innovations in resource use to add shared value. The company has discovered an innovative way to produce a preferred material for tire production, silica, from rice husks, which are an often-discarded byproduct of rice processing. This business endeavor is a true example of shared value success. Rice husks account for 20% of the total weight of raw rice and are often discarded in developing markets, resulting in excessive waste and resource inefficiencies. Pirelli's silica production process takes the husks, which are inedible, renewable, and separate from the food chain, and converts them for tire production. Using silica from rice husks is a viable alternative to the rubber plant for tire manufacturing.[30] The process utilizes less energy than traditional methods, and reduces fuel consumption by 5% to 7% when used in automobiles tires due to its low rolling resistance.[31] Pirelli's resource innovations with rice husk silica provide a low-cost material from which to produce high-performance tires, while at the same time helping to achieve fuel efficiency, CO2 reductions and enhanced safety measures.

To realize the business opportunity in utilizing energy and resources more efficiently, we need an enhanced shared value approach that considers the circular economy model that is "restorative and regenerative by design."[32] Climate conscious companies across the globe and across industries are starting to invest more in shared value strategies for business growth. In this regard, technological advancements are an important component with the ability to spur innovation, open markets and steer shared value business actions that benefit multiple stakeholders.

The electricity landscape is a prime example of this. As it undergoes a transformation, becoming more complex than ever before with rapidly evolving technologies, declining costs, and shifting regulatory landscapes, the electricity grid's shared infrastructure provides the underserved with access to affordable services. Companies such as Greenchoice are responding by stimulating people to buy into clean energy. By harnessing the rooftop potential of solar, and fulfilling the power demand of consumers on the grid, the company is on a mission to help its customers save money and transition away from fossil fuels and towards renewable alternatives (See case 45). Greenchoice is creating shared value by supplying clean energy through renewable sources to households, businesses and municipalities while helping local sustainable energy cooperatives at the same time.

45

CASE NO. GREENCHOICE

Renewable Energy for Everyone
Promoting shared value, sustainable progress
and financial gains

Case applied in: The Netherlands
Headquarters located in: The Netherlands
www.greenchoice.nl

IMPACT SDGs

SDG 7
Affordable and Clean Energy
Make access to and investments in clean energy more attractive, helping to increase the installation capacity and demand while creating a more robust market and bottom line.

SDG 11
Sustainable Cities and Communities
Stimulate people to buy clean energy by helping local sustainable energy cooperatives and consumers install solar PV-systems for localized electricity generation.

SDG 13
Climate Action
Reduce CO2 emissions by supplying alternative energy forms. The yearly carbon impact of these efforts is at least 1.4 million tons of CO2, using international standards: VCS, CCBS and Gold Standard.

SDG 17
Partnerships for the Goals
Engage with over 50 cooperatives to support decentralized renewable energy through a "bottom-up" approach to scalable energy transition.

AT GREENCHOICE, WE ARE COMMITTED TO MAKING A STRUCTURAL CONTRIBUTION TO A BETTER WORLD. THE TRANSITION TOWARDS A 100% SUSTAINABLE ENERGY-POWERED SOCIETY IS IN FULL SWING AND WE NEED TO SPEED IT UP.

EVERT DEN BOER, CEO GREENCHOICE

Greenchoice supplies sustainable energy from renewable sources to households, businesses and municipalities. The company is able to compete with its "fossil counterparts" with affordable prices, due to a low overhead structure and efficient operation. Customers value the focus on affordable and clean energy (SDG 7), as evidenced by the growth of customers served from zero in 2001 to over 400,000 in 2017 and their yearly revenue which is currently between 350-400 million euros.

Nearly 95% of Dutch households heat their homes with natural gas, resulting in around 100 TWh of gas used annually, and generating 19 million tons of CO2 each year. Greenchoice has therefore invested in raising customers' awareness of their household energy usage. Becoming energy-conscious results in behavioral changes in energy use and is the easiest way to promote energy savings measures (SDG 7). Additionally, high yield investments in efficiency measures in the individual homes, with payback in 5 years or less, could reduce heat demand (and CO2 emissions) by another 5% (SDG 13).

In the Netherlands, there is around 400 km2 of roof surface area suitable for solar PV power production. Unlocking this potential would yield a yearly power supply of 50 TWh. This is enough to cover the demand from all the buildings in the country. Harnessing the rooftop potential (SDG 11), and fulfilling the power demand of customers on the grid, is at the heart of the company's mis-

sion to help its customers save money and transition away from fossil fuels and towards renewable alternatives. In reaching this goal, Greenchoice empowers communities with services specifically designed for local energy cooperatives. Currently, the company is working with 50 local energy cooperatives, each with their own unique sustainable energy projects and ambitions (SDG 17). Greenchoice's subsidiary KiesZon is also planning to develop solar PV projects of 120 MWp capacity in the upcoming year. In total, an € 85 billion investment is needed to meet 2050 goals for the decarbonization trajectory.

Although there is more value yet to be created, Greenchoice is moving steadily towards its energy transition goals. As this is not a transition that happens overnight, they are committed to working with conservation partners to preserve ecosystems (SDG 13), spending around 2 million euros per year to stimulate Reducing Emissions from Deforestation and Forest Degradation projects, and Afforestation, Reforestation and Revegetation projects. These projects mitigate the effects of the carbon emission from the natural gas used by customers, enhance biodiversity, and support local communities in 7 countries. Greenchoice believes it is important to not only focus on realizing the CO2- and renewable energy goals, but also to ensure ecosystems are preserved while reaching these goals. Greenchoice believes in the "Trias Energetica": 1) savings, 2) sustainable energy use, 3) compensation of all fossil fuels until it is no longer necessary.

CHALLENGE

To make renewable energy affordable, readily available and widely used in the Netherlands, and help turn consumers into 'prosumers' of sustainable energy.

OPPORTUNITIES FOR SCALE

There is tremendous opportunity for Greenchoice to scale its business of helping customers transition to renewable energy. By adding value throughout the customer journey of making this switch, the company has the potential to reach a large share of the 7.6 million households and many businesses in the Netherlands. A growing number of Dutch consumers will become producers of electricity, enabling Greenchoice to grow its business as electrification of heat production becomes the norm.

Sources and further information

- http://www.pbl.nl/sites/default/files/cms/publicaties/pbl-2014-dnv-gl-het-potentieel-van-zonnestroom-in-de-gebouwde-omgeving-van-nederland_01400.pdf
- http://www.mckinsey.com/~/media/McKinsey/Global%20Themes/Europe/Accelerating%20the%20energy%20transition%20Cost%20or%20opportunity/Versnellen%20van%20de%20energietransitie.ashx
- http://statline.cbs.nl
- http://redd.unfccc.int/

" GREENCHOICE EMPOWERS COMMUNITIES WITH SERVICES SPECIFICALLY DESIGNED FOR LOCAL ENERGY COOPERATIVES. "

9.5 CAPITAL INVESTMENTS AS A SOURCE OF POWER

The environmental benefits of expanding renewable energy and conserving resources are clear. Fossil fuels contribute heavily to climate change, which has already begun to have devastating impacts on the Earth's ecosystems and financial systems. Although we know the detrimental impacts to society and the planet, there has not been enough of a shift in investments away from fossil fuels and towards renewables and conservation. A lot of money has traditionally been allocated to finance fossil fuels, but reorienting capital investments toward a cleaner future can boost profits and create jobs.

The United Nations sets out six investment areas for markets to focus on with regards to energy and resources:[33]

1. Clean technology
2. Carbon pricing
3. The energy transition
4. Risk mitigation
5. Augmenting the contribution of sub-national actors and business
6. Mobilizing finance.

Businesses are responding to this focus. As one of the largest pools of capital investors in clean energy, US businesses steered a total of US $56 billion toward the sector in 2016.[34] That is an increase of 8% from the previous year. As further proof of the upward trend, global clean energy investment has risen exponentially over the past decade from US $62 billion in 2004 to US $329 billion in 2015.[35]

Big money investors – such as banks, billionaires, and pension funds – treat investments in energy and resources just as they do in all other sectors with efficiency, innovation and reputation as integral elements to all portfolios. This is because where there is efficiency there are savings, where there is innovation there is profit, and with savings and profit come reputation, subsequently creating a positive feedback loop of growth that characterizes sustainable global investing. The renewable energy and resource efficiency sector offers all of these traits, and it is therefore why capital is being mobilized and investments have grown.

The Carbon Disclosure Project (CDP), which helps investors measure and manage their environmental impacts, found that "S&P 500 industry leaders on climate change generated 18% higher return on investment, 50% lower volatility of earnings over the past decade and 21% stronger dividend growth to shareholders than their low scoring peers."[36] As investors are always looking for big returns, clean technologies with a focus on climate action present a strong case for capital expenditures.

Even policies for putting a price on carbon have been implemented to direct capital markets and investments towards greater energy and resource efficiency measures. Carbon pricing is a method favored by many economists for reducing global-warming emissions. Reflecting the amount that must be paid for the right to emit one ton of CO_2 into the atmosphere, carbon pricing usually takes the form either of a carbon tax or a requirement to purchase permits to emit, generally known as

> **THOSE WITH STRONG CLIMATE CHANGE MANAGEMENT SECURE 18.4% HIGHER RETURN ON INVESTMENT THAN THEIR COMPETITORS; THEY ALSO HAVE 50% LOWER VOLATILITY OF EARNINGS OVER THE PAST DECADES THAN THEIR PEERS AND 21% BETTER DIVIDENDS TO SHAREHOLDERS.**
>
> SUSTAINIA

> **"I ALSO CHALLENGE GOVERNMENTS TO CREATE A LEVEL PLAYING FIELD FOR CLEAN ENERGY INVESTMENT THROUGH CARBON PRICING, REMOVING FOSSIL FUEL SUBSIDIES, AND STRENGTHENING STABLE AND PREDICTABLE REGULATORY AND INVESTMENT ENVIRONMENTS."**
>
> BAN KI-MOON, FORMER UN SECRETARY-GENERAL

cap-and-trade or "allowances." Some corporations have even developed carbon pricing mechanisms to mitigate risks associated with the climate crisis, decarbonize and reduce GHG footprints, prepare for a low-carbon economy, and increase operational efficiency. As of 2016, more than 1,200 companies globally report that they have internalized or plan to internalize carbon pricing. Among those are 210 US companies, including big names like Microsoft Corporation, Walt Disney Company, and General Motors Company.[37]

There are several companies that are starting to implement carbon pricing as a way to perpetuate the energy transition. This results in tangible benefits for both our planet and for our wallets. Since 2012, Microsoft business groups have implemented an internal fee, from US $5 to $10 per metric ton, on the carbon emissions associated with their electricity consumption and employee air travel. The revenue is used to buy renewable energy, increase energy efficiency and e-waste recycling, and buy carbon offsets. Using the funds collected by the carbon fee, Microsoft has invested more than US $2 million for 60 projects in 23 countries.[38] The company has purchased more than 14 billion kilowatt-hours of renewable energy, reduced emissions by 9.5 million metric tons of carbon dioxide equivalent (CO_2e), and saved more than US $10 million per year in energy costs. Another example of a business using carbon pricing as a solution to lead the energy transition is the ENGIE Group. As an operator in the areas of electricity, natural gas and energy services, the Group develops its businesses around a model that includes a carbon price in its investment plans. ENGIE has also set internal pricing scenarios reflecting the risks it faces with GHG emissions' impacts (See Case 46). In this context, ENGIE plans to invest €22 billion in three areas where they already hold leading market positions - renewables, supply networks and decentralized solutions – and has decided to cease new investments in coal developments and set itself concrete aims to reduce emissions by 10% by 2020. As former CEO Gérard Mestrallet rightly points out, "we cannot have business without a planet." We simply have no options – even and also from a business perspective - than to help solve the climate and resources crisis around the world.

CASE NO.

ENGIE GROUP

Universal Access to Energy and the Quest
for Innovation
Producing energy that emits no CO2

Case applied in: Global
Headquarters located in: France

IMPACT SDGs

SDG 6

Protects abundance and quality of water resources by working with local partners.

SDG 7

Committed to providing access to sustainable energy to 20 million people by 2020 as exhibited by the Terrawatt initiative, launched at COP21, and ENGIE's investment Fund "ENGIE Rassembleurs d'Energies."

SDG 11

Envisions solutions for the vibrant city of tomorrow through Terr'innove, and partners with local communities to build sustainable energy strategies.

SDG 13

Addresses the major challenges of energy transition to a lower carbon economy.

SDG 17

ENGIE is part of the Carbon Pricing Leadership Coalition, to ensure price signals to redirect investment to low-carbon technologies. ENGIE also launched the Business Dialogues, between public and private investors on climate issues.

ACCESS TO CLEAN AND RELIABLE ENERGY WILL BE CRUCIAL TO ACHIEVING THE SDGs AND TO STAYING ALIGNED WITH THE 2°C OBJECTIVE DEFINED IN THE PARIS AGREEMENT.

ISABELLE KOCHER, ENGIE GROUP CEO

The ENGIE Group has a rich history of vision and transformation. Founded as a fossil fuel energy company in the first half of the 19th century, ENGIE began focusing on Liquid Gas in 1965. Then in the early 2000s, ENGIE – then called GDF Suez - began expanding its energy reach to the point when in 2015, they changed their name to ENGIE and further expanding into renewable energy sources. The ENGIE Group is now a global leader in energy transition. It draws on three areas of expertise: electricity, natural gas, and energy services to develop innovative, effective solutions for all of its customers. The Group has launched a 3-year transformation plan aimed at being world leader in energy transition. When this plan began in 2016, 80% of the business was already on track to achieve transition to renewable low-carbon or zero-carbon energy, and now ENGIE has opted to dispose of the remaining 20% of the coal, oil and upstream gas side of its businesses. The Group aims to ensure competitive pricing for energy access as well as for climate change mitigation, so it can now move past taxation and subsidies and rely on market-based mechanisms. ENGIE invests in comprehensive strategies, and structures investments for the production of renewable or carbon-light electricity, the supply of carbon free-natural gas, and technological innovation. ENGIE aims at responsible growth and the Group is careful to to protect biodiversity(SDG 13). The Group includes a carbon price in its investment plans and has set internal pricing scenarios reflecting the risks it faces with GHG emissions' impacts. In this context, ENGIE decided to cease new in-

vestments in coal developments and has set itself concrete goals to reduce GHG emissions due to power production by 20% by 2020 (with respect to 2012). In 2014, the Group issued the largest ever Green Bond for a private company, worth €2.5 billion, to finance 77 renewable and energy efficient projects; in 2017, two additional €1.5 billion loans were successively administered (SDG 7). With those transactions, the total amount of bonds issued by ENGIE in Green Bond format since 2014 reaches €5.25 billion.

ENGIE is committed to launching innovations and partnerships that protect the planet and its people (SDG 17). ENGIE is, for instance, developing a water footprint calculation for each kWh of electricity that the power utility produces, and for each power plant in water-stressed areas, allowing it to assess the supply chain water risk based upon the extraction of the underlying fuel (SDG 6). The Group is active in the generation of distributed renewable energy, in improving energy efficiency and in the development of innovative solutions for "smart cities", including green mobility. To help cities and regions transform themselves into sustainable, efficient and attractive communities, ENGIE deploys new technologies tailored to each context as a response to the challenges of urban planning (SDG 11). ENGIE has planned to invest €14 billion to redesign its activities portfolio from 2016 to 2018, including €1 billion dedicated to digital and innovation, and a has set a €50 million fund dedicated to providing access to energy.

CHALLENGE

To overcome challenges in the transition to clean energy, while providing more power to more people and reducing global GHG emissions at the same time.

OPPORTUNITIIES FOR SCALE

ENGIE endeavors to help the world become less reliant on large-scale power plants and contributes to the development of decentralized solutions where expected by its stakeholders. In total, the Group plans to make €15 billion of asset disposals from 2016 to 2018. Over the same period, as stated above, ENGIE will invest €14 billion in three areas where they already hold leading market positions: low-CO_2 power generation, global networks and customer solutions.

Sources and further information
- https://library.engie.com/media/6c44b431-b53f-452b-9526-d2a4ac69a43d/#v=Version1&l=en&searchText=key&lc=0&p=12
- https://www.engie.com/en/news/discover-incubation-by-engie/
- https://innovation.engie.com/en/engie-new-ventures
- https://www.engie.com/en/group/opinions/groups-strategy/isabelle-kocher-changed-organizational-structure-engie/

" ENGIE IS COMMITTED TO LAUNCHING INNOVATIONS AND PARTNERSHIPS THAT PROTECT THE PLANET AND ITS PEOPLE. "

ENGIE's capital investment based on risk mitigation involving the company's environmental impacts is in line with the UN's investment focus areas. As former UN Secretary General Ban Ki-moon reminded us, "the private sector is the engine that will drive the climate solutions we need to reduce climate risks, end energy poverty and create a safer, more prosperous future for this and future generations."[39] Even the lowest cost estimates of climate-related risk, which is defined as, "the probability distribution of the present market value of losses on global financial assets" due to climate change, are in trillions of dollars.[40] For example, the Economist Intelligence Unit finds climate-related risks ranging from US $4.2 trillion to $43 trillion in discounted, present value terms, depending on the climate scenario.[41] This equates to a strong argument to develop business solutions and invest in greater energy and resource efficiencies.

Several prominent organizations, such as the Work Bank Group's International Finance Corporation (IFC), are working with clients to mobilize financing for natural resource development. In 2015, its client companies posted strong results, providing clean water and natural gas to 22 million and 55 million people, respectively, while also contributing US $7 billion in government revenues.[42] As climate-related financial risks can threaten business growth, IFC capital investment efforts will continue to be required to support augmented business contributions for sustainable growth.

Businesses will need to step in and create solutions for capital expenditures that perpetuate the circular economy. This is often realized in the form of investments allocated for reducing operating costs of energy use and resource waste through improved natural-resource management. Dow Chemical has maximized on capital returns in this regard. Reporting that it invested less than US $2 billion since 1994 to improve its resource efficiency, the company to date has saved more than US $9.8 billion from reduced energy consumption and water waste in its manufacturing processes, even as it continues to develop innovations.[43] With a 20% reduction in absolute GHG emissions, Dow has also gone well beyond Kyoto Protocol climate mitigation targets.[44] Dow is a prime example of a business responding to the UN's investment focus areas as is exhibited through capital allocations for clean technology and energy transitions, carbon pricing commitments, and contributions to resource efficiencies. The corporation, with its core business being the manufacturing of materials, also holds a leadership position in driving the circular economy by taking into account a product's entire lifecycle - from creation to use to disposal.[45]

> **"WE MUST PUT A VALUE ON THE CLIMATE RISK ASSOCIATED WITH GREENHOUSE GAS EMISSIONS."**
>
> GÉRARD MESTRALLET CHAIRMAN OF THE BOARD OF DIRECTORS ENGIE

9.6 DOMAINS OF IMPACT

The three domains of impact for energy and resources that we will explore are:

1. Climate and Energy Resources
2. Circular Economy
3. Manufacturing and Materials

1. CLIMATE AND ENERGY RESOURCES

COP21 was a turning point for the business community in its efforts to address climate change (SDG 13). The private sector was more visible and active than in any of the previous COPs, and CEOs from a range of industries stepped up their commitments. Companies pledged to decrease their carbon footprint, buy more renewable energy and engage in sustainable resource management. Global financial institutions promised to make hundreds of billions of new investments over the next 15 years in clean energy and energy efficiency.

National governments alone do not have the funds or capacity to carry out the necessary actions, they will need the buy-in and participation of the private sector. Although we know the fight against climate change will be very costly and requires a high degree of capital mobilization, we can also look to the unprecedented business opportunities that arise from solving this great challenge.

Climate change is a disruptive force and, like other investment strategies, this force is creating opportunities for companies willing to innovate. A report by IFC on climate investment opportunities in emerging markets, for example, found that Eastern Europe, Central Asia, the Middle East, and North Africa could support up to US $1 trillion in climate-related investments by 2020.2 A large drop in the price of "eco-friendly" technologies – especially renewable energy – and the rise of carbon pricing has helped trigger the shift in business models. Companies are now gravitating to climate-smart investments as a strategic move that is good for the bottom line.

Globally, renewable energy is poised for growth, primarily addressing SDG 7. Countries all over the world set ambitious targets for wind, solar, and hydro-power. Even Saudi Arabia, with one of the world's biggest oil reserves, is looking to generate the majority of its electricity from renewables and nuclear power by 2040.[46] The availability or renewables has soared, thanks to technological advances giving us the opportunity to harness it effectively, and so have the potential business opportunities. Since 2011, many global companies have realized that clean energy technologies are essential for their business models to continue to be successful.[47] Concurrently, many major electric utilities and energy companies are fundamentally changing their business models with large capital allocations to clean energy technologies. Innovations in the energy sector have spurred growth in renewables, both offsetting emissions and creating business opportunities.

> **1,700 LEADING INTERNATIONAL FIRMS FOUND THAT THE MONEY THEY PUT INTO REDUCING GREENHOUSE GAS EMISSIONS SAW AN INTERNAL RATE OF RETURN OF 27%.**
>
> WORLD BANK

Several examples of energy innovations exist all around the globe. For example, private equity fund InterEnergy invested in the development and construction of the Laudato Si wind park in Penonome, Panama.[48] As Central America's biggest wind farm, the 215-megawatt Penonome plant will eliminate 400,000 tons of CO2 emissions per year, roughly the equivalent of taking 84,000 cars off the road.[49] The private sector is also playing a key role in the construction of an immense 510-megawatt solar plant in the Moroccan desert. The project, worth US $2.6 billion, is

> **ACCORDING TO THE CARBON DISCLOSURE PROJECT (CDP) CARBON PRICE REPORT, IN 2016, 63% OF THE DISCLOSING UTILITIES AND 52% OF THE ENERGY COMPANIES REPORTED THAT THEY CURRENTLY PRICE OR PLAN TO PRICE CARBON.**
>
> CERES.COM

expected to provide power to 1.1 million people. It is significant in that it has the potential to turn North Africa into a renewable energy hub that serves as a business model for future public-private partnerships.[50] On a smaller scale, another African initiatives are underway. M-KOPA, a Kenyan solar energy company, uses an innovative financing model combining micropayments and mobile technologies to provide affordable home solar systems for rural households. The solution replaces 160,000 liters of kerosene daily, reducing CO2 by 225,000 tons since the beginning of sales in 2012. The company, while reaching approximately one million homes by the end of 2017, estimates projected customer savings of US $248 million over four years.[51]

Creating business models that respond to both energy efficiencies and people's everyday needs can render solutions with major societal impacts. For decades, pollution has been exacting severe damage on people's health and the environment. As the largest environmental cause of disease and death, air pollution has become one of the major health risks on the planet and is responsible for an estimated 9 million premature deaths worldwide.[52] Tackling the air quality crisis requires innovative business models that involve public and private sectors. The following examples are business endeavors that have turned harmful pollution into solutions.

Torre de Especialidades - Mexico City is the single most polluted city on the planet and air pollution remains a pressing concern for the city's public health officials.[53] Yet the problem has yielded some impressive innovations in recent years, one of the most fascinating of which is a building that "captures" smog. The hospital building in Mexico City is designed to transform air pollutants into harmless chemicals such as water, carbon dioxide and calcium nitrate. The building's outer layer is made up of a new type of tile called "proSolve370e," which can neutralize the chemicals produced by 8,750 cars every day.[54] According the building's inventors, the Berlin-based design firm Elegant Embellishments, the innovative lattice-like design of the tile shapes "slow wind speeds and create turbulence, for better distribution of pollutants across the active surfaces."[55] In addition to its pollution-fighting superpowers, other environmental and energy-saving benefits of the building's design include how the façade produces shadows in the inside of the building, helping to keep it cool and reduce the amount of air conditioning needed.

enVerid - Originally designed for submarines and spaceships, the enVerid⁻ cleantech solution to air pollution applies an innovative approach to material science, engineering, and operational algorithms to improve air quality and reduce energy costs in all types of commercial and public buildings. A simple solution that can be added as a retrofit to existing indoor heating and cooing systems or designed into new projects, enVerid's technology eliminates CO2 and volatile organic compounds (VOCs), stopping them from circulating in buildings. The Israel-based firm received investments from OurCrowd, a leading equity crowdfunding platform.[56] enVerid's innovation cleans the indoor air using patented reusable sorbents. By cleansing the indoor air, the unit minimizes the amount of outdoor air required to maintain the indoor air quality, thereby reducing the load on the building's system and achieving energy savings. The average energy savings enVerid's customers are achieving while maintaining or improving indoor air quality is greater a than 40% reduction in peak heating or cooling load and a 20% average energy cost savings.[57]

WATER SUSTAINABILITY

Access to clean, modern, sustainable energy as well as to resources like clean water as part of the circular economy is critical for improving the health and livelihoods of billions of people around the world. Because water is one of the most fundamental elements to human life, water management in a closed loop system offers businesses a wide range of opportunities - especially in the fields of efficient irrigation techniques, sustainable water pumping, as well as water treatment and re-use.

Water shortage is one of the biggest risks facing the planet. Over the coming decades, global fresh water demand is expected to grow by 2% annually. If we do not change course, global water demand will outpace the sustainable water supply in 2040 by 35%. Industrial water demand in particular is expected to grow rapidly, and companies are responding with innovative circular solutions. Some examples include using renewable energy, like solar and the power generated by the oceans' waves to extract water from the air, or filter water. The CETO technology developed by Carnegie Wave Energy is a large buoy that uses subsurface wave energy to generate clean electricity, as well as fresh water through desalination. It uses the

constant wave and tidal actions in the ocean to power large hydraulic pumps that drive seawater through pipes to an onshore power-generation facility, where hydroelectric turbines generate renewable electricity for the grid and deliver high-pressure seawater to a reverse osmosis desalination plant. While examples such as these continue to emerge, it will take more than linear efforts to bring about the radical systemic shift needed to achieve the Global Goals, As circular economic business models become more prevalent and consumers become more conscious about their consumption, and the production processes and effects, a systemic change will grow.

2. CIRCULAR ECONOMY

Achieving a more sustainable world will require a major shift away from the global trend of *take-make-waste* patterns of production and consumption to a circular system. The circular economy is a restorative and regenerative system where all products are designed and marketed with reuse and recycling in mind. The concept is informed by the shift in business models and policies around the world.[58] There is an undeniable business case for redesigning our entire economy to respond to SDG 12.

There are several environmental benefits of circular models, which include a significant drop in use of virgin materials, reductions in materials waste as products are designed to last, and utilization of manufacturing by-products and excess materials previously considered waste streams. The Ellen MacArthur Foundation and the World Economic Forum report that there is a strong business case for the circular economy as well. The findings show over US $1 trillion per year could be generated for the global economy by 2025 and 100,000 new jobs created within the next five years if "companies focused on building circular supply chains to increase the rate of recycling, re-use and remanufacture."[59] Also predicted is that Europe could create a net benefit of €1.8 trillion by 2030, or €0.9 trillion more than in the current linear development path by adopting circular economic principles.

> **DEVELOPING COUNTRIES WILL NEED ABOUT $100 BILLION OF NEW INVESTMENTS PER YEAR OVER THE NEXT 40 YEARS TO BUILD RESILIENCE TO THE EFFECTS OF CLIMATE CHANGE. MITIGATION COSTS ARE EXPECTED TO BE IN THE RANGE OF $140–$175 BILLION PER YEAR BY 2030.**
>
> WORLD BANK

CASE NO. **TOSHIBA**

Environmental Vision 2050
Product design for the circular economy

Case applied in: Global
Headquarters located in: Japan
www.toshiba.com

IMPACT SDGs

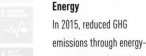
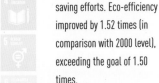

SDG 7

Affordable and Clean Energy

In 2015, reduced GHG emissions through energy-saving efforts. Eco-efficiency improved by 1.52 times (in comparison with 2000 level), exceeding the goal of 1.50 times.

SDG 9

Industry, Innovation and Infrastructure

In 2015, certified 95 environmentally conscious products (ECPs); reached sales goal of 1.8 trillion yen in 2014, one year ahead of schedule with sales totaling 2.75 trillion yen in 2015.

SDG 12

Industry, Innovation and Infrastructure

In 2015, collected 1.68 million home appliances to be recycled; the collection rate increased by about 2% compared to the previous year.

SDG 13

Climate Action

In 2015, reduced CO2e by 15.10 million tons per year by offering newly developed products throughout the world.

WE WILL PROMOTE MEASURES TO REDUCE THE ENVIRONMENTAL IMPACTS OF PRODUCTS AND SERVICES AS WELL AS OF PROCESSES.
SATOSHI TSUNAKAWA, PRESIDENT & CEO TOSHIBA

Toshiba's business model and goal is to generate a "virtuous circle" among all business activities while addressing the needs of all stakeholders. To continue to contribute to society through its technologies and business activities, Toshiba operates as a company that takes responsibility for the entire product lifecycle. Focusing on more than just take-back recycling models, Toshiba has a business plan centered on sustainability to ensure its products, people and policies all work in tandem to minimize impact on the environment. Toshiba carefully plans their entire lifecycle – from design, packaging and shipping, to considering how electronics and other recyclable products are ultimately retired.

This program promises to improve eco-efficiency by a factor of ten from base year 2000 through strict monitoring of energy usage, manufacturing process improvements and eco-conscious product development (SDG 7 & 9). The company aims to bring this vision to fruition through two approaches: while the Energy Approach "emphasizes the stable supply of reliable energy and mitigation of climate change," the Eco Products Approach "focuses on creating new value in harmony with the Earth." With stringent procurement guidelines that truly consider the circular life of a product, Toshiba strives to hold its suppliers to the same high standards it follows. This not only results in greener products, but encourages other companies to improve their practices too. In order to create a sound material-cycle society, Toshiba reduces the amount of resources extracted and dis-

charged as waste throughout the product lifecycle. Toshiba is promoting 3R initiatives (reduce, reuse and recycle) for products aimed at reducing waste, increasing incoming recycling, and improving outgoing recycling. They are also taking measures to promote design for 3Rs and implement activities to reduce the environmental impact of its products throughout their life cycles (SDG 13).

Based on the concept of eco-efficiency for the circular economy, Toshiba has built a formula to be expressed as a fraction, with the creation of new value as the numerator and environmental impacts as the denominator. The more enriched value created – or the more environmental impact is reduced and progress made toward coexisting with the Earth – the more eco-efficiency improves. Toshiba calls the degree of improvement in eco-efficiency the "Factor," and increasing the Factor leads to better business performance as well as "affluent lifestyles in harmony with the Earth."

Under the company's recent Environmental Action Plan, it aimed to further increase the amount of resources conserved to 1.5 times the 2010 level (SDG 12). In 2015, the total amount of resources used in Toshiba's major products,(estimated by multiplying the amount used for products and packaging materials by the number of shipments) was approximately 430,000 tons – a reduction of 240,000 tons, or by 30% compared to previous product models.

CHALLENGE

To reduce environmental impacts throughout product lifecycles through energy-efficiency and resource conservation methods, as well as to develop low-carbon technologies that contribute to climate change mitigation.

OPPORTUNITIIES FOR SCALE

Toshiba aims for its electronics to have a continued positive impact on the circular economy, providing energy-saving products worldwide and reducing CO_2 emissions in order to contribute to mitigation of climate change. Bringing new green products to market and expanding existing recycling programs by offering creative incentives for product take-back, Toshiba will expand on the 410% year-over-year increase in recycled products it celebrated as part of its initial "Zero Waste to Landfill" program launch.

Sources and further information

- https://www.toshiba.co.jp/env/en/products/earth_t.htm
- https://www.businesswire.com/news/home/20110425006201/en/Toshiba%e2%80%99s-E-Waste-Recycling-Program-Expanded-Accept-Spent
- https://www.toshiba.co.jp/env/en/communication/report/pdf/env_report16_all_e.pdf
- http://www.toshiba.co.jp/env/en/vision/vision2050_0.htm
- http://us.toshiba.com/green/sustainability/
- https://www.toshiba.com/csr/docs/na_report.pdf

" TOSHIBA CAREFULLY PLANS THEIR ENTIRE LIFECYCLE — FROM DESIGN, PACKAGING AND SHIPPING, TO MINIMIZE THE IMPACT ON THE ENVIRONMENT."

Circular business models have beneficial impacts on both consumers and producers. Business solutions in the circular economy employ methods of recycling and upcycling materials to reduce costs and waste. In his book *Cradle to Cradle*, William McDonough first mentions the term "upcycling" to describe "a process that can be repeated in perpetuity of returning materials back to a pliable, usable form without degradation to their latent value – moving resources back up the supply chain." Companies can implement the circular economy model by rethinking products and services using principles based on "durability, renewability, reuse, repair, replacement, upgrades, refurbishment and reduced material use."[60] By applying these principles, while implementing the recycling and upcycling methods, companies can design out waste, increase resource productivity and decouple growth from resource consumption.

Transitioning to a circular economy can unlock global GDP growth of US $4.5 trillion by 2030 and would enhance the resilience of global economies. Companies delivering economic and sustainability benefits through successful circular transformations stand to gain a competitive advantage through increased efficiencies and reduced costs. There are many benefits to implementing a circular economy and also a strong business case. The WBCSD names specifically these advantages:[61]

- **Job creation:** through circular principles, up to 500,000 additional jobs created in France alone.
- **Reduced energy consumption:** circular economy solutions could offer a 37% reduction in energy consumption in the EU.
- **Reduced greenhouse gas emissions:** in India, implementing circular solutions presents the opportunity to reduce emissions by about 40%.
- **Increased resource security:** sustainably managed forests ensure long-term availability of renewable resources for producing bio-based materials; applying circular economy principles to water management can contribute to greatly reducing water stress in key regions.

- **Innovation driver:** the potential revenue of selected circular economy business models for automotive companies could more than double by 2030, growing by $400-600 billion.

As resources become more scarce, and prices rise, circular solutions become cost effective. The report *Achieving 'Growth Within', by the Ellen MacArthur Foundation* and SYSTEMIQ, identifies the most important investment opportunities by examining three sectors for opportunities using circular models: mobility, food, and the built environment. Together, the value chains of these three sectors represent 60% of consumer expenditure and 80% of resource use. In the report, it was found that, "An additional €320 billion of circular economy investment opportunities is available to investors in the European Union until 2025 that can be unlocked through modest action by policy makers or industry." For example, remanufacturing car components at scale, scaling nutrient and energy recovery from waste, and boosting the reuse of building materials are all actions that can be taken. The report further finds that by 2025, compared with the current development path, the EU could increase GDP by an additional 7%, reduce raw material consumption by an additional 10%, and reduce annual CO_2 emissions by an additional 17%.

The opportunities for investment, business and benefits for the environment are plentiful. There are investors, companies and partnerships already aiming towards this system change. In 2017 a public-private collaboration was launched, called the Platform for Accelerating the Circular Economy. The focus is to stimulate blended finance and partnerships to scale new circular economy projects, address barriers to scaling the circular economy, and link networks and knowledge to share best practices and policies.

E-Waste is a growing issue. Some countries, like India are inundated with e-waste landfills. In addition to being overwhelmed with the amount of discarded technological waste, like laptops and old mobile phones, this can hardly be considered

GREEN SOCIAL BIOETHANOL

Green Social Bioethanol is an example of a progressive circular economic model. The social business enterprise designs, develops and installs Ethanol Micro Distilleries in rural areas of developing countries. Green's Ethanol Micro Distilleries produce bioethanol from locally grown crops in an efficient and sustainable manner that benefits society. Their projects respond to a number of the SDGs ranging from spurring rural development and innovation (SDG 8 & 12), providing a steady demand for crops (SDG 1), generating employment to increase farmers' income and improve women's income opportunities (SDGs 2 & 5), while providing a clean source of energy for the community (SDG 7).[62] The company also brings together a network of experts and investors to produce this sustainable biofuel, providing people with equal access to clean and safe energy resources (SDGs 10 & 17). Due to Green's unique closed-loop process for energy production, the distilleries add value to the chain of food production while at the same time generating energy sources.

The circular model is evident at one of Green's sites in Uruguay where it produces more than 1,000 liters of ethanol per day, equaling 330,000 liters each year. The bioethanol produced there will then be transported to another plant, and subsequently dehydrated and blended with gasoline to help diversify Uruguay's energy mix. This small-scale agricultural site of 150 hectares fosters community participation as well by giving jobs to detainees living at the nearby rehabilitation center. As they cultivate the sweet potatoes to be used in the micro-distillery, these employees are given an opportunity to earn money while being integrated back into society. Green's pioneering project serves as an example of circular investments that are both generating income and repurposing resources.

cost-effective. Not only are precious minerals and non-renewable raw materials used in the production, but CO2 emissions are generated in the production process as well. To toss these devices away when the next generation smartphone appears, or greater computer capacity is offered, is wasteful. Circular solutions for technological devices must keep pace with the advances that are made with the technological offerings.

This has already started in Japan where in 2000, they passed the pioneering "Law for the Promotion of Efficient Utilization of Resources." The law treats materials as circular goods, and covers the lifespan of a product. Manufacturers are legally required to run disassembly plants, in addition to their assembly factories. Material recovery is legally mandated which turns the issue of product disposal into an asset because the companies reuse the materials. Currently, 98% of all metals used

in production are recovered. Electronics companies like Toshiba have created successful business models that incorporate Design for Disassembly and Design for Environment principles into their product design.

3. MANUFACTURING
With the arrival of the Fourth Industrial Revolution, sustainable solutions that incorporate the accelerating and innovating power of ICT and other advanced technologies creates new markets while at the same time making exciting new production processes possible. Digital technology is a core enabler for circular business models and the key to identifying innovation models. Utilizing technology, manufacturers can change the world with their business solutions and sustainability can help unlock trillions of dollars in manufacturing opportunities.

CASE NO. **ECOMEDIAGROUP**

Forming an active network of
communication professionals with
sustainable values and knowledge

Case applied in: The Netherlands
Headquarters located in: The Netherlands
www.ecomediagroep.nl

IMPACT SDGs

SDG 3

Good health and well being

Ensures healthy lives and promote
well-being by guaranteeing 100%
IPA free print production, using
toxin free CtC bio-inks.

SDG 12

Responsible production

Pursues a model of "More is
less!" Optimizes production
processes by attaining environmental certifications.

SDG 13

Climate action

Counters the negative effects of
climate change, EMG guarantees
that all print productions and
raw materials are 100% climate
neutral.

SDG 15

Life on land

Protects and promotes the
sustainable use of ecosystems
by using FSC certificate or proven
alternative papers assuring no
loss of biodiversity in forests.

SDG 17

Partnerships for the Goals

Encourages supply chain collaboration by supporting a platform
of independent communication
professionals.

THERE IS NO NEED TO MAKE THINGS SUSTAINABLE AS LONG AS YOU DO NOT
PRODUCE THEM. **LESS IS MORE BY SETTING SUSTAINABILITY AND
DISTINCTIVENESS ABOVE QUANTITY.**
ROB WILDERS, CO-FOUNDER ECOMEDIAGROUP

There is no industry that provides more waste than the marketing communication industry. Assuming that only a fraction of the print marketing communication will be converted into an effective response, most of the efforts can be identified as waste. This leads to unnecessary environmental damage and increases social resistance.

Ecomediagroup (EMG) believes that cutting waste requires an integrated supply chain collaboration (SDG 17). It is therefore EMG's goal to build up a network of 250 active supply chain partners before 2020. Additionally, EMG has set up a local network of enterprises with the aim to reduce the carbon footprint as a collective. Data, design and production professionals need to unify their strength and share the same set of principles: quality above quantity, distinctiveness above standardization and relevancy above one-size-fits-all communication. To improve the sustainable awareness across all the supply chains, EMG offers partners a comprehensive knowledge base with (scientific) publications about sustainable marketing communication, SDG topics and practices. This also includes an online eco-calculator to compare the impact of print materials on the environment, as well as the financial implications of eco-printed products. Furthermore EMG has adapted a product information management tool. It is undeniable that data failures lead to more waste and discrepancies across all channels. This single-source of truth allows supply chain partners to improve the quality of their client's product data.

In addition to cutting waste, we focus on a sustainable printing processes, participate actively in the environmental barometer, and eliminate IPA in the production process. To ensure energy efficiency, EMG implemented an active energy monitoring system on the work floor. Eliminating the use of IPA is crucial in order to guarantee a safe and healthy work environment (SDG 3) as well as avoiding its negative impact on the environment itself (SDG 12). Using highly degradable and toxin free *Cradle-to-Cradle* bio-inks improves the recycling process (de-inking) and has significantly less impact on the environment and people.

To ensure life on land (SDG 15), EMG ensures that print is produced solely on FSC certificate paper or on sustainable alternatives. For example Agriwaste from PaperWise - highly qualified paper and paperboard made from agricultural waste. The factory is located in India, amongst the farmers. Based on a LCA calculation, PaperWise scored 47% better than FSC paper made from wood fibers and 29% better than recycled paper.

EMG promotes a 100% carbon free printed product in order to combat climate change and its impacts (SDG 13). Other measures employed in the company's operations include: optimizing sustainability in their offices and company vehicles, encouraging suppliers to supply carbon free materials, and using the latest innovations regarding production technologies and using certified renewable electricity.

CHALLENGE

Cut waste and use sustainable raw materials in the printing process to combat climate change, protect biodiversity, and contribute to a better world.

OPPORTUNITIES FOR SCALE

Ecomediagroup continues to work with industry and supply chain partners to promote sustainable options for this industry. Their goal is to build a network of 250 active supply chain partners before 2020 with the values on sustainability.

Sources and further information

- www.ecomediagroep.nl/schoon
- www.paperwise.eu
- www.green4print.nl
- http://www.cepi.org/mythsandrealities
- http://www.stofwisseling.nu/goede-praktijken-ipa-vrij-drukwerk.html
- http://www.sciencedirect.com/science/article/pii/S221078431630081X
- https://www.sciencedirect.com/science/article/pii/S2212567115004463
- http://onlinelibrary.wiley.com/doi/10.1002/hrm.20383/abstract

" ECOMEDIAGROUP (EMG) BELIEVES THAT CUTTING WASTE REQUIRES AN INTEGRATED SUPPLY CHAIN COLLABORATION."

The PWC report *Delivering the Sustainable Development Goals – seizing the opportunity in global manufacturing demonstrates this clearly.*[63]The report states that SDGs offer tremendous economic opportunities for global manufacturing players and businesses at large if these opportunities are captured and applied as part of long-term and inclusive growth strategies. With the ability to drive the transformation of economies, sustainable manufacturing has the potential to realize economic growth possibilities needed to achieve shared and sustained prosperity. According to the UN, the global manufacturing value added as a share of GDP increased from 15.3% in 2005 to 16.2% in 2016.[64]

The essence of the shift in manufacturing towards a focus on the SDGs involves manufacturing to be sustainable in conduct (the way things are produced) and in product (what is actually being produced). Manufacturing needs to become totally circular, throughout the whole supply chain, creating new business models, producing at lower costs, and using fewer resources, or even better - no virgin resources at all. With the trillions of dollars' worth of potential business opportunities, mentioned throughout the book, there is a huge shared value driver for manufacturing.

The outlook for sustainable manufacturing is promising, but bear in mind that currently both circular economy and sustainable manufacturing solutions are severely underinvested. There is a huge investment gap and thus a huge value gap as well. Of course, investment is required when making any transition, but the transition to circular, sustainable manufacturing can be coupled with technological advances and thus reduce the amount of investment that would be needed. For example, The World Economic Forum calls for "Intelligent Assets" in their report on *Unlocking the Circular Economy Potential.*[65]These intelligent assets use IoT technology to extend the use cycle length of an asset, increase utilization of an asset or resource, loop or cascade an asset through additional use cycles, and regenerate natural capital. This can be combined with one (or several) of the three main intelligent asset value drivers – knowledge of the location, condition, and availability of an asset. With this connectivity, rolled out at scale, value generation is redefined, while also helping developing economies avoid major upfront investments and resource-intensive processes. For instance, the use of solar panels and smart grids can make investments in old infrastructure obsolete. The same is seen in the use of mobile phones which already in many developing nations allow connectivity where investments in infrastructure are unavailable. If this is coupled with the circular production of these products, there is a true sustainable solution that makes a substantial impact on the SDGs. As the report states, "what is at stake is not incremental change or a gradual digitization of the system as we know it, but a reboot."

As manufacturing covers all sectors, a large part of the trillion dollar prize from transforming to sustainability will be captured by manufacturing. Examples include: producing agribusiness machinery to boost production for precision agriculture; home and office energy efficiency products like lighting, ventilation and air-conditioning based on renewable energy; and recycling machinery using renewable energy. In addition to the production of end products, the production of chemicals that are used in other products is essential in manufacturing as well. The SDGs are a compass for companies like DSM and Solvay. Jean-Pierre Clamadieu, CEO of Solvay, a large Belgian chemical firm, stated that "sustainability is crucial to the long-term survival of chemical companies." A survey further confirmed that 44% of chemical companies' CEOs said only sustainable frontrunners in chemicals will survive.[66]

Data-driven industrial production processes are expanding and creating new markets. Through updated technological innovations, customers, designers, and operators will be able to access materials on demand, collaborate with robots, and rely on virtual work instructions presented at the point of use. Breakthrough, technologically advanced, business models that offer energy and resource solutions are important turning points in the field of industrial manufacturing. There are three technology categories driving much of the change:

- **Internet of Things (IoT):** The idea of a connected manufacturing facility means using the internet to link machines, sensors, computers, and workers. For example, Stanley Black & Decker has adapted the IoT in a plant in Mexico to monitor the real-time status of production via mobile devices. This has resulted in significant energy and resource efficiency enhancements where overall equipment effectiveness has increased by 24%, labor utilization by 10%, and throughput by 10%.
- **Robotics:** China is a leader in robotics manufacturing. Since 2013, the number of industrial robots in China roughly doubled to an estimated 75,000 in 2015, with that number forecast to double yet again to 150,000 by 2018. Robotic implementation in the US and other mature economies helps drive business growth, as robots are employed to complement rather than replace workers.
- **3D printing:** Early adopters of 3D printing, also called additive manufacturing, among industrial manufacturing companies are using 3D printing to manufacture parts in small amounts for product prototypes, to reduce design-to-manufacturing cycle times and energy inputs, and to alter the economics of production. For example, BAE Systems began to use 3D printing when it could not obtain a critical injection-molded plastic part for an airplane. Through this solution, the company saved more than 60% on the cost of the part, and shrank production lead times by two months.

Sustainable manufacturing is important for large companies as well as innovative start-ups and scale-ups. And it is also crucial for SMEs, which in fact account for the largest part of all businesses worldwide. The already high costs borne by SMEs as a result of climate change and its impact on energy and resources are expected to rise dramatically. Some projected scenarios show that the cost is likely to rise 30 or 40 times by 2080.

Resource intensive SMEs, such as those in the printing and advertising business, are finding innovative ways to address the SDGs. The traditional printing process releases per ton of printed-paper 2.2 tons of carbon emissions. Based on the worldwide paper requirements for printed communication, this means 260 million tons of CO_2 emissions annually. Fifty trees per year are needed to convert one ton of CO_2 into oxygen. At this rate, 13 billion trees are needed annually to compensate the production of the worldwide printed communication. Dutch printing firm EcoMedia Group (See Case 48) is actively working to minimize their waste and curb their paper and energy use, while promoting a 100% carbon free printed product in order to combat climate change. In addition, the Group endeavors to foster relationships with supply chain partners, aiming to perpetuate their SDG commitment across their network.

WRAP UP

The sustainable use of resources and the development of renewable energy is a fundamental key to unlocking the potential of the SDGs. Technological advances in resource use, circular solutions, and manufacturing will help to accelerate and propel the transformation needed. As climate change is affecting us environmentally, socially, and economically, there is no time to waste. We need all sectors, all companies, - large and small, and all investors to support this path towards sustainability.

UN Secretary General, António Guterres remarked on the need for investors to support sustainable efforts when he said at COP 23, "Markets can and must play a central role in financing a low-carbon, climate-resilient future. Yet markets need to be re-oriented away from the counter-productive and the short-term. In 2016, an estimated 825 billion dollars were invested in fossil fuels and high-emissions sectors. We must stop making bets on an unsustainable future that will place savings and societies at risk." As, Guterres rightly concludes, "Investing in climate-friendly development is where the smart money is headed." ■

The United Nations Climate Change Conferences

COP 21

PARIS, 2015
THE CLIMATE AGREEMENT WAS CLOSED

After 20 years of negotiations, 193 countries reached a landmark agreement to combat climate change and intensify actions, and investments, to achieve lower carbon emissions. The Paris Agreement was unanimously adopted by all 193 member countries to keep global warming below 2 °C above pre-industrial levels, and continue efforts to limit it to 1.5 °C.

During the 2015 conference, delegates also launched initiatives including:
- A major scale-up of the Clean Energy Solutions Center, including the successful Ask an Expert service, which responded to more than 190 requests for assistance, providing no-cost clean energy policy support to 95 developing countries around the world.
- New Clean Energy Finance Solutions Center that provides resources to help governments mobilize clean energy finance.

COP 22

MARRAKECH, 2016
THE CLIMATE AGREEMENT INTO FORCE

On November 4 2016, the Paris Agreement entered into force. Thirty days prior, the threshold for entry into force was achieved when at least 55 Parties to the Convention accounting in total for at least an estimated 55% of the total global greenhouse gas emissions, deposited their instruments of ratification, acceptance, approval or accession with the Depositary. With this milestone, the Conference marked the implementation of the Paris Agreement.

One of the outcomes of COP22 was The Marrakech Action Proclamation which stated that "the constructive spirit of multilateral cooperation on climate change continues, signaling a shift towards a new era of implementation and action on climate and sustainable development." The proclamation declared that it was now the task of the signatories to "rapidly build on that momentum, together, moving forward purposefully to reduce greenhouse gas emissions and to foster adaptation efforts, thereby benefiting and supporting the 2030 Agenda for Sustainable Development and its Sustainable Development Goals."

Additionally, on the last day of the Conference, members of the Climate Vulnerable Forum issued a statement on behalf of 40 of the world's developing countries. These countries, which are particularly vulnerable to climate change, committed to meet 100% domestic renewable energy production as rapidly as possible, while working to end energy poverty and protect water and food security, while taking into consideration national circumstances..

The Conference Of Parties (COP) is the highest decision-making body of the Convention. All States that are Parties to the Convention are represented at the COP. These parties review the implementation of the Convention and all other legal instruments that the COP adopts, and make the necessary decisions to promote the effective implementation, including institutional and administrative arrangements.

BONN, 2017
CALL FOR SWIFT PROGRESS WHILE PREPARING THE FOUNDATION

COP 23

COP23 built on the progress made in COP21 and COP22 and prepared the grounds for COP24. The objective was to clarify the framework, and progress the shaping of the rules and principles of implementation of the Paris Agreement, which are to be adopted at the following conference in Katowice, Poland.

Significantly, after the announced withdrawal from the Agreement by US President Trump, sub-national leaders led by Gov. Jerry Brown of California and former New York City Mayor Michael Bloomberg presented a report on the ongoing efforts by American states, cities, businesses and civil society to uphold the emissions reduction target of the United States under the Paris Agreement.

This conference also saw the launch of the Powering Past Coal Alliance in which over 25 countries, states and regions, led by the UK and Canada, pledged to accelerate the rapid phase-out of coal while providing support for affected workers and communities, and maintaining grid resilience.

KATOWICE, 2018
ADOPTION & IMPLEMENTATION OF RULES AND PRINCIPLES

COP 24

This Conference will take place in a former mine in Poland, which makes the context of the site perfectly suited to the event. At COP24, the aim is to finalize the guidelines for fully operationalizing the agreement, adopt the rules and principles, assess how countries are doing collectively regarding the realization of Paris's goals for the coming years, and implement the transformation

CLIMATE CHANGE IS PREDICTED TO DRIVE 100 MILLION MORE PEOPLE INTO POVERTY IN THE NEXT 15 YEARS UNLESS ACTION IS TAKEN. WE KNOW THE MOST POOR IN THE WORLD WILL BE THE MOST AFFECTED BUT NO ONE IS IMMUNE. CLIMATE CHANGE COULD CUT THE VALUE OF THE WORLD'S FINANCIAL ASSETS BY US $2.5TN, ACCORDING TO THE FIRST ESTIMATE FROM ECONOMIC MODELING, POTENTIALLY PROPELLING US INTO ANOTHER FINANCIAL CRISIS.

MILLENNIALS-TOWARDS-SDGS

PART 4 | SCALING UP FOR A TRILLION DOLLAR SHIFT

"The scale of the business solutions must meet the scale of the Global Goals"

Throughout this book you have been reading how the SDGs need business and capital as much as business and capital need the goals. Solving the world's biggest challenges is actually as good for business as it is a good investment. However, not all societal needs are initially a firm business case. Thus, all parties - public and private - need to collaborate and mutually leverage solutions and investments.

The SDGs are the blueprint for the world we want to have, and it provides one language and one set of Goals, Targets and Indicators to guide us. But the scale of our solutions must meet the scale of our challenges, and by now it is clear; we have to significantly scale up sustainable solutions to the challenges we share, in order to achieve the Goals. Business as usual won't get us there. This means that business at scale needs to get out of its comfort zone and repurpose business as unusual.

Since the UN SDG report in 2017 was presented, we have been confronted with numbers indicating that the benefits of progress are not being equally shared. An estimated 155 million children under 5 years of age were stunted due to malnutrition. On average, women spent almost triple the amount of time on unpaid domestic and care work as men, based on data from 2010-2016.[1]

Lack of progress comes at a high price. Economic losses from natural hazards are now reaching an average of US $250 billion to $300 billion a year, with a disproportionate impact on small and vulnerable countries. Creating a more equitable and sustainable world is tough work, but failure to do so would be catastrophic for society, the environment, the economy and business itself.

Scaling up at high speed and large scale requires bold leadership, radical innovations, huge investments, and public-private partnerships, as well as collaboration, education and the supportive framework of a paradigm shift in tax, law and legislation. Nevertheless, it is a job that can be done. Let's demonstrate the leadership required and let's use the power of the new generation - the Millennials - to take us beyond 2030 towards a sustainable future.

10

SCALING UP: GLOBAL GOALS; GLOBAL SCALE; GLOBAL GOOD

The way to scale up business and capital solutions for the Global Goals is for everyone to join the movement to make the shift to a sustainable world. It needs to be the topic of conversation, and we need leaders to build the momentum and guide the way. Future leaders – the Millennials, and the generations to follow – will carry the baton as the successors, inheriting the challenges. Therefore, we need everyone to get involved, education to make young and old aware, and collaboration to drive our greatest challenge and opportunity – The SDGs. Individuals can do a lot. People have power, even more so today than ever before. With technology connecting us, we each have a louder voice with a greater opportunity to be heard. Consumers can demand that externalities should be integrated in the price of products and services. We can each be an SDG leader and inspire and support each other to build a sustainable life for ourselves and the generations to come. Achieving the Goals is a matter of leadership.

10.1 SCALING UP BUSINESS FOR GOOD

"Ours can be the first generation to end poverty – and the last generation to address climate change before it is too late." With this truthful and honest sentence by former UN Secretary-General Ban Ki-moon , we started the first chapter of the book. Equally we start the last chapter with that very statement. The world needs our business solutions, and they are needed sooner rather than later. The solutions not only need to come quickly, they need to be scaled up as rapidly as we can. The scale of our business and capital solutions simply must meet the scale of our global challenges. Inaction, or too little action, comes with a huge societal and economical price which we cannot afford.

Our Global Goals are not insurmountable. As demonstrated in this book, there are business and capital solutions that make a significant difference. The opportunities are there. Information resources are available for guidance, like this book, and the many reports referenced in the chapters. There are organizations and partnerships open to new members, as there is ample room for more leaders to join the call. The business case of both engaging with, and funding, the SDGs is a very strong business case. For instance, the Business and Sustainable Development Commission (BSDC) notes there is a US $4 trillion annual investment opportunity existing in the sectors food and agriculture, cities, and energy and materials,[2] sectors which have all been discussed extensively in this book. Their report, *Better Business Better World*, predicts that the current investment (of $4 trillion) could unlock opportunities worth more than US $12 trillion by 2030, conservatively calculated. Additional savings and revenues of trillions of dollars annually can result from the opportunities unlocked by the Global Goals. The new market opportunities can generate up to 380 million new jobs by 2030. Most of those jobs will be in developing countries which is important to control poverty and economic migration since the population is expected to grow considerably in those regions.

> "WHILE THERE ARE MANY PATHWAYS FORWARD TO ACHIEVE THE SDGs... BUSINESS AS USUAL IS NOT AN OPTION."
>
> JUDITH RODIN, FORMER PRESIDENT OF THE ROCKEFELLER FOUNDATION

> ## CURRENT INVESTMENT OF US $4 TRILLION COULD BE WORTH MORE THAN US $12 TRILLION IN 2030
>
> BSDC

The impact of business and private investments is huge. Nowadays, we live in a world where a company can command more financial capital than an entire country's GDP. Imagine for instance that Apple's finances surpass the GDP of two-thirds of the countries in the world.[3] As 50 of the largest economies on earth are corporations, and this number continues to grow as companies grow, business holds tremendous power. Companies are, for a large part, globally present and therefore have greater reach than governments. The global impact of business shows that on many levels there is a substantiated business case for embedding the SDGs. Furthermore, about 50% of all assets under management worldwide belong to the largest banks, meaning that banks alone could easily solve the SDG funding gap. There is much leverage for business and capital to drive the shift towards achieving the SDGs. But it requires leadership.

Consumers too are helping to drive the movement towards sustainability. Consumers are becoming increasingly aware of their purchasing power, and their voice. A Cone Communications study in the US shows that 87% of people will purchase a product because a company advocated for an issue they cared about, and 76% will refuse to purchase a company's products or services upon learning it supported an issue contrary to their beliefs. The study also revealed that 90% of US people surveyed would boycott a company if they discovered that the company was using dishonest or irresponsible business practices.[4]

Changing consumer behavior is becoming more widespread. Organic fresh food is outperforming its conventional offering in every core market. Demand for more natural, cleaner and healthier products drives organic sales not only in developed markets such as US and UK but also developing markets. In China for instance, sales of fresh organics increased by almost 30% in 2016 and by over 16% in South Africa despite their high unit prices.[5]

Consumers are becoming more critical of the products they buy and the companies they engage with. A study by sustainability consultancy Corporate Citizenship found the lack of tangible business action on the SDGs is causing a trust problem among consumers. This is particularly the case among millennials (those born between the 1980s and early 2000s). The consultancy's research revealed that "despite 81% of millennials believing business has a key role to play in achieving the SDGs, the majority of businesses are not yet acting."[6]

Throughout this book, we demonstrate how new markets can be unlocked and accelerated by growing consumer awareness and demands. Current and future customers want different, more sustainable offerings. Sustainability is a leading theme, even more so since our new generation – the millennials - have a much more progressive view of sustainability, as we will discuss in the last section of this chapter.

10.2 LEADERSHIP FOR THE GOALS

Achieving the goals implies bold leadership. Incremental innovation and gradual steps forward won't bring us to the destination. Business must —and can- repurpose. This can be accomplished since, like we have demonstrated throughout the book, repurposing is indeed a business case that will only improve in the future. The subtitle of this book bears the wording *Business for Good is Good Business* as it is crucial that the shared value perspective, resonating throughout this book, is picked up broadly in both business and capital, and that solutions demonstrating this, are created and scaled up.

Leadership by example is key, as is education. They both intertwine. We have some inspiring transformational global leaders like Paul Polman from Unilever, Gerard Mestrallet from Engie, Feike Sijbesma from DSM, and Henrik Poulsen from Ørsted – all sharing their leadership convictions in cases and forewords in this book. They are paving the way, and we desperately need their executive successors to follow suit as we need many, many more leaders like them.

Business leaders paving the way must be known, acknowledged and supported since building the bridge is much harder than walking on it. It is significant that UN Global Compact, as Lise Kingo points out in her foreword in this book, supports business repurposing, and puts forward the call for UN Pioneers. After the adaptation of the SDGs, Global Compact began to annually profile SDG pioneers, first in 2016 and subsequently in 2017.

True SDG-leadership must be understood thoroughly. It is not about adapting current business models within the comfort zone or within the scope on one's own company walls. SDG leadership is about responsibility at a much higher system level. It is about starting to think from a whole world's perspective and placing the role of one's own company, supply chain and customers in that perspective. In other words: it means "beginning with the end in mind" like Stephen Covey stated so accurately in many of his leadership books.

True leadership means authentic leadership. SDG leadership means principle-based leadership. The principles apply regardless the sector, regardless the company, regardless the continent or country. True leadership also means active leadership. The majority of business leaders are still mainly talking about the SDGs and its opportunities, but not taking real action or responsibility for them yet. Engaging with the SDGs is still a matter for front-runners, with 71% of leaders planning to engage, but only 13% having actually identified the tools they need to assess their SDG impact.

> **"EVEN THE MOST HARD-HEARTED CEO SHOULD UNDERSTAND THAT THERE WILL BE NO FUTURE BUSINESS WITHOUT SUSTAINABLE MARKETS AND PEOPLE WITH THE SKILLS TO PRODUCE THEIR PRODUCTS AND THE MONEY TO BUY THEM."**
>
> DOUG FRANTZ IS DEPUTY SECRETARY-GENERAL OF THE OECD

SDG BUSINESS LEADERSHIP IMPLIES NOT ONLY CREATING IMPACT THROUGH AND FOR YOUR OWN COMPANY'S ACTIONS, BUT ALSO IMPACTING AND ENCOURAGING YOUR SUPPLY CHAIN, YOUR BROADER SECTOR, AND THE BUSINESS ECOSYSTEM AT LARGE.

SDG Pioneers

2016 - 2017

CLAUS STIG PEDERSEN
Head of Corporate Sustainability, Novozymes
Denmark
2016

KERRY ADLER
Founder, President and Chief Executive Officer, Skypower Global *Canada*
2016

JOSEPH THOMPSON
CO-founder and CEO, AID:Tech *United Kingdom*
2017

ARTHUR KAY
Founder and Deputy Chairman, bio-bean
United Kingdom
2017

ULYSSES SMITH
Attorney, Linklaters LLP
USA
2016

TERESA JENNINGS
Head of Rule of Law Development, LexisNexis (RELX Group Plc) *USA*
2017

GUSTAVO PEREZ BERLANGA
CSR Senior VP, Toks Restaurant Group *Mexico*
2017

SONIA CONSIGLIO FAVARETTO
Press and Sustainability Managing Director, BM & FBOVESPA S.A. *Brazil*
2016

ULISSES SABARÁ
President, Beraca *Brazil*
2016

TÂNIA CONTE COSENTINO
President, Schneider Electric South America *Brazil*
2017

PATRICK POUYANNÉ
Chairman and CEO, Total *France*
2017

KAAN TERZIOĞLU
CEO, Turkcell Iletisim Hizmetleri A.S. *Turkey*
2017

DINA SHERIF
Chief Executive Officer Co-founder, Ahead of the Curve *Egypt*
2016

CHARLES IMMANUEL AKHIMIEN
Co-founder, MOBicure Integrated Solutions *Nigeria*
2017

PATRICK NGOWI
Founder and Chief Executive Officer, Helvetic Group *Tanzania*
2016

FARZANA CHOWDHURRY
Managing Director and Chief Executive Officer, Green Delta Insurance Company Limited *Bangladesh*
2016

SONIA BASHIR KABIR
Managing Director, Microsoft *Bangladesh*
2017

ZUBAIDA BAI
Founder and Chief Executive Officer Ayzh *India*
2016

XIAOHUI LIANG
Chief Researcher, Office for Social Responsibility, China National Textile & Apparel Council *China*
2016

JAIME AUGUSTO ZOBEL DE AYALA
Chairman and CEO, Ayala Corporation *Philippines*
2017

Figure 44 **Bueprint for Business Leadership Source: UNglobalcompact.org Blueprint for Business Leadership on the SDGs**

SDG LEADERSHIP

UN Global Compact developed the blueprint for better business, indicating the way forward to a principle-based approach. It is a comprehensive, thorough blueprint that I can recommend as it can definitely be a great help for leaders to navigate the SDG landscape. It provides a framework for companies aiming towards SDG leadership. It states clearly that business leadership on the SDGs evolves through repeating three steps:

1. Prioritize actions on SDGs
2. Act to execute those actions
3. Learn from the achieved impact in order to improve both your own company and others.

SDG business leadership implies not only creating impact through and for your own company's actions, but also impacting and encouraging your supply chain, your broader sector, and the business ecosystem at large. True SDG leadership inspires and urges others to help build the bridge and cross over to more sustainable practices and a more sustainable future.

The blueprint mentions five crucial qualities of SDG leadership, and advises on relevant actions on all of the SDGs. The five qualities clearly reinforce and substantiate the leadership responsibilities mentioned earlier.

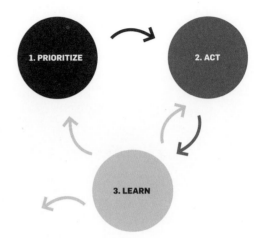

SDG leadership will come with a positive prize and so there is good business reason to be, or become, an SDG leader. At the same time, SDG leadership can only be demonstrated and pursued with a realistic view of the hurdles that will need to be overcome, and the business case that can be built. Although there is potential for all business to build sustainable business cases, not all challenges are readily a profitable business cases at the moment. And with externalities not internalized yet, sustainable business cases lack up to 40% of their real value at this time. So again, you need to be a principle-based leader to accomplish the task at hand and to be a shaper, rather than a follower.

THE FIVE QUALITIES OF AN SDG LEADER:

1. Intentional: support for the SDGs is an integral, deliberate part of a leading company's strategy
2. Ambitious: a leading company's level of ambition exceeds prevailing levels of ambition, its actions are material in the context of its end-to-end operations, and it focuses on long-term outcomes.
3. Consistent: support for the SDGs is embedded across organizational functions and external communications
4. Collaborative: support for the SDGs involves partnerships, including with business, governments, civil society and other actors
5. Accountable: a leading company is transparent, manages risks, seeks out meaningful engagement with stakeholders and is accountable for adverse impacts.

BUILDING TRUST FOR A BETTER WORLD

Another hurdle is the growing instability in many parts of the world which has a damaging effect on trust. This is, in fact, a huge threat to long term planning and tight connections between multiple parties in society. Trust however is something we need desperately, it is "a vital element of any well-functioning society," as Unilever CEO Paul Polman rightly stated. But trust has never been so low, and the lack of trust has never been so broad, related to politics, government and other institutions, as well as business. To accelerate our actions to achieve the Goals, we need trust and that trust will grow when we achieve the Goals. Both are interdependent: accelerating for the achievement of the Goals means building trust and vice versa. It is not a coincidence that Goal 17 is about the partnerships.

GUIDING CEOs TOWARDS SDG IMPACT

The encouraging news is that by now CEOs, management, and everyone else can make good use of tools and reports to guide their way. It is also the main reason for this book: to support, inspire and help to grow SDG leadership.

The World Business Council for Sustainable Development (WBCSD), released a very useful tool – The CEO Guide to the SDGs.[7] It describes the implications of the SDGs across four pillars:

1. Risk of inaction
2. Capturing opportunities
3. Governance and transparency
4. Need for collaboration

The WBCSD stresses that inaction on the SDGs will come at a price for both individual companies as well as the global economy. It describes the opportunities for business at hand, and points out the need of transparency, for example by reporting practices, and carbon disclosure.

Last but not least, it emphasizes the need for cross-sectoral and cross-stakeholder partnerships and collaborations. In fact, all the research shows that collaborative engagement with the SDGs, and bold, determined leadership, leads to a higher system-level shift than individual company transformations. One business simply cannot achieve the scale of impact needed all by itself, so collaboration is key.

ONE BUSINESS SIMPLY CANNOT ACHIEVE THE SCALE OF IMPACT NEEDED ALL BY ITSELF, SO COLLABORATION IS KEY.

In addition to Global Compact and the WBCSD, many organizations and sustainability networks around the globe are working to support you in your way forward. Consultancy firms like McKinsey, PWC, KPMG and others share crucial knowledge, and there are handy apps available to download on your phone, tablet or even your iWatch, such as the SDGs in Action app.[8] This book is also meant to serve as a useful resource, and for this reason is shared online by an open access model. Use all of the knowledge, examples and guidance available, since neither your company nor our Global Goals have time to waste.

LEADERS LAGGING BEHIND

According to a recent UN Progress report, company leaders are still lagging behind in sustainability practices and global progress on the SDGs.

In the Sustainable Development Goals Report 2017, released by the United Nations during the High-Level Political Forum on Sustainable Development, an assessment was made on where we stand on reaching the SDGs.[9] The UN notes: "While considerable progress has been made over the past decade across all areas of development, the pace of progress observed in previous years is insufficient to fully meet the Sustainable Development Goals and Targets by 2030. Time is therefore of the essence, moreover, progress has not always been equitable. Advancements have been uneven across regions, between the sexes, and among people of different ages, wealth and locales, including urban and rural dwellers. Faster and more inclusive progress is needed to accomplish the bold vision articulated in the 2030 Agenda."

SUSTAINABLE DEVELOPMENT GOALS REPORT 2017: 10 HIGHLIGHTS

- Nearly 1 billion people were lifted from extreme poverty between 1999-2013. Yet an estimated 767 million people lived below the extreme poverty line in 2013.

- The global stunting rate of children under 5 fell by 10%, from 33% in 2000 to 23% in 2016, meaning an estimated 155 million children were stunted in 2016 because they did not receive the nutrition they need.

- Fewer women and babies are dying. Between 2000 and 2015, maternal deaths dropped by 37%, and under-5 child deaths by 44%. However, still in 2015, 303,000 women died during pregnancy or childbirth and 5.9 million children under age 5 died – mostly from preventable causes.

- In 2014, only 9% of children of primary school age were out of school. The news is mixed though, as progress has virtually stalled since 2008.

- Child marriage is declining slightly, but not quickly or dramatically enough. In the year 2000, nearly 1 in 3 women between 20 and 24 years of age reported that they were married before 18 years of age, this is contrasted with figures in 2015, when the ratio was just over 1 in 4.

- In 2015, 2.9 billion people used a safely managed sanitation service, but still 892 million people openly defecate.

- The number of people with access to electricity grew from 77.6% in 2000 to 85.3% in 2014, even so, there are still more than 1 billion people who do not have access to electricity.

- The global unemployment rates fell from 6.1% in 2010 to 5.7% in 2016. However, youth (aged 15 to 24 years) were nearly three times more likely than adults to be without a job.

- From 2010 to 2015, the annual net loss of forest area globally was less than half that of the 1990s. Yet the proportion of marine stocks that are overfished has been on the rise, from 10% in 1974 to 31% in 2013.

- Official development assistance (ODA) reached a new high in 2016 at $142.6 billion, although bilateral aid to the poorest countries fell by 3.9%.

Business is crucial to solving the SDGs, but in many companies, it is still predominantly in the discussion phase. Many executives believe that the SDGs are increasingly important for their company's strategy. But while it continues to grow into an accepted and important business issue, challenges to capture its full value are not often taken on. The McKinsey study, *Sustainability's Strategic Worth*, showed, as did many PWC studies, that companies see many hurdles to incorporate the SDGs into their organizational processes. So, although there is growing recognition of the importance of repurposing towards the SDGs, it is not being ex-

ecuted enough. Fortunately, prioritizing the SDGs is gaining ground, and is moving ahead. There is evidence of increasing interest for companies to address sustainability (see figure 45), but the main challenges now are capturing sustainability's value and implementing sustainable business cases.[10]

The crucial shift is to not see sustainability as something to reckon with by conforming the existing products and services and business models, but to treat sustainability and thus the SDGs as a driver for the development of products, services and business models. We need companies to bring forward products and services that are solutions for the SDGs. If the products do not add value, or have purpose towards the achievement of the SDGs, they should actually cease to exist. Think about sugar laden refreshments, packaged foods with high fat and sugar percentages, fossil fuels and other products. You can decide yourself if they add value or not. This does not mean that a company should cease, it means the company should examine their offerings and truthfully look at whether they are contributing to a sustainable world, and if not, repurpose – as Ørsted has done (See Case 49).

Being a follower on the move towards the SDGs is not enough. We need bold leadership for the achievement of the Goals. Such leadership as is demonstrated by Ørsted, formerly named DONG Energy. This company's leadership made a strong decision, and marked their spot on the horizon. In 2017 they repurposed their company from being a traditional energy company based on utilizing fossil fuels, and made a major shift to all renewables. They made a concerted and conscientious business plan to do this, and are successfully executing it. They now have a bright future, a new future that is no longer in line with old economy practices, and thus they have rebranded accordingly to recognize that shift with their new name - Ørsted. They are also a significant investor in green bonds, recently issuing €500 million in green hybrid capital securities and €750 million in green senior bonds. They are a great example of bold and determined leadership; they made a decision, created a plan, and execute it entirely.

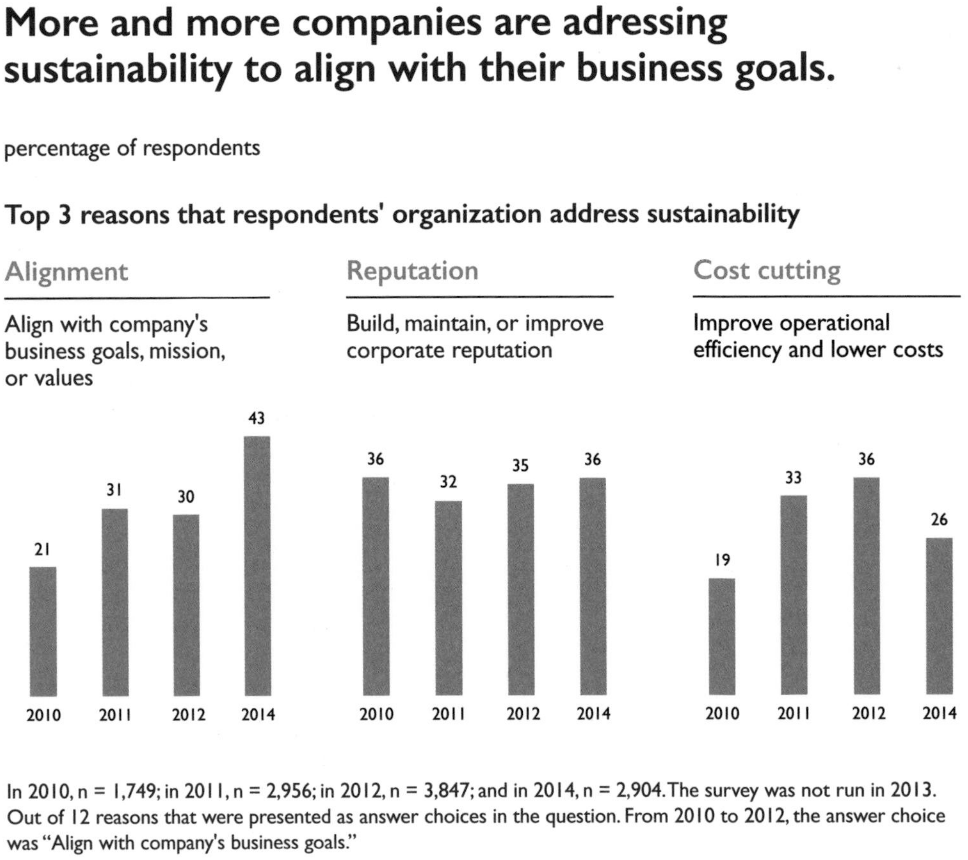

More and more companies are adressing sustainability to align with their business goals.

percentage of respondents

Top 3 reasons that respondents' organization address sustainability

Figure 45 **More and more companies are addressing sustainability to align with their business goals. Source: McKinsey.com**

Alignment	Reputation	Cost cutting
Align with company's business goals, mission, or values	Build, maintain, or improve corporate reputation	Improve operational efficiency and lower costs

Alignment: 2010: 21, 2011: 31, 2012: 30, 2014: 43

Reputation: 2010: 36, 2011: 32, 2012: 35, 2014: 36

Cost cutting: 2010: 19, 2011: 33, 2012: 36, 2014: 26

In 2010, n = 1,749; in 2011, n = 2,956; in 2012, n = 3,847; and in 2014, n = 2,904. The survey was not run in 2013. Out of 12 reasons that were presented as answer choices in the question. From 2010 to 2012, the answer choice was "Align with company's business goals."

49

CASE NO.

ØRSTED

Energy for a Sustainable Future
Leading the transformation to renewable energy

Case applied in: Global
Headquarters located in: Denmark
www.orsted.com

IMPACT SDGs

SDG 3
Good Health and Well-Being

Invests in its workforce to sustain safe, healthy, engaged and skilled employees; in 2016, the share of employees who reported experiencing stress in the workplace was 8%, nearly half the Danish average of 15%.

SDG 7
Affordable and Clean Energy

Reduced coal consumption by 73% and decreased CO2 emissions by 52% over the past 10 years. Target to reduce CO2 emission per produced kWh by 96% from 2007-2023.

SDG 9
Industry, Infrastructure and Innovation

Powering 9.5 million people, in 2016, the company surpassed 1,000 offshore wind turbines in locations around the world, making it the largest offshore wind energy developer in the world. Target to power 30 million people from offshore wind by 2025.

THE PARIS AGREEMENT BRINGS HOPE TO FUTURE GENERATIONS THAT THE WORLD WILL BREAK THE TREND OF EVER INCREASING CO2 EMISSIONS THAT ARE PUTTING GLOBAL ECOSYSTEMS AT RISK.
THOMAS THUNE ANDERSEN, CHAIRMAN OF THE BOARD OF DIRECTORS ØRSTED

DONG Energy – short for Danish Oil and Natural Gas – has changed its name to Ørsted as the company has transformed from one of the most fossil-intensive energy companies in Europe to become the greenest. The new name is a tribute to Danish scientist Hans Christian Ørsted, who discovered electromagnetism in 1820, laying the foundation for how power is produced. The energy company's move to embrace sustainable energy rather than fossil fuels has resulted in a transformation signaling they have become "too green" for their original name. With a drive to be a green energy company, the name no longer accurately described who they are, or who they want to be. The commitment to sustainability has motivated the company to critically assess its investment strategy. When the green journey was initiated almost 10 years ago, Ørsted assessed whether it was better to invest US $3 million in a coal-fired power station emitting high levels of CO2 for the next 40 years or build two offshore wind farms at the same price. In shifting from "black to green" energy, the company significantly increased its investments in renewable resources and has stopped investing coal. In fact, they have decided to fully phase out coal from its combined heat and power plants by 2023 as the first major energy company in Europe. This contributes to their vision of a planet that runs entirely on green energy (SDG 7), and responds to Ørsted's culture of fostering a world that is respectful to society, the environment and people (SDG 3).

Ørsted contributes to the SDGs through 20 sustainability programs based on four themes: 1) Energy Supply; 2) Climate and Environment; 3) People; 4) Communities. They are helping to shape the future of wind energy by working with international turbine manufacturers such as Siemens and Vestas to participate in the development process for larger, more efficient turbines. This commitment to the comprehensive process is integrated into the core business strategy where all business decisions are made with the dual objectives of value creation and sustainability. For example, all offshore wind farm investments must have a clear financial business case, with the risks as well as the best way to spend their capital clearly understood. By reorienting the business to a focus on offshore wind, Ørsted believes that it has the advantage to scale operations because they have shifted to building competencies in one technology. Offshore wind is proving to be fully competitive with other types of energy and Ørsted has been involved with some of the world's largest renewables projects in recent years (SDG 9). In spring 2017, they won the first auction on a zero government subsidy bid to the German government, which awarded Ørsted three contracts to build offshore wind power farms in the North Sea. Later in 2017, the company won the right to build the world's largest offshore wind farm at a lifetime electricity cost lower than that of new-built coal or gas-fired power plants.

CHALLENGE

To help create a world where people can use energy as a natural part of their everyday lives without contributing to climate change.

OPPORTUNITIES FOR SCALE

Ørsted Plans to become a global leader in off-shore wind, while fully phasing out coal by 2023 and decreasing CO2 emissions by 96% from 2007 to 2023. The ambition is to raise the number of people they supply from offshore wind to 30 million by 2025. Towards 2020, the company will continue to build a number of large offshore wind farms that will increase total installed capacity from 3.6GW to 6.7GW.

Sources and further information

- https://www.ft.com/content/6bef6c68-11b8-35dc-b0ef-6a964a4ed95a
- https://orsted.com/en/About-us/About-orsted/About-our-name-change
- https://www.triplepundit.com/2017/10/danish-renewables-giant-dong-energy-rebrands-ditches-oil-gas-portfolio/?utm_source=Daily+Email+List
- https://www.unglobalcompact.org/docs/publications/UN%20Impact%20Brochure_Concept-FINAL.pdf
- https://www.bloomberg.com/news/articles/2017-11-16/orsted-will-sell-first-green-bonds-as-part-of-move-away-from-oil
- https://orsted.com/-/media/WWW/Docs/Corp/COM/Sustainability/sustainability_report_en.ashx?la=en

" **ØRSTED'S CULTURE IS TO FOSTER A WORLD THAT IS RESPECTFUL TO SOCIETY, THE ENVIRONMENT AND PEOPLE.**"

To determine a company's value, the Banc of Montreal's Responsible Investment Advisory Council (RIAC) uses the "product and the conduct approach." I see that as one of the core contributions of the SDGs. It offers a clear benchmark to assess whether a company is not only doing well in conduct, but if it is also doing good for society and the environment with their product offering.

IF THE PRODUCTS DO NOT ADD VALUE, OR HAVE PURPOSE TOWARDS THE ACHIEVEMENT OF THE SDGS, THEY SHOULD ACTUALLY CEASE TO EXIST.

Applying the approach of being "SDG-proof" in both conduct and product, means employing a holistic approach. This holistic approach requires bringing about products and services that add value, and doing so in a sustainable way. I realize that if you are not an innovative start-up, or a company that already had to reinvent itself several times, this is a huge challenge. But it is, in fact, a challenge that must be taken on. Sustainability has an encompassing definition. It implies sustaining society and the environment, but it also includes sustaining business as well. Without incorporating sustainability in the heart of your company, your company will simply not sustain into the future. Engaging with the SDGs is in that sense guarding the future of your company.

MARKING THE SPOT ON THE HORIZON: TAKING BOLD DECISIONS
The point on the horizon is in focus, and leadership must drive their companies to reach it. Feike Sijbesma, leading DSM, a company that reinvented itself several times, is leading the business movement towards a fair carbon price. Sijbesma reports that this fair pricing is actually helping his business, not frustrating it. Leaders like Elon Musk of Tesla, who demonstrated that a new electrical car can be of such branding value that the price can be higher than anyone could have imagined, and keeping that price high and non-negotiable is a solid business case since people will want a car that is 'cool' and innovative. Musk has been instrumental in rebranded sustainability. Other leaders like Maurits Groen from WakaWaka, are now taking on country after country to make sure children have safe light and access to power, leading next generations towards education opportunities by providing light to study by (See Case 50).

Bold leaders like Paul Polman, who firmly decided that his company is to become energy/carbon neutral is forthright and has taken a clear step in the right direction. But he also recognizes that it will need to be taken further. Therefore, Polman has now set the course for Unilever, a multinational conglomerate with far-reaching impact, to become CO_2 negative by 2030. Huawei too, is a staunch supporter of the SDGs, and firmly believes that ICT will play a critical role in helping to implement the 2030 Agenda for Sustainable Development at scale and with quality.

We must know about these leaders and share their stories, but bear in mind there are thousands and even millions of others, not that famous, yet not less courageous. Their stories must be told as well. Many start-ups and SMEs in and for developing countries see themselves confronted with extremely difficult hurdles but they persevere. And you can see from the business cases featured in this book what perseverance can get you: a better future, and better business.

Encourage your stakeholders to create impact with your company, in collaboration with many others. And help other entrepreneurs and companies with your knowledge, experience, and network. We are all in this together, and we need all business and capital to embrace the SDGs as the point on the horizon that we are all striving towards.

" **LEADERSHIP IS NOT JUST ABOUT GIVING ENERGY... IT'S UNLEASHING OTHER PEOPLE'S ENERGY.** "

PAUL POLMAN

CASE NO.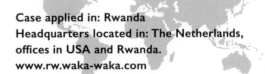

WAKAWAKA

Light for Rwanda
Generating impact through market-based
solutions

Case applied in: Rwanda
Headquarters located in: The Netherlands,
offices in USA and Rwanda.
www.rw.waka-waka.com

IMPACT SDGs

SDG 3
Good Health and Well-Being
Replaces Kerosene as a source of energy, helping to prevent injury and illness due to kerosene use.

SDG 4
Quality Education
Provides light which is crucial for education and studying.

SDG 7
Affordable and Clean Energy
Provides access to clean energy to some of the 76% of the population in Rwanda who do not have access.

SDG 10
Reduced Inequalities
Implements a unique "Robin Hood Principle" to adjust charges for the device.

WAKAWAKA FOCUSES ON AGRICULTURAL COOPERATIVES IN RWANDA. AS A GROUP THEY HELP ONE ANOTHER SAVE MONEY AND SPEND THEIR SAVINGS **ON LIFE-IMPROVING SOLUTIONS. WE CONSIDERS WAKAWAKA TO BE ONE OF THOSE LIFE-IMPROVING SOLUTIONS AND SO DO THE COOPS.**
MAURITS GROEN CO-CEO WAKAWAKA

WakaWaka is an impact driven, social enterprise that works to abolish energy poverty throughout the world. It is a leader in developing, manufacturing and marketing high-tech low-cost solar powered lamps and chargers. The WakaWaka units are durable, lightweight and compact solar device that can charge within a day of strong sunlight and provide up to 200 hours of safe, sustainable light (SDG 7). The solar power-driven device offers a clean, safe energy alternative to kerosene, every day thousands are burned by accidents with fires, and smoke and fumes of indoor kerosene lights increases the risk of respiratory diseases and lung cancer. In contrast WakaWaka provides a healthy alternative (SDG 3). With its good, safe light to study, work and travel after dark to over 40,000 people in 11 districts in Rwanda and elsewhere in the world to some 1.3 million people, among whom many refugees and victims of natural disaster.

With over a billion of the world's population living without access to electricity, WakWaka has adopted as its mission to provide energy to all (SDG 7). WakaWaka believes that access to energy is a basic need. Access to light allows children to study after dark, and access to energy to charge mobile phones provides potential access to online information and education (SDG 4). Charging mobile phones is a daily challenge for people living in rural Rwanda. The WakaWaka device helps to solve this challenge. Using a unique pricing principle called the "Robin Hood Principle," they aim to decrease inequalities (SDG 10). Meaning that proceeds made from selling WakaWaka products in developed markets at competitive prices are used to make them available to off-grid communities around the world at an affordable rate.

CHALLENGE

To abolish energy poverty by replacing the high upfront costs of solar-power through credit lines provided to cooperatives who in turn help their members to save small amount of money to pay off their purchase.

OPPORTUNITIES FOR SCALE

A nationwide rollout in Rwanda (and later in other African countries) is expected to follow, which is likely to be supported with an additional, larger funding round from investors. Already the pilot phase has been supported by the Dutch Development bank FMO as well as Angel Investors.

Sources and further information

- https://us.waka-waka.com/media/press_release_ ww_vg_.pdf
- https://us.waka-waka.com/impact/#!/project/227
- https://us.waka-waka.com/news/2014/08/ launching-the-VG/
- https://akvo.org/blog/wakawaka-rwanda-tracks- distribution-sales-of-solar-lights-chargers/
- https://sustainabledevelopment.un.org/ partnership/?p=10192

" WAKAWAKA BELIEVES THAT ACCESS TO ENERGY IS A BASIC NEED."

10.3 FAIR PRICING, FAIR TAX: THE REALITY CHECK

Although many solutions are sound business cases, we do have to bear in mind that not everything is feasible within the system we have now. The current tax, law and legislation systems frustrate sustainable business cases and the scaling up of solutions. Real change will involve a combination of both public regulation and tax shifts on the one hand and commercial pressure on the other hand.

Additionally, it is important to note that not all societal needs are a capsulated business case. Infrastructure for instance, is a domain where we desperately need public participation and investment. But here too, business can get involved as we have discussed in the chapter on cities.

NOT ALL SOCIETAL NEEDS ARE A BUSINESS CASE.

Regarding tax and legislation, it can be said that we are playing a new game, but with the same rules in place from a former game. This simply does not work, nor is it fair for those who play the new game, and it also empowers the ones with the interest to keep the old game going.
The most crucial factor holding us back is that we barely put a price on a wide range of resources, and pollution. In contrast, we subsidize the use of various finite resources. The value of resource subsidies globally is estimated at over US $1 trillion a year.[11]

Bear in mind that resources and pollution, especially CO_2 comes with a price, both societally and economically. The impact on health of air pollution is huge, and brings with it huge costs. The impact of climate change due to CO_2 emissions is also extensive, societally, environmentally, and economically. Resources are not free, and we do pay the price for resources getting scarce. Throughout the world, fossil energy, for instance, is still being heavily subsidized. Therefore, it is important and truthfully transparent to monetize externalities if we want to give sustainability a fair chance and achieve the Global Goals. Including externalities in accounting brings immense positive impact on both the world and sustainable business. The business case of sustainable solutions will improve because of internalizing costs between 8% to 92%.

> ## THE VALUE OF RESOURCE SUBSIDIES GLOBALLY IS ESTIMATED OVER US $1 TRILLION A YEAR
>
> MCKINSEY

Removing subsidies, and pricing current externalities, would accelerate the growth of business solutions to the SDGs beyond any comparison. Long-term orientated businesses, committed to the SDGs, are urging carbon pricing at global conventions, initiatives and policy negotiations. It is fair to say that it is not a matter of if, but when, carbon pricing will happen and subsidies will cease to exist.

There are many influential initiatives pushing the carbon pricing agenda forward, such as the Carbon Pricing Leadership Coalition (CPLC), which was launched to support the Cop 21 Climate Agreement. It aims to shift the social costs of climate change to the source of the pollution, encouraging polluters to reduce emissions and invest in clean energy and low-carbon growth.

The Coalition states that their objective is to "identify indicative corridors of carbon prices which can be used to guide the design of carbon pricing instruments and other climate policies, regulations, and measures to incentivize bold climate action and stimulate learning and innovation to deliver on the ambition of the Paris Agreement and support the achievement of the Sustainable Development Goals."[13]

Our global tax system should reward the social and economic behavior we want, and penalize the behavior we do not want. That applies to taxes relating to resources and pollution, it also applies to corporate income taxes. Thus, the shift to be made in terms of tax is broad and comprehensive. It implies aligning our tax system according to what we need in order to achieve the Goals. A powerful paper from Foresight Economics on corporate tax policy, written by Richard Gower, Emily Benson and Hannah Stoddart called *Aligning Corporate Tax Policy with the Sustainable Development Goals*[14] addresses the relationship between business and taxation. The report "sets out the core design principles for an effective tax system, outlines the key concerns in aligning tax systems with the SDGs, and presents a series of specific recommendations for reform." The report concludes by highlighting several reform ideas. One of the interesting points mentioned in the report is that corporate income taxes contribute 17% of the total tax revenue in developing countries, almost ten times as much as personal income taxes. Furthermore, a large number of countries raise the same amount of taxes on extractive industries (including all processes that extract raw materials for the Earth).

Aligning with the SDGs means a shift in the tax paradigm. Moving away from taxing labor, and moving towards taxing resources and pollution. When you think about it, it is actually strange to tax labor, which is one of the SDGs (SDG 8: Decent Work and Economic Growth), rather than taxing resources and pollution, which is irreversibly harming the world, societies and the SDGs.

Foundations such as Ex'Tax work to advance a transformation in the European tax system. The coniction is that "High taxes on labor encourage businesses to minimize their number of employees. Resources, however, remain untaxed; they are used unrestrained. This system causes unemployment, overconsumption and pollution." Therefore, they are raising awareness and support for establishing or increasing a tax on natural resource and decreasing taxes on labor. This would help to creates incentives to save natural resources, and it would also make services more affordable and boost manpower, craftsmanship and creativity.[15]

For business, there is an urgent need to "begin with the end in mind," to quote Stephen Covey again. But it holds true and should actually be a mantra to the achievement of the SDGs by 2030. Businesses and investors can see what is coming down the road. They can anticipate a tax shift, provide moral leadership by supporting the lobby for it no matter the country they operate in, actively engage in carbon disclosure projects, and use a price on carbon, pollution and resources in their own strategic thinking, budgeting and prioritizing. It will strengthen the future of the business as well as the world we live in.

10.4 THE NEXT GENERATION OF LEADERS: EDUCATING AND SUPPORTING THE MILLENNIALS AND BEYOND

Millennials make up a significant portion of today's target business audience. While the older generation has to adapt, sustainability, and technological savvy for that matter, is in Millennials' DNA.

It is crucial to engage Millennials, as well as the generations that follow, in the discussion of achieving and sustaining the SDGs. Education must be geared around teaching the younger generation how to be new leaders. Schools should teach children about sustainability, and excite and encourage them to be part of the movement towards achieving and sustaining the SDGs. Too much education is lagging behind, teaching "old school" methods of business and management. Millennials and the generations that follow are prime to be the flag bearers of sustainability. They are already interested in sustainability, so let's cherish that and nurture these young future leaders to make the shift that is needed in order to protect their future.

> **MILLENNIALS WILL MAKE UP 75% OF THE US WORKFORCE BY 2025.**[16]
>
> BROOKINGS

It is important that Millennials are part of the movement towards sustainability and are involved with the achievement of the SDGs. As Ahmad Al-hendawi, the UN Secretary-General's Envoy on Youth, said in AIESEC's *YouthSpeak 2016 Global Report*, "Today's generation of youth is the largest in history. We cannot hope to realize the Goals without galvanizing and working with half of the planet's population."[17]

According to the *YouthSpeak Report*, it is becoming increasingly important to engage and involve young people in discussions about the SDGs. The report found that although sustainability is this generation's DNA, only 45% of the respondents knew what the SDGs actually were.

This is a significant failing in getting the message out regarding the SDGs, which is one of the main purposes of this book, and the reason to also make the book available online as open-access. There is a pressing need for people of all ages to be aware of the SDGs and demand SDG solutions as customers, employees and leaders. Millennials tend to consult information sources online, making it all the more possible for the word to spread quickly. The SDG message must therefore be more prevalent in online media.

Despite the fact that over half of the Millennials do not know about the SDGs, according to the annual *2016 Deloitte Millennial Survey – Winning over the Next Generation of Leaders* which interviewed 7,700 Millennials across 29 countries, almost three quarters (73%) of them prefer that the businesses they work for have a positive impact on the wider society, showing an emphasized importance that the businesses they choose to engage with, behave ethically and demonstrate a commitment to helping improve society.[18]

THE MILLENNIALS SUSTAINABILITY GAP

The sustainability gap that persists today in the expectations of Millennials and their perceptions of business include:[19]

- 64% of Millennials believe that business continues to focus on its own agenda at the expense of adequately considering wider society in their decision-making.
- 54% believe that businesses are solely focused on making money, reinforced by 87% of respondents believing that the success of business should be measured in terms of more than just financial performance.

The UN Global Compact report goes on to state, "Millennials are clear that the long-term success of businesses will depend on innovative leaders who offer meaningful work, opportunities for professional development and a good work-life balance."

Millennials are not only interested in ethical businesses but in ethical work relationships. They believe in purpose beyond profit, and demand fair treatment and listening leaders, and for leaders to maintain an environment of trust and integrity. They want their views to be considered by senior management, which should be welcomed by business leaders as an opportunity to cultivate successive leaders that will accelerate change. Millennials are the stewards of change and they will champion the shift for business for good to become the norm, rather than the exception.

WRAP UP

The SDGs navigate us towards a better world. As we are well on our way towards 2030, knowing that we lack the strong progress which is needed, it is crucial to both speed up and scale up if we are to achieve our Goals in time. Leadership is the essence of what is needed for that achievement, and SDG Business Leadership specifically. This implies a responsibility not only for your company, but for society and the environment as well. Besides the business prize that SDG leadership brings, the rewards will come with deep sense of pride. The pride will be felt when solutions are working, and they are scaled up for major impact.

SDG leadership is needed for a more stable, sustainable world. Building trust is a crucial. Business can make a huge contribution and demonstrate that it is possible to improve the world by business. We must make every effort to meet the Goals by 2030. If we do, no doubt, we will be able to say we have created a more stable and fair world. I invite everyone that has read this book to engage, to find a way to be able to demonstrate real SDG leadership and to look forward to feeling that pride, knowing you are contributing to the world we all want. And just know, business for good is good business. No reason, no doubt, no hurdle should prevent you from helping to accelerate our progress towards the Goals. We can, and must, achieve the Sustainable Development Goals. Our future depends on it. ∎

Sources

CHAPTER 1

1. http://www.fao.org/resilience/resources/resources-detail/en/c/346258/
2. https://www.weforum.org/agenda/2017/01/how-much-does-violence-really-cost-our-global-economy/
3. http://www.mckinsey.com/mgi/overview/in-the-news/the-obesity-crisis
4. http://s3.amazonaws.com/aws-bsdc/Valuing-SDG-Food-Ag-Prize-Paper.pdf
5. https://www.unglobalcompact.org/what-is-gc/mission/principles
6. https://unstats.un.org/sdgs/indicators/Official%20List%20of%20Proposed%20SDG%20Indicators.pdf
7. The official list is from the Report of the Inter-Agency and Expert Group on Sustainable Development Goal Indicators (E/CN.3/2016/2/Rev.1), Annex IV includes 230 Indicators on which general agreement has been reached. Please note that the total number of indicators listed in the final indicator proposal is 241. However, since nine indicators repeat under two or three different Targets, the actual total number of individual Indicators in the list is 230.
8. KPIs are measurable values that demonstrate how effective a company is in achieving key business objectives. Organizations use KPIs to evaluate their success while striving to reach their objectives.
9. https://unstats.un.org/sdgs/files/report/2017/TheSustainableDevelopmentGoalsReport2017.pdf
10. https://unstats.un.org/sdgs/indicators/Official%20List%20of%20Proposed%20SDG%20Indicators.pdf
11. http://www.iea.org/publications/freepublications/publication/WEO2017SpecialReport_EnergyAccessOutlook.pdf
12. http://www.un.org/esa/desa/papers/2015/wp141_2015.pdf
13. http://www.stockholmresilience.org/research/research-news/2016-06-14-how-food-connects-all-the-sdgs.html
14. https://www.sdgfund.org/sites/default/files/Report-Universality-and-the-SDGs.pdf
15. http://www.huffingtonpost.ca/mel-wilson/sustainable-development-goals_b_12463124.html
16. https://www.unilever.com/news/news-and-features/2016/Why-the-SDGs-are-the-greatest-growth-opportunity-in-a-generation.html
17. http://sdgcharter.nl/about-us/
18. http://sdgcompass.org/
19. https://www.globalopportunitynetwork.org/the-2017-global-opportunity-report.pdf
20. https://www.oecd.org/std/OECD-Measuring-Distance-to-the%20SDGs-Target-Pilot-Study-web.pdf
21. https://unstats.un.org/sdgs/report/2016/The%20Sustainable%20Development%20Goals%20Report%202016.pdf
22. https://unstats.un.org/sdgs/report/2016/The%20Sustainable%20Development%20Goals%20Report%202016.pdf
23. https://openknowledge.worldbank.org/handle/10986/26306
24. http://www.ikea.com/ms/en_US/this-is-ikea/reports-downloads/index.html
25. https://www.weforum.org/agenda/2016/10/sustainable-development-goals-one-year-on-but-are-we-any-closer/
26. http://www.who.int/mediacentre/news/releases/2017/world-hunger-report/en/
27. http://edgar.jrc.ec.europa.eu/news_docs/jrc-2016-trends-in-global-co2-emissions-2016-report-103425.pdf
28. https://seeingtheworldfromanaeroplanewindow.wordpress.com/2017/01/21/goals-goals-goals/
29. https://sustainabledevelopment.un.org/vnrs/
30. http://sdg.iisd.org/news/vnr-countries-in-special-situations-report-on-sdg-progress/
31. http://online.wsj.com/public/resources/documents/NPC2017_WorkReport_English.pdf
32. https://data.worldbank.org/country/indonesia
33. http://solutions.sustainia.me/solutions/sharing-resources-to-solve-urban-challenges/
34. https://sustainabledevelopment.un.org/newsmedi/index.php?page=view&type=6&nr=184&menu=139
35. http://www.international.gc.ca/prmny-mponu/statements-declarations/2017/07/19b.aspx?lang=eng
36. https://www.usclimatealliance.org/
37. http://www.minsk.diplo.de/contentblob/5063920/Daten/7599981/Deutsche_Nachhaltigkeitsstrategie_by.pdf
38. https://www.norden.org/en/theme/nordic-solutions-to-global-challenges
39. https://wedocs.unep.org/bitstream/handle/20.500.11822/22101/EGR_2017_ES.pdf?sequence=1&isAllowed=y
40. http://www.un.org/sustainabledevelopment/blog/2017/07/pace-of-progress-must-accelerate-to-achieve-the-sdgs-finds-latest-un-progress-report/
41. http://www.duurzamerwerken.nl/media/pdf/VBDO_BB_rapport_LR.pdf
42. http://www.top1000funds.com/analysis/2017/02/01/pggm-apg-lead-dutch-sustainability-push/
43. https://www.arabellaadvisors.com/wp-content/uploads/2016/12/Global_Divestment_Report_2016.pdf
44. https://www.timeshighereducation.com/news/university-fossil-fuel-divestment-total-tips-ps80-billion-globally

CHAPTER 2

1. http://www.pbc.gov.cn/english/130721/3133045/index.html
2. http://newclimateeconomy.report/workingpapers/wp-content/uploads/sites/5/2017/03/NCE2017_ChinaGreenFinance_corrected.pdf
3. http://unepinquiry.org/wp-content/uploads/2016/09/The_Financial_System_We_Need_From_Momentum_to_Transformation.pdf
4. https://www.climatebonds.net/
5. http://newclimateeconomy.report/workingpapers/wp-content/uploads/sites/5/2017/03/NCE2017_ChinaGreenFinance_corrected.pdf
6. https://doi.org/10.1016/J.ENG.2016.04.014
7. http://www.gsi-alliance.org/wp-content/uploads/2017/03/GSIR_Review2016.F.pdf
8. https://www.weforum.org/agenda/2015/11/open-letter-from-ceos-to-world-leaders-urging-climate-action/
9. https://www.oecd.org/dev/development-philanthropy/Green_Economy_note_final_WEB.pdf
10. http://www.un.org/africarenewal/magazine/august-november-2017/private-sector%E2%80%99s-role-implementing-sdgs
11. https://www.gsma.com/betterfuture/wp-content/uploads/2016/09/_UN_SDG_Report_FULL_R1_WEB_Singles_LOW.pdf
12. https://www.gsma.com/betterfuture/wp-content/uploads/2016/09/_UN_SDG_Report_FULL_R1_WEB_Singles_LOW.pdf
13. https://www.wired.com/2017/06/even-without-paris-business-will-leave-trump-behind-climate-change/
14. http://unctad.org/en/pages/PressRelease.aspx?OriginalVersionID=194
15. https://www.mckinsey.com/global-themes/employment-and-growth/how-advancing-womens-equality-can-add-12-trillion-to-global-growth
16. https://iwpr.org/wp-content/uploads/2017/09/C459_9.11.17_Gender-Wage-Gap-2016-data-update.pdf
17. https://www.forumforthefuture.org/project/net-positive-project/overview
18. https://www.ihrb.org/pdf/state-of-play/Business-and-the-SDGs.pdf
19. http://www.hbs.edu/faculty/Publication%20Files/2011-0609_FSG_Creating_Shared_Value_20859152-c051-44dd-a2c0-761abf6bc2d1.pdf
20. http://www.hbs.edu/faculty/Pages/item.aspx?num=46924
21. http://www.nestle.com/csv/case-studies
22. https://sharedvalue.org/groups/unexpected-market-potential-sdgs

23. https://www.iisd.org/business/issues/sr.aspx
24. https://www.huffingtonpost.com/entry/csv-and-the-sdgs-creating-shared-value-meets-the_us_58eb9ceae4b0acd784ca5a63
25. http://sharedvalue.org/about-shared-value
26. https://hbr.org/2015/01/the-truth-about-csr
27. http://sharedvalue.org/about-initiative
28. https://www.clintonfoundation.org/clinton-global-initiative/commitments/establishment-shared-value-initiative
29. https://ncg.org/sites/default/files/resources/HarvardBusinessReview_Creating_Shared_Value.pdf
30. https://www.unglobalcompact.org/docs/issues_doc/development/SDGMatrix-ConsumerGoods.pdf
31. http://blog.euromonitor.com/2015/09/top-5-emerging-markets-with-the-best-middle-class-potential.html
32. http://www.hbs.edu/faculty/Publication%20Files/20130523%20-%20FSG%20Shared%20Value%20Leadership%20Summit%20-%20MEP%20Keynote%20-%20FINAL%20FINAL_d18ef7ea-e736-4da0-b3b4-e9eac61b87a8.pdf
33. https://www.unglobalcompact.org/library/3111
34. https://sustainabledevelopment.un.org/content/documents/9789CRT046599%20SDG_Financial%20Services_29sep_WEB-1.pdf
35. http://unctad.org/en/PublicationsLibrary/wir2017_en.pdf
36. https://nextbillion.net/closing-the-2-5-trillion-gap-how-blended-finance-can-help-achieve-the-sdgs/
37. https://www.mckinsey.com/mgi/our-research
38. http://www.grundfos.com/cases/find-case/water-atms-offer-low-priced-water-to-nairobis-poorest-residents.html
39. http://businesscommission.org/news/sustainable-african-businesses-can-help-unlock-us-1-trillion-in-new-market-value-in-africa-and-us-12-trillion-globally
40. http://report.businesscommission.org/report
41. http://businesscommission.org/our-work/valuing-the-sdg-prize-unlocking-business-opportunities-to-accelerate-sustainable-and-inclusive-growth
42. http://breakthrough.unglobalcompact.org/briefs/taking-sustainability-exponential-john-elkington-volans/
43. http://www.eco-business.com/news/game-changing-business-models-for-green-buildings/
44. https://hbr.org/2016/07/the-fastest-growing-cause-for-shareholders-is-sustainability
45. http://volans.com/wp-content/uploads/2016/02/the-breakthrough-forecast-market-sweet-spots-2016-2015.pdf
46. http://allafrica.com/stories/201602170661.html
47. https://www.accenture.com/_acnmedia/PDF-4/Accenture-Strategy-Corporate-Disruptors.pdf
48. http://www.sustainablebrands.com/digital_learning/tool/organizational_change/sdgs_mean_business_how_credible_standards_can_help_compa
49. https://www.businesswire.com/news/home/20160511005885/en/NIKE-Sets-Bold-Vision-Targets-2020
50. https://s3.amazonaws.com/nikeinc/assets/56158/NIKE_FY14-15_CEO_letter.pdf
51. https://www.weforum.org/agenda/2016/10/corporations-not-countries-dominate-the-list-of-the-world-s-biggest-economic-entities/
52. http://mamaope.skyapps.tech/
53. http://www.accaglobal.com/content/dam/acca/global/PDF-technical/small-business/pol-tp-esis-v1.pdf

CHAPTER 3

1. https://www.ericsson.com/assets/local/news/2016/05/ict-sdg.pdf
2. http://www.worldbank.org/en/programs/globalfindex
3. http://www.itu.int/en/sustainable-world/Pages/goal1.aspx
4. http://unctad.org/meetings/es/Presentation/cstd2016_p06_DoreenBogdan_ITU_en.pdf
5. http://unctad.org/meetings/es/Presentation/cstd2016_p06_DoreenBogdan_ITU_en.pdf
6. https://www.standardmedia.co.ke/m/?articleID=2000195647&story_title=number-of-dar-phone-subscribers-jumps-by-25-percent
7. http://www.globalopportunitynetwork.org/report-2017/
8. http://www.itu.int/en/sustainable-world/Documents/Fast-forward_progress_report_414709%20FINAL.pdf
9. http://documents.worldbank.org/curated/en/961621467994698644/pdf/102724-WDR-WDR2016Overview-ENGLISH-WebResBox-394840B-OUO-9.pdf
10. http://www3.weforum.org/docs/WEF_GAC15_Technological_Tipping_Points_report_2015.pdf
11. http://unctad.org/meetings/es/Presentation/cstd2016_p06_DoreenBogdan_ITU_en.pdf
12. https://www.economist.com/blogs/economist-explains/2013/05/economist-explains-18
13. http://www.itu.int/en/sustainable-world/Documents/Fast-forward_progress_report_414709%20FINAL.pdf
14. http://sdg.iisd.org/news/city-initiatives-contribute-to-sdg-11/
15. http://breakthrough.unglobalcompact.org/disruptive-technologies/additive-manufacturing/
16. https://yeti.co/blog/how-will-the-internet-of-things-create-a-more-sustainable-world/
17. http://www.itu.int/en/sustainable-world/Documents/Fast-forward_progress_report_414709%20FINAL.pdf
18. http://unctad.org/meetings/es/Presentation/cstd2016_p06_DoreenBogdan_ITU_en.pdf
19. http://www.itu.int/en/sustainable-world/Documents/Fast-forward_progress_report_414709%20FINAL.pdf
20. https://www.naturalcapitalproject.org/
21. http://www3.weforum.org/docs/WEF_GAC15_Technological_Tipping_Points_report_2015.pdf
22. http://reliefweb.int/sites/reliefweb.int/files/resources/NetHope_SDG_ICT_Playbook_Final.pdf?utm_content=buffer91173
23. http://www.itu.int/en/sustainable-world/Pages/goal4.aspx
24. https://www.ushahidi.com/features
25. https://www.nafham.com
26. http://www.nokia.com/en_int/about-us/sustainability/our-approach/the-un-sustainable-development-goals-and-nokia
27. https://www.ericsson.com/res/docs/2015/ict-and-sdg-interim-report.pdf
28. http://www.itu.int/en/ITU-D/Statistics/Documents/facts/ICTFactsFigures2017.pdf
29. https://www.ericsson.com/res/docs/2015/ict-and-sdg-interim-report.pdf
30. http://www3.weforum.org/docs/WEF_GAC15_Technological_Tipping_Points_report_2015.pdf
31. https://www.weforum.org/agenda/2016/01/the-fourth-industrial-revolution-what-it-means-and-how-to-respond
32. https://www.weforum.org/about/the-fourth-industrial-revolution-by-klaus-schwab
33. https://www.theguardian.com/technology/2017/jul/17/elon-musk-regulation-ai-combat-existential-threat-tesla-spacex-ceo
34. https://www.ericsson.com/assets/local/news/2016/05/ict-sdg.pdf
35. https://www.statista.com/statistics/330695/number-of-smartphone-users-worldwide/
36. https://www.statista.com/statistics/274774/forecast-of-mobile-phone-users-worldwide/
37. http://www.gsma.com/betterfuture/wp-content/uploads/2016/11/UN_SDG_ExecSumm_v03_WEB_Singles.pdf
38. http://searchengineland.com/88-consumers-trust-online-reviews-much-

personal-recommendations-195803

39. http://s3.amazonaws.com/aws-bsdc/Valuing-the-SDG-Prize.pdf
40. http://s3.amazonaws.com/aws-bsdc/Valuing-the-SDG-Prize.pdf
41. https://www.weforum.org/agenda/2016/08/why-data-is-key-to-business-action-on-the-sdgs/
42. http://www.irena.org/DocumentDownloads/Publications/IRENA_PST_Smart_Grids_CBA_Guide_2015.pdf
43. https://www.reuters.com/finance/stocks/companyProfile?symbol=KT
44. http://www.appcessories.co.uk/internet-of-things-stop-climate-change/
45. https://www.pnnl.gov/news/release.aspx?id=776
46. http://www.ab3dlabs.com
47. https://www.statista.com/statistics/261693/3d-printing-market-value-forecast/
48. https://3dprint.com/166978/mit-cellulose-3d-printing/
49. https://3dfoodprintingconference.com/
50. http://silven.co.uk/blogging/3d-printing-future-food-manufacturing/
51. http://wildfiretoday.com/2015/12/11/firefighting-robots/
52. http://www.mills-peninsula.org/robotic/procedures/robotic-procedure-list.html
53. http://breakthrough.unglobalcompact.org/disruptive-technologies/next-generation-robotics/
54. https://www.engadget.com/2017/05/17/google-launched-a-massive-open-ai-division/
55. http://breakthrough.unglobalcompact.org/site/assets/files/1630/hhw-16-0028-d_d_autonomous_road_vehicles.pdf
56. https://www.wamda.com/2012/11/the-future-of-green-technology-what-innovations-are-on-the-horizon
57. https://futurism.com/images/7-benefits-of-driverless-cars/
58. https://www.nrel.gov/docs/fy13osti/59210.pdf
59. https://www.fueleconomy.gov/feg/driveHabits.jsp
60. http://www.businessinsider.com/how-tesla-driverless-cars-see-world-2016-11/#lets-start-with-the-basics-like-before-the-car-comes-with-a-virtual-drivers-instrument-that-shows-where-the-car-is-in-relation-to-its-lane-the-car-also-comes-with-a-massive-17-inch-display-that-shows-a-map-of-where-the-car-is-in-relation-to-its-surroundings-2
61. https://www.ericsson.com/thecompany/sustainability_corporateresponsibility/technology-for-good-blog/2016/05/30/driverless-buses-mobility-as-a-service-future-transportation/
62. https://www.dbschenker.com/global/networked-trucks--db-schenker-and-man-intensify-their-partnership-for-autonomous-driving-8154
63. http://breakthrough.unglobalcompact.org/site/assets/files/1630/hhw-16-0028-d_d_autonomous_road_vehicles.pdf
64. http://breakthrough.unglobalcompact.org/site/assets/files/1630/hhw-16-0028-d_d_autonomous_road_vehicles.pdf
65. https://drones.fsd.ch/en/case-study-no-9-using-drone-imagery-for-real-time-information-after-typhoon-haiyan-in-the-philippines/
66. http://drones.fsd.ch/wp-content/uploads/2016/11/Drones-in-Humanitarian-Action.pdf
67. http://drones.fsd.ch/en/drones-in-humanitarian-action/
68. https://www.bloomberg.com/news/articles/2017-05-18/amazon-s-delivery-drone-research-focuses-on-avoiding-birds
69. http://www.businessinsider.com/cost-savings-from-amazon-drone-deliveries-2016-6
70. http://datasmart.ash.harvard.edu/news/article/how-smart-city-barcelona-brought-the-internet-of-things-to-life-789
71. https://www.ericsson.com/res/docs/2015/ict-and-sdg-interim-report.pdf
72. https://yeti.co/blog/how-will-the-internet-of-things-create-a-more-sustainable-world/
73. https://www.mckinsey.com/business-functions/digital-mckinsey/our-insights/the-internet-of-things-the-value-of-digitizing-the-physical-world
74. https://www.mckinsey.com/business-functions/digital-mckinsey/our-insights/the-internet-of-things-the-value-of-digitizing-the-physical-world
75. http://www.worldbank.org/en/news/press-release/2016/04/13/remittances-to-developing-countries-edge-up-slightly-in-2015
76. https://www.thomsonreuters.com/en/press-releases/2016/may/thomson-reuters-2016-know-your-customer-surveys.html
77. https://commons.wikimedia.org/wiki/File:Blockchain_workflow.png
78. http://blogs.worldbank.org/ic4d/world-citizen-transforming-statelessness-global-citizenship
79. https://www.cbinsights.com/research/industries-disrupted-blockchain/
80. https://guardtime.com/
81. https://www.remme.io/
82. https://www.neuways.com/neutech/cyber-security-market-to-reach-231-9-billion-by-2022/

CHAPTER 4

1. http://siteresources.worldbank.org/DEVCOMMINT/Documentation/23659446/DC2015-0002(E)FinancingforDevelopment.pdf
2. http://report.businesscommission.org/uploads/BetterBiz-BetterWorld_170215_012417.pdf
3. http://unctad.org/en/PublicationsLibrary/wir2014_en.pdf
4. http://www.undp.org/content/undp/en/home/blog/2017/7/13/What-kind-of-blender-do-we-need-to-finance-the-SDGs-.html
5. https://www.huffingtonpost.com/paul-polman/why-businesses-must-adapt_b_12132996.html
6. http://www.oecd-ilibrary.org/development/development-co-operation-report-2017_dcr-2017-en
7. https://medium.com/project-breakthrough/reorienting-financial-flows-the-12-trillion-question-7679257c2fcd
8. https://www.unpri.org/about
9. https://www.unpri.org/about/sustainable-development-goals
10. https://www.oecd.org/dac/financing-sustainable-development/development-finance-topics/Infographic%20-%20The%20Private%20Sector%20-%20Missing%20Piece%20of%20the%20SDG%20puzzle.pdf
11. https://www.rockefellerfoundation.org/blog/democratizing-finance-sustainable-development-goals/
12. https://www.huffingtonpost.com/paul-polman/why-businesses-must-adapt_b_12132996.html
13. http://www.marriott.com/MarriottInternational/CorporateResponsability/Performance_New_2016/SPG_PDFs/CDP-SP500-climate-report-2014.pdf
14. https://globalwarmingisreal.com/2014/06/26/acting-combat-climate-change-cost-benefit-analysis/
15. http://pubdocs.worldbank.org/en/943071489679764736/UAEU-Presentation.pdf
16. http://www.civicus.org/images/Summary.BusinessAndCivilSociety.pdf
17. https://www.brookings.edu/wp-content/uploads/2016/09/global_20160919_sustainable_finance.pdf
18. https://www.brookings.edu/wp-content/uploads/2016/09/global_20160919_sustainable_finance.pdf
19. http://www.worldbank.org/en/topic/smefinance
20. https://www.rockefellerfoundation.org/blog/democratizing-finance-sustainable-development-goals/
21. http://pubdocs.worldbank.org/en/394231501877501769/The-Sustainable-Development-Goals-and-Private-Sector-Opportunities.pdf
22. http://www.worldbank.org/en/topic/financialsector/brief/smes-finance
23. https://www.brookings.edu/wp-content/uploads/2016/09/global_20160919_sustainable_finance.pdf
24. http://www3.weforum.org/docs/WEF_Blended_Finance_A_Primer_Development_Finance_Philanthropic_Funders_report_2015.pdf
25. http://impactalpha.com/sizing-up-blended-finance-a-guide-to-a-new-financing-approach-to-fuel-sustainable-development/

26. https://nextbillion.net/closing-the-2-5-trillion-gap-how-blended-finance-can-help-achieve-the-sdgs/
27. http://s3.amazonaws.com/aws-bsdc/Blended-Finance-Overview_October-2017_final.pdf
28. http://www.un.org/esa/ffd/wp-content/uploads/2015/08/AAAA_Outcome.pdf
29. www.sdgfund.org
30. http://www.un.org/esa/ffd/ffd3/wp-content/uploads/sites/2/2015/07/DESA-Briefing-Note-Addis-Action-Agenda.pdf
31. http://sdg.iisd.org/news/unga-launches-global-conversation-on-financing-sdgs/
32. https://www.brookings.edu/wp-content/uploads/2016/09/global_20160919_sustainable_finance.pdf
33. http://sdg.iisd.org/news/unga-launches-global-conversation-on-financing-sdgs/
34. http://report.businesscommission.org/uploads/BetterBiz-BetterWorld_170215_012417.pdf
35. https://www.investopedia.com/terms/e/environmental-social-and-governance-esg-criteria.asp
36. https://www.duurzaam-beleggen.nl/2017/10/23/nearly-75-investment-professionals-worldwide-take-esg-factors-into-consideration-the-investment-process/
37. https://www.ncdc.noaa.gov/billions/events/US/2017
38. http://www.fao.org/3/a-i5128e.pdf
39. http://www.worldbank.org/en/news/press-release/2016/11/14/natural-disasters-force-26-million-people-into-poverty-and-cost-520bn-in-losses-every-year-new-world-bank-analysis-finds
40. https://thegiin.org/impact-investing/need-to-know/
41. https://thegiin.org/assets/GIIN_AnnualImpactInvestorSurvey_2017_Web_Final.pdf
42. http://www.undp.org/content/sdfinance/en/home/solutions/impact-investment.html
43. http://www.worldbank.org/en/topic/poverty/overview
44. https://www.cgap.org/sites/default/files/Working-Paper-Achieving-Sustainable-Development-Goals-Apr-2016.pdf
45. http://www.people.hbs.edu/nashraf/FemaleEmpowerment_WorldDev.pdf
46. http://unsdsn.org/wp-content/uploads/2015/09/151112-SDG-Financing-Needs.pdf
47. https://www.cgap.org/sites/default/files/Working-Paper-Achieving-Sustainable-Development-Goals-Apr-2016.pdf
48. http://unsdsn.org/wp-content/uploads/2015/09/151112-SDG-Financing-Needs.pdf
49. https://www.iisd.org/sites/default/files/publications/ending-hunger-what-would-it-cost.pdf
50. https://academic.oup.com/qje/article-abstract/129/2/597/1867065?redirectedFrom=fulltext
51. http://www.who.int/mediacentre/news/releases/2017/cost-health-targets/en/
52. https://www.ubs.com/global/en/wealth-management/chief-investment-office/features/un-sustainable-development-goals.html
53. https://www.cgap.org/sites/default/files/Working-Paper-Achieving-Sustainable-Development-Goals-Apr-2016.pdf
54. https://londoneconomics.co.uk/wp-content/uploads/2011/09/82-Study-on-the-returns-to-various-types-of-investment-in-education-and-training.pdf
55. http://unctad.org/en/PublicationChapters/wir2014ch4_en.pdf
56. http://www.ey.com/Publication/vwLUAssets/ey-women-investors-in-wealth-management/$File/ey-women-investors-in-wealth-management.pdf
57. http://www.catalyst.org/system/files/The_Bottom_Line_Corporate_Performance_and_Womens_Representation_on_Boards.pdf
58. https://www.pwc.com/gx/en/sustainability/publications/PwC-sdg-guide.pdf
59. https://www.globalwaters.org/WASH-FIN
60. https://www.oecd.org/tax/exchange-of-tax-information/implementation-handbook-standard-for-automatic-exchange-of-financial-information-in-tax-matters.pdf
61. http://www.iea.org/newsroom/news/2016/november/world-energy-outlook-2016.html
62. https://www.pwc.com/gx/en/sustainability/publications/PwC-sdg-guide.pdf
63. http://www.worldbank.org/en/topic/energy/brief/sustainable-development-goal-on-energy-sdg7-and-the-world-bank-group
64. http://www.sifem.ch/fileadmin/user_upload/sifem/pdf/en/Reports/Annual_Report_2016_EN.PDF
65. https://sustainabledevelopment.un.org/content/documents/11795Thematic%20discussion%209%20concept%20note.pdf
66. https://www.pggm.nl/english/who-we-are/press/Pages/Legal-and-General-and-PGGM-announce-3000-new-homes-with-%C2%A3600M-build-to-rent-partnership.aspx
67. https://www.unpri.org/download_report/24142
68. http://www.sdgfund.org/goal-12-responsible-consumption-production
69. http://sdg.iisd.org/commentary/guest-articles/2017-a-year-for-ocean-conservation-decisions-action-and-accountability-because-the-ocean-is-everybodys-business/
70. http://sdg.iisd.org/news/multilateral-programmes-focus-on-integrated-governance-of-land-based-capital/
71. http://www.thegef.org/news/two-multi-million-dollar-gef-projects-will-deliver-multiple-environmental-and-human-benefits
72. https://www.dnvgl.com/technology-innovation/spaceship-earth/peace-and-justice.html
73. http://www.sdgfund.org/sites/default/files/Report_Business_And_SDG16.pdf
74. https://www.dnvgl.com/technology-innovation/spaceship-earth/peace-and-justice.html
75. http://www.businessinsider.com/private-equity-raising-new-funds-with-long-term-horizons-2016-10
76. https://news.impactalpha.com/growth-market-private-equity-investors-look-to-2030-global-goals-for-direction-10c3c23235fe
77. https://www.mckinsey.com/industries/private-equity-and-principal-investors/our-insights/from-why-to-why-not-sustainable-investing-as-the-new-normal?cid=other-eml-alt-mip-mck-oth-1710
78. https://www.trucost.com/publication/universal-ownership-environmental-externalities-matter-institutional-investors-full-report/
79. http://www.wipo.int/wipo_magazine/en/2016/01/article_0002.html
80. https://www.alger.com/AlgerDocuments/Alger_ESG_Morningstar_Reprint_2.pdf
81. https://www.unpri.org/download_report/42251
82. http://video.morningstar.com/ca/170717_SustainableInvesting.pdf
83. https://share.ca/wp-content/uploads/2017/03/Xander-den-Uyl_PRI.pdf
84. https://www.mckinsey.com/industries/private-equity-and-principal-investors/our-insights/from-why-to-why-not-sustainable-investing-as-the-new-normal
85. https://www.top1000funds.com/analysis/2017/08/17/dutch-pension-funds-embrace-un-goals/
86. http://www.reuters.com/article/us-japan-gpif-esg/japans-gpif-expects-to-raise-esg-allocations-to-10-percent-ftse-russell-ceo-idUSKBN19Z11Y?il=0
87. http://impactalpha.com/former-world-bank-officials-launch-blueorange-for-sdg-investing-in-latin-america/
88. https://www.mckinsey.com/industries/private-equity-and-principal-investors/our-insights/look-out-below-why-returns-are-headed-lower-and-what-to-do-about-it
89. https://csis-prod.s3.amazonaws.com/s3fs-public/legacy_files/files/publication/160111_Michel_BeyondAid_Web.pdf
90. https://www.theguardian.com/global-development-professionals-network/2016/jan/26/eight-ideas-how-fund-sdgs-sustainable-development
91. http://www.un.org/sustainabledevelopment/blog/2017/02/banks-un-set-standards-on-channelling-investments-for-sustainable-development/
92. https://thegiin.org/assets/GIIN_AnnualImpactInvestorSurvey_2017_Web_Final.pdf
93. https://thegiin.org/assets/GIIN_AnnualImpactInvestorSurvey_2017_Web_Final.pdf
94. http://www.un.org/sustainabledevelopment/blog/2017/02/banks-un-set-

standards-on-channelling-investments-for-sustainable-development/

95. https://www.weforum.org/agenda/2016/08/why-data-is-key-to-business-action-on-the-sdgs/

96. https://www.standardlifeinvestments.com/WP_Impact_Investing.pdf

97. https://www.credit-suisse.com/media/assets/corporate/docs/about-us/responsibility/banking/sdg-stakeholder-workshop-report-public.pdf

98. http://www.un.org/sustainabledevelopment/blog/2017/02/banks-un-set-standards-on-channelling-investments-for-sustainable-development/

99. http://econ.lse.ac.uk/staff/rburgess/wp/aer.pdf

100. https://www.poverty-action.org/sites/default/files/publications/Banking%20the%20Poor%20via%20Savings%20Accounts.pdf

101. http://web.stanford.edu/~pdupas/SavingsConstraints.pdf

102. http://www.citigroup.com/citi/about/citizenship/download/Banking-on-2030-Citi-and-the-SDGs-Report.pdf?ieNocache=158

103. https://www.unglobalcompact.org/docs/publications/Private_Sector_Investment_and_Sustainable_Development.pdf

104. http://www.financeforthefuture.com/ClimateQEforParee.pdf

105. http://positivemoney.org/2017/04/sdg/

106. https://events.iadb.org/calendar/eventDetail.aspx?lang=es&id=5321

107. http://greenbanknetwork.org/portfolio/accelerating-green-infrastructure-financing-outline-proposals-for-uk-green-bonds-and-infrastructure-bank-2/

108. https://www.moodys.com/research/Moodys-Sustainable-investing-an-opportunity-for-asset-managers-to-generate--PR_356142

109. https://www.ipe.com/news/esg/major-european-pension-investors-commit-to-un-development-goals/10015051.fullarticle

110. http://www.univestcompany.com/about-us/introduction

111. http://impactalpha.com/sustainable-development-goals-take-hold-as-a-universal-impact-investment-framework/

112. https://www.mckinsey.com/industries/private-equity-and-principal-investors/our-insights/from-why-to-why-not-sustainable-investing-as-the-new-normal?cid=other-eml-alt-mip-mck-oth-1710

113. https://www.top1000funds.com/analysis/2017/02/01/pggm-apg-lead-dutch-sustainability-push/

114. https://www.institutionalinvestor.com/article/b14z9xw6s0h9hn/uns-new-sdgs-are-driving-the-global-development-agenda

115. http://www.un.org/pga/71/2017/04/18/opening-of-sdg-financing-lab/

116. http://www.forbes.com/sites/morganstanley/2016/12/19/new-growth-sprouts-for-green-bonds/#1cb96e3a46a6

117. http://sdg.iisd.org/news/climate-finance-update-major-emerging-market-green-bond-fund-launched/

118. https://www.txfnews.com/Tracker/Details/68676dcf-8780-4bd3-96e7-cfb15d052ae1/Orsted-issues-1-25bn-in-green-bonds-and-securities

119. https://www.climatebonds.net/2017/03/green-bond-pioneer-awards-2017-leadership-green-finance-glittering-event-london%E2%80%99s-guildhall

120. www.impact-investing.eu/download/163/eiil-sustainable-development-bonds-a4-final.pdf

121. http://sdg.iisd.org/news/stock-exchanges-highlight-role-in-promoting-sdgs/

122. http://unctad.org/en/Pages/DIAE/SSE-Initiative.aspx

123. http://unctad.org/en/Pages/DIAE/SSE-Initiative.aspx

124. http://www.sseinitiative.org/wp-content/uploads/2017/11/SSE-Green-Finance-Guidance-.pdf

125. https://wbgeconsult2.worldbank.org/wbgect/download?uuid=6bf254f8-e8c1-438a-b9fb-349cd79b5f56

126. https://www.pwc.com/gx/en/sustainability/publications/assets/pe-survey-report.pdf

127. http://www.ifcamc.org/portfolio

128. https://www.fastcompany.com/40426561/the-philanthropy-world-is-embracing-impact-investing

129. https://www.fordfoundation.org/ideas/equals-change-blog/posts/unleashing-the-power-of-endowments-the-next-great-challenge-for-philanthropy/

130. http://www.earthcp.com/sustainability/earth-dividend-tm

131. http://www.wearesalt.org/capital-for-good-the-corporate-venture-capital-solution/

132. http://www.infodev.org/infodev-files/infodev_crowdfunding_study_0.pdf

133. https://www.cgap.org/sites/default/files/Working-Paper-Achieving-Sustainable-Development-Goals-Apr-2016.pdf

134. https://www.theguardian.com/global-development/2016/sep/13/crowdfunding-development-aid-funds-globalgiving-kickstarter

135. https://www.oecd.org/dac/financing-sustainable-development/Addis%20flyer%20-%20PHILANTHROPY.pdf

136. https://sustainabledevelopment.un.org/partnerships/SDGphilanthropy

137. https://www.standardlifeinvestments.com/WP_Impact_Investing.pdf

138. https://sustainabledevelopment.un.org/index.php?page=view&type=400&nr=2017&menu=35

139. https://www.businesscalltoaction.org/news/how-data-promotes-transparency-and-helps-clean-sdg-washing

140. https://www.aircraftit.com/Uploads/eJournal/Operations/PDF/790f2a89b692418.pdf

141. http://www.ussif.org/files/Publications/GSIA_Review2016.pdf

142. https://www.robeco.com/en/insights/2016/10/sustainable-development-goals-an-opportunity-for-investors.html

143. https://sustainabledevelopment.un.org/content/documents/9789CRT046599%20SDG_Financial%20Services_29sep_WEB-1.pdf

144. http://onlinelibrary.wiley.com/doi/10.1002/smj.2410/full

145. https://www.nnip.com/UA_en/institutional/Expert-views/MindScope/view/Investing-in-the-United-Nations-Sustainable-Development-Goals.htm

146. http://www.accaglobal.com/content/dam/ACCA_Global/Technical/sus/pi-sdgs-accountancy-profession.pdf

147. https://www.journalofaccountancy.com/newsletters/2017/mar/young-cpas-help-save-world.html

148. http://businesscommission.org/our-work/papers-on-mapping-the-sdgs-corporate-taxes-and-business-accountability

149. https://theconversation.com/big-accounting-firms-taking-the-lead-on-sustainable-development-35261

150. https://home.kpmg.com/content/dam/kpmg/ae/pdf/introduction-kpmg-truevalue.pdf

151. https://drcaroladams.net/accountants-taking-a-lead-on-sustainable-development

152. http://businesscommission.org/news/release-sustainable-business-can-unlock-at-least-us-12-trillion-in-new-market-value-and-repair-economic-system

153. http://report.businesscommission.org/report

154. https://www.weforum.org/agenda/2015/07/how-much-would-it-cost-to-end-hunger/

155. http://unctad.org/en/PublicationChapters/wir2014ch4_en.pdf

156. http://apps.who.int/iris/bitstream/10665/254999/1/9789241512190-eng.pdf

157. http://www.un.org/sustainabledevelopment/blog/2016/01/global-investors-mobilize-action-in-wake-of-paris-climate-agreement/

158. https://www.pwc.com/gx/en/sustainability/publications/PwC-sdg-guide.pdf

159. https://www.calvert.com/includes/loadDocument.php?embed&fn=24532.pdf&dt=fundPDFs

160. https://news.impactalpha.com/growth-market-private-equity-investors-look-to-2030-global-goals-for-direction-10c3c23235fe

161. https://shareaction.org/press-release/investors-can-play-a-central-role-in-achieving-the-sustainable-development-goals/

162. http://www.hbs.edu/faculty/Publication%20Files/20121003%20-%20HSM%20World%20Business%20Forum%20-%20For%20Distribution%20-%20FINAL_94a553d8-ca43-4ad0-bd2b-72b5a5995548.pdf

163. http://www.un.org/apps/news/story.asp?NewsID=56075#.WjfKv0trwcg

164. http://newsroom.unfccc.int/unfccc-newsroom/financial-institutions-set-standards-for-financing-sustainable-development/

165. https://www.ipe.com/news/esg/major-european-pension-investors-commit-to-un-development-goals/10015051.fullarticle

166. http://unctad.org/en/Pages/DIAE/SSE-Initiative.aspx
167. http://www.earthcp.com/sustainability/earth-dividend-tm
168. https://uk.standardlifeinvestments.com/ifa/dynamic/article-details-editorials. html?path=shared-sli/editorials/impact_investing
169. https://www.nnip.com/Default-Display-on/Investing-in-the-United-Nations-Sustainable-Development-Goals.htm

CHAPTER 5

1. http://www.ipcc.ch/pdf/assessment-report/ar5/wg3/ipcc_wg3_ar5_full.pdf
2. The Intergovernmental Panel on Climate Change (IPCC) estimates that in 2010, urban areas accounted for 67–76% of global energy use and 71–76% of global CO2 emissions from final energy use.
3. http://www.un.org/en/development/desa/news/population/world-urbanization-prospects-2014.html
4. http://siteresources.worldbank.org/INTUWM/Resources/340232-1205330656272/CitiesandClimateChange.pdf
5. http://newclimateeconomy.report/2014/wp-content/uploads/sites/2/2014/08/NCE-cities-web.pdf
6. https://sustainabledevelopment.un.org/sdg11
7. http://unsdsn.org/wp-content/uploads/2016/07/9.1.8.-Cities-SDG-Guide.pdf
8. https://www.un.org/press/en/2017/dsgsm1080.doc.htm
9. https://sustainabledevelopment.un.org/sdg11
10. https://www.theguardian.com/sustainable-business/tackling-climate-change-copenhagen-sustainable-city-design
11. http://s-media.nyc.gov/agencies/sirr/SIRR_singles_Lo_res.pdf
12. http://www.c40.org/blog_posts/c40-mayors-support-an-urban-sustainable-development-goal
13. https://www.compactofmayors.org/
14. http://s3.amazonaws.com/aws-bsdc/BSDC-Valuing-the-SDG-Prize-Cities.pdf
15. http://newclimateeconomy.report/2014/wp-content/uploads/sites/2/2014/08/NCE-cities-web.pdf
16. https://sustainabledevelopment.un.org/content/documents/2948chairsummaryside2.pdf
17. http://unsdsn.org/wp-content/uploads/2016/07/9.1.8.-Cities-SDG-Guide.pdf
18. http://www.c40.org/case_studies/c40-good-practice-guides-johannesburg-green-bond
19. https://www.futurereadysingapore.com/2017/how-government-and-business-can-work-together-to-build-better-cities.html
20. http://www.eco-business.com/news/how-government-and-business-can-work-together-to-build-better-cities/
21. https://www.bca.gov.sg/GreenMark/green_mark_buildings.html
22. https://www.futurereadysingapore.com/2017/how-government-and-business-can-work-together-to-build-better-cities.html
23. https://www.greenbiz.com/article/what-city-sdgs-depend-answer
24. https://www.urban.org/urban-wire/financially-insecure-residents-can-cost-cities-millions
25. Peri-urban refers to agriculture practices within and around cities, which compete for resources (land, water, energy, labor) that could also serve other purposes to satisfy the requirements of the urban population.
26. http://solutions.sustainia.me/solutions/urban-voids-become-community-gardens/
27. https://www.greenbiz.com/article/reducing-food-waste-reduce-ghg-emissions-and-hunger
28. http://www.who.int/healthpromotion/conferences/9gchp/policy-brief1-healthy-cities.pdf?ua=1
29. https://www.oecd.org/pisa/pisaproducts/pisainfocus/pisa%20in%20focus%20n28%20(esp)-Final.pdf
30. http://www.buildup.eu/en/news/overview-school-buildings-leading-examples-energy-efficient-renovation-0
31. http://uil.unesco.org/lifelong-learning/learning-cities
32. http://oecdeducationtoday.blogspot.nl/2013/05/the-urban-advantage-in-education.html
33. file:///var/folders/sk/3hgdygl15wd85yhc82r2wjx80000gp/T/com.apple.Preview/com.apple.Preview.PasteboardItems/the_sdgs_what_localgov_need_to_know_0%20(dragged).pdf
34. https://www.routledge.com/Building-Inclusive-Cities-Womens-Safety-and-the-Right-to-the-City/Whitzman-Legacy-Andrew-Klodawsky-Shaw-Viswanath/p/book/9780415628167
35. https://www.devex.com/news/time-to-connect-the-dots-on-urbanization-and-women-and-girls-88958
36. https://di.dk/SiteCollectionDocuments/DIBD/BOP-Learning%20Lab/The%20Global%20Goals%20and%20opportunities%20for%20business_WEB.pdf
37. https://www.solidarites.org/wp-content/uploads/2017/05/solidarites_2017_barometre-eau_anglais_web.pdf
38. https://www.iied.org/connecting-settlements-cities-basins-realising-sdg-6-scale
39. https://www.uclg.org/sites/default/files/the_sdgs_what_localgov_need_to_know_0.pdf
40. http://pubdocs.worldbank.org/en/589771503512867370/Citywide-Inclusive-Sanitation.pdf
41. http://www.who.int/healthpromotion/conferences/9gchp/policy-brief1-healthy-cities.pdf?ua=1
42. https://www.uclg.org/sites/default/files/the_sdgs_what_localgov_need_to_know_0.pdf
43. https://blogs.wsj.com/experts/2016/04/29/why-cities-are-so-well-suited-to-renewable-energy-growth/
44. https://www.unglobalcompact.org/docs/publications/Global_Opportunity_Report_2017_SM.pdf
45. https://blogs.wsj.com/briefly/2016/07/14/the-future-of-cities-green-building-to-driverless-cars-at-a-glance/
46. http://www.irena.org/DocumentDownloads/Publications/IRENA_Renewable_Energy_in_Cities_2016.pdf
47. https://www.uclg.org/sites/default/files/the_sdgs_what_localgov_need_to_know_0.pdf
48. http://explorer.sustainia.me/solutions/electric-vehicle-car-sharing
49. https://www.uclg.org/sites/default/files/the_sdgs_what_localgov_need_to_know_0.pdf
50. http://explorer.sustainia.me/solutions/intelligent-streetlights
51. http://newclimateeconomy.report/2014/cities/
52. https://champs123blog.files.wordpress.com/2017/03/report_-business-case-for-reducing-food-loss-and-waste.pdf
53. https://www.uclg.org/sites/default/files/the_sdgs_what_localgov_need_to_know_0.pdf
54. http://explorer.sustainia.me/solutions/green-bonds-finance-city-climate-change-projects
55. http://www.globalopportunityexplorer.org/solutions/green-bonds-finance-city-climate-change-projects
56. https://www.uclg.org/sites/default/files/the_sdgs_what_localgov_need_to_know_0.pdf
57. http://staging.unep.org/urban_environment/PDFs/Coastal_Pollution_Role_of_Cities.pdf
58. http://explorer.sustainia.me/cities/yokohama-recognizing-ecosystem-services-for-climate-adaptation
59. http://explorer.sustainia.me/cities/yokohama-recognizing-ecosystem-services-for-climate-adaptation
60. https://www.uclg.org/sites/default/files/the_sdgs_what_localgov_need_to_know_0.pdf
61. https://www.bostonglobe.com/opinion/2016/08/08/building-economic-justice-america-cities/6E6V6lINwIQwXNpJ79ILQI/story.html
62. http://www.iclei.org/fileadmin/PUBLICATIONS/Briefing_Sheets/SDGs/02_-_

ICLEI-Bonn_Briefing_Sheet_-_SDGsandCities_2015_web.pdf

63. http://explorer.sustainia.me/cities/new-york-city-copenhagen-cities-collaborating-on-climate-resilience

64. http://www.irbnet.de/daten/iconda/CIB_DC26688.pdf

65. http://citiesphilanthropy.com/wp-content/uploads/2016/10/Day-1-Keynote-Prof-Porter.pdf

66. http://citiesphilanthropy.com/wp-content/uploads/2016/10/Day-1-Keynote-Prof-Porter.pdf

67. http://sdg.iisd.org/news/governments-adopt-new-urban-agenda/

68. http://report.akzonobel.com/2016/ar/sustainability/social-value-creation/note-17-human-cities.html

69. http://sdg.iisd.org/news/governments-adopt-new-urban-agenda/

70. http://report.businesscommission.org/uploads/BetterBiz-BetterWorld_170215_012417.pdf

71. https://www.retuna.se/sidor/om-retuna/

72. https://www.weforum.org/agenda/2017/04/recycled-shopping-centre-sweden-plastics-circular-economy/?utm_content=buffer1d753&utm_medium=social&utm_source=facebook.com&utm_campaign=buffer

73. http://report.akzonobel.com/2016/ar/sustainability/creating-shared-value-across-three-dimensions.html

74. http://www.mckinsey.com/global-themes/ urbanization/tackling-the-worlds-affordable-housing-challenge

75. http://report.businesscommission.org/uploads/BetterBiz-BetterWorld_170215_012417.pdf

76. http://www.who.int/gho/road_safety/mortality/traffic_deaths_number/en/

77. http://newclimateeconomy.report/2014/

78. http://www.mckinsey.com/~/media/McKinsey/Global%20Themes/Urbanization/Tackling%20the%20worlds%20affordable%20housing%20challenge/MGI_Affordable_housing_Executive%20summary_October%202014.ashx

79. http://report.businesscommission.org/uploads/BetterBiz-BetterWorld_170215_012417.pdf

80. http://www.mckinsey.com/business-functions/sustainability-and-resource-productivity/our-insights/urban-mobility-at-a-tipping-point

81. http://report.businesscommission.org/uploads/BetterBiz-BetterWorld_170215_012417.pdf

82. http://www.c40.org/ending-climate-change-begins-in-the-city

83. http://mitigationandtransparencyexchange.org/news/2017/01/19/green-bonds-for-cities-a-strategic-guide-for-policymakers-in-developing-countries/

84. https://www.forbes.com/sites/mikesteep/2016/06/27/can-smart-cities-improve-the-health-of-its-citizens/#b71618f39579

85. http://newclimateeconomy.report/

86. https://www.weforum.org/agenda/2016/02/4-ways-smart-cities-will-make-our-lives-better/

87. https://www.weforum.org/agenda/2015/10/top-10-urban-innovations-of-2015/

88. https://biztechmagazine.com/article/2017/06/businesses-rely-smart-city-infrastructure-could-be-vulnerable-after-cyberattacks

89. http://datasmart.ash.harvard.edu/news/article/how-smart-city-barcelona-brought-the-internet-of-things-to-life-789

90. https://www.vilaweb.cat/noticia/4175829/20140226/ten-reasons-why-barcelona-is-smart-city.html

91. http://datasmart.ash.harvard.edu/news/article/how-smart-city-barcelona-brought-the-internet-of-things-to-life-789

92. http://www.smartcityexpo.com/en/

93. https://biztechmagazine.com/article/2017/06/businesses-rely-smart-city-infrastructure-could-be-vulnerable-after-cyberattacks

94. https://www.mckinsey.com/business-functions/digital-mckinsey/our-insights/digital-globalization-the-new-era-of-global-flows

95. http://www.smartcitiesdive.com/ex/sustainablecitiescollective/vertical-city-concept-how-live-sustainable-life/1163942/

96. http://www.businessinsider.com/vertical-cities-future-of-architecture-2016-4?international=true

97. https://www.treehugger.com/urban-design/vertical-city-viable-solution-sustainable-living.html

98. http://newclimateeconomy.report/2014/innovation/#

99. https://globenewswire.com/news-release/2017/10/04/1140565/0/en/Global-Solar-Panel-Market-Will-Reach-USD-57-5-Billion-by-2022-Zion-Market-Research.html

100. https://economictimes.indiatimes.com/small-biz/startups/how-startups-like-attero-recycling-karma-recycling-are-making-money-out-of-garbage/articleshow/49963439.cms

101. https://www.fastcompany.com/3046428/4-cities-that-are-getting-rid-of-all-of-their-garbage

102. https://sustainabledevelopment.un.org/topics/sustainabletransport

103. https://sustainabledevelopment.un.org/content/documents/2375Mobilizing%20Sustainable%20Transport.pdf

104. http://sdg.iisd.org/news/experts-urge-mobilizing-sustainable-transport-for-sdgs/

105. https://www.tesla.com/blog/mission-tesla

106. http://newclimateeconomy.report/2014/cities/

107. http://www.ntd.tv/2017/03/02/future-urban-delivery-electric-cargo-bikes/

108. https://home.kpmg.com/content/dam/kpmg/xx/pdf/2017/05/sdg-transportation.pdf

109. https://www.theguardian.com/business/2017/sep/27/easyjet-electric-planes-wright-electric-flights

110. https://sustainabledevelopment.un.org/content/documents/8656Analysis%20of%20transport%20relevance%20of%20SDGs.pdf

111. https://sustainabledevelopment.un.org/content/documents/8656Analysis%20of%20transport%20relevance%20of%20SDGs.pdf

112. http://www.flyzipline.com/

113. https://www.wired.com/story/zipline-drone-delivery-tanzania/

CHAPTER 6

1. http://www.unwater.org/topics/water-and-food/en/

2. https://www.theguardian.com/news/datablog/2013/jan/10/how-much-water-food-production-waste

3. http://www.fao.org/news/story/en/item/196220/icode/

4. https://www.ifad.org/documents/10180/ca86ab2d-74f0-42a5-b4b6-5e476d321619

5. https://farmingfirst.org/sdg-toolkit#home

6. http://www.stockholmresilience.org/research/research-news/2016-06-14-how-food-connects-all-the-sdgs.html

7. https://farmingfirst.org/principles/

8. http://www.stockholmresilience.org/research/research-news/2016-06-14-how-food-connects-all-the-sdgs.html

9. http://www.stockholmresilience.org/

10. http://www.ifpri.org/blog/new-global-food-system-achieving-sustainable-development-goals

11. http://businesscommission.org/our-work/valuing-the-sdg-prize-in-food-and-agriculture

12. https://www.csmonitor.com/World/Making-a-difference/Change-Agent/2012/0905/Six-solutions-to-lifting-the-world-s-farm-workers-out-of-poverty

13. https://borgenproject.org/15-world-hunger-statistics/

14. https://farmingfirst.org/sdg-toolkit#section_1

15. http://www.thp.org/our-work/where-we-work/africa/benin/

16. http://weprinciples.org/Site/CompaniesLeadingTheWay/

17. http://www.fao.org/docrep/013/i2050e/i2050e.pdf

18. http://www.wateraid.org/what-we-do/the-crisis/statistics
19. http://www.un.org/sustainabledevelopment/hunger/
20. http://www.ilo.org/ipec/areas/Agriculture/lang--en/index.htm
21. http://www.ilo.org/ipec/areas/Agriculture/lang--en/index.htm
22. http://www.fao.org/childlabouragriculture/en/
23. http://www.worldbank.org/en/news/feature/2016/10/14/promoting-land-rights-to-empower-rural-women-and-end-poverty
24. http://www.worldbank.org/en/news/feature/2016/10/14/promoting-land-rights-to-empower-rural-women-and-end-poverty
25. https://www.globalfundforwomen.org/our-approach/initiatives/seeds-of-change/#.Wf76zmhSzcc
26. http://www.theguardian.com/global-development/2012/aug/26/food-shortages-worldvegetarianism?guni=Article:in%20body%20link
27. https://www.foodengineeringmag.com/articles/95493-reducing-water-usage-in-food-and-beverage-processing
28. http://www.aljazeera.com/news/2017/03/200000-die-year-pesticide-poisoning-170308140641105.html
29. https://www.ipcc.ch/publications_and_data/ar4/wg3/en/ch9s9-6-1.html
30. http://www.fao.org/sustainability/background/en/
31. http://stopwastingfoodmovement.org/our-projects/
32. http://susfood-db-era.net/drupal/
33. https://assets.kpmg.com/content/dam/kpmg/pdf/2016/02/sdg-industry-matrix.pdf
34. https://www.theguardian.com/environment/2016/jul/30/england-plastic-bag-usage-drops-85-per-cent-since-5p-charged-introduced
35. https://assets.kpmg.com/content/dam/kpmg/pdf/2016/02/sdg-industry-matrix.pdf
36. http://businesscommission.org/news/release-new-business-models-in-food-agriculture-could-create-trillions-annual-windfall
37. https://www.wfp.org/stories/10-facts-about-hunger
38. https://www.brookings.edu/blog/future-development/2017/04/03/the-sdgs-need-business-business-needs-the-sdgs/
39. http://www.worldbank.org/en/topic/financialsector/brief/agriculture-finance
40. http://www.wri.org/our-work/topics/food
41. https://www.edie.net/library/Household-food-waste-The-final-piece-in-the-food-waste-puzzle/6747
42. https://www.npr.org/sections/goatsandsoda/2015/09/28/444188475/even-poor-countries-end-up-wasting-tons-of-food
43. http://venturesafrica.com/these-10-apps-will-boost-agriculture-in-africa/
44. https://www.theguardian.com/environment/2015/feb/26/world-leaders-urged-to-tackle-food-waste-to-save-billions-and-cut-emissions
45. http://perfotec.com/
46. http://www.securefish.net/news.html
47. https://nofima.no/en/forskning/naringsnytte/keeps-salmon-fresh-for-20-days/
48. https://www.nu.nl/eten-en-drinken/4738932/bijvangst-vis-binnenkort-in-schappen-van-supermarkten.html
49. https://www.youtube.com/watch?v=tkT7oQ-hlXg
50. https://www.ted.com/talks/tristram_stuart_the_global_food_waste_scandal?language=de
51. http://www.un.org/sustainabledevelopment/takeaction/
52. https://www.epa.gov/sustainable-management-food/reducing-impact-wasted-food-feeding-soil-and-composting
53. https://en.wikipedia.org/wiki/Carbon_sequestration
54. https://www.evoconsys.com/about.html
55. http://www.globalopportunityexplorer.org/solutions/using-larvae-to-convert-food-waste-into-animal-feed
56. https://www.q-point-bv.nl/en/
57. https://www.unileverfoodsolutions.ie/our-services/your-kitchen/wise-waste-app
58. https://www.agri-pulse.com/articles/9639-opinion-the-missing-link-in-global-food-security
59. https://www.theguardian.com/environment/2015/aug/12/cutting-food-waste-enough-for-everyone-says-un
60. http://www.wrap.org.uk/content/reducing-food-waste-could-save-global-economy-300-billion-year
61. https://www.weforum.org/system-initiatives/shaping-the-future-of-food-security-and-agriculture
62. https://www.weforum.org/system-initiatives/shaping-the-future-of-food-security-and-agriculture/?utm_content=buffer8eb3f&utm_medium=social&utm_source=facebook.com&utm_campaign=buffer
63. http://www.ifpri.org/blog/new-global-food-system-achieving-sustainable-development-goals
64. https://c4rice.com/
65. https://www.technologyreview.com/s/535011/supercharged-photosynthesis/
66. https://www.tno.nl/en/collaboration/
67. https://www.pwc.com/gx/en/sustainability/publications/PwC-sdg-guide.pdf
68. https://sustainabledevelopment.un.org/topics/foodagriculture

CHAPTER 7

1. https://issuu.com/sustainia/docs/sustainia100_2016
2. http://www.globalpartnership.org/education/education-challenges
3. https://www.theguardian.com/global-development/2015/oct/20/two-thirds-of-worlds-illiterate-adults-are-women-report-finds
4. http://www.globalpartnership.org/education/education-challenges
5. http://teachforall.org/en/global-problem
6. http://unesdoc.unesco.org/images/0021/002199/219998E.pdf
7. https://www.unglobalcompact.org/docs/issues_doc/development/Business_Education_Framework.pdf
8. https://gemreportunesco.wordpress.com/2017/06/26/the-urgent-need-for-investment-in-pre-primary-education/
9. http://www.unesco.org/fileadmin/MULTIMEDIA/FIELD/San-Jose/pdf/229603E.pdf
10. http://educationaboveall.org/uploads/library/file/2a8e15847d.pdf
11. http://unesdoc.unesco.org/images/0019/001902/190214e.pdf
12. http://educateachild.org/sites/default/files/docs/2017//EAC-SDG_Infographic%20Dec%202016.pdf
13. http://unesdoc.unesco.org/images/0019/001902/190214e.pdf
14. https://farmingfirst.org/sdg-toolkit#section_2
15. http://www.thelancet.com/journals/lancet/article/PIIS0140-6736(10)61257-3/abstract
16. http://www.globalpartnership.org/blog/17-ways-education-influences-new-17-global-goals
17. http://unesdoc.unesco.org/images/0019/001902/190214e.pdf
18. https://www.unicef.org/media/media_53234.html
19. https://www.unglobalcompact.org/docs/issues_doc/development/Business_Education_Framework.pdf
20. https://www.pwc.com/gx/en/sustainability/publications/PwC-sdg-guide.pdf
21. http://siteresources.worldbank.org/EDUCATION/Resources/278200-1099079877269/547664-1099079934475/547667-1135281504040/Returns_Investment_Edu.pdf
22. https://www.pwc.com/gx/en/sustainability/publications/PwC-sdg-guide.pdf
23. http://www.unwomen.org/en/what-we-do/economic-empowerment/facts-and-figures
24. http://s3.amazonaws.com/aws-bsdc/Valuing-the-SDG-Prize.pdf
25. http://www.globalpartnership.org/blog/17-ways-education-influences-new-17-global-goals
26. http://www.educationinnovations.org/sites/default/files/%EF%BF%BCSustainable%20Development%3A%20Post-2015%20Begins%20with%20Education.pdf
27. http://www.un.org/apps/news/story.asp?NewsID=34277#.WazaKoq-Qwyk
28. http://www.who.int/en/

29. https://issuu.com/sustainia/docs/sustainia100_2016
30. https://www.msn.com/en-us/news/other/coal-is-dying-and-trump-can%E2%80%99t-save-it-but-there-are-much-better-alternatives-for-coal-country-and-our-economy/ar-BBzcTN8
31. http://www.salon.com/2017/04/02/coal-is-dying-and-trump-cant-save-it-but-there-are-much-better-alternatives-for-coal-country-and-our-economy/
32. http://www.unesco.org/fileadmin/MULTIMEDIA/FIELD/Beirut/pdf/UNESCO_Booklet_EN_v10_WEB.pdf
33. https://www.brookings.edu/blog/education-plus-development/2016/10/04/the-top-5-education-innovations-needed-to-keep-up-in-a-new-economy/
34. http://educationaboveall.org/uploads/library/file/2a8e15847d.pdf
35. https://www.brookings.edu/blog/education-plus-development/2013/02/20/improving-education-governance-and-financing-a-bigger-role-for-the-private-sector/
36. http://www.globalpartnership.org/blog/17-ways-education-influences-new-17-global-goals
37. http://unesdoc.unesco.org/images/0022/002231/223115E.pdf
38. http://explorer.sustainia.me/solutions/cash-for-recycling
39. https://edtechmagazine.com/higher/
40. https://www2.deloitte.com/nl/nl/pages/risk/articles/quality-education-and-lifelong-learning.html
41. https://www.duolingo.com/
42. https://www.noodle-partners.com/
43. https://www.knewton.com/
44. https://www.unicef.org/publications/files/Investment_Case_for_Education_and_Equity_FINAL.pdf
45. https://www.project-syndicate.org/commentary/climate-change-education-issue-by-felipe-calderon-2016-07?barrier=accessreg
46. https://www.pwc.com/gx/en/sustainability/publications/PwC-sdg-guide.pdf
47. http://educationaboveall.org/uploads/library/file/2a8e15847d.pdf
48. https://www.icsu.org/cms/2017/05/SDGs-Guide-to-Interactions.pdf
49. http://educationaboveall.org/uploads/library/file/2a8e15847d.pdf
50. https://reliefweb.int/report/syrian-arab-republic/syria-fighting-forces-hundreds-schools-close
51. http://www.globalpartnership.org/
52. https://www2.deloitte.com/nl/nl/pages/risk/articles/quality-education-and-lifelong-learning.html
53. http://www.globalpartnership.org/blog/17-ways-education-influences-new-17-global-goals
54. https://sharedvalue.org/sites/default/files/resource-files/FSG-PrintReport-Final.pdf
55. ibid
56. https://www.cisco.com/assets/csr/pdf/NetAcad_Exec_Brief.pdf
57. https://www.unglobalcompact.org/docs/issues_doc/development/Business_Education_Framework.pdf
58. https://sharedvalue.org/sites/default/files/resource-files/FSG-PrintReport-Final.pdf
59. https://sharedvalue.org/sites/default/files/resource-files/FSG%20Verizon%20Case%20Study.pdf
60. http://www.godrej.com/ensuring-employability.html
61. http://explorer.sustainia.me/solutions/parental-work-exchange-helps-to-run-schools
62. http://explorer.sustainia.me/markets/closing-the-skills-gap
63. www.Valuing-the-SDG-Prize.pdf
64. http://www.tourdestfu.com/2016/02/10-nations-that-dont-allow-girls-to-go.html
65. https://www.unglobalcompact.org/docs/issues_doc/human_rights/Investing_in_Education.pdf
66. http://unesdoc.unesco.org/images/0023/002305/230508e.pdf
67. http://www.educationinnovations.org/program/nafham
68. https://www.forbes.com/sites/joshbersin/2016/01/05/use-of-moocs-and-online-education-is-exploding-heres-why/#4013c0b97649
69. http://www.workforce.com/2017/06/01/will-take-close-skills-gap-take-educated-guess/
70. http://explorer.sustainia.me/solutions/global-labs-for-invention-through-technology
71. https://education.lego.com/en-us
72. https://www.lego.com/en-us/seriousplay
73. http://analytics-magazine.org/ibm-university-partnerships-focus-on-big-data-analytics-skills/
74. https://www.intel.com/content/dam/www/program/education/us/en/documents/stem-resources-k12-educators.pdf
75. https://www.class-central.com/report/mooc-providers-list/
76. https://www.class-central.com/report/xuetangx/
77. https://sustainabledevelopment.un.org/sdinaction/hesi
78. http://explorer.sustainia.me/solutions/parental-work-exchange-helps-to-run-schools
79. https://www.globalreporting.org/resourcelibrary/Meassuring%20Impact_BCtA_GRI.pdf
80. https://www.globalreporting.org/resourcelibrary/Meassuring%20Impact_BCtA_GRI.pdf

CHAPTER 8

1. https://issuu.com/sustainia/docs/sustainia_health_sector_guide/12
2. http://www.who.int/ageing/publications/global_health.pdf
3. http://www.who.int/nmh/publications/ncd_action_plan_en.pdf
4. https://www.ncbi.nlm.nih.gov/pmc/articles/PMC3137804/
5. http://issuu.com/sustainia/docs/sustainia_health_sector_guide?e=4517615/7911684
6. https://www.weforum.org/agenda/2015/10/how-the-sdgs-can-help-address-global-health-challenges/
7. http://www.who.int/topics/sustainable-development-goals/test/sdg-banner.jpg?ua=1
8. https://www.worldhunger.org/2015-world-hunger-and-poverty-facts-and-statistics/
9. http://www.foodaidfoundation.org/world-hunger-statistics.html
10. https://www.compassion.com/poverty/health.htm
11. https://www.icsu.org/cms/2017/05/SDGs-Guide-to-Interactions.pdf
12. https://www.franchisehelp.com/industry-reports/fitness-industry-report/
13. http://www.un.org/youthenvoy/2016/03/comprehensive-sexuality-education/
14. http://www.un.org/youthenvoy/2016/03/comprehensive-sexuality-education/
15. http://www.thp.org/issues/water-sanitation/
16. https://www.theguardian.com/environment/2014/mar/25/air-pollution-single-biggest-environmental-health-risk-who
17. http://cite.gov.pt/pt/destaques/complementosDestqs2/Decent_work.pdf
18. http://blumarble.co.in/
19. https://www.forbes.com/sites/ericagies/2012/02/22/anheuser-busch-to-join-industrial-ecosystem/#4e82cada4153
20. https://phys.org/news/2017-05-sensors-disease-markers.html
21. http://www.who.int/features/factfiles/health_inequities/en/
22. http://www.economicsonline.co.uk/Managing_the_economy/Policies_to_reduce_inequality_and_poverty.html
23. http://www.un.org/sustainabledevelopment/inequality/
24. https://www.weforum.org/agenda/2016/05/2-billion-people-worldwide-are-unbanked-heres-how-to-change-this
25. https://en.wikipedia.org/wiki/M-Pesa
26. https://en.wikipedia.org/wiki/M-Pesa
27. https://www.theguardian.com/environment/2014/mar/25/air-pollution-single-biggest-environmental-health-risk-who
28. https://www.theguardian.com/environment/2014/mar/25/air-pollution-single-

biggest-environmental-health-risk-who
29. http://www.harvestplus.org/what-we-do/nutrition
30. https://www.unglobalcompact.org/docs/publications/Blueprint-for-Business-Leadership-on-the-SDGs-Goal3.pdf
31. http://www.hindustantimes.com/india-news/heatwave-in-india-claim-4-620-lives-in-four-years/story-yDAJTaroKEUBio6uEeTcgN.html
32. https://weather.com/science/news/warm-temperatures-allow-zika-spreading
33. http://www.onegreenplanet.org/animalsandnature/marine-animals-are-dying-because-of-our-plastic-trash/
34. https://www.regenerative.com/magazine/six-problems-monoculture-farming
35. https://www.realizingglobalhealth.com/paris-declaration-action/
36. http://www.who.int/bulletin/volumes/85/7/06-033597/en/
37. https://www.biosciencetechnology.com/article/2017/04/why-we-need-culture-international-collaboration-fight-antibiotic-resistance
38. https://www.newfoodmagazine.com/news/46307/antibiotics-resistance-debate/
39. https://www.ge.com/uk/
40. https://www.sharedvalue.org/groups/how-healthcarehealthcare-companies-win-new-sustainable-development-goals-era
41. https://www.devex.com/news/opinion-more-money-alone-won-t-meet-sdg-3-90552?utm_source=website&utm_medium=box&utm_campaign=linking_strategy
42. https://www.medicalcreditfund.org/our-approach/
43. https://sharedvalue.org/sites/default/files/resource-files/Novartis%20Access%20Case%20Study_11-4-16.pdf
44. http://www.ghif.com/
45. http://www.leapfroginvest.com
46. http://www.leapfroginvest.com/videos/goodlife-redefining-access-health care-east-africa/
47. https://www.ft.com/content/413d68dc-2c22-11e7-9ec8-168383da43b7
48. https://sharedvalue.org/sites/default/files/resource-files/Insuring%20Shared%20Value_7-5-17.pdf
49. http://apps.who.int/iris/bitstream/10665/174536/1/9789241564977_eng.pdf
50. http://www.unfpa.org/publications/trends-maternal-mortality-1990-2015
51. http://www.undp.org/content/unct/lesotho/en/home/sdgs/goal-3--good-health-and-well-being.html
52. http://www.accessafya.com/
53. http://www.accessafya.com/blog/
54. https://newoldage.blogs.nytimes.com/2012/10/10/how-in-the-world-will-we-care-for-all-the-elderly/
55. https://www.1mg.com/online-consultation
56. https://www.accenture.com/us-en/insight-digital-health-digital-economy-innovation
57. https://innovation-awards.nl/themes/health-wellbeing/
58. https://www.engadget.com/2017/08/29/robot-caregivers-are-saving-the-elderly-from-lives-of-loneliness/
59. https://hbr.org/2016/03/3d-printing-is-already-changing-health-care
60. https://www.worldhunger.org/2015-world-hunger-and-poverty-facts-and-statistics/
61. https://farmingfirst.org/sdg-toolkit#section_1
62. http://www.harvestplus.org/what-we-do/nutrition
63. http://docs.scalingupnutrition.org/wp-content/uploads/2016/06/VISUAL-EN.jpg
64. http://www.who.int/mediacentre/factsheets/fs311/en/

CHAPTER 9

1. http://www.un.org/sustainabledevelopment/blog/2017/09/un-secretary-generals-remarks-at-leaders-dialogue-on-climate-change/
2. http://ar5-syr.ipcc.ch/topic_observedchanges.php
3. https://climate.nasa.gov/scientific-consensus/
4. https://sustainabledevelopment.un.org/getWSDoc.php?id=1013
5. https://sustainabledevelopment.un.org/getWSDoc.php?id=1013
6. http://www.wri.org/blog/2013/01/4-grand-challenges-energy-food-and-water
7. https://www.unenvironment.org/news-and-stories/press-release/resource-use-expected-double-2050-better-natural-resource-use
8. https://instituteforenergyresearch.org/analysis/ieas-world-energy-outlook-2017-foresees-transformation-global-energy-system/
9. https://www.weforum.org/agenda/2015/10/how-the-circular-economy-can-help-us-achieve-the-global-goals/
10. https://www.accenture.com/t20151111T221550__w__/us-en/_acnmedia/Accenture/Conversion-Assets/DotCom/Documents/Global/PDF/Strategy_7/Accenture-UNGC-CEO-Study-A-Call-to-Climate-Action.pdf
11. http://www.un.org/sustainabledevelopment/sustainable-consumption-production/
12. https://www.accenture.com/us-en/insight-outlook-environment-opportunity-sustainable-business
13. http://ceoworld.biz/2015/11/03/what-personally-motivates-ceos-to-act-on-climate-change/
14. https://www.freep.com/story/opinion/2017/09/25/guest-columnist-business-case-climate-action/105976590/
15. http://www.eesi.org/papers/view/fact-sheet-jobs-in-renewable-energy-and-energy-efficiency-2015#1
16. http://www.un.org/sustainabledevelopment/blog/2017/09/un-secretary-generals-remarks-at-leaders-dialogue-on-climate-change/
17. http://www.wri.org/blog/2017/04/numbers-how-business-benefits-sustainable-development-goals
18. http://www.wri.org/blog/2017/04/numbers-how-business-benefits-sustainable-development-goals
19. http://solutions.sustainia.me/solutions/pooling-properties-to-finance-energy-upgrades/
20. http://solutions.sustainia.me/solutions/solar-storage-community-platform/
21. http://www.marksandspencer.com/s/plan-a-shwopping
22. https://19january2017snapshot.epa.gov/sites/production/files/documents/climatehabs.pdf
23. https://www.idtechex.com/research/reports/3d-printing-materials-2017-2027-status-opportunities-market-forecasts-000516.asp
24. http://www3.weforum.org/docs/WEF_The_New_Plastics_Economy.pdf
25. http://sdg.iisd.org/news/integrated-benefits-calculator-enables-decision-makers-to-estimate-benefits-of-mitigation-action/
26. http://sustainia.me/resources/publications/The_Business_Case_for_Saving_the_Planet.pdf
27. https://assets.kpmg.com/content/dam/kpmg/xx/pdf/2017/01/SDG-industry-matrix.pdf
28. https://www.iberdrola.com/sustainability/social-contribution
29. https://ceowatermandate.org/files/IA_SustainabilityReport16.pdf
30. https://www.pirelli.com/tire/us/en/news/2016/02/26/pirelli-makes-first-guayale-based-uhp-tire/
31. https://sharedvalue.org/examples/silica-tires-made-part-rice-husks-reduce-waste-and-save-fuel
32. https://www.fsg.org/blog/advancing-circular-economy-through-shared-value
33. http://www.un.org/sustainabledevelopment/blog/2017/09/un-secretary-generals-remarks-at-leaders-dialogue-on-climate-change/
34. http://fs-unep-centre.org/sites/default/files/publications/globaltrendsinrenewableenergyinvestment2017.pdf
35. http://fs-unep-centre.org/sites/default/files/publications/globaltrendsinrenewableenergyinvestment2016lowres_0.pdf
36. www.cdp.net/CDP Results/CDP-SP500-leaders-report-2014.pdf
37. https://www.climaterealityproject.org/blog/carbon-pricing-does-it-work
38. http://www.ourenergypolicy.org/wp-content/uploads/2017/09/carbon-pricing-business-09-17.pdf
39. http://www.un.org/sustainabledevelopment/blog/2016/01/ban-ki-moons-

remarks-at-investor-summit-on-climate-risk/

40. https://www.nature.com/articles/nclimate2972?WT.feed_name=subjects_governance

41. http://awsassets.wwf.es/downloads/WWF_Climate_Guide_to_Asset_Owners_Full_version_Dec17.pdf

42. https://www.ifc.org/wps/wcm/connect/992394804ae15e6f9f8b9f34fbf4cc68/infra-cheat-sheet-2017.pdf?MOD=AJPERES

43. https://www.mckinsey.com/business-functions/sustainability-and-resource-productivity/our-insights/the-business-of-sustainability-mckinsey-global-survey-results

44. https://www.dow.com/-/media/dow/business-units/dow-us/pdf/science-and-sustainability/2010-q4-sustainability-report.ashx

45. https://www.dow.com/en-us/science-and-sustainability/2025-sustainability-goals/advancing-a-circular-economy

46. https://www.mckinsey.com/industries/oil-and-gas/our-insights/renewable-energy-evolution-not-revolution

47. https://www.ceres.org/sites/default/files/reports/2017-11/Ceres_CleanTechVentureCapInvest_110917.pdf

48. http://interenergy.com/portfolio/panama-wind/

49. https://ifcextapps.ifc.org/ifcext/Pressroom/IFCPressRoom.nsf/0/BD3D3814A76DE0FE85257DB000532C77?opendocument

50. http://www.worldbank.org/en/news/opinion/2016/01/13/climate-change-is-a-threat---and-an-opportunity---for-the-private-sector

51. http://solutions.sustainia.me/solutions/pay-as-you-go-solar-energy-to-off-grid-households/

52. http://www.thelancet.com/commissions/pollution-and-health

53. http://www.air-quality.org.uk/11.php

54. http://www.prosolve370e.com/home/

55. http://www.medicaldaily.com/mexico-city-hospital-eats-pollution-torre-de-especialidades-features-innovate-facade-tiling-265942

56. https://cleantechnica.com/2017/07/04/air-pollution-solutions-via-innovative-cleantech/

57. https://www.enverid.com/hlr-module/savings

58. https://www.ellenmacarthurfoundation.org/circular-economy

59. http://www.sustainablebrands.com/news_and_views/next_economy/sustainable_brands/wef_ellen_macarthur_foundation_project_circular_econo

60. http://docs.wbcsd.org/2017/06/CEO_Guide_to_CE.pdf

61. http://docs.wbcsd.org/2017/06/CEO_Guide_to_CE.pdf

62. http://green-social.com/concept/

63. https://www.pwc.com/m1/en/publications/documents/delivering-sustainable-development-goals.pdf

64. https://sustainabledevelopment.un.org/sdg9

65. https://www.ellenmacarthurfoundation.org/assets/downloads/publications/EllenMacArthurFoundation_Intelligent_Assets_080216-AUDIO-E.pdf

66. https://www.theguardian.com/sustainable-business/interview-ceo-chemical-firm-sustainability-survival

CHAPTER 10

1. https://reliefweb.int/report/world/sustainable-development-goals-report-2017

2. http://businesscommission.org/our-work/valuing-the-sdg-prize-unlocking-business-opportunities-to-accelerate-sustainable-and-inclusive-growth

3. http://foreignpolicy.com/2016/03/15/these-25-companies-are-more-powerful-than-many-countries-multinational-corporate-wealth-power/

4. http://www.conecomm.com/research-blog/2017-csr-study

5. http://blog.euromonitor.com/2017/03/new-2016-fresh-food-industry-data-published.html

6. https://corporate-citizenship.com/our-insights/advancing-sustainable-development-goals-business-action-millennials-views/

7. http://www.wbcsd.org/Overview/Resources/General/CEO-Guide-to-the-SDGs

8. https://sdgsinaction.com/

9. https://unstats.un.org/sdgs/files/report/2017/TheSustainableDevelopmentGoalsReport2017.pdf

10. https://www.mckinsey.com/business-functions/sustainability-and-resource-productivity/our-insights/sustainabilitys-strategic-worth-mckinsey-global-survey-results

11. https://www.mckinsey.com/business-functions/sustainability-and-resource-productivity/our-insights/resource-revolution

12. http://report.businesscommission.org/uploads/BetterBiz-BetterWorld_170215_012417.pdf

13. https://www.carbonpricingleadership.org/highlevel-economic-commission-1/

14. http://s3.amazonaws.com/aws-bsdc/Aligning-corporate-tax-policy-with-SDGs.pdf

15. http://www.ex-tax.com/

16. https://www.brookings.edu/blog/brookings-now/2014/07/17/brookings-data-now-75-percent-of-2025-workforce-will-be-millennials/

17. https://issuu.com/aiesecinternational/docs/report_youthspeak_2016

18. https://www2.deloitte.com/content/dam/Deloitte/global/Documents/About-Deloitte/gx-millenial-survey-2016-exec-summary.pdf

19. http://www.unglobalcompact.org.au/2016/02/19/sustainability-is-key-to-engaging-millennials

" REPURPOSING TO DO GOOD
FOR THE WORLD MUST
BECOME A PRIMARY MISSION
FOR ALL; IT CAN BE DONE
AND MUST BE DONE"